The

Pilgrimage

of

Life

THE
PILGRIMAGE
OF
LIFE

by Samuel C. Chew

New Haven & London

Yale University Press, 1962

PREFACE

Good wine needs no bush. A book by Samuel Claggett Chew needs no apology. But since this, his last literary work, has been published after his death, a few words of explanation are in order.

The Pilgrimage of Life, started twenty years ago, was finished on November 2, 1959. Under that date, in the tiny pocket diary my husband kept for many years, I found this succinct entry: "Laus Deo in Excelsis! I finished the book, all but a few notes. Now for revision etc."

The work was done, and he looked forward to seeing it in print. The choice of illustrations from his album of over three hundred photographs—culled from prints, woodcuts, engravings, studied so minutely by him for their inconographical, symbolic, allegorical, and emblematic interest—would be a diversion. The intricate fabric woven from so many strands was about to be presented to scholars and to all readers who have a need to learn more about the human imagination.

The twofold appeal of picture and story had long been a prime mover in Mr. Chew's literary work. For years he patiently assembled notes and pored over old books in the Huntington, Morgan, Folger, and Widener Libraries, in the rare print room of the Metropolitan Museum, and elsewhere; his sources for this particular book are too many to be listed. His particular genius lay in reducing so vast a mass into so small a compass.

The narrative of man's journey through life from cradle to grave changes from century to century, but essentially it is the same complicated tale: Time and Fortune still favor or plague him; he sinks or rises; he is guarded by angels or tormented by demons; and Death still "lays his icy hands on Kings" or commoners. When the summons came to Samuel Chew on January 15, 1960, he went forth sensing, I think, that someone would put the finishing touches to his last work. Who more naturally than I? Had he lived, he might have made revisions before the last typing; but since he could not be the final arbiter as to what to keep and what to discard, I thought it best to retain substantially his final draft. The order of the chapters has been changed, but not their contents. Quaint spellings have been allowed to remain, to give a flavor of antiquity to certain passages. Some appendices he planned to include were never written.

The great themes this book treats may satisfy that ever-present longing in man to see and feel some power greater than himself. To-day's man, intent on journeys into space, may find our not-so-remote ancestors' preoccupation with personifications, allegories, iconography, symbols, and emblems incomprehensible. Yet this narrative of man as pilgrim through life, in the world of time and fortune, is as applicable now as in the days when miniatures in Books of Hours, frescoes on walls of churches, figures woven into tapestries or painted on cloths, or later engravings and woodcuts taught men the eternal truths.

To the careful, industrious, interested, and willing spirits who contributed work and time and patience to the completion of this book, I tender my thanks for help in a difficult undertaking. Most of them I do not know even by name. David Horne of the Yale University Press has given me all the aid and encouragement anyone could ask for, and Mrs. Marian Wohl has rendered invaluable service as the editor for the Press. LaVonna Snider, who typed the final version, deserves praise for accuracy and patience. Nor do I forget the staff in each library whence came the source books, the Ford Foundation's help with publication funds, and the many others who helped in numberless ways to bring this literary work into being.
Laus Deo in Excelsis.

Bryn Mawr, Pa.   Lucy E. Chew
June 1961

CONTENTS

LIST OF ILLUSTRATIONS

Numbers in parentheses refer to the text page on which the figure is first mentioned.

INTRODUCTION

A more particularized title of this book might have been *This Strange Eventful History: The Pilgrimage of Human Life and Related Themes in English Literature of the Renaissance: With Analogues from the Arts of Design.* Analogues, not sources, are discussed. Various direct connections between verbal and visual imagery will be suggested, but in general such relationships are difficult to determine; a poem or other piece of imaginative literature and a painting, tapestry, engraving, or sculpture are more likely to be under a common obligation to a source which has been used independently. The art historian, especially if his primary interest is iconography rather than aesthetic appreciation or the discrimination of schools and styles, makes constant use of literary evidence. Historians of literature, on the other hand, with certain conspicuous exceptions, seldom take much account of evidence afforded by the fine arts. It is my purpose to bring the two categories of imagery, verbal and visual, into closer contact. Only a restricted portion of an almost limitless field of inquiry has been explored, and no claim is advanced that even within the particular area the inquiry has been exhaustive: a syndicate of scholars would have to be recruited for such an undertaking. For many years, however, I have (in the words of Graund Amour) "gathered riches as though I should live ever," and of those riches a reasonable abundance is here presented.

The verbal examples are taken almost entirely from English literature; for the visual examples I searched beyond English art. The cultural lag in England, the comparative paucity of the work of English
artists, and the artists' obvious dependence in many cases upon Continental models have led me far afield in quest of parallels. The emphasis is upon woodcuts and engravings rather than paintings and works
of sculpture because the latter generally existed only in their original
form while the former were more accessible to Englishmen: They were
re-produced in large numbers, were easily shipped abroad, and were
comparatively inexpensive. Moreover, as we shall see, a considerable
number of Continental craftsmen were at work from time to time in
England, and after ca. 1600 there were many native English engravers.
The year of the foundation of the Tudor dynasty (1485) has been taken
as the terminus a quo of the inquiry and the year of the outbreak of
the Civil Wars (1642) as the terminus ad quem. These boundaries,
however, are not strictly adhered to: There are occasional backward
glances to the Middle Ages and less frequently a forward look, even
so far as the twentieth century.

We shall have very little to do with landscapes except in those rare
cases where a symbolic intent is discernible, as when a tree in full leaf
is contrasted with a withered tree, and even less to do with genre
painting. Portraits will attract our attention only when there are symbolic details in posture or attributes. Biblical, mythological, and historical subjects will be our concern if they approximate allegory and
personification, as when Pallas is the equivalent of Wisdom, Herod of
Cruelty, or Sardanapalus of Voluptuousness. Our attention will be con-
centrated, rather, upon a large number of personified abstractions: upon
their characteristic functions and attributes, and upon the emblems suggesting them when there are no actual personifications. These, albeit
often existing independently of one another or cohering in small groups,
such as the Stoic Virtues or the Seven Deadly Sins, may be molded into
a single pattern, a continuous allegory; and I have shaped them into
a study of the great theme of the Pilgrimage of Human Life as it was
conceived in the imagination of English writers of the Renaissance and
reflected in the arts of design.

We shall watch the imagination giving to airy nothings local habita-
tions and names as it creates forms more real than living man from
the shapes that haunt thought's wildernesses. By means of these images
our forefathers sought to express their experiences of the changes and
chances of this mortal life, and we cannot contemplate them without

recognizing that these great commonplaces are still applicable to the human situation. Only to the unthinking will the subject seem remote from present actualities, and only the oversophisticated will dismiss these profound truisms as mere platitudes. Man, having through Sin forfeited the boon of immortality, passes into the World of Time, governed under God's ordinance by Fortune. A free agent, he may choose either of the Two Paths. If he chooses aright there are perils along the strait and narrow way, but clad in the armor of St. Paul he will be able to withstand the assaults of the Infernal Trinity, and though the Deadly Sins assail him a great company of Virtues counsel and protect him. Death awaits him at the Journey's End, but beyond Death is the Celestial City. This is the basic pattern of my book.

It is not to be thought, however, that the object is to preach so obvious a moral and religious lesson. Our interest centers in the theme because it was the common property of poets and artists. The corpus of symbols available to the painter, the sculptor, the engraver, the tapestry weaver, the designer of pageantry, the poet, and the writer of imaginative prose had never been unalterably conventionalized. In religious art there was, comparatively speaking, stability, but Roman Catholic and Protestant polemic and propaganda encouraged the use of fresh imagery or put to new purposes what had been inherited. In secular art the erudite and inquisitive spirit of the Renaissance discovered whole new regions of imagery. Such causes hastened the breakdown of whatever firm iconographical tradition there had been. The climate of the imagination became restless and disturbed. There is fusion and confusion; there are eccentricities and extravagances. The tendency of concepts to interpenetrate and be conflated, observable in earlier centuries, becomes more apparent. The imagery is no sooner grasped (as we flatter ourselves) than escaping from our grasp, it reappears in some new guise or with some fresh association. Sexes change: The Virtues and the Vices are sometimes masculine, sometimes feminine. Time or Fate display the attributes of Death; Death may hold the hourglass of Time or the scales of Justice. The skeleton of an embryo may be seen holding Cupid's bow and arrow. The animals, which are attributes of many personifications, are shifted about in a bewildering fashion so that, for example, the cat may be an emblem of Childhood, because it loves to play, or of Old Age, because it likes to doze by the fireside. Even Fido, traditional symbol of Fidelity, is also a snarling emblem of Gluttony. It would be amusing and not uninstructive to trace this process of disintegration beyond our period: to Hogarth, for example, who places the scythe of Time in the hands of Cupid; to Wordsworth, who conceives of Time as a shadow; to Beddoes, who likens Time to a cataract; to Rossetti, who hears the pulse of Time beating through the cosmos; to Swinburne, who gives to Time the tears of Grief and to Grief the hourglass of Time. But there is no need to look beyond the English Renaissance where the process is observable alike in literature and the fine arts.

"Whosoever loveth not Picture is injurious to Truth and all the Wisdom of Poetry." The assertion is made by Ben Jonson in his *Discoveries*. In making it he may have been moved in part by the desire to please the painters whom he numbered among his friends, but he was not one to indulge in empty compliment and the context shows he meant that those who are insensitive to visible beauty cannot apprehend the truths conveyed in poetic imagery. Such is the underlying argument of the present book which is, so to speak, a commentary upon and, within a limited range of inquiry, an expansion of the familiar Horatian theme: *Ut pictura poesis*. That "painting is silent poetry and poetry is painting that speaks" is a saying at least as old as Plutarch, and Plutarch attributes it to Simonides.[1] The apothegm was popular among Elizabethan writers. As an example of a rhetorical figure Puttenham [2] quotes the lines:

> If Poesie be, as some have said,
> A speaking picture to the eye:
> Then is a picture not denaid,
> To be a muet Poesie.

Sidney [3] quotes the phrase. Jonson [4] commends its excellence. John Davies of Hereford [5] glosses the declaration of his love of certain poets and painters with a reference to Simonides. Dekker,[6] writing of the happy collaboration of poets and architects upon the triumphal arches through which King James entered London, remarks upon those "poets who draw speaking pictures, and painters who make dumb poesie." "The secrete friendeship" and "the affinitie one with another" existing between visual and verbal art are affirmed by Lodowick Lloyd,[7] who writes in commendation of them both. There were, however, echoes in England of those discussions which in Italy sprang from the rivalry between the poets, who were recognized for their social and moral worth, and the painters, who resented their classification as mere craftsmen and defended the intellectual and moral value of their art. Joseph Martyn [8] narrates his own experience when he was called upon to act as arbitrator of a dissension between representatives of the two arts. The Painter claimed the merit of vividness; what he has accomplished is before the spectator's eyes. The Poet, speaking "in a harsh Satyricke vaine," declared that the painter was no better than a dauber. Martyn judged that whereas "painters were confin'd to mortall shape," poets were oracles of Fame, bestowing lasting names upon the long since dead. Ben Jonson [9] is more courteous and genial than Martyn's imaginary poet. "Picture," he says, "is the invention of heaven, the most ancient and most akin to Nature. It is itself a silent work . . . yet it doth so enter and penetrate the inmost affection (being done by an excellent artificer) as sometimes it o'ercomes the power of speech and oratory." Nevertheless he concludes that "of the two the pen is more noble than the pencil; for that can speak to the understanding, the other but to the sense." Painters and their advocates were unwilling to adopt this opinion; painting, they held, as well as poetry could speak to the understanding.

This rivalry is debated with great dignity in the colloquy between the Poet and the Painter in the opening scene of *Timon of Athens*.[10] The Poet is generous in praise of the portrait of Lord Timon which the Painter intends to present to his patron. This courtesy contrasts with the arrogance of the Painter who is, indeed, interested in the Poet's verses, but only insofar as he holds them to be a novel rendering of a familiar theme, that of Fortune and her clients, which one of his craft might illustrate. However, after listening to the Poet speak on the fall of the great man from Fortune's hill he brushes it contemptuously aside:

> 'Tis common:
> A thousand moral paintings I can show
> That shall demonstrate these quick blows of Fortune's
> More pregnantly than words.

At this point Lord Timon enters, and Shakespeare appears to have given the last word to the Painter. But does he really do so? In retrospect the poem is seen to be the keynote of the play. The object of this book is not to take sides but to place both arts side by side.

CHAPTER 1. MAN'S FIRST DISOBEDIENCE

1. The Tree of Knowledge and the Tree of Death

A fifteenth-century Book of Hours from the South of France contains a large miniature of the Garden of Eden [1] (Fig. 1). The Lord God with great benignity is engaged in instructing Adam and Eve in their duty of obedience. Across the greensward, upon which this group stands, and a little to one side rises a mass of jagged rocks, and waist high behind these rocks, upon which he leans complacently with folded arms, is a monstrous Satan, green and red and purple and gold, with mighty wings. He is biding his time, and he will not have long to wait. When man tasted the fruit of the forbidden tree he brought Death into the world and all his woe. Patristic commentators, recognizing the lack of antithesis between the Tree of Life and the Tree of Knowledge of

1

Good and Evil, affirmed that the Tree of Knowledge was the Tree of Death. Both manuscripts and printed texts of Book XIV of *The City of God*, in which St. Augustine expounds the doctrine of the Fall, sometimes contain an illustration of Man seated in the Tree of Life.[2] An angel on his right offers him a crown and a devil on his left offers him a money chest; and Death is sawing at the trunk of the Tree. There are paintings, for example one of the school of Lucas Cranach the Elder in the Art Institute in Chicago (Fig. 2), where Death lurks near the Tree as Eve offers the forbidden fruit to Adam. In numerous designs a skull is associated with the Tree of Knowledge as in a large and impressive woodcut by Hans Sebald Beham (1543) (Fig. 3) where a skull is placed in the crotch of the Tree. This concept is carried further in a little copperplate by the same artist (Fig. 4). Here Adam and Eve stand on either side of a tree that is formed like a skeleton, or a skeleton that is formed like a tree.[3] Different in composition and style but identical in theme is a drawing by Franz Floris (Fig. 5). St. Paul equates Adam and Death: "in Adam all die." Thus, in a manuscript of *The City of God* (Fig. 6) St. Paul is shown contemplating the Fall of Man, and at the root of the Tree of Knowledge lies a skeleton. A variant of the same subject (Fig. 7) shows the Apostle confronting Death who, wearing a shroud and holding four darts, awaits his victims without the walls of Eden.[4]

The Tree of Knowledge is the Tree of Death because it is also the Tree of Sin. The doctrine lent itself easily to the process of visualization. On the first page of the text of Johann Zainer's famous edition of Boccaccio's *De Claris Mulieribus* (Ulm, 1473) there is a superb initial S.[5] Part of this letter, along the inner margin, is fashioned as the Tree of Knowledge while another part forms the serpent's tail and finally tapers into a foliage scroll in which medallions of the Seven Deadly Sins are placed. The frontispiece of another edition of the same work (Louvain, 1487) places the Seven Sins in the branches of the Tree [6] (Fig. 8). Pride, at the very top holds a mirror; Envy gnaws upon a heart; Avarice counts coin in a box; Wrath brandishes a sword; Lechery kisses a woman; Gluttony is drinking; Sloth is sound asleep.

The fundamental Sins are Pride and Lust. Pride brought about Eve's downfall. Lust was Adam's Sin, not only in the carnal sense of Lechery, Gluttony, and Sloth, but also as Wrath, Envy, and Avarice, the Lust for Revenge, the Lust for the Worldly Goods belonging to others, the Lust to retain possessions. Such is St. Augustine's exposition of the matter. In an English mystery play [7] St. Paul delivers a sermon at Damascus

2

on the Seven Deadly Sins, and Pride and Sensuality are his principal themes, while the other five Sins receive but the scantiest mention. To be proud, says Shakespeare's Launce, was "Eve's legacy." [8] The legacy of Adam is apparent in an English woodcut of the late seventeenth century, entitled "Man's Shameful Fall," where the peacock of Pride stands by Eve, and the goat of Incontinence by Adam.[9]

2. *The Four Temperaments, the Tree of Sin, Sin on Trial*

When man was in a state of innocent perfection the four Humours, or fluids, of his body were in harmonious equilibrium, but with the Fall this balance was destroyed, one or another of the Humours predominated, and body and soul were touched with corruption, the one by disease, the other by vice. In Dürer's great and solemn engraving "The Fall of Man," the Four Humours, or Temperaments, are expressed by four animals: the choleric cat, the phlegmatic ox, the sanguine rabbit, and the melancholy elk.[1] Each Temperament was thought to be peculiarly addicted to one or another of the Deadly Sins: the Choleric to Pride and Wrath; the Phlegmatic to Gluttony and Sloth; the Sanguine to Lechery and perhaps Envy; the Melancholic to Avarice and the Despairing to Sloth. But the equating of animals with the Temperaments, which we see in Dürer's engraving, was not firmly established in iconographical tradition, and other associations were possible. Thus, in various Books of Hours,[2] in the corners of the page on which the Zodiacal Man is illustrated, the Four Temperaments are related to the Four Elements and to animals other than the ones Dürer employed. The Choleric temperament is associated with fire and a lion; the Phlegmatic with water and a sheep; the Sanguine with air and a monkey; the Melancholic with earth and a boar. The scheme of the "Complessioni" in Cesare Ripa's *Iconologia* [3] provides the same connection between the Four Temperaments and the Four Elements and gives to the Choleric man a lion, to the Phlegmatic a badger, to the Sanguine a goat, and to the Melancholic a sparrow.

Ripa adds some attributes observable in Henry Peacham's [4] four emblems of the Temperaments. Melancholia is a solitary man in a dense forest, engaged at his studies. He has no company save "Madge the Owle, and melancholy Pusse, / Light–loathing creatures, hateful, ominous." His mouth is bound up; "one foote on Cube is fix't" to secure him constancy; the purse he holds indicates avarice. Sanguis is a young man playing upon a lute and wearing a garland; a goat beside him munches on grapes. Cholera is a man with a sword and a lion. Phlegma, with a tortoise, "drinkes, spits, or nodding, in the chimney sleepes." (In this instance Ripa differs from Peacham, alloting to this Temperament a badger as well as a tortoise.)

Barten Holyday's *Technogamia, or the Marriages of the Arts,*[5] a tedious academic allegorical drama published in 1618 and performed before James I in 1621, presents a large company of personifications, among them The Four Temperaments. The Temperaments were costumed in colors approximating those in Ripa but there were some novel attributes. Choler was dressed in yellow; on the breast of his suit "were exprest two fellows wrastling;" his hat bore "a fist with a club in it." Phlegmatico was "in a pale russet Suite; on the backe whereof was express'd one filling a Pipe of Tobacco; on the brest one taking Tobacco; his Hat beset round with Tobacco-pipes: with a Can of drinke hanging at his girdle." Sanguis was all in red; on the breast of his suit was depicted "a man with his nose bleeding; on the back, one let bloud in the arme." Melancholy was clothed in black; no attribute is mentioned. Discordant colors, fantastic symbols, and grotesque actions may have served to remind thoughtful spectators of the confusion wrought in Man's nature when the original balance of the Humours was disturbed by disobedience to God's command.

Consequent upon the Fall is moral, intellectual, and physical confusion. This chaos is emblematized in a strange, complex design (Fig. 9) of the Tree of Sin in one of Father Jan (Johannes) David's books [6] which is based upon a verse in the Epistle of St. James (1:15): "Concupiscentia, cum conceperit, parit peccatum: peccatum vero, cum consummatum fuerit, generat mortem." The Soul, a forlorn woman holding a skull, is bound by a coiled serpent to a withered tree from which a devil issues, belching fire. The details, the gallows on the far horizon of the wintry landscape, the man falling through the frozen river, the man burning in the bonfire, reinforce the picture's message of warning and terror. The confusion in nature caused by the Sin of Adam is differently emblematized by Francis Quarles (Bk. I, no. 2) [7] in a design taken from the *Typus Mundi.* Amid roaring winds, tempestuous seas, and raging fire there is a globe into which the sword of Sin has been thrust and from this globe protrude the animal heads of the Seven Deadly Sins.

Two writers of the early Stuart period have told how Sin is brought to trial before God. The time of the trial is not specified; it is certainly not immediately after the Fall, and certainly precedes the Last

Judgment. The subject forms the climax of Richard Barnard's *The Isle of Man* (1627) [8] which was widely read for many years and is still memorable for its influence on Bunyan's *The Holy War*. While much of it is not germane to our purpose and need not be summarized, it should be noted that there is a trial in the court of law before Justice, who is Christ. The charges are not brought against Sin himself, however, but against Mistress Heart, Old Man Wilful Will, Covetousness, and Idolatry (who is equated with Papistry). Sin himself is brought to trial in Humphrey Mills' semidramatic poem "The Alluring Sleights of Sin." [9] The Soul complains that Sin has failed to redeem the promises of happiness which have been his instruments of temptation. Then, following a familiar medieval tradition, the Soul reproaches the Body for his downfall. An appeal is taken to God, Who requires that Sin be brought before the bar of Justice. Having been arraigned, the accused calls as character witnesses Covetousness, Lust, Pride, and Ignorance. They attempt to prove that Sin has given Man (as the Soul is now called) what was promised him, but the Divine Judge declares that such testimony makes the case all the worse. Witnesses for the prosecution are then called: Knowledge, Liberality, Chastity, and Humility, and then Saints and Angels. Man (according to a sort of stage direction) "presseth God by Argument to destroy Sin," and then (as another stage direction indicates) "the Damned are called to witnesse against Sinne," which they do at great length. In the end Sin is found guilty and sentenced with the Vices who are his assistants to hell.

This piece is followed [10] by a second semidramatic poem in which Mills reveals a power of imagination not evident in his other work. It is called "An Indightment against Death by Life, being plaintiffe." Life, appealing to God, delivers a long harangue on Death's misdeeds in afflicting families, lovers, and friends, and concludes passionately: "The world is witness what I speake is true." In refutation, Death, with a telling resort to the *tu quoque*, declares that Life, being to blame for many evils, is more guilty than he; moreover, he, Death, is God's servant: "I doe thy worke, for I am rul'd by thee." Death asks permission to have his assistants plead for him, and a strange procession of witnesses appears in court. First, the Magistrate, who argues that the fear of Death helps him to enforce the law; then, the Heir, who has strong reasons for valuing Death's services; then, the Parish Clerk, who receives a fee for every burial service, and the Sexton, who is paid for tolling the bell; then the Searchers, or corpse–winders, "two old women, weake and very poor," whose livelihood depends upon Death because they prepare the dead for burial; and then the coffin–maker, the Bearers, and the Grave–digger. Last of all, with an impressive change from character–types to a personification, the Grave speaks, urging his need for Death to bring him sustenance. Life rebuts all the testimony by demonstrating that self–interest motivates all the witnesses. God pronounces judgment, sentencing not only Death but Sin to destruction. At this moment Satan appears and sues for reprieves for both Sin and Death. God rebukes Satan but for his own purposes grants the reprieves, declaring, however, that both shall be punished in the end.

The iniquitous collaboration of the Devil, Sin, and Death forms part of the complex symbolism of a large engraving by Hieronimus Wierex after a design by A. B. Francke (1578).[11] Mundanus Homo is seen falling through a broken ceiling into a dungeon where Diabolus is ready to spring a net to entrap him. Peccatum, a naked negress, aims a dart at him and Mors, not a skeleton but a repulsive, muscular crone evidently drawn from an anatomical cadaver, has aimed an arrow at him but Divine Grace, appearing from the clouds and holding in one arm a crown, a palm branch, and a lamb, stops the arrow. The scene is of course not in Eden; this is the Fall not of Adam but of Everyman who has yielded to worldly temptations. A somewhat similar but much simpler concept is an emblem showing the Soul caught in a net spread by Death (Fig. 10) which Quarles (Bk. III, no. 9) took from Father Hugo.[12]

3. Death

There is a fourteenth–century mystery play performed at Norwich, not part of one of the cycles but a separate piece, entitled *The Temptation of Man in Paradise*.[1] In it a moving episode occurs after Adam has eaten of the forbidden fruit. Dolor and Miseria enter (Eve is not present and Adam is here really Everyman) and take Man by both arms. Dolor tells him that he "in bondage from hence shall be. / Now must thou me, Dolor, have allways in sight." Miseria declares that he must "taste and byte" of misery and Man expresses his mournful recognition of the fact that for this "ther is no remedye." Thus begins the eventful history whose last scene is enacted in the greatest of the morality plays, *Everyman*.

Exiled from Eden and companioned by Sadness and Misery, Man, who had been heedless of forewarnings of the true nature of the Tree of Knowledge, encounters Death. "The Globe of the Elements enclosed in the Orbe of the Moone," writes an Elizabethan astronomer,[2] "I call the Globe of Mortalitie because it is the peculiare Empire of Death. For above the Moone they feare not his force." The third of the preliminary cuts in Holbein's *Dance of Death* shows the gate of Paradise guarded by an angel with a sword; Death lurks nearby, ready to welcome Adam and Eve into his world. A beautiful woodcut (Fig. 11), earlier than Holbein's, is found in Raoul de Presles' French translation of *The City of God*, in Laurent de Premierfait's French version of Boccaccio's *De Casibus illustrium virorum*, in a French translation of the Bible, and elsewhere.[3] Here Death with his scythe stands immediately outside the gate from which Adam and Eve have been thrust and the grave simplicity of this design is very different from the mocking tone of Holbein's design. This motive first appears in an English book in an excessively rare volume entitled *The true and lyvely historyke purtreature of the Woll* [Whole] *Bible*, printed at Lyons in 1533.[4] Among its many quaint little cuts there is one of Death walking side by side with Adam and Eve as they emerge from Paradise. Followers and imitators of Holbein amplified this subject, exaggerating its emotionality. Thus, in a small unsigned engraving (ca. 1600) Death strums on a stringed instrument as he dances before the guilty pair.[5] In a large engraving of the seventeenth century (Fig. 12) Death hilariously conducts Adam and Eve into the world beyond the gate, and their spiritual agony seems to be shared by the troubled animals near them.[6] Death is one of the personifications appearing in Giovanni Battista Andreini's *L'Adamo, Sacra Representatione* (Milan, 1613), a choral drama well known to English scholars because it may have influenced Milton. Very effective in an operatic way is the scene where Death, rising amid flames and storm, appears to Adam and Eve.[7]

When our First Parents have been cast forth, Death triumphs not only in this world but within sullied Eden itself, as shown in the first of a series of plates (Fig. 13) by Theodore Galle in Father David's *Paradisus Sponsi et Sponsae* (1607) where the Garden of Eden and of Nature is contrasted with the Garden of Grace and of Christ. A serpent is still coiled round the tree growing in the midst of Eden; on the greensward a satyr dances to the piping of his fellows; and in the center stands a robed and sceptered Death.

Yet the contrasted Gardens also show that the Pauline promise is held out to sustain Man on his earthly pilgrimage. In paintings of the

Crucifixion (for example, one in the cloister of St. Mary's Church in Prague) the fatal fruit may be shown hanging from one arm of the Cross. The theme, it is needless to say, is an outgrowth from the Legend of the Holy Cross. From innumerable visualizations of this promise a few may be chosen for comment. A fifteenth-century French *Horae* has English connections because it is of the Sarum use and was probably exported to England. In it there is a miniature of Christ on a Cross which is placed among the branches of the Tree of Knowledge while at the base of the Tree the Serpent offers the fruit to Adam and Eve.[8] More complex is a sixteenth-century English oil painting on panel now in the Victoria and Albert Museum. Here the Tree of Knowledge and the Tree of Jesse are combined. Beside it stand Adam and Eve, above them the Serpent is coiled round the trunk, and above the Serpent Jesse lies athwart the tree, which continues to rise higher, behind rather than from his body. Kings and other personages sit upon the branches and the Virgin and Child at the top. In one of the Hugo–Quarles emblems (Bk. IV, no. 14) there is a suggestion of the traditional contrast between the *Arbor Bona* and the *Arbor Mala*, for the Soul reposes in quiet confidence in the shade of a tree at which Divine Love has been crucified. The engraved title page of an antiquarian work by John Weever entitled *Ancient Funerall Monuments* (1631) (Fig. 14) derives directly from St. Paul (I Corinthians 15:21–22). On the left is a skeleton whose foot is on a spade which suggests the grave, and the doom of Adam to dig the ground but which is also—though the association is probably not implied in this design—an emblem of Hope. The skeleton holds an apple in its hand and above him is an inscription: "Primus Adam de terra terrenus" and below: "Ut in Adamo omnes moriuntur." Opposite, on the right, is Christ, with the banner of the Cross, treading the Serpent under his feet. The inscriptions are: "Secundus Adam Dominus de Caelo" and "Ita in Christo omnes vivificabuntur."

Inappropriate though it may seem in such a setting, there must have been an awareness of the doom and the promise alike in a masque, now lost but recorded in the *Revels' Accounts*, which was presented at the court of Edward VI as part of the Easter festivities of 1553.[9] It is first referred to as "A Maske of Deaths, being medyoxes half man, half death," and subsequently as "A Masque of Medioxes being half death, half man."[10] So far as I know, no guess has been advanced as to the nature of this entertainment. I surmise that the masquers played beings intermediate between this world and the next, between life and death,

8

and further, that the performance at Eastertide was symbolic of Christ's Victory over Death. According to the Accounts, the performers wore headpieces that were "double visaged, the one side like a man and the other like death." It was not a matter of bifrontality—that is, two full faces, before and behind, as in innumerable pictures of Fortune, Fraud, and other personifications—but of contrasting profiles, as in pictures of the human head of which one half is a skull and the other covered with flesh. One cannot hope to reconstruct the complexities of the masque but one can imagine the slow entry of the line of skull-headed dancers—an elaborately lugubrious procession like that which, Vasari tells us, Piero di Cosimo designed for the Florentine court.[11] The dancers cross the platform and then, turning, reveal the faces of the living, emblematic of the triumph of Life over Death.

4. Time, before the Fall

Fallen Man, tempted by Satan to sin and therefore doomed to die, is subject to the government of Time. Time, like Death, is God's servant and has power over the temporal world. In James Day's poem "The Worldes Metamorphosis," [1] a narrative of the Creation, the Temptation, and Fall of Man, and of the changes in the natural world consequent upon the Fall, Time makes his appearance at the moment of the creation of form out of chaos:

> Then Time his houres began to measure out,
> And he most nimbly garison's about
> This new created Orbe: he tooke his flight
> And hurried restlesse on both day and night,
> His motion was so quicke, that scarce twas ey'd.
> He for ten thousand worldes won't squint aside,
> Nor once turne backe his head. . . .
> No weapon all this while for his defence
> He bore, he dealt with none but innocence.

This was before the Fall. Thereafter all things go awry:

> The Lion mild ere while for want of foode,
> Doth fill his paunch with unaccustomed blood,

and ravenous beasts would have devoured Adam and Eve had not Mercy protected them. Time takes no further part in the action of this poem.

9

But his duties in the Garden of Eden are important, as told in the Jacobean poem, too little known today, by Thomas Peyton, *The Glasse of Time, in the two first ages* (1620).[2] Written in iambic couplets, the poem moves at a leisurely pace and it is not till page twenty–seven that we come to the story. A brief account of Adam's loneliness and of his gladness when God fashions Eve leads to the abrupt appearance of Satan who questions Eve about the forbidden tree and "watches Time" preparing to avail himself of Opportunity when it is afforded him. The situation is illustrated in a little woodcut (Fig. 15) in which Time, with scythe and winged hourglass, is the central figure. Not for many pages does the poet again return to his story. After the Parliament of Heaven God pronounces judgment upon Adam and Eve.

> The Register that up this order drew
> Was Time it selfe clad all in Azure blew,
> Wing'd like an Angel, shadowed with a vaile,
> And Truth his Daughter bearing up his traile,
> Nobly attended with a lady kind,
> More quick and nimble then the swift foote hinde.
> Within his mouth a lofty Trumpe doth stand,
> And a sharpe sith or sickle in his hand.
> A glasse of sand continually that runs,
> Within his way no living thing he shuns,
> Lock't long before his head, behind all bald,
> To shew whats past can never be recal'd.

The vignette at the top of Peyton's title page (Fig. 16) shows some of these particulars. The artist has omitted the trumpet, an unusual attribute but not without parallels, for Time is sometimes conflated with Fame instead of being, as in the Petrarchan Triumphs, the destroyer of Fame. His office as "Register" is explicable when we remember that he is often associated with Memory and History. The comparison with the swift–footed hind was probably suggested to Peyton by Time's satyr–legs, though this characteristic is of different origin and need not suggest Time's swiftness.

A digression on the evils of the present time follows and when the narrative is resumed, God throws the mantle of his Mercy upon Adam and Eve, preparing them to depart from Paradise and enter the world of Time and Fortune and Death. Acting as God's messenger, Time

> mild and gently takes them by the hand,
> Shewes them the gate that to the east doth stand,

10

Leades them along lamenting of their fall,
For all their cryes, sets them without the wall,
Bars up the dore with such an iron lever,
As none alive that once can enter ever.

Time sets Justicia, Misericordia, Charitas, and Veritas as "Cherubins"
at the gate, and leaving the world to the protection of Dame Nature
he returns to heaven. The allegory is here confused, for Time's own
office is in the temporal world.

CHAPTER 2. THE WORLD OF TIME

1. Time the Destroyer

Man must pursue his journey along the Path of Life through the world of Time.[1] "I understand," says David Person,[2] "only such things to be in Time as are subject to mutations, changes, risings, and fallings, such as are all natural things below the Sphere of the Moon." Thus, when Mutability, storming the heavens to assert her claim to rule, reached the lunar circle she found sitting by the "silver gates" of the "bright shining palace" of the Moon an "aged Sire, with hourglass in hand" whose name was Time.[3] He was at the farthest boundary of his dominion; he could not enter in. But within the nether sphere he dwells in an "auncient pallace" of his own, exercising, as Abraham Fraunce tells us,[4] unchallengeable authority.

Time was a great man out of all measure, shewing a kinde of maiestie in his forehead. His face had three seuerall semblances: his browe and eyes resembling middle age; his mouth and cheekes youth; his beard, olde age. He had before him three great glasses, looking now in one, now in an other: and, according to that which he saw in them, he framed his countenance: sometimes ioyeus and mery, sometimes grave and moderate, sometimes sad and heavy. On his left side was Weeping; on his right side, Laughing. . . . About him an infinite number of seruitors: the Day and the Night, with their daughter Aurora, betweene them both . . . Peace, Warre, Plenty, Dearth, Life, Death, Pouertue, Loue, Hate, and other mighty potentates. . . . they were all ready and prest to obey him. . . . At the feete of Tyme stood Desteny, with a booke before her: which Fortune and Chaunce did tosse and turn incessantly.

Destiny writes down Time's decrees and these are put in execution by the Seasons, the Day and Night, the Hours and the Minutes, so bringing to pass all things in the world.

Oftentimes there come messengers . . . saying, such an one hath builded a fortresse against the Maiestie and dominion of Tyme: another hath erected an image, a third hath composed a booke, all intending to be masters and triumphers ouer Tyme. Tyme, perseauing this, looketh in his glasses, held by Verity and doth but smile at their attempts, willing Desteny to write his pleasure, and giuing authoritie vnto Fortune. Fortune, taking deliteth in such toyes for a time, committeth them afterwards to the power of fire or war, or else returneth them againe before the feete of Tyme, where, as soone as they are once set downe, they vanish away presently, and neuer apeare againe.

A Jacobean poet tells us how in a dream he visited the "Palace of Old Cronos." [5] There he saw Time swinging his scythe and wearying his arms "wuth killing," but his attention was fixed upon Mutation, daughter and eldest child of Time.[6] She turned a great wheel "Where millions sought with ladders to attaine / The top, but when she stird, still downe they came . . ." Logos, or Reason, a "reverend syre," tells the poet of the tasks which Mutation, working under heavenly direction, performs: the fall of the angels; the changes in the planets; the changes in the elements through the action of rivers, thunder and lightning,

winds, and seas; the fall of Adam and of princes; the changes in religion; the changes in the interior of the earth (such as the exhaustion
of mines); the destruction of great cities. "Where's stately Jericho?"
Darkness has invaded Jerusalem and there "irreligion and uncleannesse
sit." Rome likewise has fallen upon evil days. Only in the North, where
England is the dwelling–place of Humility and Peace, has True Religion a home. Logos then directs his discourse from the great world of
nature and human society to the microcosm, for in the human body
we see youth and beauty decaying to "Times map of ruine and dis-
grace." "All things taste of Mutabilitie."

The dominant motive in both these passages is that of the Destroyer—
"Tempus edax rerum," "cormorant, devouring Time." [7] "Time, that
devour'st all mortality!" exclaims a character in one of John Marston's
plays.[8] In one of the moralities Time himself appears "with a similitude
of dust and rust." [9] Thomas Andrew characterizes Time as "Thou great
consumer of huge monuments, / That mak'st stiffe marble turne to
cindry dust." [10] "I have seen Time drawn by a painter," says Henry
Peacham,[11] "standing upon an old ruin, winged, and with iron teeth."
On Willem Swidden's engraved title page (Fig. 17) of a Dutch work
on Roman archaeology,[12] Time is in the very act of gnawing upon a
ruined cornice. Personifications of imperial Rome and of Architecture
preside over the scene, and the River Tiber and the Roman wolf are
witnesses of the destruction; in the background are ruined buildings
and monuments, some of them identifiable. A similar design introducing François Perrier's treatise on those monuments of Rome which
have, as the title says, "escaped the envious tooth of Time" shows the
Destroyer gnawing at the knee of the Torso Belvedere.[13] A simpler
version of the same theme shows Time sitting atop a ruined arch; on
the ground below are an aged man and Death.[14] In a design by Otho
Van Veen a truly ferocious Time, having struck down Strength and
Eloquence, is about to attack the famous marble group of the Three
Graces [15] (Fig. 18). A painting described by Nicholas Flammel [16]
showed Mercury (that is, the Arts), and "against him there came running and flying with open wings, a great old man, who upon his head
had an houreglasse fastened, and in his hands a hooke (or sithe), with
the which, in terrible and furious manner, hee would have cut off the
feet of Mercury."

In the Garden of Adonis in *The Faerie Queene* (III, 6, 39–41) all
things would be delightful "were it not that Time their troubler is."
He is the enemy of Beauty and of everything that grows in the Garden,

mowing down flowers, flinging their glory to the ground, and with his "flaggy wings" beating down leaves and buds. "Ne ever pittie may relent his malice hard." In another passage in *The Faerie Queene* (IV, 2, 33) Spenser betrays the fact that he did not realize, as did Milton, that it was Chaucer himself who "left half-told" *The Squire's Tale*. He attributes its fragmentary condition to Time's destructiveness:

> But wicked Time that all good thoughts doth waste,
> And workes of noblest wits to nought out weare,
> That famous moniment hath quite defaste,
> And robd the world of threasure endlesse deare.

Yet the Art of Letters may escape the ravages of Time, for it is more lasting than bronze or marble. A seventeenth-century engraving by Martin Tyroff [17] shows History compiling her records as she sits among classical ruins (Fig. 19). Below her, Time, not content with his destruction of the material Past, is tearing out the leaves of a book and eating them. Love (a Cupid) is attempting to retrieve a page from his devouring jaws. Two of the title pages of the *Acta Sanctorum* of the Bollandists (Antwerp, 1643) are similar. In one, History is recording the deeds of the saints, and numerous Cupids are bringing her large tomes; there are flanking figures of Learning and Truth. Inscriptions declare that it is History's function to bring back the Past and to reveal what is obscure. But in a sort of subterranean cellar Time crouches, gnawing on the pages of a book which Love is attempting to snatch from him (Fig. 20). On the other title page Faith, attended by Truth, Study, and Probity, hold firm a pedestal inscribed "Acta Sanctorum" which Time is endeavoring to overturn. The relationship between Time and Saturn has been explained by Professor Panofsky and all that needs to be said here is that it accounts for the many designs of Time eating his own children,[18] for his lameness, and for other characteristics. The emblematic title page of Francis Bacon's *The Historie of Life and Death* (1638), an English version of the Latin text of 1623, implies a resolute confidence that great literature can withstand the onslaughts of Time. At the top, on one side, is the figure of Art with an outstretched wand and an inscription: "Art can stay Nature's decay." On the other side is a figure of Time with an inscription: "Let Time look on this book."

The treasure laid up on earth within the domain of Time is corruptible; the Soul on its journey through Life is burdened with such superfluities. Earthly renown is of no avail. Time the victor over Fame is the fifth episode in every sequence of Petrarchan Triumphs, but it is most unusual for him to be shown trampling upon a sack "dans lequel la Renommée avait entassé ses tresors." [19] But there are more or less close analogies to the sack itself. An emblem by Joannes Sambucus (Fig. 21) shows Time, who hovers above with his scythe, threatening a man and woman. With a gesture the man abandons a coffer resting on the ground behind him.[20] This object may be thought of as the chest of Time. "Alas," says Shakespeare (Sonnet 64), "that Time's beauty should in Time's chest be hid!" Most commentators accept Malone's suggestion that a play on words is intended, "chest" being in Elizabethan English both a jewel box and a coffin. I am inclined to agree, however, with George Steevens who long ago noted the parallel between this line and the words of Ulysses (*Troilus and Cressida*, III.3.145–150):

> Time hath, my lord, a wallet at his back,
> Wherein he puts alms for oblivion,
> A great–siz'd monster of ingratitudes.
> Those scraps are good deeds past, which are devour'd
> As fast as they are made, forgot as soon
> As done.

Parallels in two anonymous plays of earlier date have been overlooked. The purpose of one of these [21] is to urge London to take warning from the fate of Antwerp. Time, speaking the Epilogue, says that in order to give this warning he

> Hath stay'd his course, to rubbe the memory
> Of actions long since cast behind his back.

To rub must mean to polish or refurbish a dim memory, and casting actions behind his back is an image similar to that of putting "alms for oblivion" in his wallet. In the other play [22] there is a description of

> Ariosto's old swift–paced man,
> Whose name is Time, who never lins [ceases] to run,
> Loaden with bundles of decayed names,
> The which in Lethe's lake he doth entomb,
> Save only those which swan–like scholars take,
> And do deliver from that greedy lake.

A broadside called *The Travels of Time: Loaden with Popish Trumperies* (1624),[23] inspired by James I's proclamation expelling

16

the Jesuits, uses the image for purposes of antipapist polemic. When his daughter Truth asks him what it is "which on your back you bear so swift away," Time replies:

> I took upon my aged Back
> This load of Vanity, this Pedlar's pack,
> This Trunk of Trash and Romish Trumperies . . .
> This Burden back to Rome I'll bear again.

A woodcut in a black–letter ballad [24] conveys the same idea: Time has on his back a huge bag from which protrude a tiara and other objects (Fig. 22). In yet another ballad there is a similar woodcut.[25]

2. Time, "the nurse and breeder of all good" [1]

Ruthlessly destructive though Time is, he can be kindly and merciful. The thought is consoling to Man as he enters upon the later stages of his eventful history. The antithetical characteristics are touchingly visualized in several of the Horatian Emblems.[2] In one scene, Old Age is lying in bed and Time is driving from him Love, Sleep, Youth, and Grace; but in another, Old Age is tenderly supported by Friendship and Time, though driving off Love, Appetite, Sleep (wearing a wreath of poppies), and Play (with a tambourine), is leading up the consolers, Temperance with her bridle, Prudence with her mirror, and Divine Love with a laurel wreath (Fig. 23). Akin to Old Age is Wisdom, an elderly man, whose arm is upon Time's shoulder as he turns from Fear (a rabbit), Care, Rancor, and other troubles to philosophic studies. Time himself is not present in another scene where Wisdom, who is poignantly aware of the shortness and uncertainty of human life, is accompanied by four personifications: Hope with a flower, Fear with a rabbit, Good Times with a horn of plenty, and Bad Times with a sword and torch. Overhead are "the thin–spun" thread of life and "the abhored shears." Two other plates teach the proper deportment of Wisdom in the presence of Time or Opportunity: greeting him hospitably on his arrival and on his departure bidding him farewell without disquiet. In one design Pallas, "Philosophia Vitae Magistra," stands for Wisdom and Time aids in curing her sickness of heart by introducing to her a little child in motley, for Wisdom may on occasion condescend to indulge in a little folly.

One of the loveliest of printers' devices was used by a family at Lyons for half a century.[3] Time is hitched to a plough guided by

Virtue, and Fortune, following, scatters seed. Equally encouraging is an emblem in an anonymous English collection [4] where Learning, holding a book and the wise serpent and plodding along the path that leads to the City of Wisdom, is offered a crown by Time. But Time discriminates, evincing approval or disapproval as the case may be. Four plates by one of the Van de Passe family engraved from designs by Martin de Vos, are copied in Jacob de Zetter's *Philosophia Practica* (1644). In the first, Tempus, a kindly patron, stands by Diligence who is spinning. In the second, he crowns Felicity who holds an abundance of the fruits of her labors.[5] In the third, he flies past sleeping Negligence. In the fourth, he offers to Industry a crown and what seems to be a diploma or certificate, but he threatens Laziness with a club and scourge. In the background of this last scene are contrasting episodes of prosperity and poverty.

Time winnows the good from the bad, the false from the true. Thomas Bancroft describes how "old Herald Time" holds "dusty scales" in which he weighs the worth of gentry. Fortune tips the scales up and down; brainless gallants soar aloft but men possessing a "weight of worth" sink so that for them the earth becomes a pedestal of honor.[6] Time is an ally of Justice and may be the executioner of her decrees. Time, says one of the authors of *The Mirrour for Magistrates* (XXIV, 308), "trieth out both truth and also treason." He is "the old justice that examines all such offenders" (*As You Like It*, IV.i.203). One of his offices is "to unmask Falsehood and bring Truth to light" (*The Rape of Lucrece*, line 939). In this capacity he is "that old common arbitrator" (*Troilus and Cressida*, IV.5.225). He is the "grave Censurer of things long since ore past." [7] Corrozet and Capaccio have emblems of him holding the scales of Justice.[8] When in an English emblem he stands by an open coffin and blows upon a trumpet,[9] the trumpet is analogous to the scales, for it is not the trumpet of Fame but of the Last Judgment. In an engraving after a design by Otho Van Veen Time conducts Luxuria to hell; Vengeance (here retributive Justice) following after brandishes a whip.[10] On the title page of *The Scourge of Folly* (ca. 1610) and of *A Scourge for Paper–Persecutors* (1625) (Fig. 24), both by John Davies of Hereford, Time serves as a whipping post for Folly who, mounted on his back, is chastised by Wit. Time himself may wield the scourge. The title page of Giovanni Andrea Gilio's *Topica Poetica* (Venice, 1580) depicts a formidable Tempus brandishing a whip (Fig. 25). This is a precise visual image of Hamlet's verbal image of "the whips and scorns of Time." [11] In Act I of *The*

Sun's Darling by Dekker and Ford he enters "whipping Folly before him." [12] In a play performed by students at Oxford a figure of Time is described as holding a whip in one hand.[13]

As the ally of Justice Time "brings Truth to light." The noble theme of "Veritas Filia Temporis" [14] has been treated in scholarly articles [15] and I shall touch but lightly on it. No emblem is more familiar than that of Time leading forth his daughter from a cave or dungeon (Fig. 26). Often Envy is raving impotently behind them, or she may be accompanied by Strife and Discord or Slander.[16] A variant shows a flying, bat–winged demon labeled "Hypocrisy" vomiting upon Truth as Time is rescuing her.[17] In another, Time hovers in mid–air and reaches down to draw Truth from the cave, while Fraud, brandishing a scourge, endeavors to force her down again.[18] The anonymous writer of *The welspoken Nobody*, a broadside of the time of Edward VI, accuses the papists of having locked Lady Truth in a cage but confidently affirms that Time, "the father of Veritie," "will not suffer her to be hidden by any coloured fraude or deceit." When Time and a philosopher stand behind the coping of a well from which Truth is rising,[19] there is no suggestion of envious opposition nor, indeed, though Time is a witness of this resurrection, that he is Truth's rescuer. The paternal–filial relationship is implied in a design where Veritas, holding a book and a lighted candle, holds also a scythe and has an hourglass on her head.[20] There is no suggestion of Time's function in a device of Truth with the "Verbum Dei" and a candle and the motto: "Veritas vincet tandem." [21] Nor is Time present in a sensational illustration (Fig. 27) in one of Jacob Cats' poems where Truth rises in a blaze of glory from a tomb.[22]

The theme of Time as the revealer of Truth was useful in religious controversy and political propaganda. On January 14, 1559, Queen Elizabeth, celebrating her accession to the throne, went in procession through London. Here is part of an account of the occasion: [23] "In a pageant erected near the Little Conduit in the upper end of Cheapside, an old man with a scythe and wings, representing Time, appeared, coming out of a hollow place or cave, leading another person all clad in white silk, gracefully apparelled, who represented Truth (the daughter of Time); which lady had a book in her hand, on which was written *Verbum Veritatis*. . . . It was the Bible in English." The book was presented to the Queen, who kissed it. This pageant represented the triumph of True Religion and the "open Bible" following the death of Mary.

There are reminiscences of this in the Dumb Show which opens Dekker's *The Whore of Babylon* (ca. 1594).[24] It is introduced by a Prologue:

> Winged Time that long agoe flew hence
> You must fetch backe, with all those golden yeares
> He stole, and here imagine still he stands,
> Thrusting his silver locke into your hands.
> There hold it but two howres. It shall from Graves
> Raise up the dead.

The spectators are bidden to recall events of long ago, for it is not personified Truth which is to be raised from graves but the memory of the great dead. The Dumb Show that follows reveals Truth as well as Time, both clothed in black. Truth is sleeping and Time tries to awaken her, "but not being able to doe it, he sits by her and mourns." Then a funeral procession passes, indicating that Queen Mary's reign is over and Elizabeth's has begun, whereupon the costumes of Time and Truth are changed: Truth, now awake, is crowned and wears "a robe spotted with Starres" and Time's "properties . . . [are] altered into silver." With this transformation the Dumb Show ends and the play begins.

The Tempus–Veritas complex was for many years introduced into civic pageantry. Thus, in Thomas Middleton's Lord Mayors' Show *The Triumphs of Truth*[25] Time rode on the "frame" of Truth's chariot; but the rescue from the cave was not enacted, nor was it suggested that Truth is Time's daughter. Many years later the two appear along with other personifications in two pageants by John Tatham celebrating the Restoration of Charles II. *Londons Glory Represented by Time, Truth and Fame* included three speeches delivered from platforms, "large and good fabricks," as the King was on his way to the Guildhall. Time spoke first, craving pardon for having been "a property to slaves" (the Commonwealth government). Then Truth, who had been for so long abused, welcomed the true sovereign and afterward Fame averred that she had never forsaken Charles and promised to celebrate his future glories. In the Lord Mayors' Show that took place three months later Time drove a chariot in which rode Peace, Truth, and Plenty. He declared that as "the Register of all Mens acts" he had brought secrets to light and had requited treachery, and brought "home a *Sovereign* remedy," restoring Peace and Truth.[26]

Truth Brought to Light and Discovered by Time (1651),[27] an anonymous account of the Overbury murder, which many years earlier had shaken London society, has a title page by John Droeshout (Fig. 28). The engraving does not show Time discovering Truth; Time and Truth are, rather, fellow workers, not Rescuer and Rescued. Truth tramples upon Error and Time upon Death; and together they pull back curtains, as in Bronzino's famous painting, to reveal the past, Jacobean England represented by the dead King James. History, treading upon Sloth, records what is given her by Memory, who treads on Oblivion.

This title page may be compared with the flamboyantly cheerful title page (Fig. 29) of a poem by Jacob Cats, *Spiegel van den Ouden ende Nieuwen Tijt* (1635). Here Time is bifrons, the rearward face bearded, aged, and melancholy, the forward face young and smiling. On his head is a winged hourglass and in one hand he has an escapement. He holds a mirror up to Truth, who contemplates with evident satisfaction her reflection therein, and to Memory, who holds in her lap a broken column inscribed "S.P.Q.R.," he hands a document. By Memory sits Prudence with a mirror, not, I think, merely the looking glass that enables her to know herself but a "Mirror for Magistrates" enabling Man through his knowledge of the past to shape his course for the future. The third seated woman is Reason with the caduceus and a restraining bridle. At the top Fame blows a trumpet; her wings are bespangled with ears. Bifrons Time appears again on the title page (Fig. 30) of another of Cats' works.[28] Here he has contrasting wings, a bird's and a bat's, a characteristic we shall meet again.

It is more logical, however, that Time should be trifrons rather than bifrons, or have three heads rather than two, to represent Time Past, Time Present, and Time Future. Thus he appears in one of La Perriere's emblems,[29] which was a tribute to La Perriere's fame in the past, present, and future (Fig. 31). The design of the three animal heads has been explained by Professor Panofsky [30] and I need not pause over it, except to note two English discussions which derive from continental sources. Richard Linche [31] explains that the Wolf symbolizes greedily devouring Past Time, the Lion is the rough and stormy Present Time, and the Dog is Future Time which is full of promise and fawns upon us. Linche has also the triple heads of the Serpent, Lion, and Boar which he takes, through Cartari, from Martianus Capella. Thomas Milles [32] has this to say of the three—headed Egyptian hieroglyphic: "The Wolfes head pointed at time being past, in regarde, that Beast hath no memory, but is all for the instant. The Lyons head figured the time present because of his power and imperious command. They [the Egyptians] set downe the head of a Dogge, licking his chaps with his tongue, for evermore, our succeeding hopes do make us cherish them very carefully." Henry Peacham also states that "the most ancient picture of Eternity was expressed in the forme of a faire Lady, having three heads, signifying those three parts of time, *viz* Time past, Present, and to come." [33] This is confusing for Eternity is not Time! Again Peacham writes: "I rather allow [that is, approve of] his devise that drew him [Time] an old man in a garment of starres, upon his head a Garland of Roses, eares of Corne, and dry stickes." [34] Peacham offers no interpretation of the garland, but are not the roses the future, the ripe corn the present, and the dry sticks the past? Peacham goes on to note that in this design there are two children "one fat, and well liking, the other leane, writing both in one booke" at the feet of Time, but no explanation of these children is offered. That they write in a book identifies them with Memory or History; but why fat and lean? Are they Memory, respectively, of good times and bad?

Time's services to Memory and History are those which he performs for Truth; it is, indeed, by bringing Truth to light that he enables History, with the assistance of Memory, to record the past and to award Fame to those who deserve it. Historia, in Ripa, writes in a book supported upon the shoulders of Time. Her foot rests upon a square stone, suggestive of the incorruptible stability of History, and her head is turned towards the past. The title page of Edward Grimestone's translation of Jean de Serres' *Generall Historie of France* (1611) has, at the top, Time and Justice with their conventional attributes and, at the bottom, Fame with a trumpet and palm branch and History with a pen in one hand and book in the other. Drayton says that Time is Fame's page, bearing her stately train.[35]

3. The Divisions of Time

A character in *Respublica* (1792 f.) describes Time:

> That shuttle–brained tall man . . .
> I knowe hym; he carrieth a clocke on his heade,
> A sandglasse in his hande, a diall in his forehead.

Here as in innumerable other examples we have on the one hand the rhythmic movement of the loom and the rhythmic tick of the clock and on the other the steady, uninterrupted movement of the shadow on the dial and the like fall of the sand in the glass. The poets sometimes conceive of Time's course as continuous, without perceptible pause and renewal. "Time's thievish progress," says Shakespeare (Sonnet 77) is marked by the "shady stealth" of the dial, and varying the image he contrasts "the rough torrent of Occasion" (the opportunity for immediate action) with the quiet "stream of Time." [1]

On the other hand, it is equally, or perhaps more, natural to think of Time as divided into periods, long or short, beating rhythmically. Francis Meres writes of Opportunity: "As the Cage must bee shut, before the birds be flowne: so tide and time must bee taken, while they may be had. *Posthac occasio calva.* Time is balde behind, therefore must be taken by the forelock." [2] Meres follows this platitude with many examples of actions undertaken too late. But another moralizer argues adversely. "The proverb drops too short," says Roger Matthew, "that saieth *Time and Tide stay not:* Tides creepe on but slowly and have their interstices, stay somewhat when they have their stints, chalenge their returnes: Time is neither so, nor so." [3] When Time is emblematically associated with the heavenly bodies it is not to be thought that he has authority over them. To picture him (Fig. 32) with the sun and moon [4] or with contrasting wings, as on the title page of one of Cats' books,[5] is to convey in obvious fashion the alternation of day and night. Ripa's Horographia holds a sundial and an hourglass, and it is explained that the former is used by day, the latter by night. When, towards the close of Stephen Hawes' *The Pastime of Pleasure* (lines 5608 f.), the seven planets adorn Time with Saturn "derkely flamynge" a like rhythm is suggested (Fig. 33). The woodcut accompanying the poet's description has, despite its crudity, a massive impressiveness.

In *Time's Complaint,* one of the entertainments presented by the scholars of St. John's College, Oxford, during the winter of 1607–8, the years are said to be Time's councilors, the months his nobility, the days the common people, the hours the pages, and the minutes lackeys.[6] It would be difficult to visualize the hours individually and impossible to visualize the minutes, but the months have the twelve signs of the zodiac to represent them.[7] In the great pageant in which Spenser's Mutability demonstrates the governance and sway of Change, Time does not appear.[8] However, when the twelve Signs have followed the Four Seasons and have in turn been followed by Day and Night, and the Hours, and Life and Death, the Titaness draws the lesson:

23

For, who sees not, that *Time* on all doth pray?
But *Times* do change and moue continually.
So nothing here long standeth in one stay.

In an engraving by Philip Galle of Martin Heemskerck's "Triumph of Time," the Seasons attend upon Time's chariot: Ver is pictured with a falcon and a bow and an arrow; Aestas with a sheaf of grain; Autumn, his head bound with grapes, with a cornucopia; and Hyems, muffled up, with a brazier of coals.[9] In Hawes' description the four wings of Time are the Four Seasons. The rhythm of the Seasons is the simplest part of the somewhat complex symbolism in John Squire's Lord Mayors' Show called *The Triumphs of Peace* (1620).[10] Here the Seasons drew the chariot of Time. Spring was in green with a chaplet of flowers in her hand and a quiver at her back; Summer in yellow, her brows decked with ripe corn, a cornucopia in her hand; Autumn was naked, like Bacchus, with his temples wreathed in vines and a cluster of grapes in his hand; and Winter was dressed in a furred gown, holding a pan of burning coals. Even when the indebtedness to Ovid is admitted, this pageant is close to the engraving (Fig. 34) of Time leading the procession of the Seasons [11] in the Horatian Emblems. There are, however, differences: Time is not the traditional old man but a gay, butterflylike sprite, and Spring is not a young girl but a baby. In Chapter 6 we shall meet again with Van Veen's images, for they are suggestive of the theme of the Ages of Human Life. Even closer to that theme is Anthony Munday's Show of 1615 where Time is "coachman to the Life of Man." [12]

There are grace and charm as well as facetiousness, all doubtless pleasing to a youthful audience, in *Corona Minervae* (1635), a masque presented before the royal children at the Museum Minervae.[13] Time, a chief character, must have made an effective appearance "in a Party Coloured Robe, halfe White, halfe Blacke, fringed with Silver, with one wing of a Swan, another of a Bat." After a colloquy with Minerva, Time summons the Seasons; Spring was a female personification, the other three male. Spring wore a gown "figured with flowers"; Summer's robe was straw–colored and on his head was a garland of "Corne–flowers and blew Bottles." Autumn's garment was "Peuke–colour"; he carried a pruning knife and wore a chaplet of grapes and "Damosens." Winter had a beard of icicles and a garland of ivy and holly. After the Seasons disputed their rival merits, there followed the antimasque which was danced by the Season's four pairs of attendants, who conformed to the old tradition of grotesquerie: Spring's attendants were a Frog and a Fisherman; Summer's a Ram and a Sheepsherer; Autumn's a Pig and a Drunken Butcher; Winter's a Cat and a Chimney Sweeper. After their dance there were songs of the Seasons and the transformation scene, essential in all masques, followed: the Temple of Minerva was discovered. An intellectual feast, a banquet of books, was served to the young princes: the jellies were Aulus Gellius, the cakes were Cato, the bacon was Friar Bacon, the apples were Apuleius; and there were other simple puns. With this episode the masque ended abruptly.

Resembling the *Corona Minervae*, and quite as delightful, is Thomas Nabbes' masque, *The Springs Glorie* (1638).[14] "A curtaine being drawne, an alehouse is discovered, out of which Time drives certaine ignorant, and yet Great undertaking Almanack—makers," upbraiding them as charlatans. He bids them practice history and celebrate glorious deeds of the past instead of trying to predict the future. The Almanack—makers quaff ale, mocking Time until by Time's magic they are transformed into satyrs, "hornes growing out of their heads" (sig. F4^r.). Restored to their own shapes, Time drives them off and the scene changes to pleasant garden into which Time brings May attended by Flora and Vertumnus. After a song, a dance, and a vision of Elizium, where eight Princes of Wales appear, Time speaks an epilogue of farewell.

When Time wears a green wreath on his white hair, "manifesting that it is in his power to rebecome youth full, fresh, and blooming," [15] he is likewise associated with Seasons. The rhythm of Time may be suggested not only by the Seasons and by Day and Night but by other, shorter divisions. It is perhaps to suggest the numerical regularity of this rhythm that in a series of the Liberal Arts by Etienne Delaune Arithmetic has the very unusual attribute of an hourglass. In an engraving by Philip Galle after a design by Martin Heemskerck the Seasons run alongside the chariot in which Time rides; the chariot's wheels are cogged and have clock faces with four hands and minute hands. Two hourglasses, a sun dial, and an escapement are drawn on the chariot. The clock—faced wheels with cogs and Time with an escapement in his hand or on his head may be seen in various other illustrations of the Triumph of Time. The escapement is sometimes so sketchily drawn that it is mistaken for a cross.

4. *Tempus–Occasio–Fortuna*

George Chapman writes of "the violent wheels of Time and Fortune." [1] His separation of the wheels of Time from those of Fortune is proper for Time turns not the Wheel of Fortune upon which men rise and descend but the Wheel of Life on which revolve the Ages of Man. But the two images might, intentionally or unintentionally, be conflated. In her long diatribe against Time in *The Rape of Lucrece* (952) Lucrece declares that it is one of Time's functions to "turn the giddy round of Fortune's wheel." The earliest known Spanish copperplate (Fig. 35) shows a hieratic Time, clothed in priestly garments and wearing upon his head an enormous clock suggestive of a mitre, who, while bridled by God, turns a wheel on which figures rise or descend. [2] In a lovely anonymous woodcut the female figure who turns the Wheel is labeled "Zeit." [3] In Arthur Newman's poem "Deserts Complaint," the poet says:

> "I am not like the apes of Time
> That often for a downefall climbe"

and he begs Occasion

> "graunt thus much,
> I may no more thy baldnesse touch;
> O let me come before, that I
> May but thy lucky fore–locke spy,
> And I'll catch at it fast." [4]

Sir William Cornwallys is careful to discriminate between Time which "in it selfe is alwaies one" and Occasion which "runnes Division upon Time" and whose "note is not alwayes one." [5] Time and Occasion are fused in Archibald Symmer's *A Spiritual Posie for Zion* (1629): the forelock of "golden Opportunity" is described and Ovid's words, "Fugit irrevocabile Tempus," are quoted. One of the lovely engravings by Giulio Bonasone in Bocchi's book of emblems shows Occasion about to fall off the rim of Fortune's Wheel and the accompanying verses exhort: "Know the Time." [6] One of Jean Cousin's designs is similar (Fig. 36): "Fortuna sive Occasionis Deus," [7] Fortune in the guise of Opportunity. In an anonymous play Time is addressed as "sweet Opportunity":

"I'll bind myself
To thee in base apprenticeship so long,
Till on thy naked scalp grows hair as thick
As mine, and all hands shall lay hold on thee,
If thou wilt lend me but thy rusty scythe,
To cut down all that stand within my wrongs
And my revenge.[8]

I return to Chapman to quote these lines: "There is a deep nick in Time's restless wheel / For each man's good; when which nick comes, it strikes."[9] One has but to visualize the metaphor and the function of the escapement becomes apparent. In a printer's device Fortune has Time's escapement on her head.[10] The phrase "the nick of time" is first recorded from our period in the Oxford Dictionary. The nick of time is the immediate moment, the opportunity which if not grasped is gone forever.[11] The Tempus–Occasio–Fortuna complex presents a problem, difficult if not impossible to unravel completely. The three personifications may be completely fused, as they are in the morality *Respublica* where Time is identified with Occasion, having "a greate long tuffet of heare before, is bald behind, and "standeth with winged feet on a rolling wheel" (lines 918–949). A study of it so far as it relates more directly to Fortune may be postponed till the next chapter. It is from Occasio that both Time and Fortune borrow the attribute of the forelock.[12] Occasio with winged feet, forelock, and razor is the printer's device of Jhone Hochstraten of Malmo in Sweden who published in 1533 Jhone [John] Gau's *The Richt Way to the Kingdome of Hevine* (ed. H. F. Mitchell, Scottish Text Society, 1888; reproduced, p. 110 of that edition and in *Britwell Court Catalogue*, May 5, 1920, lot no. 205). "Occasion is bald; take her by the forelock," says Chapman[13]; and Shakespeare says: "Take the safest occasion by the front."[14] "Blest Occasion," says John Fletcher, "offers herself . . . to you. . . . Time standing still to point you out your purpose."[15] Something of this idea is conveyed in the old legend of Friar Bacon and the Brazen Head which Robert Greene dramatized in his *Friar Bacon and Friar Bungay*. By his potent art the benign English magician planned to encompass England with a wall of brass to shield her from her enemies. But this could be accomplished only at the opportune moment which was to be signalled by words spoken by the Brazen Head. For sixty days he had kept vigil by night and his colleague Bungay had watched by day. Now, wearied out, they retire to rest, leaving the servant Miles to watch, with the injunction that he wake them when the Head speaks. When it does, saying: "Time Is," Miles thinks this oracle of too little importance to warrant waking his masters. It speaks again: "Time Was," and again Miles shrugs the warning aside. For a third time the Head speaks: "Time is Past." At these words, says a stage direction, "a lightning flasheth forth and a hand appears that breaketh down the Head with a hammer." Miles cries out: "Master, master, up! Hell's broken loose!" But it is too late, and all Friar Bacon's noble plans come to nothing.[16] This crucial scene is illustrated on the title page of the second quarto of the play (1630). One of the oracles is printed sideways and one upside down, which may be intended to suggest the whirling of Time's Wheel. Certainly the triple oracles suggest the threefold aspect of Time, though the words uttered contain no reference to the future and two references to the past. However, I do not think any philosophical intent can be read into Greene's characteristic carelessness. In a contemporary allusion to the story the oracles are given, with similar carelessness, in the reverse of the proper order as: "The Time was, the Time is, and Time shall be." [17]

Far more memorable than Greene's slipshod treatment of the theme of Opportunity, more impressive indeed than anything of the kind in English literature, is Father Jan David's *Occasio Arrepta, Neglecta*,[18] one of the most attractive productions of the Plantin Press (1605). An account that embraced every detail of this book would demand more space than we can afford, and even a summary must be fairly long. The title page and the dozen plates are by Theodore Galle (Figs. 37–49). Eacn plate is followed by a "Schematis Explicatio," running from about twelve to nearly thirty pages, in which every symbol is interpreted with appropriate citations from biblical, patristic, and classical texts. A prayer follows each explanation. Among the vignettes on the title page (Fig. 37) several are noteworthy. A warrior grasps Occasion by the forelock. Occasion, unheeded, slips away. The iron is struck while hot on the anvil ("Occasio Rei"). An army drives off the enemy before the sun has set ("Occasio Temporis"). An army sallies forth from a castle and repels the besiegers ("Occasio Loci"). A seated woman holds a cornucopia and a row of crowns is strung overhead (she has grasped Opportunity). A dejected man is seated on the ground without any possessions, but chains, handcuffs, and a halter are above him (he has neglected Opportunity). The sequence of twelve plates forms a connected story for the understanding of which one must resort to Father David's explanation. It is obviously based, with a change of sex, upon the parable of the Wise and Foolish Virgins. Time and Occasion (Opportunity) are the chief characters. Time is a young man with wings but no forelock; he holds his scythe and hourglass and on his head is an armillary sphere. Occasion is a woman whose luxuriant forelock covers her face without quite concealing her features; she has a cornucopia and has many treasures to give: a crucifix, a chalice, a rosary, a book, a palm branch, a laurel crown, a globe, a scepter, and a moneybag. A guardian Angel appears in many of the episodes.

I shall now comment briefly upon each design. 1. Time and Occasion stand side by side; in the heavens above God is seen (Fig. 38). 2. With Time and Occasion nearby, an Angel summons ten young men whom one devil is endeavoring to catch with a hook, another with a net (Fig. 39). 3. The five youths who are foolish waste and mock at Time. One is plucking a feather from Time's wing. Another displays a feather he has already plucked. A third is balancing Time's sphere on his head; squatting down under its weight he exclaims facetiously that he is a new Atlas. The fourth, holding Time's hourglass, exclaims: "Quam pellucidula placet haec mihi clepsydra vitro!" The fifth rides the handle of Time's scythe as a cockhorse. Two devils are near and other devils are in the sky (Fig. 40). 4. Time is in the background, deprived of the attributes with which the youths are still playing. Occasion is walking away from one youth but he, thinking that she is facing him, reaches towards the false face which is really on the back of her bald head (Fig. 41). 5. "Tempus et Occasionem Prudentes studiose observant": Five respectful young men are being greeted by Time, Occasion, and the Angel (Fig. 42). 6. The five Prudentes have their reward: Occasion has given them a cross, a rosary, and other things they have earned. A discomfited devil slinks away (Fig. 43). 7. The Prudentes grasp Occasion by the forelock; Time hovers overhead (Fig. 44). (Logically, it seems to me, this seventh plate should have preceded number six.) 8. Time and Occasion have disappeared. The five foolish youths lament lost Opportunity and wasted Time. A devil with a whip and another with a net stand guard over them (Fig. 45). 9. The Fatui try despairingly to grasp Opportunity behind. One cries out: "Post est Occasio calva!" One devil is gloating and another dancing (Fig. 46). 10. The two devils drag in chains the five Imprudentes towards hellmouth (Fig. 47). 11. But the Angel appears and rescues them because they are penitent. Their chains have fallen off. The two devils have fallen into the flaming mouth of hell (Fig. 48). 12. Within a huge, yawning hellmouth three damned souls are in flames, and in the heavens are souls in bliss (Fig. 49). The plates and the accompanying commentaries and prayers are followed (pp. 271 f.) by a Latin play: "Occasio. Drama." The characters are Time, Occasion, the Guardian Angel, Diabolus Magnus, Diabolus Parvus, five "iuvenes prudentes," five "imprudentes," and "tres animae damnatae." There is a Chorus of the Blessed and a Chorus of the Damned. After an opening colloquy among the Angel, the Great Devil, Time, and Occasion, there follow temptations of the wise and foolish youths, and the play proceeds along the lines of the designs and accompanying commentary, ending with the woes of the three damned souls who appear only in the final scene and have had no part in the previous action. In contrast to the parable in St. Matthew's Gospel, both the wise and foolish youths attain salvation.

5. The Pace and Cycles of Time

Time is not always "swift-paced." When Rosalind speaks of "the lazie foot of time" Orlando asks: "And why not the swift foote of time? Had not that bin as proper?" "By no means, sir," replies Rosalind; "Time travels in divers paces with divers persons," and she proceeds to tell him "who Time ambles withal, who Time trots withal, who Time gallops withal, and who he stands still withal."[1] The examples she gives need not be repeated here, for the passage is familiar to everyone. In altering his speed Time may seem to be deliberately perverse.

> When we desire Time's haste,
> It seems to lose a match with lobsters;
> And when we wish him stay, he imps his wings
> With feathers plum'd with thought.[2]

Massinger varies the image when he writes that happy people "imp feathers to the broken wings of Time."[3] In a poem by Wye Saltonstall Time protests that he tries to be accommodating, to hurry to suit some people, for example a landlord waiting for the rent or a maid awaiting her lover, and to lag to suit others, for example, the tenant who cannot pay or an old man waiting for Death.[4] Human efforts to retard or hasten Time are of no avail. Just as Love may be shown attempting to bind Time in chains[5] or to stop him by holding up the weights of a clock,[6] so a man may hang by the weights of a winged clock (Fig. 50), thus trying to make Time move faster.[7] But Ripa has an Amor with drooping wings and, treading upon his bow, arrows, and spent torch, he holds an hourglass. Love, however, may attempt to resist Time who with his sickle clips Love's wings.[8]

Time never pauses though it may be almost imperceptibly slow. John Bate, who was an ingenious inventor and mechanic, designed as a "water–work" for a garden a clepsydra which he describes and illustrates with a woodcut.[9] A figure of Time (or of Death if you prefer) stands on a board fitted loosely into a tank into which water flows drop by drop. As the water gradually rises a dart held by the figure points to a perpendicular pole at the back of the tank upon which appears a series of numbers which diminish in amount as they rise: they are the hours of the day.

Bate's suggestion that, if you like, a figure of Death may be substituted for that of Time is a reminder that Death is sometimes depicted with Time's hourglass and once at least with an escapement,[10] and Time is sometimes depicted as a skeleton. Examples of such personifications will engage our attention in Chapter 8.

Time and Death, and Fortune also, are subject to the governance of God, but beneath the Moon is Time's domain, and Death's. With a most significant qualification and limitation, this concept is set forth with impressive power and dignity in the title page of George Hakewill's famous treatise, *An Apologie or Declaration of the Power and Providence of God in the Government of the World, consisting in an Examination and Censure of the Common Errour touching Natures Perpetuall and Universall Decay* (1627; second edition 1630). Hakewill's purpose is to refute the opinion that the earth as it grows older is decaying and to demonstrate how in many respects—manners, knowledge, arts, and crafts—the modern age has improved upon antiquity. One cannot, however, accept the opinion of some scholars that Hakewill sees a future of illimitable betterment; he is not really a precursor of nineteenth–century believers in "progress." Rather, he adheres to the doctrine of certain ancient philosophers that all things move in a cycle: there will be advance till a point is reached at which a return will be made to a new beginning. His argument is summarized emblematically in his title page, a complex design. At the top God, represented by the Hand and the Ineffable Name, entrusts "particulars" to Time and Death. There is ruin and destruction, and dead men and animals lie upon the ground: "Sic placuit de Singulis," thus God wills concerning individual lives and things. But (in the upper compartment of the inner margin) the Hand of God stays the scythe of Time which is directed towards the destruction of the World: "Sic manet incolumis

31

Mundus," thus the World remains unharmed. Still (opposite on the outer margin) the same Hand grasps the thunderbolt with which He will one day destroy the World with fire. Till that day comes the Four Elements, represented by animals, fish, birds, and flames, remain. (This idea is traditional: Cartari, in the *Imagini degli Dei*, and Richard Linche, translating from Cartari, had said that the four children whom Saturn does not devour—Jupiter, Juno, Pluto, and Neptune—are to be interpreted as the Four Elements "which are not perishable by the all–cutting sickle of devouring Time.") [11] Two more emblems at the foot of the title page suggest the cyclical character of the cosmic process.

There are wheels within wheels, cycles and epicycles. The concept of the wheel upon which human society passes through the successive phases of Peace, Wealth, Pride, Impatience, War, Poverty, Humility, and Patience, and so back to Peace again can be traced from the Middle Ages,[12] and was akin to the Renaissance philosophy of History as the cycle of birth, florescence, maturity, decay, and rebirth. In the Louvre there is a beautiful painting by Nicolas Poussin called "The Dance of Life," where Work, Wealth, Luxury, and Poverty perform a cosmic dance to the accompaniment of Time's music.[13] Work produces Wealth; Wealth is the incentive to Luxury; Luxury is the cause of Poverty; and Poverty necessitates Work. Thus is it indicated that Man is the author of his proper woe. This theme, which the Renaissance inherited from antiquity, is found several times in English poetry. In some aphoristic lines from the fifteenth century it is briefly summarized: "Peace maketh Plenty, / Plenty maketh Pride, / Pride maketh Plea [that is, combativeness], / Plea maketh Poverty, / Poverty maketh Peace." [14] George Puttenham quotes a version by Jean de Meun.[15] George Gascoigne [16] and Thomas Lodge [17] have the same cycle with only slight differences in the wording. It is introduced in John Marston's *Histriomastix* (ca. 1599), but this drama is so badly planned and the text is so confused that the theme is scarcely recognizable. In it the cyclical progression of society is illustrated in the experiences of a company of actors.[18] Earlier than these four versions is a drawing by Jean Cousin [19] where six personifications turn ceaselessly upon a wheel. Peace holds an object, which is curiously but indubitably and appropriately a flatiron or plasterer's tool, to smooth out differences. Wealth holds her purse; Pride holds a mirror and a peacock is beside her; War, the only masculine figure, is in armor; Poverty holds out a dish for alms; Humility, with no attribute, bows her head dejectedly. And so Peace returns. Much more elaborate is the cycle found in a commonplace book of the early Jacobean period.[20] Here the cycle is expanded from five or six stages to eleven. A description of it may be found in my book *The Virtues Reconciled* (Toronto, 1947), pp. 127–8.

There is a striking alternation of the concept in Simon Harward's description of contemporary English society.[21] He writes: "Peace hath increased plenty, plenty hath wrought pride, pride hath hatched disdain, and disdain hath brought forth such strifes and debates, such suits of law, such quarrellings and contentions, as never were heard of in any age before us." Observe that the cycle stops without being brought back to peace.

In none of these cycles, save Poussin's, do we find Time. George Wither,[22] however, has in mind the governance of Time when, interpretating the circular serpent, he describes a different cycle. Stone, he says, molders into earth; earth rarifies to water; water turns to vapor; vapor to a fiery comet; the comet to air; air becomes a cloud; the cloud drops rain; the rain turns to earth; and the earth to stone. From this dubiously scientific sequence Wither extracts the lesson of the revolution of all earthly things and especially of human life.[23]

In an elaborate piece of Elizabethan symbolism Nature and Time and Fortune perform their duties together and are associated with the spinningwheel and the web of destiny. This is George Peele's Lord Mayors' Show entitled *Descensus Astraeae: The Device of a Pageant borne before M. William Web, Lord Mayor of . . . London* (1591).[24] In these inaugural pageants it was the custom, when opportunity afforded, to pun on the new incumbent's name. Master Web's name lent itself conveniently to a play upon it. The Presenter declares in his prologue that "Time hath turn'd his restless wheel about . . . and weaved a Web." In this task Kind (that is, Nature) collaborates with Time, and Fortune, likewise cooperating, "with golden hands doth strengthen and enrich the Web." After the prologue there appeared "a child, representing Nature, holding in her hand a distaff, and spinning a web, which passed through the hand of Fortune, and was wheeled up by Time." Time expounds the symbolism:

> Thus while my wheel with ever-turning gyres,
> At heaven's high hest, serves earthly men's desires,
> I wind the web that Kind so well begins,
> While Fortune doth enrich what Nature spins.

This august vision brings together the poetic imagery of many centuries, from the medieval poets who told of Nature at her forge to the supreme modern poet who sang of the Earth–spirit weaving upon the roaring loom of Time the living garment of God.

Of equal solemnity is the title page, engraved by Theodore de Bry (Fig. 51), of the *Metaphysica, Physica atque Technica Historia* (1617) by the English occultist and Rosicrucian, Robert Fludd.[25] No comment is needed to emphasize the grandeur of this concept of Time, turning and ever turning the Macrocosm and the Microcosm, the great world of Nature and the little world of Man. Less grandiose but also concerned with the cosmos is Daniel Cramer's emblem, "Tempus." [26] Here Time, winged, sits on a pleasant hillside with a globe, which he measures with compasses, by him. The motto is: "Tempus Ego immensum spatius dimetior orbem." But, as Francis Bacon says, "it is not good to look too long upon these turning wheels of vicissitude, lest we become giddy." "As for the philology of them," he adds contemptuously, "That is but a circle of tales, and therefore not fit for this writing." [27] Still it is in this world of Time and Fortune Man must fulfill his destiny.[28]

CHAPTER 3.   THE WORLD OF FORTUNE

1. Who is Fortune?

Exiled from Paradise, Man finds himself in a world subject to the vagaries of Fortune. The allegory of the Pilgrimage is here not always clear, for vestiges of the ancient cult of the goddess Fortuna [1] survived —men still "trusted to luck"—and only gradually did the divinity merge into the personified abstraction. Her power is not absolute. Virgil expounds to Dante the function of Fortune under God's ordinance:

> Questa provede, giudica, et perseque
> Suo regno come il loro li altri dei—

she foresees, passes judgment, and carries on her government as do the other powers that work for God.[2] Chaucer likewise affirms that what blind and ignorant men call Fortune is in reality the execution of the majestic Providence Who foresees all things in His righteousness; stability is the property of heaven and this world is ever restlessly in travail.[3] So in a sixteenth—century woodcut by George Pencz of Fortune at her wheel (Fig. 52), a bridle is round her neck and a bit in her mouth, and the reins are in God's hand which reaches down from heaven.[4] A design of Fortune controlled by the hand of God was used as a printer's device.[5] The idea is carried further in an emblem showing Fortune fallen from her broken wheel which is attached to heaven by a cord. The accompanying verses declare: "Fortuitum in mundo nihil est: Deus omne gubernat." [6] In a fine design by Hans Burgkmair (to which we shall return) Fortune sits upon a throne suspended by four cords from heaven (Fig. 53), thus suggesting her dependence upon God.[7] Henry Peacham, thinking not of incalculable mundane Luck but of divine Destiny, directs that Fate shall be "drawne like a man in a faire long flaxen robe looking upward to certaine bright starres compassed about with thicke clouds, from whence there shall hang a golden chaine . . . which chaine signifieth nothing else but the conjunction of divine with human things on which they depend as on their cause." [8]

In English Renaissance literature it is frequently stated that Fortune is but a fond invention, having no existence in herself.[9] Stephen Hawes, after describing a vision of Fortune, warns that she is merely a figure fashioned by poets to explain the changes in men and declares emphatically: "The man is fortune in the proper dede." [10] The authors of *The Mirrour for Magistrates* in various parts of their work fumble after the same idea. Stephen Bateman, noting that there are as many concepts of Fortune as there are "fond heads" to invent them, remarks upon three such concepts: "One blinde that applyeth herselfe where she liste; An other Mad, that taketh away agayne the Giftes by her geven: The third is Death, that never will harken to the Prayers of the Miserable." [11] Far from being a goddess, says George Turberville, this "blinde and muffled Dame" deserves no "stool of state," for she is nothing but "spitefull cruell chance" and is indeed a "monster vile." [12] Thomas Lodge says that Fortune is a "nurse of fooles . . . supposed sovereigne" only through "our vaine construction," that is, our misunderstanding of the circumstances of life. His heroine, Elstred, denounces Fortune as a "Princesse of Paganisme . . . Folly's eldest sister, Bastard of Time . . . Mother of lyes . . . double faced shroe"; and exclaims: "It was not thou, my conscience doth excuse thee, / It was my sinne that wrought mine over—turning." [13] Another poet holds that

among Christians it is a gross impiety to think of Fortune as a deity:
" 'Tis but a word of idle wits creation / And favors fooles but in
imagination." [14] In Linche's translation of Cartari the Elizabethans
could find the authority of Cicero and Lactantius for dismissing Fortune
as "a vaine, idle, and senselesse" creation, fashioned merely to cover the
weakness and ignorance of men. [15] At a later date we find a commentator
on Du Bartas denouncing belief in Fortune as a "profane opinion." "The
Pagans have forged a certaine Goddesse with a Wheele," he writes, but
"the holy Scripture abolisheth Fortune." [16]

There are, however, poets who are not prepared to subscribe without
qualification to this denial of Fortune's existence. One of the contribu-
tors to *Tottel's Miscellany* tells us that there are people who affirm of
Fortune that

> She neither can do good nor yll,
> She hath no fourme, yet beares a name.
> Then we but strive agaynst the streames,
> To frame such toyes on fancies dreames;

but though this writer is not certain that Fortune is an authentic spirit,
he declares nevertheless:

> Well I wot, some cause there is:
> That causeth wo, and sendeth blisse. [17]

A character in a play inveighs against Nature because she knows only
how to form, not how to preserve what she has formed,

> since careless of her work,
> She leaves to giddy Fortune the whole power
> Of ruling us. [18]

Following the example of the poets and artists who clung to an
ancient concept which was part of their heritage but which had lost its
religious validity, we shall in this chapter, for the purposes of our
allegory, think of Fortune as a person, that is, an abstraction personified.

2. *The Wheel of Fortune*

Quite unexpectedly, Shakespeare's Fluellen shows himself to be a
fairly competent iconographer. When Pistol begs him to intercede with
the Duke of Exeter for the life of Bardolph, the valorous soldier who
has been sentenced to be hanged for theft by cruel fate,

37

> And giddy Fortune's furious fickle wheel—
> That goddess blind,
> That stands upon the rolling restless stone—

the Welsh captain interrupts him:

> By your patience, Aunchient Pistol. Fortune is painted blind,
> with a muffler afore her eyes, to signify to you that Fortune is
> blind; and she is painted also with a wheel, to signify to you,
> which is the moral of it, that she is turning and inconstant, and
> mutability, and variation; and her foot, look you, is fixed upon
> a spherical stone, which rolls, and rolls, and rolls. In good truth,
> the poet makes a most excellent description of it. Fortune is an
> excellent moral.[1]

The description is incomplete, but so far as it goes, the wheel, the
blindness, the restless stone, it is accurate.

No symbol attached to a personification is more familiar or more
ubiquitous than is Fortune's wheel. It is of far descent and is one of
those which, like Love's bow and arrows, Time's scythe, and the scales
of Justice, have retained a hold upon the imagination to the present day.
Yet if the number of surviving specimens is at all proportionate to the
number which existed formerly, the subject of Fortune's wheel was by
no means so prevalent in ecclesiastical murals in England as were such
other themes as Doom, Time, Death, and the Virtues and the Vices.
Only about half a dozen examples are extant. Of these the most remarkable is the thirteenth-century painting on a pier of the choir in
Rochester Cathedral. Part of this has been obliterated, but Lady Fortune
and half her wheel with two ascending figures and one at the top can
be seen.[2] A fine representation of the theme is in Hatfield Church,
Norfolk. Fortune is clothed in red with a green overmantle. The rising
king and the reigning king have been destroyed; the falling king,
with his label "Regnavi," and the prostrate king, with his label "Non
regno," are visible.[3] Comment on the other examples in Keyser's list
is unnecessary but in at least one case he may have mistaken a St.
Catherine's wheel for a wheel of Fortune.[4] Because the remains are
very scanty one wonders if the subject was frowned upon by those
responsible for the decoration of church walls because of its paganism?
Or have many examples been destroyed for the same reason? Are we
to infer that the Elizabethans had few opportunities during divine
service to contemplate this great symbol of human vicissitudes?

In numerous woodcuts and engravings Fortune indefatigably turns her wheel while foolish mortals clamber upon it, are lifted up, and tumble or, more rarely, are tossed off. Pencz's design (see Fig. 52) is typical. In Burgkmair's the goddess does not, as usual, stand at her wheel, turning it with a crank or with a cord, it is, instead, beside her as she sits on her throne (see Fig. 53). With one hand she turns it while with the other she plucks her victims from it, tossing them into one or the other of two blankets upheld by a company of poor men and a company of fiends. She is not blindfold but her expressionless eyes may be intended to suggest blindness. She has two faces (a characteristic to which we shall return), the one young and fair, the other aged, grim, and hideous. At the expense of logic Burgkmair has been loyal to the tradition of making ugliness sinister, thus he turns Fortune's foul face toward those who are attracted to her and her fair face toward those whom she is rejecting. Properly, she lures her victims with her beauty. This deceitfulness may be emblematized as a beautiful nude Fortune playing upon a flute while a young man dances before her:[5] The sweeter the music of Fortune the more one should beware of her. Somewhat similar is the concept of coming Fortune as a child and departing Fortune as a sad matron.[6]

Often a crowd of clients await their turn to ascend the wheel, as in Pencz's print, or push and jostle one another in their eagerness, as in Burgkmair's. But often their number is limited to four. This may be related to the four phases of the moon.[7] The association is as old as Boccaccio and the *Roman de la Rose*, perhaps one should say as old as human experience, for who would not draw a comparison between the changing aspects of "the inconstant moon" and the changing aspects of human fortune, between the moon's control of the tides of ocean and Opportunity's control of "a tide in the affairs of men / Which taken at the flood leads on to Fortune?"[8] "Fortune's flood ran with full stream" and "Fortune worketh as the waves," say the authors of *The Mirrour for Magistrates* (III, 71, and XII, 166). In *Bussy d'Amboise* (V.2.84 f.) Chapman draws an elaborate analogy, too long to quote, between Fortune and the sea.[9] In these passages there are no allusions to the moon, but the analogy is implicit. Elsewhere it is explicit. Thus Robert Anton writes:

> Sometimes I see the ever–turning spheare
> Of man and fortune like new–Moones appeare.
> Still waxing to a full increase of light

> Till it seem round full—circled and most bright
> To all men [sic] eyes: till by the darkesome shade
> Of some mischance, a blacke eclipse be made.[10]

Wither has a figure of Fortune holding the moon.[11] As an emblem of Inconstancy the moon is found in Ripa, and Peacham's Inconstancy holds the moon.[12] A variant of the four phases of the moon is found when the four winds of heaven buffet the riders upon the wheel.[13]

The four clients are usually kings or other persons of high estate and authority, for the height of their achievement serves to emphasize the depth of the subsequent catastrophe. "He who is down need fear no fall," sings the shepherd boy in the Valley of Humiliation, a consoling thought which Barclay expresses in a simple metaphor: "The toppys of mountayns with lyghtnyngs are brent / More oft then lowe valeys." [14] The warning to the great ones of the world is vigorously expressed by John Webster: "When Fortune's wheel is over—charg'd with Princes, / The Waight makes it move swift." [15] Substituting the image of a tree for that of a wheel the same thought finds magnificent expression in George Chapman:

> Daily and hourly proof
> Tells us prosperity is at highest degree
> The fount and handle of calamity:
> Like dust before a whirlwind those men fly
> That prostrate on the ground of Fortune lie;
> And being great, like trees of broadest sprout,
> Their own top—heavy state grubs up their root.[16]

Later in the present chapter we shall have the satisfaction of seeing Poverty triumphing over Fortune.

The simplest image of the rise and fall of those who aspire to high rank and renown is an emblem occasionally met with in which four crowns are attached to the rim of the wheel at intervals of 90°; neither Fortune nor her victims appear. Peacham labels this emblem "Status Humanus." [17] Not merely the vicissitudes of the individual man but the unavoidable, predetermined course of history may be suggested by the wheel. In a Book of Hours, now in the Pierpont Morgan Library (MS 815), which was written and illuminated in France for Henry VII of England a poor man essaying to mount the wheel and a king at the top are shown. In the background a kneeling man is threatened by Death and on the ground is a shrouded corpse. Job, not Fortune, stands by the wheel holding a scroll on which is inscribed: "For now I shall sleep in the dust." The lesson conveyed is not merely the trite caution to mistrust the vagaries of Fortune but the need to face resolutely the cycle of growth and decay, life and death. The insecurity of Fortune's favorites is emblematized by a man with a cornucopia who stands on a plank spanning an abyss while Fortune is engaged in sawing the plank.[18] With or without human figures the wheel often bears the four-fold formula: "Regnabo, Regno, Regnavi, Sum sine regno" or its equivalent in one of the vernaculars. A good small example of this scheme is a fine niello print reproduced by Hind;[19] and in a magnificent example of this version Fortune stands by her wheel, upon which there are no kings but four scrolls bearing the traditional words.[20] During the Renaissance the formula seems to occur more frequently in the arts of design than in literature. I have noted it only once in English literature, in a little play, or rather plotless dialogue, entitled *Hans Beer–Pot* (1618). The author, Dabridgcourt Belchier, an expert in the art of warfare and a very inexpert dramatist, lived for many years in the Low Countries. It has been suspected that his piece is a translation from the Dutch, but no Dutch original has been found and in my opinion it is an original English work. One of the characters is a Moor of noble birth who has been captured by the Christians and enslaved. In the course of a long speech containing various clichés about Fortune he says:

> Here may you see how fortune turnes her Wheele;
> I that before did many men commaund:
> Am now constrainde to serve. . . .
> *Regnavi, regno, regnabo, sum sine regno.*[21]

Because of Belchier's long residence in the Low Countries it is likely that he borrowed the formula (which is not in proper order) from a painting or print rather than some literary source.

Captive kings may attend upon Fortune though not actually ascending her wheel or falling from it. In *Jocasta* (1566) by George Gascoigne and Francis Kinwelmarsh the final dumb show is "a plaine Type or figure of unstable fortune." The personification has many of the usual attributes: the double face ("the formost face fair and smiling, the other behinde blacke and louring"); the blindfold, the feet resting upon a great round ball, the lap full of jewels. She rides in a chariot drawn by four noble personages. On her right hand walk two kings, crowned, and on her left two poor slaves, meanly attired, whom she leads "in a string." Presently she stays the chariot and shifts the kings to the left and the slaves to the right, placing the crowns on the slaves' heads and "casting the vyle clothes of the slaves upon the kings." [22] Did Brian Melebancke have this spectacle in mind when he described Fortune as "chopping and chaunging from right hande to lefte," that is, from prosperity to adversity? [23]

A belated morality play, *The Contention betweene Liberalitie and Prodigalitie*, which was acted at court in 1600, contains a spectacular entry of Fortune in a chariot "drawn by kings," undoubtedly reminiscent of the famous, sensational episode of the captive kings, "the pampered jades of Asia," who draw Tamburlaine's chariot in Marlowe's drama.[24] In *The Rare Triumphs of Love and Fortune*, there is another spectacular entry of Fortune, to the accompaniment of trumpets, drums, cornets and guns; but there is no chariot and there are no kings.[25] Dekker's *Old Fortunatus* opens with a procession for which the following stage direction is given: "Enter a Shepherd, a Gardener, A Smith, and a Monk, all crowned; a Nymph with a globe, another with Fortune's Wheel: then Fortune. After her four Kings with broken crowns and sceptres, chained with silver gyves, and led by her. . . . Fortune takes her chair, the Kings lying at her feet, so that she treads on them as she ascends to her seat." [26] Although there is no chariot, Dekker was nevertheless imitating Marlowe. One of the dejected monarchs turns out to be none other than the Turkish Sultan Bajazet whom Tamburlaine made prisoner; and just as Tamburlaine used Bajazet as a "block" to mount his horse, so Fortune treads on her prisoners as she mounts to her seat.

In the winter of 1607–8 the learned men of St. John's College, Oxford, ingeniously turned to a novel use the old association of Fortune and royalty. The Christmas festivities were, as usual, built up around the age–old institution of the Lord of Misrule or mock king, Christmas king, or Twelfth Night King which had come down through the various forms of the medieval winter feast, itself derived from the Roman Saturnalia whose own roots lie in prehistoric antiquity. The essential feature of this king's reign is its transitoriness; he is elected for the festive season only and is soon deposed. The scholars of St. John's took him therefore as the ruler subject to the vicissitudes of Fortune and in two Latin interludes, *Ara Fortunae* and *Ira seu Tumulus Fortunae*, they represented the rise and fall of this temporary sovereign. I know of no other instances of this juxtaposition of Fortune and the Saturnalian king. Fortune plays, however, a novel role in another Latin play, *Philomela,* performed on the same occasion. In the prologue she appears carrying a very unusual attribute, a book: "librum manu gestans." She bids the Christmas Prince who presides over the revels to open the volume at random; the story at which it opens shall be the subject of the play to be presented: "Sortire nostra pagina historiam tuam." The choice is thus dictated in a manner like that of the *Sortes Virgilianae*.[27]

The effort, so characteristic of the period, to freshen iconographical material staled by long usage, results in the case of Fortune's wheel, as in that of various other attributes of personifications, in some curious abnormalities and "unorthodox" images. We may set aside as a mere exhibition of eccentric individual taste quite without symbolic significance such a representation as that of Fortune enthroned in a temple with her wheel set high overhead in a sort of barrel vault.[28] But other vagaries may have a deliberate purpose. Francis Davison has the curious notion that Fortune's wheels (here she has more than one wheel) are the wheels of her chariot.[29] When an illuminator shows Fortune's victims lashed to the wheel it may be argued that they are bound by ambition, but since the ambitious man is all too willing to ascend it is doubtful whether it is fitting to represent him as tied.[30] The idea that the wheel is an instrument of torture is found in the Middle Ages [31] and survives in English literature of the Renaissance. A character in an anonymous play exclaims: "I am whipp'd and rack'd and torn upon the wheel / Of giddy Fortune." [32] William Drummond likens himself upon Fortune's wheel to Ixion in torment,[33] an analogy that is found in medieval literature. Wither has an emblem of a man bound in torment upon a wheel which is turned by Fortune. [34]

According to one poet the world itself is whirled upon the wheel:

> The greatest wealth is subject for to reele,
> The globe is plac'd on Fortunes tottering wheele . . .
> The waving world gives joy and sorrow,
> This day a croesus and a Job tomorrow.[35]

Another poet identifies the world and the wheel:

> The World's a Wheel, of various Timber made;
> Fortune its Course, with a high hand, does move,
> Not Regular, But sometimes Retrograde,
> Whirling, The Head below, The Heels above.[36]

A third poet says that Man is himself the wheel of Fortune, a concept which lends itself more easily to verbal than to visual imagery:

> The very wheele which Fortune turneth still
> Is Man; for him she turnes which way she will:
> He seemes of Change a Character or Map . . .
> Or like a Ship . . .
> For here, or there, the Fortunes of Man–kind
> Are blowne, and tost like Ships in storming wind.[37]

On the outbreak of the Civil Wars, when the wheel of Fortune must indeed have seemed to spin violently, John Taylor used the old convention in two satirical pamphlets, both dated 1642. One is *A Plea for Prerogative: or, Give Caesar his due. Being the Wheele of Fortune turn'd round: or, The World turned topsie-turvie.*[38] On the title page is a woodcut of a wheel with a crank upon which, had the artist possessed sufficient skill, personifications might well have been placed. As it is, there are merely eight words: centrally on opposite sides of the rim, "War" and "Peace"; opposed to one another so that evil ideas are above and good below, "Disloyalty" and "Obedience," "Sects" and "Religion," "Malice" and "Love." The satire on rebels against kingly authority which follows contains a comment on this woodcut:

> Thus vice is entred, virtue is thrust out,
> And Fortunes Wheele is madly turn'd about.
> Peace, Love, Religion, and Obedience
> Are vertues of exceeding excellence;
> Yet as the Picture in [sic; read "of"] the Wheele doth show,
> They are turn'd downwards in the spokes below,
> While Malice, War, Sects, and Disloyalty
> Are in the upper spokes, exalted high.

As a sort of refrain the second line of this passage runs, with variations, through the poem. Later it is predicted that the wheel will take another turn and virtue be exalted.[39] Taylor's companion piece is *Mad Fashions, Od Fashions, All out of Fashions, or, The Emblems of these Distracted Times.* On the title page is a crude but genuinely droll woodcut which Taylor interprets in the opening lines of his satire. It is an interesting transition between the old emblem and the modern political and social cartoon. Fortune and her wheel have disappeared, although the consequences of her vagaries remain. Everything is topsy-turvy: A man wears breeches on his shoulders, a doublet on his lower body, boots on his hands, and gloves on his feet; a horse is driving a cart, a wheelbarrow pushing a man, a mouse chasing a cat, a rabbit chasing a dog;

44

a fish and an eel fly in the sky; a candle burns upside down and a castle is upside down. Thus is the dry symbolism of the wheel in *A Plea for Prerogative* turned into fantastic humor.

3. Monstrous and Many–handed Fortune and Alexander, a famous victim

We shall come back presently to the symbol of the wheel, but for the moment let us consider certain aspects of Fortune which Fluellen, for all his iconographical *expertise*, does not interpret to Pistol.

The Pilgrim on the Path of Life must beware of the deceitful and seductive beauty of Fortune; he will learn, however, that she can be also ugly and misshapen. For the latter concept in literature and the visual arts Boccaccio seems to be chiefly responsible. At the beginning of the sixth book of Laurent de Premierfait's *Des Cas et des Ruines des noble hommes et femmes*, the French version of Boccaccio, Fortune is described as she appeared before Boccaccio in his study. She is a hideous monster: "Fortune en son corps avoit cent mains et autretent de bras pour donner at pour tollir aux hommes les biens mondains et pour abatre en bas et pour lever en hault les hommes de ce monde." [1] In *The Fall of Princes*, which is based upon Laurent de Premierfait, Lydgate tells how

> While Bochas pensief stode in his library . . .
> To him appeared a monstruous ymage,
> Parted on twayne in colour and corage. . . .
> An hundred handes she had of eche parte
> In sundry wyse her gyftes to depart.

With some hands she lifted men up and with others cast them down. The right side of this apparition was "summery," the left "wintry." Her habit was of many colors. She had an angelical mermaid's face but a serpent's tail. She was at once lamblike and wolflike, a Siren and a Charybdis. She had "no feet upon to gone," [2] a detail which evinces a misunderstanding of *Fortuna sine pedibus*. In both Laurent and Lydgate the function of exalting and depressing men is assigned primarily to Fortune's many hands; her wheel is mentioned only incidentally and later.

This scene is depicted in various manuscripts of Laurent. In a magnificent Flemish manuscript she has six arms; [3] in another manuscript she appears before Boccaccio whirling no less than thirteen arms, as though she were some Hindu divinity. [4] Many–handed Fortune is not depicted in the famous and beautiful edition of Laurent published at Bruges by Colard Mansion in 1476.[5] At the proper place in the text there is a blank space evidently reserved for an illustration of the episode, but it is not certain whether a copperplate was ever actually engraved. If made and then mislaid till too late to be used, a rough idea of the design may perhaps be obtained from the woodcut of the scene in Jean du Pré's edition of Laurent (Paris, 1484); the other woodcuts in that edition were obviously suggested by, though not precisely copied from, Mansion's copperplates. In Du Pré's illustration [6] Fortune has but two arms at the shoulders, but each divides at the elbow into a pair of forearms and hands. Seven figures are encircling the wheel. Fortune seems to be shoving to his downfall the man at the top; his crown has fallen off and there is an evident attempt to suggest his terror. With her other pair of hands she seems to be raising a man who kneels before her. Richard Pynson obtained from Jean du Pré the whole series of woodblocks of 1484 and used them in his edition of Lydgate's *Fall of Princes* (1494). Afterwards the blocks were either lost or, more likely, returned to Paris; and when Pynson reissued Lydgate's poem in 1527 it was illustrated with new woodcuts of inferior quality. These reappear in Tottel's edition of the *Fall* (1554). In this English cut [7] Boccaccio, seated at his desk, raises his hand to shield his eyes from the dazzling rays streaming from Fortune's head. She is not turning the wheel nor touching the men upon it, who include ecclesiastics as well as a crowned and sceptered monarch. She is bifrons and has two arms and six hands (Fig. 54). This concept of many-handed Fortune, to which Lydgate, Pynson, and Tottel introduced England, made very little appeal to the Tudor imagination; she does not appear in this shape even in *The Mirrour for Magistrates*. Perhaps there was a reluctance to have her use both whirling arms and whirling wheel; perhaps it was thought that her activities could best be performed by the wheel alone; perhaps the monstrous deformity was rejected by poets who preferred to think of her perilous loveliness.

A curious passage in Chapman's *Bussy d'Amboise* (I.i.113–117) runs thus:

> The old Scythians
> Painted blind Fortune's powerful hands with wings
> To show her gifts come swift and suddenly,
> Which if her favorite be not swift to take,
> He loses them forever.

Professor Gilbert has shown that this notion comes from Cartari (or from Linche), mistranslating a passage in Quintus Curtius where Fortune is said to have "manus et pennas," hands and wings, not hands with wings.[8] Cousin has a drawing (no. 193) of Fortune without hands. I cannot explain this.

The Nine Worthies are among the great personages who attend upon Fortune. In *The Example of Vertu* Youth, the hero, is admitted to a great hall where seated upon a chair of state and surrounded by kings is a lady of marvellous pride:

> Besydes her sat the Worthyes nyne
> And she amonge them a Wheele turnynge
> Full lowe to her they dyd then enclyne
> She sometyme laughynge and somtyme lourynge
> Her condycyon was to be dyssemblynge
> And many she exalted upon her Wheele
> Gyvynge them great falles that they did fele.[9]

The authority of St. Augustine, who discusses the concept of Fortune in the fifth book of *The City of God*, combined with the enormous fame in history and legend of Alexander the Great, who was struck down in his prime and pride, to make this victim of Fortune a favorite subject for illustration. Thus, in a superb miniature Fortune stands by her wheel at the top of which sits one Alexander, crowned and with orb and scepter while another is shown upon the ground with the regalia beside him. On the other side of the picture the circumstances of his death are shown.[10] In another very fine minature Alexander with orb and scepter and wearing a turban sits atop the wheel, and again, with these symbols of sovereignty discarded, sits mournfully on the ground. Fortune is not turning her wheel but with an admonitory forefinger points the lesson. Near the fallen Alexander a "roy" lies dead and two other kings are being offered poison by their ministers of state. At the extreme right a king, queen, and counsellors contemplate this "mirror for magistrates." [11]

Sir Thomas More uses Alexander as one of his object lessons. One of his earliest writings is entitled "Certain maters in engglish written by master Thomas More in hys youth for the boke of Fortune, and caused them to be printed in the begynning of that book." [12] It opens with a boastful speech by Fortune who counsels: "Better is to be fortunate than wyse." Then, as a subtitle phrases it, comes "Thomas More to them that trust in fortune." Fortune, More says, sometimes becks and smiles, but never for long:

> But lord how he doth thynk hym self full wele,
> That may set once his hande uppon her whele,
> He holdeth fast: but upwarde as he flieth,
> She whippeth her whele about, and there he lyeth.

Such was the fate of Alexander,[13] of Darius, and of Julius Caesar. Fortune glides away from former favorites but poverty is free from her domination, as the cases of Socrates, Pythagoras, and other philosophers show.

4. The two sides of Fortune and the Tree, Ladder, and Hill of Fortune

Fluellen emphasizes Fortune's inconstancy and mutability but he does not explicitly mention her characteristic bifrontality. This essential dichotomy, good and ill, favorable and unfavorable, fair and foul, is expressed in a great variety of ways in visual and verbal imagery. A typical late–medieval description is that by King James I of Scotland in *The Kingis Quair*. Fortune is said to dwell within a round, walled place. She wears a garment of divers colors. Now she smiles and now she lowers. Crowds of folk clamber on her wheel, but beneath it is "ane ugly pit depe as ony helle" into which many of them fall. Yet so fickle is she that some who are "slung" off by the whirling of the wheel she picks up and sets thereon again, safe and sound.[1] Lydgate seems to have been almost obsessed with the idea of the contrasting aspects of Fortune. She lives in a house of which one side is fair and strong, the other ugly and ruinous. In its cellar there are two vats or casks, one holding a drink of honey and spices, the other a drink of gall or poison. She has a double face [2]—a "party face," as he calls it elsewhere.[3] "Ful fayre before, but toto foule behind," one of the writers of *The Mirrour for Magistrates* exclaims.[4] Again Lydgate says that Fortune is a tavern keeper and dispenses from two vats a sweet drink and a bitter.[5] The casks or vats of Zeus and Fortune appear in various emblem books, for example, in one of Corrozet's emblems, where Zeus sits beside the casks from which Fortune blindly pours wine.[6] In one of Chapman's comedies there is a sort of farcical pageant at the close of which a servant appears "dressed like Queen Fortune with two pots in her hands." From these are drawn posies for the guests.[7]

One of the most elaborate English descriptions of Fortune is in

Michael Drayton's *The Tragicall Legend of Robert, Duke of Normandy*. The Duke's Ghost appeared attended by Fame and Fortune. Fortune "with scornfull jesture drew him by the hand." She was blind; the dusky veil which hid her sightless eyes was "Painted about with bloody Tragedies, / Fooles wearing crowns and wisemen clogd in gives." A chain of princes' crowns and broken sceptres hung from her neck and

> Her feature chang'd each minute of the hower . . .
> Now would shee smile, and suddainly would lower,
> And with one breth her words were sweet and sower.[8]

In *The Pastime of Pleasure* (ll. 3032 f. and 3107), Hawes describes "Fortune with the faces Twayne" and, using a proverbial expression we shall meet with again, says that she has "two faces in one hood."

Manuscripts of St. Augustine, Boethius, Boccaccio, and Petrarch often show Fortune with two faces, the one serene, fair, and young, the other old, ravaged, and hideous.[9] The two-facedness may even develop into complete two-headedness,[10] or a single face may be divided down the middle. Thus, two English books printed in the Low Countries in the early sixteenth century have identical cuts of Fortune with one half of her face white, the other black.[11] These contrasted sides appear in one of Cousin's drawings (no. 27), where the antithesis is carried further by placing upon Fortune's right hand a youth playing on a musical instrument who represents Happiness and on her left a cowled and drooping figure representing Misery.[12] In a splendid manuscript of Petrarch's *De Remediis* enthroned Fortune is flanked by Fear and Grief: fear of losing fortune and grief for having lost it.[13] An anonymous sixteenth-century French drawing (Fig. 55) depicts the two-sidedness of Fortune in a peculiar, perhaps unique, fashion. From throat to ankle the left side of her body is clothed, the right side is naked. With her left hand she proffers a crown, with her right she scatters feathers which are perhaps emblematic, as so often, of folly. Upon her head is a lighted candle. This attribute I have never seen elsewhere and I know no literary parallel. Is it a light, a pharos, to draw all men unto her, as moths to the flame? Behind her a hill, sloping on one side and a vertical precipice on the other, may be part of the antithesis, and the windmill at the top is suggestive of the winds of Fortune.[14] This Fortune, though a sufficiently strange figure, is no bifrontal monstrosity.[15]

We have not yet exhausted the ingenuities of the Renaissance imagination. When the Poet in *Timon of Athens* describes how Fortune beckons her favorite with "her ivory hand" is it not implied that her other hand is of ebony? There exists a copy of the *Eruditorium Penitentiale* (Paris, ca. 1485–90) which has hand colored woodcuts. The colorist has made the robe of Fortune a rosy red on the side where two clients are ascending her wheel and a somber grayish brown on the side where they are descending, and to carry the idea further he has colored the rising and falling figures correspondingly.[16] For the characteristic bifrontality other contrasts may be substituted. Thus, in a manuscript of Petrarch there are two Fortunes, one having a "belle face," the other a "laide face."[17] In one of Capaccio's emblems two Fortunes stand side by side upon a pedestal: one is confident and prosperous, with bellying sail and erect forelock, the other forlorn, with her sail tattered and her forelock drooping. On the sea behind the two figures are, respectively, a ship sailing and another ship sinking by the prow.[18] In another emblem Fortune holds a crown in one hand and a noose in the other.[19] Guido Reni's Fortune, in Rome, holds a crown and a rod. Her emblem may be a bee, as in a drawing by Bartolomeo Coriolano in the Uffizi, for the bee has honey in its mouth but a sting in its tail. The emblematists sometimes express her unreliability and inconstancy by showing her with one foot upon the ground and the other on a boat or in the water, an image which Shakespeare remembered:

> Sigh no more, ladies sigh no more!
> Men were deceivers ever,
> One foot in sea, and one on shore;
> To one thing constant never.[20]

Or, as Lydgate's Fortune had appeared long before, in a Jacobean masque she wears "a rich mantle wrought with changeable colours to express her incertainty." [21] Here the poet and the costumer have the advantage of the painters, whose fast colors cannot indicate her changeableness. The chameleon's ability to change color is the obvious reason why, as in the *Livre de Fortune* (no. 53), she holds this creature. In one of Robert Greene's tales [22] a man possesses a picture of Fortune treading upon a chameleon and a polyp; the latter creature, according to Pliny's *Historia naturalis* (9. 29), has also the ability to change its color. Elsewhere Greene says that Fortune's temples "are strewed with roses and nettles." [23] Thomas Lodge denounces Fortune as one that "profferest an eel and performest a scorpion." [24] The ups and downs of Fortune are described in what I believe is a unique image: she is said to have an hourglass and when the sand has run out she turns it upside down so that the sand runs in the reverse direction.[25] All men, says this writer, have their Time but change of Fortune turns their glass. Though the tennis ball, says Anthony Copley, when it is knocked out of the court, sometimes falls into the "dustie kennall" it may at other times "flie in at Pallace–windows." [26] From Alain Chartier comes the quite repulsive concept of Fortune with a forehead one side of which is hairy to signify prosperity and the other side bald to signify adversity.[27] The antithesis is presented in an even more unattractive way in a long, coarse comic poem published under the pseudonym of Pasquil Anglicanus and entitled *Cornu–copiae, Pasquils Nightcap: or, Anti–dot for the Head–ache* (1612). The title is a *double entendre* of which one element is based upon the attribute carried by Fortuna Abundans, Favorable Fortune. In this piece there is a description of a Temple of Fortune at Cuckold's Haven in Kent. Within it there is a "horned altar" (another double entendre) beside which Lady Fortune, "crowned with mighty Hornes," dispenses with one hand marriages while with the other she affixes horns to husbands' heads.[28] The men of Kent placate Fortune by fashioning a horned pillar. At the ceremony of dedication this pillar is borne in a chariot, as "upon that solemne day / When as the Pageants through Chepeside are carried."

To end this part of our discussion on a more pleasing note attention may be called to a beautiful engraving by Theodore de Bry in which the two aspects of Fortune are combined. In her right hand she holds a flagon and from the wrist there dangles a chain with an order of nobility. Below the extended right arm is shown the sea with two ships making safely to shore and a prosperous city in the distance. But with her left hand she leans upon a stick, and a snake enwreathes the wrist from which hangs an empty purse. Upon the sea are a wrecked ship and a drowning man, and in the distance a city is in flames.[29]

The aspirations and disappointments of Fortune's devotees may be imaged in other ways than that of the revolving wheel. Cousin's drawing (no. 33) of Fortune at the center of a seesaw on the ends of which are two clients, one high, the other low, is, I think, a unique concept. The concept of the Tree of Fortune (if we disregard the analogous but not identical motive of the Fruits of Fortune) is first found in Honoré Bonet's treatise on war and the rules of warfare entitled *L'Arbre des Batailles* (ca. 1386). The popularity of this learned work in France is attested by the considerable number of manuscripts that survive, though the only translation into a Teutonic tongue seems to be that in Scots made in the fifteenth century by Gilbert of the Haye.[30] To some of the

French manuscripts are prefixed pictures of the Tree of Battles among whose branches at appropriately different levels combats are in progress between Pope and Antipope, Emperor and King, and the lower orders of society. In some of these designs Lady Fortune stands amid the topmost branches, holding her wheel.[31] Sometimes the tree is shown growing out of hellmouth.[32] The tradition of this tree, though apparently never very popular, was long lasting. One of Ripa's half dozen specifications for Fortune shows her high up in the branches of a tree, shaking down crowns, scepters, mitres, jewels, money, musical instruments, and books, for which men below are scrambling. In the supplementary annotations to the 1615 edition of Cartari there is a picture of Fortune in mid–air, shaking from the branches of a tree gifts for her clients below.[33] In the Trevelyon commonplace book (fol. 159ʳ) Fortune is on her wheel and the wheel is in the top branches of a tree. Objects, ranging from a crown to a spade, are falling therefrom. An anonymous anti–Laudian satire, *Fortunes Tennis–ball* (1640), has on the title page a crude cut of Fortune standing upon a limb of a tree which one man is trying to climb while another is falling off and a third is prone upon the ground. Explanatory verses are in part as follows:

> See for the Frontispiece here a Cedar tree,
> Whereon sits Fortune in her Majestie.
> Those that presume t'aspire unto its top,
> She slilie gives the highest branch a lop.
> And topsie–turvie they come tumbling down.[34]

As she may be occasionally shown on a tree so even more rarely Fortune may be at the topmost rung of a ladder. Behind this motive is a long history which we could trace back to Jacob's Dream in Genesis and then follow through the various medieval concepts of the *Scala Paradisi* and the *Scala Infernalis*, but the temptation to digress must be resisted. Robert Allott takes from Pausanias the information that at Mitylene there was a temple wherein was a ladder, "a gift dedicatory to Fortune; signifying thereby, that those that clymed up with ease Fortune favoured, and came headlong down if she frowned upon them." [35] In *The Contention betweene Liberalitie and Prodigalitie* (1602) the ladder is a conspicuous stage property.[36] Having made her triumphal entry Lady Fortune ascends (by what means is not indicated) to a high place called her "bower." Presently Prodigality, a riotous and insolent youth, procures a ladder and climbs up to the bower. Fortune, says the stage direction, "claps a halter about his neck" and he tumbles down, but in his fall "he breaketh the halter" and so escapes from the despair of which the halter is the emblem.

In the medieval imagination Fortune was often thought to dwell in a palace where she holds her court. In *The Kingis Quair*, for example, she is said to dwell within a round walled place. Youth, in *The Example of Vertu*, obtains admission to the Palace of Fortune. On the title page of a Venetian book Veritas directs three men towards the "Civitas Fortunae," a stronghold set on the summit of a rocky hill.[37] This concept of the Palace of Fortune placed upon a hill is a survival from the Middle Ages. In the Jacobean translation of Ariosto's satires, attributed to Gervase Markham but actually by Robert Tofte, we read of men who toil up a hill. Too late they realize that they would have been happier had they remained in the valley below. Others envying them follow after "by troopes and flocks"; but all alike tumble down. The simple allegory is thus interpreted:

> This lofty mountaine is the Wheel of fate
> Upon whose top sits roialized in state,
> (As ignorance and follie doth suppose)
> All quietnesse, al peace, and sweete repose.
> But they (alasse) doe all mistake the ground,
> For there nor joy is, nor contentment found.[38]

Few examples could be found which better illustrate the conflation and interpenetration of imagery than does the mixed metaphor: "This lofty mountaine is the Wheele of fate."

The year in which this translation of Ariosto was published (1608) is that in which many authorities place the composition of *Timon of Athens*. In the Introduction I examine briefly the discussion between the Poet and the Painter, with which the play opens (I.1.43–94), as an example of the rivalry existing between practitioners of the two arts. Here I should like to consider the Poet's summary of the poem which he proposes to present to his patron. "Sir," he says, addressing the Painter, "I have upon a high and pleasant hill / Feign'd Fortune to be throned." The base of this hill is thronged with people, and among them "One do I personate of Lord Timon's frame, / Whom Fortune with her ivory hand wafts to her." The great man accomplishes the arduous ascent, his parasites clinging to him, and then

> When Fortune in her shift and change of mood
> Spurns down her late beloved, all his dependents,

Which labour'd after him to the mountain's top
Even on their hands and knees, let him slip down,
Not one accompanying his declining foot.

It is somewhat surprising that the Painter, ignorant of an old tradition, should commend the freshness and originality of this image of the Hill of Fortune as one that might well be delineated by an artist, even though, jealous of his own art, he presently brushes contemptuously aside the Poet's rendering of the theme.

In this account of the faithlessness of fawning parasites, the subject of the play is concisely symbolized in tragic anticipation of the catastrophe. Closely similar to the image in *Timon* are the cynical words of Lear's Fool (II.4.72–76): "Let go thy hold when a great wheel runs down a hill, lest it break thy neck with following it; but the great one that goes upward, let him draw thee after." Here the metaphor shifts in the middle of the sentence: the word "wheel" with its neuter pronoun becomes a masculine pronoun in the second clause. Shakespeare's imagination has unified Fortune's victim and her instrument. There is another link between Fortune's wheel and the heights upon which she dwells in the words of the First Player in *Hamlet* (II.2.515–18):

Out, out, thou strumpet Fortune! All you gods,
In general synod take away her power;
Break all the spokes and fellies from her wheel,
And bowl the round nave down the hill of heaven.

Is not the "round nave" or hub perhaps suggestive of the sphere of Fortune which so quickly rolls away?

To the passages in *Timon* and *King Lear* an engraving by Nicolas Guérard offers a parallel in subject but a contrast in treatment: The massive Jacobean verbal imagery of Shakespeare is replaced by the sophisticated vision of seventeenth-century France. The Great Man, Fortune's favorite, stands at the top of her wheel holding aloft an image of her whom he idolizes. From it hang fishhooks baited with coins to catch men and parasites, offering him incense, receive other coins falling from his purse. The background presents a contrast. A great wheel has run down hill, the flatterers and sycophants have turned their backs and are departing, and only Virtue remains to sustain the unfortunate man who has fallen from the wheel.[39]

5. *Fortune associated with the Fates, Nemesis, Justice, and Opportunity*

Occasionally Fortune turns her wheel not by grasping its crank but by means of a rope or cord attached to the crank. This is the method employed in a woodcut in *The Ship of Fools* where three fools are upon the wheel,[1] and again in a painting at Chatsworth where the Four Ages of Man are upon it.[2] One of Cousin's drawings (no. 123) is of Fortune holding her wheel in one hand while with the other she turns the crank with a cord (Fig. 56). A similar tiny model of the "great wheel" is carried, we remember, by a nymph in the procession with which Dekker's *Old Fortunatus* opens. In two English masques, Robert White's *Cupid's Banishment* and Thomas Carew's *Coelum Britanicum*, Fortune carries her wheel. Beham's beautiful "Fortune" holds a wheel upon which there is a king.[3] In another drawing (no. 189) Cousin almost identifies Fortune with the Fates, for she holds a distaff. In the Uffizi there is a beautiful drawing by Bacchiacca where there is a spindle on Fortune's head.[4] Ripa discusses, though he does not illustrate, the single figure of Fato which is a fusion of the Three Fates into one abstraction. Fato is not a woman but a man; his origin is proved, however, by the statement that he holds a distaff. Keeping in mind this association of Fortune and the Fates, Fortune manipulating a cord or thread and more particularly actually holding a distaff, there are several passages in English poetry to be considered.

At the beginning of the Second Tragedy in *The Mirrour for Magistrates* the ghostly speaker says:

> Among the ryders of the rollyng wheele
> That lost theyr holdes . . . forget not me,
> Whose fatal threede Fortune nedes would reele,
> Ere it were twysted by the systers three.

Eleazar in *Lust's Dominion* (V.1) says:

> I have stood upon the top of Fortune's wheel,
> And backward turn'd the iron screw of fate.
> The destinies have spun a silken thread
> About my life.

A character in one of Thomas Middleton's comedies says: "Fortune (who slaves men) was my slave; her wheele / Hath spun me golden threads." [5]

As one argument for identifying "T. M. Gent" with Middleton as the author of *The Ghost of Lucrece*, Dr. McManaway cited an allusion in the poem to "that string of Fortune's wheel." [6] Robert Southwell declares that Fortune's "loome doth weave the fine and coarsest thread." [7] In an anonymous poem Fortune is said to turn her wheel now one way and now another, so that there is "no thread so surely sponne, but that she may untwist." [8] These poets are not guilty of any ignorant confusion of the wheel of Fortune and the spinning wheel of the Fates but deliberately amalgamate the two images as certain artists had done.

Commentators on Shakespeare, including Dr. Johnson, unaware of the process of interpenetration, have brought against him the charge of confusing two separate concepts. In three of the plays Fortune is called a "housewife" or a "huswife." The editors who, in two of these passages, gloss "huswife" as hussy, a jilt, a light false woman are correct, there are parallel cases in *Hamlet* where Fortune is denounced as a "strumpet," yet it must be insisted that here, as so often in Shakespeare, more than one thought is involved in the image. One of the chief occupations of the housewife was spinning, as the term "housewife," pronounced "huzif," used for a case holding needles and thread indicates. To call Fortune a housewife is almost as much as to mention her distaff. The association with spinning is clear in some lines in *The Antiquary:*

> Next will I post unto the Destinies,
> Shiver their wheel and distaff 'gainst the wall,
> And spoil their housewif'ry.[9]

This is the concept in Celia's mind when she says to Rosalind, "Let us sit and mock the good housewife Fortune from her wheel." [10] Again, when the bearers have raised the dying Anthony aloft into the monument, Cleopatra exclaims:

> Let me speak; and let me rail so high
> That the false huswife Fortune break her wheel,
> Provok'd by my offence.[11]

On the receipt of ill tidings Ancient Pistol proclaims in his ranting vein:

> Doth Fortune play the huswife with me now?
> News have I that my Nell is dead . . .
> And there my rendezvous is quite cut off.[12]

The curious metaphor of cutting off a rendezvous is characteristic of the speaker but easily explicable if in his mind, and in Shakespeare's, is the image of spinning and cutting a thread.

Once more, the association is impressively shown in a scene in *Old Fortunatus* (II.2) where the Parcae are spinning in the background behind Fortune. In the preceding chapter I have commented upon Peele's pageant in which Fortune collaborates with Nature and Time in weaving the web of destiny.

These are but a few examples of the distinction often drawn in visual and verbal imagery between the two meanings of Fortune: unstable, fleeting, incalculable Chance and unavoidable, fixed Destiny. In an imaginary dialogue between a Scholar and his Master the former objects that dice ought to be round in order to symbolize fleeting Fortune and the Master explains that when "the die is cast" Fate is fixed and is therefore properly symbolized by a cube.[13] The contrast is impressively presented on the title page (Fig. 57) of Robert Recorde's *The Castle of Knowledge* (1556). Here we see blindfold Fortune standing upon the unstable rolling sphere and turning with a cord "the Wheel of Fortune whose Ruler is Ignorance." On the wheel is inscribed: "Corruet statim qui modo scandit," which may be paraphrased: "He who has just this instant climbed will forthwith crash down again." Opposite Fortune is Urania, the heavenly Muse. Standing securely upon a cube, she holds in one hand a compass and in the other "the Sphere of Destiny whose Governor is Knowledge." So far the iconography is simple and normal in its balanced contrast. The idea expressed in some quaint verses on the title page is, however, unusual and has some bearing upon the interpretation of Spenser's *Cantos of Mutability*. In some unexplained way Fortune seeks by turning her wheel to bring to a stop the revolutions of the celestial sphere, that is, she seeks to extend her authority beyond this nether world beneath the moon. But the Uranian sphere resists these machinations and the villainy of Fortune. Though the earth pays homage to Fortune's fickleness and men as blind as beetles advance her wheel, the heavens are not subject to her but surmount all her changes and chances. Even so Spenser's Mutability, whom most scholars do not equate with Fortune, storms the celestial spheres, seeking to enlarge her domain. At the close of Spenser's narrative Nature decrees, precisely as it is asserted in Recorde's lines, that Mutability's power is limited to the sublunary world.

In her character as Fate or Destiny Fortune approximates Nemesis and Justice. Dürer's famous engraving "The Great Fortune" is also known as "Nemesis." She holds a bridle with bit and reins. So Cousin's drawing (no. 177) of "Fortune as Nemesis" shows her with a bridle, and this attribute is assigned to Nemesis by various emblematists, among them Alciati (Fig. 58) and Whitney.[14] In fact, since, as in Dante, Fortune may be held to be one of the agents of God, her function is frequently fused with that of Justice or Nemesis. In Cousin's drawing, just referred to, the halter Fortune offers to the man is his destiny, which no man can escape. Here she is not mere Chance and we are reminded of Gonzalo's words about the rude boatsman in the midst of the tempest and the terror of shipwreck: "I have great comfort from this fellow. Methinks he hath no drowning marks upon him; his complexion is perfect gallows. Stand fast, good fate, to his hanging! Make the rope of his destiny our cable, for our own doth little advantage. If he be not born to be hang'd, our case is miserable." [15] Fortune approximates Justice or Nemesis when, as in Dürer's engraving, or on the title page by Hans Holbein the Younger of "The Table of Cebes," in Erasmus' New Testament (Basle, 1522), or on the title page of an edition of Bacon's *Life of King Henry VII* printed in Holland, she holds a bridle.[16] Abraham Fraunce describes Nemesis in terms quite applicable to Fortune: "She was figured winged: for punishment commeth quickly. She stoode on a wheele, and stearne [that is, rudder] of a ship: for she rolleth and ruleth all upside downe. She held a bridle, and a rule or measure, for we must temper our tonge, and deale justly." [17]

In the morality play *Respublica* the character Nemesis or Retributive Justice is said to possess a wheel and wings "in token that her rule extendeth far and nigh." [18] Here attributes of Fortune are given a new interpretation in order to make them appropriate to the other personifications. Alciati conceives of Nemesis as running along a path in which there are footprints; she is Retributive Justice in pursuit of Crime.[19] Jean Baudoin imagines that she is mounted upon a stag, "animal d'extreme vistesse." [20] François d'Amboise describes Nemesis as "ayant un fouet en main et une coleuvre soubs les pieds pour sa tardité." [21] And Corrozet, who provides Nemesis with a bridle and the palm of Victory, has her standing upon a snail because she is in no haste.[22] We have, thus, on the one hand the idea of the swiftness of Vengeance and on the other the idea of the remorseless slowness with which the mills of the gods do grind. Although Fortune, in her capacity as Destiny, may be slow she is sure. A device used by two Elizabethan printers fuses Fortune and Justice into one figure who blindfolded stands upon a sphere holding in one hand a sword and in the other the palm of victory. Actually labeled "Fortuna," it is obvious that she is also Justice.[23] Thomas Carew conceives her to be the surrogate for Justice. In his masque *Coelum Britanicum* (1634), Fortune delivers a long speech to the audience in which she says that since Justice has fled to heaven she is "her Deputy on

Earth," holds the scales, and with "impartial hands" dispenses the "constant lot" of men. The fault is not hers if her rewards go to men who do not deserve them:

> It is no error to conferre dignity,
> But to bestow it on a vitious man;
> I gave the dignity, but you made the vice.

Fortune further rejects any claim to being omnipotent; it has been wrongly attributed to her.[24] Richard Linche, translating Cartari, notes that some writers have identified Fortune with Nemesis and he relates both to Justice.[25] But in another context, still following Cartari, he cites authority for picturing Fortune on a galloping horse pursued by Fate or Destiny who aims an arrow at her. "These two," he says, "can never accord or agree together. . . . Where Destiny sets her foot, Fortune is there . . . inchanted . . . having no power, efficacie, or vertue." [26] In the first of these passages Fortune is God's agent; in the second she is the mere bestower of worldly wealth which Destiny may take away. We may compare an emblem labeled "Fata obstant" where, in implicit contrast to the whirling wheel of Fortune, there is a wheel which has its rim spiked so that it cannot revolve and is further impeded by being fastened by a chain to a cube.[27]

As she is infrequently identified with Justice, Nemesis, Destiny, and Fate so far oftener Fortune is identified with Occasion or Opportunity. The Fortuna–Occasio–Tempus complex of associations has been studied by Professor Patch, Professor Wittkower, and other scholars, and I have touched on it in the previous chapter, but something must be added here. Logically Fortune and Opportunity (Occasio) should of course be differentiated, because the former, though inconstant and incalculable, is not necessarily momentary; either good or evil fortune may endure for a lifetime. Yet the razor which Occasio (Fig. 59) holds in some emblem books,[28] and which clearly suggests the razor edge of the moment between the opportunity not yet come and the opportunity that is past, is sometimes an attribute of Fortune.[29] Cousin (no. 179) even assigns to Fortune a scythe as well as a razor. Again, not Fortune but Occasio may properly be likened to a footless bird constantly on the wing. At least one emblematist likens Fortune to such a bird.[30] Francis Thynne also compares Fortune to a bird and goes on to say that "the cunninge Smirnians her Image carved out / With feete cut from her legs and set on ball turninge aboute." [31] Cousin has a drawing (no. 21) of "Fortuna sine pedibus"; the figure is upright in a wide landscape but its legs end at the knees (Fig. 60). There is a similar drawing by Giorgio Vasari [32] and other examples could be adduced.[33] The two personifications, in these cases fused, are elsewhere carefully distinguished. There is a beautiful engraving by Nicoletto da Modena (Fig. 61) in which Fortune holds a wand or staff surmounted with a head or mask which has a conspicuous forelock—the head is none other than that of Occasio.[34] Fortuna, or Favore, is distinguished from Opportunity in a design where the former stands upon a pair of wheels and the latter holds the razor.[35] Again, in Robert White's *Masque of Cupid's Banishment*, Fortune and Occasion are separate characters. The latter carries "a white wand, to signify her haste; with a long lock before and bald behind, alluding to the difficulty of recalling her if she be once past." [36] Yet in countless pictures it is Fortune herself who has the forelock, just as the forelock is so familiar a characteristic of Time. One of the emblems in Corrozet's *Hecatomgraphie* is an impressive variant on the theme that Opportunity is bald behind. Occasion is also shown standing in a boat and Penitence sits behind her, lamenting for lost opportunities.[37]

Although good Fortune, unlike Opportunity, may last a long while yet Man must not count upon her favors. When we find Fortune (Fig. 62) standing on her wheel [38] or sitting astraddle it more or less in the position of a cyclist,[39] the emblem is no longer showing the ups-and-downs of life but rather the fleetingness of Chance. The same interpretation holds when instead of a wheel there is a rolling ball, as in the pictures Fluellen knew. The ball may be "infixed" upon her head [40] and then, whether intentionally or not, there is an appropriate conflation with the personification of Worldliness.[41] I am at a loss to explain what an English epigrammatist meant when he said to Fortune, "Th'arte full of mosse, and yet a rolling stone." [42] If Fortune holds the ball in her hand it may suggest the orb of sovereignty, and if the ball is made of glass, as in Giovanni Bellini's well known painting, there may possibly be a hint at divination or fortunetelling, and there is certainly an invitation to contemplate Fortune's fragility. Linche, following Cartari, reports that "with certaine people of Greece Fortune's picture or statue was made of glass, and among the Egyptians her wheel was of glass." [43] Cousin has a drawing (no. 55) of "Fortuna Vitrea," Fortune made entirely of glass, a difficult visual image but not beyond the talent of the designer of the famous stained glass windows at Vincennes. In a morality play Fortune describes herself "as brittle as the glass." [44] Robert Greene says that "her bravest seats are made of glass." [45] John Davies of Hereford has a poem entitled "Fortuna vitrea est, quae cum splendet, frangitur" [46]; the same aphorism is quoted by Sir William Cornwallys.[47] Elsewhere this glass becomes a mirror under Fortune's feet which "shewes us at once, both her instability and our inconstancy," [48] and there is a sixteenth—century German print of Fortune holding a mirror.[49] The attribute does not seem particularly appropriate till we remember that it is the traditional attribute of Pride, and Fortune's favorites are often prone to this sin.

The characteristic of blindness or, more frequently, the attribute of the scarf or "muffler afore her eyes" is a familiar feature in pictures and descriptions of Fortune. Lydgate says that she is the blind lady who sees nothing.[50] She looks not where she bestows her gifts and is thus one of the *Aveugles* along with Love and Death before whom poor humanity must dance.[51] The attribute of the scarf she shares not only with these but with various other personifications: with Ignorance and Error,[52] with Heresy and the Synagogue and Islam, even with Justice. It was some-times held that it is not Fortune but he who places his confidence in her that is blind. Sir Thomas Elyot writes: "Chilo the wyse man being demanded what fortune was, He answered: A lewde phisition, for she made many folkes blynde that trusted moche to her." [53] An emblem shows her as the blind leading the blind.[54] But at least once we find an emphatic denial of all this: "They Fortune much do wrong that cal her blind." [55] In a later chapter we shall meet with a like conflict of testimony with regard to Justice.

6. Whom does Fortune favor? With whom does she collaborate? Who triumph over her?

The court of Fortune is the setting of Ulpian Fulwell's *The Eyghth liberall Science* (1576), a series of satiric and moral dialogues directed against the devious means men employ to advance their fortunes in the world.[1] Adulation or Flattery intrudes herself into the company of the Seven Liberal Arts. Each of the Seven describes herself in a six—line stanza, and then Flattery boasts that whereas devotees of any of the Seven are always poor [2] her followers attain worldly bliss: "I spin the thread and weave the web of hap, / And none but I may sit in Fortune's lap." The author then tells how he obtained from Lady Hope a letter of introduction to her cousin Lady Fortune. When he visited her court and was admitted to her presence, "I found," he narrates, "the Poets and painters true men and not lyers, for she was muffled from her chin to the top of her temples, and it so fell out that as I came in, she was blindly . . . bestowing her guiftes. . . . She gave to[o] much to very

many, but ynough to none. Superfluity sate alofte." In a corner, solitary
and neglected, was lovely Lady Truth. Fortune tells her visitor that if
he would get on in the world he must learn to flatter and dissemble.
"Is there any universitie wherin this science is studied?" he asks; and
Fortune replies, "It is both studied and practised throughout the world."
Flatterers and sycophants must beware of the envious:

> He that lives at Court . . .
> Let him be sure of this,
> If Fortune chance to frowne,
> Envy in time will turne the wheele
> And throw him head–long downe.[3]

Cartari (ed. Venice, 1571, p. 487) has a winged man ascending the
wheel; Envy stands behind him. The wings, it is explained, are "l'ali
del favore humano."

A fool does not need study and practice in order to win Fortune's
favors. "Fortuna, quae stultis favere dicitur," says Erasmus, and his Folly,
preaching from her pulpit, declares that from the rashness and indiscre-
tion which Fortune loves it is but a step to foolishness, and "you see my
fools abounding in money, holding the helms of state, in brief, flourishing
every way." [4] One of the marginal drawings by Hans Holbein the
Younger in the celebrated copy of *Encomium Morae* (Basle, 1515) shows
Fortune emptying a bag of coins into a fool's lap.[5] No classical source
of the idea has been discovered; the extraordinary popularity of what
became a proverbial expression, "Fortune favors fools," among the Elizabethans is perhaps due to the influence of Erasmus. "Call me not fool
till heaven hath sent me fortune," says Touchstone.[6] In a form adapted
to Christian orthodoxy the saying is one of John Heywood's *Proverbs*:
"God sendeth fortune to fooles"; [7] this variant is found in Dekker's
Shoemaker's Holiday (IV.3). Thomas Nashe has the ungrammatical
form "Fortuna favet fatuos." [8] The proverb, or paraphrases of it, occurs
half a dozen times in the drama of our period.[9] Cousin has a drawing
(no. 191) of Fortune herself dressed as a she–fool with hood, bells, and
bauble. In Quarles' *Emblemes* (Bk. I, no. 10) Fortune holds aloft a fool's
cap–and–bells as the prize in a contest between Earthly Love and Mammon. Richard Brathwaite, defying Fortune, calls her an "imperious mole"
because of her blindness and upbraids her for her foolish choice of
favorites.[10] Rather wittily Taylor the Water–poet says of Fortune: "She's
bountifull to fooles, and therefore I / Have small share in her liberality." [11] Only once so far as I have observed is the more or less facetious

saying employed with real dignity and power. This is in Chapman's *The Widow's Tears* which opens with an invocation to the "blind, imperfect goddess" that delights "to converse only with fools" and ladens the "unworthy ass with gold" while "worth and merit" go unrewarded.

Asses or men with donkeys' heads appear on some wheels of Fortune in *The Ship of Fools*, and elsewhere, but these are not her favorites, for though they rise they tumble off again. These fantastic therianthropic creatures occur in different forms and in groups of two, three, or four. In various editions of *Das Narrenschiff*, in the French version, in Barclay's English version, and in the English prose version, three fools ride the wheel and beneath it yawns a grave (Fig. 63). The rising figure has a donkey's head; a donkey is at the top, either reaching for the moon or perhaps playing on a tambourine; a creature with a human head and almost entirely human figures plunges towards the grave.[12] In the Dutch version, *Dat Narren Schyp* (Lubeck, 1497) and in *Das Neue Narrenschiff* (Strassburg, 1494, and later issues) there are only two figures on the wheel: an ass–headed man rising and a human–headed donkey falling.[13] The German version of Petrarch's *De Remediis Utriusque Fortunae* pictures a man with the hind legs of an ass ascending the wheel, a crowned ass with human legs at the top, and an ass with human arms and torso falling off.[14] On the title page of Le Franc's *Estrif* (second edition, Paris, 1506) a man with ass's ears ascends the wheel, a throned ass is at the top, an altogether human figure goes downward, and another human figure lies on the ground.[15] Adaptations of the theme are found in "atouts" of tarot cards of both early and later date. In a fourteenth–century set an ass ascends the wheel, a winged monarch is at the summit, and a man is descending. All three figures have tails instead of legs.[16] Of much later date is a set of Italian "minchiate" cards one of which is a wheel of Fortune. Three of the figures are men but at the top the man has an ass's head.[17] We are reminded of these and similar designs when a Jacobean writer says that Fortune, "the purblinde witch," is apt "to set an Ass on top of all her wheele." [18] However, that Fortune's favors cannot conceal folly is the lesson to be had from a curious design of a richly dressed man with the ears of an ass from whose heart sprouts a branch bearing the heads of three fools as its fruit.[19]

In tarot cards Fortune, with or without her wheel, is sometimes shown accompanied by dogs or rabbits or apes, to indicate her indifference to merit or ability.[20] This indifference gave rise to the proverbial expression "Apes in scarlet," as when Colonel Hutchinson wrote of Cromwell's wife and children that they "were setting up for principality, which

suited no better with any of them than scarlet on the ape." [21] Otho
Van Veen has a charming emblem of Fortune resting her hand in a
patronizing gesture upon an ape that is robed and crowned [22] thus pointing out that if you are a fool not all the gifts of Fortune can conceal
the fact (Fig. 64). Another Netherlandish emblem shows an ape at the
top of a pole at whom people are looking and pointing: The higher it
is the more it exposes its ignominy. The emblematist commenting upon
this design quotes an English saying: "Offices are given but not discretion." [23] Some satires by Richard Brathwaite called "The Age for Apes"
are illustrated with a copperplate by Robert Vaughan depicting Democritus and Heraclitus. Behind the two philosophers is a garden in which
are several apes dressed as fashionable gallants. Near them a man with
a drawn sword is evidently the satirist.[24]

Man may, however, resist Fortune's blandishments. Poverty, unless
misguided by Folly, may be her implacable foe. There is an episode in
Boccaccio's *De Casibus* which came to John Lydgate through Laurent de
Premierfait. Disregarding the Latin original and the French version I
shall summarize the fable which Andalus the astronomer related to
Bochas.[25] This concerns the "disputacion betweene fortune and glad
povert" and is intended to demonstrate that "princys shoulde not atwite
constallacions nor fortune of theire unhappy fallyng but theire owne
demeritys and vicious lyvyng." Once upon a time Fortune met Glad
Poverty at a roadside and jeered and laughed at her. Poverty, a ragged,
reckless woman, replied that she preferred to be poor and happy than
wealthy and anxious. The dispute waxed bitter and Poverty challenged
Fortune to a wrestling match, the loser to obey the winner. In the bout
lean Poverty had the advantage over fat Fortune and overcame her. A
third character, Unhappy Adventure, that is, Ill Luck, now enters the
story. Victorious Poverty demanded that Fortune relinquish control over
Unhappy Adventure and bind her to a stake so only fools—and of their
own free will—need ever unbind her, and no one need ever honor
Adventure as a goddess. This fable is the subject of one of Colard
Mansion's famous engravings illustrating Laurent de Premierfait.[26] Here
several portions of the tale are grouped in a single design: Fortune carries
a shield on which is the device of a wheel; Poverty is shown first by
the wayside and then thwacking Fortune; Malheur, a male figure, the
equivalent of Lydgate's female Unhappy Adventure, appears bound to
a stake. In Jean du Pré's woodcut illustrating the fable the general arrangement is that of Mansion's copperplate; there is, however, no attempt
to differentiate between Poverty and Malheur.[27] This cut reappears

along with Du Pré's other illustrations in Pynson's first edition (1494) of *The Fall of Princes*, but when Pynson had to use new, and inferior, cuts for his edition of 1527 the scenes are radically altered: Fortune appears in colloquy with Glad Poverty and afterwards binds Unhappy Adventure, but the fight between Fortune and Glad Poverty has disappeared and in its place we have Fortune fallen from her wheel. This cut reappears in Tottel's edition of *The Fall of Princes* (1554) but the fable is not illustrated in John Wayland's edition (1554).[28] John Hagthorpe's third "Vision" is a dispute between Opulence, that is, Favorable Fortune, and Poverty. The palace of Opulence is described and also her chariot or "loftie coach," with its various allegorical details, while the children of Opulence, Boasting, Disdain, Pride, Fear, and so forth are named. Pale Poverty wears "a wreath of cammamile" for reasons which readers of Lyly and Shakespeare will recognize. The house of Poverty has its gate open, "for those that nothing have can nothing fear." There is a debate and combat between these adversaries.[29]

The theme of victorious Poverty descended to the emblematists. In the *Minerva Britanna* (no. 194) Peacham shows Fortune supine on her wheel, which lies upon the ground, and Poverty, a strong, ill-kept, uncouth man, binding her with a rope. Another example is Maurice Scève's and Martin Meyer's "Paupertas Fortunae Victrix," with Fortune prostrate upon her wheel while Poverty, a sturdy man in ragged clothes, is binding her with a rope. Meyer comments that the ethnic tradition was to make Poverty not only ragged but pallid and angry, whereas it is fitting, on the basis of Proverbs 6:11, to depict him in virile form albeit clothed in rags.[30]

When Lydgate, as we have seen, tells us that Fortune is a tavern keeper it is as much as to say that she is allied with evil, for the tavern was notoriously "the devil's church." In the manuscripts of Martin le Franc's *Estrif* there are numerous illustrations showing Fortune and Virtue in opposition, as when they dispute before enthroned Reason or when a magnificent castle rises behind Virtue and a castle in ruins behind Fortune.[31] In one of the morality plays there is the complaint:

> The time hath been, when Virtue had the sovereignty
> Of greatest price, and plac'd in chiefest dignity;
> But topsy-turvy now the world is turn'd about:
> Proud Fortune is preferr'd, poor Virtue clean thrust out.[32]

Sir Guyon in *The Faerie Queene* (II, 9, 8) declares that Fortune seldom "yields to vertue aide / But in her way throwes mischiefe and mis-chaunce." At the beginning of Dekker's *Old Fortunatus* Fortune is indifferent alike to Virtue (who wears a fool's cap) and to Vice (whose face is gilded), but as the play progresses she is seen to be herself vicious. In a quaint emblem Virtue is a tortoise which is not troubled by the buzzing of the bee Fortune.[33] The parable of the House built on the Rock and the House built on the Sand (Matthew 7:24–27) is a favorite of those emblematists (Fig. 65) who contrast the constancy of Virtue and the fickleness of Fortune.[34] This visual image receives verbal expression in a poem by Francis Kinwelmarsh:

> Upon the setled Rocke, thy building surest standes,
> Away it quickly weares, that resteth on the sandes.
> Dame Virtue is the Rocke, that yeeldes assured stay;
> Dame Fortune is the Sand, that scowreth soon away.
> Chuse that is certaine, let thinges uncertayne passe,
> Preferre the precious golde, before the brittle glasse.[35]

One of Van Veen's Horatian Emblems (p. 9) is of Virtue, armed, standing on prostrate Fortune. Virtue is surrounded by six Cupids, representing Piety, with a flame, Magnanimity with a lion, and the Four Stoic Virtues, with traditional attributes. One of Cousin's drawings (no. 87) shows Virtue standing victoriously over a prostrate Fortune whose wheel is broken; in another (no. 107), called "Fortunae Imperatrix Providentia," a similar idea is conveyed: a meek Fortune, blindfold, is at the feet of Foresight who is enthroned, crown'ed, and bifrons. Cartari (ed. Venice, 1570, p. 479) has Occasio, a masculine figure, with a caduceus and a cornucopia by him, indicating the rewards of forehandedness. These antitheses are practically identical with that in the well known fresco at Mantua attributed to Mantegna where Fortuna on a rolling ball is contrasted with Constantia who stands firmly on a square pedestal.[36] This may be compared with the illustration at the beginning of the French version of Petrarch's *Remèdes* (1523) where the goddess is on the "Sedes Fortunae Rotunda" and opposite her on the "Sedes Virtutis Quadrata" is Wisdom holding the "Speculum Sapientiae." [37] Popular among the emblematists (Figs. 66 and 67) is the theme of Fortune on her unstable sphere and Mercury standing or sitting on a cube.[38] The meaning is expounded in one of Francis Thynne's *Emblems*, "Art, the antidote against Fortune":

> On rolling ball doth fickle Fortune stand;
> On firm and settled square sits Mercury.

The god of Arts, with wisdom's rod in hand;
Which covertly to us doth signify,
That Fortune's power, inconstant and still frail,
Against wisdom and art cannot prevail.[39]

The opposition may well have been in Spenser's mind when in the *Cantos of Mutabilitie* (VI, 16–17) Mercury and Mutability confront one another. It was certainly in Chapman's mind in his recurring image of Truth associated with the firm "square" of the dice.[40] In a fine printer's device Constancy, buffeted by winds and waves, stands upon a cube.[41] Ripa directs that Constanza shall be delineated with her feet placed squarely upon a firm base. In Wither's emblem of Confidence, constant in the faith, she is seated upon a "squared stone." However, in another emblem Wither points the contrast quite differently: Fortune's victim falls headlong from the wheel while Virtue, with a human body but the head of an eagle soars to heaven. Yet another emblem has no personifications but merely a winged ball encircled by the serpent of Prudence to indicate, as Wither writes, that "Though Fortune hath a powerfull name, / Yet Vertue overcomes the same." [42] Four of Cousin's drawings convey similar ideas: Reason, Virtue, Nobility, and Patience are shown at odds with Fortune.[43] Corrozet pictures Fortune reduced to beggary because the wise have deprived her of her power; in the cut she is groping blindly and her broken wheel is slung on her arm.[44] The same emblematist shows that Hope may sustain Man under the burden of Ill Fortune: a man bowed down by a wheel on his back supports himself with a staff to which is attached an armillary sphere that, it is explained, symbolizes our Hope which is on high.[45] Wisdom knows how properly to evaluate the promises of Fortune. In one of the Horatian Emblems (p. 83) Wisdom stands upon a pedestal fearless of Fortune, Poverty (a haggard woman), Love (two Cupids shooting arrows at him), Imprisonment (a man holding up chains), and Death (a skeleton). On the title page (Fig. 68) of the Dutch edition of Bacon's *Henry VII*, a wise man, in contrast to the sycophants who render homage to Fortune, inserts a staff between the spokes of her wheel to stop its turning. The saying "Expers Fortunae Sapientia" is illustrated in an emblem where Wisdom is contentedly seated at a table in her study with her books, instruments, an owl by her, while behind her Fortune with a purse, a treasure chest and two casks is seated in a boat upon the water because she may sail away at any moment.[46] Another emblematist pictures "Sapiens supra Fortunam": Fortune is prostrate upon her wheel and a wise old man who has lashed her to it is engaged in binding her yet more tightly.[47] La Perriere draws an ingenious analogy. As the carver can make a figure out of any piece of wood, so Wisdom can apply any fortune to his profit, and the emblem shows the carver in the act of fashioning an image of Fortune.[48]

In the *Amorum Emblemata* (1608) Van Veen thrice brings Fortune and Love together. In one design (p. 157) Fortune is fastening a scarf to Love's eyes and he is standing upon a sphere, for Love may be both blind and fleeting. But in another (p. 107) she aids a brave and courageous Love to drive off Envy. In the third (p. 175) Love grasps Occasion firmly by the forelock and she, making obeisance to him, offers a cornucopia of fruit and flowers. Similar to this last is an engraving by Simone Cantarini where, as a gift to Love who controls her, Fortune pours out coins from a purse.

Instead of being hostile to them Fortune may collaborate with Virtue or with Courage or Industry or the Arts. This happy alliance of Fortune and Virtue was a concept appropriate for tributes to royalty. Thus, one of Guillaume de la Perriere's emblems shows a king above whose head Fortune and Virtue together hold a crown.[49] The allegorical title page of Dr. John Dee's treatise on *The Art of Navigation* (1577) shows, along with much else, Fortune, or rather Opportunity, standing upon the shore and proffering a wreath to Queen Elizabeth who is seated on the poop of an approaching vessel.[50] When on a triumphal arch designed by Thomas Dekker for the reception of King James there were figures of Virtue enthroned and Fortune on a turning globe, no opposition of the two personifications was intended, and Thomas Dekker explains that "his Majesty's fortune was above the world, but his vertues above his fortune." [51]

Courage, like Love, may compel a favorable Fortune. Chapman's Pompey hopes that she may cease to balance herself " 'twixt two light wings" and "on a slippery globe sustain her steps," but passing by the enemies' forces and arrived at his own may

> Displume her shoulders, cast off her wing'd shoes,
> Her faithless and still—rolling stone spurn from her,
> And enter our powers, as she may remain
> Our firm assistant.[52]

That Courage may compel a favorable Fortune is the moral of a Florentine engraving in which a wind—head blows directly against Fortune's front; that is, Good Fortune is progressing against the wind of adversity.[53]

In answering why Fortune should be depicted holding a golden apple, Alain Chartier (in the Elizabethan version) explains that "good spirits are accompanied with good Fortune." [54]

Man need not always plead with Fortune or wring concession from her. With the passage of time Virtue may bring to fruition the seeds which Fortune scatters, as in the Printer's device, referred to in the previous chapter, where Time draws the plough guided by Virtue and Fortune the sower follows after.[55] Industry may rescue Fortune when she is about to sink into the sea.[56] A beautiful *impresa* by Ieronimo Ruscelli depicts a ship with Fortune, her scarf outspread to catch a favorable wind, standing in the middle and Virtue at the helm; the motto is "Utriusque Auxilio." [57] Learning may control Fortune, "Doctrina Fortunam Regit," as in an emblem where Doctrine steers the shell in which Fortune stands.[58] Closely analagous is a printer's device showing Fortune and Mercury, the Arts, in a boat together.[59] The same concept is seen in Cartari's design of Occasio standing by Mercury's winged hat and caduceus. The moral of this emblem is that "la buona Fortuna quasi sempre andare con l'Eloquenza et con la Dottrina." [60]

CHAPTER 4. THE SPIRITUAL FOES OF MAN

1. The Infernal Trinity

Man may discipline himself to bear serenely the whips and scorns of Time and the vagaries of fickle Fortune, yet on his journey through life he is compassed about with so many and great dangers that by reason of the frailty of his nature he cannot always stand upright.[1] The captains of the hosts of hell which war against the soul are the Infernal Trinity. Explicitly in such texts as Matthew 12:24–26 and Ephesians 6:12, and implicitly in various other parts of the New Testament as well as in the Apocrypha, the Kingdom of Satan is set before us in opposition to the Kingdom of God. In John 16:33, Christ bids His disciples to be of good cheer, for He has overcome the world. St. Paul places in antithesis "the fruit of the Spirit" and "the works of the flesh" (Galatians

70

5:19–23); St. Peter beseeches the faithful, "as strangers and pilgrims," to "abstain from fleshly lusts, which war against the soul" (1 Peter 2:11). From such texts as these, elaborated and commented upon in patristic literature, the concept developed of "the thre enemys of mankinde, that is to seyn, the Flessche, the Feend, and the World."[2] These are the three beasts which (as interpreted by Boccaccio and other early commentators) Dante encounters in the dark forest near the mouth of hell; or the three may be Avarice, a worldly sin, Lechery, a fleshly sin, and Pride, a devilish sin. The three winds that buffet the Tree of Patience in *Piers Plowman* are the World, the Flesh, and the Devil.[3]

Under one or another of these commanders are arrayed the Deadly Sins. Their number and the captains under whom they serve may differ according to different patterns. The followers of the Flesh (Caro) are always Gluttony, Lechery, and Sloth. The sole attendant upon the World (Mundus) may be Avarice, but the World may have the command also of Wrath or Envy or both. Either or both of these latter Sins may be transferred to the Devil, whose principal attendant, however, whether alone or in company, is generally Pride. In *Mary Magdalene*[4] (a fifteenth-century play transitional in character between the miracle and the morality) the King of the World commands Pride and Covetousness (Avarice); the King of the Flesh has Lechery for his paramour, Gluttony for his knight-at-arms, and Sloth for his friend; and attending upon the Prince of Devils are Wrath and Envy. When her Bad Angel and the Sins fail to take the penitent Magdalene captive they are upbraided by their captains and driven off to hell. The arrangement of infernal commanders and followers is different in *The Castle of Perseverance* (dated between 1400 and 1425).[5] In the assault upon the castle within which Mankind, defended by the Virtues, has taken refuge, Belial directs the attack by Superbia, Ira, and Invidia; Caro the attack by Gula, Luxuria, and Accidia; and Mundus the attack by Avaritia. The Sins are driven off and Belial and Caro flog their followers and berate them for their defeat, but Avarice remains to assault Mankind again in his old age.

The sequence is precisely the same as the order of assault in Spenser's *The Faerie Queene*. John Livingston Lowes asserted that there is no significance in the order in which Spenser arranges the Sins, and the *Variorum* editors fail to correct him.[6] Professor Bloomfield believes that there is no point "in trying to classify Spenser's order, as it is quite obvious that he has shifted it to suit his artistic purpose." With all respect for these distinguished scholars I am sure this is an error. Spenser does not allude explicitly to the Infernal Trinity but his pattern conforms to that of the three commanders. In the pageant, first come the Sins of the Flesh (Sloth, Gluttony, and Lechery), then the Worldly Sin (Avarice), and finally the Devilish Sins (Envy, Wrath, and Pride).[7] This order cannot be accidental. Furthermore, Lowes was mistaken when he said that Pride comes first. She is described first, upon her throne, but in the pageant she comes last, in her coach. She is the climax. Much more will be said of Spenser's pageant later in this chapter; we now revert to works of an earlier period.

In the morality play *Mankind* (dated between 1461–1485)[8] the effort to devise a novel variation upon the theme of the Infernal Trinity results in some loss of lucidity. "The fiend of hell" appears bearing the name Tutivilus (that of a mocking imp in the Wakefield Mysteries). The functions of Mundus are assigned to New–Guise, Now–a–days, and Nought (the thoughtless trivialities of the worldling). Caro does not appear as a character because, as is explained in the text, this Sin is within the body of Mankind.

Stephen Hawes, in *The Example of Vertu*,[9] tells us that Sapience and Discretion led the hero, Youth, across the perilous bridge of Worldly Vanity into the country of the King of Love. Youth courted the King's daughter but was told that before he might marry her he must first engage in combat with the Dragon with Three Heads. Sapience put the Pauline armor on Youth who going forth toward the close of day, still guided by Sapience, came into a dale where he sensed "the savour of a dungyon of the foul and stynkynge dragon." Nearby was a path which led to heaven, and the dragon tried to prevent men from following that path. In the long combat that ensued—illustrated with a woodcut— Youth cut off two of the dragon's heads: the World (a sinister bearded man) and the Flesh (a smiling woman). He could draw no blood from the diabolical third head but he drove the monster "home to his darke regyon of infernall payne." The dragon in this impressive episode is obviously a variant of the allegorical interpretation of the seven–headed Hydra as the Seven Deadly Sins. It is doubtless also an intentional re- minder of the seven–headed Beast of Revelation xiii, as is the "many- headed beast" upon which Duessa is mounted in *The Faerie Queene*, I, 8, 6.

A few other examples of the Hydra or dragon of Sin may be noted. In an episode in *The Pilgrimage to Paradise* (1592), an elaborate and quite beautiful allegorical poem by Nicholas Breton,[10] the Soul encoun- ters a formidable monster, an "ougly horror" with seven heads. These heads are Ambition (which, it is explained, infects souls with filthy

Pride), Avarice, Gluttony, Sloth, Lechery, Envy, and Murder (equivalent to Wrath). An angel is sent down from heaven to sustain the Soul in the coming ordeal. The Soul kneels in adoration; the angel commends him and comforts him with these moving words: "This is the path, that patience onely treades, / Where life doth goe on pilgrimage to love." The Soul is given certain books, which are not specified either by author or title but are doubtless the several books of the Bible, and the angel departs to heaven. Each of the monster's seven heads is in turn vanquished by arguments which the Soul extracts from his reading, each becomes impotent and shrunken, and at length the monster is slain. In the course of another late–Elizabethan allegorical poem, Anthony Copley's *A Fig for Fortune* (1596),[11] the Author (for the narrative is in the first person) is conducted by an angel to the Temple of Sion which is described as a sort of conflation of the Celestial Jerusalem with the modern city of Rome. (Copley was a Roman Catholic.) There, among its saintly inhabitants, he becomes a neophyte. Presently the Temple is attacked by Doblessa and her cohorts; from an earlier passage one gathers that Doblessa is Fortune, but she is also a personification of Fraud, Riot, and other offenses. The battle is joined. A pigeon (the Holy Ghost) fluttered above the combat and the "high Sacrificator" (Christ) "Came personally himselfe unto the bickering / To cheere his men of warre." Doblessa and her forces were routed, though with characteristic deceit they "did cockadoodle it" as though they had been victorious. To celebrate the triumph the Genius of the Place (who resembles faintly the Blessed Virgin Mary) scattered roses for which the holy company "scrambled." But though repulsed Doblessa was not permanently defeated, for being Hydra–headed she returned to the attack. Copley's poem is very halting in metre and extremely uncouth in vocabulary but fairly well devised and quite lively. To it and to Breton's *Pilgrimage* we shall return in a later chapter.

In their devotional and moral manuals the Order of Jesuits made much use of allegorical material in the manner of the emblematists. One of the most attractive of these is Father Jan David's *Veridicus Christianus* (1606). One of the plates pictures the Hydra.[12] The Soul, guided by a guardian angel, pursues her way along a narrow path leading to a distant heaven. On her left are seven men wearing crowns and brandishing swords: the Seven Kings of Canaan who opposed the entrance of God's Chosen People into the Promised Land and who in typological interpretation are the Seven Deadly Sins. On her right are a coiled serpent (the Devil) and the Hydra, whose long necks terminate in the heads of animals associated with the Sins. Other plates in this volume will be discussed presently. The combat of Hercules and the Hydra is not necessarily used as a symbol of the struggle of the Soul with the Deadly Sins but rather indicates that even when Virtue has achieved some success "still new troubles and new travels" are sown by Envy.[13] Before leaving the subject of the Hydra I should like to note as a curiosity one emblem book in which the seven–headed monster is used as a symbol of good, representing Virtue resisting the assaults of Fortune: as one head is struck off another grows in its place.[14]

Variations, some of them quite fantastic, are played upon the theme of the Infernal Trinity. The Béguinage in Ghent possesses a painting called "The Fountain of Life," attributed to Lucas Horenbault.[15] The Fountain itself, from which the Precious Blood gushes forth, does not concern us here, but another part of the painting is redolent of the realistic episodes in English and Continental moralities where the protagonist, having yielded to temptation, runs riot in the world. The World does not appear personified but the scene is set therein, and the Flesh and the Devil play prominent parts. Heretics who have rejected Divine Grace turn toward a shop kept by Satan and Lechery, the latter a finely costumed girl with horns sprouting from her head and with the clawed feet of some dreadful creature. "Come hither! Buy of me!" she cries. Gewgaws and vanities and the writings of Mahomet, Luther, Calvin, and Menno (the founder of the Anabaptists) are sold in this shop, and beneath it the gates of hell open.

A large engraving from a design by Heinrich Vogtherr the Younger (Fig. 69) presents the contrast between "The Death of the Righteous and the Death of the Unrighteous." [16] In the upper part Christ sits in judgment and six Works of Mercy are shown in rondels. Below are two deathbed scenes. On Christ's right hand (the spectator's left) the Righteous Man is attended by Faith, Hope, and Charity; and Thankfulness, behind the bed, holds out a wreath of Victory. In the background is a flock of sheep. On the opposite side of the print the Unrighteous Man writhes in agony while behind the bed a gloating skeleton holds an hourglass; the devil, issuing from the flames of hell, clutches at the dying man's arm; and a young woman, personifying the Flesh and wearing an orb–like halo labeled "Die Welt," hastens away. In the background are goats. To look at this fine engraving is to sense an imagination like that which inspired *Everyman*.

Further removed from normal renderings of the Infernal Trinity theme but not unrelated to it is a woodcut which appears in three reli-

74

gious tracts by Henrick Niklaes (Henry Nicholas), the founder of the Family of Love.[17] These tracts are in English but were printed at an unnamed place in the Low Countries. The cut shows the Devil (labeled "Sinne") supine on the ground with a globe, half hidden in a dragon's jaws, crushing him. On the dragon is a skeleton, and on the skeleton the triumphant Lamb of God. Christ's overcoming of the World and the Devil and his victory over Death are clearly, if crudely, symbolized, but the third member of the Unholy Trinity does not appear.

Two designs in Father David's book must now be mentioned.[18] In one (Fig. 70) a kneeling Christian is being tempted by the World, wearing a false face and an orb on her head, who offers him gifts with one hand but in her other hand holds a bit and bridle which she conceals behind her back; by the Flesh who, with bare breasts, and a pillow or cushion on her head, a symbol of Lechery or Sloth with which we shall meet again, offers a flower but conceals the flames of hell; and by the Devil brandishing in one hand a pronged weapon but plying with the other the fan of temptation, a variant of the more usual bellows.[19] The design contains two subsidiary episodes. In the background a stronghold on a hill is besieged; in the foreground a bristling hedgehog (the Soul) is worried by three dogs. The following plate shows the Christian Knight in full armor, trampling on a globe, a woman's head, and a serpent. Flanking him are a guardian angel and Freewill, the latter holding a winged mallet which, when it appears again in a later plate, is explained: "Apud fukros ipsos nostrâ linguiê (Willeken) Voluntus; malleus ipse appelatus, quod quaecumqua vult faciat, nihilque ei obsistat."

A French volume containing a series of religious emblems includes an illustration of the assault of the Infernal Trinity upon the Soul.[20] Psyche is asleep with her arms embracing the Cross. Divine Love wards off the World, a woman with a globe upon her head and holding a musical instrument; the Flesh, not the usual seductive woman but Cupid shooting his arrows at the Soul; and the Devil, with the bellows of temptation. Analogous to this is Van Veen's design (Fig. 71) answering St. Paul's question: "Quis nos separabit a Charitate Christi?" The Soul snuggles up to Divine Love, secure from a warrior, a woman with crown and scepter, a man with a chain and gyves, and Death.[21]

The Infernal Trinity along with several individual Sins are allegorized but not personified in a sermon by Thomas Adams entitled *The Spiritual Navigator Bound for the Holy Land* (1615). The Sea is the World, the waves are Pride swollen by the wind of Vainglory, the foam is Lust, and the turbulent waters Wrath. Satan is the great Leviathan, and just as the swordfish is the enemy of the whale so is the Sword of the Spirit the enemy of Satan. "There be Sirens in the Sea of this world. Syrens? Hirens, as they are now called. . . . In plaine English Harlots swimme amongst us." [22]

A tiny vignette on the title page of John Haywarde's *The Sanctuarie of a Troubled Soule* (1616) derives from the theme of the Infernal Trinity but does not conform strictly to it. Here the Christian is not triumphing over Evil but is in flight from it. Sitting side by side are a flamboyantly costumed woman and a black Devil who holds a moneybag. Antithetical to them is the Good Samaritan coming to the aid of the victim of the thieves.

Renold Elstrack's engraved title page (doubtless suggested by George Wither himself) to *Wither's Motto. Nec habeo, nec Careo, nec Curo* (1621) employs our usually lugubrious motif in a unique and quite charming way (Fig. 72). A prefatory "Explanation of the Embleme" helps us to understand the motto: "I do not possess, I do not want, I do not care." A contented man, clothed only in a mantle embroidered with heart's–ease, sits upon a firm rock, his head resting against the column of Fortitude and Constancy, with a cornucopia by him, showing that he does possess a sufficiency. He points downward to a landscape of abundant prosperity into which there drops a scroll with the words "Nec habeo," and with his foot spurns a globe (the World) beneath which a scroll reads "Nec Curo." His gaze is directed upward to the Tetragramaton from which a great ray of light streams down into his heart and a scroll issuing from his mouth reads "Nec Careo," that is, possessing Divine Love he needs nothing else. Angels, or rather the heads of angels, hover over him and Devils in the air and an armed band of men upon the ground hurl javelins at him, but they glance harmlessly aside. Thus the contented Christian is impervious to the assaults of the Devil and the temptations of the World and the Flesh—the last emblematized not, as usual, by a woman but by the superabundance of food being grown on the farm below.[23]

William Hall's *Mortalities Meditation: or, A Description of Sinne. With a Definition and plaine setting forth of Mans three chiefest and greatest Enemies, to wit, the World, the Flesh, and the Devil* (1624) is a dull poem in 183 six–line stanzas. The three enemies are described, but not in terms of personification, and war upon them is urged, but not in terms of allegory.

Thomas Cecill was the engraver of the plate (Fig. 73) on the *verso* of the title page of Joseph Fletcher's poem, *The History of the Perfect-*

Cursed–Blessed Man (1628).[24] A Christian in full armor is threatened by a snarling four–footed Devil. To the left of him stands a fair woman with bare breasts and with a globe upon her head. In one hand she holds a scepter and a money bag, in the other a crown, and from her mouth issue the words "All these things will I give thee if." In this personification the World and the Flesh are obviously conflated. To the right of the Christian stands Death, a skeleton, holding an hourglass and a scythe. From this same year dates a German engraving of a Christian Knight whose flaming sword is labeled "Gottes wort." He confronts the Devil, the World (a woman with a globe on her head), and the Flesh (a grossly fat, nude man—an unusual personification, for the Flesh is almost always female).[25]

For the reprint in 1631 of Sir Richard Barckley's *The Felicitie of Man, or, His Summum Bonum* originally published in 1598, William Marshall supplied an engraved title page. The Christian stands upon a globe beneath which lie a naked woman and the Devil. Faith, Hope, and Charity are in the background. Antithetical to the Christian is a turbaned Moslem engaged in fondling a woman who sits at a bountifully spread table. The margins of this design are decorated with appropriate objects.

John Payne was the engraver of the fine title page (Fig. 74) of John Downame's *The Christian Warfare* (1634).[26] At the top stands the Christian in full armor. A bat–winged, goat–footed demon hurls javelins against his shield and another demon, with scaly tail, whispers in his ear while pointing enticingly at a woman who has one breast bare. In one hand she holds a money bag and in the other a scepter and what seems to be a costly receptacle; at her feet are a globe and an open bag from which coins spill. Above her is the inscription: "Omnia haec tibi dabo." In this personification we have once more a conflation of the World and the Flesh.

How intimately these two members of the Infernal Trinity are allied is shown in another way in Richard Brathwaite's Latin dialogues entitled *Novissima Tuba* (1632) which John Vicars translated into English verse.[27] In the First Dialogue Flesh, who is the maidservant in the house of the Soul, hears a knocking at the door, opens it, and is confronted by Death, an ugly monster, "blinde of both eyes, without or lippes or chin." Death says: "I am a Ghost, yet am thy Looking–Glasse." (The ominous words recall the "Warning to Beauty," the subject of many paintings and engravings, where Death holds up a mirror to a woman who sees reflected therein not her own face but a skull.) Into the Dialogue is now introduced the familiar motif of "Death and the Maiden": Death woos

77

fair Flesh who shrinks shuddering from his courtship. The Second Dialogue is carried on by the World, the Flesh, and the Devil. The colloquy of Flesh with Death has converted her to godliness and the World, who is closely attached to Flesh, also quarrels with the Devil and both part company with him. The four Dialogues that follow contain nothing to our present purpose, but it may be noted that the general pattern of Brathwaite's book is vaguely that of the Pilgrimage of Human Life, ending with the Soul's arrival at the City of God.

The engraved frontispiece by John Droeshout to "E.B.'s" (Edward Browne's) *A Description of an Annuall World* (1641) [28] contains, along with much else not germane to our subject, a Christian kneeling at a table on which are a skull and crossbones, an hourglass, and a candle. From above an angel extends toward him an olive branch and a crown. At his feet are three small figures: two devils and a finely costumed woman who has a globe beside her. An inscription reads: "Contempt of the World, Flesh, and Devil."

The last example I have found within our period is one of the unsigned engravings in Thomas Jenner's *A Worke for none but Angels and Men* (1653 ?).[29] This shows an artist with palette and brushes sitting before an easel and engaged in painting a human heart within which is the Infernal Trinity: an orb, a woman, and a devil. The design is labeled "Fancie." The ambiguity is probably intentional, for the artist is following the dictates of his fancy and the fancies of the heart lay it open to temptation.

The lack of rigid uniformity in traditional material permits the poet or artist to exercise, if he will, much freedom in his treatment of such subjects. We have seen that with the Infernal Trinity may be grouped some other personification such as Death or some type figure such as the Christian; that two demons may be substituted for a single Devil; that the World and the Flesh may be conflated in a single personification; that one member of the Trinity may be absent. An example of extreme freedom is Christoff Murer's fantastic design [30] in which the Soul (Anima) is molten metal upon a sort of crucible (Homo) which rests upon a tripod (the World). The fire symbolizes Tribulation and the smoke Vanity. The Devil blows the fire with the bellows of Temptation while Finis (Death) beats upon the metal with a hammer. On one side stands a Good Angel and on the other Caro, a naked woman.

2. *The Deadly Sins and the pageant in* The Faerie Queene

In an overwhelmingly large number of instances, both in literature and in the arts of design, there are seven Deadly Sins. This is due to the "pull" of that "mystic" number.[1] But there may be fewer and frequently there are more than seven, as when Pride, Queen or Mother of the rest, is exalted above them, leaving room for Vainglory or Worldliness or Vanity; or when Avarice and Prodigality both appear; or when Gluttony in food and Intemperance in drink are differentiated. All the Sins may be of one sex or some may be male and others female. All may be personified or some personified and others represented by typical figures. Sometimes it is not the Sin but the typical Sinner who is portrayed throughout an entire sequence. Pagan divinities such as Venus or Mars or Bacchus may be substituted for personifications. A story or an individual from the Bible, classical mythology, or secular history may represent a Sin. Sometimes a personification is placed against the background of a typical incident, as when a house afire is shown behind Wrath. A great variety of animals emblematize the Sins, and an animal associated with one Sin in one sequence may be associated with another in another; or the animal may appear alone with no personification. The possible permutations and combinations are, in sum, very numerous. Occasionally, but not so frequently as might have been expected in an age of religious controversy, the Sins are used for purposes of polemic, Roman Catholics and Protestants insulting each other. This is especially true of the surly imagination of Stephen Bateman, and in the case of one of the Sins in Spenser's pageant there is evidently a similar intent.

No one will dispute the opinion that by far the finest and most memorable of all treatments in art or literature of the theme of the Seven Deadly Sins is the pageant in *The Faerie Queene* (I, 4, 13–38). It is fitting therefore to base our discussion upon it and to group other versions more or less loosely round it. First let us note that from this magnificent achievement of the poetic imagination some motifs employed by one or another author or artist are either omitted altogether or barely touched on.

The Castle, the Wheel, Hell, whatever he may imply, Spenser does not consign the Sins to hell or each particular Sin to a region or circle of the Inferno. At the very time when he was composing the earlier books of *The Faerie Queene* there was published Giovanni Paolo Gallucio's *Theatrum Mundi et Temporis* (Venice, 1589) which contains an interesting scheme, vaguely reminiscent of Dante and more closely related to the *Ars moriendi*, of the Deadly Sins in Seven of twelve concentric circles within the earth. In descending order these circles are Terra et aqua, Limbus, Purgatorium, Accediosi, Vanagloriosi, Gulosi, Luxuriosi, Iracundi, Avari, Superbia, Proditores (tormentors), and in the bottom circle the Devil. Pride is personified but in the other six circles typical sinners' figures writhe in torment. At the foot of the page is a text from Job 7:9: "Sicut consumitur nubes, et pertransit: sic qui descenderit ad infernos non ascendit." Nor does Spenser suggest any such notion as we find in inscriptions on the title page of Giuliano Dati's *La Magnificantia del Prete Ianni* (Florence, n.d., ca. 1502) where Pride is associated with earth, Lechery with wood, Gluttony with lead, Envy and Wrath with iron, Sloth with silver, and Avarice with gold.

Spenser makes no use of biblical texts nor does he draw analogies from incidents or persons in the Bible. Such texts and analogies occur frequently in other versions of the subject. Three examples may be given. In a series of copperplates engraved by Crispin de Passe from designs by Martin de Vos [2] each Sin has in the background two *exempla* from the Bible. With Pride are Nebuchadnezzar eating grass (Daniel 4:33) and Herod struck dead by the angel of the Lord "because he gave not God the glory" (Acts 12:23). With Lechery are Amnon committing rape upon Tamar (II Samuel 13:14) and the Israelites committing whoredom with the daughters of Moab (Numbers 1:1). With Envy are Joseph put into the pit (Genesis 37:24) and the daughter of Herodias receiving from Herod the head of John the Baptist (Mark 6:28). With Wrath are Jonathan warning David that Saul seeks to kill him (I Samuel 19:2) and Simeon and Levi slaying the Shechemites (Genesis 34:25). With Avarice are Ahab taking possession of Naboth's vineyard (I Kings 21:16) and Achan hiding the spoils in the earth in the midst of his tent (Joshua 7:21). With Gluttony are Lot made drunk by his daughters (Genesis 19:33) and Nabal refusing to give food to David's followers (I Samuel 25:11). With Sloth are David in idleness watching Bathsheba washing herself (II Samuel 11:2) and the disobedient prophet slain by a lion (I Kings 13:24).

An anonymous engraving of the early seventeenth century has as its principal subject the torments of hell and there are supplementary representations of each of the Seven Deadly Sins.[3] Three—Pride, Envy, and Wrath—are personified; the other four are illustrated by typical actions. In only one case (Envy) is there a parallel from biblical story, but biblical texts (all but one taken from the New Testament) serve as commentaries. It is noteworthy that Avarice, not Pride, comes first. For Avarice we have a man and a woman seated at a table on which there are money bags: "Ye cannot serve God and mammon" (Matthew 6:24). Pride is a woman with a peacock and a looking glass: "God resisteth the proud, but giveth grace unto the humble" (James 4:6). Gluttony shows two men at a table, one drinking and the other vomiting: "Burden not your heart with filth and drunkenness" (Luke 21:34). Lechery is represented by a naked man and woman on a couch: "He that commiteth fornication sinneth" (I Corinthians 6:18). Envy is a woman gnawing upon a heart and in the background Cain is slaying Abel: "By envy of the Devil Death came into the world" (Wisdom 2:24). Wrath is a woman in armor, with a sword, a torch, and a shield with a lion's head, and in the background is a burning city: "He who is angry with his brother shall be judged" (Matthew 5:22). Sloth is illustrated by two men sleeping under a tree: "The tree that bringeth not forth good fruit is hewn down, and cast into the fire" (Matthew 7:19).

Anthony Munday's *The Mirrour of Mutabilitie* (1579),[4] a close imitation of *The Mirrour for Magistrates*, contains as its first series of tales seven drawn from the Bible. They are written in a variety of stanzas. Introducing each is a short poem in which the initial letters of each line spell out the name of a Deadly Sin. Then follows the "Complaint" of a biblical personage whose ghost appears. When that is finished there is a brief colloquy between the ghost and the author. And so the pattern is repeated. Pride is exemplified by King Nabuchodonozor, Envy by King Herod, Wrath by King Pharao, Lechery by King David, Gluttony by Dives (the only case where a parable is used), Avarice by Judas, and Sloth by Jonas. The other stories in this book are not attached specifically to the Sins.

There are other concepts of the Sins which have no biblical analogy yet are quite dissimilar from Spenser's. Several of the plates in Francesco Pona's *Cardiomorphoseos sive ex Corde Desumpta Emblemata Sacra* (Verona, 1645) have to do with the Sins. These 101 emblems are concerned with the adventures of the human heart. Many are fantastic and grotesque to the degree of repulsiveness, e.g. no. 34 where the Heart rests upon a stove which is heated by bellows manipulated by Divine Love. In another (no. 61) Divine Love sits upon the Heart, which is at the center of seven jets of flame, each labeled for a Sin. In no. 11 the Heart is shown with castelated battlements on which a crucifix is erected while from a projecting rampart Divine Love shoots arrows at undifferentiated demons below. But in no. 89 the fortress of the Heart has been taken by seven demons; one is climbing the scaling ladder, and another is already inside the ramparts. Three hold labels marked respectively Spes, Fides, and Caritas. This seems odd, but as they are obviously devils it indicates that they have triumphed over the Christian Virtues, capturing their standards, or that they are disguised.

Spenser's Sins are loosely linked together in that six of them ride upon the animals which draw the coach of Pride, but each is busily engaged with his own concerns, and they do not form an intimate group. However, such groups are found elsewhere, notably in some of the Horatian Emblems designed by Otho Van Veen. The sins combine most closely when they cooperate in an attack upon an individual victim. This they do in many pictures of the Temptation of St. Anthony, two of which I shall scrutinize now. The first is of the School of Hieronimus Bosch in the Colonna Gallery in Rome. The casual observer may fail to note that along with the outlandish goblins all the Sins are here. Four are behind the kneeling saint, whose attention is steadfastly directed to his book of devotions. A repulsive, nondescript creature, huddled up and swathed from top to toe, can be identified as Sloth only because he (or she?) rides upon an ass. Avarice is, however, easily recognizable: He proffers a purse with one hand and his other hand is in a wallet by his side, he wears a gaberdine, and his features are unmistakably Jewish. Gluttony is a nightmarish monstrosity with table legs instead of lower limbs, a table cloth for a skirt, a balloonlike belly, a serpent's head, and in place of a nose a flute, upon which he is playing (music and jollity are often associated with this Sin). At his side dangle fruits and vegetables, a frying pan, and a carving knife. Envy is a more conventional figure: a brooding, dog-headed demon with pendulous breasts, and a snake entwined round her. In front of the saint are the other three sins. Closest to him is Lechery, a beautiful young woman with bare breasts, an extravagant headdress, and tightly curled locks which, I should like to suggest, if it is not carrying interpretation beyond plausible limits, resemble the horns of a goat. By her a little devil is eagerly pumping the bellows of desire and the man on her left, not a personification but a type of pander figure, presents her to the saint. Next to her is Pride who rides astraddle upon a creature that cannot be identified because its head is a skull and its body is covered with drapery which trails behind it. Pride wears a false face, she looks into a mirror, a peacock is under her arm, and peacock feathers are in a vase balanced upon her head. Wrath is a shocking demon, all head and no body; legs ending in fierce claws protrude from its jaws and its nostrils are pierced by an arrow. Accompanying Wrath are two armed warriors carrying an enormous knife with which they mutilate three animal—

shaped demons. (There is a similar knife employed in like fashion in a print of Wrath which is one in a series of the Sins formerly and erroneously attributed to Peter Brueghel the Elder.)

With this *fantasia* may be compared a painting by David Teniers in the Prado. Despite its horrors there is a homely earthiness about it that is almost genial. Demons and goblins (more than thirty of them in the shape of mammals, birds, reptiles, amphibians, serpents, and what not) swarm in the Hermit's cave, on the ground, and in the air. Small wonder that patient Saint Anthony is distracted from his prayer book and the Crucifix! Amid this devilish crowd are personifications of the Sins. Pride is a young gentleman from whose wig pointed satyr's ears protrude. He carries a peacock under his arm. Lechery is a prim, modestly dressed young *hausfrau* whom even a saint would not recognize as a Deadly Sin were it not for the terrible talons of a bird's foot which are exposed below her gown. (One is reminded of the episode in the fresco of the Thebaid in the Pisan Campo Santo where the true nature of soberly dressed Lechery is revealed by the bird's feet). Avarice, again with these revealing feet, is an elderly woman, seated on the ground weighing coins in a pair of balances. Three large sacks of coin are beside her, and behind her a man with greedy eyes holds a coffer. Sloth is a woman seated sound asleep upon an ass. Envy is a woman lying prone and eating a heart. Gluttony is a stout young man who, astride a skull–headed swine, holds in one hand a ewer and in the other a flagon, while across one shoulder and over his chest (as though it were the riband of an order of knighthood) there is a chain of sausage links. The expression on his face evinces jolly contentment but once more there is a revealing bird's foot with ferocious claws. Only by the figure of Wrath is something akin to genuine spiritual terror evoked. Her frenzied eyes are unforgettable. She runs beside a lion which she guides by its mane. Her ears are pointed, and in her hand she brandishes a bloody knife. This painting and others like it [5] are in intention and tone far removed from those renderings of the Sins in which there is a sincere ethical purpose.

Spenser's Red Cross Knight is in quest of holiness under the guidance of Truth, but he does not seek protection by clinging to the Crucifix. A contrast may be seen in an engraving by Hieronimus Wierex which illustrates St. Paul's question: "Quis ergo nos separabit a charitate Christi?" and his impassioned affirmation of confidence (Romans 8:35–39). A Christian is assailed by Death, a skeleton, a male personification holding two scourges who may be Tribulation, and by five of the Deadly Sins. Envy has her snaky locks and waves writhing snakes

above her head. Wrath brandishes his sword. Pride lays her hand upon
the Christian's shoulder, Gluttony (a male personification) throttles him,
and Lechery (also a male figure) clutches at the genitals beneath his garment. But the Christian with calm assurance embraces the crucified
Christ (Fig. 75). Wierex made also a simpler version of the same
theme in which the Christian is attacked by four enemies ("Kitto" Bible,
53, 9742). Illustrations similar in sentiment appear in various books
of devotions, as, for example, a design by Otho Van Veen entitled
"Amoris Securitas" where the Soul assaulted by Worldliness, the Burden
of Possessions (?), Wrath, and Death seeks safety by embracing Divine
Love.[6]

One or another of the Sins is occasionally used to exemplify disobedience to one or another of the Commandments. I have found, however, no parallel to a colored Bavarian woodcut (ca. 1480) in which
twenty–two small tondi illustrate the Seven Deadly Sins, the Ten Commandments, and the Five Senses.[7] The Sins are not personified but are
symbolized by a peacock (Pride), a wolf with a goose in its jaws (Envy),
a boar (Avarice), a lion (Wrath), two dogs (Gluttony), a cock (Lechery),
and an ass (Sloth). In Spenser the association of the Sins with violations
of the Commandments may be implicit but is not stated outright. Two
of his Sins of the Flesh, Gluttony and Lechery, naturally involve Taste
and Touch but he does not otherwise symbolize the Senses.

There is no trace of the Psychomachia in Spenser's pageant, though
this great theme was undoubtedly known to him. Abraham Fleming's *A
Monomachie of Motives* (1582) [8] is a charming Elizabethan survival
of it. In it no less than twenty–five Virtues and twenty–five Vices, divided into five groups, are "at mutual hatred and strife." The pattern
of each "Assault" and "Repulse" is repeated twenty–five times: Each
begins with a "golden sentence" of St. Bernard against a Vice, then
the Vice addresses Man, a prayer follows against the Vice, then St.
Bernard is quoted commending the opposing Virtue, and that Virtue
achieves the "Repulse." Each combat is an argument rather than an
allegorized clash of arms. Although all the participants in the combats
are personified, there is no attempt to describe their appearance, costumes, or attributes. But they speak convincingly in character, the sophis-
try, cynicism, and self–indulgent worldliness of the Vices being admirably rendered in vigorous, homely English. I need not list them all; suffice
it to note that among them are all the Seven Deadly Sins. There is
little or no system in the ordering and subdivisions of the groups. The
classifications owe something to the refinements of analysis in earlier

treatises and to the "trees," and analogous patterns, of Virtues and Vices. An example of the trees with "daughter" Vices is an Italian engraving (ca. 1470–80) in which there are eight Sins—Regina Superbia being exalted above the rest, to which Vanagloria is added. The eight control a total of no less than sixty–four daughters.[9] Some details survive from the older tradition, as when, in the fourteenth combat, Hope, replying to the arguments of Desperation, cites the examples of Mary Magdalene, St. Peter, the Penitent Thief, and St. Paul. Another Elizabethan Psychomachia is "T.A.'s" *The Massacre of Money* (1602).[10]

The strange, hideous figures called "Frau Welt" or "Frau Sünde," in which several of the Deadly Sins are combined in a single personification, have nothing, save their repulsiveness, in common with the Sins in *The Faerie Queene*.[11] The woman has bat's wings, and a crown of feathers, and holds a cup, a forked stick, and, most oddly, an ass (Sloth) which is upon her right arm. Her single leg ends in a bird's foot. She stands upon a globe, her posture symbolizing Insecurity, with Death gnawing at her leg. In another version the chief difference is that she has two legs: One leg represents the dragon of Death which is gnawing at the other, bird–footed limb, which represents Life. The scholars who have commented upon these fifteenth–century prints have not noted their resemblance to the composite monster designed by Stephen Bateman in which various Sins (but not precisely the traditional Seven) are conflated.[12] Bateman's explication of this deformed creature is as follows: "The long schull betokeneth Craftie imagination: The pleasant countenance, Flattery, The long Necke, Excess in eating and drinking; The right arme being shorter than the left, betokeneth small Devotion: The bagge of money Covetousnesse: The left arme Wilfulnesse: The Sworde Crueltie; The straunge disguising in apparell, Pride." This explanation is for the most part lucid and provokes but one question: Are the arms of different length so that the hands cannot be clasped in prayer? Emblematists invented similar but less grotesque conflations. Thus we have the Tree of Vice and its fruits: half–length figures of Death and the Devil protrude from its trunk and growing on it are a peacock, a sword, and other emblems. Again, we have the fingers of a man attached by cords to a sword, a purse, a peacock feather, a globe, and a man and woman kissing.[13]

The concept of the Sins in William Dunbar's vigorously grotesque poem *The Dance of the Sevin Deidly Synnis* [14] is much coarser than any part of Spenser's pageant. On "the feist of Fasternis evin" (that is, Shrove Tuesday) the poet dreamt that Mahoun (that is, Mahomet, who was popularly thought to be a devil) held a dance of unshriven shrews (rascals). The first to leap were the Seven Deadly Sins. Pride was a gallant, and many a proud deceiver, grimacing hideously, danced with him through scalding fire. Yre (Wrath) brandished a knife; his partners were braggarts accoutered for war. Next came Envy with flatterers and courtiers. Cuvetyce (Avarice) was accompanied by usurers and such people who shot molten gold out of their mouths at one another, and as they rid themselves of it fiends filled them with more gold. Sweirnes (Sloth) resembled a sleepy sow just out of a midden; with him were many lazy, well-fed fellows whom Belial lashed on the loins. Lechery, roaring like a stallion, was led by Idleness, and many a stinking corpse that had died in sin was with him. Gluttony with "unsasiable" belly was followed by drunkards with cans and cups and quarts, crying "Drink!" There being no minstrels for the dance, Mahoun called out for a "Heleand padyne" (a "Highland pageant"). A fiend ran far Northward and fetched Macfadyne and other Ersemen. Such a clatter of Erse ensued that the Devil smothered them in smoke in the deepest pot of hell.

How different from this demoniacal roistering is the solemnity of the Sins who speak over the tomb of Graunde Amour [15] in *The Pastime of Pleasure*. Though personified, no particulars of their characters are given. Their function is to remind the Soul of the protagonist of the offenses of which he has been guilty during his mortal life. Spenser had probably read Hawes' poem, but there is nothing in his episode to suggest that he borrowed from it for his pageant. There are various departures from the traditional Seven which are, however, evidently suggested by the old convention. John Hagthorpe envisions the Sin as four altars erected to Ambition and Cruelty, Ignorance and Idolatry, Avarice and Oppression, and Lust and Luxury. At the Last Judgment these altars will be destroyed.[16] Elsewhere Hagthorpe likens Man to a "cittadell" or fortified town in which Malice, Ambition, Despair, and Fear are what we should today call fifth columnists.[17] On his visit to England in August 1604 King Christian IV of Denmark entertained James I on board one of his ships. On a lighter near the ship was "a beautiful and well-contrived firework" consisting of a cube upon whose sides were "eight capital Vices." These were not quite the "orthodox" set since eight, not seven, were needed for the eight corners of the cube. They were Iracundia, Desidia, Luxuria, Fallacia, Invidia, Superbia, Injustitia, and Gula. "This firework very methodically, one part after another, continued burning and cracking for the space of three quarters of an hower." [18] A curious and, so far as I know, unparalleled use was

86

made of the Sins when Johanne Gayler, a famous divine who enlivened his sermons with colloquialisms and homely anecdote, preached at Strassburg in 1499 a series of sermons on the general text of Ephesians VI, the Pauline Armor. These, when published, were illustrated with woodcuts by Hans Burgkmair. One cut [19] has seven demons each with a sword marked on the blade with the name of a Deadly Sin. Apart from the labels there is no attempt to differentiate among the demons and swords. Another cut [20] shows seven scabbards, a striking device to warn the faithful that the Sins are unsheathed and dangerous. Having passed in review a number of versions of our theme (selected from a larger number) which have little in common with the pageant of the Sins in *The Faerie Queene*, we must now direct more particular attention to that pageant.

3. *The Deadly Sins and the pageant in* The Faerie Queene *cont.*

The source—hunting commentators (among whom I am not to be numbered, for our concern in this book is primarily with analogues, not sources) have studied literature primarily and have generally neglected the arts of design. I begin, therefore, with some examples from the Fine Arts where there is the possibility, though not a demonstrable probability, of a connection, at first or second hand, with Spenser's pageant. Of such, perhaps the earliest in date is the series of now destroyed murals of the Triumph of the Virtues over the Vices in the "Painted Chamber" in Westminster Hall.[1] Originally there were probably seven opposing pairs, though shortly before their destruction by fire in 1834 only two were recognizable: Generosity trampling upon Avarice and Meekness trampling upon Wrath. Does it not seem likely that Spenser was acquainted with murals so close at hand? It is, furthermore, likely that he had seen one or more of the wall paintings of the Sins in English churches.[2] These sometimes portray personifications, sometimes typical sinners, sometimes both Sins and sinners. Three patterns may be distinguished. First, when a wheel is painted, spokes divide it into seven segments in each of which is a Sin; the hub may be hell. Secondly, there may be a tree with seven branches at the top of which a crowned figure, Superbia, may be seated or from which she may be falling, dragged by demons. Finally, the sins may be shown in hellmouth, sometimes upon a tree protruding from its yawning jaws. Whether the pattern is a circle, a tree, or a hellmouth, it is noteworthy that symbolic animals seldom appear. The Sins sometimes are engaged in activities, as when Wrath stabs himself or Lechery kisses a woman. The problem of the identification of figures in these paintings, which are almost always in a much deteriorated condition, is an interesting one and often defies solution. The most interesting of these murals is the Wheel in Ingatestone Church, Essex,[3] where the Sins are between the spokes. Pride is at the top: a seated woman with an attendant, who holds a mirror up to her. For Wrath two men are shown brawling while a demon eggs one of them on. Lechery is represented by a man embracing a woman; Sloth by a man sleeping; Avarice by a man counting coins. In Gluttony's compartment one man is drinking, a second vomiting, and a third seems to be remonstrating with them. In the seventh compartment, where Envy ought to be, four men are disputing before two judges. This may be Calumny, as in Apelles' lost painting, which is close to Envy. Three details in other murals may be noticed. In Trotton Church, Sussex, the Tree of the Sins is contrasted with a Tree of the Works of Mercy.[4] In Brooke Church, Norfolk, the Prodigal Son is shown as the type of repentant sinner with representations of the Sins beside or beneath him.[5] In Hoxne Church, Suffolk, two devils are sawing through the trunk of the Tree of the Sins.[6] It is noteworthy that very rarely in church murals are animals found as attributes.

When Professor Lowes argued for the indebtedness of Spenser to the procession of the Sins in Gower's *Mirour de l'omme* (lines 241–300, 757–9720), he did not know of the existence of a French "livre de miniatures" dating from about 1390 and therefore almost immediately contemporary with the *Mirour*.[7] In this manuscript each Sin is depicted riding on an animal and holding a bird. In six of the seven cases (all but Avarice) animal and bird are those in Gower's description. The parallels are too close to be fortuitous; it would seem, therefore, that neither Gower nor the French artist chose his emblematic creatures at random, but that both went back to some common source. I shall comment later upon these miniatures for the sake of their possible indirect relationship, through the *Mirour*, to Spenser.

Behind the German series of woodcuts in *Die Siben todsünden* (Augsburg, 1474) and their Dutch derivatives (Magdeburg, 1490) [8] are the miniatures in a manuscript in the Pierpont Morgan Library (ca. 1460).[9] In these three closely related sequences the Sins, in addition to being provided with steeds, display supplementary emblematic creatures on their helmets, shields, and banners. The opposing Virtues are similarly mounted and equipped. These designs influenced the artists who planned the grandiose tapestries produced in Brussels about the beginning of the sixteenth century in which are shown the Fall of Man, the Parliament of Heaven, the Plan of Redemption with Christ as the Christian Knight, and the Combat of the Virtues and Vices for the possession of the Soul. In these tapestries the Sins are riding upon appropriate creatures and other such emblems are on their shields. Such a set of eight pieces, of which fragments survive, was purchased by Cardinal Wolsey for Hampton Court.[10] Being so near, Spenser may have heard of them or even seen them. Less close to *The Faerie Queene* is a set of "hangings" at Hardwick Hall, depicting the triumph of the Virtues over their contraries, who are shown, however, not as personifications but by historical or mythological characters.[11]

In chapter I, I discussed the illustrations in two editions of Boccaccio's *De Claris Mulieribus* in which the Seven Deadly Sins are in the branches of the Tree of Knowledge of Good and Evil. It is conceivable but improbable that either of these books, or both, may have been known to Spenser. The first part of Jacques le Grand's *Livre de bonnes meurs* (Paris, 1487) contains woodcuts of the Sins riding upon animals.[12] The English version, however, *The Boke of good maners* (Wynkyn de Worde, 1507), does not include these illustrations, and as there are no personifications in the text it is the less likely that it influenced Spenser. The *Eruditorium Penitentiale* (Paris, ca. 1485–1500) has cuts of the Sins riding,[13] but of this there was no English version. The illustrations in the *Ars moriendi* and in the *Kalendrier des Bergers* show with fantastic imagination the punishment of each type of sinner but there are no personified Sins.[14] The tortures of the damned are reported by Lazarus after his resurrection. Of more importance to the student of Spenser is the lovely series of the Psychomachia in Pierre Gringoire's *Le Chasteau de Labour* (Paris, Simon Vostre, 1499).[15] Here the Virtues on horseback subdue the Sins on their several creatures. Copies of these metalcuts appear among the embellishments at the foot of the pages of the *Horae ad Usum Sarum* (Paris, ca. 1506) which Antoine Vérard printed for the English trade.[16] It is unlikely, however, that Spenser, toward the close of the century and long after the Reformation, knew this Book of Hours. But Alexander Barclay translated Gringoire's work into English. Of the first edition of his *Castell of Labour* (Paris, ca. 1503), printed by Vérard for importation into England, only a single leaf is known to be extant and from that we can learn nothing about the illustrations, which were probably from the French plates. A second edition (London, Richard Pynson, ca. 1505) exists only in fragments; the cuts therein are fairly close to the originals. For a third edition (Wynkyn de

Worde, 1506) a craftsman was employed who made debased copies on wood from the French metalcuts.[17] Of a book associated with so famous a name as Barclay's, a book, moreover, which went through three editions, it may be said with due caution that it may have been known to Spenser.

No such caution is necessary when we look at *A Booke of Christian Prayers* either in John Daye's original edition of 1578 or in the reissues of 1581 and 1590.[18] It is almost inconceivable that so ardent a lover of beauty as Spenser did not admiringly contemplate this most beautiful of Elizabethan books (Fig. 76). Among its marginal ornamentations are twenty–one designs of Virtues standing in triumph either upon prostrate or crouching Vices or their equivalents. The scheme is larger and looser than that of the two hostile groups of Seven. All the Virtues are female personifications; the Vices, however, are mostly historical devotees of a particular sin, or emblematic creatures, or objects emblematizing the sin. Of the Vices only five belong among the "orthodox" Seven; of these only two are personified: Pride and Wrath. Sloth is represented by an ass and Lechery by a goat, and for Intemperance (equated with Gluttony) we have the typical action of a man vomiting.

There are Continental precursors of this prayer book, but another volume from Daye's press is completely English. This is Stephen Bateman's *A christall glasse of christian reformation* (1569),[19] a series of coarse and bitter attacks upon the Roman Catholic Church based for the most part upon the motive of the Seven Deadly Sins and illustrated with many cuts, with accompanying explanations, and other comments. Spenser may well have known this book, but that question is almost beside the point because its range of imagery makes it the most ambitious of all English treatments of our theme. The symbolism of many of the crude woodcuts is obscure, and Bateman's prose commentary, though an aid to interpretation, is not itself always easily understood. The summary that now follows must be lengthy, even though many insignificant details are omitted. Each of the Sins is represented four times.

1. Covetousness is a purse from which hangs a globe (the World). These objects and three swords (Mischief) a devil proffers to a fool in motley. 2. A judge receives from two litigants coins in a lower pair of outstretched hands, while an upper pair delivers to the litigants his decrees. The antipapal meaning is: "No peny, no Pater noster." 3. A richly clothed man (Usury) rides upon an elephant (Force). He is laden with purses, a coffer, boxes hanging from his shoulder, and a banner on which is shown a wolf devouring a lamb. A shabbily dressed man

90

(Niggardship) leads the elephant by a rope (Deceit). 4. Three men on horseback (three states of the worldly minded: the Gentility who are not content with a sufficiency, the Popish Spirituality, and the Yeomanry who "desire to have") ride toward the Devil who spreads before them a net (Unsatiable Desire).

1. Wrath is a boar whose rider (Mischief) carries a banner displaying the portrait of a pope. Before goes a man stabbing himself (Desperation) and behind is a woman with arms upraised in a wild gesture (Madness). Bateman explains that the flag is "uncertain religion," thus implying his confidence in the certainty of the Reformation. 2. A seated ass (Wrathful Justice) wears robes and an ermine cope. Behind the ass stand a monk (Lies) and an associate (Perjury). A man (Truth) is being drawn away by two other men (Flatterers). 3. A man dressed as a "prophet" (Godliness) confronts a monk (Treason) who holds a chalice from which rises a serpent (poison). In the background one man stabs another in the back. 4. A pope (Oppression) is enthroned. An executioner (Cruelty) is decapitating a man (Constant Religion). Three men (Love, Forbearance, and Truth to the Gospel) are kneeling.

1. Lechery is a goat upon which a fine lady (Whoredom) rides. The goat is led by Meretrix, a bawd. A devil, Nicticorax ("a blinde guide or deceaver") is in the air above them. 2. Fallax, a friar, caresses a nun (Infamy or Shame). Nearby is a devil garbed as a friar (a "rayler against Truth"). 3. Two armies oppose each other (the Flesh strives against the Spirit). 4. Two pairs of lovers embrace. Nearby is a woman (Lechery) whose feet are claws. A devil playing upon a mandolin is conducting toward the jaws of hell a man and a woman wearing feathers in their hats.

1. Gluttony is a typical scene in which five men are depicted: One is pouring wine upon the floor; two are fighting; one is escaping through a door; the fifth lies dead. A skeleton holding a dart (Death) is entering through a window. Drunkenness makes men forget reason and causes bloodshed and death. 2. Podagra (the gout), a fat old woman with swollen legs, leads two fat men by a rope attached to their noses. One of the men is Prodigus, a Bacchuslike figure, crowned and girt with vine leaves and carrying a tankard and a bunch of grapes. The other man, said to be Ravin, fully clothed, wears a crown of vine leaves and carries grapes. 3. A Bacchus ("insatiable Desire") clad only in a barrel is shown in a cloister. From holes in the barrel his hands reach out, proffering a flagon to a tonsured priest (characterized as "Newter, neither hoate nor

colde") and a nun (Credulity). 4. Bacchus, mounted upon a bear (Force), is preceded by a king (Maintenance) and a friar, and followed by a popish priest (Careless Diet) and a servingman (Riot).

1. Sloth is a man asleep upon a bed ("Sloth in hearing of the worde"). On the floor lies a dead man covered with vermin (the miserable end of filthy behavior and an idle life). Flames (God's wrath) are licking round the window of the room. 2. A teacher is asleep at a table with books upon it. Children are playing with a windmill, a cat, and a dog. The moral drawn is obvious. 3. A man with folded arms leans against a tree with his tools, a hammer, saw and so forth, on the ground before him. (Bateman says the man is a dissembling laborer who only works when the eye of the master is upon him, but the design is suggestive of Melancholia.) 4. A friar holding a huge rosary is riding on an ass.

1. Envy is an "envious deceaver" who wastes the seeds of Verity by emptying them into a stream. Nearby a "true labourer" seeds a ploughed field while birds ("faithful followers of the verity") fly overhead. 2. A priest and a friar ("enemies of God's word") try to force a "furtherer of the gospel" from a pulpit. A group of people seated quietly near at hand (the Nullifidians who desire only to live according to their own wills and minds) make no protest against this outrage. 3. A man, behind whom is an angel, slays another man who has Death behind him. Victory is the reward of him who preserves constant faith in Christ, and Death the consequence of enviousness of the Faithful's quiet state. 4. A cardinal (Persecution) rides on a dragon (the enemy of all that profess the word of God); a friar (Murder) slits the throat of a sheep ("Professours of Christ from the beginning to the end of time").

1. Pride is a woman looking into a mirror (Flattery or Deceit). Her foot rests upon a skull (forgetfulness of the destruction awaiting her in the life to come). A horrid devil (Temptation) has one clawed arm upon her shoulder. 2. A rich man in fine attire meets a poor man in rags. 3. A knight on horseback (maintenance of popish ceremonies) is attended by a monster (popish ceremonies) with a cockatoo crest, sheep's ears, a human torso, bird's legs and claws, and a peacock's tail. This uncouth creature discharges from a gun a rosary, asperger, bishop's crook, censer, crucifix, chalice, and a skull. An angel with a flaming sword (God's wrath against persecutors) bars the way of the horseman. 4. A pope (Pride), riding on a lion ("forceable Strength") is pursued by a devil (Dreams) with a bow and arrow (Feigned Holiness). The pope bestows his blessing upon kneeling people (those ignorant of the Truth).

Bateman has thus offered, along with a commentary, no less than twenty–eight representations of the Seven Deadly Sins. He then, with much fuller commentary but fewer illustrations, turns his attention to a few Virtues. Among them is Charity—a Virtue of which he himself certainly stood in need! Finally the book trails off into an attack upon the doctrine of Purgatory and a discourse on the Last Doom. Throughout, Bateman cites an abundance of biblical, historical, and mythological anecdotes to support his polemics and exhortations.

4. *Vanity, Folly, and the banquet in* The Faerie Queene

When the Red Cross Knight enters the House of Pride he is guided through the throng of courtiers and to the lowest stair of Lucifera's throne by the gentle usher, Vanity. Spenser does not describe Vanity's appearance, but it is easy to visualize him. In an English morality play Vanity appears "dressed all in feathers." [1] Thomas Lodge says that Cupid's wings "are plumed with the feathers of vanitie." [2] In an anonymous German emblem book a beautifully engraved tondo shows a peacock whose spread tail almost fills the entire circle; it is labeled simply "Vanitas." [3] Vanity is more often a female personification than a male. Shakespeare speaks of Vanity as a "puppet"; [4] Marlowe alludes to Lady Vanity and Ben Jonson does so twice. [5] In another morality Wit comes perilously close to mistaking Lady Vanity for Lady Wisdom. [6] She may hold a looking glass, and often she is associated with bubbles. In a scene of the Prodigal Son (Fig. 77) dining with various evil personifications Vanity is a woman blowing a bubble. [7] A charming design in the *Pia Desideria* shows Divine Love with his hands over the Soul's eyes lest she behold Vanity, a finely dressed woman with bubbles and a fan. [8] In one of Wither's emblems weights are being heaped into one pan of a pair of scales and a boy is blowing a bubble into the other. The bubble outweighs the other pan, the moral being that the burden of worldly possessions is less than vanity. [9] Ripa's "Vanità" has no feathers, mirror, or bubbles; her care for outward appearance is shown by her painted face, rich clothes, and her heart which lies exposed upon a dish on the top of her head. [10] But Vanity may be something other than mere foolish and ostentatious conceit: It may be the Preacher's awareness that "all is Vanity." A mezzotint, "Vanitas," by Pieter Schenck of Amsterdam (1645–1715) shows a skull, a candle burnt almost to the socket, a scallop shell (Life's Pilgrimage), and several floating bubbles. [11]

Vanity is practically identical with Folly. The guide and "governesse" of the Wandering Knight is Folly, "apparelled . . . lightly in a cloack of feathers." [12] Both personifications are closely allied to the Deadly Sins. In a morality play Conscience explains: "These seven synnes I call foly"; the Seven Sins thus mentioned do not appear separately but are amalgamated in the character of Folly.[13] In the Horatian Emblems (pp. 16–17) Van Veen groups Folly, a woman dressed in motley, with the Sins. Folly, like Vanity, may be male. In a drawing by Mantegna, Folly is a man with the ears of an ass.[14] A very surrealistic emblem portrays Folly as a finely dressed man with ass's ears from whose heart sprouts a branch of a tree which bears the heads of three fools.[15] Had Spenser thought fit to describe the "gentle usher" it is valid to surmise that Vanity would resemble one or another of these concepts of him, or his fellow, Folly.

The denizens of the House of Pride "entertain" the newly arrived guest in "goodly" fashion. He, however, considers their "glory" vain and "that great Princesse too exceeding prowd." Two fine prints offer striking analogies to this banquet. In the *Exercitium super Pater Noster* [16] there is a woodcut (Fig. 78) to illustrate the petition "Deliver us from evil." A man, an Everyman, dines with three ladies who are dressed alike but are labeled individually, Superbia, Gula, and Avaricia, and have different attributes: the first holds a crown, the second has many dishes before her on the table, the third holds two purses. Death touches Everyman upon the shoulder, a hovering Devil extracts his tiny soul from his head, and two kneeling angels pray for him. Resembling this woodcut but lacking any reference to Man's mortality, is the second print (see Fig. 77), probably by Cornelis Anthonïsz, Tennissen (ca. 1540), the Prodigal Son. Filius Prodigus is consorting with a fearful company. At the head of the table sits Mundus, wearing an orbed crown, with a backgammon board and two dice on the table before him. His foot is upon the head of Conscience who lies beneath the table. The Prodigal sits close to Caro, the two hold the same wineglass and food and a wine flask are before them. Next to Caro sits Avaritia, a wrinkled hag, drinking from a large goblet (an action uncharacteristic of this personification) and beyond her is "Proprium commodum," a man rising from the table and making off hastily with a big purse. Behind this group are three other personifications: Vanitas blowing a bubble; Heresis, with what seems to be a scorpion on her head, holding in her arms what seems to be a fox; Ratio (that is, trust in mere human reason) playing upon a bagpipe. Overhead there is a dreadful demon with seven heads. On an imaginative level much beneath these two prints is a description in Thomas Adams' *The Divells Banket* (1614) where a harlot acts as hostess for the Devil, Vices bid guests to the banquet, and the guests must pay "the shot or reckoning." These three analogues enable us to picture the manner in which the Red Cross Knight was entertained. In William Rankins's attack upon the stage, *A Mirror of Monsters* [17] (1587), a very different banquet is shown in an episode in which Pride and Lechery appear. Pride and Lechery, it is said, are married in the theatres, and a marginal gloss [18] runs: "The Theater and Curtine may aptlie be termed for their abhomination, the chappel *Adulterinum*." The "doore keepers" and "boxe–holders at Playes" are the servants of this wicked pair. Rankins tells [19] how Pluto sent up from hell in honor of them "a Maske chose from the most famous fellowes of all hys dominion." The masquers were Idleness, Flattery, Ingratitude, Dissention, Blasphemy, and Impudency, each characterized with historical examples.[20] Pride and Lechery welcomed and thanked them, and there followed a banquet in the Hall of Misery [21] where they were all feasted with "delicate dysshes, of continual vexation, guilty conscience, worlds of woe, and never dying torments."

In almost all cases in literature and the fine arts Pride is the chief of the Sins. Let us take notice at once of an exception. In Francis Sabie's poem "The Olde Worldes Tragedie," in which the wickedness of the world before the Flood is accounted for by the activities of the Deadly Sins, Envy rules the earth as "supreame Queene," and Pride is merely the "standard–bearer" to Injustice.[22]

5. *Pride*

Reigning in the House of Pride is Lucifera, daughter of Lucifer, a "mayden Queene." In emphasizing her virginity Spenser does not intend any disrespectful allusion to Queen Elizabeth, such an implication would have been perilously close to *lèse majesty*, but rather indicates that Pride brooks no consort, no rival; she reigns alone. As the *fons et origo* of the other Sins, Pride, whether a masculine or feminine personification, is often of royal blood and may wear a crown or carry a scepter, baton, or warder.[1] The King of Life in the morality play *The Pride of Life* stands for Pride. Protestant polemic sometimes equated Pride with the pope. There is of course no such parallel implied when in a fifteenth–century tapestry she wears a triple crown; [2] this is simply symbolic of her supreme power. But we have seen Bateman fusing the two ideas; and Pride was so presented in an interlude, now lost, which was performed at the court of Edward VI.[3] The concept is close to such "daughter" Vices as Worldliness, Vainglory,[4] or merely Fashion. Thus, in one design Worldliness is a gorgeously costumed woman wearing a globe on her head and holding a mirror adorned with peacock feathers.[5]

"Proud as a peacock" is still a cliché. Six of the Deadly Sins are among the potent princes who surround Satan during a council in hell and here Pride wears a peacock's plume, an embroidered gown, and is perfumed.[6] In scenes of the Fall of Man a peacock is sometimes standing by Eve.[7] The ostentatious bird is present in innumerable pictures of Pride, for example, in those by Burgkmair, Ripa, Martin de Vos, Furnius, and Callot,[8] and in Trevelyon's commonplace book.[9] We may glance at a few such designs. The title page (Fig. 79) of Philip Galle's series of the Sins [10] shows Death and the Devil lifting a curtain and exposing seven naked children, each a Sin. Pride with a peacock and holding a scepter is at the top. Seven metalcuts (Figs. 80–86) of women's heads follow and in the corner of each design are *putti* who generally, but not invariably, display attributes of the Sin. Superbia holds a mirror ornamented with peacock feathers, and two of her putti wear headdresses of such feathers. In a series published by H. Cock in 1558 and falsely attributed to Peter Brueghel the Elder,[11] Superbia is associated not only with a peacock but with half–hatched fledglings. The frontispiece, engraved by Thomas Cockson, of John Taylor's *Superbiae Flagellum, or, The Whip of Pride* (1621) shows Simplicity, a naked youth, treading on a peacock's tail and scourging the creature.[12] This motif is close to that of Heavenly Love and the Soul performing the same act in Otho Van Veen's *Emblemata Divini Amoris* (1615). In an earlier volume, *Amorum Emblemata* (1606), Van Veen had pictured (Fig. 87) Cupid stepping on a peacock's tail, accompanied by the motto: "Amor hayt l'orgeuil." The bird appears in many other emblem books, sometimes standing for Pride, sometimes for one of the "daughter" Vices. Ripa's Arrogance, which springs from Pride, has a peacock, and, in an engraving to be described presently, Satan himself wears peacock plumes, and the peacock of Vainglory is one of the creatures harnessed to his chariot. When Marlowe's Pride (a masculine figure) tells Faustus that "like a fan of feathers" he kisses a wench's lips,[13] we may easily guess from what bird the feathers came. Spenser does not assign the peacock to Pride, but presently in likening her coach to "Junoes golden chaire . . . Drawne of faire Pecocks," he implies the association. The turkey cock is another bird that spreads its tail ostentatiously; Pride's hand rests upon one in an English tapestry (ca. 1565).[14]

Under the feet of enthroned Pride, Spenser tells us, lies a "dreadful dragon." Perhaps the poet had in mind an image of the Infernal Trinity such as that in *The Pastime of Pleasure*, or one of the many Hydras we have discussed; but it is so unusual to associate a dragon with Pride that I suggest he may have seen one of the Horae or Offices of the Blessed Virgin Mary in which the Sins illustrate the Penitential Psalms and the beast accompanying Pride is a dragon.[15]

Spenser tells us that in her hand Pride held a "mirrhour bright," an attribute he may have observed in some English church wall painting or in Bateman or in the *Booke of Christian Prayers*.[16] Continental parallels are innumerable: for example, in designs by Burgkmair, Philip Galle, Golzius, Furnius, and Callot. Trevelyòn's Pride has a mirror. Fynes Moryson writes of French gentlewomen: "They use a strange badge of pride, to weare little looking glasses at that [their] girdles." [17] The mirror may also be an attribute of "daughter" Vices such as Vanity, Worldliness, and Frivolity; and Lechery may hold it.[18] Philautia (Self–Love) in Henry Peacham's *Minerva Britanna* (ca. 1620) is gazing at her reflection in a looking glass. The mirror is, of course, a good attribute also, held by Prudence who looks before and after and obeys the injunction "Nosce te ipsum." I have suggested elsewhere [19] that when in the deposition scene in *Richard II*, the King dashes a mirror to the ground two symbolic meanings may have been intended: Richard has not followed the injunction of Prudence and his Pride is shattered.

Pride takes her place in a coach, drawn by the beasts on which her "six sage Counsellors," the other Sins, ride, and driven by Satan, who sits upon the wagon beam. The concept descends from one medieval form of the Psychomachia, from the Petrarchan Triumphs, and from ambulatory pageantry.[20] In Tudor–Stuart literature the coach or chariot is often overloaded with allegorical detail, with names given to the vehicle, the harnessed beasts, the wheels, the charioteer or coachman, the whip he wields, and even the lashes of the whip.[21] Spenser's reticence is in marked contrast to this habit; he suggests the opulence of the coach but refrains from allegorizing its parts. Closest to Spenser's pageant is a plate (no. 84) in Father David's *Veridicus Christianus* (Fig. 88) where fond and foolish Man is being driven in a chariot straight into hellmouth. The peacock feathers of Satan, the charioteer, identify him with Pride, and the chariot is drawn by the dog of Envy, the peacock of Vainglory, the ass of Sloth, the pig of Gluttony, the goat of Lechery, the lion of Wrath, and the camel of Avarice. In this design the creatures are the Sins but Spenser enriches the allegory by personifying the Sins and having them ride upon emblematic animals. Otherwise the allegory is strikingly close, save that Spenser's Sins are not (for the nonce) journeying to hell. Variations may be found upon this motif. In another of Father David's designs (no. 11) Satan and a heretic drag toward hellmouth a triangular sled, or hurdle, on which are Death and seven sinners, their backs turned to the way they are traveling, looking into a convex mirror bordered with peacock feathers, the distorting mirror of their own vanity and vainglory. A seventeenth-century copperplate by Conrad Meyer [22] is a portentous variant of the idea (Fig. 89). Hateful monsters have pursued to the brink of a terrible waterfall a boat in which are the Seven Sins, each identifiable by an attribute or action. They utter the apocalyptic cry: "Woe, woe, woe!" On the shore are the pious, and Virtue points towards a vision of Christ. The accompanying text is from St. Paul (Galatians 5:19) on "the works of the flesh." The same lesson is taught in one of Quarles' emblems (Book I, No. 11) showing the World, a globe, trundled in an ornate chariot drawn by a boar and a goat. A devil brandishes a whip and Divine Love pulls hard upon a cord attached to the World. "Pull, gracious Lord!" is the ejaculatory prayer.

Even when the Sins are depicted in separate miniatures or cuts it may sometimes be inferred that they are riding processionally. In French ecclesiastical wall paintings there are ten surviving examples of such processions.[23] It is remarkable, in contrast, that not a single painting of the Sins in English churches follows this pattern. Spenser's pageant, however, is not the only vestige of the processional convention to be found in England. In the morality play *Wisdom who is Christ* (ca. 1480–90), where in place of the Seven Sins there are no less than eighteen Vices, those attendant upon Mind are ushered in by a trumpeter, those attendant upon Understanding by a bagpiper, and those attendant upon Will (who has become Lechery) by a hornpiper.[24] It seems likely that in *Doctor Faustus* the Seven Deadly Sins paraded about the stage; certainly they were piped on and off, for at the end of the episode Lucifer gives the command: "Away, to hell, away, on piper!" [25] There is a cavalcade of the Sins in John Lane's poem *Tom Tel-Troths Message* (1600) [26] where seven "Mincing maides and fine-trict truls ride past" on their way to Pluto's palace. John Day pictures Sin, in ceremonial progress, walking under a canopy borne by her "seven kinsmen." [27]

When Pride is riding, the emblematic mount is a lion, and whether riding, walking, or seated a lion is often near her.[28] Or the lion may be shown upon a banner that she carries, as in *Die Siben todsünden*. The lion, however, may be not Pride's emblem but her retribution. In a Florentine engraving (ca. 1470–80) [29] we see two ladders, one is climbed by Meekness, a fair youth, followed by a lamb and from the other Pride falls into the yawning jaws of a fierce lion. But the convention of Pride's animal was not completely stabilized. She may, as in *Die Siben todsünden*, ride upon a dromedary (because upon its hump she is perched so high) or, as in *The Pastime of Pleasure*, upon an elephant (which is a regal beast) [30] or even upon an ass (for, when all is said, Pride is a stupid Sin).[31] Thomas Trevelyon places a horse beside Pride.

Pride is the only female personification in Spenser's company of the Sins and she is the only one not afflicted with some disease. Among her retinue and close to the coach rides "that false Lady Faire the fowle Duessa," who had brought the Red Cross Knight to the House of Pride. Duessa has a major role in Book One of *The Faerie Queene* and, although her identification is important for the interpretation of the political allegory of the poem, we are not here concerned with it. In the moral allegory she is Fraud. Deceit, Dissimulation, Lying, Hypocrisy, and Flattery may be grouped together with Fraud in literature and the visual arts. They all have one characteristic in common: they show themselves under two aspects. Fraud in Bronzino's famous painting in the National Gallery, in London, miscalled "Venus, Cupid, Folly, and Time," is a pretty girl, but the close observer notes that she has two left hands and no right hand, and she may be wearing a false face. Ripa has a number of concepts which must be considered.[32] His Fraud is a *bifrons* woman, one face young and beautiful, the other old and ugly. She holds in one hand two hearts, in the other a mask. She is naked to the waist, and her lower garment is yellow, the color of deceit. Her feet are eagle's talons and she has a scorpion's tail. In a second concept, Fraud holds a fishing rod with which to catch the unwary. Ripa's Adulatione, or Flattery, is again a young woman with two faces: fair and alluring, ugly and evil. Bees swarm from her hands because they have honey in their mouths and stings in their tails, and a dog beside her suggests that Flattery fawns. Ripa's Hypocrisy is emblematized by a swan with white feathers and black flesh. He has no less than four concepts of Inganno, or Deceit. 1. A man dressed in gold and with serpents' tails in place of legs has beside him a panther hiding its head between its forelegs; it is the panther's habit to hide its terrifying head and display its pretty back. 2. A woman wears a beautiful mask, but part of her face is showing and it is ugly and withered. 3. A man whose face is barely visible and in whose hand is a net with fish. 4. A man holding fishhooks and a bunch of flowers from which a serpent is crawling. In the French and English translations of Ripa there is a conflation of images: the man with serpents' tails holds fishing nets or hooks and a panther is at his feet.[33] Bugia, or Lying, in Ripa is an ugly woman. She wears no mask, but her dress of changeable colors is painted all over with masks and tongues. Other emblematists play but minor variations, if any, upon these motives. Jean Jacques Boissard's Hypocrisy, with a false face and snaky hair, is fishing for the unwary.[34] Georgette de Montenay's Hypocrisy is a woman holding a tongue in an outstretched right hand (proffering fair words), but she trails her heart far behind her.[35] John Marston denounces "this Janian bifront, Hypocrisy." [36] Peacham, borrowing from a Continental source, has a bifrons Dissimulation who, with Avarice as a partner, catches Pallas (Wisdom) in a net. His Deceit, a reverend and pious old man with coiled serpents' tails and a panther beside him, is close to Ripa's image but not identical with it.[37] Henry Peacham describes Dissimulation as "a lady wearing a vizard with two faces, in a long Robe of changeable colour." [38] Wye Saltonstall likens a waterman on the Thames to "the embleme of deceite, for he rowes one way and lookes another." [39] One of Daniel Cramer's emblems is a bifrons "Mendacium." [40] One of Quarles' (Book I, no. 15) shows Truth scourged by bifrons Fraud, "sweetlipt Fraud, with her divided face." In the *Mundorum Explicatio* (p. 159) Deceit is "a twy–fac'd Hag." In a woodcut which possibly derives from a tapestry, Fraud, enthroned, dominates three women (Justice and Reason bound fast and Truth with a padlock on her lips) with their legs in the stocks.[41] There are innumerable pictures of Fortune in which her two faces betray her deceitfulness. When Humfrey Gifford says that Fortune "in one hoode a double face doth beare," [42] he draws his image from an English proverbial expression. John Skelton uses it twice,[43] and Francis Kinwelmarsh writes: "Abhorred is that false dissembling broode, / That seemes to beare two faces in one hoode." [44] Spenser implies the antithetical characteristics of Duessa by barely mentioning her fairness and falseness, but this antithesis becomes shockingly apparent when in a later episode her hideously obscene hinderparts are exposed.

What, now, of the "six Wisards old," the "six sage Counsellours," who ride upon the animals that draw the coach of Pride?

6. *Sloth or Idleness*

Idleness or Sloth (Spenser uses both names) "all the rest did guide." Does not Satan find mischief for idle hands to do? In the Prologue to *The Second Nun's Tale* Chaucer had called Ydelnesse the minister and nurse of vices and "the porter at the gate" of sensual pleasures. Lydgate several times in his poems calls Idleness the Mother or "chief porteresse" of Vices, and in his *Assembly of Gods* (lines 666 f.) Idleness leads the Vices. John Day likens Pigritia (Sloth) to a castle without walls or moat, and therefore unprotected from assaults. It is noteworthy, however, that among Van Veen's Horatian Emblems [1] there is a tempestuous design, "Il Tempo vola, e va di mal in peggio," of Time hurtling through the air dragging after him six infant Sins but Sloth is not among them. To this design is attached the despairing comment: "Nos peres passoyent en malice leurs ayeux, et nous pire qu'eux." Again, Sloth does not appear among Satan's counsellors in the *Mundorum Explicatio*. Similarly Wrath does not appear among the Sins in Acheley's *Massacre of Money*, perhaps because the other six are all wrathful. Perhaps Sloth is absent from both examples because it lacks the evil energy with which the other Sins are filled.

Spenser's Idleness rides upon "a slouthfull Asse" which Satan whips when, bogged in the mire, it brings the pageant to a standstill. The ass is the most nearly consistent of all the emblematic animals. Unless all the Sins ride horses, the ass is always Sloth's mount, except in *The Ancren Riwle* where Sloth is assigned a bear (because it hibernates?), and, when not mounted, Sloth is often in proximity to an ass. In one of the Horatian Emblems Sloth is an ass, though all the other Sins are shown with human forms.[2] Very tentatively it may be asked whether there is any emblematic intention in the fact that Bottom the Weaver, hitherto so energetic, goes to sleep when the ass's head is put on him and when awakened promptly goes to sleep again. Titania loves him in that guise, and we recall the emblem in which Love affixes angel's wings to an ass.[3] Another emblematist pictures a man with an ass's head sprawled upon a Globe; the motto is: "Homo iners gravissimus Mundi Onus." [4] Sloth is placed in proximity to an ass in pictures by Fanti, Burgkmair, Martin de Vos, Callot, and Trevelyon. Crispin de Passe places a staff in the hand of Pigritia, perhaps to suggest that he is too lethargic to walk without support. In *A Booke of Christian Prayers* (sigs. 47ʳ and 67ᵛ) Industry stands upon an ass. Other examples might be cited but these will suffice. Occasionally Sloth is represented by another animal, as when Edgar, conforming to an old tradition, characterizes himself as a "hog in sloth." [5] Gower and the French manuscript fancy that an owl accompanies this Sin, probably because it sleeps by day. Ripa assigns to Accidia a torpedo–fish because, according to Pliny and Plutarch, this creature causes anyone who touches it to become inert.

Idleness as he rides upon his ass, is, Spenser tells us, so "drownd in sleepe" that he can scarce "uphold his heavie hed." Sometimes there is no animal or other attribute and Sloth is merely shown sluggish or sleeping. Acheley's Idleness moves at a snaillike pace, his eyes are sunk in his head; "snorting he lies all night, dreaming all day." In Philip Galle's series of the Sins Sloth is asleep and of all the Sins only she and her sleeping putti have no attribute. Marlowe's Sloth tells Faustus that he has lain "on a sunny bank" ever since he was begotten, complains of having been brought thence to Faustus' study, and asks to be carried back by Gluttony and Lechery. Thus he drowses quietly on Boccaccio's Tree of Knowledge. Dekker's Sloth in *The Seven Deadlie Sinnes of London*, 1606, is the only one of London's Deadly Sins who does not ride in a chariot. He is instead borne along in a litter carried between "a couple of unshodde Asses"—i.e. without iron shoes they walk softly. One is reminded of the stupidly somnolent Sin lugged along by two companions in Mantegna's "Triumph of Minerva" in the Louvre. When, as in a design by Peter Furnius and in one of the Horatian Emblems,[6] Sloth reclines upon a pillow, an association with Lechery is perhaps suggested.[7] If, as in concepts of Sloth by Virgil Solis, Ripa, and Callot, this Sin is sitting upon the ground among ruins, we have to do not with mere Idleness (as in Spenser) but with Accidia, Spiritual Lethargy, Wanhope. This is surely why Trevelyon places Slouthe by a tomb. So interpreted, the Sin may be identified with Despair. But the Red Cross Knight's encounter with Despair is another and very terrible adventure.

Idleness is the only Sin which Spenser connects with the Roman clergy: He "caries a Portesse" (a breviary) and is 'arayd in habit blacke, and amis thin, Like to an holy Monck." We have, however, observed Bateman's obsession with this idea; and in the lost Edwardian interlude to which I have made reference every one of the Sins is a Roman ecclesiastic. One can only guess what considerations dictated the equations. These are my guesses: Pride is a pope, for obvious reasons; Wrath is a bishop (because he wields angry authority); Envy a friar (because he is vowed to poverty); Avarice a parish priest (because he collects tithes); Gluttony a chantry priest (because the endowment sustains him in comfort); Lechery a monk (violating the vow of chastity); and Sloth a hermit (who dwells in idle solitude). Spenser also says: "A shaking fever raged continually" through the limbs of Sloth but I cannot explain why Spenser imagined Sloth to be afflicted with this disease; it does not seem appropriate.

7. Gluttony

In picturing Gluttony as riding upon "a filthy swine" Spenser follows
a convention appropriate indeed but not so well established as that of the
ass of Sloth. Ripa's Gula is so mounted, and Burgkmair, Martin de Vos,
Callot, and other artists introduce a pig or hog in this Sin's emblem.
However, in Gower and elsewhere he rides upon a wolf, and Edgar in
King Lear describes himself as "wolf in greediness." In the *Chasteau
de Labour* he is mounted on a boar (not a pig, for its tusks protrude).
Die Siben todsünden places this Sin on what is described as "an animal
or worm called Ratus" (whatever that may be, the text does not correspond to the woodcut); on her helmet is a fox, on her shield a fish
(a pike), and on her banner "a beast called Parchrio" (which I am at a
loss to explain). The Bavarian woodcut (see note 7, Chapter 4, Section 2)
represents Gluttony by two dogs snarling over a bone. Elsewhere, for
example, in Lydgate's *Assembly of Gods*, in Bateman, and in Thomas
Nashe, the animal chosen is a bear.

Spenser's Gluttony has an "up–blowne" belly, his eyes are swollen
with fatness, and "like a crane his Necke was long and fyne." Spenser
may have observed these characteristics in Alciati (as the *Variorum* notes),
and they are found elsewhere.[1] Poliphagus, a character in a poem by John
Davies of Hereford, expresses the wish that man's neck were like a crane's
so that meat and drink "would longer passe, with pleasure to our
mawes." [2] Ripa assigns to Gula the ostrich as an emblem. Even nastier
than his swollen belly and greedy neck is Gluttony's vomiting: he "spued
up his gorge," says Spenser. In a mural in an English church Gluttony
is vomiting, as does a putto in a corner of Philip Galle's "Gula." Of
Gluttony Acheley tells us that "his house is nought but Kitchen" and
his followers are "smel–feasts." In Spenser's description the association
of Gluttony with Bacchus is suggested by the garment of "greene vine
leaves" and the "yvie girland." We have noted the parallels in Bateman,
and in at least one Brussels tapestry Gluttony is a winged Bacchus.[3] The
"bouzing can" held by Spenser's personification is an attribute so obviously
appropriate that parallels need not be cited: Tankards, kegs, barrels,
cups, glasses, flagons, and the like abound. In two Horatian Emblems
Gluttony is so immoderate that even while drinking from a glass she is
pouring more wine into it. Emphasis is, in fact, more often laid upon
drinking than eating, though one of Philip Galle's putti is gnawing on
a joint of meat. Sometimes, as in Trevelyon's design and in Day's

Peregrinatio Scholastica, Drunkenness, or Ebriatas, takes the place of Gluttony (greediness for food) among the Sins. In the *Mundorum Explicatio* Drunkenness and Gluttony are "brothers," thus making up the number seven in a company where, as I have noted, Sloth does not appear. In Anthony Van Worms' design, though all seven of the Sins appear, there are only six compartments, Luxuria and Gula being represented together. Gluttony is "full of diseases," Spenser tells us, mentioning particularly that "a dry dropsy through his flesh did flow." Falstaff's reference to Dives as "the Glutton" [4] is an example of a biblical character verging into a personified abstraction. Nashe in *Pierce Penilesse* associated "Master Dives" with Gluttony.[5]

8. Lechery

Lechery, or Luxuria, is closely allied to Idleness. We have seen that it was idleness that prompted David to commit adultery with Bathsheba and that in Dunbar's *Dance* Lechery is led by Idleness. In the seventh satire of *The Letting of Humors Blood in the Head–Vaine* [by Samuel Rowlands] ed. 1613, occurs a passage (sig. D5 ᵛ) beginning:

> Seaven graund Divels, bred and borne in Hell,
> Are grac'd like Monarches on the earth do dwell.

The Seven Deadly Sins are thus characterized, but as types rather than personifications. Lechery is said to spend all his time "In Two wheeld Coatch, and Boson ocupation." This description seems to associate Lechery with Luxury in a wider sense, embracing Sloth, Ostentation (Vainglory), and Gluttony. In a Triumph of Love tapestry in Vienna Idleness and Volupté push Cupid's chariot.[1] The anonymous Florentine engraving (ca. 1460) in which six women are defeating three demons is a kind of Psychomachia or Combat of Luxury *vs.* Chastity. The chief devil lies bound upon a large cushion (emblem of Luxuria); a second is being driven off, crying "Oime!"; a third hangs in chains. Only a dwarfish mocking imp is apparently unconcerned.[2] Spenser's Lechery rides upon a goat, the usual emblematic animal. The goat of Incontinence may stand by Adam in scenes of the Fall. Among innumerable examples of the goat of Lechery, we find it in Gower; Lydgate; the *Livre de bonnes meurs*; the *Eruditorium Penitentiale*; Stephen Hawes' *The Example of Vertu* (Fig. 90); Bateman; *A Booke of Christian Prayers*; Philip Galle; the Horatian Emblems; and Callot. An engraving by Heinrich Aldegraver (1528) of Intemperance (of which Lechery is one manifestation) shows a woman whose hand rests upon a goat. In the *Mundorum Explicatio* Lust wears a goat's skin and has sparrow's down instead of hair. In Ripa's various concepts of Libidine she is associated with a goat, a crocodile (because of its reputed fecundity), a dove or partridge (notoriously amorous), a leopard (its spotted skin analogous to a spotted mind), vine leaves (suggesting her friendship with Bacchus), a lolling posture (since Libidinousness springs from Idleness), and a scorpion (the sign of the Zodiac ruling the genitals). In the Bavarian woodcut a cock is her emblem. Trevelyon places by "Riotous or Adulterie" a camel as well as a goat. In *Die Siben todsünden* she rides on a bear.[3]

Special attention may be directed to a sixteenth-century anonymous German print illustrating "the Power of Woman." [4] This, though not one of a series of the Sins, suggests the personification of Lechery. The woman riding on an ass approaches four men who wear fool's caps. Behind her are four reluctant apes which she drags along with ropes round their necks. A scroll on the print begins with the words: "Eynen essel reyden ich wan ich weil." Does she ride the ass as Phyllis rode Aristotle? Does the fact that she, certainly no virgin, leads apes in this life cast any light upon Shakespeare's metaphor that old maids are destined to "lead apes in hell"? [5] "Amor, carnalis" is a blindfold, nude, winged female with bow and arrow. Skull, sword, and hellmouth are shown beneath and cautionary saints and moralists in surrounding compartments.[6]

For Lechery's "greene gowne" I have no parallel except (as is noted in the *Variorum*) Lust clad in green in *The Court of Love*. By the burning heart which Lechery carries does Spenser intend to suggest an antithesis to the familiar attribute of Charity or Heavenly Love? He has, says Spenser, many ways "to bait his fleshly hooks." It is just possible that these are the fishhooks of Dissimulation but it is much more likely that claws are implied. Spenser's Mammon has "nayles like clawes" and Envy, appearing for a second time much later in his poem, has "long nayles . . . like puttocks clawes." [7] In the *Mundorum Explicatio* Avarice has claws like iron teeth and "his pawes [are] continually convext." The Tyrant in Lorenzo Leombruno's version of the "Calumny of Apelles," in the Brera, has terrible talons for fingernails.

Spenser tells us that Lechery "joyd weake womens heart to tempt." Only here in the pageant does a personified abstraction almost become a type figure. The abstraction would tempt both men and women but because his Lechery is masculine the poet imagines the temptation to be directed against women. Elsewhere more consistently than any other Sin, Lechery is imagined to be female. In *Doctor Faustus* she is apparently the only female Sin; Faustus addresses her as "Mistress Minx." In Acheley's poem Vice commends "mine own darling, hight licentiousness" whose "brests lay open . . . the perfect mirrour of formositie." It is my impression that more frequently than any of the other Sins, Lechery is visualized, not as a personified abstraction, but by a typical situation. Perched on Boccaccio's Tree of Knowledge, all the other Sins follow their several activities in solitude, but Lechery is represented by a pair of lovers kissing. Embracing lovers symbolize this Sin in wall paintings in English churches, in the Horatian Emblems, in designs by Burgkmair, Furnius, and other artists. In a German woodcut (ca. 1480) a woman riding on a goat turns to kiss a young man who sits behind her.[8] Fanti has a satyr approaching a woman. Lechery, Spenser tells us, is afflicted with "that foule evil . . . That rots the marrow and consumes the brain" (syphilis).

9. Avarice

There seems to have been no agreement as to the emblematic animal appropriate to Avarice or Covetousness. Spenser's Avarice rides upon a camel. Christ's words established the connection between the camel and the rich man and consequently the hump may become emblematic of the rich man's burden of superfluities. An engraving in an English book shows Avarice (or an avaricious. man) standing beside the animal, with his hand resting upon its hump; a great needle let down from heaven attracts the camel's puzzled attention.[1] In an impresa, however (and therefore applied to an individual only), the camel with its hump signifies the cheerful bearing of the tribulations of the Christian life.[2] The accompanying motto is: "Il me plaint le trouble." The burden, however, may be too heavy to be borne, as is suggested by an emblem of a crouching camel.[3]

Avarice is often found with some other animal attribute. Lowes considered the horse on which Gower mounts Covetousness "a rather inept assignment"; however, Covytise so rides in an English poem of earlier date,[4] and the same animal is conspicuous in the *Ars Moriendi* illustration of the temptation of Avarice, where the theft of his horse and the tapping of his wine vats distract the thoughts of the dying man.[5] Since there was no generally accepted animal convention, the Sin may be found with various creatures, more or less appropriate. An ape may appear, perhaps with a purse hanging from its neck.[6] A variety of burrowing and hoarding animals are obviously suitable: a mole, badger, hedgehog, squirrel, or toad.[7] The ass of Avarice, laden with a bundle of bread, meat, and wine but feeding upon thistles, was one of the most popular of Alciati's original emblems.[8] Tenacity, who is Avarice, rides an ass in the interlude of *The Contention of Liberality and Prodigality* (ca. 1565). Ripa's wolf of Avarice is justifiable for the Sin may be ravenous, but it is more frequently assigned to Envy. According to Pliny (Bk. VIII, chap. 25) only death can stop the crocodile's growth and this is perhaps the reason Jacob Cats makes a skeleton sitting astride a crocodile an emblem of Avarice. In Cats' *Silenus* all the emblems are repeated three times, first with an amatory interpretation, then a moral, and finally a doctrinal one. Consequently a skeleton rides and controls the crocodile,[9] first because only death can stop the growth of true love, then because Avarice grows with advancing years, and finally because the soul of the Christian continues to expand till death. This explains why on a silver beaker, a wedding cup, in the Yale University Museum of Art made by Cornelius Vanderburg (1685), the skeleton–ridden crocodile, an emblem seemingly so inappropriate, appears.

Encumbered with "two iron coffers," a "heape of coin," and some "bags," Avarice is one of the most uncouth figures in Spenser's pageant. So vividly is he pictured that watching him count his coin as he sits precariously upon his tall beast, a reader is almost anxious lest he topple off! Treasure chests, wallets, and purses are attributes so obvious that they are always adopted, and I need not give a list of artists. Occasionally one discovers ingenious or amusing variations: In *Piers Plowman* (A: Passus V, 188 f.) the cheeks of Coveytise sag like purses; a chest through which large holes have been bored becomes the stocks in which a rich man sits.[10] When wings are attached to the money bag of Avarice, the emblem seems confused, for this is suggestive rather of Prodigality.[11] Once it is Pride not Avarice who offers a purse to a man [12] because as the design makes clear, it enables him to indulge each of the Five Senses and self–indulgence is not a characteristic of Avarice. With the object of accumulating riches, Avarice, Spenser tells us, sacrifices his "backe and belly," goes clothed in threadbare garments, and in all his life has scarcely tasted a "good morsel." Alciati's ass, neglectful of good provender, is found elsewhere. The meaning is the same when Avarice is pictured in mean clothing though rich garments hang near,[13] or gnawing on a bone though an abundance of food and drink is at hand.[14]

The satiric interlude *Respublica* (belonging to the reign of Mary Tudor) accords a special prominence to Avarice. He is the only Deadly Sin among the dramatis personae, and the other Vices (Insolence, Oppression, and Adulation) hail him as "our Founder and chief, Mr. Avarice," although in their final discomfiture they lay the blame on him. The theme is, in general, that the love of money is the root of all evil and, in particular, that extortion and corruption had been rife during the reign of Edward VI. In order to deceive Respublica and People, Avarice assumes the name "Policy" and turns his coat so as to hide "these same purses that hang att my backe." Though People is suspicious of him, for long he beguiles Respublica; but in the upshot Truth forces him to disclose his ill–gotten gains and he is condemned by Nemesis (Queen Mary).[15] It is to be noted that in this play Avarice is not, as are the Sins in the older moralities, a psychological characteristic of the protagonist, intent upon serving him, but a type figure, intent upon his own interests. Unlike Pride or Sloth and notwithstanding scriptural authority, Avarice is seldom conceived as the root of all evil. It is true, however, that Nicholas Breton in his list of the Seven Deadly Sins at the beginning of *Pasquils Mad–Cap, And Mad–cappes Message* (1600) places Money (i.e. Avarice) first. This, however, is exceptional; this satiric poem is an onslaught upon riches, which dominate every phase of English life.

Spenser says of Avarice that "accursed usurie was all his trade." There are parallels: in Dunbar's *Dance* Cuvatyce is accompanied by usurers; Bateman calls Avarice Usury; Richard Barnfield likens Covetousness to a usurer, clad in a cassock "made of poor men's skins." [16] Yet ethically the concept is somewhat confused, for whereas usurers are avaricious, the avaricious man is not necessarily a usurer. We are further told that Avarice weighs right and wrong in an "equal ballaunce." The Sin is depicted with a pair of balances in an edition of the *Roman de la Rose*.[17] The attribute is unusual, but the thought is clear enough: unlike Justice, but like Time and Death (when they are provided with scales), Avarice takes no account of the rightfulness or wrongfulness of claims. Spenser might have conveyed much the same idea by depicting Avarice as blindfold, though he does not. The Sin is so shown by Virgil Solis, Burgkmair, and Trevelyon. There is a seventeenth–century engraving (Fig. 91) of a miser sitting at a table on which are moneybags and heaps of coins; a devil from behind him dangles two purses before his eyes, so that he cannot see Justice and Death.[18] On the other hand, it may be Avarice who seeks to blindfold Pallas: "Sapientiae deceptrix Avaritia." [19]

This is the only Sin whose age Spenser implies: his "life was nigh unto death's door yplast." In *The Castle of Perseverance*, after the assault of the Sins has been driven off, Avarice persuades Humanum Genus, who is now Old Age, to leave the Castle, and at the foot of the bed upon which Humanum Genus dies is (according to the plan of the setting in the manuscript) "Coveytyse copboard." Similarly, in another morality, *Mind, Will, and Understanding* (ll. 532 f.) Lucifer says of the protagonist:

> So to covetyse he shall wende,
> For that enduryth to the last ende.

In *The Pastime of Pleasure* Policy introduces Graund Amour to Avarice, whereupon Graund Amour casts aside fleshly pleasures and, as he tells us, "gadred [gathered] ryches as I should lyve ever." The episode is a long one, covering lines 5350–5473. Avarice in *Respublica* (line 113) is the Sin of Old Age. In the *Contention* Tenacity is an aged rustic. One of the Horatian Emblems (p. 84) shows Avarice as a woman riding astride an old man on all–fours. With perhaps a suggestion of the rich man's burden, this scene is related iconographically to that of Aristotle and Phyllis: the philosopher was senile when he submitted to this indignity. "In foote and hand a grievous gout tormented him," says Spenser of Avarice; and gout is a disease of later years.[20]

10. Envy

In Spenser's pageant Envy rides upon a wolf. There are analogous concepts in the Bavarian woodcut and in engravings by Fanti, Furnius, and Callot, among other artists. A wolf attacking a sheep is near the many–headed monster of Detraction on the title page (Fig. 92) of a pamphlet by John Dee.[1] The wolf emblematizes not Envy but Cruelty in *A Booke of Christian Prayers*. Occasionally other beasts appear with her: Furnius' Envy has a wolf and a dragon; in *Die Siben todsünden* and in Bateman there are dragons. In an anonymous seventeenth–century Dutch print (an example is in the Metropolitan Museum of Art) Envy is accompanied by a leopard. In one of Middleton's Lord Mayors' Shows Envy rides on a rhinoceros [2] (I do not know why). Thomas Nashe in *Pierce Penilesse* says that "Envie is a Crocodile." John Swan assigns to Envy a peacock and a lynx.[3] Acheley's Envy, a masculine personification, keeps an owl, a terrifying spook in whose "iron pawes" are poisonous snakes and "balls of wild–fire," whose shrieks awaken him to work revenge. Of the most usual animal emblem, the dog, there are more examples than there is space to note them. Æsop's dog-in-the-manger probably suggested it. Spenser tells us that Envy "chaws" upon a toad (just as in the *Mundorum Explicatio* Envy's garments are "speckled" with toads), but Spenser does not forget the "hatefull snake"; it lies secretly in Envy's bosom. In his second personification of Envy (V, 12, 32) it is a snake that is gnawn upon. When, as so often, this Sin is personified as female, she may have wild, lank, snaky locks or else wear a wreath of snakes. Among the best known of countless Continental examples are Giotto's Envy in the Arena at Padua and Poussin's painting "Time and Truth," in the Louvre. In the familiar emblem of Time leading forth Truth from a cave Envy with the attribute of snakes sometimes appears.[4] The attribute is of such common occurrence that I limit myself to some English instances and assemble them in a note.[5]

This Sin is closely affiliated to Slander, Detraction, Calumny, and Deceit.[6] Ripa's Detraction has a snakelike tongue protruding from her mouth. In the various "Calumny of Apelles" paintings there are similar concepts. In the *Mundorum Explicatio* poison drips from the lips of Envy. Spenser says that Envy hates good works and virtuous deeds, and "backbites" the "verse of famous Poets witt," spewing poison "on all that ever writt." Of his second personification of Envy, a hag, Spenser tells us that she delights to hear of harms that have come to men. This is why Giotto's Envy in the Arena has huge ears. An emblematist shows Envy gnawing at the robe of a woman holding a *caduceus* (the Arts) while to one side a spider's web overhangs three beehives: Poison hostile to Sweetness and Light.[7] So Envy tells Faustus: "I cannot read, and therefore wish all books burned." In a play performed by amateurs at Oxford in 1607 the actor who took the part of Detraction was "planted" in the audience and hissed so realistically that the spectators began to handle him roughly and had to be assured that he was one of the players.[8] Thomas Bancroft has the conceit that this Sin is so contemptible her own snakes hiss at her.[9] In a great spectacle devised by Thomas Dekker Envy "raged" against the Four Stoic Virtues and against King James' four kingdoms, "for very madnesse . . . feeding on the heads of Adders."[10] She hates those whom Fortune favors and is pleased when Fortune frowns.[11] She is the opponent of Love. Wither has a charming emblem (Bk. I, no. 5) showing Cupid (Human Love) whipping a top-shaped spinning World, for 'tis love that makes the world go round, while opposite him Envy, a crone with snaky locks, whips the World with a lash made of three writhing snakes. Ignoring the poor, she rails against the rich.[12] In Venetian editions of Ovid's *Epistolae Heroides* a lean, flaccid-breasted Envy appears to the poet as he sits at his writing table.[13] Boissard shows Envy gnawing at the robe of a female figure who holds a caduceus and represents the Arts.[14] John Day's Envy, "a leane and meager hagg" (Day has forgotten that earlier in the *Peregrinatio* all the Sins are masculine) with sore eyes, is likened to a worm in a tree or a moth in a garment. In her company Learning, the protagonist of Day's narrative, is corrupted and envies "that any mans pen should be praised" or any man's labors rewarded save his own.

The chiefest enemy of Envy or Detraction is Fame. John Dickenson tells how Beldame Envy "did belch foule gobbets with a hell of snakes" upon Apollo's laurel tree. The tree began to wither, whereupon a second hag, Oblivion, began to "rake" it toward her, and Ignorance tried to get for her pupils some of the laurel. But Fame, the winged goddess, blew so shrill a note upon her silver trumpet that Envy, Oblivion, and Ignorance fled. Fame assigned to Desert the guardianship of the laurel tree, now green again.[15] "No tace invidia quando gloria crida," is the motto of a fine emblem which shows Envy springing from a cavern behind the back of a venerable sage, but Fame blows a trumpet overhead.[16] Spenser's Envy has a "leprous mouth"; the disease is appropriate.

11. *Wrath*

Any ferocious beast would be a fitting emblem for Wrath. The lion, albeit so often found with Pride, occurs frequently with Wrath. In Spenser's pageant this Sin rides upon a lion. Wrath tells Faustus: "I leapt from a lion's mouth when I was scarce an hour old." John Lane's Wrath, tearing with "Wolvish" teeth the hearts which he holds "butcherlike" in his hands, is "attired in a roring Lions skin." [1] In the *Mundorum Explicatio* the demon Wrath has a lion's face. In various Horae where the Four Temperaments are depicted in the corners of the page of the "Zodiacal Man," a lion represents Choler.[2] Similarly, in Peacham's emblems of the Temperaments Cholera is a young man with a lion by him.[3] Joachim Camerarius illustrates "Iram Prudentia Vincit" with a man throwing a cloth over a lion's head and about to catch the beast in a noose.[4] A less specific concept is that in *A Booke of Christian Prayers* where the Christian Knight stands triumphantly upon a lion's head, labeled "Hell Temptation Overcome." [5] In place of the lion, however, some other animal may be found: a bear, a wild boar, a wolf, a camel, a dog, a dragon, or an unidentifiable creature.[6]

Wrath brandishes a "burning brond." In like manner, later in *The Faerie Queene* (III, 12, 17), Fury tosses a firebrand about her head.

This brand is conspicuous in the Horatian Emblems and elsewhere. Antithetical to it is the inverted torch sometimes held by Concord or Peace.[7]

Fire, the element connected with the choleric temperament, is characteristic of this Sin even when there is no torch. Spenser tells us not only that Wrath's eyes "did hurle forth sparkles fiery red" but that he is afflicted with "Saint Fraunces fire," a curious error (not noted in the *Variorum*), for the poet must intend St. Anthony's fire, or erysipelas, of which a symptom is a reddish or fiery skin. The frame of the chariot in which Thomas Dekker's Cruelty rides is made of flints which "strike one–another, and beate out fire that is able to consume Citties." [8] Ripa's Wrath is a woman of red complexion, red eyes, and reddish clothes. In the French version of Ripa (1698) Wrath's dragon spews forth flames. In the *Mundorum Explicatio* the demon Wrath belches fire. Ben Jonson's Rage is "flame–ey'd." [9] In contrast to such emphasis upon the eyes of Wrath there are two Horatian Emblems which show Wrath blindfold; we still attach the epithet "blind" to rage. Spenser likens Furor to a "blindfold Bull" (*Faerie Queene*, II, 4, 7). In John Day's allegory Ira is the only Sin that blinds his victims.

The raiment of Wrath is "all to rags yrent." Even so, later in the poem (*Faerie Queene*, III, 12, 17) Furor tears the garments from her own back and tears her hair. Giotto's Ira in the Arena Chapel is a woman rending her clothes; and Spenser may have observed Wrath tearing her hair on the wall of the "Painted Chamber" at Westminster, or in a mural in Hoxne Church. He tells us (*Faerie Queene*, II, 4, 7) that Furor often hurts himself unawares, and in the pageant an allusion to "fretting grief the enemy of life" carries the implication that Wrath wounds himself "with rancours rusty knife." Marlowe's Wrath exhibits to Faustus a "case of rapiers" with which he says he wounds himself when he can find no one else to fight with. On the wall of Brooke Church Wrath stabs himself with two daggers. In *A Booke of Christian Prayers* Wrath, crouching under the feet of Patience, is in the act of stabbing himself, as he is in Nicolas Poussin's "Time and Truth," in the Louvre, to which I have alluded on page 110, and other parallels could be cited. There are more instances than there is space to note of this Sin brandishing a sword or bloody knife even when he does not turn the weapon against himself.

Finally, it is noteworthy (though all the commentators seem to have passed over this memorable detail) that Wrath "often would repent . . . his cruell facts." This is the only Deadly Sin with which Spenser associates repentance. In John Lane's *Tom Tel–Troths Message* Repentance follows Wrath but no other Sin. The chariot of Cruelty (who is the equivalent of Wrath) in Dekker's *Seven Deadlie Sinnes of London* is followed, as this Sin's only attendant, by Repentance, but so fast does the chariot move "that Repentance being lame (and therefore slow) tis always very late ere he comes to him."

A "foggy mist" covers all the land as the Seven Deadly Sins parade futilely in the "fresh flowering fields" outside the House of Pride. This fog is that "general mist of error" which, says John Webster, is Man's life.[10] Ben Jonson conceives of Error as "clad in mists." [11] An English engraving shows Falsehood wearing a head–covering of cloud.[12] Ripa's Error is blindfold and his Falacious Hope holds in one hand a cloud. In an English printer's colophon depicting the Liberal Arts, Rhetoric is shown with smoke or cloud or mist issuing from her mouth.[13] This must mean that Rhetoric may be employed to confuse or becloud the truth. Does it not cast light upon Shakespeare's "sweet smoke of Rhetoric" [14] (upon which the commentators are silent)? Thomas Middleton describes Error's head as "rolled in a cloud" and mists are "hanging at his eyes," but Truth chases away Error with a fan of stars.[15]

12. The Purple Island

Among the most faithful followers and most ardent admirers of Edmund Spenser were the two brothers Phineas and Giles Fletcher. With the younger and far more gifted of these poets we are not here concerned; but Phineas Fletcher's *The Purple Island* [1] (published in 1633 but certainly begun and perhaps completed at a much earlier date) demands our reluctant attention. A short account of it, omitting innumerable details, will serve as an epilogue to this chapter.

The poet adopted the well–worn medieval allegorical concept of the body of man as an island or fortress in which dwells the Soul. His taste for pastoral poetry suggested to him a most inappropriate framework: Thomalin, a shepherd lad, describes to his fellow shepherds the characters in the story and narrates the action. The first six cantos are an anatomical and physiological allegory in which every organ, artery, vein, muscle, and bone of the body are described and their functions explicated. For his anatomy Fletcher certainly depended upon Vesalius and for his physiology probably in the main upon Galen and his followers. The poet thus erected a monument of exhaustive and misdirected erudition and enthusiasm. In literary history these six cantos are notorious; to even the most devoted admirer of the extremes to which seventeenth–century poets carried their liking for "conceits" they are intolerable. The princely master of this island is Intellect who is "Shut in a tower where thousand enemies / Assault the fort." He has eight counsellors: the Five Senses, Common Sense, Fancy, and Understanding. His queen is Voletta, Will, and upon her attends a damsel, Conscience.

With Canto VII we come to an account of the forces of the enemy which is continued in Canto VIII and requires no less than 142 seven–line stanzas. These armies are under three commanders. The first is a two–fold dragon or Devil which I find most difficult to visualize. He is at once a "monstrous beast" with seven heads dwelling by the Tiber, i.e. the Pope, and a "black vulture" which "o'er shadows half the earth" and has "frighten'd the Muses from their native spring," i.e. the Turk. With this compound Devil are allied (as my readers will have guessed) Caro and Cosmos. All three, as in medieval genealogies and trees of the Vices, have many followers. By careful reckoning, the accuracy of which I do not guarantee because there is some overlapping, the entire host numbers some sixty–two personifications. To each of these an erudite name deriving from the Greek or Latin is generally given, but some names are in plain English that might have won Bunyan's approval. Never was baroque fancy put to a greater strain than in the presentation of these Sins and Vices—their appearance, physical characteristics, clothing, armor, actions, and attributes. Much that is by now familiar to my readers will be found here, employed with painstaking particularization and very rarely any originality whatever. There are many beasts, not accompanying the personifications but as devices upon their shields. There are foul diseases and hearts that are gnawn upon, cranelike necks and fat paunches, Fancy's feathers and Bacchus' grapes, masks and painted faces, claws and a skeleton, swords, daggers, darts, and other weapons, veils and strange disguises, fire, mists, and fogs. Phineas Fletcher pored over not only earlier allegories but many emblem books also.

One concession must be made in his favor. Spenser and Shakespeare (in *Pericles*) had made some slight use of the old motif, deriving from battles and tournaments, of the motto or "word" inscribed upon the combatants' shields. In emblem books such "words" are always part of the pattern, whether or not a personification is involved. To almost all Fletcher's Sins and Vices one is assigned. The very compactness of these mottos gives them a crispness, clarity, and freshness deplorably lacking in the poet's descriptions of his characters. We even observe occasionally a touch of humor. Strife so persistently did "chide, rail, bark, and bawl" that her tongue made use of every word in the language and "her shield no worde could finde." Gluttony had no "word" because he "could but grunt." 2

At the conclusion of Canto VIII Thomalin says to the other shepherds who are his hearers:

> But if I all this rout in foul array
> Should muster up, and place in battle ray,
> Too long yourselves and flocks my tedious song would stay.

Did ever poet judge himself more candidly? He has mustered up more than a sufficiency, and his song is certainly tedious.

In Cantos IX and X there is a like catalogue of the Virtues, who are not so numerous. We shall meet with them in the next chapter. Then follows the Psychomachia, so confusedly narrated that in the hurly–burly the reader is often uncertain as to which Virtues are fighting with which Vices. Needless to say, the forces of good are victorious. Finally, and not very clearly connected with all the anatomical, physiological, ethical, and theological matter that has preceded it, there is a narrative of the mystical marriage, the Heavenly Bridal, of Christ and the Church. This subject Giles Fletcher, at the close of his poem *Christ's Victory and Triumph*, had modestly but perhaps too confidently entrusted to his brother's genius.

CHAPTER 5.   THE SPIRITUAL GUARDIANS OF MAN

1. Patience

The flight of Time is beyond Man's power to control, but given Opportunity and the aid of certain Virtues he may compel Fortune to his service (unless she be thought of as mere blind Chance) whether she be a goddess or a demon or a power working under the governance of God. We have seen that he can summon to his aid Wisdom, Learning, Prudence, Foresight, Love, Courage, Industry, Humility, and Patience. Rising above any dependence upon Fortune, Wisdom may, like Horatio, be prepared to accept "with equal thanks" her buffets and rewards. Some of the emblematists [1] find in the Caspian Sea, which, it was reported, neither ebbs nor flows, an image of the constant mind that is above the sway of Fortune. Man must be prepared for either eventuality: for Good

Fortune or for Bad. Very popular in emblem books is the motto or "word": "In utrumque paratus." Whitney takes the Virgilian tag as the title of an emblem showing two hands, one holding a sword and the other a trowel: be prepared for the exertions of war or peace.[2] Closer to our theme is the emblem of the ox between the plough and the altar: ready for labor or for sacrifice.[3] William Martyn, who in instructing the young makes much use of emblematic material from natural history, cites Pliny as the authority for "a kind of Eagle who (having one claw–foot, & the other flat) is armed and provided; and useth to take her prey, both upon the water & upon the land also."[4] Capaccio uses this strange fowl as an emblem.[5]

Patience and Perseverance may triumph over adverse Fortune. No other emblem was more popular and ubiquitous than that of the weighted palm tree. This derives from Pliny. To the obvious question why this represents Constancy Alain Chartier replies: "Because the more it is oppressed, and the greater weight it hath the better it is."[6] Samuel Daniel, translating from Paolo Giovio, draws the analogy of the weight to "the fury of Fortune" and explains: "A Palme, having the top thereof weighed downe with the heavie poise of a great Marble tied thereunto, to signifie . . . that it returneth to the former fashion be it depressed with never so greate a waight."[7] John Lyly says: "It is proper for the Palm–tree to mount; the heavier you load it the higher it sprouteth."[8] A character in one of Massinger's plays says: "I will, like the palm–tree, / Grow under my huge weight."[9] The promise held out is not, however, necessarily an assurance of mundane success; often the reward will be in the life to come. In a curious mystical romance the hero, Alector, describes a picture of such a palm tree hanging in a temple; it bore the inscription: "The lower fortune dooth thee abace, / The higher to heaven lift up thy face."[10] Robert Aylett draws the same moral lesson:

> As Branches of the Palm, the more opprest
> With burthens, nearer Heav'n themselves doe raise,
> So Fortitude in valiant Christians brest
> The more assaulted, merits greater praise.[11]

George Wither's interpretative comment upon this emblem is: "No inward grief nor outward smart / Can overcome a Patient Heart."[12] He uses it again to draw a different lesson: "Truth, oft oppressed, wee may see, / But, quite suppressed it cannot be."[13] Even after more than three centuries one cannot remain unmoved by the appearance of the same emblem as a detail (Fig. 93) in the famous portrait of King Charles

I at his prayers in the *Eikon Basilike* (1649), and the many editions through which this book passed must have made it familiar to countless thousands of people.[14] In the versified explanation accompanying the portrait are the lines: "Though clogg'd with weight of miseries, / Palm—like depress'd I higher rise." Here the motto is "Crescit sub pondere Virtus." This is the motto most usually selected, but we also find "Inclina resurgat," [15] "Obdurandum adversus urgentia," [16] "Onerata exsurgit in altum," [17] "Depressa resurge," [18] "Sursum deflexa recur-rat," [19] "Adversus pondera surgo," [20] "Ponderibus virtus innata re-sistit," [21] and other gnomic aphorisms. The burdened palm tree is a family crest still existing today,[22] and it was a printer's device. Once at least it is combined with the familiar emblem of victory, "a token of victory," says John Swan, "because [palms] are of this nature, viz. that they will shoot upward, though oppressed with never so great a weight: neither do the leaves of it ever fall." [23] Peacham uses the palm branch as an emblem without reference to its burden; this is from Ripa, and signifies Perseverance. In his Second Vision in memory of Henry, Prince of Wales, he likens the Prince to a palm upon whose boughs hang crowns, but at its root a serpent gnaws.[24]

Occasionally some other tree or some crop may be substituted for the palm. Peacham has a cypress, upon which he comments: "The Cypresse tree; the more with weight opprest, / The more (they say) the braunch will upward shoot," and he draws the analogy of Constancy and Virtue resisting the frowns of Fortune.[25] Another variant is that of a tree into which a sickle has been driven, with the motto: "Per vulnere crescit." [26] We also find a pollarded tree bound with a chain at its top, and the motto is "Per vincula crescit." [27] We have also the analogous example of the crop which flourishes the richer the more it is trodden under foot. Famous because Falstaff parodies it is Lyly's observation that "the Camomill, the more it is trodden and pressed downe, the more it spreadeth." [28] Hag-thorpe imagines that Poverty wears "a wreath of cammamile," obviously suggesting her superiority to the buffets of Fortune.[29] Thomas Combe's emblem of a man stamping upon a crop is explained: "The more that Saffron troden is with feete, / The more it still doth flourish on the ground." [30]

The lesson taught by the palm tree, the cypress, the camomile, and the saffron, that Man may rise the higher the greater the burden put upon him, is taught also by the tennis ball, which rebounds "with greater force" the harder it is dashed to the ground.[31] "Like Tennis—bals, throwne downe hard highest rise," says William Browne.[32] A variant of the figure is John Bodenham's "Even as the racket takes the balls rebound, / So doth good fortune catch ill fortunes proof." [33] When in the *Horatian Emblems* (pp. 16–17) Virtue with her sword sheathed is shown escaping from the Deadly Sins, Van Veen's intention is not to depict her as pusillanimous but to illustrate Horace's precept: "Virtus est vitium fugere."

Of all the Virtues who support Man on his toilsome pilgrimage, Patience is recommended notably often in the visual and verbal imagery of the Renaissance and to her (or very rarely him) particular attention must be devoted here. I begin with Chaucer's curious personification, curious because it is quite out of accord with the customary concept and is, I think, unique. Before the door of the temple described in *The Parliament of Foules* Chaucer tells us that he found Dame Patience sitting "upon an hill of sand." [34] Why should Patience occupy a seat so unstable, so different from her customary sturdy cube, pedestal, or monument? The "hill of sand" is a detail added by Chaucer to his source–passage in the *Teseide*; Boccaccio says nothing about it. Skeat suggested that it was intended to convey the idea that Patience endures even in the most comfortless and insecure situation. Or may the image be analogous to that of the slow, patient piling–up of sand in the hourglass? Long after Chaucer's time that sand, rising into a little mound and ever and anon sliding down again, was used by John Hall as an emblem of the slipperiness of Man's life. [35] We cannot say whether or not Chaucer had some such image in mind.

The meek endurance of Patience is symbolized in various ways. Ripa's personification wears a yoke in conformity with Christ's words: "Take my yoke upon you." Upon the manacles with which she is bound water falls drop by drop, an assurance that little by little she will triumph over adversity. Another emblem shows the heart resting upon an anvil with three hammers beside it, [36] or, since the Passion of Christ is the supreme example of Patience, the anvil may have the instruments of the Passion resting upon it. [37] The lamb which she may hold or which, as in Heemskerk's design, is at her feet is a symbolic animal of obvious appropriateness. Beham's engraving of Patience (1540) clasps a lamb. A devil is near her, but she sits securely on the drum of a column and two cherubs hold a crown over her head. [38] In a *Horae* in the Huntington Library (MS. 1088, fols. 225^v–226^r) Christ and eleven poor people, artisans, nuns, a monk, and a child, are together bearing the Cross. Following Christ's injunction: "Take up My cross and follow Me," she and the seven biblical *exempla* whom Heemskerk pictures for us all carry banners with a cross. In an English treatise on Patience her banner bears Constantine's inscription: "In hoc signo." [39] In one of the illustrations in the English version of *The School of Patience* (1640) by Henry Drexelius she stands upon a mound of crosses,[40] and on the title page of the same work she stands beside the column of Fortitude. A fantastic engraving formerly attributed to Peter Brueghel the Elder shows Patience holding a Cross and sitting upon a cube, thus linking her with Constancy.[41] Elsewhere she rests her elbow upon a column.[42] One of Capaccio's emblems is of special interest to students of Shakespeare for the analogy it affords to the famous passage in *Twelfth Night* (II.4.117–118) where Viola tells the Duke about her lovelorn "sister." Capaccio's Patience stands upon a pedestal (one might say a "monument") and has a bandage across her mouth,[43] an emblem of silent endurance but also reminding us of the "sister" who "never told her love."

> She sat like Patience on a monument,
> Smiling at grief.

Here is a nice example of the relationship between verbal and visual imagery. In most texts "Patience" is capitalized, that is, personified, but "grief" is not. In other words, it is not one personification who smiles at another but the girl who sitting like Patience smiles at her own grief. The question is whether there are two emblematical figures or only one. Malone thought there were two, but the consensus of editors and commentators follows Halliwell–Phillipps who asserted roundly: "Patience is personified but grief is not." This may of course have been the image Shakespeare intended. But in *Richard III* (III.7.25) he employs the simile of two "dumb statues" staring at one another. Half a dozen passages in the plays show that he had often in mind a complex of associations of Patience with Grief. Closest to Viola's description of her "sister" are Pericles' words (V.1.137 f.) to his daughter Marina:

> Thou doest look
> Like Patience gazing on kings' graves and smiling
> Extremity out of act,

that is, with a smile curbing the extremity of Grief from rash action. When the dethroned and humiliated Richard II was brought to London (V.2.5–33) and "rude misgoverned hands . . . Threw dust and rubbish" on his head, "with gentle sorrow" he shook off the dust, "His face still combating with tears and smiles / (The badges of his grief and patience)." When Cordelia read the letters telling her of Lear's plight, a messenger reports (IV.3.18–21) that she was moved

> Not to a rage. Patience and sorrow strove
> Who should express her goodliest. You should have seen
> Sunshine and rain at once: her smiles and tears
> Were like, a better way.

The antithesis is further developed in *Cymbeline* (IV.2.51–58), where the wronged and slandered Imogen (disguised as a youth) is said to yoke smiling with a sigh, "the smile mocking the sigh," and grief and patience mingle their roots together. May patience grow, hopes one of the brothers, and may "the stinking elder, grief" "intwine his perishing root" from the "increasing vine" of patience. There is a colloquy in *Othello* (I.3.202–219), too long to quote, where the Patience–smiles–Grief complex receives elaborate treatment. When Tybalt is enraged to see Romeo at the Capulets' ball (I.5.91) his antithetical emotions are different, for Patience meets not with Grief but with Choler. This catena of passages supports the view that in Viola's simile both Patience and Grief are statues and that Shakespeare had in mind the contrasting abstractions adorning funeral monuments, as Michaelangelo's Night and Day, Dawn and Twilight in the chapel in San Lorenzo.[44]

The Triumph of Patience is celebrated in a series of eight plates engraved by Johannes Galle after designs by Martin Heemskerk.[45] Hope and Longing draw a car in which sits Patience with the attributes of the lamb and anvil and a banner bearing the device of a rose between two thorn bushes. To the car's rear is tied blindfold Fortune with a broken wheel. In the succeeding plates seven devotees and examples of Patience are depicted. Isaac rides on a camel which drags a little car carrying the ram caught in the bushes. Joseph rides on a bullock with Invidia (his brothers' envy) and a nude woman (Potiphar's wife) dragged behind him. David on a lion drags Saul and Shimei. Job on a tortoise drags his wife, his three friends, and Satan. The fifth example is somewhat confused; the principal figure seems to be a conflation of Tobit and his son Tobias. He is plainly labeled "Tobias," but far from being a youthful prospective bridegroom he is elderly and bearded. He rides on a donkey, and behind him are blind Poverty and a woman, unidentified by any label, who may be Tobit's wife. Poverty has with her a small dog, an animal elsewhere always associated with Tobias rather than with his father. St. Stephen rides on an elephant, the animal probably being intended to suggest his fame as the protomartyr. Two men, carrying stones, the instruments of his martyrdom, are dragged behind him. Last of all comes Jesus Christ in a car decorated with the symbols of the Gospels. The World, Sin, Death, and Tartarus are led in captivity behind Him.

On a minute scale when contrasted with the overwrought and fantastic magnificence of these engravings, is the device of an Antwerp printer which makes use of biblical exempla: Patience with a cross is grouped with Job with his boils and Daniel in the lions' den.[46] As examples of Patience and the Cross may be cited an illustration in an English book where she stands upon a pile of crosses [47] and a print in which she holds a cross and is sitting upon a cube.[48]

So far we have observed Patience struggling towards her triumph in solitude or almost alone. But she has many allies. "Patience," writes William Cowper, Bishop of Galloway, "is never alone, all the remanent Graces of the Spirit frequent the Palace of Patience." [49] He goes on to say that the Virtues "march in battaile against the spirituall Enemy." "Truth goeth before . . . bearing the Lanterne of the Word." Faith follows Truth and is flanked by Charity and Holiness. Then come Humility and Meekness. In the midst of this procession is Patience, "Lady and Queen of Virtues," with Constantine's banner bearing the Cross and the motto: "In this sign conquer." [50] Experience and Hope attend upon her, the former having as his "badge" a book registering the Lord's "deliverances" (by which seems to be meant a record of examples of salvation through faith in Christ), the latter with the "badge" of a brazen pillar (a curious aberration from the traditional iconography of this Virtue). The good bishop then becomes confused in his allegory, for when Patience is "sore put out" she leans back upon the pillar of Hope and reads from the book of experience. Pillar and book have ceased to be "badges"! Last of all comes Perseverance holding a crown. Accompanying all these gallant warriors is Prayer, flying overhead like a winged Cupid.

2. Several Series of Triumphant Virtues

Among the embellishments with which John Daye expanded his earlier compilation, the *Christian Prayers and Meditations* (1569), into *A Booke of Christian Prayers* (1578), a repository of traditional and new iconographic material unique among publications of the Elizabethan period,[1] is a long series of triumphant Virtues. Each is represented by a female figure trampling upon a corresponding Vice. Patience, like the other Virtues, is almost always conceived of as feminine. However, in *The Pastime of Pleasure* (2472–3) Hawes makes her the sister of Prudence, who is, most unusually, masculine, a "leach" or physician. And in *The Faerie Queene* (I, 10, 23–24) Patience is masculine, himself the "leach" in the House of Holiness, curing the "disease of grieved conscience." The conquered Vices are sometimes personified abstractions, sometimes human types, sometimes individual historical characters, sometimes animals, and sometimes objects. For the theme there was ample precedent in Continental *Horae*, where, however, the Virtues are generally seated upon thrones with their foes at their feet.[2] The iconographic tradition is not that of the Psychomachia in which opposing abstractions fight one another on foot or tilt at one another, riding appropriate animals. Nor is it that of the *Trionfi* where the chariot of each Virtue rolls over supine enemies. It is that of Gothic sculpture and of such medieval murals as those in the "painted Chamber" in the Old Palace at Westminster. Another example is the representation of the Four Stoic Virtues at the wedding of James IV of Scotland to Margaret, daughter of Henry VII (Edinburgh, 1503). The Virtues were figures on a gate. Justice trod on Nero, Fortitude on Holofernes, Temperance on Epicurus, and Prudence on Sardanapalus.[3] This tradition was precisely adapted to the vertically long, horizontally narrow space provided in the prayer book's margins. The Virtues who triumph over one or another Deadly Sin have been remarked upon briefly in the preceding chapter. Now the entire series of twenty–one designs must be passed in review.

Knowledge of God with a lighted candle and an open book—both favorite Protestant attributes of Truth—stands upon Mahomet. Love of God holds a heart and stands upon Idolatry which is represented by a crucifix, a chalice and host, a crozier, a reliquary, and other objects associated with Roman Catholicism. This is the only design that is openly antipapist in intention. Faith with a flaming sword and a shield bearing a device of clasped hands stands upon Cain who "dispaireth of Mercy." Hope with an anchor stands upon Judas who was "ashamed, and hanged him selfe."

Patience with a Cross stands upon Wrath who is stabbing himself. Humility holds the olive branch of Peace and stands upon Pride, a crouching woman who is looking at herself in a mirror. Mercy with a lamb stands upon a wolf which symbolizes Cruelty. Concord holds a crown.[4] A pair of love–birds is on a branch above her head. Discord is symbolized by the pieces of armor on which Concord stands. Love with a child at her breast and two children clutching at her dress stands upon

Herod who "murthereth infants." Chastity with lilies in one hand and a swan in the other stands upon a goat, for "Uncleanes is like a Goate." Wisdom with an open book stands upon Sardanapalus who was "an imprudent king." Understanding has a sextant and an armillary sphere, for she "reaches the heavens." She stands upon Ignorance, a man with ass's ears. Industry with a carpenter's square and a pair of compasses stands upon Sloth, an ass. Memory with pen in hand and about to write in a book stands beside an open grave, for "Oblivion is as a grave." Justice is blindfold and holds the sword and scales. She stands upon Tyranny, a prostrate monarch who is not identified. Strength, her arm around a column which is broken in the middle, stands upon Holofernes, "slayne by Judith." Courage with a crown and scepter stands upon a prostrate man who is Cowardice. Temperance with a bridle in one hand and a clock in the other, because she "watcheth and bridleth," stands upon Intemperance, a man who is vomiting. Measure, that is, Moderation, pours wine into a drinking vessel, for "Measure in wine comforteth," and she stands upon a prostrate man who is Excess. Sobriety "watcheth her mouth," says the inscription. A large key rests upon her right shoulder and in her left hand is a fish. The two symbols are not interpreted; the key may be that with which, as we have seen in earlier chapters, the lips of Truth or the Good Wife may be locked; the fish probably suggests fasting. Sobriety stands upon Voluptuousness, a fat, gross Bacchus with a jug, a drinking vessel, and a cluster of grapes.

The sequence is now interrupted by a type–figure of a Christian soldier standing upon a lion's head labeled "Hell Temptation overcome." It concludes with Perseverance which "indureth to the end." She carries a tiny fish on a line and a larger fish dangles from her hand. The attributes obviously draw their appropriateness from Luke 5:5: "Master, we have toiled all the night, and have taken nothing; nevertheless at thy word I will let down the net." Success followed the disciple's perseverance. Perseverance stands upon "Revolting, a Sow in the mire." The appropriateness of this I do not see. In sum, the defeated Vices, among whom are only four of the "orthodox" Seven Deadly Sins, are represented by four unindividualized type–figures, three personifications, four animals, three objects, one classical divinity, two characters from secular history, and four from the Bible. A variety of interest is thus gained, relieving the monotony of the parade of the twenty–one Virtues.

In the same year in which John Daye published the *Christian Prayers and Meditations* he published also Stephen Bateman's *Christall glasse* (1569), a book which engaged our prolonged attention in the previous chapter. Bateman follows his representations of and comments upon the Seven Deadly Sins with an account of eight Virtues.[5] Here there is a great deal of exhortation but, whereas the Sins had been emblematized in no less than twenty–eight woodcuts, only one cut is allotted to each of the Virtues. (Bateman's grim imagination seems to have been less moved by virtuous living than by iniquity.)

Love is a woman who clasps a heart and stands upon hellmouth. Above her a lamb, interpreted as the "quiet conscience of the faithful," stands upon a supine skeleton. Faith is a man in armor who tramples upon the prostrate devil of temptation. The accompanying commentary interprets his cross–bearing shield as "lively faith," his spear as "continuance" (that is, perseverance), and his sword as "the word of God." The pieces of his armor have no such labels as we shall observe in other representations of the Christian Knight later in the present chapter, but St. Paul's great words in Ephesians 6:13–17 are quoted in the commentary along with other texts. The knight gazes upward at the Tetragramaton. Hope is a ship much battered on the sea of temptation. Conforming to the medieval tradition, Bateman explains that the ship is the Church. This is curious since the ship is wrecked. Men are swimming, or floating on a raft, or mounting a gangway to "the rock of felicity" at whose summit is a castle where Christ receives them. One man is tumbling off the rock.[6]

Bateman's representation of Charity does not conform to the usual convention of a woman nursing babies and is an interesting example of the tendency to conflate personifications. He manages to combine in one design six Works of Mercy (Burial being, as so often, omitted). A charitable man holds in one hand a flagon and with the other passes a loaf of bread to a woman who is a prisoner behind bars. A second charitable man is in the act of clothing a sick man who is sitting on a doorstep. Thus, one recipient of charity is hungry, thirsty, and in prison and the other is sick, naked, and a stranger. Justice is enthroned and has the usual attributes of the sword and the scales. She has but one eye, in the middle of her forehead. Cambices sits beside her with the skin of the flayed Sisamnes before him. It may be noted that Thomas Preston's drama, *Cambises King of Persia*, is precisely contemporary with Bateman's book. The design of Verity is curious, complex, and confused. Truth is not personified but is identified with Christ.[7] He is shown on a rainbow above a globe upon which a pope and a cardinal are endeavoring to climb. The globe is upheld by Death, a skeleton, and from it a devil is falling headlong into hellmouth.

For Wisdom we have the contrast between the House built upon a rock, the strong castle of "stedfast belief," and the House built upon the sand, "the Church of Antichrist." No people are shown in or around the strong castle, but from the windows of the other house, which is crumbling and tottering, papist clerics gesticulate frantically. Peace is represented by a dignified man who holds a book, doubtless the Scriptures, and a woman with a lamb in her arms. The woman is "the spouse and congregation of Christ." In sum, Bateman includes the three Christian Virtues, but the Stoic Virtues of Prudence and Fortitude do not appear, and Truth and Peace, which are not Virtues but the consequences of virtuous living, seem to be intrusions from the theme of the Four Daughters of God.

The Seven Virtues, or "seven vertuous women," as he calls them, in Trevelyon's commonplace book (fols. 154^v–157^v) all have traditional attributes and offer no points of interest except the proof of the survival of old conventions. The same comment holds for the Seven Virtues on the engraved title page of John Reynolds' translation (1622) of Denys de Refuges, *A Treatise of the Court or Instructions for Courtiers.*

Unique, so far as I have been able to discover, is Richard Niccols' poem "Vertues Encomium," [8] which is not in praise of abstract, personified Virtue but, as he says in his dedication, presents an image of the Lady Honoria Hay. Was ever a lady so praised? The poet draws analogies between twelve Virtues and twelve different parts of her body. Her forehead is Faith because it is open and candid. Her eyes, which are raised towards heaven, are Hope. Her cheeks, which resemble roses scattered on snow, are Charity. Her lips are Prudence because she is silent when it is prudent to be so. Her teeth are Justice because they are in even rows. Her columnlike neck is Fortitude. Her breasts are Temperance, for they yield in moderation the milk of goodness. Her bosom is Chastity, her lap Modesty, her legs Patience, her feet Humility, and her hands are Concord because she plays upon the lute or viol.

No less than twenty—five Virtues and followers of the virtuous life engage in the Psychomachia in Phineas Fletcher's *The Purple Island.* The Commanders of this "holy train" are the Holy Spirit and Urania. The long descriptions of each in Cantos IX and X are so much clogged with frigid, erudite detail as to present few points of interest, and I shall not enumerate them all. In three instances a Virtue is associated with a biblical type figure: Humility with David, Faith with Joshua, and Love with Jonathan. As in the case of Fletcher's Sins and Vices, each personification has a shield adorned with a device and a motto or "word." Hope, for example, has an anchor on his shield. Temperance's device is a hand from heaven pruning the "superfluous boughs" in an orchard. Upon the shield of Patience (X, 15)

> a Palm-tree still increased,
> Though many weights his rising arms depressed:
> His word was Rising most, by being most oppressed.

3. *The Three Christian Virtues*

The Three Christian Virtues who are Man's strongest supporters and guardians on his pilgrimage are found so frequently in Renaissance literature and fine arts that an exhaustive treatment of them is unnecessary and, in fact, impossible. I shall limit myself to some samplings, emphasizing unusual attributes or activities.[1]

First we may note the quite beautiful idea, which occurs in an English sermon [2] (and perhaps elsewhere), of associating them with the three great Feasts of the Church: Faith with Easter ("I am the Resurrection and the Life"), Hope with Whitsunday ("Lo, I am with you always"), and Charity with Christmas (with its gifts to the poor). There is little to our purpose in Gervase Babington's *Brief conference betwixt mans frailtie and faith* (1583), a long dialogue on poverty, injustice, sorrow, and temptation, for though there are whimperings from Frailty and robust reassurances from Faith the personifications are very frigid. More memorable is Joshua Sylvester's *The Triumph of Faith* (1592), a translation from Du Bartas. In a dream the poet sees Faith borne through the air in a chariot drawn by an eagle. Her body is full of eyes to pierce the heavens and of tongues to praise God. Virtues, saints, and martyrs attend her, and "groveling in the dust" or driven before her are Mahomet, other Moslems, and victims of the cloaked and vizarded beldam misnamed Reason.

The most beautiful evocation of Faith in English poetry is in *The Faerie Queene* (I, 10, 13). Dwelling in the House of Holiness she holds in one hand a golden cup of mingled wine and water, the chalice, which also appears elsewhere as an attribute of Faith.[3] Spenser tells us that in this cup "a Serpent did himselfe enfold." The serpent is a promise of salvation through Faith, this serpent being the one which Moses lifted up in the wilderness. It is also an attribute of Wisdom and of Prudence. Iconographically the serpent in the cup is identical with the snake issuing from a cup in some portrayals of St. John, but there is no relationship in theme, for in the latter case the allusion is to the legend of St. John's miraculous escape when he drank from a poisoned vessel. Spenser says further that in her other hand Faith grasped "a booke that was both signed and sealed with blood," the blood of the martyrs with which the Scriptures are signed and sealed.

The book is an attribute which Faith shares with Truth; often it is labeled "Verbum Dei." In an interlude from the time of Edward VI the personification of Religion was "a Woman with a bible in her armes." [4] Upon the book which Faith holds in a pseudo–Brueghel print there is perched a dove with a halo, suggesting the inspiration of the Scripture by the Holy Spirit.[5] In the same print she wears the Tables of the Law on her head; in a design by a German artist, however, the Tables of the Law are discarded in the background, in conformity with various New Testament texts.[6] The Faith in the Arena Chapel holds a scroll upon which are legible the opening clauses of the Nicene Creed. In a lovely sixteenth–century French manuscript Faith wears a twelve–pronged crown (the twelve articles of the Creed); she carries a closed book (the Old Testament) and an open book (the New Testament); she touches the eyes of a blind boy, Reason.[7] Occasionally she may be depicted holding a miniature church; [8] in one of Ripa's concepts Religion holds "a beautiful temple." Trevelyon's Faith holds a cross. At Hardwick Hall, where a series of "hangings" represents the triumph of the Virtues over historical or mythological types of the Sins, the "contrary" of Faith is Mahomet. (In features and costume Faith is said to resemble Queen Elizabeth.) With this piece of embroidery one may compare (Fig. 94) a Low Countries copperplate (ca. 1580) where Faith, spurning the Koran, is opposed to Mahomet, who is bowed in thought.[9] The antithesis is a usual one. We have just noted that in the *Booke of Christian Prayers* Knowledge of God stands upon Mahomet. The same antithesis occurs on title pages where Christianity and Islam are contrasted.[10]

In Sylvester's poem, as we have seen, Faith is full of eyes and an eagle draws her chariot. In Mathias Holzwart's emblem she holds aloft the keen–eyed eagle.[11] In view of the definition of Faith as "the evidence of things not seen" (Hebrews 11:1) and of Christ's reproof to Doubting Thomas (John 20:29) it is surprising that Faith is not often represented blindfold. She is so depicted in one emblem book, with the motto: "Fides, quod non videt, credit." [12] The two contradictory concepts are in a way reconciled in John Hall's emblem which shows Faith at the bottom of a dark well but able to see the stars.[13]

One of the most pleasing of attributes attached to personifications is still familiar to us in the name "Fido." The idea certainly goes back to the dog which accompanied the young Tobias on his adventurous journey to seek his bride. The dog lies at the feet of the recumbent effigies on the tombs of many faithfully wedded pairs and it is an affirmation of fidelity between man and wife in the famous Arnolfini double portrait by Jan Van Eyck. At the feet of Faith in the so-called "tarots of Mantegna" is a dog. Holzwart's emblem of Fides holds a tiny dog on her bent arm. A Spanish emblem shows a dog lying upon a tomb, and the motto is "Post Fata Manet Fides." [14] It is somewhat odd that this emblematic pet does not occur in English literature of our period. And yet, having said this, one wonders whether Proteus in *The Two Gentlemen of Verona* did not send to Silvia the dog—that "little jewel," only one-tenth the size of Launce's dog Crab—as a "present" because it was an implicit earnest of his fidelity. And was Shakespeare mocking at the emblem when Launce tells us that he took upon himself the blame and punishments for Crab's misdemeanors, thereby showing himeslf more faithful to the cur than the cur was to him? [15] With this perhaps too frivolous question I leave the subject of Faith.

The anchor, the usual attribute of Hope, derives from the great words in Hebrews (6:19): "Which hope we have as an anchor of the soul, both sure and stedfast." In the House of Holiness Hope appears with a silver anchor lying along her arm. Ruskin, commenting upon this passage in *The Faerie Queene* (I, 10, 14) and forgetting his New Testament, criticized the symbol as both inaccurate and vulgar; [16] and the editors of the *Variorum* Spenser, who quote Ruskin, fail to correct him. Hope figures prominently in Thomas Geminus' huge copperplate portrait of Queen Elizabeth.[17] The Queen's likeness is framed by the columns of a temple upon whose pediment are figures of Justice and Hope. Some lines of verse in a cartouche refer to the anchor; actually, however, in the engraving Hope has no anchor but a spray of roses, a spray of thorns, a cross, and two keys. Trevelyon's Hope has an anchor and the dove which Noah let fly from the ark. In one of the fantastic pseudo-Brueghel prints (published by H. Cock in 1558), Hope stands upon an anchor floating, absurdly, on a tempestuous sea in which shipwrecked people are struggling towards the land. Her votaries surround her: a blazing fire is being extinguished and "prisoners of hope" are in the stocks or looking through the bars of a jail. Hopeful of the harvest she carries a sickle and a spade, and hopeful of the honey which is the reward of industry she wears a beehive on her head.[18] Somewhat similar to this is an engraving by Heinrich Vogtherr (1545) where her votaries are a man in the stocks, a sick man in bed, and a monkey attached to a ball and chain. She stands upon a bird cage, emblematic of the hopeful captivity of Man in this world, and on her head is a large ship. A miniature in a French missal (ca. 1500) shows Hope holding a beehive and a spade and wearing an immense ship on her head.[19] In one of Cousin's designs (no. 175) Hope, holding a ship, stands by Fortune. A ship coming to port is an emblem of Hope;[20] we still use the expression "When my ship comes in." As for the spade, in the morality play *Mankind* (ll.526 f.) the protagonist digs hopefully in the earth till his spade encounters a board or plank which Tutyvillus, the fiend, has maliciously concealed beneath the surface of the ground in order to bring Mankind from hope to despair. Hope has the emblem of the spade in the engraving entitled "Le Reveil de Paix Endormie."[21] Hind (E.III.5) reproduces an early Italian engraving of the Seven Virtues. Six have their customary attributes; Hope, however, has flames in her hand. This I cannot explain.

Ripa recommends that Hope be dressed either in yellow, the color of the dawn, or in green, the color of Spring, the hopeful season of the year. "Hope," says Peacham, "by the Ancients was drawne in the forme of a sweete and beautiful child . . . standing upon tiptoes."[22] In one of the Horatian Emblems Spring is such a child and in the same posture. But Spenser's Hope wears a blue garment, the color of the sky towards which she looks. In the Arena Chapel she reaches upward to a crown held by an angel. Elsewhere she stands on a winged ball, which can soar aloft, and gazes skyward;[23] or the phoenix on the burning nest may be at her feet;[24] or she may have as her emblem an armillary sphere because she looks to heaven.[25] To represent Faith we also find an emblem of a man with a wheel upon his back (the burden of ill fortune) who sustains himself upon a staff to which such a sphere is attached.[26] This brings us back to Proteus, who says that "Hope is a lover's staff."[27] At Hardwick Hall Hope stands upon Judas, the type of Despair.

In visual and verbal imagery Charity is not always easily distinguishable from the kindred Virtues of Mercy, Pity, Clemency, and Generosity (Largesse). All these have much in common in their offices, characteristics, and attributes, and there is a good deal of conflation and interpenetration in the iconographical formulae. I have dealt so fully with Mercy as one of the Four Daughters of God, and consequently with her sister Charity, in *The Virtues Reconciled* (pp. 101–110) that a brief condensation of that discussion will suffice here.

The attribute of Charity may be a heart, emblematic of the abundance of Divine Love.[28] She may be shown pouring money from a purse,[29] or holding a box for alms, or even clothed in a garment embroidered with alms boxes.[30] Often her symbolic creature is the pelican which feeds its young from its own wounded breast.[31] Spenser follows the most usual tradition when he describes her as surrounded by a number of infants;[32] Trevelyon's concept is similar; in the fine arts there are innumerable examples in which she has a baby at her breast and children beside her. In the pseudo–Brueghel print the Seven Works of Mercy are around her.

In agreement with Christ's words (Matthew 25:35–36) there are properly Six Works of Mercy, not Seven, and sequences of six are common,[33] but the influence of the mystic number was strong, and the example of the charitable Tobit was at hand, so that a seventh Work, the Burial of the Dead, was generally added. In *The Pastime of Pleasure* (5411–12) it is Lady Mercy who buries the body of Graund Amour. But there were difficulties because this merciful act cannot conceivably be performed for the Divine Judge, the King of Glory. Robert Aylett, in his long account of the Works of Mercy, solves the problem by substituting for Burial the charitable work of Comforting the Sorrowful.[34] That the convention was not stabilized is apparent from a Florentine engraving in which Burial is the Sixth Work and the Visitation of Prisoners the Seventh, the latter is obviously based upon the last words of Christ's discourse: "I was in prison, and ye came unto me."[35]

Spenser, who may well have seen representations of the Works of Mercy in murals in English churches,[36] has given us the most beautiful treatment of the theme in English poetry.[37] He personifies "seven beadsmen" in the House of Holiness, each engaged in an act of charity. The poet exhibits an effective independence of tradition. The first beadsman receives "all who came and went," whereas in Matthew Hospitality to Strangers is the Third Work. The second gives food and drink, thus combining the First and Second Work. The third clothes "bare wretched wights," which in the Gospel is the Fourth Work. The fourth visits prisoners and redeems captives, an expansion of the Sixth Work which is of poignant significance at a time when so many Christians were held captive by the Turks or by the Barbary pirates and when collections of funds were being made in England and throughout Christendom for their ransom.[38] The fifth beadsman attends upon the sick and comforts the dying. The sixth buries the dead. The seventh gives aid to orphans and widows, an office not referred to in Christ's discourse, paraphrasing one of the Spiritual Works of Mercy

The seven "beadsmen" are not differentiated by Spenser save by the act which each performs. The Works could not easily be personified and

are generally represented by appropriate incidents, characteristic deeds
of kindness. A famous example of this treatment of the theme is the series
of reliefs, wonderful in their clarity and realism, by Giovanni della Robbia
on the exterior of the Ospedale del Ceppo in Pistoia. On the De Bry
title page two of the episodes are taken from the Old Testament, "Suscipe
Peregrinos" showing Abraham welcoming the three angels and "Invise
Aegrotos" showing Job, his three friends, and his wife. The Six Works
ornament the borders of twelve pages in *A Booke of Christian Prayers*.[39]
Each is illustrated three times, two episodes on the outer margin and one
at the bottom of the page. These incidents contain some charmingly
realistic details, as when a charitable person tucks two strangers in bed
and when he gives medicine to a sick person from a spoon. In these cuts
each injunction from the Gospel is reinforced with an appropriate text
from the Old or New Testament or the Apocrypha. In this series Mercy
is explicitly equated with Charity by labels reading, for example, "Charity
clotheth the naked," and "Charity visiteth prisoners."

A large engraving by Philip Galle (1577)[40] represents the Works
neither by personification nor by incidents but by objects used in performing them or associated with them (Fig. 95). There is a pleasant,
homely realism in these objects. For the Hungry we have fruit, grain,
bread, a broiler, and a pot of soup; for the Thirsty, a barrel, jar, mug,
glasses, and a bunch of grapes; for the Naked, a cap, a hat, a shirt, shoes,
boots, and a pair of tailor's shears. Captives are represented by the things
they must endure: swords, shields, chains, gyves, a padlock, and so forth.
For the Sick there are vials, a pill box, a warming pan and other utensils.
The Stranger's staff and pilgrim's hat are shown, and a three legged stool
for him to rest on, and a candle to light him to bed. For the Dead there
are spades, a skull, coffins, and a tomb.

In a series of small Flemish engravings (ca. 1600)[41] the number of
the Works is expanded from seven to eight quite without scriptural or
iconographical warrant. Burial of the Dead is omitted, its place being
taken by the Consolation of the Mournful, and there is added the Teaching of the Ignorant. Both examples are transfers from the Spiritual Works
of Mercy to the Corporal. The Seven Spiritual Works do not rest upon
any single passage of Scripture. They are: Correct the Sinner, Instruct
the Ignorant, Counsel the Doubtful, Comfort the Sorrowful, Bear wrongs
patiently, Forgive all men, and Pray for others, even our enemies. It is
obvious that these injunctions cannot be personified; and if illustrated
with typical episodes how is the artist to distinguish among the first four?
The charitable person with his auditor must be in much the same posture

whether he is correcting a sinner, instructing an ignorant person, counseling one who is doubtful, or comforting one who is sorrowful. In a little volume of brief moralizing and pietistic poems by Ralph Crane entitled *The Workes of Mercy both Corporall and Spirituall* (1621) the poet draws a series of parallels between the members of each group. For example, to give drink to the thirsty is equated with the instruction of the ignorant. In an undated reissue of this book the title is changed to *The Pilgrimes New–yeares Gift, or, Fourteene Steps to the Throne of Glory. By the 7. Corporeal and 7. Spirituall Acts of Charitie*. The so happily altered title brings with it a keen awareness that every deed of kindness is a step in the right direction as the Pilgrim pursues his way along the Path of Life.

4. The Four Cardinal or Stoic Virtues

Allied with the Three Christian Virtues are the Four Cardinal or Stoic Virtues: Temperance, Prudence, Justice, and Fortitude. The Four appear in Ulpian Fulwell's strange historico–moral panegyric *The Flower of Fame. Containing the bright Renowne, and most fortunate raigne of King Henry the VIII* (1575). In mingled verse and prose it tells how at the battle of Bosworth Lady Concord came down from heaven to unite the houses of York and Lancaster. At the birth of the future King Henry VIII the Cardinal Virtues descended to attend on the Prince. There are woodcuts of the Four, bearing shields on which are emblazoned the scales, the column, the mirror, and the flagon and cup.[1] The episodic story proceeds, with the death of James V at Flodden,[2] the Field of the Cloth of Gold, and the death of Henry. The recumbent figure on the tomb of the first Earl of Salisbury at Bishop's Hatfield is borne up by kneeling figures of the Four Cardinal Virtues.[3] Nicholas Stone fashioned the four Stoic Virtues on two tombs.[4]

Sir R. G. Knight's "Characterisme of the Foure Cardinall Vertues" contains no allegory but subdivides each of the Four in a manner reminiscent of the "daughter" Vices of the Deadly Sins. Prudence is three–fold: of Heart, Tongue, and Work; Fortitude encompasses Magnificence, Confidence, Patience, and Perseverance; Temperance is shown by Continence, Clemency, and Modesty; and Justice is found in Religion, Piety, Gratitude, Revenge, Obedience, and Truth.[5] In *The Country–mans Commonwealth. Containing divers golden Sentences* by W.S. (n.d.; early 17th century) there are seven little chapters on the Virtues, which sometimes hover on the brink of personification, as when Temperance is called "a sad and sober matron." Their opposites are also discussed: all obvious save that Folly is made the opposite of Prudence. There are no attributes suggested. *Vertue Triumphant, Or a lively description of the Foure Vertues Cardinall* (1603), with a dedication signed, "Sir Walter Leighton," contains a poem in which the Cardinal Virtues are described:

> four Elements, four rivers, of Paradise;
> four Colors; four spices.
> four wheels of Elijah's chariot;
> four living creatures of the Apocalypse:
> Prudence—eagle—watchful
> Temperance—calf—sacrificial
> Fortitude—lion—brave
> Justice—man—"the band of true societie"
> four Gospels.

After these generalities each Cardinal Virtue is analyzed into its parts, opposing Vices given, and instances of illustrious practitioners noted.

John Lydgate declares that Temperance governs her three sisters.[6] John Higgins, who in the history of English poetry is a descendant of Lydgate, depends not upon him but upon Aristotle, Cicero, and other moralists for the idea, which he sets forth with some eloquence, that of the Four Cardinal Virtues only Temperance is independent.[7] Questioning Aristotle's naming of Prudence as "the mother of vertues," he warns that "for wante of Temperaunce, those whiche were counted the wisest that euer were, fel into wonderfull reproche and infamie." Of Justice, "that incomparable vertue," Higgins says: "If she be not constant, which is the gift of fortitude, nor equal in discerning right from wrong, wherin is prudence: nor use proportion in judgement and sentence which pertaineth to temperaunce, she can neuer be called equitie or iustice, but fraude, deceate, iniustice and iniurie." And of Fortitude it is said that "if hee whom we suppose stoute, valiaunt, and of good courage, want Prudence, Iustice, or Temperaunce, he is not counted bolde, manly and constant, but made beastly and desperate." In the series of tragic narratives with which Higgins expanded the original *Mirrour for Magistrates* a basic cause of downfall is a refusal to submit to the guidance of Temperance.

In the Huntington Library there is a unique fragment of an otherwise unknown English book, without title and of uncertain date it is undoubtedly of the early sixteenth century. The two leaves contain two discon-

nected portions of a dialogue in which Disobedience on the one hand and
Temperance and Humility on the other are the interlocutors. The sex
of the personifications is not indicated but the violence of the behavior
of Disobedience suggests that this is a masculine abstraction. The fragment
begins [8] in the middle of a speech by Disobedience who boasts of his
power and freedom. Temperance utters a reproof and is struck by Disobedience who demands to know what Temperance is doing in England.
(There is, however, no specific topical allusion in the piece.) A break
then occurs in the text and when it begins again on the second leaf Humility has joined in upbraiding Disobedience. To none of the three characters is any attribute assigned. Is this a fragment of an unrecorded and
otherwise lost morality play?

Giotto's Temperance in the Arena bears a sword, which is unusual.
The more customary iconography is represented in English literature
by Henry Peacham who gives to this Virtue a bit and bridle and a cup
in which she mixes wine and water.[9] She is the only one of the Stoic
Virtues to be represented ordinarily on tarot cards,[10] and she is the subject
of one of the so—called tarots dubiously attributed to Mantegna.[11] In these
engravings she is shown mingling wine and water. In the Cambio in
Perugia, Perugino's Temperance is engaged in this action, as she is in
Trevelyon's design. Ripa plays a variation on this motif when he recommends that she be depicted holding pincers with which she plunges hot
metal into water, thus tempering it. Ripa also assigns to her a clock,
explaining that Temperance knows the proper times and seasons for all
things and that the clock's escapement is a regulator. Sometimes, as in a
pseudo—Brueghel print [12] and in a French manuscript of ca. 1500,[13]
she may wear the clock on her head. In the Hardwick Hall embroidery
Temperance tramples upon Sardanapalus. In Simon Vostre's *Horae* she
treads on Tarquin and, somewhat strangely, holds a skull and a mirror.

Lady Prudence, says Alexander Barclay, following Aristotle, is "the
mother of all virtue." [14] The iconographical conventions of this Virtue
were firmly established, though one finds variations, permutations, and
some eccentricities. Very frequently she is bifrons because looking before
and after she takes into account the experiences of the past in shaping her
course for the future. Thus she appears in the Arena in Padua, in the
allegory of Obedience in the Lower Church at Assisi, in the Luca della
Robbia terracotta tondo in the Metropolitan Museum, on the tomb of
Francis II of Brittany in Nantes, and in countless other places. Robert
Allott misunderstands the significance of this bifrontality when he explains that painters so set her forth "that on what side soever anyone

beholding her did stand, either before her, or behind her, he had a full sight of her."[15] When one of her faces is young and fair and the other old and ugly, as in an engraving by Hugo Goltzius,[16] we have what seems to be a rather pointless conflation with Fortune Bifrons. Equally pointless is the conflation with Time when, as in a design in Guillaume de la Perriere's *Le Miroir Politique* (Paris, 1567), one face is that of a beautiful young woman and the other that of an elderly bearded man, for the image of contrasting ages and sexes does not properly belong to Prudence. The characteristic of two faces she may share not only with Time or Fortune but with Wisdom.[17] Rarely she may be found with three faces.[18] In the romance of Alector a statue of Prudence "had three heads that she might be better brayned and more sage" and also that she might behold the past, the present, and the future.[19] In Simon Vostre's *Horae* she has a lighted candle and a book.

Lydgate in his "Devyse," without mentioning the bifrontality of Prudence, assigns to her a mirror for hindsight and foresight.[20] More frequently, especially when the mirror reflects her own face, this attribute is a reminder of the injunction: "Nosce teipsum." In the lost Edwardian interlude Wisdom held not one but two mirrors, one in each hand; these must have been intended to suggest regardfulness of the past and future. Perugino's Prudence has a mirror with three surfaces, reflecting the past, the present, and the future. She may also have the serpent of Wisdom, as in various emblem books,[21] and this may be, not very logically, the circular serpent of Eternity,[22] or in the form of a dragon.[23] Trevelyon assigns to her the mirror and serpent. In Francesco de Alegri's *Tractato* and in an engraving by Burgkmair she holds a compass with which to steer her course. Ripa in addition to the mirror and the serpent gives her other attributes, notably a skull because she keeps the end in view and a stag because, as he explains, this prudent animal never travels without due thought for the breadth of its antlers, lest they get entangled in the underbrush. With the skull one may compare the coffin which she wears on her head in a French manuscript [24] and which she holds in a pseudo–Brueghel print.[25]

In the last mentioned print there is a sieve on the head of Prudence, an indication that she sifts the true from the false, the good from the bad, before reaching a decision. The statue of Prudence described in the romance of Alector holds a touchstone, which enables her to make the same distinctions. Achille Bocchi pictures her with scales; in one pan is the rounded stone of Fortune, in the other the cube of Virtue.[26] In the niello print already referred to she holds a cornucopia, symbolizing the fruits of a prudent life. The skull, coffin, sieve, touchstone, scales, and cornucopia are all aberrations from the traditional iconography of Prudence.

In a design by Luca Penni, engraved by "L.D.," the retributive function of Justice is finely emblematized: each of seven chains from her waist is attached to the neck of one of the Deadly Sins.[27] In Linche's translation of Cartari Englishmen could read of Jupiter as the equivalent or representative of Justice or just government, as reported by Plutarch and Pausanias. Statues of Jupiter sometimes had no ears, for Justice is unswayed by "private conference, or glosing insinuations"; sometimes four ears, to hear and understand all sides of every question. When he has three eyes it is because he is ruler of heaven, hell (*sic;* we should expect earth), and sea. Jupiter without hands means that Justice receives no bribes.[28] The usual attributes of Justice, the sword and the scales, are to this day familiar in courthouse sculpture. Spenser's Sir Artegall, the knight of Justice, was entrusted with a "steely brand" "that all other swords excelled" and was taught "to weigh both right and wrong / In equal ballance." [29] The sword and the scales represent two different though not necessarily contradictory concepts of this Virtue: the sword is emblematic of retributive Justice, the scales do indeed weigh right and wrong but also emblematize equitable distribution. These attributes appear in a cut on the title page of Stephen Hawes' *The Example of Vertu*,[30] a poem in which Justice hears the arguments of four plaintiffs, Nature, Fortune, Courage, and Wisdom, and delivers a compromise verdict (Fig. 96). We have seen earlier in this chapter that Justice is the enemy of Tyranny. Barclay declares that Fear, Money, and Favour are three "fell tyrans" who "oft tymes use to brake the balans of justyce." [31] An odd conflation with a New Testament parable is found in the following Jacobean epigram:

> Some doe paint Justice sitting in her state,
> With Scales and Ballance to give each his waight:
> Surely her Scales are even, so thinke I,
> And that the beame hangs not in Justice eye.[32]

The beam that must be pulled out before the man in the parable can "see clearly" is equated with the beam of the scales!

But must Justice "see clearly"? Here we meet with contradictory traditions as to whether she should have all–seeing eyes or be blind or blindfold. Her eyes are wide open in the statue described in the romance of Alector.[33] Thomas Peyton in *The Glasse of Time* emphasizes her "blazing eyes." But later he tells us that she wore a scarf before her eyes. When Ripa gives to Justice the emblem of the ostrich it is not because it hides its head in the sand but because its feathers are all of equal length (the impartiality of Justice) and because it ruminates its food as Justice should the testimony put before her. The illustrator of *The Ship of Fools* supplements the assertion in the text that only a fool would attempt to blind Justice.[34] We have already noted that in Bateman's concept Justice is a Cyclops, her one eye seeing only the truth. Similarly in one of Ripa's concepts she wears a necklace with a pendant which is a sculptured eye. Elsewhere a Prince, who is the embodiment of Justice, holds a scepter full of eyes, and his hand, extended to grasp another hand in friendship, has eyes in each finger tip and in the palm.[35] The famous "Rainbow" portrait of Queen Elizabeth shows her wearing a robe embroidered with eyes and ears to symbolize the vigilance of royal Justice.[36] In Thomas Geminus' portrait of Queen Elizabeth, where she is flanked by two Virtues, Justice has a crane perched upon the point of her sword. Similarly in an engraving dubiously attributed to Mantegna Justice has at her feet the crane of Vigilance, grasping its stone. Again, Wither places a crane on the top of a crozier as a symbol of the watchfulness of the bishop, the overseer of the Church.[37] No explanation of this familiar emblem is really needed, but because the notion is so pleasant it may be recalled that the crane was thought to stand guard upon one leg while holding in its other foot a stone because in this way if it should sleep it would be roused by the stone's falling. The cock also, but for a different reason, may symbolize Vigilance.[38]

Justice, however, may be depicted as blind or with a scarf before her eyes. Lydgate describes her as blind that she may see no favorites, and armless that she may receive no bribes. Nicholas Ling explains that "Justice is painted blinde, with a vaile before her face, not because she is blinde, but thereby to signifie that Justice, though she do behold that which is right and honest, yet will shee respect no person." [39] She is blindfold on the title page of *The Example of Vertu*; on the title page of the English edition of the Latin text of Vesalius; [40] she wore "a silver veil before her eyes" on one of the triumphal arches in London in 1604; [41] she is blindfold (Fig. 97) when she brings the Soul to trial before Divine Love.[42] Holding the sword and scales she is blindfold in Trevelyon's design.

The antithesis of armless Justice appears in one of Bateman's designs, where an unjust judge has four hands; with two he delivers scrolls of judgment to two petitioners while with the other two he receives their bribes. But in *The Faerie Queene* (V, 9, 24) it is vigorously asserted that "just judgments" may not be broken "for any bribes or threats." Even so, in an engraving (Fig. 98) by Johannes Galle,[43] blindfold Justice upon her throne is offered by her petitioners a scepter and crown, bags of coin, and costly dishes, and one man is threatening her with a sword while another man lights the fuse of a cannon aimed at her. Displayed on banners on either side of Justice are the words: "Nec Spe" and "Nec Metu."

Fancy extended itself very far in the portrayals of Justice. Richard Brathwaite describes "certaine images of Judges . . . having neither hands nor eyes."[44] The notion is commonplace but the application to judges, not. Justice herself shows the fluctuation between personification and the typical. Robert Aylett, telling the story of the chaste Susanna, evinces a feeble effort to make her stand for justice.[45] This is absurd: Properly she is the protégée of Justice, whom Daniel should represent. The Egyptian hieroglyphic of a headless figure was interpreted by Pier Valerian as Justice,[46] as was the armless Hermes of ancient Roman sculpture.[47] Because she is as remorseless to the guilty as is Death to every man, Ripa recommends that she be portrayed as a skeleton holding a pair of scales.[48] In a London pageant she held a touchstone to distinguish between the innocent and the guilty.[49] This antithesis is less clearly visualized in the "Hatfield Seasons," where Justice stands between a tree in leaf and a withered tree. To typify Justice Father David has a man sawing the withered branches from a tree.[50] Once we have her engaged in giving suck to two infants who are said to symbolize Justice in war and peace.[51] This conflation with the image of Charity is an iconographical monstrosity! A less questionable conflation is the device of an Antwerp printer in which a woman is at once Justice, Pity, and Faith: She holds the scales; she gives alms to a beggar; she stands upon an orb (the World) and a devil.[52] After passing in review all these varied appearances and attributes of Justice one is ready to agree with Robert Aylett, who writes:

> Some Painters Justice without eyes describe,
> That she might know no Man in doing right;
> Some without hands, that she may take no Bribe;
> Some without pockets, that may gifts invite . . .
> But vaine it is to thinke by likelinesse
> Of earthly things, to type out things Divine.[53]

The attributes of Fortitude are simple, and there is no need to linger over this Virtue because I have not found her personified in English literature of our period, except in Lydgate's "Devyse" where she has a sword. Often she stands by a column or may encircle it with her arm, and this column may be broken, signifying Courage even in disaster. She may hold a mace or club.[54] Once at least she holds the model of a strong fortress or castle in her arms.[55] Fully armed, she may wear, like Hercules, a headdress fashioned from a lion's skin.[56] A lion may be at her feet, as in the engraving attributed to Mantegna and in the emblem by Mathias Holzwart. Trevelyon's Fortitude is associated with a lion and a column. Giotto's Fortitude in the Arena Chapel has a shield embossed with a lion. But the pseudo-Brueghel print shows her standing upon a dragon and she has an anvil on her head.

"Spiritus Fortitudinis" is one of the Seven Gifts of the Holy Ghost and appears in a series of copperplates depicting that cycle by Adrian Collaert after designs by Martin de Vos.[57] A lion's skin is on her shoulders and she carries a mace. No distinction is drawn between this representation of her as one of the Gifts and representations of her as one of the Seven Virtues. Man is protected not only by the Virtues but by his Guardian Angel. Curiously, to no one of the Nine Orders of Angels is this function specifically assigned. It is true that the Order of Powers are often depicted as chaining or subduing devils and the Archangels are sometimes the protectors of cities, but the Order of Virtues are associated with miracles and the divine mysteries, and the Order of Angels generally appear as pilgrims or messengers.[58] A fine example (Fig. 99) of the theme of the angelic Guardian is an anonymous Flemish engraving (ca. 1600). Here Humanity is championed by the Guardian Angel who fights against fiends and has shattered to pieces a globe of vanities: playing cards, a stylish hat, and a jug.[59] The engraving has the text: "Angelis suis Deus mandavit de te, ut custodiant te in omnibus viis tuis." In one of Father David's designs a Guardian Angel leads the Soul along the straight and narrow way between the powers of Evil.[60]

5. The Pauline Armor

Against spiritual enemies the Pilgrim is protected not only by the Virtues and by his Guardian Angel but, if he be indeed an Eques Christianus or a Miles Christianus, by the Pauline armor of the magnificent exhortation in Ephesians 6:13–18. The "Armatura mystica christiana" is a subject inherited by the English Renaissance from earlier centuries and it has its place not only in many sermons and homilies but in imaginative literature, from the heights of *The Faerie Queene* to the depths of wellmeaning but talentless poetasters. Medieval preachers had exercised their ingenuity by giving names to additional pieces of armor (such as the spurs) not mentioned by St. Paul.[1] In John Lydgate's "Henry VI's Triumphal Entry" seven virgins gave to the king a crown of glory, a "septre of clennesse and pytee," a "swerde of myht and victorie," a "shelde off ffeyth," a "helme of helthe," and a "girdyll of love and parfyte pees." [2] Elsewhere the same poet departs widely from St. Paul, for it is the goddess Pallas who wears the "helm of temperance," the "lance of righteousness," and the "shield of patience." [3] In one of the miracle plays the Holy Ghost gives to Adam "the brest plate of righteousness," "the shylde of fayth," "the hellmett of salvacion," and "the sworde of the Spright," and there is a typically anachronistic reference to St. Paul's words.[4] Preparing a youth for his fight with the three–headed dragon in Hawes' *Example of Vertu* Sapience puts upon him "the armour for the soul / that in his epystle wrote saynt Poule." Hawes has a briefer allusion to the theme in *The Pastime of Pleasure* (3376–80).

Erasmus' small work of pious morality, the *Enchiridion* (1503) did not attain wide popularity till after the appearance of the second edition (1518).[5] It was then translated into various languages and in these vernacular versions went through many editions. Between 1533 and 1576 there were no less than nine editions of William Tyndale's English version: *A booke called in latyn Enchiridion militis christiani and in englysshe the manuell of the christen Knytht*. Its influence must have been wide; already, however, shortly before the appearance of Tyndale's first edition, Thomas Paynell, translating a French book, described the Knight's armor in *The assaute and conquest of heven* (1529). Here there are wide departures from St. Paul's allegory. The Knight wears the shirt of Chastity, the coat of mail of Justice, the "legge harneis," boots of iron, of Patience and Constancie, the "helmet of helth," and he carries the sword of the Spirit. His umbraces, gauntlets, gorget, shield, dagger, and spear are all allegorized in like fashion.[6] Later (chapter 12) we learn that the horse on which he rides is Man's body, the spurs with which he pricks his steed are the Hope of Glory and the Fear of Damnation, and that the saddle is Knowledge of Man's Fragility. The four horseshoes are "the four pryncipall affections . . . love, hevynesse, hope and drede." And so on through all the harness. This treatise ends before the assault begins, but the warrior is armed and ready.

The simplicity with which the theme is introduced into George Wapull's morality play *The Tyde tarryeth no Man* (1576 but probably written much earlier) may be due to the exigencies of stage performance. The character Christianity carries a sword called God's Word and a shield called Faith, but because of the evils of the time the sword has on its reverse side the name Policy and the shield on its reverse the name Riches. Faithful–few turns the proper names outward and promises to endow Christianity "with such weapons as Saynt Paule hath ordayned." [7] We have already noted that in one of Bateman's concepts of Faith an armed man has a sword, spear, and helmet with allegorical names, and that the "Christian soldier harnassed" intrudes himself rather effectively into the procession of the Virtues in *A Booke of Christian Prayers*. Notwithstanding its title, there is little to our purpose in Thomas Becon's *The Christen Knighte*, a dialogue in which Satan attempts unsuccessfully to bring the Knight to desperation.[8]

In the course of my discussion of the Infernal Trinity (Chapter 4) we met with the Christian, whether armed or unarmed, avoiding, defying, or triumphing over various powers of evil. Not all of these make any specific reference to the passage in Ephesians. A detailed, not to say pedantic, treatment of St. Paul's word may have been suggested to English engravers by the so–called "Christian Knight Map" of the world engraved by Jodocus Hondius (ca. 1596–7).[9] Hondius, a Fleming, had lived in England (ca. 1584–95) and had illustrated some English books. The map is dedicated to three English friends, one of them Edward Wright, the cartographer and reformer of the laws of navigation. The Knight stands in the empty space where the South Atlantic or the Antarctic ocean' should be, near "Terra del Fogo." Is there any symbolic intent in this location? Upon the pieces of his armor or close to them are words from Ephesians and other Pauline texts. His enemies are Caro, Peccatum, Mundus, Mors, and Diabolus.

On a much lower level of technical expertness the same theme was essayed by two English engravers. One of them was Thomas Cecill who made the "Christianus Militans" illustration for Joseph Fletcher's poem, *The History of the Perfect–Cursed–Blessed Man* (1628). Six pieces of the Christian's armor are inscribed with parts of the text in Ephesians. Obviously deriving from this design but even cruder in technique is a vignette on the title page (Fig. 100) of the *Workes* of Bishop William Cowper (second edition, 1629).[10] Here too the parts of the armor are labeled with St. Paul's words. A poem entitled "The Illustration of the Frontispiece" interprets each detail. "A Christian Knight" appears in the Trevelyon commonplace book (fol. 161ᵛ). He carries "The Sheild of faith" and wears "The helmet of helth," "The girdeill of trueth," "The brest plate of Justice," and "The clothinge of preparation to peace." At his feet are written the names of the Seven Deadly Sins.

Five examples, chosen from among others of even less note, may be given of the employment of the theme by writers. In *The Whole-Armor of God* (1616) William Gouge offers an elaborate analysis of the exhortation in Ephesians, most of it quite unnecessary, for where is to be found a more lucid allegory? Despite its promising title, *The Christian Knight Compiled by Sir William Wiseman, Knight* (1619) is not directly concerned with our theme; it is a piece of hortatory prose directed against dueling and avarice.[11] The Pauline armor is described in painstaking, plodding detail in William Hall's poem, *Mortalities Meditation* (1624).[12] Robert Aylett, without mentioning other pieces of armor, says that the "leg-armor" of St. Paul are "the brazen Bootes of Patience." [13] Genuinely fervent are some lines in a poem by Thomas Collins:

> I'le now put on the Armour of my God,
> The helmet of salvation I'le take:
> My feet shall be with preparation shod,
> Of righteousnes I will my brest-plate make:
> Sword of the spirit which mak'st sin to shake,
> Ile gird thee on, and most couragiously,
> Use thee against my spirituall enemie,
> Thou many-headed-monsterous Hydra sin.[14]

CHAPTER 6.   THE PATH OF LIFE

1. *"One man in his time plays many parts"*—As You Like It

As the Pilgrim, strengthened by desire and hope, burdened with anxiety and fear, beset by temptations and guarded by spiritual powers, pursues his way along the Path of Life, seeking ever "a better country," he finds that with advancing years the character of the landscape through which he moves undergoes a succession of changes: "One man in his time plays many parts." (Shakespeare was *nel mezzo del cammin* when he composed the familiar account of one such "strange eventful history." [1])

The lines are spoken by Jaques; and they are spoken in character. It is always a mistake to seek for the poet's opinions in the words of his dramatis personae; and it is particularly erroneous when they are put into the mouth of a jaded libertine, an affected malcontent, a comic character. The theatrical tradition is quite mistaken which permits an actor to deliver these sententious commonplaces as though they were a profound epitome of human experience. In his description of the Seven Ages of Human Life Jaques seems to be elaborating upon his own report (two scenes earlier) of Touchstone's words: "And thus from hour to hour we ripe, and ripe, / And then from hour to hour we rot, and rot." "And thereby," Jaques adds cryptically, "hangs a tale." Is not that "tale" the "history" subsequently narrated? For all his experience of foreign lands, for all his sophistication, Jaques' knowledge of life was limited. The seven parts played by man upon the great stage of the world are, according to him, the mewling and puking infant, the whining schoolboy, the sighing lover, the boastful soldier, the prosing justice, the shrinking pantaloon, and the decrepit old man. There are no toys in infancy; no playmates in boyhood; no hunting or hawking or jousting in youth; no commerce or industry in middle life; no "honour, love, obedience, troops of friends" such as should attend upon old age. Nowhere (as John Palmer remarked [2]) is there any indication that "anyone has truly striven, aspired, suffered, meditated, or seen beyond the end of his nose." Plainly, this is Jaques speaking; this is not Shakespeare's reading of life.

Here as everywhere in the plays the commentators have busied themselves with *quellenstudien*.[3] The quest is futile; no convincingly precise source has ever been found. Shakespeare was doubtless acquainted with various renderings of the great theme of the Ages of Human Life —in poetry, in prose, and in the arts of design. And once that assumption is made, surely we may attribute to his own powers of observation the knowledge that babies mewl and puke, that boys go unwillingly to school, that lovers are wont to express their passion in verse, that soldiers —some soldiers—swear, that justices—some justices—are pompous and rotund, that elderly folk like their slippered ease, and that the very aged lose their memory and their teeth. He did not need to consult solemn and bulky treatises to assemble such information.

But he must have had some knowledge of contemporary discussions of the physiological, psychological, astrological, and metaphysical aspects of the problem of the division of man's life span. Did he place any reliance upon his audience sharing in that knowledge? The "spontaneity of response" which he sought always to evoke came, in the case of Jaques' speech as in so many other incidents in the plays, not only from the pleasure of surprise but from the pleasure of recognition. There were probably among the spectators at the Globe some, the very ignorant and the very young, who had never heard of the problem of the Ages; their ears were tickled by mere novelty. But the dramatist did not aim to please only the groundlings. There were the wiser sort who would catch overtones of meaning and association and would recognize, as they listened to Jaques, that here was something that had oft been thought but ne'er so well expressed. Some of them may have seen the Ages depicted in stained glass windows or in murals or in engravings. Others may have been reminded of morality plays patterned upon the scheme of the Ages. Others may have recalled the learned writers who discussed the problem of the proper number of the Ages, their division into periods of years, the number of years included in each period, the characteristic indications of demarcation between each and the next following, the physiological and psychological mutations, the control exercised by the four seasons and the seven planets, and so forth.

Learned inquirers and theorists appealed to the authority of antiquity.[4] Aristotle had made three divisions; Pythagoras, Horace, and Ovid, four; Marcus Varro, five; Solon, Saint Augustine, Avicenna, Isidore of Seville, and the Venerable Bede, six; Hippocrates, the famous seven. Philo Judaeus, Galen, Proclus, and other writers—philosophers, astronomers, physicians, poets—were cited in support of this, that, or the other opinion. Medieval England had not neglected the problem.[5] Analogies had been found in the apocalyptic divisions of world history;[6] in the parable of the workers in the vineyard;[7] in the steps or stages in the education of the young.

Time has enriched the associations attaching to Jaques' speech. We have an advantage over the original audiences at the Globe Theatre, the accumulated advantage of three and a half centuries. To us the lines suggest associations (not, for the moment, to mention parallels in literature) stretching from the carved portals of the Baptistry in Parma, through the many and various renderings of the theme during the Renaissance (with which we shall be chiefly concerned), to Currier and Ives and the Waldorf Hotel in New York[8] and that most beautiful of twentieth-century buildings, the Town Hall in Stockholm. The Swedish artist of our own day was well versed in traditional iconography. In the great room called the "Golden Hall" (which rivals Monreale in glistening, subdued splendor) are the Ages of Human Life, one of many symbolic, stylized representations of ideas: An infant is shown in its cradle; children come playing, one of them chasing a butterfly; a youth rides on horseback while another youth makes love to a girl; an older man is shown bowed down with the weight of responsibility symbolized by a rock upon his shoulders, and leading a child by the hand; an aged man and woman hobble on crutches through the last years of life; and finally a hearse is drawn by black horses. We shall meet with sequences of earlier date in which the Ages, whatever their number, are followed by this inevitable *coda*.

Many artists have illustrated Jaques' speech in sequences of seven separate designs. The Victorian painter William Mulready, greatly and absurdly daring, grouped the Seven Ages into one company, showing a chaotic variety of incidents, from suckling an infant to ministering to the dying, all going on in the same place at the same time! [9] Tourists in Victorian days could purchase at Stratford models of Shakespeare's birthplace in which little figures representing the Ages were assembled on the lawn in front of the house. Our concern, however, is not with these and other parasitic growths upon Shakespeare's fame but with the great tradition of which Jaques' speech forms a part.

2. The Bridge, the Stairway, and the Circle as Symbols of the Path

In the simplest visualizations of the theme the Ages may be designated merely by numerals. Thus, in a German woodcut (ca. 1488) [1] Life is represented as a bridge. A Pilgrim is crossing it; a fiend clutches at him from behind; and Death awaits him at the farther end. The bridge rises to the middle and then declines again, according to the pattern of Life, and its planks are numbered by half decades from five to ninety–five. Here the motif of the Ages is obviously conflated with that of the Pilgrimage of Human Life, much as it appears in some of the morality plays. In *The Castle of Perseverance* [2] the protagonist, Humanum Genus, first enters as an infant, announcing that "this night I was of my mother born." Later on, his age is twice specified: at one point he is forty years old and at another sixty. In *Mundus et Infans*, another morality, the protagonist does not possess throughout life a single generic name, such as Humanum Genus or Mankind or Everyman, but has different names during different stages of his pilgrimage: His mother named him Daliance, when he was six years old the World named him Wanton, at fourteen his name was changed to Love–Lust–Liking, and at twenty–one to Manhood. Later, Folly imposed upon him the name of Shame, and in old age Conscience bestowed upon him the name Repentance. In this text, then, the two themes—the Ages and the Pilgrimage—are completely fused.

The rising and falling pattern made by the humped bridge in the German woodcut and suggested in the morality plays is frequently observable in designs of the ages. In the upper semicircle of a round window in the cathedral of Amiens there are seventeen figures (the number is without significance), undifferentiated except that those on the upward slope are young and beardless and those on the downward old and bearded. The scheme is related to that in the magnificent rose windows in the cathedral of Trent and in the church of San Zeno in Verona.[3] Each depicts a Wheel of Fortune round whose rim we see the mounting and descending figures of ambitious and disappointed men.

More closely resembling the bridge pattern is the rising and declining stairway, an image of the course of Life so obvious and impressive that it remained popular from the sixteenth century till the nineteenth. The earliest example of the stairway seems to be a *Memento Mori* print (dated 1540) by Jorg Breu the Younger.[4] Human life proceeds from babyhood upward to the topmost step (the fifth) and then downward to extreme old age. The number of years in each Age is not indicated, as it is in some analogous prints, and the abrupt, unmodulated change from infancy to young manhood is in contrast to the usual attention devoted to early years. The infant's hand is raised in aspiration, a symbolic gesture we shall meet with again. At the knees of the oldest man is another infant, perhaps suggestive of "second childishness" but perhaps also representative of the next generation just as when, in *The Castle of Perseverance*, Death comes to Humanum Genus he is accompanied by Garcio.[5] At the top of the stairway, behind the stalwart man in the prime of life, Death threatens, and beneath the central arch the Last Judgment is depicted. In recesses beneath the human figures are nine animals, each symbolic of an Age: a kid, a calf, an ox, a lion, a fox, a wolf, a poodle, a cat, and an ass.[6] Breu balances a cradle before the first Age with a bier that follows the last.

A stairway of the Ages (Fig. 101) designed by Christofero Bertello (or Bertelli) [7] shows a man of eighty with one foot in a coffin, a contrast to the cradle of infancy.[8] Besides the appropriate beasts there are here subsidiary symbols: Cupid appears at the age of twenty, the column of Fortitude at forty, the ominous hourglass at fifty, and so on. The steps rise and fall over a rocky cavern in which Death is whetting a scythe. The same artist did a companion print (Fig. 102) of the Nine Ages of Woman,[9] with birds instead of four-footed beasts as symbols. Obvious to the point of sentimentality is the hen with her chicks at the age of motherhood. A peacock takes the place of the lion as the symbol of the pride of maturity, and the goose the place of the ass in extreme old age.

One of these prints, or some other like them, must have been in the mind of the English epigrammatist Thomas Bancroft when he wrote the lines: [10]

> We climbe the slippery stairs of Infancy,
> Of Childhood, Youth, of middle age, and then
> Decline, grow old, decrepit, bed–rid lye,
> Bending to infant–weaknesse once agen,
> And to our Cophines (as to Cradles) goe,
> That at the staire–foot stand, and stint our woe.

This stairway remained for a long while a popular theme in prints. Sometimes with, but generally without, satiric intent, they are edifying and cautionary. There is a seventeenth–century "ballad" entitled *The Age and Life of Man Perfectly Showing his Beginning of Life and the Progress of his Dayes, from Seaven till Seaventy*.[11] It has a woodcut of the ascending and descending stairs. The poem proceeds through periods of seven years each, but there are actually not ten Ages but eleven, the eleventh is said to last till "the end" after an unspecified number of years.

Of the later seventeenth century is a fine Dutch print of the Ages of Woman,[12] where though only nine Ages are numbered there are actually twelve, for the first is subdivided into three: a babe in swaddling clothes, a tiny tot learning to walk, and a girl child with an embroidery frame under her arm; and at the other end of the sequence, beyond a tottering old woman who, as the number indicates, is the ninth Age, there is an unnumbered figure, a helpless old woman who, lying upon pillows, balances the cradled infant at the beginning of life. The antithesis is further developed in the figures of Love and Death in the foreground, and in two trees which frame the central composition, one in full leaf, the other dry and withered. The stairway reappears in the eighteenth century.[13] In the early nineteenth century it was used in a popular colored lithograph in France,[14] in which a man and a woman are companions on the journey through life. Not long afterwards it is found in two prints by Currier and Ives [15] of the Ages of Man and the Ages of Woman.

But we must return to the Renaissance. A *Memento Mori* print (Fig. 103) by Hans Schäufelein [16] develops the appealing subject, so conspicuously absent from Jaques' speech, of the companionship of two friends through life. This composition is circular, clockwise from the bottom. At the start of their pilgrimage they have not been drawn closely together but are indistinguishable in a group of five children of various stages of growth. Presently this group is reduced to three, and then to two boys, spinning tops. In the fourth Age one of the friends devotes himself to bodily labor (the *Vita Activa*) and the other to study (the *Vita Contemplativa*), later both become warriors, and then afterwards, older, they enjoy together a quiet game of draughts. In the next scene they are elderly; in the next, bowed with years; and in the last scene of all one watches by the other's deathbed. In the center of this print a company of Deaths is destroying representatives of poor humanity. Here the circular pattern moves counterclockwise, in the direction opposite to that of the cycle of the two friends. The contrast between the serenity of the peripheral episodes and the violence of the central scene is impressive.

One of the miniatures in a famous manuscript [17] of much earlier date than Schäufelein's print is an equally complex and beautifully stylized circle (Fig. 104). In the center is the head of Christ and in the four corners beyond the circumference are the Four Ages: Infantia with his aspiring hand; Iuventus, crowned and sceptered; Senectus, leaning upon a staff; and Decrepitas, reclining. Episodes in ten small tondi which together form the circle subdivide the Four Ages: A nurse sitting before a fire holds an infant; a frivolous youth gazes into a mirror while he combs his hair; he holds a pair of balances, probably to indicate that he has begun to acquire judgment; he enjoys life to the full, riding and hawking; he boasts: "Rex sum; rego seculum; mundus meus totus"; [18] he is dressed as a religious, having withdrawn from the world; the younger generation appears, for Decrepitas leans upon a boy's shoulder, the lad's gesture is perhaps in mockery of his elder; there is a deathbed with a physician in attendance; and finally in two more tondi we see the funeral rites and a tomb.

The circular pattern is approximated in one of the finest of all versions of the Ages, in a compartment of the marvelous Cosmati pavement in the cathedral of Siena (1476).[19] Familiar to Shakespearian scholars because it has been cited as a parallel to Jaques' lines in *As You Like It*, it is, I think more agreeable than they, for it has not been contaminated by the dramatic necessity of suggesting an unpleasant character. The Ages are represented thus: Infantia rides upon a hobbyhorse, Pueritia is a schoolboy, Adolescentia is an older scholar garbed in a long cloak, Juventus has a falcon on his wrist, Virilitas is robed in dignified fashion and carries a book, Senectus, leaning upon a staff, holds a rosary, Decrepitas, leaning upon two staves, looks into his tomb. Six of the seven scenes are set in a garden, the Garden of the World; only Decrepitas stands upon barren ground. The emphasis is upon the years of growth, which take up four of the seven episodes, and in this respect the design is suggestive of those humanistic interludes in which the journey is not from the cradle to the grave but from Ignorance to Education.[20] It is noteworthy also that Love and Commerce and War have no part in this quietly uneventful history. The composition is further remarkable for its simplicity at a time and in a milieu which usually invited the introduction of astrological and other recondite ideas.

The Schäufelein print, the Arundel miniature, and the Siena pavement all show the theme of the Ages isolated, so to speak, from other motifs. But, as we have seen, Wheels of Fortune may exemplify not only her favorites and her victims but also the ascending and descending course of life. The two concepts are fused in an anonymous fifteenth-century German woodcut [21] which bears the label: "Rota vite que fortuna vocatur," although it is not a conventional Fortune's Wheel. Round the rim runs an inscription which may be translated: "Thus adorned, they are born into this mortal life. Life decaying, they glide like water away." The cycle proceeds from Generation to Corruption. Seven Ages are depicted, the number of years in each being given: the swaddled baby and the child learning to walk (till the age of seven); the boy with a toy windmill and a pet dog (till fifteen); the adolescent, hawking (till twenty-five); young manhood, jousting astraddle the wheel at its top (till thirty-five); mature virility in a countinghouse (till fifty); old age, leaning upon a staff (till seventy); and "Decrepitas usque ad mortem," represented by a corpse. In the center of the design a figure manipulating the wheel is suggestive in its starkness and masculinity of a personification of Death rather than of Fortune.

But Lady Fortune appears unmistakably and in regal dignity in a miniature on the single surviving leaf of a lost thirteenth-century English manuscript. (This miniature is known, from the artist's name, as the "De Brailes Wheel of Fortune." [22]) She is seated behind her wheel. Small semitondi within the large circle illustrate the legend of Theophilus, perhaps because it presents a famous example of the reversal of Fortune through the intervention of Our Lady. The rim of the main roundel is cut at intervals of ninety degrees by four small circles. Between each pair of these are three semitondi. The entire series of four plus twelve makes up a pageant of sixteen Ages of Human Life. But the four principal members of the series are distinguished from the rest in that they represent the rise and fall of a king or magistrate—the most notorious subject of Fortune's incalculable activities. The sequence runs clockwise from the lowest semitondo on the left to the fourth complete circlet at the very bottom of the design: an infant; a little child learning to walk; a boy with bow and arrow; a youth mounting towards kingship; then three further stages of growth; a king enthroned at the top of the picture; then an elderly man gazing downwards; then in a crouching posture; then falling headlong; and thereafter the artist shows only various tumbling postures till the last complete tondo is reached, which encircles a corpse. A wall painting in Rochester cathedral (which I have not seen) is said to be related to this picture.

The fusion of Fortune and the Ages may be managed more simply. Just as in many paintings of the Adoration of the Magi the Three Kings represent not only the three traditional races of mankind but also the Three Ages,[23] so the four kings who are Fortune's clients may also represent the Four Ages of Human Life. This conflation is found in some manuscript miniatures of the *Roman de la Rose*,[24] and a good example is a painting by Hans Schäufelein [25] which has been in England since Tudor times. In the latter the contrasting ages of the kings upon the wheel are conspicuous, and in particular we note the gesture of the youth who is about to mount, an arm raised in aspiration.

Death, personified as a skeleton, appears in some sequences of the Ages, as we have already observed, and in murals of Les Trois Vifs et les Trois Morts, the three Living occasionally represent the Three Ages, all confronting their destiny.[26] There is an anonymous English poem of the early sixteenth century in which Death threatens each of the Four Ages.[27] To the Twentieth Year he says: "Deth biddith beware, this day a man, to—morow non!" To the Fortieth Year his message is: "Man, beware! thou shalt not tary long." He warns the Sixtieth Year that he stands at the brink of the pit and bids him drink of his cup. And in "the last age of mankynd . . . called Decrepitus," Death strikes him with his sword, shouting: "Man! it shal be thus." Upon the title page of J. J. Boissard's *Theatrum Vitae Humanae* (1596), engraved by Theodore de Bry (Fig. 105), are four scenes, showing Death striking an infant in its cradle, tapping a bridegroom upon his shoulder, creeping up upon a middle—aged merchant engaged in enterprise, and digging a grave for an old man. From this fine design we may descend to the lowest level of English folk art to note a broadside of the time of the Great Plague.[28]

In a woodcut at the top (Fig. 106) Death, brandishing his dart against the Four Ages, exclaims: "I kill you all!"

3. The Three Ages of Man

Just as Man on his pilgrimage must accept the favors or bear the blows of kindly or adverse Fortune and must face the inevitability of Death, so is he subject to the rule and guidance of Time. Into a piece of civic pageantry Anthony Munday [1] introduces Time as the "coachman to the Life of Man," driving a chariot which "runneth on seven wheels, describing the Seven Ages."

With the passage of Time in mind, Shakespeare, in his seventh sonnet, likens youth, manhood, and old age to the sun at morning, at noonday, and at evening. The authority of Aristotle, reinforced by universal human experience, made three a favorite number of the Ages, manhood being the mean between the extremes of childhood and old age. So in the medieval examples of the Ship of Life the forecastle is Youth, the "top–castle" is Maturity, and the hindcastle is Old Age. Death's black flag is on the mast, but the pilot of the Ship is Christ or Holy Church.[2] The Earl of Surrey wrote a poem [3] in which a small boy wishes to be a tall man so that he may escape the rod; the man, feeling in his bones the pains of toil, wishes to be a rich old man; and the old man, seeing his end draw nigh, wishes to be a boy again. The simplicity and logicality of the scheme of Three Ages made it widely popular, as is attested by many paintings. Titian's version in the Palazzo Doria in Rome is perhaps the best known; it represents two children asleep, a pair of lovers nearby, and in the background an old man meditating upon bones and skulls. Sassoferrato's painting in the Borghese Gallery is close to Titian's except that Cupid stands by the sleeping children. A similar sequence by Dosso Dossi is in the Metropolitan Museum of Art. In Vandyke's painting in the Museo Civico in Vicenza there are a sleeping child, a warrior and a young woman, and an old man. The warrior points to roses in the woman's hand; the old man points to an unknown bourne beyond the picture's limits. In a fresco by Giulio Romano in the Palazzo del Tè near Mantua are depicted the successive stages of Birth, the Age of Love, and the Decline of Life. With truly terrifying force and candor Hans Baldung delineated the Three Ages in a painting now in the Prado: upon the ground a child is asleep; near by stands a buxom, young, naked woman; and beside her is a hideous, withered crone. Behind this group is Death with his scythe and an hourglass.[4] Ripa directs that the Three Ages shall be represented in art as a woman whose dress is of three colors: changeable, because youth is unstable; golden, to indicate the perfection of strength and reason in maturity; and for old age the color of faded leaves about to fall. This is very academic and theoretical; I have not noted that any artist attempted to follow Ripa's directions. In the *Minerva Britanna* (no. 80) Peacham emblematizes the Three Ages by a plant with three branches, bearing respectively a bud, a flower in full bloom, and a withered flower.

In none of these paintings does Time appear, but he is present in a tiny design, touching in its naïveté, at the top of a title page border [5] often used in English books immediately contemporary with Shakespeare, where he leads a stalwart man while a child goes before him and an old man follows after (Fig. 107).

4. *The Four Ages of Man*

Time may be found also conducting the Four Ages of Human Life, as he does in a lovely engraving in the "Horatian Emblems" (p. 207), where Time—not the familiar, venerable, paternal figure with his scythe, but a sprite with butterfly wings to signify his ephemerality—leads on the Seasons. The four figures wear or carry emblems that are seasonal but they are also clearly representative of the four periods of life: the child with hopefully outstretched arms; the debonair youth; the sturdy bearded man; and the muffled elder with his staff. At a much earlier date Barthelemy Aneau [1] emblematized the equation of the Seasons and the Ages in a circle divided into four quarters, each containing a tiny seasonal scene: Thomas Tusser [2] has a quatrain entitled "A Description of Time and the Seasons" which runs:

> The yeere I compare, as I find for a truth,
> The Spring unto childhood, the Sommer to youth,
> The Harvest to manhood, the Winter to age:
> All quickly forgot as a play on the stage.

Tusser found this "truth," needless to say, in the famous passage in the fifteenth book of the *Metamorphoses*. Elizabethans who had "small Latin" had to be content with Arthur Golding's [3] rendering in clumsy "fourteeners":

What? seest thou not how that the yeere as representing playne
The age of man, departes itself in quarters fowre? first bayne

And tender in the spring it is, even like a sucking babe.
Then greene, and voyd of strength, and lush, and foggye, in the blade,
And cheeres the husbandman with hope. Then all things florish gay,
The earth with flowres of sundry hew then seemeth for too play,
And vertue small or none to herbes there dooth as yit belong.
The yeere from springtyde passing foorth too sommer, wereth strong,
Becommeth lyke a lusty youth. For in our lyfe through out
There is no tyme more plentifull, more lusty whote [hot] and stout.
Then followeth Harvest when the heate of youth growes sumwhat cold,
Ripe, meeld, disposed, eane betwixt a youngman and an old,
And sumwhat sprent with grayish heare, Then ugly winter last
Like age steales on with trembling steppes, all bald, or overcast
With shirte [short] thinne heare as whyght as snowe. Our bodies also ay
Doo alter still from tyme too tyme, and never stand at stay.
Wee shall not bee the same wee were too day or yisterday.

Sixty years later George Sandys [4] did somewhat better:

> Doth not the image of our age appeare
> In the successive quarters of the Yeare?
> The Spring–tide, tender; sucking Infancie
> Resembling: then the juycefull blade sprouts high;
> Though tender, weake; yet hope to Plough–man yeelds.
> All things then flourish; flowers the gaudie fields
> With colours paint: no vertue yet in leaves.
> Then following Summer greater strength receives:
> A lusty Youth; no age more strength acquires,
> More fruitfull, or more burning in desires.
> Maturer Autumn, heat of Youth alaid,
> The sober meane twixt youth and age, more staid
> And temperate, in Summers waine repaires:
> His reverent temples sprinkled with gray haires.
> Then comes old Winter, void of all delight,
> With trembling steps: his head or bald or white.
> So change our bodies without rest or stay:
> What wee were yester–day, nor what to day,
> Shall be to morrow.

Closer to Van Veen's picture because the Seasons are clearly personified
is a short passage in the second book of the *Metamorphoses*. This is translated by Thomas Heywood [5] in the course of his discussion of the various
proposed divisions of the Ages:

Now Spring stood there, a fresh wreath girt his braine,
And Sommer, naked, with a crowne of graine:
Autumn, from treading grapes, in torne attyre;
And rugged Winter, new come from the fire.

The parallel between the Seasons and the Ages which (taken from Clément Marot) forms the pattern in the December Eclogue of Spenser's *Shepheardes Calender* (1579) is so well known that only one detail, apparently overlooked by the commentators, must be noted here. Autumn, traditionally and in experience the time of fruitfulness and abundance, is in Spenser's imagination, and in keeping with Colin Clout's "complaint," bare and barren; the fruit has fallen to the ground and rotted before it was ripe: "the eare that budded faire is burnt and blasted." When in the *Cantos of Mutability* (VII, 28–31) Spenser again uses the motive of the Four Seasons, only in the cases of Winter is there an analogy with the Four Ages. The pattern of the Seasons and the Ages is found again in the masquelike play, *The Sun's Darling*, written by Thomas Dekker probably about 1598 and revised by John Ford probably about 1623, though not published till 1656. Here, however, it is somewhat obscured by a crowd of supernumerary mythological characters and personifications. Dekker may have derived suggestions from Spenser. Robert Farley, who in the history of pastoral poetry is an interesting intermediary between Spenser and James Thomson, combines verbal and visual imagery in his *Kalendarium Humanae Vitae* (1638). Here in crude and hearty woodcuts (Figs. 108–111) Robert Vaughan depicts Spring (Fig. 108), the time of budding; Summer (Fig. 109), the seed–time, hopeful of the harvest; Autumn (Fig. 110), the harvest of ripened years; and Winter (Fig. 111), the time of chilly old age. But in his poems Farley divides each season into its three months, and beginning with March the life of man is traced till December, not February. Thus the fourfold scheme is expanded to ten. January ("Mors Janua Vitae") is a meditation upon death, and February is devoted to "Epitaphs on the Dead."

This is very simple, but the pattern of four may be very elaborate, as in the now destroyed frescoes in the cathedral of Anagni south of Rome where in a complexity of quartets the Seasons, the Elements, and the Cardinal Humors were all fused with the Ages. Childhood was related to Spring, to the air, and to the sanguine temperament; Youth to Summer, to fire, and to the choleric temperament; Manhood to Autumn, to earth, and to the melancholy temperament; and Old Age to Winter, to water, and to the phlegmatic temperament.[6] In one publication the seasonal theme is developed in a manner so amusing and fantastic that it must be described. This is *Theatrum Temporaneum Æternitati Caesaris Montii* (Milan, 1636), a set of engravings published by Ottavio Boldoni in honor of Cardinal Monti when he was consecrated Archbishop of Milan. The Seasons here emblematize the four stages in Monti's ecclesiastical advancement—nuncio, patriarch, cardinal, and archbishop. It strikes one as not a little strange and silly to see, for example, Autumn holding his grapes in one hand and a cardinal's hat in the other, or Winter with his brazier of coals, wearing a miter and grasping a crozier. Yet the intention seems to have been entirely serious.[7] English literature and art offer no parallel to this baroque extravaganza.

The Four Ages may be discussed in scholarly fashion or made the subject of imaginative treatment without reference to the Seasons. Dürer represents the so–called Four Apostles in accordance with the criteria of the Four Temperaments and the corresponding Ages.[8] The Four Ages may be the solution of the riddle which the Sphinx propounded to Œdipus.[9] Thomas Tusser,[10] playing a variant upon his lines already quoted, attaches to each Age an appropriate animal:

> The Ape, the Lion, the Foxe, the Asse,
> Thus sets foorth man, as in a glasse.
> Like Apes we be toieng [toying], till twentie and one,
> Then hastie as Lions till fortie be gone:
> Then wilie as Foxes, till three score and three,
> Then after for Asses accompted we bee.

With no emblematic ornament Robert Allott [11] asserts: "They that devide the age by seven most commonly say amisse, but it is rather meete to follow the devision of nature": childhood, youth, manhood, and old age. From translations of Juan Huarte,[12] the Spanish physician and psychologist, came some reflections on the four divisions of man's life more "scientific" in tone than we usually find. Noteworthy is his uncertainty as to the terminal year of childhood which might be, thought Huarte on the basis of his own observations, the age of twelve, fourteen, sixteen, or eighteen. On the same basis he rested his assertion that those who complete their childhood early are shortlived.

The painted cloths which Sir Thomas More designed for his father's house in London have long since vanished, but we have More's own description of them.[13] Apparently of his own invention and, so far as I know, unique, was their curious intertwining of the motif of the Four

Ages with that of the Petrarchan *Trionfi*.[14] Each of these "nyne pageauntes" had accompanying verses composed by More. The scheme which painters, tapestry weavers, and engravers expanded from Petrarch's vision of the Chariot of Cupid, whereby all six personifications (Love, Chastity, Death, Fame, Time, and Eternity) are pictured in triumphal cars, was not followed, but in its stead was the pattern, familiar from imagery of the conflict of the Virtues and the Deadly Sins, of one type or personification lying beneath the feet of another who is the conqueror. This was adhered to in all More's pageants save the first and last. "In the first pageant was painted a boy playing at the "top [whip] & squyrge"; an inscription declared that while Childhood delights in quoits, ball, top, and all kinds of play, all books are hateful to him and he would like to burn them. In the second a youth (called Manhood) appeared on horseback, with hawk and hounds; his delight, ran the verses, is to hunt and hawk and to bestride a lusty steed. The child of the first episode lay under the horse's hooves of the second. Into the third design the Petrarchan theme intruded, for now we have the Lover, and the fact that he may be a type of one of the Ages (as in Jaques' speech) afforded the opportunity to amalgamate the two themes at this point. This was a Triumph of Love. The goodly young man of the second pageant now lay prone and upon him stood Venus and Cupid of the third. To Cupid were assigned verses boasting of his power. Intermediate years were then passed over, and the fourth pageant showed "an old sage father sittyng in a chayre" with Venus and Cupid beneath his feet. Old Age declared that he is "of our short lyfe, the last and best part," marked by devotion to the public weal, and he bade Cupid withdraw his fiery dart and give over his "childish game and ydle bysinesse." With this episode the theme of the Ages terminated, but the pageants continued. Death trampled the "sage father" under his feet and ironically bade him set aside his pride and lend "to me, a fole [fool], some of your wise brayne." Then Lady Fame, "with tongues . . . compassed all rounde," was shown with "cruel Death" beneath her feet and saying that despite Death she causes a noble man to live in the perpetual memory of posterity. But Time "with horyloge in hande" trampled upon "simple Fame," scoffing at her promise of an eternal name to any man; how can man have a name eternal in the world "when I shall in proces distroy the world and all"? And then Lady Eternity, crowned and "sittyng in a chaire under a sumptious clothe of estate," was shown with Time beneath her feet, to whom she says:

Thou mortall Tyme every man can tell,
Art nothing else but the mobilitie,
Of sonne and mone chaungyng in every degree,
When they shall leve theyr course thou shalt be brought,
For all thy pride and bostyng into nought.

These four pageants were in precise accord with the Petrarchan tradition, but there was still a ninth and final episode in which the Poet himself appeared. In Latin verses he drew the lesson that since the eye feeds on pictures and since figures of make-believe mirror the truth, from these scenes we may learn that the world is fragile, that honor quickly fades, and that man's hopes must be fixed on immortality.

The contrast is extreme when we turn from the poetic feeling and admonitory purpose of More's painted cloths to the cynical, satirical worldliness of four French engravings [15] of the late seventeenth century (Figs. 112–115) which are, I think, among the most memorable of all interpretations of our theme. In each print a figure stands in a formal center from which several paths radiate. First (Fig. 112), there is a boy encircled by paths which lead to the Church, the Law, the Sciences, War, the Trades, or a career at sea—"De Tout Côté Peine." The boy's fingers are being rapped, his ear pinched, and his bottom birched, for "la bonne correction fait la bonne education." In the background the old emblem of the spinning top: the more you whip it the faster it goes. Second (Fig. 113), a young man, holding a bottle and a wine glass, spills rivulets of coins upon paths leading to Love, Fashion, the Theatre, Gaming, Equipage, and Crime—"De Tout Côté Dépence." Third (Fig. 114), the middle-aged man, bearing an hourglass upon his head (he is conscious of the passage of Time) and a house upon his shoulder (he is burdened with an establishment), is surrounded by Debts, Lawsuits, Bankruptcy, "la Marmite" (keeping the pot boiling), Marriage, and the Misbehavior of his children—"De Tout Côté Chagrin." One of his feet is winged (the old emblem of the desire to escape), but the other is chained to his wife and children.[16] In the last stage (Fig. 115), fear is shown on every side—"De Tout Côté Peur." The old man has a treasure chest under his arm, for Avarice is the sin of old age. The paths now lead to Fear of Heat, of Cold, of Robbery, of Poverty, of Sickness, and of Death. In all four engravings there are placed upon the paths vividly appropriate symbols.

A like lugubriousness and something of the cynicism of these engravings are concisely conveyed in one of the emblems in Peacham's *Minerva Britanna* (no. 119), called "Humanae Miseriae." A young woman holding a bunch of birch twigs in one hand and a bottle in the other stands beside a globe. The Four Ages of human misery are the rod in childhood, a wife in youth, the worldly cares of middle age, and the diseases (represented by the medicinal flagon) of old age.

5. *The Five Ages of Man*

The analogy of the Three Ages to Morning, Noon, and Evening was easily drawn, as was the analogy of the Four to the Seasons. When we come to the sequence of Five Ages the metaphor of Life as a theater [1] is available. When Shakespeare likened the Ages to the seven acts of a play he started some source hunters on a wild—goose chase after dramas in seven acts. In some fine lines formerly attributed to Sir Walter Raleigh [2] the figure is handled better, for birth is the Prologue to the play and death the Epilogue, and between them come five acts:

> Man's life's a tragedy: his mother's womb,
> From which he enters, is his tiring—room;
> This spacious earth the theatre; and the stage
> That country which he lives in: passions, rage,
> Folly, and vice are actors: the first cry
> The prologue to the ensuing tragedy.
> The former act consisteth of dumb—shows:
> The second, he to more perfection grows;
> I' th' third he is a man, and doth begin
> To nurture vice, and act the deeds of sin:
> I' th' fourth declines; i' th' fifth diseases clog
> And trouble him; then death's his epilogue.

Apart from this poem I have found but one instance, and that a very forlorn one, of the occurrence of the Five Ages in English imaginative literature. This is a tedious, jog trot, moralizing poem by "V.L." entitled: *The pleasaunt playne and pythye Pathewaye leadynge to a vertues* [*sic*] *and honest lyfe, no lesse profytable then delectable* (1550?).[3] On "the eleventh day of the floryshynge Moneth of May" the poet, a young man, chanced to encounter a grave elder who proceeded to give him valuable and voluble counsel to the effect that he should fear God, follow Virtue, and shun Gluttony, Pride, hot Rage, and above all lewd Lusts. This discourse modulates into one on the miseries of human life into which is introduced [4] characterizations of the Five Ages: Infancy comes weeping into the world; Childhood experiences grief, travail, fear, and pain; "Ignorant frail Youth" leaves Reason and is ruled by Vice, refusing to heed good warnings; "Then cometh man's state, grave and sage," but "he laboureth with paine . . . his house to sustaine," and his care is to feed and clothe his wife and family, thus "spending his best age with miserye"; at length "wearye rude age" comes, "his senses shrinke away," without the aid of a staff his senses fail him, and this "last age" does not leave him till the grave. There follows an emphatic warning against unwise love, which is the greatest of all perils that assail man, and this leads to Part II of the poem in which the old gentleman tells the young poet of his own unfortunate love affair long ago. (In his Preface "V.L." explains that he introduced this "merry invented matter" in order to "quicken the spirits and to avoid tediousness"!) Part III passes through more general counsel to the final precept: prepare for Death.

It is likely that "V.L." obtained suggestions for his fivefold sequences from a Latin work widely used as a text in English schools. This is the *Zodiacus Vitae* of Pier Angelo Manzoli (Venice, ca. 1531).[5] Barnabe Googe translated this as *The Zodiake of life* (1560). At the beginning of the discussion of the Five Ages [6] Life is likened to a pageant, and Googe adds a marginal gloss: "the world a stage play." Infancy weeps, "disturbing all men night and day with voyce and waylings shrill"; Childhood suffers threats and lashing stripes, not only at school but from his brothers or mother or stepmother; Youth is amorous, brainsick, and brawling; with Man's Estate come gravity and wisdom but also cares and ambition; lastly comes wrinkled Age with its failing senses and fading strength. Other discussions of the Five Ages may be consigned to a footnote [7] with the exception of a sequence suggested by Ripa which seems to be unique. He links Childhood with the Hour, Adolescence with the Day, Young Manhood with the Month, Maturity with the Year, and Old Age with Time in general. This curiously inept notion seems never to have been accepted by any artist.

A particular application of the pattern of five to the experiences not of life as a whole but to the love life of woman is the subject of a French engraving (Fig. 116) of the time of Louis XIV.[8] It is called "Folie du Temps," bears the inscription: "Le Temps détruit tout, hormis la Folie," and displays a large figure of Time. Time is the master of woman's fate in love, as is shown in five small vignettes: Between the ages of fifteen and twenty the young lady scorns her suitors, between twenty and twenty–five she gives ear to her lover's plea, between twenty–five and thirty she accepts him gladly, at thirty years of age she takes whom she can find, and at forty she buys a lover. This variation upon our general theme suggests in its cynicism the mood of Jaques.

6. The Six Ages of Man

Quite without cynicism, indeed somewhat sentimental, is an analogous sixfold cycle of woman's married life as set forth by the Dutch poet Jacob Cats.[1] The sequence is Maidenhood, Courtship, Bridal, Pregnancy, Parenthood, and Widowhood. This last scene shows the husband departing while the wife weeps and children cling to him. A concluding vignette shows effigies of husband and wife upon a tomb. A small dog in the lower corner of the whole engraving symbolizes fidelity.

The domesticity of married life may be pictured in six episodes, but we must look far to find the whole of life so divided. A sixfold sequence is carved on the porta maggiore of San Marco, Venice (Figs. 117–120). It shows carefree childhood, the sports of youth, the perils of manhood, marriage, the authority acquired by experience, and the wisdom of old age and its consolations found in family affection (a child offers a flower to an old man). The authority of Saint Augustine in the *De Civitate Dei* supported the parallel between the Six Ages of Man and the Six Ages of the World. A series of windows in the clerestory of Canterbury Cathedral illustrates the parallel. In *The Treasurie* (1613),[2] a huge Jacobean miscellany of information on all sorts of subjects, Augustine, along with Bede and Isidore of Seville, are cited in support of this parallel although the analogy is here drawn between only three of the stages of world history and the history of human life. A series of six engravings, doubtfully attributed to one of the Van de Passe family, entitled *Ætates Hominum secundum Anni Tempora* (Cologne, 1599) [3] associated all the Six Ages, except the last, with animals. The first plate shows a naked infant with the lamb of innocence; at the top is an inscription: "Miseriae humanae ingressio." In the second two children are playing with a cat; in the background other children are at play, and a monkey sits at a nearby window.[4] In the third a young man holds a dog by the collar; in the background is a hunting scene, and a man and a woman are making music. In the fourth a man with a falcon on his fist demonstrates his strength by tying a lion to a tree. The fifth plate shows an elderly man with a coffer containing coins and jewels; behind him is the wolf of Avarice, which has caught a lamb, and in the background a harbor with much traffic. In the last plate, against the background of a church, Death takes "Aetas Decrepitas" by the arm, showing him an hourglass, and the old man holds a scroll upon which one reads: "Humanae miserie egressio."

The only English poem of our period which contains the Six Ages is Rachel Speght's *Mortalities Memorandum* (1621),[5] a pedestrian but touchingly sincere memorial to her mother. Meditating upon the swift passage of human life, she lists the Ages as Infancie, Childhood, Iuventus, Adolescency, Virilitie, and Old–age. The order she adopts is incorrect, for Iuventus should follow Adolescency. Whether or not she was aware of the fact, under Old–age she conflates Senectus and Senilitas.

7. *The Seven Ages of Man*

A special prestige attaches to the pattern of Seven Ages[1] not only because Shakespeare adopted it but because of the connotations of that number. That which most influenced the emphasis upon seven as the number of the Ages of Human Life is the number of the planets. A convincing argument[2] equates Jaques' Ages with six, not seven, of the planets: Sol must be omitted. The scheme then becomes: Infancy and the Moon, the Schoolboy and Mercury, the Lover and Venus, the Soldier and Mars, the Justice and Jupiter, the lean Pantaloon and Saturn, Second Childishness and the Moon again. The "pouch on side" and the "hose a world too wide" of the Sixth Age are attributes of Saturn and Melancholy, but "childishness" is not. In extreme age Man is again subjected to the unstable planetary influence under which he set forth upon his pilgrimage, so Sol, if included among the planets, distorts the entire pattern. The question remains whether Shakespeare deliberately planned the survey of life in this way or whether it is a mere coincidence.

The influence of the planets upon the Ages was the subject of the now destroyed frescoes by Guariento di Arpo[3] in the church of the Eremitani in Padua. Here the planets were personified, and each was accompanied by a pair of human beings: boy and girl; swain and sweetheart; man and wife; and so on.

Probably the most elaborate version of the Ages in the arts of design was the long since vanished fresco on the exterior wall of a house in Florence, painted in 1554 from designs by Giorgio Vasari. Vasari, who was proud of this work, describes it in detail,[4] because, as he says, "it may not enjoy a long life, being in an exposed position, and it was scarcely finished before it suffered serious damage by a heavy rain and hail." Vasari's text is easily accessible, but the fresco was so remarkable

163

that I summarize his description and add a few comments. Each Age was associated with a planet, one of the Seven Virtues, one of the Seven Liberal Arts,[5] one of the Seven Deadly Sins, and with a miscellaneous assortment of other personified abstractions. 1. Infancy was represented by a woman in childbed, with nurses near. The Moon was figured as the goddess Diana. Charity suckled her infants. Grammar taught children to read. The Human Will was a subsidiary personification. 2. Boyhood showed some children at play and others going to school. Mercury carried his caduceus. Faith baptized a boy. Logic wore a veil and held the serpent of Wisdom. Truth and Falsehood were subsidiary figures. 3. Adolescence was not a single figure but two youths one of whom was climbing a mountain while the other, lingering behind, was lured by Fraud towards a precipice. The Sun appeared under the form of Apollo. Hope was there with her anchor, and Music with her musical instruments. Labor and Sloth were both present. 4. Youth showed a young man with books and instruments of music, while other young men were occupied with games, banquets, or love—making. Venus was embracing Love (Cupid). Temperance held her bridle. Rhetoric was the Art but with no attribute or symbolic posture described. (The confusion between Music and Rhetoric in the third and fourth parts of the design is apparent: Rhetoric as part of the Trivium should come before Music, part of the Quadrivium. I doubt whether the error was perpetrated in the painting; more probably Vasari's memory of it played him false.) Subsidiary personifications were Self-knowledge and Fraud. 5. Manhood had Memory and Will as his companions. Mars was in armor and displayed trophies of war. Prudence held her mirror. The Art was Philosophy. (Properly Philosophy should not have appeared among the Liberal Arts, being a *Summa*, not one *inter pares*. Here she took the place of Arithmetic which, unless Vasari's memory was again at fault, did not appear in the sequence at all.) 6. Innocence and Hilarity were shown. Old Age was garbed as a priest and knelt before an altar, acompanied by Religion and Compassion. Jupiter appeared with his eagle. Fortitude, with a fragmentary column, was in the act of taming a lion. The Art was Astrology. 7. Decrepitude had as his companions Felicity and Immortality. Saturn, in the act of devouring his children, had as an emblem the serpent with its tail in its mouth, a familiar symbol of Eternity. The Art was Geometry. On a lower level of the fresco Leah, representing the Active Life, was grouped with various industrious persons, and Rachel, the Contemplative Life, with philosophers and astrologers. The "conclusion of the whole invention" was Death on a lean horse, accompanied by the other three Horsemen of the Apocalypse. Vasari enters into much painstaking detail regarding the arrangement between windows, doors, and so forth of this truly monumental work.

In comparison with its intricacies Shakespeare's lines seem simple to the point of ingenuousness. But the essentials of the planetary pattern can be presented without complexity, as they are in an eloquent passage from the pen of Sir Walter Raleigh:

> Our Infancie is compared to the Moon, in which we seem only to live and grow, as plants; the second age to Mercury, wherein we are taught and instructed; our third age to Venus, the days of love, desire, and vanity; the fourth to the Sun, the strong, flourishing, and beautiful age of man's life; the fifth to Mars, in which we seek honor and victory, and in which our thoughts travail to ambitious ends; the sixth age is ascribed to Jupiter, in which we begin to take accompt of our times, judge of ourselves, and grow to the perfection of our understanding; the last and seventh to Saturn, wherein our days are sad and overcast, and in which we find by dear and lamentable experience, and by the loss which can never be repaired, that of all our vain passions and affections past, the sorrow only abideth.[6]

This grand sentence may be compared with sundry other sequences of which I note only a few that contain some individuality of treatment. The emblematist Guillaume de la Perriere [7] follows the usual conventions with some pleasant variations of his own. Adolescence, holding a flower, stands with Venus in the Garden of Love. Apollo, holding a sun–faced monstrance, leads a vigorous man who has a falcon on his wrist: "Comme au mylieu des cieux Phoebus regente, / Ieunesse tient le mylieu de la vie—" Iuventus, that is lasting, in the sense deriving from Roman law, till somewhat over forty years of age. In the Fifth Age Mars, carrying a spear, leads a slightly bowed man who is distinctly not a warrior and does not suggest ambition or the desire for honor; at this age, says the emblematist, the mind increases in subtlety but "le corps . . . commence à decliner." This does not seem appropriate to Mars. La Perriere places all his scenes out of doors except the last, where Saturn and a decrepit old man are standing side by side at a fireplace.

The chariot of Time in Anthony Munday's Lord Mayor's Show "runneth on seven wheels, describing the Seven Ages [listed] . . . all of them subjected to the power of the Seven Planets, as on each wheele they beare their characters." [8] Ripa's directions for grouping the Ages and the planets are without originality, for the association of the Ages with the days of the week is merely a variation upon the same idea. However, on the same page he emblematizes "Vita Humana" as a woman standing upon a wheel that has seven spokes and he makes the lyre an emblem of life because it has seven strings.

In England William Vaughan's *Directions for Health* (1600), a popular medical treatise,[9] may have instructed many people who otherwise might not have been informed regarding the combination of the Ages with the planets. The connection between the two supplies one method of "secret writing" in John Willis's *Art of Stenography* (1602).[10] Willis suggests that the sign for each planet may be used to indicate not only an Age of human life but also a day of the week, a part of the body, a temperament, a metal, a precious stone, a color, a plant, an animal (quadruped), and a bird. It is not to be supposed that he intends any metaphysical or esoteric association between all the members of each of these groups; he is merely teaching a system of shorthand. Many of his connections are traditional, some ingenious, a few quite puzzling. Is the owl attached to Infancy because it sleeps so much of the day and keeps people awake at night? The yew is the tree for Mars and for "Firmage" probably because bows are made of it. Is the hart the animal for Old Age because it desires the water brooks as the Soul longs after God? Other such questions might be asked. Henry Cuffe,[11] in his very prolix book, *The Differences of the Ages of Mans Life* (1607), first accepts the Aristotelian "tripartite division" which he relates to Childhood and Spring, Prime and Summer, and Old Age and Winter. These three principal Ages he proceeds to subdivide, allotting to Childhood Infancy (with the Moon), Boyhood (with Mercury), and both Adolescence and Youth together (with Venus); to Prime ("our flourishing and middle age") two subdivisions, Youth (the name is repeated, "for so the penurie of our English toong warranteth me to call it"; attached to the Sun) and "Man–age" (with Mars); to Old Age two subdivisions also, Old Age (again the name is repeated; with Jupiter) and Decrepit Age (with Saturn). These subdivisions add up to a total of eight Ages, but he remarks that seven is arrived at by "compromising our Pubertatem and Adolescentiam under one." After this juggling Cuffe is ready to discuss the Seven Ages and the Planets. A section of David Person's [12] *Varieties* (1635) is entitled "How the seven Planets are said to rule severally over the seven ages in the life of man." This offers no novelty either in arrangement or in the attribution of different emotional characteristics to each Age, but it is noteworthy that Person, ignoring the biblical "three score and ten" or "four score years," carries Decrepit Old Age to no less than ninety–eight years. As in various other treatments of the subject, Person's does not allot an equal number of years to each Age; his "Youthead" is but eight years long, while "Adolecencie" lasts for twenty years and Old Age for twenty–two.

The most memorable and most attractive of English versions of the theme proceeds decade by decade to the "three score and ten." This is Francis Quarles' *Hieroglyphikes of the Life of Man* (1638). Engravings by William Marshall (see Figs. 122–126) supplement and illustrate Quarles' poems, pithy moralizing sentences, and appropriate quotations from the Bible, the Church Fathers, and other writers. Here the planetary scheme of the Ages is combined with the emblem of the candle of life.[13] But before describing these plates I must note the first eight, which play other variations upon the motif of the candle. The first is an unlit candle; the second is lighted by a flame held in the hand of God; the third is blown upon by envious winds; a physician snuffs the fourth (a warning, as Quarles explains, against too much care: trust Nature!); the fifth candle flame is protected from a darting bee by a guardian angel who holds a shield, Time restrains the hand of Death who seeks to extinguish the flame of the sixth candle before its allotted hour; in the next design the flame is dimmed by the light of the sun (Quarles' accompanying words are "Great God, I am thy tapour, Thou my sunne"); the eighth and final plate shows a dark lantern resting upon a coffin.

Quarles had already, a year earlier, devised a title page (Fig. 121) for a posthumous volume by his friend, Arthur Warwick.[14] Here a central memorial column is depicted, a guttering candle smokes, and Death with his sickle cuts a fading rose. Above, however, the candlelight has become a star, and for the earthly rose there is a heavenly crown of fadeless flowers. One of the plates in Robert Farley's [15] *Lychnocausia* (1638) is similar: A skeleton lies in a coffin, a hand reaching into the picture holds a candle burnt to the socket, the flame is in mid–air, mounting to heaven. Farley's book is the closest English analogue to Quarles'. Light is the moral emblem and among the various motifs are: "Better to burn out than to mould away"; "Passing the torch on"; "Lighting others does not make my light less"; "Burning the candle at both ends"; "A candle is no help to a blind man"; Diogenes and his lantern; the woman of the parable searching her house for the lost penny; Leander swimming the Hellespont, guided by Hero's candle; and so forth.[16] Farley does not introduce any sequence of the Ages.

In Quarles' concept of the Seven Ages of Human Life the candle diminishes with each Age, the point to which it has declined being indicated by a numeral upon it. The Moon governs weak and unstable Infancy (Fig. 122); the emblems are an embryo, a cradle, a baby's rattle, and a rosebush in bud. For the second decade, Mercury, the emblems are a peacock, a prancing horse, primroses in bloom, and a tree in leaf. For the third, Venus (Fig. 123), they are the bow, arrows, and quiver of the God of Love, a goat, and a grapevine which suggests the alliance of Venus and Bacchus. The fourth decade, the Sun, shows an oak tree, Apollo's bay tree and lyre, and a boar, emblematic of virility. In the fifth decade (Fig. 124) the flame of the candle is guttering in wind blown by Mars; there is a lion, a sword is shown, and fruit is falling from a tree. In the sixth decade, Jupiter (Fig. 125), a serpent ("Invidiosa Senectus") darts its tongue at the candle flame, and Death is shaking the leaves from a tree. It is the time "When yellow leaves, or none, or few do hang / Upon those boughs which shake against the cold." And lastly, Saturn (Fig. 126), the sun is setting, the foundations of a house are crumbling, there are withered flowers and a leafless tree, and the candle is almost spent.

Two small books of later date are of interest for a few departures from the traditional iconography of the Seven Ages. In 1688 there was published *The Vanity of the Life of Man. Represented in the Seven several Stages thereof, from his Birth to his Death. With Pictures and Poems exposing the Follies of Every Age.*[17] This was by a certain Robert Burton. The woodblocks for this were used again in *Meditations on the Several Ages of Man's Life: Representing the Vanity of it, from his Cradle to his Grave. Adorned with proper Emblems. To which is added Scriptural Poems* (1701). The author's name is given as John Bunyan, but the work is, I am sure, spurious.[18] In an introduction the analogy of the Ages to the Seasons and the planetary associations are discussed, and a definition is offered: "An Age is such a Period or Term of Man's Life, wherein his Nature, Complexion and Temperature is [*sic*] evidently (and yet naturally) changed." A scriptural quotation, some lines of verse, and a prose meditation accompany each illustration. The text appeals to the lowest level of literacy, taste, and pietistic morality; and the cuts are equally degraded. There is no novelty in the emblems and animals depicted, but I know of no other sequence where the fifth Age (Mars) is personified as a conqueror wearing a laurel wreath and riding in a chariot attended by a herald and a trumpeter. In a few other details there are also signs of an effort to refurbish the old theme.

The Seven Ages are occasionally found, as in the Siena pavement, without any hint of the influence of the planets. Woodcuts in three incunabula are closely related because they all illustrate the text of Bartholomeus Anglicus. The earliest of these (Fig. 127) comes from Lyons in 1482 in both the Latin *De Proprietatibus Rerum* and the French *Proprietaire des Choses*.[19] In an indoors setting a baby is shown in a cradle, a little child is learning to walk, a boy rides a hobbyhorse, an older boy wears a scholar's gown, a young man has a sheathed sword at his girdle, an elderly man lifts an admonitory finger, and an old man has a rosary and a staff. In the Dutch *Boeck van den proprieteyten der dinghen* (Harlem, 1485)[20] the upper part of the design (Fig. 128) which is divided into two levels, shows the Seven Ages out of doors. In their iconography there is nothing to remark except that the artist is quite unequal to the task of differentiating among the last three reverend, soberly garbed gentlemen. John Trevisa's English version of Bartholomeus[21] (1495 ?) contains a crude copy of the same design. Long afterwards it reappears in Stephen Bateman's huge expansion of Bartholomeus's original work.[22] Trevisa and Bateman both include the secondary scene of the original Dutch woodcut, an indoors scene showing a woman on a sickbed, a physician scrutinizing a vial, and in a courtyard a surgeon performing an operation. Thus, the misery of human life is suggested, and the inevitable end also, for a corpse lies at the feet of the Seven Ages. The cut (Fig. 129) in the French version (Lyons, 1500)[23] differs in two details: the child of the third Age is eating, and the young man of the fourth is ostentatiously dressed with no suggestion of the warrior. In all these designs the emphasis upon the very young is remarkable, and the more conspicuous because it does not correspond to anything in the text of Bartholomeus.

Unlike any other treatment of our theme in English Renaissance literature is that found in *Delectable demaundes*[24] (1596), an anonymous translation of a work by Alain Chartier, the fifteenth–century French poet. Here a question is posed: "How ought every age of man to be governed?" and answers provided for the first six Ages: the Babe with milk, the Infant with rods, the Child with shame, the Young Man with good discipline, the Man with arms, and the Old Man with good counsel. But no reply is forthcoming when the seventh is reached, for "the Latter Age is deceit and twise childish."

8. The Ages of Man Divided into Eight, Nine, Ten, Eleven, and Twelve Stages

My survey of the Seven Ages has been a complex business. In contrast, the Eight Ages can be dealt with in a brief paragraph, for such a sequence is, so far as I have discovered, almost nonexistent. It is true that, as we have seen (p. 166), Henry Cuffe did, by a system of divisions and subdivisions, arrive at the number eight, but no sooner had he done so than he joined two of his Ages together and reduced the total to seven. In *The Touchstone of Complexions* [1] (1565), translated from the Latin of Levinus Lemnius by Thomas Newton, the phrasing is so obscure that the Ages may be counted as seven or eight. That is all there is to say about this number.

A search for the Nine Ages is scantily rewarded. At Verdings in Tyrol there is a mural showing a gigantic Death turning a wheel on which revolve figures representative of the Nine Ages.[2] There is also a series of roundels engraved by a member of the Van de Passe family [3] which show the Nine Ages. The sequence is divided into decades, and some of the subjects are handled in an unusual or even unique manner. I note a few of these innovations. The embracing lovers of the twentieth year are near a calf; we still have the phrase "calf love." In the thirtieth year a warrior bids farewell to his weeping wife. The fortieth year finds domesticity restored: the man is at work, a pair of compasses in his hand, the wife is sewing; a child is reading. At fifty a lord and lady are waited upon by two servants. At sixty a man and woman are weighing gold pieces and putting them in a coffer; a madman is present who points to a marriage ceremony taking place in an adjoining room. The note of cynicism apparently intended here is conspicuous in the design for the seventieth year, for a man is placing the horns of cuckoldom upon an old man's head while nearby a young wife is in the company of a young gallant. At ninety an aged man, leaning upon a boy's shoulder (that representative of the next generation whom we have met before), drags himself feebly towards a church; Death, a skeleton playing upon a violin, accompanies him. This is the only instance I know of where the Ages are conflated with the Dance of Death.

Again, as when we watched the stages of a woman's love and the stages of matrimony, we are led into a digression. There are treacherous and perilous roads to tempt the Pilgrim from the Path of Life. A warning against nine stages on such a road is given in a very curious English book of the mid–seventeenth century. This is *The Ages of Sin, or Sinnes Birth and groweth. With the Stepps, and Degrees of Sin, from thought to finall Impenitence*. No date and place of publication are given nor the author's name.[4] Nine "ages" are illustrated, each supplemented with six lines of verse and each is emblematized by an animal. The texts as well as the emblems are engraved on copperplates which have been impressed on one side of the paper only. Altogether a singularly amateurish production, perhaps not intended for publication, it is nevertheless impressive in its fashion. Without the expository verses the intention of the emblematist would not always be apparent. The Nine Ages of Sin are as follows. 1. Suggestion: a snake with her brood crawling from her belly.[5] 2. Rumination: a bear licking her cubs into shape (a familiar emblem). 3. Delectation: a she–ape hugging her young (another familiar emblem). 4. Consent: two wolves sucking the blood of a lamb, i.e. the Soul and Sin consent together. 5. Act: a tiger swallowing a man whose legs dangle from the beast's mouth, i.e. the Soul swallows Sin. 6. Iteration: "flesh–flies" swarming over a pile of meat in a butcher's shop can be driven off, if at all, only by Divine Grace (represented by a boy with a fly–tap). 7. Gloriation: a lion attacking an ass, i.e. the saucy sinner is as boastful as a rampant lion. 8. Obduration: a tortoise being thwacked by a man with a sword i.e. the sinner's heart is as hard as a "Tortess–back." 9. Final Impenitency: a leopard (which cannot change its spots) jumping from a cliff into the sea. Even so "Conscience, headlong, casts Impenitence, / With horrid frights of Hellish Recompense."

Two sequences of the Ages are, as it were, connecting links between the idea that there are nine and the idea that there are ten Ages. One is a woodcut dated 1482 and probably produced at Augsburg.[6] It consists of twenty small rectangles set in two rows: the upper row exhibits the Ages, the lower the emblematic creatures appropriate to each. Although it is unnecessary to describe them all, it is interesting that the tenth Age is a corpse upon a bier, and the creature below this scene is a goose. Obviously there are here not ten but nine Ages of Life. Precisely the same sequence appears in a curious little volume entitled *Der Dieren Palleys* (Antwerp, 1520) which is chiefly concerned with animal lore. One poem in it, adorned with an extremely crude woodcut, tells how and why each of the Ten Ages resembles one or another creature: The kid is never tired of play, the calf has no wisdom, the bull is quarrelsome, the lion is noble and wise, the fox is full of sharp practices, the wolf is greedy and avaricious, the dog gnawing a bone is symbolic of man's gnawing anxiety for his soul, the cat lies sluggishly by the fire, the ass is a stupid laughingstock, and finally, man, like a goose, has all his worldly possessions plucked by Death. I suspect that the association of Death with a goose is not so much a matter of plucking but may be connected with the old superstition that when one shudders or shivers involuntarily a goose is flying over one's future grave.[7]

The full Ten Ages may appear without the intrusion of Death as the final stage of Life. So they appear in a fifteenth–century Dutch woodcut,[8] in a sequence by the Master of the Banderoles, and elsewhere. A set of ten plates (ca. 1575–1590), engraved by Philip Galle after designs by Gerhard Van Groeningen (Paludanus) shows Ten Ages which proceed by decades to the age of a hundred. Play, hunting and music, the military life, scientific studies, and financial affairs occupy, respectively, the first five decades. (Love, courtship and marriage do not appear). In the sixth decade an elderly man charitably puts coins in the purse of a poor woman. In the seventh, an old man is served food and drink by attendants. In the eighth, he points an admonitory finger towards two children who have their hands raised in aspiration. In the ninth he is extremely old. And in the tenth he is dying, comforted by two attendants, while another person is peeping into a money box. Each Age has a distich in Latin and French commenting upon it. That for the tenth reads in part: "Les biens aux hoirs, et le corps en terre." An impressive version of the Ten Ages is a German poem entitled *Die Zehn Alter dieser Welt* (Augsburg, 1518) which is a series of dialogues between a hortatory hermit and each of the Ages.[9] Each dialogue has an accompanying woodcut of an Age with the appropriate animal. To the best of my knowledge the Ten Ages never appear in English poetry.

Earlier in this chapter, in the course of a survey of the ascending and descending stairways, we noted the English "ballad" which, dividing the Ages into periods of seven years each, shows the progress of Man's days from seven to seventy, and it was remarked that actually not Ten Ages but Eleven were shown, since beyond the seventh period Life might continue "till the end," an unpredictable term. This "ballad" is, then, a link between the concepts of Ten Ages and Eleven Ages. I know of no reason why a sequence of eleven should ever be employed; the number has to my mind no suggestiveness other than that of the apostles after the treachery of Judas Iscariot—and the eleven faithful apostles have no connection with the Ages of Human Life. But Eleven Ages do, as we shall see in moment, actually occur.

As the Ages may be joined to the three periods of the day or to the four seasons of the year, so they may be connected with the Labors of the Months. Appropriate quatrains appear in the margins of the Calendar of various French Books of Hours, especially in those published by Thielman Kerver.[10] The verses are a condensed popular redaction of a fourteenth–century poem. In the original poem each Age is said to last six years, seventy–two in all. But of these, thirty–six pass in sleep (men must have slept long in the Middle Ages!), fifteen are wasted in childhood, while sickness and imprisonment account for five more. Consequently Man can count on only about fifteen years of productive labor. After this somewhat melancholy prologue the poem proceeds to attach each Age to a month. It is this portion of the poem that we find condensed in the Calendars of some *Horae*. Not all Books of Hours have congruous woodcuts or engravings, but when these appear they are as follows: January—children's games; February—a schoolroom scene; March—hunting in a forest; April—lovers' promenade; May—lovers on a horse, the girl riding *en croupe*; June—a wedding; July—a family: father, mother, and children; August—a prosperous farmer paying a laborer his wages after the harvest; September—an improvident farmer with empty barns and barrels; October—the man of property dines with his family; November—he is ill, seated in an armchair with a physician in attendance; December—he is dying, with a priest and weeping women nearby. The conflation of the Ages with the Labors of the Months, though pleasantly suggested, is not realized, for at no period of the year is the protagonist shown toiling. But what is more remarkable is that in the month of September (contrasted with August) another theme is introduced—the theme of Industry *vs.* Idleness. For this we are not prepared by what has gone before, and we hear nothing more of it in what follows after. However, the story is really in eleven stages, not twelve, since one month is devoted to a second, contrasting person. Though based squarely upon the Months, this is a series of Eleven Ages, not Twelve.

Thomas Tusser's poem [11] "Mans age devided into twelve seavens" is based rather pointlessly upon the idea of twelve seven–year apprenticeships (Man passing through successive stages of experience as he goes through life) and suggests neither the months nor their labors, which is surprising considering Tusser's special interests. The complete pattern of twelve is found in a simple and beautiful emblem entitled "Omnium rerum vicissitudo." [12] Here the Twelve Ages are conflated with the Wheel of Life. This wheel has twelve spokes. To the rim at equal distances are attached twelve roses, from earliest bud through full bloom to falling petals and dessicated remains.

CHAPTER 7.   STRANGERS AND PILGRIMS

1. Philippians 3:20 and Hebrews 11:10–16

Students of English literature who have concerned themselves with the theme of the Pilgrimage of Human Life have generally centered their attention upon the sources and analogues of Bunyan's *Pilgrim's Progress*. George Offer, John Brown, James B. Wharey, and more recently Dr. Owst may be mentioned among the many scholars who have pursued this inquiry.[1] The paramount question has been the relationship between Guillaume de Guilleville's *Pelerinage de la vie humaine* and Bunyan's book; investigations, however, have extended backwards to Lucian and to the so-called *Tabula* or *Tablets* or *Table* of Cebes, have ranged widely through medieval and Renaissance allegory, and have considered various (but not all) Tudor and Stuart examples of the allegorical journey through life. Not much attention has been paid, however, to analogues in the arts of design. We have here little or nothing to do with the Bunyan problem; it is mentioned only because it is bound to be in the recesses of the reader's thoughts and may be exorcised by being brought into the open. Our interest is in the parallel appearance of the allegory in English Renaissance literature and in the fine arts. The parallels have not been studied before, and, moreover, the examples themselves are often beautiful and moving and have been undeservedly forgotten by all but special investigators because they are obscured by Bunyan's masterpiece.

As in the preceding chapters of this book, the question of sources is not our concern, but a few essential passages in the Bible should be recalled. The two Old Testament texts (Leviticus 25:23, and Psalm 39:12) which declared that men are "strangers and pilgrims" *with* God support the opinion of historical criticism that as Jahweh was limited spatially to the land of Israel, so was he limited temporally to this present life; he was a God of the living, not of the dead. But these texts were subjected to a new interpretation by St. Paul when he affirmed (Philippians 3:20) that "our citizenship is in heaven," and by the author of Hebrews in the great passage (11:10–16) on "the city which hath foundations, whose builder and maker is God," a city prepared for those "elders" who "confessed that they were strangers and pilgrims on the earth" and desired "a better country, that is, an heavenly." This text in Hebrews is the basic inspiration for the countless figurations in Christian literature of Life as a Journey to a Better Country. A prefiguration of this idea was discerned in the Old Testament narrative of the entry of the Chosen People into the Promised Land. During the Renaissance there were even manuals of practical instruction for pilgrims to Jerusalem which supplemented the account of the actual mundane city in Palestine with an edifying allegory of the journey to that true Jerusalem which is above.[2] Other portions of Holy Scripture were similarly interpreted: for example, the parable of the man who went down from Jerusalem to Jericho, fell among thieves, and was ministered unto by the Good Samaritan (Luke 10:30–36).

2. *The Choice of the Two Paths*

The theme of the Pilgrimage was naturally associated with that of the Choice of the Two Paths which, grounded upon Christ's words (Matthew 7:13–14) about the strait gate and narrow way which leadeth unto life and the wide gate and broad way which leadeth to destruction, was expanded in the early Christian document called the *Didache* and in the apocryphal *Epistle of Barnabas*,[1] and, from these and other sources, was spread widely through medieval edifying literature. Biblical and Christian strands were interwoven with others from classical antiquity. In particular there was the myth of Hercules confronted by Virtue and Pleasure at the Parting of the Ways.[2] Times beyond number this scene appears in emblem books but we may limit ourselves to four examples. Whitney shows Hercules standing in a street in a city as he makes his choice.[3] In Maurice Scève's design Venus stands in a rose wreath but behind her are dark clouds, and Virtue in a wreath of thorns but behind her the sky is bright.[4] Christoff Murer shows the "Via Vitae" with an angel behind Virtue and the "Via Mortis" with Death behind Pleasure.[5] In Corrozet's rendering of the myth, however, Hercules has made his choice and is following Virtue, and Pleasure is retiring, discomfited.[6] Linche (sig. Ti[v]), following Cartari, discusses the Choice of Hercules, noting its origins in Xenophon and Cicero. Thomas Bradshaw notes that Xenophon's *Memorabilia* is the source of his poetical "Dialogue betwixt Hercules and the two Ladies, Voluptuousness and Virtuous." [7] Wither's fine emblem is unusually complex (Fig. 130). A nude youth labeled Hercules stands between a venerable bearded man with a book in his lap and a caduceus resting against his knee and a hideous crone who holds a false face to hide her withered face. At the right of Hercules grows a barbed thistle; at his left is a vase of flowers. His right hand points skyward, his left hand down. Behind him on his left Death, a skeleton, crouches.[8]

Though Hercules is the representative man, in interpretations of the Choice which Man must make this Greek myth frequently is only implied. Exceptional but typically humanistic is Stephen Hawes' description of the two "highways" between which his protagonist must choose: the "sharpe" way of contemplation and the "more plain" way of "worldly dignity, of the active life." [9] But almost always Man is offered the option not between the Vita Contemplativa and the Vita Activa but between Virtue and Vice, Virtue and Pleasure. In *Reson and Sensuallyte* (664 f.) Lydgate tells how in a dream Dame Nature offered him the choice between the Road of Reason and the Road of Sensuality, but later in the same poem (2071 f.) the poet, apparently forgetting that a choice has been already made, re–enacts in his dream the Judgment of Paris, choosing Venus. A marginal gloss at this point reads: "Per istam fallaciam trium deorum clare significatur quod Iuuenis cum venerit ad annos discretionis sibi potest proponi triplex modus vivendi vel triplex vita, scilicet contemplativam activam et voluptuosam."

Lydgate is careful to remark that the choice is made when Youth has reached the years of discretion. This is of course why the symbolic letter which tradition associates with Pythagoras is not a V but a Y. The trunk of the letter represents the irresponsible years of childhood and the two paths branch off when discretion has been gained. As, respectively, an ethical and a religious symbol, Stephen Bateman notes that the letter Y is said to be "a figure of Virtue" and the letter X is of course the Cross.[10] The two ways, says Abraham Fleming, were set forth "by a profane Philosopher, in a letter of the cross-row, namelie Y." Fleming develops the idea with many examples of wayfaring from Scripture.[11] The distinction is usually made between the broad and narrow branches of the letter, the broad arm being sinister. Boissard introduces Pythagoras pointing with a wand to the letter, one arm of which is festooned with thorns but is topped with a crown, and the other arm is festooned with roses but is topped with flames, the primrose path that leads to the eternal bonfire.[12] Elsewhere the Y occurs without the philosopher. Somewhat surprisingly it is found, rendered very simply, in Cousin's *Livre de Fortune* (no. 30). A beautifully engraved emblem (Fig. 131) shows one arm of the letter surmounted by a crown, from it hang various objects promising rewards, an orb, a scepter, a palm branch, a book, and the other arm ending in flames, from it hang such threatening objects as a knife, a gibbet, and a wheel.[13] This was the device of the famous printer Geoffrey Tory, and Tory designed a similar one for the bookseller Nicholas de Chemin.[14] The Choice of the Paths may be conflated with another very popular emblem, that of the figure, child or man, having a wing attached to his right arm but a weight tied to his left foot, the figure aspires to heaven but is bound to earth. Thus a drawing in the British Museum said to be copied from Correggio shows Hercules between Virtue and Pleasure. Pleasure, who has a flute player beside her, has fastened his left leg to a heavy weight. The same choice and the same impediment, though without reference either to Hercules or the Pythagorean letter, is the subject of two woodcuts by Tobias Stimmer in Reusner's book of emblems. One is called "Aut Deo aut Mundo," the other "In Philoplutum." In both a man with hands raised in aspiration has his ankles fast bound to a moneybag.[15]

The actual letter may disappear though an explicit reference to it may remain, as in an emblem by Giovanni Ferro called "Strada Y," where one path leads through thorns to a flower garden and the other through smooth and clear fields to a dark wood.[16] In a design by H. V. Bael engraved by Hieronimus Wierex (Fig. 132) the Y pattern is clearly discernible though the letter itself does not appear. Here the Two Paths are delineated in much detail. On one side a thin line of pious folk ascend a hill past several churches and chapels, and so skyward to the Heavenly City where an angel stands proffering a crown. On the other side a crowd of men and women are engaged in feasting, music, love-making, and other carnal pleasures while close behind them yawns the flaming mouth of hell in which sinners are writhing. But hope is held out for the worldly, for some avoid hell and having passed through a dark forest come to the rude huts of Humility and Repentance. Between the branching paths is a crucifix, and sitting threateningly in the middle distance are four skeletons, two with darts, one with a scythe, and the fourth with an hourglass.[17]

The Choice, so critically important for Man's destiny, may be illustrated in other ways. In some manuscripts of *The City of God* the theme is conflated with that of the Tree of Life (from Book XIV): Man, sometimes conspicuously youthful, stands or sits at the top of the tree, an angel offers him a crown and a devil a money coffer, a dragon gnaws at the root of the tree and Death is sawing through its trunk.[18] In a variant there are two dragons, one white, labeled "Jour," the other black, labeled "Nuit." [19] Obviously related to these Augustinian designs is a fifteenth-century German print showing Youth standing on a treetop, flanked by an angel and a devil. There are no dragons but Death and the Devil, using a two-handed saw, are cutting through the tree's trunk.[20] Father David combines the "Y" with the "Arbor Bona" and "Arbor Mala." Here there are the customary branching ways; an unusual feature, however, is a tree in the background which bears leaves and fruit on one side while the other side is withered.[21] The same conflation is effected in a more complex way in the engraved title page by Robert Vaughan of Richard Brathwaite's *Lignum Vitae* (1658), a devotional book in Latin. The Pilgrim has already chosen the right path and a hand from heaven holds out to him the promise of a crown as he climbs a hill on whose top grows the "Arbor Vitae." On the plain below, which the Pilgrim has left behind him, is a second tree, not precisely what we should have expected but the "Arbor Scientiae," the tree of Science or Worldly Wisdom. But the wrong path may be chosen. Linche (sig. Tiii[r]) describes an image of Lady Voluptia seated in a "pontificall and majestike chaire," with Virtue, "dejected, troden downe, and despised by her," beneath her feet.

George Wither, as we have seen, criticized William Marshall for not engraving "a plain invention" for the title page of his *Emblemes* (1635) and he invited his readers to puzzle it out for themselves. Essentially it is a Choice of the Two Paths and, excluding subsidiary details, we recognize the following scheme. At the bottom there is a cavern which seems to be the Cave of Birth. Above it Fortune and the World stand upon a hill. Two men are drawing lots from an urn. On one side the Narrow Way leads past the Seven Virtues and a church to upland slopes. In the distance from the top of a mountain an eagle (traditionally a symbol of Divinity) is soaring aloft bearing on its back a Christian soul. On the other side the Way of Destruction leads not downward but likewise to a mountain and passes the Seven Deadly Sins and a temple of Venus. On the mountain are gibbets and wheels of torment, murders and duels are in progress, and at the top stands Death.

Two English poems to which we shall recur later must be glanced at here. In John Davies of Hereford's *Humours Heav'n on Earth* (1609) the subject of the Two Paths is strangely confused, for the Parting of the Ways occurs beyond the House of Death. When William Browne's protagonist Riot, who has become the type of Fallen Humanity, leaves the palace where he has been tortured by Remorse, he comes to forking paths, the Way of Repentance and the Way of Despair and Death. Although he starts down the wrong path, an angelic warning dissuades him and he chooses the proper one. It should be noted that here there is not the traditional choice between Virtue and Pleasure.[22]

That it is never too late to "mend one's ways," that Man wandering astray may regain the right road, is the lesson implied in the sequence of five charming engravings which precede the five books of Father Drexel's devotional treatise *Heliotropium* (1627).[23] The first plate has for its principal subject the Conversion of St. Paul; on one side a heliotrope is in bud and the sun's rays are pouring down upon it and on the other a winged human heart on earth is attached by a chain to the Heart of Christ in heaven. In the second plate the Soul is embraced by Christ; the heliotrope is expanding and the human heart has risen to heaven. In the third David kneels in prayer while an angel holds a crown over him; the heliotrope is in fullest bloom and the two hearts, both wearing crowns, are side by side in a tondo of cherubs' heads. But in the fourth plate troubles and temptations have come: The human heart, with the chain which had linked the human heart to Christ's broken and the feathers of Pride piercing it, falls to earth, pulled down by a devil; a cloud obscures the sun, the heliotrope has withered. The final plate shows

Moses, a type of Patience, leaning upon the rock (an emblem of Constancy and Virtue) whence flows the living water; the heliotrope, watered by an angel, is reviving and another angel carries the human heart aloft to rejoin Christ's.

I return to simple renderings of the Choice in order to note degenerations of the theme, the intrusion of cynicism and pessimism. There is nothing of this in the vignette by Robert Vaughan on the title page of Richard Brathwaite's *The English Gentleman* (1630), where Youth stands between Virtue, holding a palm branch, and Pleasure, a naked siren with a mirror and comb. No hint is given as to what the choice will be, but knowing Brathwaite and English gentlemen we may assume that it will be the right one. Nor has the choice been made in the emblem by Schoonhovius of Youth flanked by Virtue with a book and Voluptas with flowers. Behind the former a thorny path leads to a temple on distant heights; behind the latter a flowery path leads to deep woods in a distant vale. The moral should be obvious, but the title of the emblem, "Lubricum Iuventutis," is ominous.[24] There is little doubt as to the choice in Theodore de Bry's "Adolescentia." Youth sits astride a globe. On his right a monk wearing a church upon his head pulls him by a chain; on his left a fair lady pulls him by a slender cord.[25] There is cleverness as well as cynicism in an amusing print by Nicolas Guérard called "La Sourde Oreille." In the foreground the "Chemin de la Vertu" and the "Chemin de la Joye" branch off from one another and at the point where they separate stands a modishly dressed young man. On his right a young woman named Plaisir is speaking into an ear trumpet which he holds attentively while with the other finger he stops the other ear into which Vertu, a reverend gentleman, is speaking through a megaphone. At the top of the engraving is the legend: "Il n'est de pire sourd que celuy qui ne veut pas entendre." This sentiment is expanded in some lines of verse below the picture.

From the various pious writings of the Tudor–Stuart period which discuss the Choice, I select as a sample an eloquent passage in Henry Crosse's *Vertues Commonwealth* (1603):

> Two waies are proposed and laide open to all, the one inviting to vertue, the other alluring to vice; the first is combersome, intricate, untraded, overgrowne, and many obstacles to dismay the passenger; the other plaine, even beaten, overshadowed with boughes, tapistried with flowers, and many objects to feed the eye; now a man that lookes but only to the outward shewe, will

easily tread the broadest pathe, but if hee perceive that this smooth and even way leads to a neast of Scorpions: or a litter of Beares, he will rather take the other though it be rugged and unpleasant, than hazard himselfe in so great a daunger.

Crosse goes on to sound a warning against the lamias and sirens lying in wait to entrap the unwary traveler along the Path of Vice. "As many waies crosse the Queenes high—way, so Vertue is . . . thwarted with many smoothe paths, if by exact care they be not avoyded." He reaches, however, the secular, rather than otherworldly, conclusion that the man who "goeth streight to his journies end shall arrive at the house of Fame." [26]

3. *Fame and Rumor*

In the words of a great poet, "Fame is the spur that the clear spirit doth raise . . . To scorn delights, and live laborious days" and when the poet laments that the "thin spun life" is slit by the blind Fury, Death, at the moment when we hope to find the "fair Guerdon," Phoebus replies: "Fame is no plant that grows on mortal soil . . . nor in broad rumour lies," but is the reward to be expected in heaven. Even so Shakespeare says of true Fame, "that all pant after in their lives," may be "register'd upon our brazen tombs," for Honor "bates" the keen edge of Time's scythe and may "make us heirs of all Eternity." [1] The need for Man to "live laborious days" if he would win renown is the theme of a prose "Dialogue between Fame and the Scholler" by Thomas Fenne. Here Fame, scarcely personified save with the gift of speech, describes herself as the scholar's mentor, and by way of encouragement she cites an abundance of examples from classical antiquity and other historical characters.[2]

The distinction must be drawn between Good and Ill Fame. Raffaello Borghini suggests that the two trumpets which she is often shown blowing are "per dimostrare forse che hora suona la tromba per rapportare il bene e il vero, ed hora la tromba con cui rapporta il male ed il falso." [3] Drayton points the same contrast in his description of Fame upon whose breast are two "tables" (tablets), the one of crystal which is "the fair booke of heavenly memory," the other of ebony which is "the black scrowle of infamy." [4]

The distinction is not always so clearly drawn between true Fame and mere Rumor. Thus Ripa takes from an antique medal a design of Mercury and Pegasus as the emblem of Fama Chiara, Illustrious Fame, Mercury being the messenger of Zeus and the god of Eloquence and Pegasus being winged and hence symbolic of the swift passage of Rumor through the world. Peter Pett imagines that "a prease of rumours and reports" enters constantly the wide open doors and windows of the Palace of Fame, and these she makes known to all the world with a "trompe of brasse." [5] But Ripa, in his discussion of Rumore, differentiates this personification sharply from true Fame, for Rumore is depicted as an armed knight hurling darts. In the French version of Ripa this figure is called "Rumeur ou Discorde," whence it is but a step to the "flying Reports among the Multitude" of the English version, and thence to the many–headed mob–monster. The most famous example of Rumor is of course found in the Induction to *Henry IV, Part Two*, spoken by "Rumour painted full of Tongues." [6] Here Rumor is definitely slanderous, spreading surmises, jealousies, and conjectures, a "pipe" upon whose stop "the blunt Monster with uncounted heads" can play. Similarly Ripa's Detrattione, Detraction, may be associated with false Rumor and scandalous gossip. She has a protruding serpent's tongue, she may have as attributes a dagger and a rat, she is poorly clothed, for base circles of society are given to detraction, and she is seated because laziness encourages her.

Ripa implies a like connection between Rumor and Curiosity. His Curiositá is a woman whose dress is embroidered with ears and frogs— with frogs because of their bulging eyes, or as the English version quaintly explains: "Frogs are Emblems of Inquisitiveness by reason of their goggle–eyes." In Thomas Campion's masque at the marriage of the Earl of Somerset there appeared "Rumor in a skin coate full of winged Tongues, and over it an antick robe; on his head a Cap like a tongue, with a large paire of winges to it." Attending upon him were Curiosity whose coat and cap were both "full of eyes" and Credulity with a coat and cap "full of eares." [7] Similarly in Ben Jonson's *Time Vindicated* Fame—who is nothing else than mere Rumor—is accompanied by "the Curious: The Eyed, the Eared, and the Nosed." The text subsequently makes it clear that the performers' costumes displayed these attributes. The action is grotesquely comical.

The immense prestige of Virgil fixed firmly in men's imagination the attributes of Fame's many "watchful eyes" ("tot vigiles oculi"), her many tongues ("tot linguae"), and her "pricked up ears" ("tot subrigit aures"). [8] From Virgil came also her trumpet and her wings. In the French translation of *Bocace de la Genealogie des Dieux* (Paris, Verard, 1498), which is the first illustrated edition, there is a cut (fol. Xii^v) of Fame with eyes, ears, and tongues. An engraving of Fama in the Virgil *Opera* (Strassburg, 1502) shows her with cloven feet, wings on her feet and shoulders, and several pairs of ears clustered together.[9] This rather repulsive design is suggestive of False Report rather than of True Fame. Virgil Solis' engraving of Fame (ca. 1550) has her entire body covered with eyes but no tongues or ears; in an accompanying poem there is a reference to the description in the Æneid. Richard Linche, following Cartari, notes that Fame's mantle is so girt round her that she may run swiftly. She is winged and blows upon a "cornet." By some, he goes on, she is "depainted" with many eyes in her face, or she may have ears and tongues all over her body. Linche does not neglect to add that in this guise she is "most excellently delivered" by Virgil.[10] Very similar is Peacham's description. Fame's garment is "open to the middle thigh, that she might runne the faster"; it is "embroydered with eies and eares"; she is winged and carries a trumpet, "as she is described by the Poet Virgil." [11] Peacham also has an emblem of Virtue handing a scroll to Fame. The latter's dress is open to mid–thigh and is adorned with what may be—the drawing is defective—eyes or ears or tongues, or all three. She also has a trumpet at her lips. Here Peacham makes no reference to Virgil.[12] Of various other emblematic renderings of the concept two may be noted here as samples. Daniel Cramer's Fame is winged and has a trumpet; her dress is full of eyes. An engraved inscription reads: "Voca, oculis, alis, toti sum cognita mundo." [13] Jean Baudoin's Fame wears a robe adorned with eyes, ears, and tongues, and she has two trumpets.[14]

Glancing farther into the past than is usual in this book, the reader may like to have a paraphrase of Chaucer's description in *The House of Fame* (1, 356–392). In that house there was no crowding though there was a great press of folk. Upon an imperial throne sat "a feminyne creature" who seemed at times very small and then again so large that her feet touched the earth, while her head reached to heaven. She had as many eyes as there are feathers on birds, and she had also tongues and up–standing ears, and on her feet were partridge's wings. In *The Pastime of Pleasure* (155–196) Graund Amour tells of a meeting:

> I saw come rydynge in a valaye ferre
> A goodly lady envyronned aboute
> With tongues of fyre. . . .
> Her palfraye swyfte rennynge as the wynde. . . .
> My name quod she in all the worlde is knowen
> Yclypped Fame in every regyon

For I my horne in sondry wyse have blowen
After the dethe of many a champyon
And with my tonges have made aye mencyon
Of theyr grete actes.

This is not Rumor or Report, still less Ill Fame, but, rather, what Ripa was later to call "Chiara Fama." It should be noted that Hawes emphasizes the speed of Fame, her palfrey is, he says, Pegasus. After the death of Graund Amour, Dame Fame reappears and associates him with the Nine Worthies (5495–5606). At the beginning of this episode there is a woodcut of Fame in which the fiery tongues are apparent. One of the "pageants" (actually a set of tapestries or painted cloths) devised by Sir Thomas More, of which I have already given an account (pp. 157–59), showed Lady Fame "with tongues . . . compassed all rounde." The distinction between Fame and Rumor, or Report, is, as I have remarked, not always made. Thus, in a royal entertainment of 1519 there appeared a character named Report who was garbed in "crimson sattin, full of toongs," [15] but for another entertainment in 1553 payment was made "for paintinge of a Cote and a Capp with Ies [eyes] tonges and eares for fame." [16] Rumor is not necessarily ill–founded or malicious, and sometimes might as well be denominated Fame but for the lack of any suggestion of renown. Thus, Rumor, in a play by John Phillip, enters "blowyng and puffing," indicative obviously of speed, and the news announced is true.[17] In an anonymous play Rumor enters "running." [18] In neither of these instances is there any indication of attributes. Similarly, in an Italian design a winged Fame with her two trumpets is shown running.[19] John Higgins takes a simile from the circles that widen in water: "So fame in flight increaseth more and more." He also says that "a monster swifter none is under sunne"; the epithet need not carry an evil implication but, rather, suggest the monstrous apparition of "plumes" from top to toe and many eyes and tongues and ears.[20] I have found but one instance in Tudor–Stuart literature of Fame and Rumor as separate characters. In an anonymous pageant they both appear; Fame has her trumpet, Rumor no specified attribute.[21]

Fame—that is, Chiara Fama, not Scandalous Rumor—appears frequently and appropriately in Lord Mayors' Shows, generally with no record of her attributes though the trumpet is occasionally mentioned. Often she is associated with Antiquity or Memory or History.[22] The engraved title page of William Burton's *Description of Leicester Shire* (1622) groups Fame with Truth, Antiquity, and a personification of the county. Fame, whose robe is full of eyes and ears, holds with one hand a trumpet to her lips while, kneeling, she holds in the other a garland over the towery head of Leicestershire. On another title page Herodian the historian weighs in scales the "fruit," heads of a lion, a goat, a peacock, a serpent, etc. which are symbolic of different emperors, fallen from the tree of the Roman Empire and recommends these "rip'ned Monarchs" whether for shame or glory to Fame who holds a scroll inscribed: "Non ficti parique tenax sed nuntia veri." The branches of the tree are shaken by Fate, a skeleton. In one pan of Herodian's scales is a book, in the other the head of a goose.[23]

Sufficient, perhaps more than sufficient, examples have been given of actions, postures, and attributes that have more variety when seen than when read about, and I close this part of our discussion with an attempt, unique so far as I know, which was made to give novelty to old concepts. Thomas Scot says that the House of Fame has been enlarged by the poets of all ages since Homer, one adding this detail and another that. His contribution is the novel idea that the eyes and tongues of Fame are on her house, not on her body or her garments; her house is now "glazde with eies" and "hangd round about with nimble tongues." [24]

4. Love

Man has, or may have, various companions upon his journey. Fortunate indeed is he if accompanied by friends. Occasionally the emblem of Friendship is found: a figure with the words "Hiems. Aestas" inscribed upon his forehead; "Procul. Prope" upon his heart (which is shown within his breast); and "Mors. Vita" on the hem of his garment.[1] Thus, the true friend does not change with the changing seasons, is the same whether far off or near, and is loyal in death as in life. Reciprocal aid is given by friends, as shown in the emblem of a lame man leaning upon the shoulder of a blind man, the one guiding his companion, the other giving support.[2] A variant shows the lame man being carried by the blind man.[3] This theme of "Mutuum auxilium" is easily transferred to emblems of blind Love carrying lame Love (both personifications being Cupids), a charming idea of frequent occurrence.[4]

That Love is dominant over sea and land is the meaning of the emblem in which Cupid holds a fish and a flower.[5] That "Love altreth Nature" and is blind to any defects in the loved one is an experience emblematized by Cupid affixing wings to an ass,[6] even as Titania loves Bottom and strokes his ass's head. Love is a beacon to the soul, as Shakespeare's magnificent lines: "It is an ever–fixed mark . . . / It is the star of every wandering bark" declare. Closely parallel is the design of Cupid standing at night on a wharf with a beacon flaming above him, and a ship sailing towards him.[7] Shakespeare goes on to declare that "Love's not Time's fool." Even so Alain Chartier in answer to a question had said that Love is free and is not subject to Time,[8] and the first emblem in Van Veen's *Amorum Emblemata* is of Love (Cupid) sitting in "the endless serpent ring" of Eternity since "No tyme can ruin Love." [9] This occurs again in the *Fons Amoris* (no. 61), yet in Van Veen's volume (p. 237) there is also the design, to which I have referred in my discussion of Time, of Time clipping the wings of Love. The symbolism is somewhat obscure when Robert Greene describes Cupid's "winges plumed with Time's feathers least [lest] hee might let slip occasion." [10] Love is hindered by this present life: A familiar motif is that of Cupid with a weight attached to one wrist and wings to the other; the aspiring arm is generally raised.[11]

That extravagance in Love leads to Grief is emblematized by a weeping Cupid who holds a sieve into which a young man is pouring water.[12] This is close to the theme of Amor Carnalis. A German print (ca. 1475) of a nude, winged female figure shooting an arrow with a skull, a sword, and a hellmouth below her and saints and philosophers, some with admonitory pointing fingers, on either side, warns against Carnal Love.[13] No such moral warning is conveyed in the frivolous illustrations of the saying "Sine Baccho et Cerene friget Venus." These designs, showing a sullen and lethargic Venus, sometimes with Cupid by her, and Ceres and Bacchus disappearing in the distance, are of such frequent occurrence that no examples need be cited. Not so common is the contrary emblem of Venus standing between Ceres, who offers to her blades of corn, and Bacchus, who offers her a bowl.[14] Again, a man and a woman are embracing as they sit at dinner table. Cupid shoots his arrow at them, Ceres offers food, and Bacchus is pouring wine.[15]

When Lysander suggests to Hermia that they should meet in the wood a league beyond Athens she promises to do so, swearing "By Cupid's strongest bow, / By his best arrow, with the golden head." [16] It is true that, as Shakespeare says, the gods smile at lovers' vows, and in Van Veen's *Amorum Emblemata* (pp. 140–141) Jupiter and Venus smile as Cupid takes an oath on a book. But why has Cupid's "best arrow" a "golden head"? The answer is implicit in the line itself: his other arrow has a leaden head. The theme of Cupid's two arrows derives from Ovid,[17] and in Golding's translation is rendered:

That causeth love is all of golde with point full sharp and bright.
That chaseth love is blunt, whose steele with leaden head is dight.

George Turberville acknowledges his debt to Ovid, where he (addressing Cupid) had

> read of thy shafts and of thy golden Bow,
> Thy shafts which by their divers heads their divers kindes did show.[18]

The two arrows do not occur, so far as I have observed, in the arts of design, probably because of the difficulty, even impossibility, of depicting the contrast between the two metals. The subject is, however, extraordinarily prevalent in literature. Disregarding the use of it in Boccaccio's *Amorosa Visione* (XV) in the *Roman de la Rose*, and in the French poem *De Venus la Deesse d'Amor* (stanzas 247–250), we may limit ourselves to English literature. It is found in Chaucer's *Knight's Tale* (A. 1963–6) and in Gower's *Confessio Amantis* (III, 1701–5), where Phoebus is wounded with a golden dart and Daphne with a leaden. In the anonymous *Court of Love* (I, 315 f.) "the Golden Love and Leden Love," not precisely arrows, however, are referred to. Lydgate gives to Cupid not only two arrows but two bows. With a bow made of ivory he shoots arrows having golden tips, five in number, to wit: beauty, symplesse, sothfastnesse, companye, and beausemblaunt. With a black bow he shoots five lead–headed arrows tipt with venom: pride, felonye, shame, diesperaunce, and "chaunge of thoughtys new." [19] William Neville is content with the simple form of the tale: Cupid pierced Phoebus with a golden dart and Daphnys with one "ledyn blont and hevy." [20] An anonymous early Tudor poem wanders far from this simplicity. It tells how the Heart accused the Eye of entrapping him and how the Heart issues a challenge that results in a combat in the lists of Love. Presiding over the list is Love himself, winged and crowned, and holding "a bowe of unycorne" which has two strings.[21] The material from which the bow is fashioned indicates Chaste Love, for the unicorn is an emblem of Chastity. Why there are two strings is not explained; the connection with the golden and leaden arrows must be assumed. The subject is found twice in *Tottel's Miscellany* (1557). There is a "Description of the fickle affections . . . of love": "He makes the one to rage with golden burning dart, / And doth alay with leaden colde agayn the other hart." [22] In the second poem it is told how Apollo borrowed from Cupid his bow and two arrows, but by mistake shot Daphne with the shaft "which headed was with lead." The poet compares his own case: he has been shot with the golden shaft, his lady with the leaden.[23] Thomas Preston introduces the motive in a stage direction in *Cambises* (ca. 1570), though it has no part in the action of the play. The direction reads: "Enter Venus leading out her sonne, Cupid, blinde: he must have a bow and two shafts, one headed with golde and th'other with lead." [24] There are several other Elizabethan versions. One is in an anonymous poem:

The quivers which thou doost behold, which stand this God in stead,
The one is full of golden shaftes, the other full of lead,
The golden strike the fervent wights which pas their daies in love.
The lead doth wound the brasen harts whom no complaint can move.[25]

Thomas Watson varies this only in phrasing:

> Love hath two shaftes, the one of beaten gold,
> By stroake wherof a sweete effect is wrought:
> The other is of lumpish leaden mould,
> And worketh none effect, but what is nought.[26]

In the anonymous ballad of "Cupid's Courtesie" (ca. 1595) it is said that no physician can cure the wound from the golden arrow in the lover's heart, but the lady's heart, pierced by the leaden arrow, is frozen.[27] It is noteworthy that almost invariably it is the man whom the golden arrow strikes and the woman the leaden. This is probably because the writer is in all cases a man. However, it is not in accord with universal experience. Spenser, having just touched on the theme in *Colin Clouts Come Home Again* (807), returns to it in the splendid "Masque of Cupid" in *The Faerie Queene* (III, 12) on which the *Variorum* edition commentary is so full that it need not be discussed here.[28] John Fletcher introduces into his play *A Wife for a Month* (acted 1624), a masque (II.5) which is obviously a simplified borrowing from Spenser. Here, however, there is no allusion to the two arrows. Instead, Cupid is attended by various personifications, among them the Graces, whom he commands to remove the scarf from his eyes that he may see the beautiful ladies among the spectators, and being satisfied, he has his eyes covered again. A dance of masquers, the consequences of Love, follows: Fancy, Desire, Hope, Fear, Distrust, Jealousy, Care, Ire, Poverty, and Despair.[29]

The foregoing survey of the theme of the two arrows is surely ample enough to satisfy the most exigent reader. I turn now to other renderings of Love. A seventeenth–century ballad is illustrated with a woodcut of Cupid holding a book.[30] Similarly on the title page of an anonymous collection of model love letters there is a cut depicting two lovers whom

Cupid is shooting with an abnormally long arrow pronged like a fork which has on its tip a book.[31] In neither case is the volume identified, but it is undoubtedly Ovid's *Ars Amoris*.

The early Elizabethan play *Tancred and Gismunda* has a prologue spoken by Cupid, who, according to the stage direction, "cometh out of the heavens in a cradle of flowers, drawing forth upon the stage, in a blue twist [cord] of silk, from his left hand, Vain Hope, Brittle Joy; and with a carnation twist of silk, from his right hand, Fair Resemblance, Late Repentance." [32] We need not bother about the lack of clear-cut antithesis between the two pairs of personifications for what is interesting here is the association of Love with flowers. Similarly Thomas Lodge describes Cupid as having a milk-white wreath over his eyes; [33] and we remember that in the "Allegory of Chastity" at Assisi Cupid wears a wreath.

It is not only in the famous "Masque" that Spenser introduces Cupid into *The Faerie Queene* but also in another episode (IV, 12, 13) where the poet consciously or unconsciously suggests the lay of Phyllis dominating Aristotle by riding on his back. When Marinell heard Florimell lamenting in the cave of Proteus his stony heart was touched and—

> Dame Venus sonne that tameth stubborne youth
> With iron bit, and maketh him abide,
> Till like a victor on his backe he ride,
> Into his mouth his maystring bridle threw,
> That made him stoupe, till he him did bestride:
> Then gan he make him tread his steps anew,
> And learne to love.

The adventures of Love (Cupid) or of lovers are popular subjects in many emblem books, and the specialized love-emblem books are a distinct subdivision of this literature. It is unnecessary to record them all here, nor in what now follows do I give precise references. Probably the best known is Van Veen's *Amorum Emblemata* (Antwerp, 1608) from which I have already taken various examples. It was available to English readers in an issue which had the texts in English.[34] The exquisite "miniature" volume *Fons Amoris sive Emblemata Amatoria*,[35] the *Emblemes Sacres* of "Monsieur Brunet Chanoine d'Auxerre" (Auxerre, 1687),[36] the *Typus Mundi*, which was one of Quarles' sources, Father Herman Hugo's *Pia Desideria Emblemata*, which was another, are among the most attractive collections. Van Veen led the way in adapting the Human Love series to the purposes of religious teaching, Cupid becoming Divine Love and the object of his solicitude the Soul. Among the most attractive themes are two already noted: Love changes Nature (affixing wings to an ass) and Blind Love carying lame Love. Others are: The shadow cast by Love is Envy; Love finds a way (his quiver is a boat, his bow is an oar, and he is rowing towards the Beloved); Love fashions unpromising material into shape (he watches a mother bear licking her cub); he scatters seed and the heads of infants protrude from the ground; Love is slow to depart (halting upon one leg and supported by a crutch he takes leave of a lady); two Loves hold torches, one lit from the other; his thoughts turn ever towards the Beloved (he holds a heliotrope), yet Love is changeable (he may hold a chameleon); from Love comes Eloquence (Love holds Mercury's caduceus); Love knows no bounds (an amusing design, for he is upsetting a Terminus with a violent kick); he tames Strength (Hercules is spinning); he conquers Fear (he is standing upon a dead rabbit); it is impossible to conceal love (he hides his torch under a barrel but the light shines through); he stops his ears so as not to hear the trumpet of Ill Fame; he hates Pride (he is stepping on a peacock's tail), and Avarice (he is forcing coins out of Avarice's purse); he tames Wrath (he is wrenching a sword from the hand of a man in armor). To these examples may be added a few motifs occurring in one of another series in which a religious lesson is taught. Love and Hate make the world (a top–shaped orb) go round by spinning it with whips. Love and Avarice (an old man with moneybags) fall from an orb upon which stands the peacock of Pride. From the hub of a wheel blown upon by four winds protrudes a cross upon which Love securely stands; this design has the motto: "In Cruce stat securus Amor." Divine Love, armed, approaches a fortress, guarded by devils, in which Human Love is imprisoned. Human love is nursed by Hope while Divine Love is near at hand. Divine Love and Human Love play together a game of pocket–pool, the latter aiming through a laurel crown, the former through an arch surmounted with a crown of thorns. Divine Love, hiding his sweet face behind a wrathful mask, chastises Human Love. Death cuts the chains binding Human Love who yearns towards Divine Love. Many designs of this sort are adaptations of the story of Cupid (equivalent to Divine Love) and Psyche (the Soul or Human Love).

Apart from all these allegories is the famous story of how Love and Death, having by mistake exchanged their arrows, pierce the wrong victims, Cupid transfixing an aged doting man and Death slaying two young lovers. In some versions Love and Death have slept side by side and on awaking each picks up the other's arrow and in other versions they have become drunk at an inn or in Bacchus' house, quarrel, and the arrows are by oversight exchanged. The story derives from Jean le Maire de Belges,[37] from one of the *Elegies* (II, 6) of Johannes Secundus, and from a poem by Joachim du Bellay.[38] Alciati does not show the meeting at the inn, the drunkenness, or the sleeping together but only the shooting at the wrong victims. In the edition of 1531 all four characters are standing, Cupid and Death at the right, their victims at the left.[39] In a French version, however, Cupid and Death hover in the air and their victims are on the ground below.[40] In another French version the artist has curiously confused the story, for Cupid has shot his bolt and a child is transfixed, while Death is aiming his dart at an old man.[41] Maurice Scève, followed by Peacham and Meyer, combines two parts of the story in one design: In the foreground Cupid and Death are asleep under a tree; in the background they aim the arrows.[42] Several English poets refer to the story. It is hinted at in *Venus and Adonis* (lines 947–948): "Love's golden arrow at him should have fled / And not Death's ebon dart to strike him dead." Into his translation of the *Jerusalem Delivered* Edward Fairfax introduced two lines that are not in the Italian original: "Death hath again exchanged his darts with Love, / And Cupid thus lets borrow'd arrows fly." [43] Richard Barnfield tells how the two, having become drunk "at swilling Bacchus' house," get into a fray in the course of which the arrows are exchanged and subsequently are wrongly aimed.[44] One of William Strode's characters says: "You know sometimes / That Death and Cupid do mistake their shafts." [45] Thomas May introduces a variation of the theme; one of his characters says:

> Black is Cupid's colour: Death and he
> Have chang'd their liveries now, as in the fable
> They did their quivers once.[46]

Thomas Collins' *The Teares of Love: or Cupids Progresse* (1615) has as its central motive the story of Cupid and Death exchanging arrows.

The most pretentious treatment of the story in English literature is James Shirley's masque *Cupid and Death* where large and curious liberties are taken with the theme. The two protagonists meet at a tavern, where their darts are exchanged not accidentally but by a mischievous Chamberlain. There follows the customary transformation scene, thus described: "The scene is changed into a pleasant Garden, a fountain in the midst of it; walks and arbours delightfully expressed; in divers places, Ladies lamenting over their Lovers slain by Cupid, who is discovered flying in the air." Presently "Old Men and Women with crutches" are struck by

Death with Cupid's arrow, and "they, admiring one another, let fall their crutches and embrace." In a grotesque antimasque the Chamberlain is smitten with love for two apes, but at the close the mistakes are rectified.[47]

A curious analogue to the Cupid and Death story is found in John Dickenson's poem "Cupid's Journey to Hell." Cupid escaped from his mother's care, posted to the Stygian lake, was welcomed by the bloodless ghosts, and was entertained by Pluto. Having quaffed much wine both host and guest fell asleep and while Cupid slept Proserpine stole his bow and quiver and gave them to Plutus. "Since then the god of gaine usurps loves roome." [48]

5. *The Five Senses*

Other companions along the Path of Life are the Five Senses. If controlled they are a help to Man; if given free rein they may be a peril to his immortal soul, often by leading him to Folly. In countless Netherlandish paintings and other designs the Five Senses are depicted, but there is by no means always a satirical or monitory intent in these examples. Before surveying in more detail English versions of the theme we may consider a few continental examples.

A colored Bavarian woodcut (ca. 1480) represents them in a very simple form. The Five Senses here occupy five of twenty–two little *tondi*, the others containing the Ten Commandments and the Seven Deadly Sins. Sight is a man's head before a mirror; Hearing is an ear with a flute and a lute beside it; Taste is a man licking a spoon; Smell is a rose; Touch is a hand. In this print there are no personifications; in four cases there are symbols, and Taste is represented by a typical action.[1]

Various editions and derivatives of *The Ship of Fools* contain illustrations of the folly of each of the Senses.[2] Particularly lively are those in Jean Drouyn's (Figs. 133–37) *La Grand Nefs des Folles, Composee suyvant les cinq sens de nature, selon l'Evangile de Monseigneur S. Matthieu, des cinq vierges qui ne prindrent point d'huylle avec elles pour mettre en leurs lampes* (Lyons, 1583). As the title indicates, this is an ingenious conflation of the original Ship of Fools with the Five Senses and the Five Foolish Virgins. Each cut illustrates a short poem, and each poem is followed by a long prose commentary. The satire is directed chiefly against women: Eve is said to have been the first fool, "la plus folle et mere de toutes follies," and all the Senses are female

personifications, each is in her own ship. Sight (Fig. 133) is a woman
with a comb and a mirror. A masculine fool assists other fools to climb
aboard. Hearing (Fig. 134) is personified by two women playing on
musical instruments. A he–fool beckons to other fools ashore. Smell (Fig.
135) is a woman with flowers in her hand. A he–fool has an open box
of perfumes on his knee and two women on shore are plucking flowers.
Taste (Fig. 136) is a woman presiding at a banquet where five male
fools are her guests on the ship. Touch (Fig. 137) is a woman kissing
a male fool. In the prow and in the stern other couples are embracing.[3]

The Senses usually have appropriate objects as attributes and this convention is quite firmly fixed, though there are occasional exceptions.
There are often symbolic animals also, and each Sense may be supplied
with both object and animal or one may have an object and another an
animal. As examples of the Senses and their attributes may be cited the
series in the tapestry of the "Dame a la Licorne" (ca. 1530) in the
Musée de Cluny, a set of five engravings by Frans Floris (ca. 1565),
and a sixteenth–century Swiss embroidered coverlet in the Victoria and
Albert Museum.[4] These all show, respectively, women with flowers and
a dog, musical instruments and a stag, fruit and a monkey, a mirror and
an eagle, and a parrot and a tortoise. This last, Touch, has no object.
Identical with these in four of the five personifications is the Barcheston
tapestry of the Five Senses.[5] Hearing, however, does not conform to the
convention. Placed in the center of the design and on a larger scale than
the other four, it is, instead, depicted by three women playing upon musical instruments. Perhaps this was a tapestry made for a music room.
Among the murals uncovered not long ago in a room in the tower of
Longthorpe near Peterborough is an interesting and, so far as I know,
unique representation of the subject: a wheel of the Five Senses. There
are no personifications; each sense is symbolized by an animal, in all but
one case (Taste which is a monkey) differing from the continental examples described above. Smell is a vulture, Touch a spider, Hearing a
boar, and Sight a cock. Behind the wheel is a majestic full–length figure
which has been tentatively identified as Reason, who controls the Senses.[6]

The Five Senses may indeed be controlled, but Pride and Riches all
too frequently tempt man to excess. In an engraving by Coornhert
Superbia offers a purse to a man from whose head six fine lines direct
attention to six details in the picture: a parrot, a dog, a vase of flowers,
a banquet, a painting on the wall, and some horses. The meaning of
the first five objects is obvious; the sixth probably represents luxurious
living.[7]

The most attractive of English versions of the theme is the series, occurring twice, in *A Booke of Christian Prayers* (1578), a beautiful volume to which I have referred in earlier chapters and which is a delight to the iconographer. All Five Senses are women, standing full-length in the outer margins. Each cut has on it a reference to a biblical text; only the book and chapter are given but in all but one case the verse intended is unmistakable. I now pass the series in review, quoting the precise verses.

Sight holds a mirror; an eagle is at her feet; the sun is above her. "Let thine eyes look right on, and let thine eyelids look straight before thee" (Proverbs 4:25). Hearing holds a lute; a drum and a trumpet are at her feet. "The ear of jealousy heareth all things; and the noise of murmurings is not hid" (Wisdom 1:10). Taste has a basket of fruit. "The ear trieth words, as the mouth tasteth meat" (Job 33:3). Smell is smelling flowers; a dog with its head raised is at her feet. "Give ye a sweet savour as frankincense" (Ecclesiasticus 39:14). Touch has a parrot on her wrist biting her thumb; a tortoise is at her feet. The accompanying reference to I Corinthians (6) is appropriate only in a general way, for St. Paul is there giving counsel against fornication and no single verse can be selected.[8]

The text of Richard Brathwaite's *Essayes upon the Five Senses* (second edition, 1635) consists of mere moralizing, uninteresting though edifying, but the engraved title page by William Marshall has some individuality of treatment. Around a globe on which a naked man is seated are five women, none labeled but all identifiable: Smell, Hearing, and Taste have the customary flower, lute, and fruit; Sight has no attribute and stares fixedly at the man; Touch holds a heart pierced with arrows, the appropriateness of which is obvious when we remember how often this Sense is represented by embracing lovers.

Thomas Jenner's shabbily manufactured book *A Worke for none but Angels and Men* (ca. 1655) [9] contains illustrations of the Five Senses some of which depart widely from the norm. Smell is a woman with a basket and a bouquet of flowers; in a corner of the plate is a dog's head. Hearing is a gallant. Sight is a woman with a mirror and a telescope. Taste is a female gallant, a "roaring girl," smoking a pipe. Touch, which is called "Feeling," is a woman whose hand is being bitten by a parrot. To some of the plates deplorably crude verses are attached, an example is Feeling's quatrain:

> When Hearing, Seeing, Tasting, Smelling's past:
> Feeling (as long as life remains) doth last.

Mayde reach my Lute, I am not well indeede:
O pitty—mee, my bird hath made mee bleede.

It is a relief to turn from such jejune amateurishness in order to mention the robust designs of the Senses by George Glover and the even
more attractive tapestries woven at Mortlake (at the time of Charles I)
from designs almost certainly by Cleyn. The only novelty here is that
Feeling is represented by a reclining woman who has by her a squirrel.
The popularity of this series in England is evinced by the publication of
a volume of engravings with the oddly bilingual title: *Quinque Sensum
descriptio. In co picturae genere quod (Grotesche) vocant intali. F. Clein,
inv. 1646. Sould by Thomas Howlett at his Shop neere Temple Barre.*
These highly ornamented baroque plates follow the established conventions and introduce no novelty in actions or attributes.

The well planned and well written allegorical drama *Lingua* is the
most ambitious treatment of the theme of the Five Senses in English
literature.[10] Probably performed at Cambridge (ca. 1603–4) it was
first published in 1607 and by 1657 had gone through six editions,
evidence of a popularity rather surprising considering its academic tone
and merciless length. All the editions are anonymous but the author was
probably John Tomkins. The plot, involving two rivalries, is ingenious
and amusing. Lingua, the Tongue, a female personification, claims a
place among the senses and manages to involve the Five in a quarrel for
precedence among themselves. The case is adjudicated by Common
Sense who announces that Sight and Hearing are of higher rank than
Taste, Touch, and Smell, for the former pair serve the Commonwealth
by exercising vigilance while the latter trio benefit only individuals.
Lingua's place among them is partially allowed, it being conceded that
the Sense of Speech is an endowment possessed by women. Among numerous other personifications are Memoria who repeatedly interrupts
the dialogues to tell of his reminiscences of times and events long past,
and Tobacco who delivers himself of a few short speeches in incomprehensible gibberish.

6. *The Seven Liberal Arts or Sciences*

The Seven Liberal Arts or Sciences—the alternative term was employed to embrace all knowledge based upon Reason and independent
of Revelation—are not only preparations for the Pilgrimage but companions on it. They are, however, not always personified; Dante, for example, conceives them as the seven walls of the Castle of Learning. How-

ever, Dante, as well as Boethius, *The Seven Sages of Rome*, the great
fresco in the Spanish Chapel of Santa Novella, and other medieval
renderings of the subject, must be omitted from a brief discussion limited
to English literature and a few samplings from the arts of design. I begin
with Lydgate, who is a connecting link between the Middle Ages and
the beginnings of the Renaissance. At the Triumphal Entry of Henry VI,
designed by Lydgate, there was a "richly arrayed" tabernacle in Corn-
hill in which were Dame Sapience and "the seven sciences called lyberall."
Each was accompanied (as in the Spanish Chapel and in many other
representations of the subject) by a famous patron and practitioner of
the art. Music was particularly attractive, for along with Boethius there
was a company of scholars who played upon stringed instruments and an
organ to exhibit their craft to the king.[1] In Lydgate's *A Pageant of
Knowledge* Logic and Arithmetic do not appear, their places are taken
by Philosophy and Metaphysics.[2] In *The Court of Sapience* (Chap. II),
which is perhaps by Lydgate, a castle is described in which dwells the
Lady Divine Theology, attended by seven ladies, the Arts. Contemporary with the poet were two Arras tapestries woven in silver thread
and representing the "Seven Sciences." [3]

The two sets of the so-called "tarots of Mantegna" include, with
much else, the Seven Arts.[4] One set is much like the other save in the
case of Arithmetic. Grammar holds a vase and has a three-sided ferule;
Logic holds a little dragon beneath a semi-transparent veil; Rhetoric,
in armor and with a sword, has at her feet two *putti* blowing on trumpets;
and Geometry, a three-quarter figure, floats on a cloud with a square,
a circle, and a triangle in the sky beside her. In one of the designs Arithmetic is counting coins; in the other she holds a tablet upon which
are numerals. Music plays upon a pipe, musical instruments and a swan
are by her, and Astrology, wearing a starry crown, holds a book and a
wand. Following Music and preceding Astrology the two series are enlarged with two more personifications (Hind, nos. 27 and 28): Poetry,
piping by a fountain and holding a vase turned downward, and Philosophy, in armor with a spear and a shield marked with a gorgon's head.
Culminating the series is Theology (Hind, no. 30) rising three-quarter-
length behind a hemisphere spangled with stars. This figure is *bifrons*,
male and female. To attempt to interpret the details of attributes and
postures in these exquisite engravings would lead us too far afield.

The woodcuts in Gregorius Reisch's *Margarita Philosophica* (Basle,
various editions between 1496 and 1583) are well known but they must
be described both because they are representative of the established convention and because they influenced an English poet. There are sepa-

rate illustrations of each of the Arts. 1. Grammar leads a child into a Tower, the famous "Tower of Doctrine," or "Tipus Grammatice." On its lower story are Logic, Rhetoric, and Arithmetic; on a higher, Music, Geometry, and Astronomy; above them are Natural and Moral Philosophy, and at the apex is Theology. Rhetoric has a scroll, Grammar a hornbook, Arithmetic an abacus, Music a lyre, Geometry a compass, and Astronomy an armillary sphere. Logic with no attribute gesticulates argumentatively. Philosophy, a winged woman with three heads, presides over the Arts. In the lower corners of the design Aristotle represents Natural Philosophy, Seneca Moral Philosophy, and at the top Divine Philosophy is represented by the Four Fathers of the Church. (Three of the other six Arts are attended by famous practitioners and three are not.) This cut is copied on the title page of Stephen Hawes' *Pastime of Pleasure* (1517).[5] 2. Logic, a woman equipped with a sword, "Syllogismus," and a bow, "Questio," and blowing a trumpet, stands near a forest called "Sylva opinionum" into which a winding path marked "Insolubilita" leads while Logic's path is straight and does not enter the forest. A dog, "Veritas," is chasing a hare, "Problem," and another dog, "Falsitas," is sniffing. 3. Enthroned Rhetoric has issuing from her mouth a sword and a palm branch. Cicero and other devotees surround her, and among them two turbaned figures in postures of abasement remind us not only of such paintings as Traini's "Triumph of St. Thomas" in Pisa but also of the many Christian controversies with Islam. 4. Arithmetic's dress is embroidered with numbers and signs, and she holds two books. Boethius and Pythagoras sit at two tables below her. 5. Music holds a tablet with musical notes. Four unlabeled figures play upon instruments, a fifth holds a baton, a sixth a balance indicating measure or rhythm. 6. Geometry is using a compass. Five unlabeled persons are engaged in measuring land or holding a quadrant or a right–angle rule. 7. Astronomy is with Ptolemy, who is taking an observation. An armillary sphere is near him.[6]

In the narrative of Graund Amour's progress through the Arts which occupies so much of *The Pastime of Pleasure* (348–2,913) Hawes imagines Grammar, Logic, Rhetoric, and Arithmetic to be in separate chambers of a single tower; Music is in a tabernacle in another tower; Geometry in yet another tower; and Astronomy in a pavilion. The separation of Arithmetic from the other members of the Quadrivium and her association with the Trivium is noteworthy. The Seven Arts are said to be the daughters of Dame Doctrine, but Hawes does not lead up and beyond them to Theology.

Contemporary with Hawes is a series of German engravings (ca.

1500) which have some unusual features. Grammar is a man sowing a ploughed field; Rhetoric a miller with a sack on his back, entering his mill; Logic a baker reaching with his *pêle* into an oven. Thus the Trivium holds together grain, flour, and bread. Arithmetic is a merchant at his counting table, Geometry a carpenter measuring a building, Music six smiths beating upon an anvil (compare Tubal Cain in the Spanish Chapel), and Astronomy an artist engaged upon a painting of the heavens. Thus all the Arts are visualized in terms of trades and crafts.[7]

Richard Grafton's device shows the Arts in an entirely conventional fashion except that, as I have noted in another context at the end of Chapter 4, Rhetoric has a cloud or mist or smoke coming from her mouth.[8] There are few features of interest in an Italian series (1544) by the engraver who signs himself "B." However, each Art is a nude woman, which is unusual. Dialectic (that is, Logic) holds a pair of scales; Rhetoric has her fingers in the position of argument.[9]

Limited to a single Art but amusing, though over ingenious, is the engraving of "The Tower of Grammar" by Heinrich Vogtherr the Younger (1548). A child is climbing steps labeled "alphabet," "syllabary," and so forth, and then ascends the stories of the Tower, each representing one of the parts of speech. Grammar as the necessary support of more advanced disciplines is clumsily emblematized by Joannes Sambucus, a crouching woman who has on her head and shoulders three women: History with an hourglass and a lighted torch, Rhetoric gesticulating and brandishing a spear, and Dialectic searching (as the text explains) for Truth in a well which yawns before her.[10] Several refreshing novelties may be observed in a series of the Arts by Frans Floris the Elder. No patrons or practitioners appear; however, with the exception of Music, there are books nearby and, with the exception of Geometry, these bear labels indicating writings appropriate to the Art. There are other eccentric features which I cannot explain: One of Arithmetic's books is entitled "Abraham"; Dialectic has a bird perched on her head and there is a frog on her books and on the floor; another frog reaches up the surface of a globe that Geometry is measuring. It may also be noted that behind Rhetoric three actors are performing on a scaffold while spectators stand round and that Astrology, winged, with the signs of the planets on the hem of her garment, and an eagle beside her, takes the place of Astronomy.

In the previous chapter I have remarked that the Arts, like the Ages of Life, are sometimes under the patronage of the Planets. Raffaello Borghini follows this tradition when he links Grammar with the Moon,

Dialectic with Mercury, Rhetoric with Venus, Arithmetic with the Sun, Music with Mars, Geometry with Jupiter, and Astrology with Saturn.[11] These companionships are not based upon any logical connection between each pair; they merely follow the ascending order of the two sequences. Since I have quoted in the Appendix Weever's description of the adornment of Sir Nicholas Bacon's banqueting house at St. Alban's with paintings of the Liberal Arts, no more need be said about this version. Nor is it necessary to do more than mention the Liberal Arts on one of Stephen Harrison's Arches of Triumph. The forlorn, neglected state of the Arts at Oxford and Cambridge, lamented by John Lane in *Tom Tel–Troths Message,* and the sneering boastfulness of Flattery, who is more influential than the Arts, which is the subject of Fulwell's *Eyghth liberall Science,* have received attention in an earlier chapter. George Glover's series of prints is quite conventional and offers no opportunity for comment.

One of the eight small compartments surrounding the central representation in Robert Vaughan's engraved title page of Brathwaite's *English Gentleman* (1630) is called "Education." A grave, bearded man holds in one hand a shield on which are two human breasts (Nourishment) and in the other a bundle of rods (Correction) and surrounding him are the Liberal Arts, quite conventionally portrayed except that Logic has two keys, a rare attribute. But when we come to Brathwaite's discussion of the Arts we note one surprising irregularity: Astronomy is not mentioned and for it Medicine is substituted, with Hippocrates as a patron.[12]

It might have been expected that the famous Cambridge University play, *The Pilgrimage to Parnassus* (acted 1598), would contain much matter germane to our subject, for the way to the Hill of the Muses leads through the Liberal Arts, but the Arts are not personified. Philomusus and Studioso pass through the island called "Dialectica" where their feet may be blistered by the crags. In the land of Rhetoric they find a "smoother pathway" and rejoice to hear the nightingale "Don Cicero" sing sweetly and many another bird "make tunefull melodie." In the land of Poetry they are tempted to linger rather than spend their "blooming age / In sadd dull plodding on philosophers." Repeatedly they are warned by disillusioned sceptics that Learning is not a path to prosperity or preferment. And that is all.[13]

Less interesting to the literary historian but far more rewarding from our special point of view is another University play, Barten Holyday's *Marriages of the Arts,* performed by the students of Christ Church College, Oxford, in 1618.[14] This is confusedly allegorical in its action and contains a tedious amount of erudite jocosity but the costumes of the Arts are described in detail and as they were both striking and costly they command our attention. The traditional Seven were enlarged to twelve, as we shall see.

Grammar's breeches were "close to his thigh" and "his stockings garter'd above knee." One wonders if this was a fashion for boys. "A Ferula at his back" is a little puzzling: Does it mean strapt to his back or, more likely, embroidered on his jacket? Rhetoric wore a green silk gown. Her coronet was "beset with red and white roses" which perhaps, by recalling the Wars of the Roses, suggested rival disputants. In the coronet's front "was exprest a garland of bayes with a palm of a hand in the middest, and round about the border, above the roses, were describ'd palmes of hands." With these palms one may compare the argumentative gesticulation often given to Rhetoric. Logic, a man, wore a wide–sleeved gown and a square cap. Arithmetic wore a green silk gown. On her coronet was a "Table of Multiplication" with the nine radical figures and a cipher about its border. Geometry was a man wearing a pyramidal hat. On his clothes geometrical figures, and the embroidery on his cloak depicted a man measuring the height of a tower with a Jacob's staff. Music was "a merry wench" dressed in "red–branched velvet." Her coronet was very ornate: At its front was "the Table of the Gammut, with the first sixe Musicall notes"; above was a bagpipe and a harp; on its border were other instruments; and at the top of the crossed arches of the coronet was a figure of Fame sounding a trumpet. Astronomy wore an azure gown and a mantle "seeded with stars." The tiara upon her head had the sun and moon on opposite sides, the "seven stars" (that is, the planets), "and behind, starres promiscuously."

Of the Arts, then, three were men and four were women. With the Seven Arts were five other Liberal Studies or Disciplines; three of these were women, two men. Astrology was a woman wearing "a dark starry Mantle." Her tiara had round it dim stars, on its front was "the Scheme of a Nativity" (a horoscope), and on either side the sun and moon in eclipse. The differentiation from Astronomy, the dimness, darkness, and eclipses, is interesting testimony to the growing discredit of Astrology at this period. Geography, a man, wore clothes of green, white, red, and blue, symbolizing indubitably (though it is not so stated) the Four Elements: green for Earth, white for Water, red for Fire, and blue for Air. His cloak was embroidered with the two hemispheres and his cape with the two poles. Physics, Physica, that is "Natural Philosophy," a woman in a green gown, held "Ceres horn" in her arms. On the front of her coronet was shown a woman giving suck to two infants, and on its border were beasts and trees. History's gown was of green velvet. Her coronet was bordered with the Nine Worthies and on its top stood a figure of Time. Ethics was a man with a gray beard, dressed in black, with a velvet pouch and a walking staff.

7. *The Ladder of Life*

Having made the choice of the Right Path, Man, assaulted by temptations, guarded by the Virtues, with companions or solitary, sets out upon his Pilgrimage. There are other routes than the Path by which he may journey from Birth to Death—and beyond Death to the Celestial City. I have already described the "Spiegel der vernuft," or "Speculum Rationis," the impressive German print showing a bridge across which a Pilgrim is making his way and at whose further end is Death. There is here room but to glance at the analogous subject of the Ladder of Life. This is grounded upon interpretations of Jacob's dream (Genesis 28:12), popularized in an "instruction" called the "Scala Paradisi" sometimes attributed to St. Augustine or St. Bernard,[1] and best represented in English literature in Walter Hilton's moral and gently mystical treatise *The Scale of Perfection* (fourteenth century). Among many allegorical engravings of the Scala Paradisi four may be noted as examples. One is in Antonio Bettini's *Monte Sancto di Dei* (Florence, 1477) which shows a young monk climbing a ladder. Each rung is named, Humility, Fear, Piety, Knowledge, the Stoic Virtues, and so forth, the uprights of the ladder are "Oratione" and "Sacramento," and between the upper six rungs are the letters of the word "Perseveranza." [2] A fine large cut in Johannes Junior's *Scala Coeli* (Strassburg, 1483) shows the nine steps of the ladder, each labeled, from Confession, Satisfaction, and so forth, up to Contemplation of Perfection. Angels are assisting Man to ascend and devils are attempting to seduce him.[3] An Italian allegory shows Meekness ascending the ladder with a lamb following her while Pride is falling headlong down another ladder into hellmouth.[4] The ladder may be set on rocks amid a stormy sea, but the climber is steadied by a hand reaching from the sky.[5] The concept is simplified into a mere diagram without any personifications in Domenico Benivieni's *Scala della Vita Spirituale* (Florence, ca. 1490–1500) where a ladder ascends through the elements and spheres to heaven.[6] A similar concept is that of the Hill of Virtue. Thus, in Father David's *Veridicus Christianus* (no. 31) the Seven Virtues sit upon a hill up which three men are toiling on hands and knees; a fourth is tumbling down (Fig. 138). A fine emblem of much later date brings together the hill and the ladder. A man with a heavy burden on his back—and we think of Bunyan's Christian—pauses to rest, looking meanwhile at a winding path that leads up a hill at the top of which another man is beginning to mount a ladder which he has placed against the sky.[7]

Two fifteenth–century works of French literature are among the antecedents of the Tudor–Stuart allegories of the Pilgrimage and of *Pilgrim's Progress* and may have influenced them. They have attracted the attention of students of Bunyan and need receive here no more than a bare notice. One is Phillippe de Mézières' *Le Songe du Vieil Pelerin* (of uncertain date), a long and tedious prose narrative of the Way of Salvation in which the Pilgrim encounters various adventures along the road. There are some personifications but none of much interest.[8] The other is Olivier de la Marche's allegorical poem *Le Chevalier Délibré* (Gouda, 1486–90).[9] The Author ("l'Acteur") tells his own story, which does not encompass his entire life but his latter years. He is warned by Thought that in the Forest of Fate he must meet Accident and Weakness. He receives instructions from the hermit Understanding, engages in combat with Age, is tempted near the Palace of Love, and is welcomed at the Manor of Good Hap. At a tourney he witnesses the death of Charles of Burgundy, overcome by Accident—an incident conflating allegory and history in a manner to which there are English parallels. At the close of the poem l'Acteur returns to the hermit to make preparations for his encounter with Death.

Quantities of English sermons, homilies, and pious meditations are, as would be expected, concerned with the Pilgrimage. Of these many have been described by Wharey in his monograph on Bunyan's sources, by Professor William Haller, or by other scholars. I limit myself to those I know at first hand, sometimes merely quoting the significant title, in other cases adding brief comments. The title suffices to give an indication of the subject of Abraham Fleming's *The Footepath of Faith, leading to the Highwaie of Heaven. Whereunto is annexed the Bridge to blessedness* (1581).[10] A certain "I.D." who has not been identified compiled a series of apposite biblical texts entitled *A Hedgerow of Busshes, Brambles, and Briers: or a Fielde full of Tares, Thistles, and Time: Of the vanities and vaine delightes of this Worlde, leading the way to eternall Damnation* (1598) which is, needless to say, a warning to those in danger of choosing the wrong Path. There is no allegory save in the title of *The Narrow Way and the Last Judgement* by an unidentified "G.B." (1607); and the scholar in quest of allegory is again disappointed, despite its promising title, when he reads William Attersoll's *The Pathway to Canaan: or an Exposition upon the xx and xxi Chapters of the Book of Numbers. Wherein is declared, how the Faithful behaved themselves in their Journey: Their lets and stumbling-blockes in the way* (1609). Edward Chetwind's *The Strait Gate and the Narrow Way to Life* (1612) is a series of sermons on Luke 13:24, and the epigraphs below the title are from Jeremiah 6:16 and John 14:6—all texts occurring often in sermons on the Path of Life. More interesting is Thomas Cheaste's *The Christian Path-Way* (1613) where the theme of the Choice of the Two Paths is carefully developed. The warning (p. 16) that "If thou wander out of this way, into the pleasant paths of sinn . . . Sathan will take thee prisoner" reminds me of Jan de Cock's impressive panel painting (ca. 1522–1530?) of a Pilgrim encountering the Devil. Satan, attempting to disguise himself, has a staff, a dish, and a rosary, but his bloodstained feet have claws, and the blank, sinister expression on his face is unforgettable.[11] A sermon of really impassioned eloquence is Immanuel Bourne's *The True Way of a Christian, to the New Jerusalem* (1622), preached at Paul's Cross in 1617. This is not allegorical but often hovers on the verge of allegory, as in a passage (p. 119) on the blessed state of the man who resists "those three entizing harlots, the world, the flesh, and the devil."

The theme of the Path crops up in many places. Thus, in George Turberville's version of Mancinus, *A plaine Path to perfect Vertue* (1568), the translator supplies a prologue of commendation, not paralleled in the earlier English rendering by Alexander Barclay,[12] in which the allegory is developed. Turberville counsels: "March on, let Mancine be your guide, if he the banner beare / And stately standerde in the fielde, you neede not stande in feare" [13]—he will steer you clear of labyrinth of loathsome sin and lead you to the lodge and palace of Lady Virtue, to Justice, and to that "famous Dame" Fortitude. Richard Robinson's remark that "Mannes life is a waifarying or travillyng" introduces the story of a young man put up for the night in an inn where by his bed were a lion, a dragon, a bear, serpents, and toads: "This bed mans life is likened to, / Where in a short time he doeth lye." The creatures are symbolic, the toads and serpents, for example, Man's guilty conscience, and the bear is Death.[14] A variant of the same metaphor is Walter Colman's curious conceit that different types of men put up at different inns:

> The World's the rode, and we the passengers
> Are billeted at severall Innes: the Crowne
> Some entertaines, and for Embassadors
> The Angel is reserv'd; others goe downe
> Unto the Miter or the Cardinals Hat;
> Some to the Plough, some unto this, some that.[15]

Richard Brathwaite's theme of the prodigal Pilgrim's return, under the guidance of Repentance and Humility, to the right homeward path connects our allegory with the parable of the Prodigal Son.[16] The Pilgrimage is the subject of a charming design in Wither's *Emblemes* (Bk. IV, no. 1). Here the Soul is guided by Divine Love through the maze or labyrinth of Life by a cord with which Divine Love, in a tower high above the maze, pulls her in the right direction. But the sluggishness of the human Will is emblematized by Quarles (Bk. I, no. 13) as a man mounted upon an ass (Sloth) riding slowly up a hill on whose top is a celestial globe, with a snail crawling before him. A pretty couplet imparts the lesson: "When our dull soules direct their thoughts to Thee / The soft-paced Snayle is not so slow as wee."

Turning now to more elaborate treatments of the theme of the Pilgrimage in Tudor and Stuart literature, we note first Hawes' two major poems to which I have already made many references, *The Example of Vertu* [17] and *The Pastime of Pleasure*. The pattern of both is that of the Path of Life; it is, however, often obscured by erudite digressions. In the former poem Youth, who at the age of forty receives the new name Virtue, tells his own story. At the outset Lady Discretion guides him across the waters of Vainglory to a fair island where they visit the palace of Dame Fortune, the tabernacle of Dame Hardiness (Courage), the tower of Dame Sapience, and the "solemn and royal mansion" of Dame Nature. These four ladies are engaged in a lawsuit and Youth sees and hears them pleading at the bar of Dame Justice, who pronounces a compromise verdict: all four are of service to Man and all are to help him in his need. They accept the verdict, and while three of the ladies vanish Dame Sapience lingers to give counsel to Youth as to his further journey. She tells him of a fitting bride for him and then entrusts him to Lady Discretion. The narrative, which had moved with tedious slowness during the trial scene, now picks up momentum. Youth and Discretion enter a wild wood; the sun has set and the moon is "horned and nothing clear"; ferocious beasts are abroad: the lion, the wolf, the bear, and a panther must be close by, for though he is not seen his proximity can be detected by the sweetness of his breath. With startling, dreamlike suddenness and clarity—and Hawes is here displaying genuine imaginativeness—"a lady excellent," young and lusty, appears riding on a goat and invites Youth to pleasure. When "Nay sayd dyscrecyon that may not be," Lechery vanishes. Then the old lady Pride, riding on an elephant, boasts of her riches and invites Youth to accompany her, but he rejects her advances. Notwithstanding the companionship of Discretion he then finds himself in the maze of Worldly Business where he wanders to and fro. His best mentor reappears: "Sapience!" he exclaims, "Who thought to have found you here!" She replies, very beautifully: "I have bene nere you oftentymes syth my departynge / And have ben cause of your good gydynge." She and Discretion now lead Youth across the perilous bridge of Worldly Vanity and they come to the Kingdom of Grace. Sapience presents him to the King of Love and tells the King that Youth desires to marry his daughter, Dame Cleanness. The King replies that the suitor must first slay the three–headed Dragon and the combat follows, of which I have given an account in an earlier chapter. Youth, returning in triumph, is met at the gate of the King's palace by a company of fair ladies: Perseverance, Faith, Charity, Prayer, and Love. The wooing of Dame Cleanness follows; the King gives his consent; and Youth, whose name is now changed by decree to Virtue, is conducted to rest in the chamber of Clean Conscience where a little barking whelp kept awake those whose conscience was uneasy, but Virtue slept soundly. On the following day there was the wedding, attended by various saints and personifications— a slightly ridiculous but naively sweet piece of narrative, and the marriage feast at which St. Peter served the company "our swete lordes body." We are then suddenly reminded that we have to do with the Pilgrimage of Human Life, for

> By this tyme was I .xl yeres olde
> And desyred for to lyve in peas
> For I beganne to growe two folde
> And my feblenes dyd sore encrease.[18]

An angel shows him a vision of "the peynes of hell full of great wo," a place of darkness, where were "black and tedious" devils and some "chrysten soules" burned while others were in ice. At the close of the narrative Virtue is guided to heaven, "the realm of delectation," "the land of infinite gladness," filled with sweet tunes and azure air, and he joins the company of the saints. There is a concluding prayer for

Henry VII and for the hopeful Prince Henry, the heir apparent, and with a modest comparison of his own work to that of Gower, Chaucer, and Lydgate, Hawes apologizes to his readers for his "rudeness." Admitting the validity of an apology for halting rimes and rhythms, for "aureate" vocabulary, and for tedious divigations, I cannot but hold that modern scholars, even Mr. C. S. Lewis in *The Allegory of Love,* have not done justice to this beautiful poem.

The same qualities and defects are apparent in Hawes' second and better known poem, *The Pastime of Pleasure.* Graund Amour's courtship and marriage to La Bel Pucell is the center of whatever plot there is, but that story, deliberately imitative of the chivalrous romances of the Middle Ages, is repeatedly interrupted by the hero's experiences with each of the Liberal Arts and by the conflicts in which he engages with the three–headed and seven–headed giants and with the fiery monster, Privy Malice. After their marriage the hero and heroine live happily for many years, till Age intrudes accompanied by Avarice. Then, as in *The Castle of Perseverance* and in *Everyman,* comes the summons of Death, and there follows the solemnly impressive pageant of Fame, Time, and Eternity. Here the poet attains his best poetry, and the only lines which posterity has held in fond memory:

> For though the day be never so longe,
> At length the belles ringeth to evensonge.

Precisely contemporary with the publication (1530) of *The Example of Vertu* was the publication of the first English version of *The Table of Cebes the Philosopher.* The name of the translator, Sir Francis Poyntz, is not given on the title page but is supplied in the preliminary address of "The Printer to the Reader." The book is not dated; as, however, Poyntz died in June 1528 the guess in the Scottish Text Society that it appeared ca. 1530 is near the mark, if it was a posthumous publication. The number of editions, translations, and paraphrases [19] recorded in the British Museum Catalogue testifies to the popularity of this apocryphal treatise during the Renaissance.

The most famous treatment of the "Table" or "Tablet" is, however, the great woodcut by Hans Holbein the Younger.[20] This adorned the title page of Froben's edition of Erasmus' New Testament (Basle, 1522), Froben's address to the reader in his edition of the *De Civitate Dei* (1522), and is found in other works of the same press.[21] Holbein generally did not sign his woodcuts but he evidently considered this too important for anonymity and it bears his double "H." To recreate or reconstruct the fictitious lost picture described in the *Table* was a more difficult and less rewarding undertaking than the analogous case of the lost painting by Apelles, descriptions of which inspired Botticelli and other artists to recreate the "Calumny." Holbein's design is crowded and is well nigh incomprehensible to those who have not read the *Table*, and the text is very arid without the accompanying life and movement of the great woodcut. Holbein conformed so closely to his literary source that a summary of the text, to which we shall come in a moment, will serve as the best description of the cut.

Holbein was in England in 1527–8. Among the works he accomplished during this visit were an oil painting and two drawings of Sir Nicholas Poyntz who was a nephew of Sir Francis Poyntz the translator of the treatise. The conjecture is therefore not only pleasant but valid that since Holbein was in touch with this family it was probably knowledge of the cut, and possibly a suggestion from the artist, that led to the English version.

The "table" was a picture set up in a temple of Saturn; the description of it is in the form of questions and answers [22] addressed to and given by a "fatherly man" who explained "what the invencion of this Table betokeneth." As he gave his interpretation he pointed out details with his staff. A circular "place" within a wall is called Life, the wall represents the limits of life and the children outside it are souls not yet born. By the entrance is an old man, Genius, who counsels all who enter. Within the gate is a path leading from the center of the picture and zigzagging uphill to Felicity who is at the top center. Hard by the entrance sits Deceit, a woman of alluring countenance who proffers a drink of which all comers take more or less, thus imbibing Ignorance and Error with the consequence that "they cannot find whiche is the trewe way in the life, but wander unadvisedly." Fortune, surrounded by many men and women, some rejoicing, others mourning, is mentioned:

> But that woman, what is she, the whiche seemeth as it were one blind and madde: and standeth upon a rounde stone? She is called, quod he, Fortune [;] she is not only blynde, but also madde and deaffe. What doeth she? She walketh every where, quoth he, and from some she taketh rychesse: to some other she geveth: and from them by and by she taketh agayne that, that she gave them before. . . . What token is that, quoth I, that she standeth upon [,] a round stone? what betokeneth that? Marie that her geftes be bothe uncertaine and unstable.

Beyond the gate are four women resembling harlots: Incontinence, Riot, Covetise, and Flattery. Those who yield to their enticements consume all that Fortune has given them, and thereafter they are delivered to be tormented in a cave at whose mouth are the sluttish, ragged women, Punishment with whips, Heaviness with her head between her knees, Sorrow plucking her own hair, lean and pale Sluggishness "or lacke of courage," and her brother Wailyng. With these Man must pass his life unless Repentance be sent by Fortune. If she comes and he harkens to her, she will set him in the path to True Learning but even so, there is danger lest he be beguiled by False Opinion, also called Untrue Learning, a woman who, seeming "veraie nette and pure," deceives foolish folk such as some poets, orators, logicians, astronomers, and philosophers of different sects. Only by drinking a "pourgeyng vertue" may anybody escape from False Opinion, and though they may escape "thei shall never be without some evill, for these studies sake."

Above this level of the picture there is a desert through which the path leads to another gate. This is the way to True Learning, steep, rough, stony, and strait; few are shown climbing it and from it it is easy to fall headlong. Those who toil upwards are encouraged by two godly women, Continence and Sufferance, who giving the aspirant strength and boldness draw him on. At the summit of the steep cliff is a fair meadow, the habitation of blessed folk, and in its midst is yet another gate by which on a square and securely set stone stands True Learning with her daughters, Truth and Persuasion, beside her. To all who arrive she gives a drink that purges them of ignorance and error, and she brings them to the Virtues, fair women simply dressed, Knowledge, Strength of Mind, Justice, Goodness, Temperance, Soberness, Liberality, Continence, and Meekness. The Virtues bring the traveler to their mother, Felicity, who sits in a porch on a high place at "the toppe of all the other compasses" (that is, the circuits of the winding path). Him who has attained this height Felicity crowns "as a man the whiche hath overcome marveilouse great battailes" against Ignorance, Deceit, Sorrow, and other enemies. The crown imparts to its recipient a clearsighted realization of the wretchedness of surrendering to the temptations through which he has passed. Here the allegory, both text and woodcut, ends, but the sage who has expounded it to the inquirer has more to say, particularly of the functions of Genius, and he concludes with philosophical, ethical, and educational advice.

It is difficult or in fact impossible to determine the influence of either the text or the woodcut in Tudor and Stuart England, for allegories of the "Scholastic Pilgrimage" are necessarily more or less similar and the likeness may be due rather to identity of theme than to direct borrowing. The only design by an English artist that is even remotely suggestive of Holbein's is William Marshall's title page of Wither's *Emblemes*. At all events Poyntz's version of the *Table* sufficed to supply any English demand for eighty years; the Jacobean version by John Healey is quite independent of Poyntz.[23]

In chronological order we have next to note a poem, *The Travayled Pilgrime, bringing newes from all partes of the worlde, such like scarce harde of before* (1569).[24] The author's name is not given, but the dedication is signed "S.B." and there is no doubt that Stephen Bateman wrote it. In the dedication he writes: "I have painted forth the fonde devise of man, and the straunge Combats that he is daylie forced unto. . . . The sayde Pilgrime bringeth newes out of all partes of the world, by which newes is signified the straunge inventions of man. . . . I write this . . . by way of friendly exhortation, exhorting every faythfull Christian, to have such regarde to this their Pilgrimage here on earth, that in the lyfe to come, they may enjoy the happie gaine of endelesse felicitie." The story, told by the Pilgrim himself, is illustrated with several woodcuts. At the opening of the poem is a cut showing the Pilgrim clad in armor, with the spear of Good Government, the shield of Hope, and the sword of Courage. Reason and Truth stand by him. The poem begins as he sets out upon his travels riding upon his horse, Will. He meets with Understanding who entertains him at a banquet, served by Diligence, where the bread is Sobriety and Peace and the wine is Love, and in Understanding's house he sleeps and is refreshed. Guided by his host he visits the House of Reason where he sees the Seven Virtues and wishes to remain, but Understanding urges him to pursue his journey, for he has not yet sufficient knowledge of life. His restive horse "beginnes to runne in the fielde of Worldly pleasure" but the vext Pilgrim forces him back into the road, and there follows an encounter with Age who counsels him to avoid the Forest of Lost Time and obey the dictates of Sapience. "The Author agreeth to the counsel of Age." Presently, however, he rides deliberately into the Path of Deceit and comes to the Palace of Disordered Lives, "A thousand sounds of instruments most musicall I harde / Whose harmonie was callde Deceit." In the Palace dwell "a thousand counterfeited shapes, fresh Ladies fit for Pan," who draw their victims "into most filthy life." Memory, however, comes to his aid, he escapes their wiles, and thence passes into the Desert of Age where he witnesses the conquest of many fair women—

Dame Daintie, Dame Coy, Dame Pickthanke, Mistress Nice—by Old Age: "of force he made them bow." The *Ubi sunt?* motive is now introduced into the allegory and it impinges upon history: Memory and the Pilgrim talk of the dreadful combats in which mighty champions have perished at the hands of Death. A long digression follows on the death of King Henry VIII and (in less detail) King Edward VI. A woodcut shows Henry, announced by Death's herald with a skull and crossbones, entering the lists presided over by Thanatos where he engages in a combat with Defiance and where Dolor, Despair, and Debilitie are among the champions. After Henry and Edward are both slain the Pilgrim and Memory behold "the auncient showe and Funerals of mighty Conquerours past." At this point in the poem a cut shows a knight sitting on a tomb, a skeleton at his feet, and crowns strewn on the ground. Then, surprisingly, there is a triumphal entry of Queen Elizabeth whom Dolor and Debilitie are "as yet not able to resist." [25] From this historical and topical digression the allegory then returns to its authentic theme. Memory counsels the Pilgrim to provide and arm himself against Thanatos. The Pilgrim retires to the chamber called Pain, whence he issues out for the final combat with Death.

Far finer than Bateman's clumsy allegory, very popular in its own day and for long afterwards, and lately brought back into notice is *The Voyage of the Wandering Knight* (1581),[26] a prose narrative translated by William Goodyear from the French of Jean de Cartigny. The story is told by the protagonist with two chapters containing comments by the actual author. "When I had passed," the Knight begins, "three weekes of the yeares of mine age: that is to say, my Infancie, Childage, and Youth, which make together one and twentie yeares, I entred into the age of a young·man," [27] and minding to make a voyage to discover true felicity he took counsel with Folly, "a damosell which ruled my house." She engaged an armorer named Evill–will to furnish the Knight with a shirt of lasciviousness, the armor of ignorance, the gauntlets of idleness, the sword of rebelliousness, and the lance called hope of long life. Folly herself put upon him a cloak of "Vaine–glory which is of such a property, that the greater it grew the lesse I perceived it," and Pride supplied the Knight with a horse named Temerity. As they rode forth Folly told him of her many successful exploits since first she counseled Lucifer and Eve and the builders of the Tower of Babel. Her boastful discourse runs on for many pages of biblical and classical story with some more recent examples of her influence: "I governed," she says, "the false Prophet Mahomet and counsailed him to make a Booke, to entitle it Alcaron, and to expound things in the holy Scriptures carnally, which hee did, and that Law is yet continued in the greatest part of the World."

They came (Part I, chapter 6) to a Parting of the Ways where the Knight met Lady Virtue and Lady Voluptuousness. He harkened to each; Folly warned him of the hardships he would undergo if he followed Virtue, and he elected to follow Voluptuousness. "Alas (poore perplexed Pilgrime!) if I had had but the wit of a Wodcocke . . . I had followed Vertue." So they went on to the Palace of Worldly Felicity where Lady Lust and Lady Wantonness entertained them with delicious food and beautiful music. Wearing the cap of Curiosity he was shown over the Palace, seeing Prince Lucifer, Dame Drunkenness, Lady Venus, and a blind boy who shot an arrow into his heart but he declines to tell of what he saw in "the very secret lodgings of Voluptuousness" because such a relation would offend reverend readers. The walls of the palace had seven towers within each of which lodged a Deadly Sin, each with its attendant Vices: "My purpose was to goe into them all one after another." He dwelt in the palace eleven days—eleven being, as the writer, not the Knight, explains a wicked number because it is one more than the Ten Commandments; at this point the Commandments are printed entire! The Knight then resumes his tale but how he and Folly escaped from the palace is not made clear. However, scarcely had he ridden out into the surrounding forests and warrens when there was an earthquake and looking back he saw the palace sink into the ground. Presently he found himself, his companion, and his horse floundering in mire and he cried out desperately in that "beastly bog." (The resemblance to Bunyan's Slough of Despond is obvious.) Once more the author interrupts the Knight's tale, this time to deplore the notions of felicity in the minds of worldlings and citing examples from history, among them Bajazet King of the Turks who was encaged by Tamerlane. So ends Part One of the allegory.

In response to the Knight's penitent tears a fair lady, God's Grace, descended from heaven and having rebuked him reached forth a golden rod which he grasped and so extricated himself from the bog, leaving "Temeritie my horse and Folly my governnesse, to fish for frogges." His filth does not stain the garments of Divine Grace but her whiteness cleanses his. She leads him to the place where the Palace of Worldly Felicity had stood and where there was now a yawning chasm, the pit of hell, in which he saw the damned. Over this terrifying gulf she carried him by a narrow plank and brought him to the School of Repentance, where Conscience brought him almost to despair. (It is noteworthy that despair is not personified). Remembrance, however, read to him stories of God's mercies, and he listened to a sermon on Mary Magdalene preached by the hermit Understanding. He was then guided by Grace to the Palace of Heavenly Virtue. Part Three begins with a description of that Palace. It had seven towers, each the abode of a Virtue; all are described. From the Tower of Faith the Knight saw afar off the Celestial City. Grace left him in the care of Lady Perseverance; Understanding instructed him how to keep Perseverance always at his side; and so with prayers and a repetition of the Ten Commandments this lovely and often quite moving allegory comes to a close.

We descend to a far lower level of the imagination when we turn to two poems immediately contemporary with *The Wandering Knight,* James Yates' *Castell of Courtesie* and *Holde of Humilitie,* which are actually a single narrative in two parts.[28] At the beginning of the first piece the poet tells how he walked abroad, "damped all with dumpish doubtes," lost his way among thorns and and thickets, and lay down "howling." An old man called Ayde asked Youth (the poet's name) why he, so young, ranged abroad; he replied that he was seeking novelty. Ayde conducted him to the Castle of Courtesie over whose entrance was engraved: "No hoggish hob, nor currish carle may once presume so bolde / To enter here within this Gate, this Castle to beholde," and so forth, to the effect that it is for the pleasure of "courteous wights." The place where the Castle stood was named "None–such"; its Captain was Clemencie. Youth, expressing his gratitude to Ayde, desired to remain there, for he had ever loved courtesy, but Ayde tells him that their journey is not yet done; he has yet to show Youth "a noble Houlde." So they set forth again. At this point Yates, who on his title page describes himself as a "Serving-man," introduces "the Authors Farewell to the Castle of Courtesie." If only, he says, Pallas, Cicero, and Virgil were alive instead of being "consumed in ground," he would hasten to them for counsel as to how to make himself a better poet. He certainly needed advice from someone!

At the beginning of *The Holde of Humilitie* he confesses he is tempted to write about "the frailtie of our present Time," but a voice has told him "flat" that the subject would be out of his way, so he returns to the story of Youth and Ayde. After passing through the forest, which is inevitable in these allegories, they came to the towery "Hould," or fortress, so huge and high that Parnassus cannot compare with it. Over the gate was inscribed:

I am humilitie, the holde, the humble to receive:
The stubborne I renounce them quite, the froward I do leave.
Approach not nigh you currish carles, lest that my battering shotte
Discharged be to coile your coates, and make your stomackes hote.

"These verses carry fire; their sense is tart!" Youth exclaimed. Resistance, the porter, let them in; Salutation received them; Gratulation, the Captain of the Castle, welcomed them and bade his servant Diligence show them all over the place. Its wonders are not described, however, for the poet says he must be brief. They gave thanks for the hospitality they received, and prompted by Ayde Youth gave Diligence what we (and Yates, too, had he known the word) call a tip. Having left the Palace Ayde told Youth that he must return "to my Cottage poore, to rest my Aged spright, / Untill such time as fatall Mors bereaves my drudging dayes." Youth bade his guide a grateful farewell, declaring that Ayde has been as true to him as ever Dido was to Æneas. In conclusion, the poet celebrates the virtues of Ayde as a protector against amorous toys and the uncertainties of Fortune; prays that God may forgive us all our "filthie facts"; and urges his readers "to thinke the best of this his worke." Poor Yates! His pitiable effort is of interest merely to illustrate to what a low level a great ethical and romantic theme may descend when treated by incompetent poetasters.

The allegory is admirably managed in Nicholas Breton's poem, *The Pilgrimage to Paradise* (1592),[29] which is strangely overlooked in Wharey's study of Bunyan's sources. A certain Lord (the Mind or Soul) set out upon a perilous journey, taking with him five servants, the Five Senses. Their master charges them respecting their duties, and they obey: When Venus, "a light of little worth," appeared, Sight shaded his master's eyes from temptation; when enchanting music was heard, Hearing stopped his ears; Flora and Ceres tempted him, but they were repulsed by Smell and Taste; Devils attempted to impede his progress, but Feeling spurned their obstructions. So also when Diana, who is unaccountably equated with "worldes delight," solicited him, she was rejected. Breathing unwholesome and infected air, the Lord and his servants came to a wood full of brambles and briars where "All beastly mindes, that coulde not be reformed, / Were to the shapes of their own shame transformed." But these horrible monsters could not stop the Pilgrim on his way and presently he encountered a seven–headed "ougly horror," which, aided by Patience, he overcame. (Of this triumph over the Seven Deadly Sins

I have given an account in an earlier chapter.) He has many subsequent adventures: He crosses a stormy sea in a boat managed by an humble fisherman, Humility; he makes his way through crowds of worldlings and followers of "Machavile," and of silly fools who are slaves of love; an ill–favored monster, Jealousy, "mopping and mowing like an olde she Ape," accosts them; they pass through a City of the Plague," the plague of Blasphemy; visiting a university, Human Reason, they hear scholars disputing all day long; in a court of stately and gracious living (a sort of Abbey of Theleme) the Pilgrim worries lest the Senses should be tempted to desert him; in a camp he observes the activities of the martial life. At length he arrives at a Church at whose door sat the porter, Penitence, who admitted the lordly Pilgrim, and the poem closes with a rapturous and very beautiful description of Paradise.

Halting in meter and uncouth in vocabulary but fairly well devised and not uninteresting is Anthony Copley's poem *A Fig for Fortune* (1596).[30] This narrative in the first person is informed with an unusual sympathy for Roman Catholicism and the imagery is often taken from papist ceremonial. At one point in the story a Hermit expresses his surprise on being visited by the narrator: "All too rare are now a dayes / Elizas subjectes seen to passe this wayes." With this sympathy, however, are combined fervent loyalty and praise of Queen Elizabeth; with a pleasant play on words the author describes himself as an "Elizian." The allegory (with various long speeches of counsel omitted almost altogether) is as follows.

Exiled from joy and riding on the black jade Melancholy the author one night, in a savage desert, encountered a terrifying beast whose upper shape—it should be noted that the personification is female—was angelical, the lower serpentine. This "mongrel–lumpe" was the ghost of Cato and constantly stabbing herself was an image of Despair. In a long speech she glances at the story of Cato's suicide and similar examples, and counsels self–destruction as the best remedy against Fortune, for Death is an "eternal Sanctuarie from unrest and woe": "Deferre no longer then thy doome of death, / But Champion–like confound Calamitie." So much impressed was the author that he drew his "emboldened blade," being resolved to "massacre [his] loathed life." The resemblance here to the experience of the Red Cross Knight in the cave of Despair is so close as to be a pastiche, but no Una comes to the rescue, and the beastly ghost vanished, leaving behind a stench of sulphur. Quite understandably he "misdoubted some illusion" and remounting his horse was of two minds, thinking to follow Cato's counsel "and then anon reflecting on his stink."

In a gloomy dale scowling Revenge, with blazing eyes and "snake–incurl'd" hair, appeared and boastfully citing the examples of her illustrious clients she counsels vengeance as the best remedy against Fortune. But "suddenly she vanisht out of sight / Because now in the East it dawn'd day–light." The Day of Grace (so the author makes clear in his brief prose introductory "Argument to the Reader") is at hand and when the steed Melancholy vanishes like mist, he sees a white jennet named Good Desire. Mounting her he rode to the Rock of Devotion where in a "penall place" dwelt the Hermit Catechrysius who possessed a crucifix, skull, hourglass, scourge, "map of doomsday," and other appropriate objects. At great length he instructed the author against Despair and Revenge and showed him that Virtue is the best remedy against Fortune. An angel then equipped the author with the helmet of Reason, the crest of Vigilance, and other pieces of armor analogous to, but not identical with, the armor of St. Paul, and with a standard bearing the motto "In hoc signo vinces"; and thus prepared he was conducted to the Temple of Zion. In the description of this temple with its liturgical ceremonies are rather attractively combined impressions of the actual city of Rome and visions of the celestial Jerusalem. Among its saintly inhabitants the author becomes a neophyte. Of the attack upon the temple by Doblessa and her cohorts and of the celebration of victory over these forces of evil, I have given an account in an earlier chapter. Suddenly the "Elizian" author was "rapt home againe to Elizium"—England, that "demi–paradise" as John of Gaunt calls the "dear, dear land"—and the poem ends.

I digress now from my chronological presentation in order to bring together Copley's poem and another later secularization of the theme of the Pilgrimage. This is Robert Carlyle's *Britaines Glorie, or An Allegoricall Dreame: with the Exposition thereof* (1618). The dream is a poem of forty–two six–line stanzas; the exposition is an enormous prose commentary appended thereto. An angel conducts the poet to a strange country which, as the commentary informs us, is Heathendom. Thence they pass to a land "where huge deformed ugly Giants breed," black fiends who smoke tobacco, "that foul stinking weed." Tobacco, it is explained, "causeth men to evacuate a noisome choaking smoake," and "maketh the body of Man blacke and uncleane within," and it therefore represents the blasphemy of the Moslems, especially the Turks. The poet and his guide then enter (as my readers will have expected) a thick forest where the trees grow all sorts of fruit, some sweet and some bitter. This wood is Protestant Variety, "the confused mixture of opinions and sects in religion in Amsterdam." Thence they travel to "a goodly Vine—yard kept by a Tyrant," the Church of Rome and its ruler the Pope. Finally they reach a "goodly Paradise," which is none other than England, Scotland, and Ireland, expounded by the poet as "a comprehensible Type of the incomprehensible excellence of the holy Jerusalem." The title page had announced that the poem was "conceived and written . . . for the love and honor of his King and Country."

I revert to an earlier date to consider a much more important poem, John Davies of Hereford's *Humours Heav'n on Earth* (1609).[31] This allegorical poem, which extends to no less than 246 stanzas of ottava rima, is a gnarled and rugged work, confused in concept and pattern, turgid in style, and evincing hesitations between clear—cut personifications and the delineation of types of humanity. It possesses, however, much power and energy. The allegory of the Pilgrimage is but one of its complex strands, and since I have touched on some parts in earlier chapters, a certain amount of repetition is unavoidable. In it Truth, Justice, Time, Death, and other famous and formidable abstractions are portrayed with interesting variations upon familiar relationships, sometimes in traditional, sometimes in novel settings.

The poem opens with a description of three men who, as a gloss notes, are the "three sins most familiar with mens nature": Poliphagus the paunchy glutton, Epithymus the dandified lecher, and Hyselophronous the proud man. They debate the question as to what is the "dearest sin." Glutton expresses the wish that men's necks were long like a crane's so that meat and drink "would longer pass, with pleasure to our mawes" (were he a personification of Gluttony he would *have* such a neck) and through eight stanzas the pleasures of taste are described. Lecher describes the pleasures of touch, citing the example of famous devotees of lust. The proud man, however, remarking disdainfully that such gratifications are shared with the beasts, asserts that to rule over other men is godlike. Yet each of the three is in agreement as to the delights celebrated by the other two, for (as a marginal gloss nobly expresses it) "the concord of the Evil condemns the discord of the good." Meanwhile Reason (Logus) has been endeavoring to rouse the Soul (Psyche), urging her to "leave your Gluttony, your Lust, and Pride," but the three Sins (Davies having tacitly transmuted his types into personifications) drive off Reason who protests to Nature (Phusis) and Custom (Praxis), for

Nature is the mother of the Sins and Custom has made them worse. Though it is a question which of these two is the more responsible for the plight of the Soul, there is no question of the need to rescue her and Reason advises Nature to call upon Truth (Lady Aletheia) for aid.

Where may Truth be found, Nature asks; and Reason replies:

> She is seene about the Mansion old
> Of father Chronos, which he did erect
> For him, and her (his daughter deare) to hold:
> Or Thanatos, his Man, who riddes away
> That which his Master bringeth to decay.[32]

Reason proceeds to describe Time, and, among other attributes that are not clearly visualized, we note the familiar scythe, horologe, and "upon [his] Head in stead of hat" the hourglass.

> His Haire was white as was the driven Snow,
> And from his Head it seem'd to hang, by drifts
> Turn'd up againe, ev'n as the same doth show
> When it doth hang, so driven upon Clifts.

The forelock, which in countless pictures flares upwards and backwards from Time's forehead, is impressively likened to the snow driven back from some cliff by the wind. The description of Death that follows is in solemn accord with the long tradition of emblems of mortality; the poet is indeed found in the very act of rendering into verbal imagery the *Memento Mori* wall paintings, where Time and Death are associated together, which he must have seen so often—and we know that Davies was attentive to pictures—in English churches. Thanatos,

> bare to the bones,
> Was more than naked from the toppe to toe:
> All hairless, toothlesse, eielesse, stocks or stones,
> Are all as quicke, though he much more can doe:
> And all he said, *I was as you are, once*;
> Which was in sullen silence spoken to[o]:
> Upon a Spade he leanes, as if he did
> By his day labour live, call'd *Wincke, all hid.*

Here the poet's harsh style is appropriate to his theme; there is genuine imaginative power in the concept of Death uttering "in sullen silence" the old warning, *Hodie mihi, cras tibi*, and in the name "Wink–All–Hid," or "Hide–and–Seek," given to his spade.

Acting upon Reason's counsel, Nature seeks out Time. The description that follows is reminiscent of Spenser and of Sackville's *Induction*, which is behind Spenser. Time dwelt in a rocky cave, covered with moss and nettles and hemlock, a place of dripping water, echoes, and darkness. The porter at the gate was Sickness (Nosus), a thin, panting, fault-finding wight, bundled up in many clothes and leaning on a staff. Nearby was the House of Death, roofed and paved with skulls and bones. Love shuns that dwelling, though Christ, the Lord of Love, "once three days lay there." "Zijm and Iim" (the mysterious goblins of Isaiah 34:14) inhabit it; there Sense lies in a lethargy; and Silence keeps Death company. Sometimes men, for pride, cover this abode with a stately tomb or pyramid; "But Chronos' spite that Cover doeth undoe, / Which cannot brooke the pompe of Thanatos." [33]

In the Cave of Time Nature encounters Truth [34] who makes complaint of churchmen, philosophers, lawyers, and merchants who seek to conceal or destroy her; "Upon poore Poets I can least complain," she says, because "they best know, that have best eyes to see." Of Truth Nature solicits counsel touching her three children, Gluttony, Lechery, and Pride, for she fears lest when they have passed through the House of Death they will choose the wrong path, that which leads to hell.[35] (I have already remarked upon the curious confusion of the allegory at this point: The choice of the Two Paths is not to come till after the passage through the abode of Death!) Truth consents to warn Nature's children of their danger and sets out upon this mission, leaving Nature and Reason at the gate of Time's cave. On her return she gives a depressing report of her experiences while traveling throughout the world to caution Nature's children against vice: princes stabbed her; judges expected to be given "golden scabberds" in which to sheathe the sword of Justice; poor poets, whom she pitied in her heart, were filling the world with their fables and living on their even more fabulous hopes of obtaining favors from the great. Nature, she advises, should employ Truth's sister Justice to govern her turbulent sons. At this point Truth disappears from the allegory; we hear no more of her.

Nature then implores Time to warn her children by giving them examples from his long experience. He consents to do so, but returning from this mission he reports that few have heeded him. Each of the Five Ages of Man he has tried to guide and discipline:

> In Childhood I did teach, in Youth did threat:
> In Manhood I reprooved: and in Age,

> With their own bones, their bones I sore did beat:
> And in Decrepitenesse, I worse did rage . . .
> Yet for all this, they worse and worse became.

The allegory now becomes slipshod and hurried, as though Davies were weary of it and had lost the thread of his design. We find Time reveling with Gluttony, Lechery, and Pride, for (as a marginal gloss explains) "All times [are] apter to Vice then Vertue." Then Thanatos summons Nature's children away, praying to Justice for them, where allegorist leaves her. Why this weighty, ambitious, impressive, and untidy poem is called *Humours Heav'n on Earth* I do not know. Its slight but discernible connection with the theme of the Pilgrimage is my justification for summarizing it here.

William Browne of Tavistock in *Britannia's Pastorals* (1613–16) combines, as had Davies, the subject of Truth's wanderings with that of the Pilgrimage.[36] Disregarding complexities in the narrative, we may glance briefly at the former theme, for it is not really part of our present inquiry. Truth, seeking shelter, was refused admission to an abbey, where she saw Idleness, Drunkenness, and Gluttony welcomed, while Lust climbed over the wall by night. She comes to a prince's court, but Greatness turns her away on the ground that Adulation would quit his service if Truth took up her abode there. She decides not to go to the City for, she realizes, she would not be known but to "homely townes" where she meets with a miller, a tailor, and a weaver who likewise reject her. At length she meets Idya (England) who from her horn of plenty gives her nourishment, knowing that Truth is "the chiefest consort of the Fairy Queene." With this story is interwoven that of Riot who is cruel, bloody, and blasphemous. This allegory, though clogged with pastoral similes, is truly moving and is obviously much indebted to Spenser. Riot comes to a palace whose portress is Remembrance, with a "back–bent eye." In an inner court he sees a lady, Remorse, who, groaning, grasps her own heart with pincers (as in various emblems). She subjects him to torments, and we sense that he has become the personification of Man in his fallen state. Lame and full of wounds he creeps to the postern door of the palace beyond which he sees two paths, one the way of Repentance leading uphill, the other leading down to "the soules black homicide, meager Despair," and to Death. By Despair's abode men were dashing out their brains, or leaping from the rocks, or hanging themselves, or taking poison, or drowning themselves, to "die in water to revive in fire." None had a tear with which to appear at Mercy's seat. Riot starts down the wrong path, but a heavenly choir warns him (in a beautiful lyric) to choose the other way, and oft stumbling and sliding back he at length reaches the House of Repentance. Upon its floor he sees many penitents, garbed in sackcloth and camel's hair and scourging themselves; by them are vials of tears. Humbleness (who reminds us of Humility, the portress of Spenser's House of Holiness) brings him to Repentance, Metanoia, who restores his innocence and changes him into a shepherd lad, a metamorphosis characteristic of the pastoral poet.

Almost certainly imitated in part from *Britannia's Pastorals* and obviously indebted to some episodes in *The Faerie Queene* is John Day's *Peregrinatio Scholastica*.[37] This narrative in prose remained in manuscript till printed by Bullen in 1881. It seems to be a synopsis or outline of an intended poem that was never written and is too much condensed to provide much of the quaint realistic detail that endows some such allegories with vitality. The plan, if indeed it is merely a plan, is, however, interesting. Learning or Philosophus, the youngest son of Cosmos, set out upon a journey to the shrine of Worship or Religion, Latria, accompanied by his servant Time and his page Truth. They came to the country of the Cosmophili where the townsmen barred the way, a butcher, baker, cheesemonger, haberdasher, cook, draper, and jailkeeper all refusing to admit Truth on the ground that she would certainly "blab" about their dishonesty and cheating. Learning then "turnd the streame of his jorny another way" and he and his two companions came to a meadow where they were met by a dwarf mounted on an elephant who brought an invitation from Diana, the lady of a nearby castle. Truth was dubious about accepting this but Learning did so nevertheless, and in order not to put too great a charge upon the lady he bade Time wait for him at the next village along the road. Now the dwarf's name was Error, and he had blinded Truth to the fact that the lady was really Sin, an old beldam, daughter of Eve by the Serpent "and mother of seven desperate sonns." Error gave Learning and Truth to drink of an enchanted cup and they fell asleep. Carrying sleeping Truth to prison and there robbing him of his clothes, Error disguised himself in them and returned to Learning, who, waking, was deceived.

Sin met Learning under a tree festooned with tablets that were inscribed with the choicest verses, for she knew how to adapt her bait to the taste of every victim of her wiles. Thence she accompanied him to her castle where revels followed: a masque of Bacchus drawn in his chariot and an antimasque in which were represented the several stages of drunkenness.[38] The revels ended, Sin conducted Learning to his lodgings for the night, hostess and guest walking under a canopy upheld by her seven sons. These, Error whispered, were the Seven Liberal Sciences—a lie rousing poor Learning to intense expectations when Error told him they were to serve him. Thus he resolved to remain in the castle, and he quite forgot that Time was waiting for him down the road. Meanwhile Truth had spied through a loophole in his prison and saw that Sin's domain was "a bare and blasted wilderness" inhabited by ugly monsters and ignorant idiots under the rule of that hideous hag. Each of the Seven Deadly Sins is recognized by Truth,[39] but Learning, separated from Truth, slept that night in Sin's bosom. Learning himself, even without Truth's guidance, might have identified them by natural instinct had he not been reassured by Error, disguised as Truth, who made light of his offenses in this bad company.

How he escaped from the castle is not made clear, but we next find him continuing his journey, still under the guidance of Error. Presently he was cast upon an island where dwelt a grim and aged matron named Necessity. Above her cave there was a cliff upon whose top "sat an ill–favored creture, braydeing and twisting halters, scowreing and sharpeneing knives, which she through [threw] down to desperate and discontented passengers." Error told Learning that this was "the next and onelie waie to finish his pillgrimadge," but as Learning was about to hang himself Necessity beckoned to him and bade him follow her counsel. She sent him to her workhouse where people of all ranks and ages were toiling and there he set himself to work, writing tractates of philosophy. With these in hand he went to a prince's court but was refused admission: Masques and entertainments, satires and invectives would have won him entrance, but not philosophy! At a city's gate his experience was the same: "Lord have mercy upon us! that a scholler should have noe more witt but to think he should finde entertainement in the City!" A merchant, yes, or a traveler, a dancing master, or a fiddler, but "a scholler, and a poore one to[o], they had no use for him except it were once in a coronation to make a speech." [40] And so, despite the warnings given him by Industry, whom he has met upon his way, Learning came to Beggars Bush. Experience now showed him that his guide was really Error in disguise, and having cast off that deceiver he arrived at Weeping Cross and sent Industry to save lost Time and set Truth free. Once more with these good companions, Learning came to the House of Humility where we leave him preparing to climb the mountain to the shrine of Worship.

I revert for a moment to the various encounters we have witnessed of Man with Despair.[41] Incomparably the finest of all the many versions of this encounter is that in *The Faerie Queene* when the Red Cross Knight, tempted by Despair, is about to kill himself and is rescued by Una. This is one of the supreme achievements in all English poetry and is so famous and universally admired that no account of it is needed here. The post–Spenserian poets who personify Despair are one and all influenced by this scene. Very close to Spenser is the episode in Giles Fletcher's *Christ's Victory and Triumph* (II, 23 f.): Satan led Christ to a "baleful bower" where the light was "like clowdie moonshine" and bones were strewn upon the ground and the bodies of suicides were hanging, Despair lived there, a pale wight with disheveled hair and deep–sunk eyes. In *The Apollyonists* (I, 15) Phineas Fletcher's Despair is a woman, a "sad ghastly Spright," sitting close to Sin, the portress of hell. "Fayne would she die, but could not," even as at the close of Spenser's scene Despair is attempting vainly to do away with himself. Also reminiscent of Spenser is the episode in Richard Corbet's "Somnium" where Melancholy, having been taken by the ferryman Despair across the Lake of Lament, is about to slay herself when Hope intervenes. How startling (in an anonymous piece) is the sharp cry: "I know him now by the Halter about his Necke: it is dull, dismal Despair!" [42] George Wither draws an image of "Despair: with gastly looks he stands, / And poysons, ropes, or poyn–yards fill his hands." [43] Into his masque of *Cupid and Death* James Shirley introduces the character of Despair, carrying a halter and in quest of Death.

The dreadful personification is found long before Spenser; I cite but a few examples. A fiend hovers by the woman who has hanged herself in Giotto's representation of Despair in the Arena Chapel. An illustration in Petrarch's *De remediis* shows a fiend dragging a stool from under the feet of a woman who has hanged herself to the rafters of a house.[44] A "desperate fool" hangs himself in *The Ship of Fools*.[45] More famous and far finer than any of these is the concept of the sin of despair in the *Ars Bene Moriendi* in the original Latin and the vernacular derivatives.[46] Here Despair is not personified, but devils tempt the dying Christian by reminding him of his sins: "Thou hast lived in avarice!" "Thou hast committed fornication!" and so forth. He resists them, however, by contemplating scriptural *exempla* of the plenitude of God's Mercy: St. Peter (represented by a cock perched on the head of the bed), Mary Magdalene (with a box of ointment), the Penitent Thief (on his cross), and St. Paul (falling from his horse on the road to Damascus).[47] There are similar reminders of God's Mercy in the morality play *Mundus et Infans* where, when Sinful Age longs for death and seeks to kill himself, Perseverance bids him beware of Wanhope and take comfort in the thought of Doubting Thomas, Paul who "dyde Crystes people grete vylany," Peter who "at the Passyon forsoke Cryst," and Mary Magdalene who "lyved longe in lechery": "Yet these to Cryst are derlynges dere, / And now be sayntes in heven clere." [48] In *The Castle of Perseverance* Humanum Genus, though he lapses into sin, never despairs. On his deathbed he prays for protection against this worst of sins, and his last words are: "I putte me in Godys Mercy." But in another morality Mankind, brought to desperation by his sins, cries out for a rope; Mischief proffers him a rope and has a gallows prepared; in the nick of time Mercy appears, drives off Mischief, and brings the protagonist to repentance.[49] Again, the encounter of Magnificence with Despair and Mischief is the most memorable incident in Skelton's play. When Good Hope appears the two evil personifications take flight, Magnificence is brought into the right way by Redress (that is, Restitution for injuries committed), and is kept in that way by Perseverance.[50] A similar scene in George Wapull's morality play *The Tyde tarryeth no Man* is the high point of a mediocre but intensely serious piece. Wastefulness, the protagonist, is saved from Despair, an "ougly shape," by Faithful–few who prays with him and bids him trust in God's Mercy. There follows the stage direction: "Dispayre flyeth, and they arise." [51]

Sackville's portrait of Despair in the Induction to *The Mirrour for Magistrates* is too famous to require more than a bare mention here. In one of the narratives in John Higgins' continuation of the *Mirrour*, Despair provides Cordelia with a rope and with the sword with which Dido slew herself.[52] In another pre–Spenserian allegory Dido is herself among the unfortunates imprisoned in a dungeon by Despair, "a wofull wretch whose greedy gorge delighted much in wrong." [53]

This digression has not led us so far from the Pilgrim's road as the reader might infer, for our next version is Sir William Denny's *Pelecanicidium: or the Christian Adviser against Self–Murder. Together with A Guide, and the Pilgrims Passe To the Land of the Living* (1653).[54] The work is in harsh, abrupt, uncouth verse with prose comments and explications and, as the title implies, it is in three parts. The Book I is a series of overwrought, ejaculatory poems against suicide; from them one might gather that self–murder was as common in England as continental commentators upon the *maladie anglaise* believed. Book II is closely conected with Book I but has a fresh subtitle: "A Guide to the Land of the Living for the Discontented, That are in the Dangerous

Path to Self–Murder. Comfort to All in Distress; by Way of Divine Poem, Perspective, Moral, Prospect, Consolatory Essay." Each of the following six cantos conforms to this pattern. There is first the "Divine Poem," charged with allegory; then the "Perspective," a prose paraphrase and interpretation of the allegory; then the "Moral," drawn from the writings of theologians and moralists; then the "Prospect," a short poem of good counsel; and finally the "Consolatory Essay" in prose, which is what its title promises. In the allegory the Pilgrim journeys from the Den of Idleness, through the Grotto of Repentance, the Wilderness of Tribulation, the Fruitful Vale of Tears, and the Cell of Humility to the House of Prayers. This much constitutes the "Guide," but in Book III the itinerary continues as the Pilgrim travels from the Mount of Faith, through the Camp of Resolution, the Lodge of Patience, the Ruins of Mortification, and the Farm of Self–Resignation to the Holy Hill of Contemplation. Each of these twelve localities (six in each book) occupies a canto. The final canto is, however, sub–divided and there are descriptions of the Downs of Cogitation and the Promontory of Meditation before the Pilgrim reaches the actual Holy Hill.[55] The plan is descriptive, not narrative; we hear scarcely anything of the Pilgrim's adventures or his thoughts. In an engraving by Francis Barlow, used as a frontispiece to both the "Guide" and the "Pilgrim's Passe," a godly person, who is a divine, or moralist, and not a Guardian Angel, points out to an eager Pilgrim the Celestial City. Also shown are the road hitherward, winding uphill, and a snarling dragon protruding from its den (Fig. 139). At the bottom of this plate are the lines:

> Wise Traveller through Wildernesse does lead
> The Christian Pilgrim, teaching where to tread:
> From Feind in Worlds Way Foes he warnes his Freind,
> Through Deepe, up Steepe, shewes Heavn's his Journeys end.

For the most part the many personifications are not very vividly delineated. One remembers, however, Faith wearing the Pauline armor with a shield exhibiting a golden cross upon a bloody field, Charity from whose breasts flows forth not milk but "cream," and Contempt of the World who is the porter at the gatehouse of the Ruins of Mortification. Strikingly anticipatory of Bunyan is the Slough the Pilgrim must wade through before reaching the open barren country where is the Lodge of Patience. Much allegorical use is made of paths, groves, caverns, chambers, stairways, foods and drinks, and there are various temptations to wander from the right path; many analogies are drawn from nature lore, both faunal and floral; and the poet was also well versed in emblem literature.[56]

My final example (for I pause short of *Pilgrim's Progress*) is the *Mundorum Explicatio* (1661) by "S.P.," [57] who is identified by some authorities with Samuel Pordage, by others with his father. Lodowick Lloyd, who published it, issued in English translation various works by Jacob Behmen, and this monstrously dull and, to me, in parts incomprehensible poem is based on Behmen's writings. A large folding copperplate called the "hieroglyph" displays the Worlds of Phantasy, Light, and Darkness; Trees of Good and Evil; Life and Death; and much else. Above the "Mundus Tenebrosus" where Satan is enthroned the Lamb of God is crushed beneath the World, the Devil, Death, and a dragon. Opposite, Satan is crushed beneath the "Mundus Luminosius," Death is sprawling, and the Lamb is triumphant. Only two portions of the poem are of interest to us. One is the Council in Hell where the Seven Deadly Sins are among the potent princes. I have noted their characteristics in my discussion of Man's spiritual foes. The other is the story of the progress of the Pilgrim (who is so called) in Part II. Patience is his attendant, and as he pursues his way, often singing, the Virtues protect him from many Vices: When accosted by Lust, a satyr whose sword changes into a naked nymph, Chastity rescues him; from Wrath he is saved by Meekness; from Envy by Charity. Deceit, "a twy–fac'd Hag," attempts to direct him into the wrong path, but Truth guides him aright and shows him a picture of the heavenly Jerusalem, after which Zeal carries him in his chariot. He is vouchsafed a vision of Sophia, the Holy Wisdom, and at length he meets Death and passes into the "Locus Purgatorius inter Mundus" and thence to Paradise.

CHAPTER 8.   THE JOURNEY'S END

1. The Dance of Death, the Three Living and the Three Dead

In the Litany there is a moving and terrible petition for deliverance from lightning and tempest, plague, pestilence, and famine, from battle and murder, and from sudden death. Modern Western man, for reasons which cannot be explored here, has endeavored with greater or less success to remove the awareness of the inevitability of death into the background of his consciousness. Not so the Renaissance where, as in so many other aspects of thought and expression, there is no break with the later Middle Ages. The rudimentary state of medical and surgical knowledge and practice, the ever–present threat of pestilence, the prevalence of diseases that have since been eradicated by the advances of knowledge, the shortness and uncertainty of "life's fitful fever," the dread of

Judgment to come—all these and other factors contribute to this persistent fear: Life is "a pilgrimage, that every step treades on a Coffin." [1] So thick are London's burials that the worms "are curious," that is, fastidious, "where they picke and how they feed," and a new meal is ready for them e're the old be eaten.[2] Sermons, homilies, meditations, morality plays, poems all sound the warning perpetually, and in the minds of a pious, church–going people it was re–enforced by the abundant opportunities to look at the *Memento Mori* themes in ecclesiastical mural paintings. Woodcuts and engravings also served as reminders.

The few surviving specimens of such cautionary subjects in churches are of three conspicuous sorts. First, there is the theme of Time and Death, to which we shall return later in this chapter. Second, there is the Dance of Death, a subject already so thoroughly explored [3] that a few comments will suffice here with a more extended account of a memorable English series. Third, there is the related subject of the Three Living and the Three Dead which has also been abundantly inquired into.[4] There is no way to estimate the number of such murals that formerly existed. Of paintings of the Dance of Death only two series survive in English churches, and neither of these is anywhere near complete. Two or three other paintings are in so ruinous a condition it is a question whether they are examples of the theme or not. A painting of Death and a young nobleman in one church is probably the one extant member of another series, as is the stained glass window of Death and a bishop in Norwich. The Dance still exists, albeit in so ruinous a state as to be almost unrecognizable, in carvings in Rosslyn Chapel near Edinburgh. Of one knows not how many lost examples, the earliest and most famous was the Dance in the Cloister of Old St. Paul's.[5] It seems to have been inspired by the even more celebrated Dance in the Cemetery of the Innocents in Paris. When John Lydgate (ca. 1440) described the London Dance [6] he generally followed the verses that accompanied the Paris murals and acknowledging his indebtedness to Frenchmen who gave him aid in his translation, he records also that he had seen the Dance painted on a "wall" in Paris. In his poem Death addresses in turn thirty–six persons, each representative of one of the ranks of society, Pope, Emperor, King, Cardinal, and so on in descending degrees, and each person replies to Death. To the French roll–call Lydgate added a new character, not a type but an individual, an Englishman, "Mr. John Rikill, Tregetour." "Tregetour" means juggler; Rikill was Henry VI's jester. How close we are to Hamlet's "Alas, poor Yorick!"

Lydgate's epilogue is spoken by "Machabre the Doctoure," who was supposed to be the originator of the Dance. (It is needless to attempt here a résumé of the many discussions of how it came to be attributed to him.) From the last two decades of the fifteenth century block–books, woodcuts, and engravings spread through Europe a knowledge of the Dance. Illustrations of the *Danse Macabre* were issued from the presses in Paris and Lyons and in smaller numbers in Germany and elsewhere.[7] Especially memorable is Guy Marchant's series in folio of 1485. The types of humanity were at first limited to masculine figures, but in 1490 there appeared Marchant's *Danse macabre des Femmes*, followed (ca. 1500) from a Lyons press by *La Danse Macabre des Hommes et des Femmes*, the only version bringing the two sexes into a single volume. From Lyons also came *La Grant Danse Macabre* (1500) which includes the scene of Death breaking into a printing room, the earliest illustration of this metier that we have. All these and other versions culminated in the best known of all, the *Dance of Death* by Hans Holbein the Younger (Lyons, 1538). Meanwhile the idea had been borrowed by some designers of *Horae* where the episodes of the Dance decorate the margins of some pages.[8]

England produced no volume devoted wholly to the Dance till long after our period,[9] but it is found in two beautiful books printed by John Daye, *Christian Prayers and Meditations* (1569) and *A Booke of Christian Prayers* (1578 and other editions in 1581, 1590, and 1608).[10] Behind both books is the long history I have briefly summarized. In the volume of 1569 the Dance of Death follows the cuts illustrating episodes in the Life of Christ and is introduced with casual abruptness and with no relation to the text of the prayers on the same pages. On each page the outer lateral margin has two scenes of the Dance, the bottom margin, a supine skeleton or emaciated body or shrouded corpse or an effigy upon a tomb; and the other two sides of the frame, formal decorations having no reference to the theme. Following the familiar formula, Death holds before his victim an hourglass, or tolls a passing–bell, or brandishes a sword or scythe, or carries a spade or a broom on his shoulder. Occasionally he is garbed in a shroud. He gesticulates mockingly or seizes the doomed one with violence or leads him gently away. Thirty–six types of men are represented, ranging downward in social rank from Emperor and King to Beggar, Fool, and Infant, but the ecclesiastical hierarchy, conspicuous in some French sequences, is not represented at all. The entire series of masculine figures is repeated, and then follows a female Dance of Death, with twenty–six types. In many of the episodes, male and female alike, an effort has been made to adapt the scheme to English society. The old notion that in these cuts we may have a record of the general pattern and appearance of the Dance of Death in Old St. Paul's or of the Dance, long since lost, which Holbein painted in Whitehall has little to recommend it, for the plan and many particulars obviously follow the margins in some French *Horae*. It is conceivable, however, that the grimly vigorous couplets addressed by Death to his victims may derive from one or another of the Dances on the walls of English churches. These couplets, though rough and homely, are never quite doggerel, and it is not without emotion that we hear Death addressing the Aged Woman (in words paraphrasing Stephen Hawes' famous lines): "Be the day never so long: / At length commeth Evensong." The initial "G" is on about half of the cuts, a detail leading to the inference that Daye employed at least two craftsmen. That these men were trained on the Continent, probably in Germany or the Low Countries, seems certain, for their technical skill is above the level of native English work of the period. But the Last Judgment with which the Dance concludes differs markedly in style and is so nearly identical with one frequently used by Pigouchet in Paris as to support the suspicion that it comes from a tracing.

The Dance of Death in the *Christian Prayers* of 1578 contains all the ranks and types represented in the volume of 1569 and adds a dozen more. The ecclesiastical hierarchy now appears, an Archbishop, Bishop, Doctor, and Preacher, although there is of course no Pope, and the Protestant element is sufficiently apparent. A Printer appears twice, once seated at his type and again working at his press. Music is likewise represented twice and in a manner differing from all the rest of the series: Instead of summoning an individual, Death comes to two men and two women who are singing while they sit at table and then to two men and two women who are playing upon musical instruments. The female Dance is enlarged by the representation at the very end of a second infant and a She–fool. I have noted that in 1569 there are two sequences of the male Dance and one of the female. In 1578 both occur there times, though the third is slightly truncated by the omission of the second infant and the She–Fool. These deletions provided space for the insertion of a new cut: the Triumph of Death, showing, above, Death striding over a heap of victims and, below, Death in a chariot drawn by stags. This new cut is signed "G." Furthermore, Daye enhanced the lugubrious impressiveness of the sequences by substituting for the formal decorations of the top and inner borders of 1569 a great variety of erect or prostrate skeletons, emaciated bodies, or heaps of skulls and bones. The whole concludes, as in 1569, with the Last Judgment.[11]

Closely related to, and sometimes combined with, the Dance is the legend of the Three Living and the Three Dead.[12] It is found, however, at a much earlier date and its origins have been traced to folklore. Dating from the thirteenth century are four French poems on the subject and, deriving from one or another of the French, four German, one Italian. and one Latin. In the fourteenth century the legend is sometimes a vision of St. Macarius who in many designs of later date becomes the Hermit. Succinct summaries are found on bas–reliefs on tombs: "Such as ye be, such wer we; / Such as we be, such shall ye be."

The greatest and best known of all versions of the legend in the arts of design is the fresco in the Campo Santo at Pisa, reduced to a ruinous condition by a bomb during the Second World War. Other murals are found at Subiaco and elsewhere in Italy. The subject seems to have come to England by way of Calvados and the Channel Islands. Known because they are still in existence, albeit more or less deteriorated, or else from descriptions or copies made when they were still visible, are no less than two dozen murals in English churches. Most are dated to the fifteenth century; a few to the fourteenth; at least one so late as the sixteenth. Slight but interesting variations occur in these paintings. Generally the Three Living are kings, while the Three Dead who confront them are occasionally crowned skeletons. Once at least the living kings represent the Three Ages of Life. The mise–en–scène (as at Pisa) is often but not always a hunt, and a huntsman, greyhound, and hare may be depicted. The Three Living may be on horseback and the Three Dead standing in arresting attitudes, but in one example two of the Living are on foot while the third, wearing a triple crown, rides a horse. Once the Three Living are crowned old men, two with scepters and the third with a battle–ax. Instead of three kings there may be a king, a queen, and an ecclesiastic. In one case this third person seems to have represented the lower orders of society, for on a scroll we read: "Mors sceptra ligonibus equat." An unusual feature of one mural is the representation of the Three Living by a youthful king and two elderly attendants. Elsewhere (as in Huntington MS 1132, Fig. 140) the Three Living do not meet with the Three Dead but with a single skeleton. Once the subject is expanded to include Our Lady of Pity accompanied by her devotees and St. Michael standing upon a seven–headed dragon and weighing souls in his balance.

Traces of inscriptions are sometimes discernible, but in only two instances are they in part decipherable. Once above the skeletons are scrolls reading: "So were we." And once, in a very striking scene in another church, three equestrian kings are separated by a cross from three standing skeletons and labels accompany each of the Living. The first king's is: "O benedicite, what want ye." The second, shielding his eyes with his hand, is saying: "A marvelus syte ys that I se." The third has turned his horse to gallop off, and the portion of the damaged label that is legible reads: "wyl I flee." To the Three Dead corresponding labels were probably attached but they have been obliterated.

This fragmentary dialogue suggests that I penetrate behind the insecure *terminus a quo* of the present book in order to call fresh attention to the impressive version of our subject in Arundel MS 83 (ca. 1308) in the British Museum. A miniature [13] of the confrontation of the Three Living by the Three Dead shows the first king grasping impulsively the wrist of the second king, and the third shrinking away. Inscriptions above the six figures suggest with great power the emotion of the affrighted kings in the presence of these awful apparitions, and the murmured voices of the Dead are like a soft wind blowing over graves.—

First King:	Ich am afert.
Second King:	Lo what ich se.
Third King:	Me thinketh hit beth develes thre.
First Dead:	Ich wes wel fair.
Second Dead:	Such scheltou [shalt thou] be.
Third Dead:	For godes love be war by me.

A fifteenth century manuscript provides an interesting contrast in that the admonition comes not from the Dead but from the Living; one king says: "What we are, those skeletons had been; and we shall become what they are now." [14]

Of the many miniatures in manuscripts there is room here to mention but one more. This is a *Decretals of Gregory* (early fourteenth century) [15] which has an Italian text but miniatures of English workmanship which illustrate various adventures of the Three Living who are all kings. They appear in about a score of episodes: They sit in judgment, hunt, pray, approach a hermit, and meet with the Three Dead. In the fifteenth century this manuscript belonged to St. Bartholomew's Priory, Smithfield. A fair number of Londoners, inmates or visitors to the Priory, must have had opportunities to see it.

By means of woodcuts and engravings the grim subject was further popularized. We find it in Caxton's so-called *Fifteen Oes* (1491), and this cut reappears in eight books up to 1506.[16] Wynkyn de Worde used a woodcut of the legend in several books: in *The doctrynale of dethe* [17] (ca. 1498) where it appears both on the preliminary title page and on the first page of the text; in Richard Fox's *The Contemplacyon of Sinners* (1499); and at the end of *The Ordynarye of Crysten Man* (1502). As far as I know the subject disappeared in later Tudor England with the exception of the Hugh Singleton reprint of *The Contemplacyon of Synners* in 1578 where Wynkyn de Worde's cut was again used.

Illustrations of the legend are found in Books of Hours from the Paris presses of Pigouchet, Caillaut, and Jean du Pré. It is not in the original edition (1491) of Guy Marchant's *Kalendrier des Bergers* but that printer inserted it in the edition of 1499. In all the examples hitherto mentioned the Three Dead are standing, with the exception of the frescoes at Pisa and Subiaco. This fact gives interest to two other versions. In a Venetian print they are in their coffins; two lie supine, the third is in a sitting posture.[18] A drawing by Jacopo Bellini in the Louvre has the Three Living riding, their horses are shying and there are dogs sniffing or turning away, and opposite this group are three graves with portions of the slabs removed showing the center one empty and crowned skeletons standing in the other two.[19] A design by Hans Wechtlin (early sixteenth century) in the Albertina conveys an authentic spiritual terror; it is perhaps the most memorable of all renderings of the legend.[20]

The dread warning conveyed by *Les Trois Vifs et les Trois Morts*— "Hodie mihi, cras tibi"; "Fui, non sum; es, non eris"—is expressed in various simpler forms having an implied relationship to the legend. Thus, there is an emblem of a youth standing by a tomb from which a skeleton steps; [21] another emblem shows a human head of which one half is living, young, and fair, and the other half a skull.[22] An English black–letter memorial broadside of 1570 has a woodcut of Death with a dart in his hand and a coffin on his shoulder and his foot resting on a tomb. Round this illustration run the lines:

> I death this Coffyn beare
> For you that lyving are
> The dead are past my feare
> Therfore ye lyving prepare.[23]

In both the Dance of Death and the Three Living and the Three Dead we rarely have to do with personifications of Death. It is the Dead who warn the Living; it is with the Dead that the Living dance.

2. Personifications of Death

So familiar from innumerable tombstones, monumental effigies, *Memento Mori* paintings and prints, epitaphs, elegies, and other sources is the personification of Death as a skeleton that a single quotation will suffice, and I choose Sackville's portrayal of Death in the *Induction* (stanza 48) whose "bodie [is] doght with nought but bones." The strength of the influence of this personifying convention is evidenced by the fact that in various Renaissance treatises on anatomy, such as the *De humani corporis fabrica*, though cadavers are merely anatomical plates, skeletons are often represented as Death personified, in the postures of living men and with familiar symbols. Thus, in a huge treatise by Helkiah Crooke three skeletons lean respectively on a reed, a spade, and a scythe; the skeleton of a woman holds an hourglass; and that of a newborn child has a bow and arrow—this last a most curious conflation with Cupid or with the First Age of Life! [1]

The skeleton may have wings, as in an exquisite little engraving (1544) by Hans Sebald Beham where such a figure stands behind a woman.[2] It is possible that concepts of this kind are influenced by the biblical theme of the Angel of Death. An anonymous print, probably Flemish (ca. 1600), illustrates 2 Samuel 24:15–16. The two hands of the Angel of Death appear from heaven, holding a sword and a scourge, and beside these hands sits Death, a skeleton, upon a cloud, holding a javelin.[3] A terrifying apparition, which in the "Triumph of Death" at Pisa is heedless of the prayers of the poor, the ailing, and the aged to release them from their miseries and makes ready to strike the young, the lusty, and the prosperous, is flying above these two groups. The concept may be simplified into that of a winged skull.[4]

The Pisan Death is a woman, "Pallida Mors." When, albeit rarely, we find this female personification the choice of sex may be due in part to association with Atropos, the third of the three sisters who are the Fates.[5] Petrarch in the *Trionfi* describes Death as a woman in a black robe. In a series of Florentine engravings illustrating the *Trionfi* Death has long hair and wears a woman's dress; her head is a skull but the body retains its flesh.[6] In a design of "Senex et Mors" Death, hovering over the Old Man, is a female figure with bat's wings.[7] In an anonymous English poem we read:

> Death is come to pay her due,
> With all the paynes that shee can well invent . . .
> death hath spit her spight.[8]

A passage in the Countess of Pembroke's translation of Philippe de Mornay's *Discourse of Life and Death* (1600) is another example of the same concept: "Beholde, now comes Death unto us: Behold her whose approach we so much feare. . . . We are afrayde of her: but like little children of a vizard, or of the Images of *Hecate*. We have her in horrour: but because we conceive her not such as she is, but ougly, terrible, and hideous: such as it pleaseth the painters to represent unto us on a wall." Two of Ripa's four concepts of Death are female. That there was a hesitating bewilderment in the minds of some poets is evident when within four lines Death is feminine and then masculine: "sleep doolfull *sister* . . . claymed, that [what] *he* bought: and took that erst *he* gave." [9]

Death, whether male or female, winged or wingless, skeleton or shrouded corpse, may be imagined as blind. The Gaoler in *Cymbeline* (V.4.184) had never seen him pictured with "eyes in's head." When in *Richard II* (I.3.223–4) John of Gaunt, lamenting for the banishment of Bolingbroke, says that by the time he returns "My inch of taper will be burnt and done, / And blindfold Death not let me see my son," all the commentators are led astray. The image is not of Death wearing a scarf before his eyes, still less of Death covering the eyes of his victims with a scarf, and certainly not of Death as himself the scarf. "Fold," here, as often in similar contexts, has been misunderstood because scarfs are "folded." It is, however, etymologically the past participle of the verb to fell: Death is stricken with blindness, a fitting epithet for the sightless skull. My readers will remember that in Pierre Michault's *Danse aux Aveugles* Death, Love, and Fortune are the three blind powers before whom mortals perform their dance. Death in Milton's tremendous words, is "the blind Fury" who "with the abhorred shears" "slits the thin–spun life." Twice in the *Horatian Emblems* (pp. 211 and 265) Van Veen depicts a hand cutting with large shears a slender thread. In the first of these designs various personifications are wailing by a corpse.

Death appears in many shapes. Ripa directs that he shall be drawn wearing a mask over the face of the skull because he has so many guises. At the battle of Shrewsbury "hateful Death put on his ugliest mask." [10] Holbein portrays him in a variety of costumes. Death, in his triumphant mocking of Man, is suggested in a tiny copperplate by Beham where he wears a fool's costume with a bauble and cap–and–bells.[11] In a sequence of the *Todten–Dansz* published at Frankfort so late as 1725, no. 39 shows Death dressed as a fool. Were these examples, or others like them, in Thomas Lovell Beddoes' mind when he wrote *Death's Jest–Book*? Sleep bears a close resemblance to him, "Heavy Sleepe, the cosin of

Death," writes Sackville,[12] and Samuel Daniel says that Sleep is "brother to Death." [13] The relationship between the two comes from Seneca's *Hercules Furiens* (line 1069) where Sleep is "frater durae languide Mortis." Elsewhere more fantastic analogies are drawn. Thomas Bancroft describes Death as "a strange Miller" who grinds flesh to dust.[14] George Wither, with an unjustified backward glance at the Gunpowder Plot, says that when Death struck the Prince of Wales, he was "disguised like a murthering Jesuite." [15] Another poet, relying upon what was thought to be natural history, composed an extravagant "Comparatio Mortis et Hyenae." [16] The hyena has a wolf's face, a viper's neck, an elephant's back, and a man's voice. Similarly, Death is ravenous as a wolf, nimble and gliding as a viper, stronger than an elephant, and crafty as a man. Death, he concludes, comes in many shapes.

3. *The Messengers of Death and Death's Arrival*

Often Death despatches his Messengers to admonish Man and give him warning of his coming. In De Guilleville's *Pelerinage de la vie humaine* Old Age and Sickness meet the Pilgrim on his way.[1] In the extant fragment of *The Pride of Life*, probably the earliest of the English moralities, we know from the Presenter's prologue that a Messenger warns the King of Life that Death is about to come. Languor and Sickness are Death's beadles or sergeants, says Lydgate.[2] "My minstrel Sickness pipes the tune," says Death in a mid–sixteenth–century broadside ballad.[3] "These grey locks, the pursuivants of Death," says Shakespeare.[4] "Hairs of Age are messengers," says William Harris, "of Death the harbingers." [5] "Doth the summons of Death appear in your gray head?" asks Robert Greene.[6] Sickness and Old Age, says Nicholas Ling, "are the two crouches whereon Life walketh to Death." [7] An anonymous poem in the *Gorgeous Gallery* is reminiscent of *Everyman*, for when Sickness summons Worldly Desire to come away, Worldly Desire exclaims: "Thy paines doe pearce my hart, / Thou messenger of death" and pleads for permission to linger awhile with Friends and Goods, but Sickness is adamant in refusing him. "The Fall of Folly," a poem by Thomas Proctor in the same collection, tells how Old Age, the messenger or "page" of Death, "attaches," that is arrests, Folly.[8] Rachel Speght assigns to Death three, not two, "monitors," adding Casualtie (Accident) to Sickness and Old Age.[9] Thomas Flatman imparts to this theme a rhetorical dignity and power that suggest the influence of Sir Thomas Browne and recall, not unworthily, the mighty periods of the great prose master:

Consider well, and every place
Offers a ready road to thy long home,
Sometimes with frowns, sometimes with smiling face
   Th' embassadors of Death do come.
By open force or secret ambuscade,
   By unintelligible ways,
   We end our anxious days,
And stock the large plantations of the Dead.[10]

But frequently Death, dispensing with any messenger or ambassador, appears suddenly. No emissary ever invites the various types of humanity to his Dance, and the Three Living are never warned in advance that they are to meet the Three Dead. Death the skeleton is generally shown in the arts of design standing, sitting, or supine, or hovering in the air, or, as in many versions of the *Trionfi*, riding in a chariot. Sometimes he rides upon an animal, most frequently (with a recollection of the pale horse of Revelation 6:8) upon a horse. Graund Amour tells us how "When I thoughte longest to endure, / Dethe with his darte a rest me sodaynely"; and an accompanying woodcut shows Death on horseback holding in one hand a dart and in the other a coffin lid.[11] Triumphing Death appears on horseback in sets of tarot cards.[12] William Bullein tells with considerable power of the coming of Death: "The fearful horseman lighted in the valley. . . . He casteth forth his three dartes. . . . It is merciless Death most fearful." The black dart is the pestilence, the pale dart hunger, the red dart war. Presently Death speaks: "I have no respect of any persons; be thei never so noble, riche, strong, wise, learned, or connyng in Physicke, they shall never prevaile againste me. . . . I come into the Kynges chamber at the time appointed. . . . I overthrowe the Daunser, and stoppe the breathe of the synger, and trippe the runner in his race. . . . I am the greatest crosse and scourge of God." [13] A curious eccentricity, which I am unable to explain, may be observed in the *Heures a l'Antique* (Paris, Geoffrey Tory, 1527) where at the Office of the Dead a cut shows Death astride a horse and facing backward! Is this intended to suggest the "longing, lingering look" which the dying cast behind upon "the warm precincts of the cheerful day"?

The horse is not the only animal on which Death may ride. In my discussion of Love as a companion of Man on his Pilgrimage I interpreted the emblem showing Death riding upon a crocodile, and no more need be said about that beast here. The Office of the Dead in the famous manuscript, the *Tres Riches Heures du Duc de Berri*, has a little *tondo* showing Death riding on a unicorn. This seems to be reminiscent of the prayer in Psalm 22:21 for salvation from "the horns of the unicorns," coupled as it is with the prayer for deliverance from "the power of the dog" and from "the lion's mouth." It seems reminiscent also of the threat in Isaiah 34:7 that "the unicorns shall come down" upon the enemies of the Chosen People, along with other predictions of blood and dust, destruction and death.[14]

In various paintings of the Triumph of Death dating from the first half of the fifteenth century or earlier, for example that by Matteo de' Pasti in the Uffizi and that by Lorenzo Costa at Bologna, Death is in a chariot drawn by bulls or bullocks. But never in such paintings does Death ride on one. This is not surprising since in paintings inspired by Petrarch all six personifications are in chariots. Then, about 1460 or somewhat later, in the Office for the Dead in certain *Horae*, where hitherto had been depicted various other scenes such as the Last Judgment, the administration of the Sacraments, a funeral procession etc., we find illustrations of Death astride a bullock. The proximity of dates makes it possible, as the Comte de Laborde argued,[15] that this new motif derives from Pierre Michault's *Danse aux Aveugles* (ca. 1460) where Death is described and illustrated as so riding.[16] But it should be noted that in Books of Hours where Death is depicted on a bullock he is never blindfold while his sightlessness, a characteristic shared with Love and Fortune, is a principal theme of Michault's *Danse*. If we turn again to Isaiah's dire prophecy against the Lord's enemies we find that in the same verse in which unicorns are named agents of slaughter, bullocks and bulls are named also. Surely we need look no further for their association with Death.[17]

While awaiting the arrival of Sir John Falstaff, Justice Shallow and Justice Silence chat together, the former boasting of his youthful prowess when a student in the Inns of Court, and his memories take on the character of a homely and lowly *Ubi Sunt ?* as he realizes "how many of [his] old acquaintances are dead."—

> *Silence:* We shall all follow, cousin.
> *Shallow:* Certain, 'tis certain; very sure, very sure. Death, as the Psalmist saith, is certain to all; all shall die. How a good yoke of bullocks at Stamford fair?
> *Silence:* By my troth, I was not there.
> *Shallow:* Death is certain. Is old Dooble of your town living yet?

Silence: Dead, sir.

Shallow: Jesu, Jesu, dead! 'A drew a good bow—and dead! [18]

How simple, how realistic, and how touching is this talk! When Shallow shifts the subject so abruptly from Death to the price fetched by bullocks and then back again to Death is he merely seeking an escape from painful thoughts or does Shakespeare intend that the idea of Death carries with it the image of the bullocks? Or if the association is not intended dramatically, was it perhaps unconsciously in the mind of the dramatist? My suggestion is probably merely fanciful; no Shakespearean scholar to whom I have mentioned this interpretation has accepted it. But it is attractive.

Horse, crocodile, bullock, there is an illustration of Death astride yet other beasts. The engraved frontispiece of Joannes Weichardus Valvasor's *Theatrum Mortis Humanae* (Salzburg, 1682) is a Triumph of Death that is far from the usual iconographical tradition. In the upper part there are Roman ruins. Beneath, Adam and Eve are bound captive; two men are digging graves; the fatal tree is in the midst. On a central hill is a crowned Death, flanked by a second Death riding on an elephant, a third riding on a camel, and other Deaths on horseback. Whence come the elephant, a beast symbolic of regality and conquest, appropriate to Death imagination desiring to impart a new flavor to an old theme? Or is the elephant, a beast symbolic of regality and conquest, appropriate to Death the King and Conqueror? Is the camel, a beast symbolic of Avarice, appropriate to Death who sooner or later seizes everything? [19]

For a last time we must turn to Isaiah's prophecy. When the Lord's enemies have been slaughtered their land shall become a desert wilderness inhabited by cruel birds, among them the owl and the raven. During the hours preceding Duncan's arrival at Macbeth's castle there had been ominous phenomena of nature, and among them a falcon, a kingly bird (often associated with the three kings who meet the Three Dead), "was by a mousing owl hawk'd at and kill'd." A Florentine print (ca. 1465–70) shows a young man with a pipe and drum approached by Death carrying a bier and with a scroll proclaiming his insatiable desire. On the gallant's sleeve is embroidered the impresa of a hawk descending upon its quarry.[20] When Lady Macbeth receives the message that the King is on his way to Dunsinane she mutters:

> The raven himself is hoarse
> That croaks the fatal entrance of Duncan
> Under my battlements.

There is a woodcut (1524) by Urse Graf of Basle showing Death in the crotch of a tree pointing, with a grimacing smile, to his hourglass on which a raven is sitting.[21] The Office of the Dead in a Parisian *Horae* is illustrated with a cut of a winged Death holding a dart and a clock and striding over prostrate victims. Nearby in a withered tree a black raven croaks "Cras, Cras." [22]

4. Death Conquers All

Graf's woodcut is but one of countless examples of the fear that Death, though he may come as a release to infirm and poverty stricken Age, is the implacable foe of Youth and Love and Beauty. Van Marle and other iconographers provide many illustrations of these aspects of Death in the arts of design, and I limit myself to a few, some famous, others not well known. A sixteenth–century engraving shows Death swathed in a dark cloak, with one foot in a coffin beside which lie his scythe and spade. He clutches at the short cape worn by a young man.[1] In an early, anonymous Italian engraving Death, who has a bier on his shoulder, is bearing a lady's train. Nearby is a man with a pipe and drum who seems not to be her lover but to represent the *joie de vivre*.[2] Death threatens or destroys sensual pleasure, as seen in a drawing in the Uffizi by Pietro Testa called "The Garden of Worldly Delight." Labels enable us to identify most of the abstractions here depicted. Pride, a naked woman with a peacock on her arm, leads Free Will into this Garden where Luxury, Lasciviousness, Idleness, and other personifications, all represented as naked women, are dancing in a ring in the center of which is Death. Ruthlessly he triumphs (Fig. 141) over the Lust of the Flesh, the Lust of the Eyes, and the Pride of Life.[3] Poignant for all its fantasticality is Daniel Meisner's "Iuventus proposuit, Mors disposuit," where Death thwarts the hopes of Youth (Fig. 142). From a young man's heart there grows a tree on which are a purse, a woman, and a house: wealth, love, and domestic happiness, and the trunk of this tree Death is cutting with his scythe.[4] An anonymous German print (fifteenth century) shows Death confronting Youth who wears armor, but to no avail, for the apparition holds up his hourglass and Youth is saying: "Ich hab ain geding gemacht mit dem tod." [5] In another German print Death has slain three men who lie at his feet and he is about to strike with his scythe Youth who has a falcon on his wrist.[6] A Flemish print (ca. 1470–80) shows Death and Youth playing at chess; it requires no intuition to know who will lose the game.[7] Similarly in an early copperplate Death plays chess with a king while an angel holds up an hourglass and a crowd of people watch the contest.[8] England produced no such designs, but there is a ballad of genuine power entitled "A dialogue betweene death and youthe" (1563–64). This is a colloquy in quatrains: Death utters his summons, Youth pleads vainly for delay, but Death is intransigent.[9] The contrast may be presented between the very beginning of life and its inescapable end, as in a small unsigned engraving (Flemish, sixteenth century) showing an infant asleep beside an hourglass and a skull. This bears the motto "Mors Omnia Aequa [t]." [10]

All too frequently Death is the enemy of youthful lovers. Dürer's print called "The Promenade" (ca. 1510) is so well known that only a bare reminder is here called for: Death with an hourglass on his head spies from behind a tree upon two lovers. In an engraving by Peter Flettner (ca. 1535) Death with his hourglass sits upon a tree watching the lovers.[11] Hans Burgkmair made a truly ferocious print (1510) of a winged Death who tears at the face of a prone warrior while a woman flees in terror.[12] A variant of this is Beham's woodcut called "Death and the Courtesan" (1522). A nude woman is kneeling upon a bed; a warrior lies dead upon the floor; Death with a spear and hourglass is entering at the door.[13] In both these prints Death has in jealousy deprived the woman of her lover because he is eager to take possession of her.

The theme of Death amorous of Beauty—the "Death and the Maiden" motif—was often used by painters, especially in Northern Europe, and is also in the repertoire of engravers.[14] Romeo, gazing upon the dead body (as he thinks) of his beloved, and seeing Beauty's ensign in her crimson lips and cheeks, addresses her:

> Why are thou yet so fair? Shall I believe
> That unsubstantial Death is amorous,
> And that the lean abhorred monster keeps
> Thee here in dark to be his paramour? [15]

In an earlier chapter we have noted the episode in Brathwaite's *Last Trumpet* where Death woos Flesh and Flesh shrinks shudderingly from his courtship. Elsewhere we read that Beauty wears beneath her surface "Death's pale–fac'd Livery" and no "wanton glance of an alluring eye" can divert "th' inevitable fury of his Lance," even though she is cozened by "the deceitfull Index of a glasse." [16] William Habington in his poem "To Death, Castara being sicke," attempts not very successfully to touch lightly on this grim subject. "Away, grim man!" the poet exclaims (I paraphrase). "Come not near my fair! Perhaps a dart from her eye has singed thy wings and thou art forced to hover nigh her. But I beware lest 'thou shoulds't murder with a kisse.' " [17] A late ballad (ca. 1680) which survives in a fragmentary condition is entitled "Beauties Warning–piece." In the lost opening Death's coming was probably narrated; in the remaining part he tells the "fair one" that her glass has run, her thread of life is spun and though she pleads for delay: "Take another and set me free. . . . Cut me not off in my prime," Death "fiercely at her beauty strikes." [18] As an example of this "Warning to Beauty" motif in popular art may be cited a print by Daniel Hopfer. Two women are looking in a mirror and behind them Death holds a skull at such an angle that the reflection in the mirror is of it and not their faces. A fiend is behind Death.[19] Nor is this warning addressed to women only. An impressive printer's device, perhaps used in England during the visitation of the plague in 1603, shows a reverend old man holding up to his young companion a looking glass in which the youth sees not his own image but that of Death who stands behind him. This device bears the motto: "Behoulde your glory." [20] Unexpected novelties are occasionally found. Thus, a late–fifteenth–century French *Horae* has in the Office for the Dead a kneeling Death—not a skeleton but a skull–headed cadaver—who holds a mirror in which is reflected his own grim visage; no living person is present.[21] Another French *Horae* (ca. 1500) conflates the legend of the Three Living and the Three Dead with the theme of Death and the mirror. The Three Living are all young. One of the Deaths holds up the mirror to one of the Living, and there is reflected therein not a skull but his own face, just as he is, with red cap and golden hair. The warning to be conveyed is certainly obscured.[22]

In contrast to the theme of Death's partiality for Youth and Beauty is the other theme, of his supreme impartiality. In my chapter on the Ages of Life we have seen Death destroying the infant in its cradle, the bridegroom at his wedding, the merchant at his business, the old man beside a grave. Death, in a mural at Verdings in Tyrol, manipulates a Wheel of Life upon which the Nine Ages, numbered and carefully delineated, are being turned.[23] Man may cling to Hope and long to continue to enjoy his worldly possessions, but Death hurls his dart at him.[24] An emblem shows Man riding on a horse at whose traces, which are fixed to a globe (worldly possessions) drawn behind him, Death slashes fiercely.[25] In one of the most dramatic of the Horatian Emblems (pp. 196–97) Death parts a father from his child and his weeping wife;

Death bears a cypress tree on his shoulder to be planted upon the grave
(Fig. 143). Other emblems in Van Veen's fascinating volume show
(pp. 202–3) Death selling to all ages and conditions of humanity tickets
for the passage across the Styx, and (pp. 204–5) Death, who has just
slain a poor shoemaker, knocking with the handle of his scythe at the door
of a king's palace. A ballad first printed by Professor Rollins has the very
specific title: "Deth with houreglasse in the one hand and speare in the
other threateneth all estates." It begins:

> Loe heare I vaunce with speare and shield,
> To watche my pray, to spoyle, to kill.

Gloating over his destruction of Croesus, he warns all men:

> I depend on Jove's decree,
> And forth will walke with glasse in hand
> to slay, to spoile, by sea and land.[26]

That all ranks are subject to Death's sway is the warning conveyed in
more designs than can be mentioned here. Three anonymous fifteenth–
century German woodcuts in color show a Pope, an Emperor, and a
Peasant confronted by a skeleton. Scrolls bear such warnings as "Gedenck
was wir sein." [27] A fantastic engraving, perhaps by the Master of the
Banderoles though Lehrs assigns it to an anonymous artist, and deriving
in part from the legend of Barlaam and Josefat, shows (along with much
other symbolism) a tree in whose branches are the ten orders of humanity, from Pope down to Churl. In the foreground Death lies supine
in a coffin, but he holds a rope that is attached to the tree. Among the
immense number of illustrations in an Italian treatise of nearly six hundred pages are many, largely derivative from Holbein, showing Death
coming to all types of humanity.[28] One of the plates (no. 85) in Father
David's *Veridicus Christianus* depicts Death, wearing a crown that is
topped with a winged hourglass, standing upon a heap of corpses: bishops
and warriors, young and old, representatives of various types of men.
In the moralizing text accompanying this plate Father David quotes
the famous lines from Horace: "Pallida mors aequo pulsat pedo pauperum
tabernas Regumque turres." The thought inspired many emblematists.
It may be expressed by crossing a scepter with a hoe, and this design is
called "Dell' ugualita dopo la morte." [29] In another emblem a scepter
and a mattock are crossed; the inscription reads: "Mors sceptra ligonibus
aequans," or, as it is rendered in the English version, "Death maketh
Kings scepters equall to pore mens mattocks." [30] An English emblem,

borrowed from the Continent, shows a scepter and spade crossed one on the other and lying upon a grave.[31] Because he is impartial Death may hold the scales of Justice; the pans of the scales are in equal balance, one with a crown and scepter, the other with a rake, a pitchfork, and a mattock.[32] Ripa recommends that Death be depicted with a hook to pull down the mighty and a sickle to mow down the lowly. Inadequate to the subject in style but precise in meaning are two lines by an un-identified Elizabethan writer who says of Death that "He steemes [esteems] no more a mightie Prince, his Scepter or his port, / Then Mattocke of a laboring man, one of the poorer sort." [33] Of such designs and verses the first hearers and readers of James Shirley's poem, which King Charles I so rightly commended as "noble," must have been re-minded:

> Sceptre and crown
> Must tumble down,
> And in the ground be equal made
> With the poor scythe and crooked spade.

One of the plates in the English translation of Jean Puget de la Serre's meditations on death shows Diogenes challenging Alexander to distinguish between the Great and the Mean in a heap of skulls.[34] In the simplest form of the "Ubi sunt?" one or two great men of olden times may be named, as when Hamlet meditates upon the possibility that "Im-perious Caesar, dead and turned to clay / Might stop a hole to keep the wind away," or that the "noble dust of Alexander" may stop a bunghole. In a ballad quoted above Death boasts of his triumph over Croesus, but in another ballad the roll call of his illustrious captives is long. He comes riding on a "barbed horse, with couler pale." "I am that champion, greate of power," he announces, and he cries: "Yeeld, princes! . . . Come breake a staffe with me who dare!" Nimrod, Samson, Alexander, Caesar, Hector, David, Josias—"Theise all ar now in dusty plight."

> Looke, therefore, look alwayes for me;
> For when thy glasse is full runne out,
> I come with speare, be out of doubt.[35]

A solemnly macabre and quite powerful poem by W. Parkes called "A meditation upon the vanity of all vanity" contains no names of the fa-mous dead but the theme is there, and is of special interest because the inspiration is drawn from Westminster Abbey.

> Go but unto that ancient teeming mother . . .
> Whose royall bordered honourable wombe
> So many Kings and Nobles doth intombe.

The poem continues, pointing out that their pomp is now nothing, the guard has forsaken them, the worm may seize them though they call out treason, Death has made equal the scepter and the spade. There follows the motif of "Worms' meat, worms' meat!" which I quoted at the beginning of this chapter. And then with genuinely fine effect there is a change from pentameter couplets to tetrameter and Death speaks:

> You gallant dames behold your doome,
> To me at length you all must come. . . .
> You, carelesse you, looke well on me,
> For as I am, so shal you be.
> I am that Death, at length that must
> Lay all your glory in the dust.[36]

We find the "Ubi sunt?" again in Rachel Speght's memorial poem on her mother. In a dream she sees Death, the "fierce insatiable foe," and having meditated upon his different aspects, upon the swift passage of the Ages of Life, and upon the failure of the Five Senses, she asks: "Where are now Absalom, David, Salomon, Cressus, Dives, and Sampson." [37] For a far finer rendering of the theme, comparable indeed in its poignant quality to Villon's two ballads of which the reader needs no reminder, we must turn to an illustration in a work of the Dutch poet Jacob Cats. It is entitled "Sic transit gloria mundi." A company of men and women have removed the marble slabs from five tombs within which lie five skeletons. Inscriptions in Dutch read: "Here lies Solomon, the world's wisest man"; "Here lies Samson, the world's strongest man"; "Here lies Alexander the Great, the greatest conqueror"; "Here lies Croesus, the world's richest man"; and in the center of the row of tombs: "Here lies Helen, the beauty of the world." Overhead Fame blows her trumpet but Time attacks with his scythe a warrior's sculptured portrait. The central inscription calls to mind the lines in Thomas Nashe's beautiful lyric: "Queens have died young and fair; / Dust hath closed Helen's eye." I turn from this motif to call attention to two other impressively macabre illustrations in Cats' poem. In one there is a company upon the Ship of Life, enjoying wine, women, and song; but Time is at the prow and Death, blowing a trumpet, is on the poop. In the other Death reaches his hourglass across a table to an old man who continues his studies though one of his feet is in the grave that yawns beside him.[38] For a final example of the lesson that human nature is subject to Death and that no eminence or glory can withstand his power let us revert once more to Stephen Hawes. Youth visits "the solemn and royal mansion of Dame Nature."

> She sate as a fayre goddess
> All thynges creatynge by her busynesse.
> Me thought she was of merveylous beaute
> Tyll that dyscrecyon ledde me behynde.

There Youth saw the "privity" of her work, for

> at her backe than dyd I fynde
> Of cruell dethe a dolefull image.

A woodcut (Fig. 144) shows Death standing behind Dame Nature.[39]

5. Death as God's Agent and Nature's Companion

The ruthlessness of Death is not motiveless; he is the agent to carry out God's just decrees. Without introducing a personification an engraving in the Albertina, possibly by "Master I. A. op Zwolle," implies this by showing Moses with the tables of the Law flanked by two skulls with a third above his head and below him a prostrate skeleton. A plate in the English translation of Drexelius shows Death exhibiting to mortals the fatal apple and a parchment—the contract they must abide by, having violated God's command.[1] An engraving of much later date shows Death striking a rich old man; his weapon is a rolled document with three seals.[2] Romeo "seals with a righteous kiss" upon Juliet's lips "a dateless bargain to engrossing Death."

"That fell sergeant, Death," says the dying Hamlet, "is strick in his arrest." The image has many parallels. Graund Amour, speaking after his own death, tells us that "whan I thoughte longest to endure, / Dethe with his darte a rest me sodaynly." [3] One of the morality plays contains the warning: "Whan Deth with his mace dooth you areest . . . / From the ladder of lyfe downe he wyll the [thee] thruste." [4] Two Jacobean poets express precisely the same thought. William Hornby in a warning to drunkards writes:

> Then grim—faced Death comes with his Mace in's fist,
> And at Gods suit doth sudden them arrest. . . .

He is Gods Sargeant, and no kind of baile
Can any whit in all the world prevaile.[5]

Of this there seems to be a direct echo or imitation in William Hall's lines:

Our hoorded wealth will naught at all prevaile
When we are summon'd by deaths fatall call:
Who uncertaine, yet certaine will meet us,
And with, Sir I arrest you, it will greet us
Like a bold Sergeant with his Mase in's fist.[6]

Two of the dramatists vary the metaphor or simile. According to George Chapman it is not God but Dame Nature who sends "her sergeant John Death" to arrest an old man who owes her a debt.[7] According to Dekker it is not Death but Sickness, "the Sergeant with the Black Rod," who "arrests us." [8] Elsewhere we come across a grimly humorous pun, when Death is called "Squire Katch," for as everybody knows Jack Ketch was the name of the public hangman.

6. Death with Parcae, Fortune, and Time

Death is not only God's servant and an inevitable companion of Nature, he is also to be found with the Parcae, with Fortune, and with Time. The first of these associations seems not to have appealed to the English imagination. It is found, so far as my reading goes, only in Lydgate's *Assembly of Gods* where the office of Atropos is "all [men] with my dart fynally to chastyse" and who, desiring to serve the Lord of Light, has his name changed to Death.[1] Four examples from the arts of design may be cited. In the Albertina there is an anonymous drawing which may be a "Triumph of the Pestilence," for there is no indication that it survives from an otherwise lost series of the Petrarchan *Trionfi*. Death with robe and crown and holding a saw—toothed sickle stands at the front of a car with one foot on the rump of a buffalo and behind him in the car are the Parcae. Corpses strew the ground.[2] In a series of French tapestries of the early sixteenth century, now in Vienna, illustrating the *Trionfi* "The Triumph of Death" does not conform to the norm. Death himself does not appear. Instead the parcae stand in a car which runs over Chastity. The car is drawn by oxen, and Vieillesse lends aid by pushing one of the wheels while Pandora goes before. In "The Triumph of Divinity" in the same sequence the car in which ride the Holy Trinity runs not over Death but over the Parcae.[3] Of about the same date is a tapestry of The Triumph of Death woven in Brussels. There is no Death and no chariot or car but, rather, the three Fates stand upon the prostrate body of a fair woman.[4] In an emblem engraved by Theodore de Bry death and the Parcae all appear and a tiara, crowns, and scepters lie scattered on the ground, but to one side, isolated, stands Virtue opposing Death and the Fates with sword and shield.[5]

Death is often found with Fortune. We have just noted the Tyrolean mural where a gigantic Death turns a wheel closely analogous to a Wheel of Fortune. An anonymous German woodcut (ca. 1470) shows Death actually turning her wheel (Fig. 145). On it there are seven figures of whom the two topmost are crowned; and one of several inscriptions reads: "Your Wheel of Fortune must go round; you must leave wealth behind you." [6] An engraving (1464) by the Master of the Banderoles combines in one design Fortune at her wheel and Death shooting his dart at men and women who are thickly clustered in the Tree of Life. On the wall of the cloister of Corpus Christi Church in Cracow a late-seventeenth-century painting conflates the Wheels of Life and Fortune with the Triumph of Death. On either side is a Death crowning himself, and in the middle is a wheel between whose spokes are deathheads wearing, respectively, a crown, a miter, a cap, or other headgear indicative of social rank.[7] I have described earlier the disputations in the *Danse aux Aveugles*, *The Rare Triumphs of Love and Fortune*, and *Soliman and Persida* in which Death engages with Love and Fortune and discomfits his opponents.

The most memorable of all versions of the rivalry is John Davies of Hereford's *The Civile Warres of Death and Fortune*, a massive poem in 109 stanzas of ottava rima in the volume of 1609.[8] At a marriage feast (in whose honor is not made clear) the gods were among the guests and Death and Fortune among the dancers. Fortune preferred as partners those who flattered her while Death danced with his foes, for all were his foes. They danced to Time's music, albeit Fortune, turning, "kept no time, thogh Time his turns did serve." She danced lavoltas because they rise and fall, but Death danced "the passing-measure" or "the shaking of the sheets," and now and then he would drive his partners "from dancing into Winck-all-hid." The dancing done, they fell into a dispute: Death boasted of his universal authority, to which Fortune replied that if he were not blind [9] he would see that "Tyranny is no true Sov'raigntie," whereas her subjects follow her willingly. They agreed to have Jove arbitrate between them, and the debate was conducted in "this round world's spacious theatre." Fortune's devotees were there, among them rulers, fools, and philosophers in search of the "stone." Crowds followed and fawned upon her, but Death could persuade no one to follow him, not even the galley–slave.[10] The debate ended, Jove gave the verdict to Fortune, and

> ever since Death rageth more and more:
> That now all men false Fortune doe preferre,
> Before just Death.

The same rivalry is the subject of one of Thomas Bancroft's epitaphs and one of his epigrams. The conceit in the former is that when "Death, the great gamester" gambled with "sightless Fortune" for the life of one of Bancroft's friends, Death won, but Fame sided with Fortune and so won the "after–game." The epigram is that Life is "a cheating game at cards" in which Fortune stacks the pack but Death cuts last and wins the game.[11]

While Death is the enemy of Fortune he is almost never conceived as hostile to Time, and though he may be Time's servant he is more frequently his partner. The two personifications are frequently closely linked. Of this relationship the greatest and most famous example in literature is the scene at the close of Molière's *Don Juan* (1666) where the Specter is transformed into a likeness of Time with his scythe. However, examples of much earlier date are to be found. Without these personifications and depending wholly upon the emblem there is the device of a skull which rests upon a crossed scythe and bone; on the skull is an hourglass and on the hourglass an escapement.[12] In 1537 Cornelis Anthonisz (Tennissen) designed a print (Fig. 146) in which a skeleton "Tempus," leans against the shoulder of a grave, bearded man and points to an hourglass.[13] An engraving by Marius Kartarius (1563) places Time and Death side by side.[14] Half a dozen, or perhaps more for the subject of one or two is doubtful, murals of Time and Death survive in English churches. The same figures are to be seen on the title pages of English books. Each standing upon a globe, signifying their dominance over this life, they flank the title of *The Crums of Comfort*. At the top of the page men and women are kneeling round "The Hill of Joy" and "Crummes of Comfort" fall from heaven; at the bottom is "The Valley of Tears," where the sun is setting and people gesticulate and weep.[15] The engraved title page of Colman's *La Dance*

Machabre (ca. 1633) has Death seated on a cornice, his bony foot thrust through a laurel wreath held by two Cupids. Is this intended to suggest Death's contemptuous conquest of Love (the Cupids) and Fame (the laurel wreath)? At the bottom of the page Time sweeps his scythe over the globe. Four marginal panels depict four types of humanity, all subject to Time and Death, one is an artist at his easel engaged in drawing a skeleton. Some verses interpret, not very lucidly, "The Mind of the Front." The anonymous designer (probably a Hollander) of the title page of John Paget's *Meditations of Death* (1639) was content with simple flanking figures of Time and Death.[16] On the margins of the title page of Edward Buckler's *A Buckler against the fear of Death* (1640) are Death transfixing a heart with his dart and Time about to cut a flower with his scythe. A printer's device (1637–40) shows Time and Death holding between them a large book.[17] A woodcut depicting both decorates a ballad called "Time and Death's Advice to all Wicked Livers." This begins:

> Beware of Time, too High don't Climb
>   For Fear you catch a Fall,
> For if you do, 'tis even True
>   Squire Katch will pay you all.[18]

The same woodcut is used in "A Description of Plain–Dealing, Time and Death." [19] In all these examples from literature and the arts the two formidable abstractions cooperate or are grouped together. But elsewhere Time is the master of Death, for, as the Moslems say, every man's hour is written in his forehead and until that hour strikes he is not subject to Death. We are once more reminded of Quarles' emblem of Time staying the hand of Death and of John Davies of Hereford's concept of Death as the servant of Time. With Davies' description we may compare lines by another poet:

> "Ah why should Painters limme Death with a dart [?],
> Time with a Syth before him cuts all downe,
> Death doth but lance, and play the Surgeons part,
> Time fells the Corne, that's ready to be mowne
>   Alas! what Cruelty hath Death us showne?
> Thou [*i.e.*, Death] art but as a Servant unto time,
> To gather fruits which, he [*i.e.*, Time] saith, ripe by growne:
> In Wine–presse thou but treadest out the wine,
> To barrell up in Tombes that there it may refine." [20]

Once we find them not engaged as equals in their respective offices or as master and servant but as foes. This is in Samuel Rowlands' poem, *A Terrible Battell betweene the two consumers of the whole World: Time and Death*. In this debate each protagonist heaps abuse upon the other and boasts of his own powers and achievements. In lines quoted in the Appendix, Time reproaches Death because his picture on the ale house wall is a *Memento Mori* to the brawlers. Death denounces Time as

> a foul misshapen monster,
> Behind all bald, a lock ell–long before,
> With cloven feet.

This poem is decorated with a woodcut, on the very lowest level of popular imagery, showing Death about to hurl his spear at Time and Time with his scythe threatening Death.[21]

7. *Death as a Release from Life*

It is with relentless Time leading him on and inescapable Death behind him that the Pilgrim pursues his way and reaches the journey's end. As Rowlands in another poem expresses it: "Time runs before, and instantly forsakes us, / Death posts behind, and sodaine overtakes us." [1] With an accompanying motto: "Il tempo va, la morte viene," an illustration in one of Jacob Cats' poems conveys the same idea more impressively. A young gallant, flamboyantly attired, is in the center of the picture. Turning away from him is Time with an hourglass on his head and an escapement in his hand and Death with his dart poised to strike taps the man on his shoulder.[2]

"O wretched man that I am!" exclaims St. Paul; "who shall deliver me from the body of this Death?" (Romans 7:24). The Soul under the ribs of Death, imprisoned in the bony torso and looking yearningly from between the bars, is an emblem (Fig. 147) borrowed by Quarles from a French source and found again in a French collection of much later date.[3] A variant depicts a castle in which the Soul is imprisoned, with devils on guard and Divine Love coming to the rescue.[4] Divine Love may reconcile the Soul to Death, as in an emblem where he entrusts the Soul to his formidable servant.[5] Death may be shown cutting the chains that bind the Soul to the World,[6] or he may release Man who is sitting in the stocks of this mortal life.[7] One English writer has the image of Death as an inn where Man finds repose at the end of his Pilgrimage; [8] but another says that Death is "a packhorse to carry [Man] from earth to heaven, from pain to pleasure, from misery, vexation, grief and woe, to endless mirth." [9] In one of La Perriere's emblems Death leads the Soul—a Pilgrim, for she has the staff and scrip—away from Envy and Fortune. The motto is: "J'ai un confort, cest que Envie et Fortune / Ne me pourroit apres mort nuyre plus." [10] A design often found is that of kindly Death assisting weary Man to step out of the world (Fig. 148). In the background a path winds upward, its further reaches hidden in the cloud of Divinity. The motto is: "Desiderans dissolvi." [11]

Another of La Perriere's emblems shows the Soul, laurel–wreathed and seated in a chariot. The coachman of the Chariot is Death and it is drawn by the bees signifying Virtue,[12] for "the actions of the just," in Shirley's famous words, "smell sweet and blossom in the dust." An early Elizabethan black–letter memorial broadside has a woodcut of a skeleton lying upon a tomb. From the skeleton grows a tree in full leaf and entwined among its branches is a scroll bearing the words: "Post funera Virtus vivet tamen." [13] This is the device of John Daye and is found, for example, as the colophon of such volumes as William Cunningham's *The Cosmographical Glasse* (1559) and *A Booke of Christian Prayers* (1578). There are variants such as an emblem of wheat sprouting from dry bones with the motto: "Spes altera vitae." [14] A more elaborate concept is found among Wither's emblems. In the background is a grave marked with a cross, and nearby men are cutting ripe wheat at harvest time. Into this setting is placed the emblem, an hourglass upon which rests a skull which has full ripe blades of wheat growing from its eyes and jaws and a burning candle resting on its top. Accompanying verses declare that "Death is no Losse, but rather, Gaine; / For wee by Dying, Life attaine." [15] Elsewhere the lesson "Sola mori nescit Virtus" (Fig. 149) is drawn from the design of the sprouting tomb.[16] But it may be that Good Fame is all that survives the grave. This idea is implied in the title page of *Truth Brought to Light and Discovered by Time* where a tree growing out of a coffin bears books and documents as its fruit. Loosely attached to this concept, for there is no tomb or tree, is a printer's device of Time cutting with his scythe a sheaf of wheat. In the foreground is a book bearing the words: "Verbum Dei manet in aeternum" and round the oval frame of the design are the words: "Non solo pane vivet homo." [17]

Death, however, is not the end. Quarles has an emblem of the Soul with a spyglass (Fig. 150). In the distance stands Death, behind him are the flames of hell, but above Christ sits on the rainbow.[18] In the first illustrated edition of St. Ignatius Loyola's *Spiritual Exercises* there is an engraving of a blindfold man creeping forward upon his hands and knees with two baskets containing a devil and symbolic animals resting on his back. They are the burden of his sins.[19] Among the emblems of Jacobus Bornitius is one of a Pilgrim, weary because the burden is still on his back, resting for a moment from his travels along the path which stretches steeply up a precipitous mountain. At the summit is another traveler, his citizenship in heaven, "Nostrum Politeuma in Coelis," who is about to climb the Scala Paradisi extending onward and upward.[20] An engraving by Robert Vaughan on the title page of an English book is of a Pilgrim, unmistakably identified by the scallop shell on his hat, who also bears a burden, but it is the Cross (Fig. 151). The path he must ascend is indeed steep, but upon the mountain top grows the Tree of Life,[21] which has beside it the inscription: "De Ligno Vitae emanavit balsamum omni vulneri Saluferium." A version of the same theme in an engraving in Sir William Denny's *Pelicanicidium* contains two figures: the Pilgrim with his scallop shell and a cruciform staff, and his godly mentor. Beside the path on which they stand is a dark cavern from whose recesses protrudes a horrible dragon, but they heed not this demon. Below the picture are verses: "Wise Traveller through Wildernesse does lead / The Christian Pilgrim, teaching where to tread." [22]

APPENDIX. KNOWLEDGE OF THE ARTS

1. Some Analogies between Shakespeare and the Fine Arts

Answers, tentative at best, can only be found by piecing together a large number of bits of evidence.[1] By this means I shall here attempt to show what knowledge of the arts of design people of culture during the English Renaissance possessed, and to what extent this knowledge was shared by those who lacked an opportunity to refine and enlighten their taste.

It seems likely that in dramatizing the rivalry between the Poet and the Painter in *Timon of Athens* (scene 1) Shakespeare may not have depended only upon his own evaluation of the comparative merits of the two arts but may also have reported what he heard and said in private intercourse. In Elizabethan London the world of writers and artists was small, and it is probable, albeit undemonstrable, that he numbered painters among his friends. It can at least be shown that a poet who may have been his friend was a friend of painters. This was John Davies of Hereford who twice in cryptic marginal glosses attached to poems alludes to "W.S." Whether these are complimentary references to Shakespeare is a problem that has been much debated and can never be settled. Both times these initials are associated with the initials "R.B." which probably refer to Richard Burbage; and in one of these two cases John Davies seems to be referring to Burbage's talent as a painter rather than to his genius as an actor.[2] Davies addressed an epigram to his "approved friend and good neighbor," Rowland Locky the portrait painter. It was perhaps in Locky's workshop that Davies watched the process which furnished him with the conceit for another epigram whose title describes the artist in the very act of changing the subject of a portrait: "Upon the making of one friends face on the Bord [i.e. a panel] where anothers was made; the first being put out with coulor, for the second thereon to be painted." In a third epigram he expresses the resolution to praise a friend with moderation, for to be too lavish in praise would be to act like those who "lay upon a curious Print fair Coulors thick" with the consequence that "each principall Deliniament is drownd in Coulor of lesse ornament." [3] Again Davies describes a painting

> Which, one way, had a fair–Maides Phisnomy,
> The other way, an Apes, which seemed to talk:
> So, that Face had two Faces, in one hood:
> A faire Maides, and an Apes: which seem'd to me
> The Painter was not mad, in mirry mood:
> That, under mirth, hid grave morrality.[4]

The "grave morrality" of the painting lay in the antithesis of maiden and ape, an emblem of lasciviousness, which suggested Fraud, Deceit, Hypocrisy.[5] The poet thus lends his support to the painters' claim that in their art they were not limited to "sense" but could convey a moral meaning.

This painting was one of those oddities, entertaining as a display of technical skill but of little or no aesthetic worth, that are still occasionally met. Contrasting subjects are painted on opposite sides of a set of parallel, vertical slats attached at right angles to a base. One of this sort was done by Nicholas Hilliard, showing from one direction a woman

and from the other a figure of Death.[6] Shakespeare may have been thinking of such a tour de force when Cleopatra says of Anthony (*Anthony
and Cleopatra*, II.5.116–7): "Though he be painted one way like a
Gorgon, / The other way's a Mars." The image here, however, may
have been suggested by the designs, not uncommon in emblem books,
of a face or figure with right and left sides contrasted: beautiful and
hideous, young and old, peaceful and warlike, man and woman, even
alive and dead. There is, however, no doubt about the origin of the
image when one of Chapman's characters speaks of "a couzening picture, which one way / Shows like a crow, another like a swan." [7] A
composite trick picture might be not merely double but threefold, a
third subject being painted on the baseboard. One such is described
by Chapman:

> A picture wrought to optic reason,
> That to all passers–by seems, as they move,
> Now woman, now a monster, now a devil,
> And till you stand and in a right line view it,
> You cannot well judge what the main form is.[8]

From a painting of this sort, in which three contrasts are presented, Ben
Jonson draws an elaborate metaphor of swindling.[9] He calls it a "perspective," a term which he uses elsewhere in the more ordinary sense
with which we are familiar from the distorted portrait of King Edward VI and the distorted skull in Holbein's portrait of "The Am-
bassadors." To see such an object aright the position at which the viewer
must place his eye is sometimes indicated on the border of the painting,
or the painting may have to be squinted at through a hole. Of this
Jonson must have been thinking when one of his characters says: "I
brought some dozen or twentie gallants this morning to view 'em (as
you'll doe a piece of Perspective) in at a keyhole." [10] Shakespeare, too,
had seen

> perspectives, which rightly gaz'd upon,
> Show nothing but confusion—ey'd awry,
> Distinguish form.[11]

However, he was thinking not of such bizarre paintings but of trick mirrors when he makes the Duke, wondering at the resemblance between
Viola and Sebastian, exclaim: "One face, one voice, one habit, and two
persons! / A natural perspective, that is and is not!" [12] Either of these

optical illusions, the distorted painting or the trick mirror, may have been in his mind when Bertram explains to the King how his admiration of Helen had been corrupted:

> Contempt his scornful perspective did lend me
> Which warp'd the line of every other favour . . .
> Extended or contracted all proportions
> To a most hideous object.[13]

The problem of Shakespeare's acquaintance with the arts of design has been so frequently and so thoroughly investigated [14] that further discussion of it may here be brief. Almost as notorious as the Bohemian seacoast in *The Winter's Tale* is the passage in the same play (V.2.104–7) where the statue of Hermione, described as "a Peece many yeares in doing," is said to be "newly performed by that rare Italian master Julio Romano." It is not to be assumed that Shakespeare was ignorant of the fact that Giulio Romano was a painter, not a sculptor. The statue having been carved by other artists, the master "performs" the work—that is, completes it by painting it. Being in reality Hermione herself it must needs be flesh–colored.[15] In an often quoted passage in his letters Sir Henry Wotton deplored the fashion of coloring statuary as an English barbarism. This was, however, a common practice not only in England but on the Continent. An anonymous traveler who was a closer observer than Wotton and who had visited the College where Jesuits were trained for the English mission wrote: "After the Carver hath most artificially finisht his Arte, comes the Painter, and daubes it over with his lively colours." [16] Actually polychrome sculpture descends uninterruptedly from antiquity.

Other passages in Shakespeare's plays present smaller problems. No one has identified the picture to which Feste alludes in *Twelfth Night* (II.3.16) when, joining Sir Toby and Sir Andrew, he asks merrily: "Did you never see the picture of We Three?" The allusion is probably to a painting on some alehouse or tavern wall depicting perhaps three roistering boon companions but more probably two persons with a looking glass between them, the point of the feeble joke being that the third person was the viewer. Commentators on the play supply parallel passages from other writers, and to these may be added the description of Mad Laughter in Phineas Fletcher's *The Purple Island* (1633), Canto VIII. This personification has on his shield the device of "two laughing fools." The polished shield reflects his own face; his motto is: "We Three."

In *Love's Labour's Lost* (III.1.20) we find the simile: "Your hands in your pocket, like a man after the old painting." The use of the definite article suggests that Shakespeare had some particular painting in mind, but it is unidentifiable. When Ariel in *The Tempest* (III.2.136) plays upon a tabor and pipe, Trinculo, because Ariel is invisible, exclaims marveling that the tune is "play'd by the picture of Nobody." A large woodcut of Nobody occupies the upper half of an undated (early Elizabethan?) black—letter broadside entitled "The Welspoken Nobody." The allusion, however, cannot be to this cut, for the man shown is of entirely normal shape. There is little doubt that it is to the woodcut on the title page (Fig. 152) of the anonymous play *Nobody and Somebody* (1606) or else to the sign on the shop of John Trundle, who issued the play. The grotesque figure has no body, the head rests on the thighs and arms attached to the hips. It is likely that the cut is a more or less faithful reproduction of the sign. A theater audience would have more probably caught a reference to the sign than to the title page of a play several years older than *The Tempest*.

2. *Murals and Paintings, Religious and Secular*

There is reason to believe that many of the wall paintings which once adorned most English churches and various secular buildings had been neglected and had fallen into disrepair through neglect before the Reformation hastened their decay and obliteration. It is impossible to determine what percentage of the total number surviving from earlier centuries were still undefaced or not covered with whitewash in Elizabethan times. Prejudice again Romish subjects led to much deliberate destruction. The prejudice was, however, directed chiefly against subjects whose doctrinal content was considered dangerous or disputable.[1] Hostility was certainly not so much inflamed against traditional moral subjects as against theological ones. At later dates, however, Puritan iconoclasm and neoclassic scorn of the Gothic past were responsible for many losses, as were the late—eighteenth and nineteenth—century restorers. Fortunately a good many paintings have been recovered from beneath whitewash or behind interior structural alterations, and though later reconstruction work again obliterated some and destroyed others, sufficient remain, either more or less intact or in copies made by enlightened antiquarians, to give a fair idea of the range of subjects with which people of our period were familiar. Among them were various personifications.[2]

On the west wall of many church naves the Last Judgment was depicted. All commentators agree that Shakespeare must have remembered "the great Doom's image" with its "painted devil" which had perhaps frightened him as a child at Stratford.[3] With the Doom were associated other cautionary and hortatory themes. More than a score of murals of the Seven Deadly Sins have either survived or are known from records. Sometimes personifications, sometimes type figures represent the Seven Deadly Sins. They may be shown in combat with the Virtues or subdued by them or thrust into hellmouth; or arranged schematically upon a wheel or as the limbs of a tree. Half a dozen examples of the Wheel of Fortune are extant in churches. Of the Ages of Human Life but three specimens have been recorded. One of these is so ruined that the subject is doubtful; the other two are in secular buildings. A *Scala Salvationis* has been uncovered on the wall of a church in Surrey. Fragments of the Dance of Death have been found in five churches. No less than twenty–three murals depicting the Three Living and the Three Dead are known.[4] An isolated figure of Time or Death serves sometimes as a *Memento Mori*, and elsewhere these two solemn abstractions appear together. Philippe de Mornay, urging the penitent to trust in God and arguing against the fear of death, wrote, as translated by the Countess of Pembroke in *A Discourse of Life and Death* (1592): "Wee have her [Death] in horror: but because wee conceive her not as she is, but ougly, terrible, and hideous, such as it pleaseth the Painters to represent unto us on a wall." In contrast to such admonitions there are subjects encouraging the faithful: various sequences of the Works of Mercy set edifying examples; the parable of the Prodigal Son taught repentance.[5]

Secular buildings, both public and private, might be decorated with murals or tapestries or those cheap substitutes for tapestries known as "painted cloths." In that day when pictures were still often "the poor man's Bible" (*Pictura est laicorum Scriptura*) Biblical histories and parables were often popular. In a description of ale houses we read that "you shall see the History of Judith, Susanna, Daniel in the Lyons Den, or Dives and Lazarus, painted upon the walls." [6] Two murals of this last subject are extant in a manor house in Hampshire: In one Dives is feasting with his guests; in the other he is about to buffet Lazarus. These date from ca. 1580. Some years ago there were discovered a late–Elizabethan sequence of murals on the Prodigal Son. Originally it occupied five panels but the first, which doubtless showed the Prodigal's departure from his home, has been destroyed and the fifth, which doubtless showed the fatted calf and the sullen brother, has been badly cut into by a door of later date. In the second panel the Prodigal is feasting with fine ladies; in the third he kneels at the swine's trough; in the fourth he is welcomed home by his father.[7] Falstaff speaks of both Lazarus and the Prodigal. He says his conscripts are "as ragged as Lazarus in the painted cloth, where the glutton's dog licked his sores." The room he was assigned in the Garter Inn at Windsor was "painted about with the story of the Prodigal, fresh and new." He recommends this subject to Mistress Quickly for her walls.[8] Murals illustrating the Book of Tobit have been discovered in the White Swan Inn at Stratford–on–Avon.[9] The Nine Worthies were popular subjects; they might be seen in taverns, where they exemplified both heroism and the subjection of great men to Fortune.[10] Other themes provided similar admonitions. Sir William Cornwallys says that tavern paintings cry out to the guests: "Fear God!"[11] In a poem by Samuel Rowlands it is said of Death:

> Thy picture stands upon the Ale–house wall,
> Not in the credit of an ancient story,
> But when the old wive's guests begin to braule,
> She points, and bids them read *Memento mori:*
> Looke, looke (saies she) what fellow standeth there.[12]

When Doll Tearsheet counsels Falstaff to leave fighting and foining and "begin to patch up thine old body for heaven," the two were in a tavern which might have had such a painting on the wall. Does this not add poignancy to Falstaff's protest: "Peace, good Doll! Do not speak like a death's head. Do not bid me remember mine end"?[13] and did the paintings of the Prodigal and of Dives the Glutton impress him because he felt something like remorse?

Fortune with her

> painted turning wheele . . .
> Which after one selfe manner everywhere
> Is drawne by painters[14]

was a familiar sight to Londoners for her figure adorned the main entrance of the splendid new Fortune Theater on the Bankside. In one of Thomas Heywood's plays a character, refusing to budge from his place till he has obtained a pardon, declares:

> I'll rather stand here
> Like a statue in the fore–front of your house,
> Forever, like the picture of Dame Fortune,
> Before the Fortune Playhouse.[15]

In Elizabethan English the word "picture" refers also to statues; Heywood employs both words in this single sentence. It is less likely that a carved figure of Fortune stood before the playhouse than that a painted one was seen upon a sign thrust out at right angles to the façade. We can at any rate be confident that so famously fine a building had a conspicuously handsome ornament. By analogy we can assume that a representation of Hope with her anchor adorned the Hope Theater, and Atlas supporting the globe was probably outside the playhouse of that name.

In a few places direct evidence of indebtedness to Continental masters survives. The remains of a series of wall paintings of the story of Cupid and Psyche were brought to light during reconstruction work at Hill Hall in Essex.[16] These are copies of Italian engravings by the "Master of the Dye" which are based on designs by Michiel Coxie. A tradition that Sir Thomas Smith, the owner of Hill Hall, helped with the decoration warrants the assumption that, since he had traveled on the Continent, he may have brought home the engravings to be copied. A small banqueting house built by Sir Nicholas Bacon in an orchard of Gorombery manor near St. Albans has disappeared, but we know that it was "most curiously adorned," for round about it "the liberall Artes [were] deciphered, with the pictures of some of those men which have been excellent in every particular Art." The antiquarian to whom we owe this information [17] lists the practitioners, three or four being associated with each art. Had the designer seen or heard of the fresco in the Spanish Chapel or some other Italian rendering of the subject?

The most memorable paintings to be seen in Elizabethan London were undoubtedly the canvases by Hans Holbein the Younger in the Steelyard, illustrating "The Triumph of Riches" and "The Triumph of Poverty." [18] These great paintings were lost long ago, but a sketch by Holbein himself for the "Riches" and several other sketches of both "Triumphs" survive and from them we can obtain an idea of their rhythm and movement and magnificent effect. In general the moral lesson is imparted by the contrast between honest Poverty and Riches, unstable and in thralldom to Fortune.

We have a number of inventories of paintings and other works of art in the possession of the royal family, of church dignitaries, or of the nobility and gentry. Two such lists (1590 and 1609) are of paintings at Lumley Castle and at Lord Lumley's other residences.[19] They whet the appetite for all that is lost beyond recovery. They record a vast number of portraits, contemporary, earlier Tudor, historical, and pseudo-

historical; paintings of Biblical and mythological subjects; some paintings by Italian or Netherlandish masters. A "statuary" (i.e. a full–length
painting) of "old tyme" and a "table" (i.e. a painting on panel) of
"the Ficklenes of Fortune" attract our special attention.

The casual allusions of dramatists and other poets show us that there
was an easy familiarity with the fine arts. A young woman in a play, apparently hoping to give birth to twins, exclaims: "O, how like the picture of Charity should I look with two sucklings at my breast!" [20] "Look,
where they come," exclaims a character in another play, "just like the
picture of Knavery betwixt Fraud and Lechery!" [21] Another comments:

> You seem like the issue
> The painters limn, leaping from Envy's mouth,
> That devours all he meets. [22]

Yet another character remarks: "You never saw Pride pictured but in
gay attire." [23] In a poem by Richard Brathwaite Death says that "Painters doe me a mans dead karkasse paint without eyes." [24] When Posthumous tells the Gaoler that he knows where he will go after dying, the
Gaoler comments: "Your death has eyes in's head then. I have not seen
him so pictured." [25] "Death," says Thomas Nashe, "is ne'er pictured
but with an upper chap only." [26] The designers of pageantry, state en-
tries, Lord Mayors' Shows, and similar spectacles could count upon the
spectators' ability to recognize many of the personifications. For example,
Thomas Dekker, writing of the triumphal arches of 1604, says of a figure
of Justice: "I hope you will not put me to describe what properties she
held in her hand, since every painted cloth can inform you." [27] One of
the conventions in masques and other courtly entertainments was the
personification of abstract ideas. [28] In a play by John Marston [29] there
is such a performance by amateurs.

There are also allusions to Biblical and mythological subjects which
are included here not only because they afford further evidence of a
knowledge of the arts but because they sometimes impinge upon allegory.
Thomas Kyd, in his testimony concerning the blasphemous remarks and
atheistical opinions uttered by Christopher Marlowe, accuses Marlowe
of joking irreverently about the small "portion" allowed the Prodigal
Son by his father who "in all pictures" is represented as grasping his
purse so near the bottom that it must have been almost empty. [30] In a
play the hairiness of a child is accounted for by the fact that before
his birth his mother had been "thinking on a picture / Of Saint John

Baptist in his camel's coat." [31] Elsewhere a character refers to "the picture of Hector in a haberdasher's shop." [32] This may have originally been one of a series of the Nine Worthies. Among the rarities which were "snatched from the jaws of Time" by the Antiquary in Shakerley Marmion's play of that title were twelve "portraitures of the Sibyls, drawn five hundred years since by Titianus of Padua, an excellent painter and statuary." The blunders in this description are those of the speaker; one must not infer ignorance on the part of the dramatist. The Antiquary also possessed a naked Venus and Cupid, drawn by Apelles, and a collection of statues and busts, including three made by "Jacobus Sansovinus the Florentine." [33] William Browne of Tavistock imagines the juxtaposition of subjects from Biblical and classical antiquity. These are the paintings on the wall of the Cave of Famine showing the conquests achieved by Limos. Hagar and Ishmael in the wilderness were shown, several episodes of the siege of Jerusalem as told by Josephus, and the tale of Erisichthon from Ovid's *Metamorphoses*.[34] Michael Drayton describes elaborately a queen's bedchamber decorated with "shapes" "wrought by skilfull Painters." Among the subjects were a death of Hyacinthus with Apollo and the wood nymphs, an Io viewing her "heyfere shape" in a brook, a "landskip" of Mount Cynthus with "half–naked Nymphs" and Phaeton falling from the sky, and a Mercury and Hebe by a fountain. Of this last Drayton provides a very Flemish detail: "On their Browes he [the painter] made the drops so cleare, / That through each Drop, their faire skins did appeare." [35]

The taste for narrative poems on classico–erotic subjects to which Marlowe, Shakespeare, and Marston catered was paralleled by the popularity of the erotic in the arts of design. Everyone will remember that as part of the practical joke played upon Christopher Sly in the Induction to *The Taming of the Shrew* he is offered three paintings for his entertainment: one of the maiden Io beguiled and surprised, one of Apollo weeping to see the scratches upon Daphne's legs as she roams through a thorny wood, and one of Venus spying on the bathing Adonis. This episode of the paintings does not occur in Shakespeare's source (or was it his own first version?), *The Taming of a Shrew*. That he added it surely indicates a greater interest in the visual arts than he is sometimes credited with. The purely pictorial quality of the descriptions has often been remarked; there is no action, no motion, no narrative. A collection of paintings described in a play by Jasper Mayne [36] included two that Christopher Sly would have admired: a "Mars and Venus in a net" and "a naked nymph lying asleep and some lascivious satyr taking her lineaments." In the same collection was "the finest ravish's Lucrece," a subject perhaps suggested by the popularity of Shakespeare's poem. Michael Drayton's Fair Rosamond tells her royal lover:

> As in the Gallerie this other day
> I and my woman past the time away,
> 'Mongst many Pictures, which were hanging by,
> The silly Girl at length hapt to espie
> Chaste Lucrece Image, and desires to know,
> What shee should be, herself that murd'red so.[37]

Two writers who were something of authorities on the arts of design protested against the sale of lascivious pictures; they were thinking of prints as well as paintings. Henry Peacham's disapproval is so intense that his syntax becomes confused:

> What lewde art is there showne in many prints and peeces that are daily brought over out of Italy, Flanders, and other places, which are oftener enquired after in the shops then any other, little use is there in most of the wax pictures of Curtizans in Rome and Venice being drawne naked, and sold up and down as Libidinis Fomenta, surely I cannot but commend art in them, as many times there is excellent good, but verily do hate their wicked makers and abhominable ends.[38]

William Sanderson, an art critic of later date, utters a similar caution: "Forbeare Obscene Pictures, those Centaures, Satyrs Ravishings, Jupiter—scapes in several Shapes, though often done by rare Artists." [39]

Occasionally we find one or another quite unprovocative detail of the painter's art rousing interest. Peacham, discussing the absurdities committed by some artists, tells us that in an inn he once saw a painting of a siege in antiquity, with ordnance and small shot, and he protests against this gross anachronism.[40] From the phenomenon of a portrait "following the eye" of a beholder William Browne takes this simile:

> As in a picture limb'd [sic] unto the life,
> Or carved by a curious workman's knife,
> If twenty men at once should come to see
> The great effects of untirde industry,
> Each sev—rally would thinke the pictures eye
> Was fixt on him, and on no stander by.[41]

By way of introduction to his *Little Bartas* (1620), a condensation of his translation of *Les Semaines*, Joshua Sylvester develops an elaborate and quite charming simile from the practice of "wanton lovers" who, not content to gaze upon the objects of their idolatry, must needs have their portraits painted, and then, not content with the portraits, must have been copied "in little" (miniatures), so that they may carry them about with them. Even so, says Sylvester, his translation is a full–size copy of the French original, and now he is going to copy that copy "in little." Sylvester brings in half a dozen artists by name; lovers, he says, are not satisfied with portraits

> Done by De–Creets, Marcus, or Peake at large . . .
> They must have Heliard, Isaac, or his Sonne,
> To do in Little what at large was done.[42]

There were some shops in London, generally kept by the artists themselves, where paintings were sold, and of these we have a few vivid glimpses. Samuel Rowlands has an anecdote of a woman who had her portrait painted and then refused to pay for it. To put pressure on her the artist changed the dog which she held in her arms into "a filthy Catt" and hung the portrait in his shop "where gazers swarm." The woman had to pay him an additional fee for altering the animal into a dog again.[43] In one of his epigrams Peacham notes how an artist who has newly set up his place of business attracts customers:

> A late–come Painter to the Strand
> Doth formost place the Pourtraicture in sight
> Of some remarqued Statesman of our Land,
> To grace his Shop, and buyers to invite.[44]

A citizen sauntering through the London streets so long ago is brought vividly to mind when we read in Robert Burton of the passer–by who pauses to gaze at "an antick picture in a painter's shop." [45]

References to named painters are disappointingly bare and jejune. We have just quoted Sylvester's brief list. Francis Meres, who offers the crudest imaginable comparison between Greek and English artists, includes natives and foreigners indiscriminately in his list of eighteen painters and three engravers. Six of the painters and two of the engravers are foreigners employed in England; of the native artists five are miniaturists.[46] Peacham was probably moved by patriotism and friendliness when, after his discussion of some great foreign artists, he added: "Mine owne countriemen . . . have beene, and are able to equal the best, if occasion served." Is there a hint of doubt in the vague qualification? He commends Peake, Hilliard, Isaac Oliver, and "many more unknowne to me." If they could "equal the best" how did it happen that they were unknown to a connoisseur? [47] We look now a few years beyond the usual terminal date of this study in order to note William Sanderson's interesting, rapid review of no less than thirty–four English painters.[48] "Although some of them," he says, "be strangers born, yet for their affection to our Nation we may mixe them together." He classifies them as portrait–painters ("in the life"), "story" (that is, narrative pictures, historical or imaginary), "copying after the Antique" (by which he probably means after the great Italian masters of the Cinquecento), "Fowl and Fish," "Flowers and Fruit," "Sea–Pieces," portraits "in little," and water colorists. Of the names on his list nearly a score are readily identifiable, a few are well known, and one, Sir Peter Lely, is famous. Among those whom posterity has forgotten are four gentlemen who were "ingenious in their private delight," that is, they were amateurs. The list ends abruptly: "Quaere, Haines and Thorne." Had someone read the author's manuscript and made a marginal suggestion which crept in this odd fashion into the text? Sanderson has strong likes and dislikes: He is half–hearted in praise of Dürer and dubious about Rubens and Netherlandish painters in general except Vandyke; Michael Angelo and Raphael receive unstinted praise. His summary (p. 17) of Italian art before Raphael is worth quoting as indicative of the low estate of English art history in the mid–seventeenth century: "The ancient Italians, who first began in figures, were Cimubes, and he was farre surpassed by Gotto, famous untill the time of Perugino, who was infinitely out–done by his excellent Scholler Raphael Urbino." That is all.

The masterpieces of Italian and North European painting in England in Elizabethan and Jacobean times were in the royal collections or in the possession of the nobility and wealthy gentry. Probably few poets and other writers had adequate opportunities to see them. Ben Jonson was one of the privileged few, and consequently when, in *Discoveries*, he commends Michael Angelo, Raphael, Titian, Correggio, Sebastian del Piombo, Andrea del Sarto, and Giulio Romano we cannot always be sure whether he is writing from firsthand knowledge of some of their works, or from acquaintance with engraved copies of famous paintings, or merely from a knowledge of the reputation of these artists. But when Robert Burton recommends rectifying melancholy by the pleasure to be derived from pictures by Michael Angelo, Raphael, and Francesco Francia he is almost certainly referring to engravings after their works rather than to originals, which would be inaccessible to his readers; and this is the more probable because he goes on to recommend "excellent landskips, Dutch-works, and curious cuts by Sadleir of Prague, Albertus Dürer, Goltzius, Vrintes, etc." [49] The "landskips" and "Dutch-works" he has in mind may have been paintings, since he seems to differentiate them from the "curious cuts."

3. Tapestries

Of tapestries there was an enormous, almost incredible abundance in Tudor and Stuart England. They primarily interest us because personifications were so frequently delineated in them. Many inventories have survived of royal, noble, and ecclesiastical collections.[1] Records of gifts by European dignitaries to English kings go back as far as the reign of Richard II. Among the tapestries presented to that monarch by the Duke of Burgundy was a series of the Seven Virtues with a virtuous king at the feet of each appropriate personification and of the Seven Deadly Sins with vicious kings similarly placed. An inventory compiled after the death of Henry V in 1422 includes two pieces which seem to have formed part of a series based upon the Apostles' Creed. Were they similar in subject to the several episodes of the lost "Creed Play"? From the reign of Edward IV dates an inventory of Ewelme Almshouse, Oxfordshire, in which, among many other tapestries, were a "xv signes of the Doom" and two sets illustrating the "Seven Sciences." A poem entitled *The Life of Saint Werburgh* by Henry Bradshaw (who died in 1513) describes tapestries in the hall of the Abbey of Ely on scriptural subjects and on the Nine Worthies.

The tapestries owned by Henry VIII were numbered literally by thousands.[2] Some of them are described as "counterfiet," by which "painted cloths" are meant; but most were woven, and the king kept a staff of "arras-makers" to mend and darn them and keep them in repair. There were several sets of the Petrarchan Triumphs and of the Deadly Sins; a set of the Cardinal Virtues; "6 peces of Synne and Vertue;" "Amor and Prudence" in a set of eight; "3 peces of the three fatall Ladies of Destenye;" "2 peces of Pleasure;" "3 peces . . . of the Seven Sciences;" "1 pece of Vertue and Vice fighting;" and many sets illustrating the parable of the Prodigal Son. The royal collections, from which much had been eliminated since early Tudor times and to which much had been added, were dispersed by sale after the execution of Charles I.

Without attempting an exhaustive survey of personifications in tapestries, extant or recorded, I may note a few other items. In 1522 Wolsey procured from the Continent the famous sets of hangings for Hampton Court, including the "Story of the Seven Deadly Sins" in nine pieces. In the following year he bought the "Petrarchan Triumphs" in eight pieces, four of which (Time, Fame, and two Deaths) are still in Hampton Court. A "Triumphe of Veritie" in eight pieces which belonged to Mary Queen of Scots is inventoried though the set is lost. An armorial tapestry of English workmanship (ca. 1565) shows the coat of arms of William Herbert, first Earl of Pembroke, flanked with seated figures of Pride (a woman with a turkey cock) and Luxuria (a man embracing a woman).[3] Still at Hardwick Hall are two "hangings" which well exemplify the association of mythological or historical individuals with personifications: Penelope standing between Patience and Perseverance, and Lucrece, in the act of stabbing herself, attended by Chastity and Liberality.[4]

A milestone in the history of tapestry weaving in England is the setting up of looms at Barchester Manor in Warwickshire about 1561. William Sheldon, the founder of this establishment, had already done weaving since about 1550 and had sent Richard Ryckes to learn more about the craft in the Low Countries. Hitherto there had been practically no English weavers, and the trade had depended upon the Flemings and French; Arras was in fact, as everybody knows, a synonym for tapestry of the finest quality. For more than half a century the Sheldon looms were the best in England, and though it is uncertain how the business terminated it seems to have been carried on by the Sheldon family down to the outbreak of the Civil Wars. Not many of these tapestries can be identified indisputably, but there is fairly general agreement that the Pembroke coat of arms; a Faith, Hope, and Charity now in Edinburgh;[5] and the splendid "Seasons" at Hatfield are achievements of the Sheldon organization. The "Seasons" will engage our attention later in this chapter. In 1619 about fifty Flemish weavers were brought over and established at Mortlake in Surrey. For some of their earliest and finest works they borrowed motifs from Raphael, Dürer, and Lucas Van Leyden. In borders designed by Vandyke there are various abstractions, for example, blindfolded Justice. About 1623 the Mortlake works began to employ Francis Cleyn, who came to them from Germany, as a resident designer. His "Hero and Leander" was a popular subject, woven again and again. Cleyn also decorated houses, etched, and collaborated with Wenceslaus Hollar.

Some dramas contain brief references to tapestries. That which adorned

Imogen's bedchamber was "wrought in silk and silver" and showed "proud Cleopatra when she met her Roman." [6] When in Jonson's *Cynthia's Revels* (IV.1.50) a character is likened to "a Venetian trumpetter i' th' battaile of Lepanto, in the gallerie yonder," the allusion is almost certainly to a tapestry rather than a painting. In a play by Jasper Mayne [7] Aurelia says to Timothy: "Sir, I took you for a mute i' the hangings," and he replies:

> Do I look like one of them Trojans?
> . . . Why, lady, do you think me
> Wrought in a loom, some Dutch piece weav'd at Mortlake?

We are reminded of the long description of the "piece of skilful painting" of the Siege of Troy adorning the home of Lucrece in Shakespeare's poem (lines 1366–1456). That this was a series not of wall paintings but of "painted cloths" is almost certain. Two passages in *The Faerie Queene* have been exhaustively studied in the endeavor to associate them with tapestries that actually existed.[8] The walls of the House of Busyrane (III, 11, 28–46) are "yclothed . . . with goodly arras of great majesty" portraying "all Cupid's Wars"—the loves of Jove, Apollo, Neptune, Saturn, Bacchus, Mars, and many mortals of various degree, from kings and queens down to the "rankest rablement." Of like splendor are the "clothes of Arras and of Toure" adorning the walls of an inner room in the Castle Joyeouse (III, 1, 34–38) which depicted the love of Venus and Adonis. Is there a reminiscence of Spenser in a play where the "very fair hangings" of a "pretty lodging" are described as portraying "the poetical fiction of Venus kissing Adonis in the violet bed" while Vulcan "stands sneaking behind the brake to watch 'em"? [9]

Twice we catch glimpses of visitors looking at such works of art. In a play by William Cartwright [10] a servant says politely to a visitor:

> Pray y', entertain yourself awhile, until
> I give my mistress notice of your presence. . . .
> You'll find
> Some pretty stories in the hangings there.

One of the engravings in Sir John Harington's translation of Ariosto shows a Lord of the Castle with a group of ladies and gentlemen in a great barrel–vaulted hall. Attendants with flambeaux are illuminating the walls on which are six tapestries (or perhaps they are paintings?) with scenes of the Wars of France and Italy. We see an Italian hall but it suggests what must have often taken place in England when a nobleman or gentle-man exhibited to guests the decorations of his residence.[11]

Unless painstakingly preserved tapestries became faded, mildewed, tattered, "fly–bitten," as Falstaff describes some (*II Henry IV*, II.1.159); "decaied dead arras," in Jonson's words (*Cynthia's Revels*, Induction, 101), no longer worthy of a place in great collections. They might pass from hand to hand and end their days in humble surroundings. It is inconceivable that Mistress Quickly could have afforded to purchase hers fresh from the looms, and judging from Falstaff's contemptuous description those she possessed were in a wretched state. We have no in-ventories of Elizabethan and Jacobean inns and taverns, but it is likely that in many of them, as well as in many homes of the less well to do, secondhand hangings were used to keep out the cold and to conceal damp or decayed walls. When old tapestries were discarded the wealthy would replace them with fresh ones. In a play [12] a lady gives orders for the renovation of her bedchamber: The old hangings are to be removed and a new set is to be commissioned, done in silver work with gold borders, the subject to be the Civil Wars in France. In another play [13] a lady is dissatisfied with her hangings, which she describes as "Jewish stories stuffed with corn and camels," obviously the story of Joseph. In their place she commands her steward to procure new hangings in silk and silver with "stories to fit the seasons of the year" so that they can be changed at appropriate times. Her distaste for "Jewish stories" reminds one of Robert Aylett's narrative poem on the life of Joseph in which is found the quaint notion that the "stately Parlour" of Joseph's house in Egypt where his brethren are received is "all hang'd with curious Arras richly wrought." The subjects depicted are Biblical, from the Deluge down to Joseph's own adventures, with such episodes as his "party coloured" coat, his dreams, and his betrayal by his brothers. Small wonder that the brothers stare on each other in amazement, for as yet Joseph has not revealed his identity.[14]

4. *Prints*

Prints, whether woodcuts or from metal plates, existed in great num-bers in Elizabethan and Jacobean England. Some were issued separately, others are illustrations in books. Easily obtainable, comparatively inex-pensive, generally of no great size, they could circulate freely from hand to hand. It is a priori likely that there will be many parallels between their visual imagery and the verbal imagery of literature, and this turns out to be the case.

From the earliest days of printing woodcuts fashioned on the Continent were used in England.[1] Some blocks were borrowed and afterwards returned to their owners; others remained in England and of these a few underwent strange vicissitudes. A striking example of this is the title page of Herman Bodius' *Unio dissidentium* (Cologne, 1531). The border has figures of Pride, Justice, Avarice, Prudence, Hope, Envy, Fortune, and Suspicion. It is copied in nine books printed by John Byddell between 1534 and 1538,[2] but liberties have been taken with the original. The Fortune has disappeared, to make room for Byddell's imprint, although Justice, Prudence, and Hope remain. The Vices, however, had been so vaguely and feebly personified that Byddell made them do duty as Virtues, labeling Pride as Charity, Avarice as Faith, Envy as Obedience, and Suspicion as Patience. The posture of Urania on the title page of Robert Recorde's *The Castle of Knowledge* (1556) is closely reminiscent of the Urania in the frontispiece of the *Sphaera Mundi* by Johannes de Sacro Busto (Venice, 1488).[3] Some late fifteenth-century Continental blocks were still being used in England in the early seventeenth century.

After the Reformation Settlement some Romish subjects were suppressed. On New Year's Day, 1561, Queen Elizabeth attended the service in St. Paul's Cathedral. Dean Nowell caused a special copy of a book of prayers to be placed at her prie–Dieu, enriched (or extra–illustrated, as we say) with pictures of saints and martyrs. The Queen, displeased, taxed the Dean for his failure to heed the proclamation against Romish images. "How came you by these pictures?" she demanded. "Who engraved them?" "I know not who engraved them; I bought them," replied the Dean. "From whom bought you them?" she asked. "From a German," he replied. Had Nowell been to Germany? Or did he procure them from an itinerant German salesman? Or was there a German dealer in prints already established in London? We do not know. There is no record that prints by Dürer or Lucas Van Leyden or, for that matter, the Italian Marcantonio Raimondi were imported into England in their lifetime; they had all died long before the reign of Elizabeth.[4]

The first English book to be illustrated with engravings seems to have been *The Byrth of Mankynde* (1540), a treatise on midwifery. These copperplates were copied from Continental woodcuts by an anonymous craftsman. Thomas Geminus' debased copies of the anatomical plates of Vesalius followed in 1545. The brothers Franciscus and Remigius

Hogenberg were working in England around 1569–79. The former did the title page of the Bishops' Bible (1569) and his plates of Gresham's Royal Exchange are the earliest "views" engraved in England. The latter, besides making two portraits of the Queen, was the chief engraver of Christopher Saxton's maps of England (1574–79). One of his English assistants was Augustine Ryther who did the famous maps of the Battle of the Armada.[5] Of the three engravers mentioned by Francis Meres, the only Englishman is William Rogers, who engraved portraits, title pages, and maps. With him Meres associates "Christopher Swetzer and Cure." Switzer (undoubtedly a Swiss settled in London) worked chiefly in woodcut (as in John Speed's *History of Great Britain*) but engraved the title page of Sylvester's translation of Du Bartas (1605). By the name "Cure," Meres probably intends Pieter van den Keere, who engraved the title page and three maps for John Norden's *Speculum Britanniae* (1593) and whose view of London has been often reproduced.

Two curious instances of English use of subjects popular on the Continent date from the last decade of Elizabeth's reign. In 1595 there appeared an anonymous pamphlet entitled *The Brideling, Sadling, and Ryding, of a rich Churle in Hampshire, by the subtill practise of one Judeth Philips, a professed cunning woman, or Fortune teller*. This woman, who was a Londoner, visited a town in Hampshire and there cheated a wealthy and foolish countryman "that was somewhat fantastical and given to beleeve every tale he heard." His cupidity roused, he consented to cooperate with Mistress Philips. Part of her faked magic was to saddle and bridle him and ride on his back three times between his house and a tree within his grounds. This episode is the subject of a large cut on the title page; it is precisely the episode used in illustrations of the *lai* of Aristotle and Phyllis.[6] This notorious example of the wiles of women must have been known to the author of the pamphlet and he may have invented the tale of the cozened churl from Hampshire in order to make use of the popular design.

Another problematical case of Anglo–Continental interrelationships is presented in William Broxup's poem *Saint Peters Path to the Joyes of Heaven* (1598). The only known copy is in the Folger Shakespeare Library. It was probably subjected to rigid censorship because of its non–Scriptural and very Romish religious theme. In it (sig. B^r) there is a finely executed engraving of the crucifixion of St. Peter which is recognizable as one of a series of illustrations of the martyrdoms of all the Apostles. Technically the plate is far above the level of native English work and cannot be a copy of the original; yet it is not pasted into the book or otherwise inserted. It is paged in as part of the foliation with the signature printed at the bottom in correct sequence, showing that the picture was printed off at the same time as the letterpress. Therefore the book must have been printed in the Low Countries or else, which is more probable, the original copperplate had been brought into England.

Two mystical treatises by Hugh Broughton involve us in a more complex story. His *Moyses Sight on Mount Sinai* (of which the only perfect copy is in the Folger) is engraved throughout, not only the illustrations but the text. The colophon reads: "Graven in brasse by I.H. 1592." We may confidently identify the initials as those of Jodocus Hondius who was in England at this time. It is likely, therefore, that Hondius had engraved the unsigned copperplates in Broughton's *A concent of Scripture* (1588 or 1589). In a new edition of the *Concent* (ca. 1592) the designs have been freely adapted in larger and coarser form by an engraver who signs himself "WR." He was undoubtedly the Englishman William Rogers. Not without some ingenuity he has combined in one plate two visions of Daniel which in the earlier edition are illustrated separately. Several times labels are added to parts of the designs, as when the Scarlet Woman is named "Rome" and her attendant animals "Satan," "Pope," and "The belly God Clergy." The rarity of metal cuts in England and of tastes and standards sufficiently disciplined to distinguish between good work and bad may be deduced from the "Advertisement to the Reader" prefixed by Harington to his translation of Ariosto. With pride he commends the plates adorning his book: "all cut in brass, and most of them by the best workmen in that kind that have been in this land this many years. . . . I have not seen any made in England better, nor (indeed) any of this kind in any book," with the exception, he adds, of "Master Broughton's book on Revelation" (that is, the *Concent*). He notes that other English books with illustrations have the figures "cut in wood and none in metal."

After the turn of the century the number of English engravers increased; ten of them may be considered briefly here. Laurence Johnson illustrated heavy-handedly Richard Knolles' *Generall History of the Turkes* (1603). William Kyp was one of the engravers of the fine plates in Stephen Harrison's *Archs of Triumph* (1604). The coarse and ugly work of Renold Elstrack is of importance to the iconographer. Francis Delaram, who was probably of foreign descent, was influenced by the Wierex family of engravers and by the Italians. Almost alone among his contemporaries in England he has charm, as may be seen in the dainty plates in Sandys' *Relation of a Journey* (1615). William Hole, most favorably remembered as an engraver of music, had connections with many men of letters. There are portraits by him of Chapman, Florio, and Wither. He illustrated Coryat's *Crudities*, Drayton's *Poly—Olbion*, and Browne's *Britannia's Pastorals*. Title pages which he engraved for the installments of Chapman's *Iliad* he adapted in enlarged form for the complete Homer of 1616. To the same year belongs his most interesting title page, that of the Ben Jonson folio. Of native engravers during the Caroline period the most important were Thomas Cecill, William Marshall, John Payne, William Faithorne, Robert Vaughan, and George Glover. The last two may be ignored here for we have met with some of their work before. Cecill's allegorical portrait of Queen Elizabeth is probably from a lost painting of about 1588. His title page to Sir William Cornwallys' *Essayes* (1632) is, as we shall see, admirable for its good taste and serene restraint. Among his other title pages is that to Thomas Heywood's *Hierarchie of the Blessed Angels* (1635). Marshall is of interest to the historian of literature because of the portraits he supplied to books (portraits of Shakespeare, Fletcher, Bacon, Herrick, Suckling, Quarles, and Milton) but they are of no value as works of art. He has, however, an important place in our inquiry because he did work for Francis Quarles; and his emblematic portrait of Charles I is known to everyone. A couple of Payne's title pages have been referred to. Three plates in Heywood's *Hierarchie* are by him and his huge engraving of the great ship "The Sovereign of the Seas" is a celebrated document in British naval history. Payne's later work is in a transitional style, plainer than was fashionable in the early Stuart age. William Faithorne, who did his best and most characteristic work in the Restoration period, ranks far above any of these men.[7] Before his death the older art of line engraving was passing out of vogue, yielding to the new art of mezzo—tint.

Two Continental families are of importance in the history of English engraving. Crispin Van de Passe the Elder lived in Cologne and Utrecht and may never have visited England, though, as Colvin has suggested, he may have had an agent in London to procure him drawings to be engraved and to sell his prints. His eldest son, Crispin the Younger, probably never came to England either but the second son, Simon, was in England in 1613 and was established in London from about 1615 till 1622. Besides many portraits Simon engraved a few title pages, the best known one being for Bacon's *Instauratio Magna* (1620). His chief occupation was, however, the engraving of coats of arms on silver plaques;

many examples of these still exist. Willem, the youngest son, came to England about 1621 and remained till his death in 1637. He did the title page for Chapman's *Batrachomyomachia* (1624–25) and an equestrian portrait of Buckingham, but his engravings are so few that one assumes he had other means of livelihood, perhaps as a goldsmith. The work of the Van de Passe brothers obviously influenced John Payne, who may have been their pupil. Three of the Droeshouts, a family of Low Countries origin settled in London, were engravers. Michael, who was probably the father of the other two, is of no consequence. John did nothing to interest us save the title page of *Truth Brought to Light and Discovered by Time* (1651), a crude piece but, as we saw, of iconographical interest. Martin Droeshout is world famous (or should we say notorious?) for his portrait of Shakespeare in the folio of 1623, although it is a very poor specimen of his craftsmanship. There is much dignity in the architectural design of his emblematical title page of the third edition of Florio's translation of Montaigne (1632). Other foreign engravers at work in England permanently or more or less temporarily were Cornelis Boel, Jan Barra, Lucas Vorsterman, Robert Van Voerst, Frederick Van Hulsen, and the elder Cornelis Van Dalen.

Between the last fifteen years of Elizabeth's reign and 1642 we know of more than a dozen print dealers in London. We rely largely on Colvin for our information about them. During this period Englishmen had ample opportunities to acquaint themselves with, and purchase, prints brought in from abroad. Unique testimony to this is furnished by a "Harmony" of the Gospels in the British Museum (a "Harmony" is made by clipping and rearranging two copies of the texts, a matter of scissors and paste) which is abundantly illustrated with German, Flemish, French, and Italian prints put together by the community at Little Gidding about 1631. From it we can infer that such small works of art were easily come by in England, unless Nicholas Ferrar and his associates, employing no intermediary, imported them directly from the Continent, which does not seem likely. The industry of native engravers and foreigners resident in England was almost wholly limited to portraits, title pages, and illustrations in books which did not come into competition with the imported Continental prints. Of these prints by far the greatest were Dürer's, and it is unfortunate that the early history of that great artist's fame in England has not been fully explored.

The London dealers seem to have limited themselves to a retail import trade. When at the time of the publication of his *Graphice. Or the Use of the Pen and Pensil* (1658) William Sanderson was afflicted with the loss of the cuts and prints which were to illustrate the book—they were stolen en route by a "watchful Pirate" who plundered the ship's passengers and made off with "that Cargasoon of papers"—he could not make good his loss in England because "so many thousands of Prints as the Presse of this Edition would contain" were not to be had. All that he can do is advise the learner who wishes to copy and imitate the masters to furnish himself with prints from the stock "at Mr. Fatherns (a Graver, without Temple–bar) or at other Print–sellers." Lacking the plates, the text is often rather pointless, a fact Sanderson regretfully notes at several places in his book. The only illustrations are Faithorne's fine portraits of Sanderson himself [8] and of King Charles I.

At an earlier date John Bate, another writer on the fine arts, had advised the student of drawing and painting to imitate "good prints," and "be private in his designes, for he himselfe may print them when they are cut, nor shall they be exposed to the view of every stationer that frequent upon all occasions the howsen of common workmen, whereby one receiveth much injury and vexation." In other words: Do not entrust the plates you have engraved to a professional craftsman because you run the risk of theft or plagiarism. Bate goes on to say that of all genres of woodcut or metal engraving he considers that "Emblem or Empresse worke is the most hard or difficult . . . and the most to be commended" because of the demand such work makes for the rendering of the finest details of expression.[9]

5. Continental Emblem Books

Bate wrote when the popularity of emblem books in England was about at its peak with the publication of Quarles' and Wither's collections (both 1635). The history of the origins and growth of emblem literature has been so competently explored and set forth by excellent scholars [1] that only a summary, for purposes of orientation and with emphasis on certain aspects important to our subject, is here needed. Before beginning this summary, however, I should like to quote four writers of the period who discuss the definition of the word "emblem" and cognate words. William Camden distinguishes as follows between the *impresa* and the *emblem:* [2]

> An *Imprese* . . . is a devise in picture with his Motto, or Word, borne by noble and learned personages, to notofie some particular conceit of their owne: as Emblems (that we may omitte

other differences) doe propound some generall instruction to all. . . . There is required in an Imprese . . . a correspondence of the picture, which is as the bodie, and the Motte, which as the soul giveth it life. That is, the body must be of faire representation, and the word in some different language, wittie, short, and answerable thereunto; neither too obscure nor too plaine, and most commended, when it is an Hemistich, or parcell of a verse.

The distinction made here is not entirely accurate: Although it is true that an *impresa* is personal and an *emblem* general, in both a picture and a "word" are combined. Camden refers by name to but one Italian designer of imprese, Ruscelli, but he describes many examples, admitting at least once his inability to interpret a very enigmatic design.[3]

Thomas Jenner, recommending his collection of spiritual emblems, expresses the hope that "because men are more led by the eye, then, eare, it may be, thou looking upon their little Prints, mai'st conceive of that which many words would not make so plaine to thee." [4] Proper emphasis is here laid upon the visual image and there is an implicit repudiation of "naked" emblems, but no definition is offered. The Roman Catholic emblematist Henry Hawkins defines an emblem as a device in action. In his series in honor of the Blessed Virgin Mary each concept requires two designs: in the first (the device) the animal, plant, or other object is merely depicted; in the second (the emblem) the representation reveals its symbolic meaning. Thus, for example, we have first simply a well drawn bee, nothing more; and then we see it flying between the flower and the hive.[5] Quarles' definition, "An Emblem is but a silent Parable," is curiously incomplete, for he is thinking only of the design and disregarding the accompanying motto, poem, and commentary.[6]

The amplest discussion to appear in English within our period is Thomas Blount's translation of Henri Estienne's *L'Art de faire les devises* (1645).[7] The terminology in this somewhat technical treatise is at times confused, the word "device" being used both in a broad sense covering any and all such symbolic designs and in the proper, narrow sense when and as it is appropriate to a particular person, having regard to his rank, fortunes, achievements, and character. In this restricted sense it is correctly called an "impresa." As it is a highly individualized invention which is not inheritable it differs from the designs in heraldry, which are attached to families, not to persons, and pass on from generation to generation. But like a coat of arms or a crest an impresa was often used as an ornament.[8] Details of designs, motives, and mottoes occupy much of this treatise but there are also interesting general observations and some definitions. The distinction is drawn that "in speaking by a Metaphor you demonstrate the thing, which you intend to signify, by the words onely, when as in discoursing by Devises you explicate the matter partly by words and partly by figures." Four classes of images are distinguished from each other. A *Symbol* imparts a grave meaning in great brevity and its property is "to be concealed and enveloped in Labyrinths of obscure sentences." An *Aenigma* is "an obscure sentence, expressed by an occult similitude of things." [9] An *Emblem* is "a sweet and morall Symbole, which consists of picture and words, by which some weighty sentence is declared." A *Devise* is "a rare and particular way of expressing oneself, the most compendious, most noble, most pleasing, and most efficacious of all other that humane wit can invent." It is at this point in the work that Estienne, through Blount, voices a stern protest against the employment for devices of such "vile and abject things" as a kettle, frying pan, chafing dish, or pair of bellows and against any recourse to obscenity. An inconclusive discussion of the origin of devices involves the question: Are they from Egypt? The influence of medals from classical antiquity is recognized and it is noted that themes from the Holy Scriptures, such as the Lamb of God, set examples to designers.

From the too succinct or too verbose and always somewhat fumbling efforts of these old writers to define an emblem and to differentiate it from other species to which it is more or less allied it is possible, especially if aided by actual inspection of innumerable examples, to arrive at a satisfactory definition, which may be given in the words of Professor Praz: "An emblem is a symbolic figure accompanied by a motto, an explication in verse, and sometimes a prose commentary." [10]

The roots of emblem literature penetrate deep into the past. There is a universal tendency to attempt to discern in human beings, organic creatures, inanimate objects, words, and events profounder significances than appear on the surface. The sixteenth century inherited from the Middle Ages the tradition of allegory as a dominant type of expression in literature and the Fine Arts. The accepted method of interpreting Holy Scripture in accordance with the theory of prefiguration prepared men's minds for the application of an analogous method of exposition in other departments of human experience, in morals, psychology, social relationships, and the study of the world of nature. Survivals of prefigurative exegesis are occasionally found in emblem books, as when Jacob's Ladder is the antetype of the "Scala ad Coelum Christus." [11] Such impressive concepts as the Spies and the Grapes or the Mystic Wine Press were still employed in the seventeenth century.[12] Many of the parables of Christ could be visualized: the Good Samaritan, the Sower, the Wise and Foolish Virgins, Dives and Lazarus,[13] and (most popular of all) the Prodigal Son.[14] Some other parables, however moving in the immediacy of their verbal imagery, were not adapted to visualization. Still the emblematists could not be discouraged from attempting the rationally impossible, sometimes with fantastic results. Thus, Father Jan David [15] shows a Christian "heaping coals of fire" into a grate which is formed by a crown worn by his meekly kneeling enemy (Fig. 153). The parable of the Mote and the Beam is depicted not only in New Testament illustrations and in paintings and in separate prints but in various emblem books. The mote, a wisp of straw, protrudes from the eye of one of the brothers and the beam, often a massive joist, thrusts forth a yard or two from the other's eye. The effect is ludicrous and grotesque.[16] Amusing, unintentionally so for it is found in a very serious book, is the picture of the Camel confronted with the job of passing through the Eye of a Needle.[17] Some of the metaphorical texts in the Epistles of St. Paul were beautifully adaptable to this type of visual literalness. The sown grain that cannot quicken unless it die is the inspiration for countless emblems, memorial broadsides, printers' devices, and so forth in which the wheat sprouts from a corpse or skull or tomb. Impressive use was made of the great passage in Ephesians on the spiritual powers against whom the armed Christian must make a stand. The yearning to escape from "the body of this death" is visualized as the Soul "under the ribs of Death" and looking forth through the grim bars.[18]

The typological interpretation of Scripture was adapted by students of profane literature to Homer, Virgil, Ovid, and other classical authors whose works were scrutinized for their supposed hidden doctrinal and ethical content. Typical of such ingeniously misdirected scholarship is the *Ovid Moralizé* which became a rich source of emblematic material. Classical mythology and fable were sought in texts other than the great poets; it is not merely a coincidence that the style of illustrating Æsop's *Fables* is often so similar to that of some emblem books. Many themes came from the medieval bestiaries and lapidaries, from astrology, from the *Physiologus*, and in general from the traditions of "natural history" descending from Pliny, Ælian, and other ancient writers. From heraldry various themes were derived. The emblem literature had not developed very far before we begin to find subjects taken from domestic life in town and country; and machines such as clocks, pumps, and printing presses suggested novelties. These point the way towards vulgarizations, such as the use of kitchen utensils, against which some sensitive devotees of emblems protested in the seventeenth century.

All these sources were confluent. The immediate inspiration of the emblematists was a Greek word entitled *Hieroglyphica* which purported to be a translation from an Egyptian original by Orapollo or Horus Apollo of whom, even if his name is not purely fictitious, nothing else is known. It is based upon the belief held by Pliny, Plutarch, Apuleius, and other writers that the hieroglyphics of Egypt were ideographs in which the priests and wizards of Egypt recorded the divine secrets and wisdom into which certain Greek philosophers were held to have been initiated. In 1419 the manuscript of this work was brought from the Ægian region to Florence, where it excited the interest of the humanists. Motives from it were taken for medals, columns, triumphal arches, and other works of art.[19] Orapollo was expounded and enormously expanded with materials from the *Physiologus* and other sources by Giovanni Piero Valeriano in his *Hieroglyphica sive de Sacris Ægyptiorum aliarumque gentium literis* (1556).[20]

Many years before Valeriano's treatise, however, the first emblem book had appeared, the product of the learned leisure of the eminent Pavian jurist Andrea Alciati.[21] In its original form the *Emblemata* dates probably from about 1522 but the earliest extant edition is of 1531. In successive editions Alciati added to his collection and expanded his commentary. It is noteworthy that in the edition of 1551 he lays emphasis on the value of emblems for the decoration of houses, costumes, and so forth. To this use they had already been put, and Gilles Corrozet, one of Alciati's earliest followers, had recommended his own collection in these words:

> Aussi pourront ymagers et tailleurs,
> Painctres, Brodeurs, Orfeoures, esmailleurs,
> Prendre en ce livre aulcune fantasie,
> Comme ils feroyent d'une tapisserie.[22]

Alciati's book was translated, newly illustrated, supplemented, imitated, and subjected to more and more elaborate and erudite commentary. Before the close of the sixteenth century it had passed through some 150 editions in the original or in translation. The edition with the commentary of Luigi Pignorio (Padua, 1621) runs to more than a thousand pages. No English version appeared but the English emblematists are heavily indebted to it.[23]

Upon the firm foundation laid by Alciati the vast, fantastic edifice of the emblem literature was erected. The later history of the fashion need not be repeated here, but some remarks may be offered on a few books, either because English publications offer parallels to them or because they are of a sort not imitated in England.

Adrian Junius (De Jonge) was a Dutch physician, a commentator on Plautus and Martial, the writer of other learned works, and the compiler of a multilingual vocabulary. His *Emblemata* (Antwerp, 1565) [24] was printed and published by the house of Plantin who became enthusiastic and expert in the field of emblem literature. De Jonge recommends such books as his as appropriate "Strennae," New Year's gifts. This is a significant admission of the essential triviality of at least some of them; they are for amusement. Some later emblematists, George Wither among them, shared this opinion. Giovanni Andrea Palazzi's *Discoursi sopra l'imprese* (1575) is weighty and serious, making no concession to the opinion that the invention of devices is but a pleasing and frivolous social convention. Giulio Cesare Capaccio's *Delle Imprese* (1592) is a work of larger scope. A beautiful book intended for an aristocratic and wealthy circle of readers, it contains along with many refined and elegant woodcuts much information on three topics: the manner of making imprese; how to fashion them from hieroglyphics, symbols, and other "mystic material;" and how to use natural objects for the same purpose. Much of the material in Scipion Bargagli's *Dell' Imprese* (1594) exploits themes already, or destined to become, widely known: the bird in the cage as the emblem of the Soul imprisoned in this life; the candle whose flame is an emblem of the brevity of life; the lantern as the emblem of Faith guiding us, and the like. His inventions are often farfetched and not seldom puerile in ingenuity, and his book is a precursor of the extravagances and absurdities of some later emblematists. Often he draws symbols from homely objects such as carpenters' tools. We have read Henri Estienne's protest against the use of "vile and abject things" in this noble art. But in Germany and the Low Countries much interest was taken in mechanical ingenuities, domestic utensils, farming implements, and the tools of various crafts as subjects for symbolic interpretation.

It was in Germany that Joachim Camerarius applied emblematically enormous stores of natural and pseudonatural lore and learning. The first installment of his great work was *Symbolorum et Emblematum ex Re Herbaria Centurie Una Collecta* (date 1590 on the title but 1593 in the preface); the second, *ex Animalibus Quadrupedibus* (1595); the third, *ex Volatibus et insectis* (1596); and the fourth, *ex aqualitibus et reptilibus* (1604). All four are illustrated with lovely copperplate medallions. The four installments were brought together in one volume in 1605.

England produced no book on so ambitious a scale, but there are four books which though without illustrations are quite charming. Archibald Simson's *Hieroglyphica Animalium* (Edinburgh, 1612) is a moral treatise on beasts, birds, and fishes with a lesson drawn from each. It is not an emblem book but covers ground familiar and useful to the emblematists. Richard Brathwaite (or Brathwayte) in *The Schollers Medley* (1614),[25] having urged that a knowledge of living creatures is needful to divines who desire to dilate upon the wonders of God's creation, continues: "The witty Emblematist also draines his pretty inventions from these resemblances; portraying the creature and annexing his device to the Portray," and citing Alciati's use of material taken from Pliny he remarks: "We have many such witty Emblemes well befitting the most Christian understanding." Brathwaite draws from natural history a number of emblematic parallels, generally well worn and obvious enough, as of the goat and the wanton amorist. Twenty years later this writer returned to the subject in a quaint book entitled *A Strange Metamorphosis of Man, transformed into a Wildernesse. Deciphered in Characters* (1634). The World is pictured as a Wilderness, and Man, having left the path of Rectitude, has "entered into the desert way of Jericho." In this desert Man, like Ulysses' crew, undergoes a strange metamorphosis. This simple parable is to be taken as a "clew" to the meaning of forty little essays that follow: on beasts, birds, trees, flowers, bushes, a lake, an echo, and other phenomena. The moralist, however, is often distracted from the quality symbolized by the charm of the symbol itself; he has so warm an affection for objects of the natural world that he forgets they are intended to be parts of a *Speculum Moralis*. What moral lesson is to be drawn from so delightful a description as that of the squirrel?—"He is a foure-footed bird that is kept in a cage, not to sing, for he hath no voice that is worth the hearing, but to dance only." Or of the parrot?—"A Jew among Birds, because he hath no proper language of his own" and must "accommodate himself to our Languages of Europe." Brathwaite is equally attractive when writing of the dog, the bat, the goose, the horse, or the elephant; and he nearly always leaves to his readers the discipline of extracting emblematic significance from his creatures. A somewhat similar book is John Swan's *Speculum Mundi or A Glasse Representing the Face of the World* (Cambridge, 1635). Treating of the Six Days of Creation, this contains a great variety of curious "natural history" taken from

Topsell, Sebastian Munster, and other authorities classical and modern. Swan is an engaging writer, for he too loves his creatures without regard sometimes for their moral significance; but generally he adheres to his purpose, which is to extract new emblems from this natural lore or to play fresh variations on old themes.[26] Thus, the Dog of Egypt which for fear of the crocodile laps water from the Nile while running is "a fit pattern for us in the use of pleasures," for the danger lies in lingering over them.[27] The Mole which, blind all its life, begins to see when dying, is an emblem of worldly men. We have already encountered Swan's covetous and envious creatures in an earlier chapter.

The four books just described are unpretentious English analogues, if not direct imitations, of the huge work by Camerarius. But on the Continent fashions developed that in England were imitated but faintly, if at all. A deliberate effort to cater to coarse tastes is evident in the *Emblemata Saecularia, Mira et Jucunda Varietate Saeculi huius Mores ita exprimentia* (1596) where poems in Latin, German, Dutch, and French are followed by fifty copperplates by John Theodore and John Israel de Bry. These are arranged in a logical sequence, introduced by Heraclitus and Democritus, the weeping and the laughing philosophers, and ending with the confrontation of Man and Woman by Death. The emphasis is on sexual attraction, and the treatment is cynical, often vulgar to the verge of obscenity, very Brueghelesque, and sometimes extraordinarily anticipatory of surrealism. There are only a few personified abstractions but there is a vivid variety and vitality in these plates. England produced nothing like this book.

We shall see later that the Jesuits adapted to the purposes of religious instruction the method of the emblematists and that their style was imitated, sometimes with modifications, in England. But no English book rivals the extravagances of devout emotionalism seen in Daniel Cramer's *Emblemes Sacrez* (Frankfort, 1622). It is concerned with the amazing adventures and sufferings of the human Heart (depicted with anatomical accuracy), sometimes alone, sometimes incongruously associated with a human figure. The Heart is tied to the World, tested in a furnace, roasted on a gridiron, set in thorns, weighed on scales, afloat upon a stormy sea, nailed to a cross, hung from a palm tree, placed on a skull, pecked at by birds, pursued by a fiend, aflame, quenched, squeezed, rent, wounded, subjected to all manner of indignities, severed from the World, tied to a tomb, carried to heaven. For English parallels, and they are comparatively restrained, we must turn to a few title pages and to a few poems by Richard Crashaw.

England offers us no specimen of the emblem book published for a special occasion. Of limited but intense appeal, such books were in vogue in Germany, where a scholar or group of scholars would invent and issue one to celebrate the anniversary of, say, a hospital or a school of medicine or law. Festival books of this kind were produced in honor of distinguished personages. An Italian example celebrates the consecration of Cardinal Monti as Archbishop of Milan; [28] the engravings in it have been described in an earlier chapter in connection with the Four Seasons and the Four Ages of Human Life. Like honor might be paid to a great person lately dead. From Italy comes one of the most fantastic specimens of the extremes to which the ingenuity of the emblematists could go. This is a memorial tribute to Pope Gregory XIII (died 1585) and contains no less than 254 handsome copperplates by Natale Bonifazio di Giroloma.[29] It is, as is stated on the title page, an allegory of the Dragon. Each plate is explicated in a sonnet. There is a remarkable conflation and interpenetration of heraldry (the Dragon being on the coat of arms of this Pope), the impresa (the design's being applicable to a great individual), and the emblem (the design interpreted in a broader ethical and religious sense). The Dragon appears in nearly all the plates and is always a symbol of good. He is seen with the Virtues, with the Seasons, and in many other combinations. He is identified with the serpent lifted up by Moses in the wilderness. He swims with the Ship of the Church on his back. Two of him (so to speak) are entwined round Mercury's caduceus. He is an amusingly ubiquitous creature, though in the long run one grows tired of him. The excesses of baroque fantasy seldom went further than this.

James Cleland, a writer on educational theory and practice, suggests that one way to "allure" young gentlemen to their books is to entertain them with emblems, and he mentions one of Alciati's designs as suitable for this purpose; [30] but though instruction, as well as entertainment, was one of the objects of English emblematists it was generally limited to the fields of religion and morals and no English emblem books were concerned with instruction. However, several such came from Germany. Composed with pedantic care is a volume published in Nuremberg in 1597.[31] This contains problems set for students whose task it was to compose and deliver orations and panegyrics suggested by animals, plants, ships, a candle, and other objects, and by a few classical myths. Attractive little copperplates with an emblem on one side and an inscription on the other illustrate the text. Many are on familiar themes, often in ingenious new arrangements.[32]

There is a loose connection between emblem books and *tarocchi* or tarot cards; both employ personified abstractions which have symbolic and esoteric meanings.[33] How popular tarots were in England it is difficult to determine. John Florio in his *Worlde of Wordes* (1598) defines tarocchi as "a kinde of playing cardes used in Italy, called terrestrial triumphes;" in his revised edition (1611) he adds the English form of the word, "tarocks." [34] In a French–English conversation book tarots are grouped with dice, chess, and other games.[35] James Cleland assures his readers that King James' "permission of honest house games, as Cardes, French Cardes, called Taraux, Tables, and such like plaies, is sufficient to protect you from the blame of those learned men, who thinke them Hazards."

In the strict sense only the twenty–one cards above the suits are tarocchi. The suits themselves contain four sets of ideas: Coins; Cups or Chalices; Swords; and Clubs: In terms of the several ranks or states of society they represent, respectively, the Nobility, the Clergy, the Military, and the Commonalty; in terms of the Virtues they are Charity, Faith, Justice, and Fortitude; [36] in terms of Sins they are Greed, Drunkenness and Gluttony, Hate and Strife, and Ferocity. The fame of tarocchi among connoisseurs is not due, however, to the suits, which though often beautifully designed are somewhat monotonous, but to the twenty–one cards ranking above them.[37] Here personifications are represented, among them the Four Stoic Virtues, Fortune at her Wheel, and Death appear in all packs. Time does not appear; the figure sometimes mistaken for him is properly called the Hermit. It is obvious that while playing this game contestants would be constantly reminded of a few symbols and personifications.

To the best of my knowledge no tarots were made in England, or if they were they have been lost. An anonymous imitator of Samuel Rowlands managed, however, to extract symbolism from an ordinary pack of cards.[38] Lucifer, a cunning juggler, discards the four Kings, representing Truth, Mercy, Justice, and Temperance. The four Queens are four queans: a punk, a doxie, a scold, and a bawd. The Knaves are four types of rascality and they are also related to the Four Temperaments: Spades to the Melancholy, Hearts to the Sanguine, Clubs to the Choleric, and Diamonds to the Phlegmatic. In the Trevelyon commonplace book in the Folger Library (fol. 160ᵛ) the four suits represent the Four Ages of the World in descending order: hearts, spades, diamonds, and clubs, or love, labor, wealth, and violence.

Some of the devices used by printers as colophons or placed on title pages call to mind the emblem books. Many are attractive, a few quite exquisite. Prudence with her mirror and serpent and Justice with her sword and scales often appear. Fortune is a favorite device, sometimes with Mercury to contrast her fickleness with the stability of learning and the arts. Very popular is the device of Father Time. English printers often took ideas from Continental sources or copied foreign designs. William Ward, whose shop was "At the Sign of Time," borrowed from a Parisian printer a device showing Time rescuing Truth from the cave. The prolific printer Thomas Creede generally used a personification of Truth, doubtless in allusion to his own name.[39]

6. English Emblem Books

Having focused attention on diverse continental developments with but fleeting glances at a few English parallels, we have now to look more closely at English books. Close connections existed between the comparatively few English emblematists and some of the publishers on the Continent. Of this relationship the earliest example is John Van der Noodt's *Theatre for Worldings.* The Dutch original and the French translation were both published in London in 1568 and the English version in the following year.[1] That all three versions appeared, surprisingly enough, in London and not in the Low Countries may have some bearing upon the problem of authorship. Each of the score of woodcuts has an accompanying poem and the collection as a whole is followed by a commentary. The little book is a humble and not entirely typical example of its genre, being limited in scope to antipapal propaganda and to meditations upon the swift decay of earthly glory; but the question of its relationship to Spenser's *Complaints* and the probability that the English version is in part by Spenser have attracted the attention of scholars.

Though Stephen Bateman is not to be numbered among the emblematists, he gives signs of an awareness of their methods. The long throat and monstrous paunch of Gluttony in one of his books [2] may have been taken directly from Alciati. His most celebrated work, *The Doome warning all men to the Judgemente* (1581), "Batman's Doome," as it came to be called, was for generations popular among the semiliterate chiefly because of its crudely vigorous woodcuts. It is a large chronological catalogue of eclipses, triple suns, comets, earthquakes, hurricanes, floods, pestilences, monstrous births (both human and animal), and other portents. Of the occasional efforts to extract an allegorical or emblematic meaning from the monsters a single example will suffice (p. 295); some details of this very nasty example may be conveniently passed over.

The lack of arms is interpreted as the lack of good works and an eye in the knee as the "bending of the minde only to earthlie things." But the monster is marked with a "Y" and an "X" which Bateman says are good signs, "for Y is a figure of Vertue" (that is, the "Y of Pythagoras," symbolizing the Choice of the Two Paths) and "X" is the Cross.

Geffrey Whitney's *A Choice of Emblemes* (1856) [3] is truly representative and was never rivaled as the amplest and most wide ranging of English collections. It was printed in Leyden by the great firm of Plantin which not only had much experience with books of this kind but had in store large supplies of woodblocks. Whitney's originality consisted in the invention of but a small fraction of these emblems, of the 248 designs only twenty–three are by him; the rest are taken from Alciati, Sambucus, and other Continental sources. He follows foreign theorists in his threefold classification of emblems: the historical, which have to do with the deeds of noble persons; the natural, which deal with the properties of creatures; and the moral, which pertain to virtue. (This system stems through intermediate growths from the three "Mirrors" of Vincent of Beauvais.) For definitions of Emblemata, Symbolum, and Ænigma with the distinctions to be drawn among them Whitney refers somewhat casually in his address "To the Reader" to the discussion by Alciati, La Perriere, Bocchius, and other authorities.

A year earlier than Whitney's book Samuel Daniel had published a translation of Paolo Giovio's *Dialogo* on military and amorous imprese.[4] Apart from his preface Daniel made no original contribution. The theory and practice of emblems is learnedly discussed in Abraham Fraunce's *Insignium* (1588),[5] where many examples are cited from the authors of classical antiquity, illustrating "Figure" (that is, the design), "Vox" (that is the motto, "word," or "mot"), and the accompanying text. Fraunce quotes or refers to many Continental emblematists, among them, Alciati, Scipion Bargagli, Ruscelli, Sambucus, Gabriel Simon, Beza, Adrian Junius, Reusner, and Paradin. The *Devises Heroiques* (1551) by Claude Paradin appeared in an English version, *Heroicall Devises* (1591) by P.S., who has not been identified. The translator added material from other sources. William Wyrley's *The True Use of Armorie* (1592) is on the closely related subject of heraldry. Dating from as early as 1593, when it was entered in the Stationers' Register, and known to Meres in 1598, 1614 is the date of the earliest extant edition of Thomas Combe's *The Theatre of Fine Devices, containing an hundred morall Emblemes* which is a translation of Guillaume de la Perriere's *Le Theatre des Bons Engins* (1539). Andrew Willet's *Sacrorum Em-*

blematum Centuria Una (Cambridge, 1596) is the first extensive English collection of so—called "naked emblems," a subsidiary genre about which something will be said presently. These Elizabethan publications point the way towards the emblem literature of the Stuart age.

Cultural ties and exchanges in this specialized department of intellectual and artistic life became more intimate in the seventeenth century. The attractive English Roman Catholic exile Richard Verstegen (born Richard Rowlands), who for many years lived generally in Antwerp, became, like Whitney, a link between London and that city. It is practically certain that he was the author of the English versions of the poems in Otho Van Veen's *Amorum Emblemata* (Antwerp, 1608) when that charming book was prepared for the English market with a dedication (also probably by Verstegen) to the Earls of Pembroke and Montgomery.[6]

Meanwhile Jacob Cats, Dutch poet, scholar, and diplomat, had as a young man studied at both Oxford and Cambridge.[7] After his return home he took up emblems as a hobby and in them made frequent use of English proverbs and pithy phrases, while also drawing upon other tongues to display this sort of gnomic wisdom. To his *Silenus Alcibiadis, sive Proteus* (1618) Joshua Sylvester contributed a commendatory sonnet in French.[8] Thomas Heywood was another of Cats' English admirers. In the prose apparatus following each book of *The Hierarchie of the Blessed Angels* (1635) there is a section entitled "An Emblem." Each is a description of some person, object, or scene with a moral "Application" attached. All are taken from Cats' writings but they are "naked" —that is without the woodcuts or engravings of the Dutch originals— and are tedious and dreary. The same criticism holds for Heywood's "Emblematicall Dialogue, interpreted from the Excellent and most learned D. Jac. Catzius; which sheweth how Virgins in their chaste loves ought to beare themselves." [9] This is a quite faithful and therefore pedestrian version of Cats' *Maechden—Plicht* (1618); lacking the forty—eight copperplates which add some vitality to the mawkishly moralising counsel given jeunes filles on the affairs of the heart it is intolerably boring. That emblems thus stripped of their adornment (and hence called "naked") could get into print is an indication of interest in the genre. Further evidence of the Dutch poet's popularity in England is found in the 1627 edition of his *Proteus*. The texts in the first part, accompanying fifty—one emblems of Love, are in Dutch, Latin, and French. Then comes a half title: *Emblemata D. Iacobi Catsii in linguam Anglicam transfusa*, introducing fifty—one little English poems, whether composed by Cats himself or by an anonymous Englishman is not known.

George Wither's relations with the Low Countries were commercial rather than personal. The plates used for his *Emblemes* (1635) were those made by Crispin Van de Passe the Younger for Gabriel Rollenhagen's *Nucleus Emblematum selectissimorum* (Arnheim, 1611). In his prefatory "To the Reader" Wither, writing not of the metal cuts themselves but of a copy of Rollenhagen's book, states that "these Emblems, graven in Copper by Crispinus Passaeus . . . came into my hands, almost twentie years past"—that is, not long after they were published. For his own pleasure he made "illustrations" (expository poems) to go with some of the designs. "Some of my Friends . . . requested mee to Moralize the rest. Which I condiscended unto: And, they had beene brought into view many yeares agoe, but that the Copper Prints (which are now gotten) could not be procured out of Holland, upon any reasonable Conditions." He does not say whether he negotiated for them directly with the Dutch owner or through an English agent. He implies that he got them at a bargain price, and a comparison of Rollenhagen's book and Wither's makes plain why this was possible, for by 1635 the plates, so fresh and crisp in 1611, were worn and dark. Originally each copperplate had engraved beneath the emblem two lines of Latin verse, but, says Wither, "the Verses were so meane, that they were afterwards cut off from the Plates." This amputation reduced them from rectangles taller than their breadth to squares.[10] In his text Wither is quite independent of the Dutch book. "I have not so much as cared," he says, "to find out their meanings in any of these Figures, but, applied them, rather, to such purposes as I could think of, at first sight; which, upon a second view, I found might have beene much bettered, if I could have spared time from other imployments." There are some admissions that he cannot comprehend the purpose of a design, as when he begins one set of verses: "What in this Emblem, that mans meanings were / Who made it first, I neither know nor care." [11] Not only does he cut loose from the Dutch text, he adapts his own book to purposes of recreation that were no part of Rollenhagen's intention. To the last leaf of each copy were attached metal spinners pointing to circles of numerals. The lower spinner directed the player's attention to one of the four books into which the collection is divided; the upper spinner to one of the poems and designs in each book.[12] The player was supposed to obtain information about his character and fortune. Wither admits the childishness of this lottery game but expresses the hope that he may attract readers to his serious moral purpose.

Like Wither, Francis Quarles was indebted to Continental sources for the designs in his *Emblemes* (1635).[13] He did not, however, import directly but had copies made or adaptations devised by William Marshall, William Simpson, and John Payne. Those for Books I and II are by Marshall and derive from an anonymous volume, *Typus Mundi*, published by the Jesuits of Antwerp in 1627. They treat of the calamities and perils of the Soul. Books III, IV, and V are almost entirely limited to the Cupid and Psyche myth, allegorized as the relationship between Christ and the Soul, with a close dependence upon the Song of Songs. The designs for this second series are taken from the woodcuts by Christofell Sichem the Younger in the second edition of Father Herman Hugo's *Pia Desideria Emblematis . . . Illustrata* (Antwerp, 1628). Most are close copies but in a few there is considerable freedom of treatment.[14] In his text Quarles follows Father Hugo in a general way only, substituting a puritanical moral emphasis for the Jesuit's emotional mysticism.[15] When in 1686 Edmund Arwaker published a new version of the *Pia Desideria* (with debased copies of the cuts) he followed the original text quite closely, albeit deleting and expanding, whereas Quarles, as Arwaker remarks in his preface, "only borrow'd his Emblems, to praefix them to much inferior sense."

Wither and Quarles were the most popular of English emblematists and remained so for long after they died. Henry Peacham never attained to such renown, though his *Minerva Britanna or a Garden of Heroical Devices* (1612) was reprinted. He depends partly upon his classical erudition and partly upon Continental predecessors; only rarely is he original. A prefatory remark of his upon the paucity of English books of the sort is interesting, suggesting as it does the great expense involved and the lack of inventive talent, "for except the collections of Master Whitney and the translations of some one or two else beside, I know not an Englishman in our age, that hath published any worke of this kinde." He might have added that the English trade did not have the facilities and outlets to wide markets possessed by some foreign publishers.

A final example of a borrower from abroad is Christopher Harvey, the disciple and imitator of George Herbert. All the plates (with the exception of the first three, which are by William Marshall) in his *Schola Cordis or the Heart of it Selfe, gone away from God; brought back againe to him; and instructed by him, in 47 Emblems* (1647) are taken from the *Schola Cordis* of the Dutch emblematist B. Van Haeften (1629). Some, being in reverse, seem to have been traced on new plates from original impressions; for others the original plates, worn and much retouched, were probably used.[16]

From the foregoing survey collections of emblems in manuscripts have been omitted. They seem to have been made for presentation to noble patrons, and except in cases where parts of their contents were borrowed for books of later date it is not likely that they exerted any wide influence[17]

7. *Personifications and Emblems in Various Arts*

The "Bed of State wrought and embroidered all with gold and silk" by Mary Queen of Scots which Drummond described to Ben Jonson [1] was adorned with many imprese and emblems. The remarkably early date of this lost treasure is of course explained by the influence of the French culture that Mary brought when she fled to England in 1568. The finest of all surviving memorials of the English vogue for tapestries is the famous set of the "Seasons" at Hatfield, probably woven on the Sheldon looms.[2] Venus represents Spring, Ceres the Summer, Bacchus the Autumn, and Æolus the Winter and the Labors of the Months are depicted. To the iconographer the borders are the most interesting parts of the tapestries. Each of the four has forty–two little roundels, no less than 168 in all, each with a Latin motto. Some are heraldic but most are emblematic. Whitney is certainly the principal source, but other emblematists are drawn upon, although the origin of some has not been traced, and it is possible that a few are fresh inventions. To give an exhaustive account of this vast series would occupy a volume. Four emblems, all familiar from one collection or another, may be described briefly as examples. "Concordia Insuperabilis" is a crowned king with three heads and six arms. "Mutuum Auxilium" is a blind man carrying a lame man who guides him. "Scelerum Conscientia" is a man fearful of his own shadow. "Despair" is a man falling on his sword.

Another great creation was the series of arches erected for the state entry of James I in 1604. The original structures have disappeared, but we know them from famous engravings [3] as well as from descriptions in *The Magnificent Entertainment* by Thomas Dekker and *The Time Triumphant* by Gilbert Dugdale (both 1604). Among the decorations were many personifications (the Liberal Arts, the Cardinal Virtues, Fortune, Fame, Zeal, Peace, Wealth, Quiet, Safety, and so forth) generally quite conventional and unimaginative, though the ensemble must have made a fine show. We observe the overlapping of the long–standing tradition of representation of abstract concepts with the newer fashion of emblematizing.[4]

As on occasions of public rejoicing so on occasions of public mourning emblems and devices were called into service. The funerals of Sir Philip Sidney, Queen Elizabeth, and Henry Prince of Wales are examples.[5] The housings and trappings of such processions are known from engravings that have been often reproduced but the figures on some monumental tombs are more interesting because they are still extant. Charity, History, and other personifications appear on the Thomas Sutton monument by Nicholas Stone in the Charterhouse, and above the tablet are bas–reliefs of Time and of a child blowing bubbles. The latter is certainly Vanity, though the pair have been misinterpreted as Youth and Old Age. The Four Stoic Virtues are found on two other tombs by Stone.[6]

The display of devices, on helmets, shields, or banners, in tournaments or warfare was a custom still so well remembered that a few instances from literature will suffice to illustrate it. Let the reader refresh his memory of the "triumph" of the six knights in *Pericles* (II.2). Each has upon his shield a device with a motto or word. Five of these inscriptions are in Latin, one in Spanish. In Marlowe's *Edward II* (lines 810 f.) Lancaster and Young Mortimer describe their devices and mottoes. In *Richard II* (II.3.25) one of the accusations brought by Bolingbroke against Bushy and Green is that they "razed out [his] imprese," thus leaving to the world no sign that he was a gentleman. In *The Partial Law* (I.5), an undated, anonymous Stuart tragedy, five knights bear shields on which are devices and mottoes. Each is described, as, for instance:

> A man sunke in the Sea, only his head
> Borne above water by a Scepter, which
> Is by a hand supported from the skyes,
> His word *Hinc sola Salus*.

The personifications in Phineas Fletcher's *The Purple Island* have shields with devices. That of Covetousness (VIII, 29) is no proper shield but a pot lid. On it the impresa is a securely sealed bag; the word is "Much better sav'd, then spill'd." The squalor of this is appropriate to the context.

In Elizabethan portraits naturalistic representationalism is sometimes sacrificed for the sake of symbolic meaning. Two exquisite little portraits by Marcus Gheeraerts the Younger [7] show a lady standing upon a tortoise. She holds the forefinger of her right hand to her lips; the left hand, with a dove perched on the wrist, is pressed to her heart; a bunch of keys is at her waist. The two paintings are sweetly contrasted: one is of a young woman with the motto "Sis tu talis" and the other of an older woman with the motto "Haec talis fuit." One portrait gives counsel to a young woman; the other offers tribute to an older. The theme is that of the Perfect Wife: She stays at home (the tortoise); she is silent (the finger to her lips); she is loving (the dove); she is a good housekeeper (the keys). The symbolism is in part traceable to Greek antiquity and was used in some emblem books.[8]

Three portraits by Hans Eworth invite our scrutiny.[9] There is a great contrast between the winning restraint of the two paintings just described and the fantastic exuberance of Eworth's portrait of Sir John Luttrell who quite naked wades waist deep through a stormy sea where the face of a drowned man is seen and a ship is tossed. Luttrell's raised right arm is lightly touched by the hand of Peace who, naked and with her olive branch, issues from a cloud. Latin inscriptions on his two bracelets imply that separation has not altered him nor love of gain tempted him. On a rock protruding from the sea is another inscription: "More then the rock amydys the raging seas / The constant hert no danger dreddys nor fearys." Sufficient is known of Luttrell's life to explain the appropriateness of all this. In another painting by Eworth a man and a woman join hands upon a skull which rests on a tomb. In the foreground a corpse lies on a sheaf of wheat. Over the joined hands of the pair is the inscription: "W.I. Behowlde ower ende. I.I." The initials are certainly those of a husband and wife, and on the evidence of armorial bearings that appear Cust identified the family as Judd. On the tomb are these verses: "The worde of God / Hath knit us twayne / And Death shall us / Devide agayne." Cust was, I am confident, wrong in describing this as a "memorial painting." It is a conflation of the *Memento Mori* theme with an asservation of fidelity in marriage (as in Jan Van Eyck's "Arnolfini Portrait"). A third portrait by Eworth exemplifies the difficulty of determining in some cases whether an object depicted is a "moral emblem" or is simply an indication of the subject's calling. A man holds a mariner's compass and from his neck hangs what seems to be a magnet. Is this a seaman with the instruments of his profession? Or is the compass a symbol of Constancy and the magnet the point towards which it is always directed? One cannot be sure.

The emblematic suggestiveness in many portraits is, however, beyond doubt. One by George Glover [10] (probably a self–portrait) has on one side of the figure a pair of balances on which a compass (craftsmanship and proportion) outweighs a coat of arms i.e. art is of greater worth than pride of birth. A portrait of Sir Thomas Chaloner [11] shows him holding scales; in the higher, lighter pan is a winged globe and in the lower, a book from which issue rays of light. A Latin inscription reads in part: "The mind alone has weight; all other things fly upward like the empty scale of the balance." This emblem, so consoling to an artist or scholar, is found elsewhere with variants, as when a pen and a laurel wreath outweigh a cannon.[12] In William Rogers' engraved portrait of Essex,[13] the Earl is flanked by personifications of Constancy and Envy. Constancy holds over him a wreath with the Devereux motto: "Basis Virtutum Constantia." Envy plucks away part of the Laurel, and an inscription: "Virtutis Comes Invidia" is a "word" found in some emblem books. Symbolic meanings are here used for purposes of personal and political propaganda, the engraving perhaps reflecting the situation in 1599 when dangers were gathering round Essex. It may have been intended to invite sympathy for him.

Portraits of Queen Elizabeth are rich in symbolic meanings. They have been the subject of much study and I shall deal with them briefly without becoming involved in problems of authenticity, attribution, and chronology. She is depicted with Justice and Prudence;[14] with Justice, Mercy, Fortitude and Prudence;[15] with the three goddesses, ascribing to the Queen the power of Juno, the wisdom of Pallas, and the beauty of Venus;[16] with the rainbow of Hope, the eyes and ears of Vigilance, and the serpent of Wisdom;[17] with Peace and Plenty;[18] with the olive branch of Peace, the sword of Justice, and the dog of Fidelity;[19] with Victory and Plenty and the pomegranate of Constancy.[20]

The title page of George Carleton's *A Thankfull Remembrance of God's Mercy* (ed. 1627)[21] is a connecting link between emblems in portraits and emblematic title pages. Ecclesia Vera is shown seated with her feet upon a pope, a monk, and a devil. On one side is Queen Elizabeth, labeled "Debora," with a banner depicting the Battle of the Armada and a shield that bears the motto "Semper Eadem." On the other side is King James I, labeled "Salomon"; his banner portrays the Gunpowder Plot and on his shield is the motto "Beati Pacifici." Beneath the Queen's portrait is the Ark with the words "Per Aquas" and beneath the King's a burning bush with the words "Per Ignem." The old Biblical typology has been turned to political account: dangers but also salvation have come to England by water and by fire.

When in *II Henry IV* (I.1.60–61) Morton enters to bring news of the defeat at Shrewsbury, Lord Bardolph exclaims: "This mans brow, like to a Title–leafe, / Fore–tels the Nature of a Tragicke Volume." The commentators assume that the image refers to the black bordered title of elegies, such as the one which appeared on the death of the Prince of Wales in 1613. Examples of this funerary fashion dating from the time of Shakespeare's plays have not been found, but he must have known at least one. In general, prologuizing or epitomizing title pages are rare in Elizabethan books and did not become the fashion till the Jacobean age, when they ranged from the plainest representationalism to the most recondite symbolism. Often authors thought themselves obligated to interpret titles for their readers' better understanding, so often, in fact, that it is refreshing to come across these verses "Upon the Frontispiece": [22]

> Hee that in words explains a Frontispiece,
> Betrayes the secret trust of his Device:
> Who cannot guesse, where Mottos and Emblems be,
> The drift, may still be ignorant for me."

That is, it is the reader's business to interpret the design for himself.

However, there were not always new, and therefore puzzling, inventions; instead reliance might be placed on inherited, traditional, and easily apprehensible material. Thus, the title page of Samuel Rowlands' volume of religious verse, *The Betraying of Christ* (1598) [23] has the instruments of the Passion. An English translation of a French *Summary* of Du Bartas (1621) [24] shows at the top the Fall of Lucifer, on the lateral margins the Six Days of Creation, and at the bottom The Sabbath. In the third edition (Oxford, 1628) of Burton's *Anatomy of Melancholy* [25] the author's portrait appears along with the four types of Melancholy: the Inamorato, the Hypocondriacus, the Superstitious, and the Maniacus, which are represented not as abstractions but as individuals, each in a typical costume, posture, and situation. Burton supplies a verse "Argument to the Frontispiece" which is really not needed. Thomas Cecill's design for Thomas Johnson's translation of *The Workes of that most famous Chirugion Ambrose Parey* (1634) [26] has a like simple literalism. At the top is a portrait of Paré flanked by two scenes: a surgeon trepanning a patient and a physician compounding a drug. On the lateral borders a skeleton and an anatomical cadaver are represented and retorts, surgical instruments, and three monstrous births are placed at the bottom. In the four cases just discussed there are no personifications or genuine emblems; no more is meant than meets the eye.

On the other hand, sometimes the subject is not so simple as at first glance it appears to be. Cecill's engraved title page of the "newly corrected" edition of the *Essayes* of Sir William Cornwallys (1632) [27] presents an interesting problem (Fig. 154). Its philosophic serenity and the relative excellence of its craftsmanship make it the most pleasing of all early Stuart works of its kind. In this double portrait the man who is writing wears the Elizabethan ruff and the man who is reading wears the Jacobean falling collar. To some observers the writer appears to be older than the reader. Because of these two differences between the portraits the Dictionary of National Biography holds that a father and son are portrayed. But objections to this view may be raised. First, the fancied difference in age is due to the direction of the light and, moreover, the older Cornwallys was not a writer and therefore not connected with the book. Secondly the piped ruff did not immediately go out of fashion in Jacobean times, though it is conceivable that the ruff was used to suggest that the *Essayes,* first published in 1600, go back to Elizabethan times. Furthermore, while a father might closely resemble his son, we have here not similarity but identity: the portraits are obviously of the same man. It has also been suggested that Sir William is portrayed at two periods of his life but, as I pointed out above, the portraits show no real contrast between the ages of the two men. I think the title page shows the essayist at his two favorite occupations, reading and writing,[28] and one may compare this work with John Payne's title page to the *Workes* of John Boys (1622) [29] which shows the learned author reading, writing, preaching, and praying.

To read into a design something that was not intended is a temptation that not all iconographers are always able to resist. (Such a tendency is analogous to the interpretations advanced by some contemporary critics of poetry, particularly seventeenth–century poetry.) Although aware of this temptation, I must confess that in the past I have committed errors of this nature, and yet one cannot help being puzzled by curious details such as appear in William Hole's title page to the folio edition of Ben Jonson's *Workes* (1616).[30] It is a view of a "Theatrum" (Fig. 155) based on Italian views of surviving Roman structures, or upon theoretical reconstructions. To these is added a superstructure of gabled roofs. Is this hybrid due to the artist's assumption that in ancient theaters the machinery depended from "huts" such as he was familiar with in London playhouses? Or is there an intention to symbolize the union in Jonson's dramas of classical and native elements? The latter alternative is unlikely but conceivable. Personifications on this title page represent different kinds of drama, and since we know that Jonson supervised the printing of the folio, it seems probable that Hole consulted with him when making this design.[31]

Two other designs by Hole require attention. The excessive emotionality of the title page of John Haywarde's *The Sanctuarie of a Troubled Soule* (ed. 1616) [32] (Fig. 156) is an unpleasant invention but does foretell the nature of the volume. To understand it we must remember that Haywarde's *Life and Raigne of King Henrie IIII* (1599) had been dedicated to the Earl of Essex, both the subject and the dedication had cast suspicion on him, and for a time the charge of high treason hung over him. The *Sanctuarie* is a series of prayers and meditations. From the center of a heavy architectural structure the Contrite Heart is suspended by chains held by Faith and Hope. Love pierces the Heart with a fiery javelin but at the same time pours upon it healing balm. Grief torments it with briars and Fear stabs it with a sword. There are subsidiary symbols. The epitomizing title page is again exemplified by Hole in Michael Drayton's *Poly-Olbion* (1616) [33] where, however, the concept is better than the execution. In the midst sits Britannia holding the cornucopia of Prosperity and wearing a robe embroidered with the fields and rivers and hills and cities of England. In the architectural frame are four men, representing four periods of the past: the prehistoric when "vast earth-bred giants" woo'd Albion, the Roman, the Saxon, and the Norman. Preliminary verses expound all this. Here is a visual prologue to Drayton's topographical and historical poem.

That there could be sympathetic collaboration between an artist and a poet is evident when we compare Renold Elstrack's title page of Sir Walter Raleigh's *The History of the World* (1613) [34] with Ben Jonson's accompanying poem "The Mind of the Frontispiece to a Booke." No emblematic title page is better known, but because it is so rich in meaning it cannot be passed over without comment. History, the "Magistra Vitae" because she searches the hidden springs of Truth and guided by the Past controls the Future, standing proudly upon Death and dark Oblivion holds the great globe of the terrestrial world; above it is the Eye of Providence and on either side are Fama Bona encircled with light and Fama Mala in a spotted robe. In recesses framed in pairs of pillars are Wisdom, or Experience, with a rule and plummet, and naked Truth with a "beamie hand." The pillars of Wisdom are the Testimony of Time, of which the surface is adorned with books, and the Herald of Antiquity, adorned with hieroglyphics. Of Truth's pillars one has the streaming flames of the Light of Truth and the other the laurels of the Life of Memory. The taste for such heavily charged pieces of imagery is an acquired one, but to one who has it there is evidence of a thoughtful harmony.

Another example of an artist's intelligent grasp of the subject of a book is Robert Vaughan's title page of Richard Brathwaite's *The English Gentleman* (1630) [35] which is an excellent visual summary of the treatise. In the center stands an English gentleman; over him is the inscription: "Spes in Caelis" and below: "Pes in terris"—his hope is in heaven but his feet are firmly fixed upon earth. Eight surrounding compartments prepare the reader for the eight divisions of the book. Youth is confronted by the Choice of the Two Paths; Disposition plucks an apple in an orchard; Education is represented by the Seven Liberal Arts; Vocation shows implements of mental and physical labor; Recreation is a hunting scene; Acquaintance shows two men embracing one another; Moderation is an old man with a halcyon (calm) and a tortoise (firmness); and Perfection is a man standing upon clouds with rays of light about his head and in his hand a palm branch. The harmony between the engraving and the book is absolute. Yet oddly enough there was some misunderstanding between author and artist. In his interpretation of the design he confesses at one point that he is uncertain of the engraver's intention: in the vignette of the Choice is the branch held by Virtue a palm or an olive? Had Brathwaite given Vaughan no instructions? And if not, could he not have asked him what his intention was?

A few more title pages are worth mentioning for one reason or another. That by William Marshall of Wither's *Emblemes* [36] is an example of poor cooperation between artist and author. In a foreword Wither complains that the "graver" did not follow his recommendation of "a plain invention." He thought of casting "this piece" aside but decided to retain it because though obscure and complicated it would exercise the reader's wits. A "plain invention" was often intelligently achieved, as in Hole's design for Aaron Rathborne's *The Surveyor* (1616) which is severely and appropriately architectural in pattern. There are flanking figures of Arithmetica and Geometria with their attributes, and Artifex (a surveyor at work) stands upon two prostrate men, one with asses' ears, the other wearing a fool's cap—Learning dominating Ignorance. Marshall's design for *The Resolver; or Curiosities of Nature* (1635), an anonymous translation from the French of Scipion de Plesis, is also architectural. On a cornice are Time and Death; below stand Plato, laurel wreathed, holding a scroll, and with eyes directed heavenward, and Aristotle with his arms thrust commandingly before him. Are these two figures distantly reminiscent of Raphael's "School of Athens"? George Glover's exuberant talent was better suited to his several series of the Seasons, the Senses, the Arts, the Worthies, and similar subjects than to a meditative mood, but he is not unsuccessful in introducing

William Austin's *Devotionis Augustinianae Flamma or Certayne Devout, Godly, and Learned Meditations* (1635) with some small vignettes on the title among which we note Patience with her heart, yoke, anvil, and hammer, and David contemplating the Path of Life. Robert Vaughan's title page of Robert Farley's *Lights Morall Emblems* (1638) is in strict and detailed keeping with the text, where, as we have seen, variations are played upon the theme of light.

Lastly, I note the frontispiece (in the modern sense, not a title page) which Thomas Cecill engraved for *The Tragedie of Ludowick Sforza* (1628), an anonymous play. This picture is a curiosity unique in the history of Tudor–Stuart drama in that it is an emblematic prologue to, and summary of, what follows. In the foreground a wolf is slaying a lamb. On a higher level of the plate the wolf is shown enthroned and dead lambs lie before him. But from behind him a lion, with a banner displaying fleurs–de–lis, is snatching the crown from his head. The wolf is Sforza; the lambs are his victims; the lion represents the invading forces of France.

NOTES

Abbreviations

CBEL	*Cambridge Bibliography of English Literature*
DNB	*Dictionary of National Biography*
EETS	Early English Text Society
ELH	*A Journal of English Literary History*
MLN	*Modern Language Notes*
OED	*Oxford English Dictionary*
PMLA	*Publications of the Modern Language Association*
STS	Scottish Text Society
TLS	*Times Literary Supplement*

Unless otherwise noted, all English titles were published in London.

1. In the *De Gloria Atheniensium* and in the *De Audiendis Poetis.*

2. George Puttenham, *The Arte of English Poesie* (1589), ed. G. D. Willcock and Alice Walker (1936), p. 209.

3. Sir Philip Sidney, *The Defence of Poesie* (1595), ed. A. S. Cook (1901), p. 16.

4. *Discoveries* (posthumously published, 1641), in *Ben Jonson*, ed. C. H. Herford, Percy Simpson, and Evelyn Simpson, *8* (1947), 609.

5. John Davies of Hereford, *Microcosmos. The Discovery of the Little World* (1603), p. 215.

6. Thomas Dekker, *The Whole Magnificent Entertainment* (1604), in *Dramatic Works*, ed. J. Pearson, *1* (1875), 276.

7. Lodowick Lloyd, *The Pilgrimage of Princes* (ca. 1590), p. 25.

8. Joseph Martyn, *New Epigrams and a Satyre* (1621), no. 29.

9. *Discoveries,* in *Ben Jonson,* p. 610.

10. See Anthony Blunt, "An Echo of the 'Paragone' in Shakespeare," *Journal of the Warburg Institute, 2* (1938–39), 260–62.

Chapter 1. Man's First Disobedience

1. THE TREE OF KNOWLEDGE AND THE TREE OF DEATH

1. Huntington Library, MS 1104, fol. 191^r. The Preparation for Confession is in langue d'Oc. The scene is suggestive not only of the influence of St. Augustine but of a survival of sympathy with the heretical dualism of Albi.

2. Reproduced in Le Comte de Laborde, *Les Manuscrits à peinture de la Cité de Dieu, 3* (Paris, 1909), pl. 25. Ibid., pl. 136, has the same scene from the French translation (Abbeville, 1486) for which see also the J. Pierpont Morgan *Catalogue of Manuscripts and Early Printed Books, 3* (New York, 1907), 85.

3. The two are reproduced in Gustav Pauli, *Hans Sebald Beham* (Strassburg, 1901), nos. 7 and 687.

4. Reproduced in Laborde, *3,* pls. 119 and 92.

5. Reproduced in the Morgan *Catalogue, 1,* 194, and in Albert Schramm, *Der Bilderschmuck der Frühdrucke,* 23 vols. (Leipzig, 1924–43), no. 15.

6. Reproduced in the Morgan *Catalogue, 3,* 104; in A. J. J. Delen, *Histoire de la gravure dans les Anciens Pays-Bas* (Paris, 1924); and elsewhere.

7. *The Digby Plays,* ed. F. F. Furnivall, EETS, 1896.

8. *The Two Gentlemen of Verona,* III.i.342.

9. "Kitto" Bible (an extra-illustrated folio in the Huntington Library), *1,* no. 79. A similar German print of about the same date is in ibid., *2,* no. 355.

2. THE FOUR TEMPERAMENTS, THE TREE OF SIN, SIN ON TRIAL

1. Erwin Panofsky, *Albrecht Dürer*, 2 vols. (Princeton University Press, 1945), *1*, 85, and 2, pl. 117.

2. For example, Pigouchet for Simon Vostre, *Horae* (ca. 1502); Thielman Kerver, *Horae* (1505); Hardouyn, *Horae*, Paris, 1514.

3. Ed. 1630. This is the edition used throughout the present book.

4. *Minerva Britanna, or a Garden of Heroical Devices* (1612 ?), nos. 126–129.

5. *Technogamia*, I.3, 5, and 9; II.3. The edition by Sister M. J. C. Cavanaugh (Washington, D.C., 1942), though abundantly annotated, almost ignores the Temperaments.

6. *Veridicus Christianus* (ed. Antwerp, 1606), pl. 23. Three of Father David's works are referred to so frequently in the present book that a brief account of him may be given. Jan (Jean or Johannes) David, S.J. (1545–1613), born in Courtrai, was active in controversy against the Reformers. The first edition of *Veridicus Christianus* came from the press of Plantin in 1601. The 100 copperplates engraved by Cornelius Galle were also issued separately as *Icones ad veridicum christianum P. Ioannis David* (Antwerp, Philip Galle, 1601). The work appeared also in Flemish (1603) and there is a Flemish issue of the plates. I have used the Latin "Editio altera auctior" of 1606. In the accompanying commentary marginal references direct attention to details in the plates. Theodore Galle did the engravings in David's *Occasio Arrepta, Neglecta. Huius Commoda: Illius Incommoda* (Antwerp, 1605). Of this there is an Italian version (Rome, 1606 ?). Of David's *Paradisus Sponsi et Sponsae* (Antwerp, 1607) with plates by Theodore Galle there are versions in Polish, German, and French. Father David published many other works, most of them in Flemish. See further A. and A. De Backer, S.J., *Bibliothèque de la Compagnie de Jésus*, 2 (Brussels, 1891), columns 1844–53.

7. *Emblemes*, 1635.

8. *The Isle of Man, or the Legal Proceedings in Man-shire against Sinne, Wherein, by way of a continued Allegorie, the Chiefe Malefactors disturbing both Church and Commonwealth are detected.* Before the appearance of Bunyan's *The Holy War* this book had passed through 16 editions. For a summary see J. B. Wharey, *A Study of the Sources of Bunyan's Allegories* (1904), pp. 78–91.

9. "H.M." [Humphrey Mills], in *Poems occasioned by a Melancholy Vision* (1639), sig. 12[r].

10. Ibid., sig. M3[r].

11. This picture has a trilingual title: "Smenshen val," "Casus hominis," and "La Cheute de l'homme."

12. Father Herman Hugo, *Pia Desideria Emblematis* (Antwerp, 1624).

3. DEATH

1. *Non-Cyclical Miracle Plays*, EETS, *104* (1909), p. 17. A skeleton with scythe and hourglass on the title page of Arnold Weickardid,

Thesaurus Pharmaceuticus (Frankfort–a–M., 1626), is labeled "Dolor."

2. Thomas Digges, augmenting and correcting his father Leonard Digges' *A Prognostication Everlasting* (ed. 1576), sig. M2ʳ.

3. Reproduced in John MacFarlane, *Antoine Verard* (1910), pl. 45; in A. M. Hind, *Introduction to a History of Woodcut*, 2 (1935), 626, fig. 369; in Willard Farnham, *The Medieval Heritage of Elizabethan Tragedy* (1936), frontispiece; and elsewhere.

4. Sig. B2ʳ. This is a translation from the French of Claude Paradin by Peter Derendel, himself a Frenchman. A copy of this book is in the Folger Library.

5. Huntington Library, "Kitto" Bible, 4, no. 512.

6. Ibid., 3, no. 449.

7. Act IV, Scene 7 (p. 120 of ed. 1617). This is the subject of one of the copperplates from designs by Carlo Antonio Procaccivi. He evidently drew from an actual performance: the characters stand on the boards; the backgrounds are backdrops; the front edge of the stage is shown.

8. Huntington Library, MS 1125, fol. 81ʳ.

9. Albert Feuillerat, *Documents relating to the revels at court in the time of King Edward VI and Queen Mary* (Louvain, 1914), pp. 131, 134, 145.

10. The word "mediox," which is not in *OED* or Webster, is formed from the Plautine word "mediozumi." In Martianus Capella's *De Nuptiis Philologiae et Mercurii* "Medioxumi" are demons dwelling in the middle region between earth and heaven.

11. Giorgio Vasari, *Lives of the Most Eminent Painters, Sculptors, and Architects*, translated by G. De C. Vere, 4 (1912–14), 128. Some of the performers wore "masks that represented a death's head both in front and behind."

4. TIME, BEFORE THE FALL

1. In *A New Spring of Divine Poetrie* (1637), pp. 3–4 and 11–12.

2. The second edition (1623) is not a continuation as it is described in *DNB* but a reissue of the sheets of the first edition with a new title page and a new poetical address to James I. There is a reprint (New York, 1886) but without the woodcuts. The *CBEL* classifies the poem under emblem books, where it does not belong.

Chapter 2. The World of Time

1. TIME THE DESTROYER

1. Some parts of this chapter are taken from my article on "Time and Fortune," *ELH, A Journal of English Literary History*, 6 (1939), 83–113. So far as possible I have avoided a mere repetition of what is expounded with admirable erudition by Erwin Panofsky, "Father Time," *Studies in Iconology* (New York, Oxford University Press, 1939), pp.

69–93 and plates. Hence my disregard of such aspects of the subject as Time's relationship to Saturn, the many designs of Time eating his own children, his lameness, and so forth.

2. *Varieties: or, A Surveigh of Rare and Excellent Matters, necessary and delectable for all sorts of persons* (1635), Bk. I, p. 28.

3. Spenser, *Two Cantos of Mutabilitie*, VI, 8, 5–7. There is no comment in the *New Variorum*, ed., Baltimore, 1932.

4. *The Third Part of the Countess of Pembroke's Ivy-church* (1592), fols. 58ᵛ–59ʳ. The visit to the Palace of Time forms the climax and conclusion of Fraunce's work.

5. John Hagthorpe, *Visiones Rerum. The Vision of Things* (1623), First Vision.

6. "Time is the Father of Mutabilitie," Nicholas Ling had said, in *Politeuphuia* (ed. 1598), fol. 227ʳ.

7. *Love's Labour's Lost*, I.1.4.

8. *The Insatiate Countess*, III.4.1.

9. *The Trial of Treasure*, in *Dodsley's Old English Plays*, ed. by William C. Hazlitt, 3 (1874–76), 299. Hereafter referred to as Hazlitt's Dodsley.

10. Commendatory sonnet to Samuel Rowlands, in *A Theater of Delightfull Recreation* (1605), p. 10.

11. *The Gentleman's Exercise* (ed. 1612), p. 111.

12. *Voornaamste Gebouwen Vande Tegenwoordige Stadt Romen*, n.d., seventeenth century. I know this only from a detached leaf in the Huntington Library's extra-illustrated Bryan, *Dictionary of Painters and Engravers*, 2 (ed. 1816), 450, pl. 3. Note Time's contrasting wings, a bird's and a bat's.

13. *Segmenta nobilium signorum et statuarum quae temporis dentem inuidium* [sic] *euasere* (Rome, 1638); reproduced in Panofsky, "Father Time," *Studies in Iconology*, fig. 60.

14. An engraving signed "I.H.W." in "Kitto" Bible, 24, no. 4590. Death holds an hourglass surmounted by the contrasting wings.

15. Otho Van Veen (Vaenius), *Quinti Horatii Flacci Emblemata* (Antwerp, 1612), p. 191. My many references to this delightful book are to the "Horatian Emblems." The plates, not numbered, are on the pages with uneven numbers. Each text begins with a passage from Horace, followed by parallels from other classical authors. Then come verses in Spanish, Italian, Dutch, and French. There is a brief exposition of each plate in Latin prose. In *Othonis Vaeni Emblemata Horatiana* (Amsterdam, 1684) the designs have been reengraved on a smaller scale and for the Spanish verses others in German have been substituted. A direct "steal" from Van Veen is Marin Le Roy de Gomberville, *La Doctrine des Moeurs. Tirée de la Philosophie des Stoiques: Représentée en cent tableaux et Expliqués en cent discours pour l'instruction de la jeunesse* (Paris, 1646). Daret, the engraver, claims to have done the "figures" but they are merely debased copies in reverse of Van Veen's designs. Thomas Manington Gibbs translated this book: *The Doctrine of Morality; or, A View of Human Life . . . Exemplify'd in One Hundred and Three Copper-plates done by the Celebrated*

Monsieur Daret Engraver to the late French King (1721). Both volumes are handsome folios, the English much larger than the French because it retains the French text in parallel columns with the English. Van Veen receives no credit at all.

16. *Nicholas Flammel: His Exposition of the Hieroglyphicall Figures which he caused to be painted upon an Arch in St. Innocents Church–yard at Paris* (1634), pp. 11–12. This claims to be a translation by "Eirenaeus Orandus," obviously a pseudonym.

17. Huntington Library extra-illustrated Bryan, *Dictionary of Painters and Engravers*, 2, pl. 4, preceding p. 497.

18. For example, Jean Mercier, *I. C. Emblemata* (1592?), fol. 13ᵛ: Time gnaws upon the arm of a wretched child.

19. This is one of six stained glass windows (ca. 1502) depicting the Triumphs. See Prince D'Essling and Eugène Müntz, *Petrarque* (Paris, 1902), p. 201.

20. In *Emblemata* (Antwerp, 1564), p. 23.

21. *A Larum for London, or The Siedge of Antwerp* (1602), ed. W. W. Greg, Malone Society, 1913.

22. *The Return from Parnassus Part Two*, IV.3, in Hazlitt's Dodsley, *4*, 199, and later editions. For Ariosto's description of Time see Sir John Harington's translation (1634) of the *Orlando Furioso*, XXXIV, 90 f. and XXXV, 17 f. An engraving in Harington, p. 289, shows Time casting his "whole load of names" (on scrolls) into Lethe. Time elsewhere travels toward another river. Richard Linche, translating from Vincenzo Cartari (who goes back to Boccaccio) says: "Time so soone as wee are borne . . . doth carrie us along by little and little unto our deaths, and setteth over the river of Acheron." See *The Fountaine of Ancient Fiction. Wherein is lively depictured the Images and Statues of the gods of the Ancients, with their proper and perticular expositions. Done out of Italian into English* (1599), sig. Q1ʳ.

23. The unique copy of the original (which I have not seen) is in the Library of the Society of Antiquaries in London; it is reprinted in *Old English Ballads*, ed. Hyder Rollins (Cambridge, Mass., 1920), pp. 184 f.

24. "Poor Robin's Dream," *The Bagford Ballads*, ed. J. B. Ebsworth, 2 (1878), 973. A note in the Arden edition of *Troilus and Cressida* compares this cut of Time with a bag with Time's wallet in Ulysses' speech.

25. "Roome for a Ballad, Or, a Ballad of Rome," *The Roxburghe Ballads*, ed. W. Chappell, *4* (1877), 100.

2. TIME, "THE NURSE AND BREEDER OF ALL GOOD"

1. *The Two Gentlemen of Verona*, III.1.243.

2. Van Veen, Horatian Emblems, pp. 89, 163, 169, 171.

3. R. Laurent–Vibert and M. Audin, *Les Marques de libraires et d'imprimeurs en France* (Paris, 1925), nos. 17–21, 40–42, 206, 207.

4. *The Mirrour of Majestie* (1612), no. 28.

5. Time and Abundance are the central figures in an Elizabethan petit–point panel. On one side there is a banquet; on the other, a group of well

to do people are playing at draughts. Near the banquet is a beggar. Reproduced in *The Connoisseur*, *99* (1937), op. p. 148, fig. 2.

6. "To Time," in *Two Bookes of Epigrammes and Epitaphs* (1639), sig. A3⁴. Time is called "Herald" because it is a function of the College of Heralds to decide on claims to the rank of gentleman.

7. Joseph Martyn, "To Time," in *New Epigrams and a Satyre* (1621), sig. A3ʳ.

8. Gilles Corrozet, *Hecatomgraphie. C'est a dire les descriptions de cent figures et histoires* (Paris, 1543), sig. Niiᵛ; Giulio Cesare Capaccio, *Delle Imprese* (Naples, 1592), Bk. I, fol. 4⁴.

9. Robert Farley, *Lychnocausia* (1638), sig. Iᵛ, no. 57.

10. Reproduced in F. H. Haberditzl, "Die Lehrer des Rubens," *Jahrbuch d. . . . Sammlung d. . . . Kaiserhaus*, *27* (1907), 228, pl. 53.

11. *Hamlet*, III.1.70. The line is generally taken to refer to the times in which Hamlet is living, but I am confident that the parallels show that Time is personified and that the "whips and Scorns" are those of the World of Time.

12. In *Dramatic Works*, *2*, 298 f. The play may be four years later in date. When Time leaves the stage Folly says "Farewell 1538." This is odd but explicable. It seems to identify the play with *Phaeton*, first recorded by Henslowe in 1598. That is, in Folly's eyes Time is an old man of sixty.

13. Barten Holyday, *Technogamia* (1618), II.1. Time is not one of the dramatis personae but a small figure. A stage direction reads that the character Historia wore "on her head a coronet, about the border whereon stood the nine Worthies, and on the top of two crosse arches arising from the circle of the coronet stood Time, an old man with a long beard, at his feet lay a sithe, holding in one hand a crowne, in the other a whip."

14. I have not seen *Temporis filia veritas. A mery devise called the Troublesome travell of Tyme* (1589), of which the unique copy is in the Cambridge University Library. See STC, 23875. On the title page of Richard Linche's *Fountaine of Ancient Fiction* (1599) and on both the title and last page of the same writer's *An Historicall Treatise of the Travels of Noah into Europe* (1601) occurs the astonishing statement that "Tempo è figliuola di verita." This can be nothing else than a pointless individual eccentricity. D. Franken, *L'OEuvre gravé des Van de Passe* (Amsterdam and Paris, 1881), nos. 1034–7.

15. F. Saxl, "Veritas Filia Temporis," in *Philosophy and History: Essays presented to Ernst Cassirer* (Oxford, 1936), pp. 197 f.; Donald Gordon, "Veritas Filia Temporis," *Journal of the Warburg Institute*, *3* (1939–40), pp. 228 f.; S. C. Chew, *The Virtues Reconciled* (Toronto, 1947), pp. 69 f.

16. Adrian Junius, *Emblemata* (Antwerp, 1565), p. 59, no. 53. Compare Geffrey Whitney's *A Choice of Emblemes, and other Devices, For the moste parte gathered out of sundrie writers, Englished and Moralized. And Divers Newly Devised . . . herein by the office of the eie and the eare, the minde maye reape dooble delighte* (Leyden, 1586), p. 4 where Time releases Truth from a dungeon in which she has been imprisoned by Envy, Strife, and Slander.

17. Reproduced in Edward Hodnett, *English Woodcuts, 1480–1535* (1935), fig. 232.

18. Thomas North, *The Morall Philosophie of Doni; drawne out of the auncient writers* (1570), ed. 1601, fol. 91ʳ. Cf. R. B. McKerrow, *Printers' and Publishers' Devices* (1913), no. 306. This arrangement is in a cut, occurring three times, in Francesco Doni, *Inferni* (Venice, 1553). The motto is "La Verita Figliuola e del gran Tempo."

19. Guillaume de la Perriere, *La Morosophie* (Lyons, 1553), sig. H4ᵛ, no. 48.

20. Jan David, *Veridicus Christianus*, pl. 43.

21. Truth with the "Verbum Dei" and a candle is the device of John Ros, Edinburgh printer. The motto is "Veritas vincet tandem." Time does not appear. See, e.g., title page reproduced in *Britwell Court Catalogue*, Dec. 16, 1919.

22. *Spiegel van den Ouden ende Nieuwen Tijt* (3rd ed. Dordrecht, 1635), Part III, p. 44. Truth, laurel wreathed, is heaving up a huge slab upon which is inscribed "Veritas." On the wall is a tablet with the inscription: "Hier Leyt Bargraven Vrovw Waerheyt." Following the engraving are two pages of proverbial lore and the dicta of classical authors about Truth.

23. John Nichols, *The progresses, and public processions of Queen Elizabeth. Among which are interspersed, other solemnities, public expenditures, and remarkable events during the reign of that illustrious princess, 1* (1788–1805), 35. Another account, ibid. *1*, 48, says that Time was represented by a child.

24. In *Dramatic Works*, 2, 191. The play dates from ca. 1594 and was clumsily revised ca. 1606–7.

25. In *Dramatic Works*, 8 vols. ed. A. H. Bullen, 7 (1885–86), 244 and 249.

26. John Tatham, in *Dramatic Works*, ed. J. Maidment and W. H. Logan (1879), pp. 293 f.

27. Reproduced in Chew, *The Virtues Reconciled*, pl. 9. This narrative has nothing save the title in common with Richard Brathwaite's collection of poems, *Times Curtaine Drawne, or the Anatomie of Vanitee* (1621). The dead king's hand rests upon a skull. The posture conforms to the fashion occasionally observed in family group portraits where those who have died are designated by a skull beside them or held in the hand. A curious example of this is an engraving by Willem Van de Passe which exists in two states. In the earlier James I, regnant, sits upon his throne. On his right stand Queen Anne and Prince Henry, each with a hand resting upon a skull. (This dates the print 1619, the year of Anne's death, or later.) Two royal children who died in infancy sit upon the steps of the throne, leaning against skulls. In the foreground stands Prince Charles. His hand is upon two books which lie on a table: "Biblia" and "Opera Regis." (He depends for guidance upon the Scriptures and his father's writings.) Opposite him are Frederick and Elizabeth of Bohemia and their seven children. In the second state King James' hand is upon a skull; Charles wears a crown and Queen Henrietta Maria stands by him. Frederick and Elizabeth now have three more children, and one of the original

children is provided with a skull. My guess is that this second state appeared shortly after King James' death, to meet an immediate demand. Otherwise the new king would surely have been shown upon his throne. Both states of the engraving are reproduced in G. S. Layard, *Catalogue Raisonné of Engraved British Portraits from Altered Plates* (1927), no. 63 and pl. 23.

28. *Tafereel van de Belacchende Werelt* (Amsterdam, 1635).

29. *La Morosophie* (1553), sig. B3ᵛ. The accompanying poem is a compliment to La Perriere by a friend who commends his glory in the past, present, and future. Time holds a palm branch and a laurel crown.

30. The three faces and the three animal heads are associated not only with Time but with Prudence, Good Counsel, Fortune, Apollo, Serapis, etc. See Erwin Panofsky and Fritz Saxl, "A Late-Antique Religious Symbol in Works by Holbein and Titian," *Burlington Magazine, 49* (1926), 177 f. and Panofsky, "Titian's Allegory of Prudence: A Postscript," *Meaning in the Visual Arts* (Garden City, New York, 1955), pp. 146 f. and accompanying pls.

31. *The Fountaine of Ancient Fiction* (1599), sig. Diiᵛ. This is a somewhat condensed translation of Vincenzo Cartari, *La Imagine degli Dei* (Venice, 1571, and later editions.)

32. *The Treasurie of Auncient and Moderne Times* (1613), p. 37.

33. *The Gentlemans Exercise* (ed. 1612), p. 105. Peacham cites the authority of Petrarch, quoting from the Trionfi.

34. Ibid., pp. 111–112.

35. Michael Drayton, *Tragicall Legend of Robert, Duke of Normandy* (1590), line 79, in *Works*, 5 vols., ed. John Hebel, *1* (Oxford, 1913–41), 256.

3. THE DIVISIONS OF TIME

1. *II Henry IV*, IV.1.70–72.

2. Francis Meres, *Palladis Tamia. Wits Treasury* (1598), fol. 154ʳ.

3. Roger Matthew, *The Flight of Time Discerned By the dim shadow of Jobs Diall* (1634), sig. B4ʳ. This is a sermon on Job 9:25.

4. The sun and moon, labeled "Dies" and "Nox," appear in the print of Time with a whip in G. A. Gilio's *Topica Poetica* (Venice, 1580) and in Francis Quarles, *Emblemes* (1635), Bk. III, no. 15, where Time is taking flight from the Soul. In Philip Galle's engraving of "The Triumph of Time" one of the horses drawing the wagon has on its collar the sun, on the other's is the moon.

5. *Tafereel.* The antithetical wings of Day and Night sometimes appear on the hourglass, as in the one held by Time in cuts in Thomas Peyton's poem of which an account is given in Chapter 1. This device occurs on seventeenth–century English memorial portraits and on tombstones as late as the eighteenth century. There is an hourglass with bird's and bat's wings in a painting by Frans Floris, reproduced in H. W. Janson, "The Putto with the Death's Head," *Art Bulletin, 19* (1937), fig. 29. In John Hall's *Emblems* (1658), Bk. II, no. 7, an hourglass with these wings rests

on a skull; and in the engraving ("Kitto" Bible, *24*, 4590) of the ruins wrought by Time which I have already described Death himself holds such a glass. Ripa directs that the Spring Equinox ("Equinottio della Primavera") shall be depicted with wings on his feet, one white, the other black—black for the departing winter, white for the blossoms of the spring. Two English poetasters, straining after novelties beyond the potentiality of their feeble fancies, attach these wings surprisingly to other personifications. Anthony Sherley in his poem "Of Feare," in *Witts New Dyall: or, a Schollers Prize* (1604), sig. H3ᵛ, tells us that

> Feare has two Winges, a Blacke one, and a White;
>   The White flyes high, and shuns Dishonour more
> Than death or greife; the Blacke wing hands down-right
>   And by base Cowardes are his Fethers wore.

Richard Niccols' epigram "In Amorem," in *The Furies with Vertues Encomium, or The Image of Honour* (1614), sig. B4ᵛ, describes, without mentioning any color, the two wings of Love. With one he flies from those who pursue him and with the other he pursues those who fly from him. In the entire range of Renaissance imagery I know no concepts more inept and unvisualizable than these; in fact, till airplanes flew with one wing shot off these images of Fear and Love were surely without a parallel!

6. *The Christmas Prince* (anonymous), ed. W. W. Greg and F. S. Boas, Malone Society (1922), p. 111.

7. In a Leipzig Almanac (1492), reproduced in Schramm, *Der Bilderschmuck der Frühdrucke*, *13*, no. 44, Saturnus, as Time, with a star on his forehead, looms behind the Signs of the Zodiac which he embraces with widespread arms.

8. *Cantos of Mutabilitie*, VII, 28–47. The commentators pass over an interesting detail in the description of the month of January (Aquarius). The pageant is of course moving and eleven of the Signs either ride or walk. But January stands in an "earthen pot" and there is no reference to his means of locomotion. September marches on foot, carrying "a paire of waights"; why could not January have walked, carrying some sort of wateringpot? Did Spenser's powerful visual imagination for once fail him? It may be further noted that from the "wide mouth" of the pot in which January stands "there flowed forth the Romane floud." The commentators have been puzzled by the epithet "Roman." Might not Spenser have heard or seen prints of the fountain in Rome on which there is a statue personifying the River Tiber?

9. For the entire series of Petrarchan Triumphs of which this Time is one, see Thomas Kerrick, *Catalogue of the Printes which have been engraved after Martin Heemskerck* (Cambridge, 1829), pp. 81 f. and the listing in F. W. H. Hollstein, *Dutch and Flemish Etchings, Engravings and Woodcuts, ca. 1450–1700, 8*, Amsterdam, 1953. For the latter reference I am indebted to Miss Janet S. Byrne of the Metropolitan Museum of Art.

10. John Nichols, *The progresses, processions, and magnificent festivities,*

of King James the First, his royal consort, family, and court . . . , 4 (1825), 624.

11. Van Veen, p. 207; crudely reproduced in Henry Green, *Shakespeare and the Emblem Writers* (1870), opposite p. 491.

12. *Metropolis Coronata*, in Nichols, *Progresses of James I*, 3, 114.

13. *Corona Minervae. Or a Masque Presented before Prince Charles His Highnesse, The Duke of York his Brother, and the Lady Mary his Sister, the 27th of February at the Colledge of the Museum Minervae.* This anonymous piece has been ascribed to Sir Francis Kynaston. The ascription is plausible, for Kynaston, a well to do and public spirited gentleman and member of Parliament, had recently founded the Museum Minervae, which seems to have been a sort of academy for young people. As a poet he is memorable rather for a few graceful lyrics than for his more pretentious work.

14. *The Springes Glorie. Vindicating Love by temperance against the tenent Sine Cerere et Baccho frigit Venus. Moralized in a Maske*, sig. F^r f.

15. Linche, *The Fountaine of Ancient Fiction*, sig. Dii^r.

4. TEMPUS–OCCASIO–FORTUNA

1. *Bussy d'Amboise*, II.2.115. In *Works*, ed. by M. Parrott, 1910.

2. To the four kings on the Wheel are attached the words so frequently found with Fortune's favorites and victims: "Regnabo," "Ego regno," "Regnavi," and "Perdidi regnum." At the top center are the first two lines of the liturgical hymn: "Rector, potens, verax Deus, / qui temperas rerum vices." This engraving, which dates from before 1454, is reproduced in *Revista de archivos*, *1* (1897), opposite 4.

3. See R. Campbell Dodgson, *Catalogue of Early German and Flemish Woodcuts in the British Museum*, *1* (1903), 341–2. Formerly attributed to Dürer this woodcut is now generally held to be by the Master of the Illustrations of Celtis, sometimes called "Dürer's Doppelganger." The fact that the bird at the top is crowned shows that this is a Wheel of Fortune, though turned by Lady Time; it is odd, however, that the birds mount on both sides of the Wheel and none is descending. The fox assisting Lady Time to turn the Wheel seems to relate the print to one of the romances of Renard. This problem does not concern us, but compare the conclusion of *Renard le Nouvel*, where Fortune stops her Wheel with Renard, crowned, seated forever at the top. Note that the noble eagle and falcon are at the bottom, the ignoble jay, magpie, and pheasant are ascending, and another magpie is king. To the personification of "Zeit" as female there are parallels in English literature. Henry Crosse wrote a discourse with the formidably long title: *Vertues Commonwealth: or the Highway to Honour. Wherein is discovered that although by the disguised craft of this age, vice and hypocrisie may be conceald: yet by Tyme (the triall of truth) it is most plainly revealed* (1603), R2^r f.: "There is nothing so precious as time, which being wilfully or willingly overslipt, it is impossible to be recalled, for that she is deaf and cannot heare . . . and the louder she is called, the faster she flyeth." John Carpenter's poem *Time Complaining, giveth a most*

godly admonition and very profitable instruction to England in this our dangerous Tyme (1588); and has on the title page a cut of Father Time, but it is "Lady Time" who calls upon England to repent. The poem is headed: "Tyme complaineth for that she is so vainely consumed of worldly men, as wearie of continuance." She implores England to be wise and "repent with ancient Ninevie," "Els Ladie Time yet will implore / That she might sleepe, and wake nomore." In the Epistle Dedicatory the poem is dated June 30, 1588, a month before the Battle of the Armada. That Time is feminine is implied in a poem "To Time" in Francis Davison's anthology, *Poetical Rhapsody* (1602), ed. H. E. Rollins, *1* (Cambridge, Mass., 1931–32), 195: "Eternal Time, that wasteth without waste . . . / Thy wombe that doth all breed, is Tombe to all." Cf. "The never barren, ever breeding womb of Time," Samuel Speed, "Time's Travel," *Prison ∙ Pietie: or Meditations Divine and Moral* (1677), p. 160. David Person, in *Varieties: or, A Surveigh of Rare and Excellent Matters, necessary and delectable for all sorts of persons* (1635), Bk. I, pp. 28 f., says that Time is "the endest daughter of Nature."

4. In *Pleasures Vision: with Deserts Complaint, and a Short Dialogue of a Womans Properties, betweene an Old Man and a Young* (1619), sigs. C6ʳ and ᵛ.

5. In *Essayes . . . Newly corrected* (ed. 1632), Essay 24, sig. K4ᵛ.

6. Achille Bocchi, *Symbolicarum Quaestionium . . . Liber Quinque* (Bonn, 1555), no. 79.

7. *Le Livre de Fortune* (1883), no. 17. Cousin's drawings, made in 1568, were first published from the originals in the Bibliothèque de l'Institute by Ludovic Lalanne (1883). The title of the originals reads in part: *Liber Fortunae centum emblemata et symbola centum.* The 100 figures of Fortune alternate with 100 scroll–like frames, each with a device at the top and the center blank, probably for the insertion of a family coat of arms or a personal *impresa*.

8. *Lust's Dominion*, I.2, in Hazlitt's Dodsley, *14*, 104.

9. *Bussy d'Amboise*, I.1.134–5.

10. See G. Van Havre, *Marques typographiques des imprimeurs et libraires Anversois, 2* (Antwerp, 1883), 201.

11. Samuel Gardnier [sic], *Doomes–Day Booke: or An Alarum for Atheists, A Watchword for Worldlings, A Caveat for Christians* (1606), p. 6: "The verie nicke and exegent of time"; p. 36: "The nicke and exegent of the direfull day of doome."

12. Thus, Giles Corrozet, *Hecatomgraphie* (1540), ed. 1543, no. 84, fols. Miiᵛ–Miiiʳ, shows Occasion standing in a boat, but in the stern sits Penitence lamenting for lost Opportunity; and J. J. Boissard, *Emblemata* (1584), no. 34, shows an armed man seizing Occasion by the forelock; behind her is Repentence, an old woman with a scourge.

13. *May–Day*, III.3.118.

14. *Othello*, III.1.52. Shakespeare has Occasion in mind in passages where he does not use the name: "Let's take the instant by the forward top" (*All's Well that Ends Well*, V.3.39); "Take the present time [that is, the

immediate opportunity] by the top" (*Much Ado About Nothing*, I.2.15);
"Time and the Hour runs through the roughest day" (*Macbeth*, I.3.147).
In this last passage the distinction is clear cut between Time in general and
the Hour which is the opportune moment.

15. Because she may provide opportunity for wrongdoing Occasion is
sometimes conceived as a malign being. Spenser's Occasion (*The Faerie
Queene*, IV, 2, 4 f.) is a "wicked hag" in "filthy disarray" whose hoary
locks grow "all afore." This concept differs in several respects from the
"orthodox" abstraction; highly individualized, she is, as the commentators
note, Occasion in a particular aspect: Occasion for Wrath. Shakespeare's
Lucrece (881 f.) describes the "secret cell" of Opportunity within which
"sits Sin, to seize the souls that wander by him." When, however, in *King
John* (IV.2.125 f.) the King pleads with "dreadful Occasion" to "with-
hold [her] speed" the epithet does not imply malignancy.

16. *Friar Bacon and Friar Bungay*, IV.1.

17. William Terilo, *A Piece of Friar Bacons Brazen–Heads Prophecie*
(1604), sig. A2ʳ.

18. *Occasio Arrepta, Neglecta. Huius Commoda: Illius Incommoda.*
The Shakespearean analogues are discussed by Green, *Shakespeare*, p. 265.
See also Rudolf Wittkower, "Chance, Time and Virtue," *Journal of the
Warburg Institute*, *1* (1937–38), 318.

5. THE PACE AND CYCLES OF TIME

1. *As You Like It*, III.2.322–351.

2. John Tomkis, *Albumazar* (1615), II.51, in Hazlitt's Dodsley, *2*, 346.

3. In Massinger's *The Great Duke of Florence*, I.1.244, a lover says
to his lady that they will "imp feathers to the broken wings of Time."
Massinger uses the same metaphor from falconry in *The Roman Actor*,
V.2.22, and in *The Renegade*, V.8.7–8.

4. [Wye Saltonstall]. *A Description of Time: Applied to this present
Time. With Times merry Orders to be observed* (1638), sig. A3ʳ f. Time
declares that he is ashamed of the sights he sees, such sights as "make his
old gray Fore–lock stand on end." Following this poem comes "Times
Orders," a rather lively and interesting satire in prose on the abuses to be
observed in London: drinking, beggars, the filth of the streets, and so forth.

5. In a Brussels tapestry, 1684, from a design by David Teniers III,
reproduced in Heinrich Göbel, *Tapestries of the Lowlands* (1924), no.
185.

6. Cousin, *Le Livre de Fortune*, no. 69.

7. Thomas Combe, *The Theatre of Fine Devices* (1614), no. 68.

8. Otho Van Veen, *Amorum Emblemata* (1608), p. 237.

9. *The Mysteries of Nature and Art* (1634), 2nd. ed., 1635, p. 46.
With Bate's clepsydra contrast one designed by Holbein which depended not
upon rising but upon falling water, the hours being marked on an upright
tablet down which an arrow moves as the water runs out. This design is
reproduced in *Burlington Magazine*, *58* (1931), 227.

10. Theodore de Bry, *Emblemata Nobilitatis et vulgo scitu singularis historiis symbola adscripta* (Frankfort–a–M., 1593), unnumbered pl., p. 88.

11. *The Fountaine of Ancient Fiction.*

12. See Howard R. Patch, *The Goddess Fortuna in Medieval Literature* (Cambridge, Mass., 1927), pp. 170–171.

13. Reproduced in Panofsky, *Studies in Iconology*, fig. 68.

14. Quoted by Thomas Wright and J. O. Halliwell, *Reliquae Antiquae*, 2 (1845), 315, from two fifteenth–century manuscripts.

15. *The Arte of English Poesie* (1589), ed. G. D. Willcock and Alice Walker (1936), p. 208 and p. 332, note.

16. "Dulce bellum inexpertis," stanza 9, in *The Poesies* (1575) in *Works*, ed. J. W. Cunliffe, *1* (1907), 42.

17. Thomas Lodge, *A Fig for Momus* (1595), Satire V, 21–24.

18. *The School of Shakespeare*, ed. Richard Simpson, *2* (New York, 1878); Tudor Facsimile Texts, ed. J. S. Farmer (1912). Marston worked over a lost, anonymous play of earlier date.

19. *Le Livre de Fortune*, no. 119. Reproduced in Chew, *The Virtues Reconciled*, fig. 17. Cousin may have taken this subject from a poem by Clément Marot. This poem is given in English translation in *The School of Shakespeare*, ed. Simpson, *2*, 87–88, in the course of comment on *Histriomastix*.

20. In the Folger Shakespeare Library there is an unpublished manuscript commonplace–book (ca. 1608), the work, as seems likely, of a certain Thomas Trevelyon.

21. *The Solace for the Souldier and Saylour* (1592), sig. B3ᵛ.

22. *Emblemes*, Bk. I, no. 45.

23. Daniel Price, *Prince Henry His Second Anniversary* (1614), p. 19: "Time is fixed on a wheele, that incessantly whirleth, and draweth with it us, and all our actions."

24. In *Works*, ed. A. H. Bullen, *1* (1888), 361 f.

25. The title page was recalled to general notice when Sir Charles Sherington reproduced it in *Man on his Nature* (1941), facing p. 54.

26. In *Emblêmes des differens Etats de la Vie* (ca. 1630), p. 94.

27. *Essays*, no. 58: "Of Vicissitude of Things."

28 For Time in the sense of Occasion, the opportune moment, see further the following chapter, and for Time and Death, Chapter ·8. Four pleasant trivialities may be noted here. Nicholas Breton has a poem entitled "A pretty toye written upon Tyme," in *A Flourish upon Fancie* (1577), sig. Liiiᵛ f. "Tyme is set out with head all balde, save one odde lock before." If you hold him fast he will do you good service. If you let him stand idle he will do knavish work. His scythe cuts down all things save Virtue. I, says the poet, saw him standing idle this morning, and put pen and paper in his hand, and made him write these verses. Michael Drayton, "Idea" (1619), Sonnet 17, in *Works*, ed. Hebel, *2*, 319, pays tribute to his lady's looks. There Time may see, as in a mirror, his own youth: "the World's Beautie in his Infancie"; and passing on Time is to tell to Posterity "that thou once hast seene, / In perfect humane shape, all heav'nly Blisse." Another lover's compliment is a quite pretty piece in William Habington's

Castara (1634), p. 14, called "Time to the moments, on sight of Castara." Time bids the moments stay and wonder. Nature waited till he was weakened by age before fashioning Castara. Were he younger he would throw away his scythe, break his hourglass, and body himself in clay in order to love her. Since that cannot be, his revenge is that Castara "shall like me grow old." In the same author's drama *The Queen of Arragon* (1640), I.1 (in Hazlitt's Dodsley, *13*, 329–330), there is an even more extravagant notion. A lover tells his lady that when that "old bald man, call'd Time" begins to steal away the lady's beauty Fate will have a care to "stop the motion of envious Time." The lady comments sensibly: "Fate hath more serious business." Despite its title John Hanson's *Time is a Turne–Coate* (1604) contains nothing to our purpose. It is not an allegory but an account of Queen Elizabeth's death and the accession of James I. The general theme is "Post tristia, laeta."

Chapter 3. The World of Fortune

1. WHO IS FORTUNE?

1. On the classical origins of the cult and its medieval developments see Howard R. Patch, *The Goddess Fortuna in Medieval Literature* (1927). Consult also Professor Patch's subsidiary studies listed in his bibliography. Fortune's Wheel and Death a variant shows a King is at the top of the wheel; a poor man essays to climb; at its base is a shrouded corpse. In the background a man, praying, is threatened by Death. Job stands beside the wheel holding a scroll: "For now I shall sleep in the dust." *Hours of King Henry VII of England*, French MS 15th cen., Morgan 815.

2. *Inferno*, VII, 67–96.

3. "Fortune," ll. 65–70.

4. Raimond Van Marle, *Iconographie de l'art profane*, *2* (The Hague, 1932), 199, fig. 225.

5. Van Havre, *Marques typographiques*, pp. 25–26.

6. Jacobus Bornitius, *Emblematum Ethico—Politicorum Sylloge posterior* (Heidelberg, 1664), Second Series, no. 5. The wheel with no figure of Fortune but broken by a hand from heaven is an emblem of Patience in Georgette de Montenay, *Emblemes, ou Devises Christiennes* (Lyons, 1571), no. 31.

7. This design appears in the German translation (Augsberg, 1532) of Petrarch's *De Remediis Utriusque Fortunae* and was used again in several mid–sixteenth–century German books. Reproduced in Arthur Burkhard, *Hans Burgkmair* (Berlin, 1932), pl. 56, in Van Marle, *2*, 199, fig. 224, and elsewhere.

8. *The Gentlemans Exercise* (ed. 1612), p. 117. For the familiar symbol of the golden chain Peacham refers to the *Iliad*, Bk. VIII, and to Plato. The flaxen robe is explained, with a reference to Valeriano, on the ground that "Flax was the hieroglyphick of Fate among the Ægyptians."

9. How this denial of the actuality of such a being developed gradually

into the Elizabethan concept of tragedy is demonstrated in Willard Farnham, *The Medieval Heritage of Elizabethan Tragedy* (1936).

10. *The Pastime of Pleasure*, ll. 3207 f.

11. *The Golden Booke of the Leaden Goddes. Wherein is described the vayne imaginations of Heathen Pagans, and counterfaict Christians* (1577), fol. 28ᵛ (misnumbered). With Bateman's third Fortune, Death, compare Cousin's "Ultima Fortuna," in *Le Livre de Fortune*, no. 199, where Death grasps the rim of Fortune's wheel and stops it. John Lydgate, *A Thoroughfare of Woe*, ll. 130 f., in *Minor Poems*, 2 (1911), 822 f., says that Death "casteth down princes from Fortune's wheel."

12. "Pyndara's Answer," in *English Poets*, ed., Alexander Chalmers, 2 (ed. 1810), 594.

13. *The Complaint of Elstred* (1593); in *Works*, ed. Sir E. Gosse, 2 (Hunterian Club, 1883), second pagination, 74–75.

14. Richard Niccols, *The Furies, with Vertues Encomium* (1614), sig. D2ʳ.

15. Richard Linche (from Cartari), *The Fountaine of Ancient Fiction* (1599), sig. Ziiᵛ f. In *The Treasurie of Auncient and Moderne Times* (1613), the Jaggard–Milles translated compilation from Pedro Mexia and other continental sources, there is a long discussion of Fortune, Bk. VII, chap. 12, pp. 655–658. Some philosophers, it is remarked, hold that Fortune is "the mirror and instrument of the Divine providence; as if God should stand in need of some other to performe his workes for him"; but the counsel is given to good Christians to forsake their bad custom of making complaint on Fortune. In this discussion will be found, with ample citations from ancient authorities, comments upon Fortune bearded ("Fortuna Virilis"), blind, without feet, with the horn of abundance, with the wheel, standing upon a ball, guiding a ship, made of glass, and so forth. Fortune is likened to a comedy in which the actors often change their parts and to a theater in which the best persons often get the worst seats.

16. *A Learned Summary Upon the famous Poeme of William of Saluste Lord of Bartas Wherein are discovered all the excellent secretes in Metaphysicall, Physicall, Morall, and Historicall Knowledge . . . Translated out of French by T.L.D.M.P.* (1621), p. 307. I do not know the French original and have not identified the translator.

17. "Of Fortune and Fame," in *Tottel's Miscellany*, ed. H. E. Rollins, 2 (Cambridge, Mass., 1928–29), 129, no. 176.

18. Joseph Rutter, *The Shepherd's Holiday*, I.i, in Hazlitt's Dodsley, *12*, 367.

2. THE WHEEL OF FORTUNE

1. *Henry V*, III.6.2640. Note how swift is the shift in this short passage from visual to verbal imagery; the painter of the first sentence becomes a poet in the second.

2. Reproduced in Tancred Borenius and E. W. Tristram, *English Medieval Painting* (Florence and Paris, 1927), pls. 38 and 39 (detail), and in Frank Kendon, *Mural Painting in English Churches during the Middle*

Ages (1923), pl. 15 (in color). The discovery of the Rochester Fortune was announced in *Gentleman's Magazine*, New Series, *14* (1840), 137–8. It is strange that Halliwell–Phillipps, in a note on Fluellen's speech, reproduces a Fortune said to be in Rochester Cathedral that is quite different from that described in my text and reproduced by the authorities cited above. Fortune stands on her wheel which floats upright on water. Towards it walks a tonsured cleric. Opposite another cleric has fallen backward into the water and is sinking. Were there at one time two Fortunes in Rochester Cathedral?

3. *Norfolk Archaeology*, *1* (1847), 133 f.; *Victoria County History*, *Norfolk*, *2* (1901–06), 536–7.

4. See below, p. 336, note 2. *Victoria County History*, *Buckingham*, *4* (1905–27), 214, mentions two St. Catherine's wheels in Padbury Church, Buckinghamshire but does not record a wheel of Fortune.

5. La Perriere, *La Morosophie*, no. 91.

6. Linche, *Fountaine*, sig. Aaiv^r f.

7. On the medieval association of Fortune with the moon see Patch, *The Goddess Fortuna*, p. 51, note 6, where abundant references are given, and for the "formula of four," ibid., pp. 164–6. For examples see Chaucer's translation of the *Romaunt*, 1.5331 and Lydgate's *Reson and Sensuallyte*, 1.48.

8. *Julius Caesar*, IV.2.218.

9. In two letters Albrecht Dürer tells of a great whale which has been washed ashore "mit einer grossen Fortuna und Sturmwind." See K. Lange and F. Fuhse, *Dürer's Schriftlicher Nachlass* (Halle, 1893), p. 144. A footnote, with a reference to Schmeller's *Bayrisches Worterbuch*, p. 762, defines "Fortuna" as "Flut," that is, high tide. Professor Panofsky kindly called my attention to these passages in Dürer's letters.

10. In *The Philosophers Satyrs* (1616), Satire 7, "Of the Moon," p. 73.

11. *Emblemes*, Bk. III, no. 40.

12. *Minerva Britanna*, no. 147. Here Inconstancy has one foot on a crab, which, as Peacham explains, is "so doubtfull in his waies." The crab is from Ripa.

13. On the title page by Hans Weiditz of the German Petrarch, *Von der Artzney bayder Glück* (Augsburg, 1532), four wind–heads blow upon the riders. A copy of this very rare book is in the Pierpont Morgan Library. Wind–heads blow on the wheel in a cut in the German version by Hieronymo Ziegler of Boccaccio's *De Casibus* (Augsburg, 1545); reproduced in Weiss and Company's *Catalogus Librorum Rarorum*, Part V (Munich, 1929), no. 57.

14. Alexander Barclay, *A Treatyse intitulyd the Myrrour of good manners* (ca. 1520), sig. C3^v.

15. *The Duchess of Malfi*, III.5.112–113.

16. *The Conspiracy of Byron*, III.3.24–30.

17. *Minerva Britanna*, no. 76. For another wheel without the figure of Fortune see Julius Wilhelm Zinkgref, *Emblematum Ethico–Politicorum Centuria* (Heidelberg, 1616), no. 94, where the motto is "Rien n'est Constant."

18. Jacob de Zetter, *Philosophia Practica* (Frankfort, 1644), no page ref.

19. A. M. Hind, *Nielli, Chiefly Italian of the Fifteenth Century . . . in the British Museum* (1936), no. 284.

20. Martin le Franc, *Estrif de Fortune et de Virtue*, Bibliothèque Royale de Belgique, MS 9510. Reproduced in Paul Durrieu, *La Miniature flamande* (Brussels, 1921), pl. 35. In other manuscripts of the *Estrif* one notes interesting variations: in one the wheel has both the "Regno" formula and the kings; in another a Pope, a King, and a Cardinal sit at the top of the wheel, Fortune stands on six prostrate victims, but no client is either going up or coming down; in the third the wheel is turned not by Fortune herself but by an attendant. See further Alphonse Bayot, *Martin Le Franc L'Estrif de Fortune et de Vertu* (Brussels, 1928), on the Brussels MS where the Fortune is reproduced in full color. For variants in other MSS of the *Estrif* see Bayot, pls. 4, 8, 10, 12, 15–18.

21. *Hans Beer–Pot His Invisible Comedy of See Me and See Me Not. Acted in the Low Countries by an honest Company of Health Drinkers* (1618), sig. B3ᵛ.

22. *Early English Classical Tragedies*, ed. J. W. Cunliffe (Oxford, 1912), p. 139.

23. *Philotemus: The Warre betwixt Nature and Fortune* (1583), sig. Aiiʳ. A character in this euphuistic romance says: "I can sitt the whole day long, and make me spoorte at the spyte of the dizarde muffled Godesse, to see what game shee makes at the grefe of her subjects, this day lyfting them up to her loftiest throne, and tomorrowe throwing them downe to her lowest footestoole, chopping and chaunging from right hande to lefte, giving him a fanne that bore a Scepter before, and laying a yocke on his neck that had a diademe on his head."

24. *Liberality and Prodigality*, I.6, in Hazlitt's Dodsley, *8*, 341. The date of this piece is uncertain; the original version may belong to the fifteen–sixties, but whether genuinely archaic or archaistic, it was certainly refurbished after the appearance of *Tamburlaine* (1587).

25. *Love and Fortune*, end of Act IV, in Hazlitt's Dodsley, *6*, 227.

26. There is some confusion here, for the trades of the four men who enter first do not correspond to the trades indicated in a subsequent speech by Fortune. But this is of little consequence, for all that matters is that these are humble men raised to exalted station.

27. *The Christmas Prince*, ed. W. W. Greg and F. S. Boas, Malone Society (1922). This general title was given by an editor in the early nineteenth century who first published, from the manuscript at Oxford, the account of these festivities.

28. Reproduced in D'Essling and Müntz, *Petrarque*, p. 87.

29. *Poetical Rhapsody* (1602), ed. Rollins, *1* (1931), 243.

30. Reproduced in Bayot, pl. 13.

31. See Patch, *The Goddess Fortuna*, pp. 167–8.

32. *Lust's Dominion*, I.4, in Hazlitt's Dodsley, *12*, 110.

33. *Poems* (Edinburgh, 1616), sonnet beginning "Let Fortune triumph now."

34. *Emblemes*, Bk. I, no. 6.

35. James Day, "On Contempt of the World," in *A New Spring of Divine Poetrie* (1637), p. 42.

36. Henry Delaune, **PATRIKON DERON**, *or a Legacy to his Sons, Being a Miscellany of Precepts* (2nd ed., 1657), p. 66.

37. Arthur Newman, *Pleasures Vision: with Deserts Complaint, and a Short Dialogue of Womans Properties, betweene an old Man and a Young* (1619), sig. B3ᵛ.

38. Reprinted in *Works*, Spenser Society, First collection, 1870.

39. *A Plea for Prerogative*, p. 2.

3. MONSTROUS AND MANY–HANDED FORTUNE AND ALEXANDER, A FAMOUS VICTIM

1. *Les Cas des nobles hommes et femmes infortunes* (Paris, Nicholas Couteau, 1538), fol. cxxiii.

2. *The Fall of Princes*, ed. Henry Bergen, EETS, *6*, 1–77.

3. British Museum, MS Royal 14.E, fol. 271; reproduced in Durrieu, *La Miniature flamande*.

4. Geneva, Bibliothèque de l'Université, MS français, 190, tôme 2, fol. 30ᵛ. So far as I am aware this has not been reproduced. I owe my knowledge of it to a description by Professor Millard Meiss transmitted to me by Professor Panofsky with an accompanying sketch. The illuminators did not always follow the accounts of Fortune's many–handedness. See, e.g., a reproduction in Sir E. Maunde Thompson, "The Rothschild manuscript in the British Museum of 'Les Cas des Malheureux Nobles Hommes et Femmes,'" *Burlington Magazine*, 7 (1905), pl. II b. In a manuscript of St. Augustine in the British Museum Fortune has only two hands and points with an admonitory finger; reproduced in Le Comte de Laborde, *Les Manuscrits à peinture de la Cité de Dieu*, *3* (Paris, 1909), pl. 59. In the Rothschild manuscript, it may be remarked, Fortune does not stand by her wheel or carry it; it is embroidered on her headdress.

5. See Henri Michel, *L'Imprimeur Colard Mansion et le boccace de la Bibliothèque d'Amiens* (Paris, 1925), i.e. the copy of the edition of 1476 now at Amiens. The book is probably the earliest to be illustrated with copperplates. The engraver has not been identified; he may have been Colard Mansion himself.

6. Reproduced in Van Marle, *Iconographie*, *2*, 201, fig. 228.

7. *The Fall of Princes* (Tottel, 1554), sig. Cciiʳ.

8. A. H. Gilbert in *MLN*, *52* (1937), 190 f. See Vincenzo Cartari, *Le Imagine degli Dei degli Antichi* (ed. Venice, 1571), p. 482, where Fortune's entire arms have wings attached. Professor Gilbert refers to the French translation of Cartari (Lyons, 1581), p. 557.

9. Stephen Hawes, *The Example of Vertu*, III, 10. A woodcut illustrating this scene is in Wynkyn de Worde's edition, *Here foloweth a compendyous story and it is called the exemple of vertu in the whiche ye shall fynde many goodly storys and naturall dysputacyons* . . . (1530), sig. Aiiᵛ. It

appears also in Thomas Berthelet's edition of Lydgate's *The Temple of Glasse* (n.d.).

10. In Jean de Courcy, *Cronique dite La Bouquechardiere* (mid fifteenth century); reproduced in Jacques Meurgey, *Les Principaux Manuscrits à peinture du Musée Condé à Chantilly* (Paris, 1930), pl. 68. In other manuscripts of this Chronicle there is the same scene (Morgan Library, MSS 214 and 224). Here the monarch is not labeled but is certainly Alexander.

11. This miniature, which is (or was) in Berlin has been cut from a lost manuscript of *The City of God;* reproduced in Laborde, *Les Manuscrits, 3,* pl. 30.

12. *Workes* (1557), in preliminary leaves with no signature. On "The Book of Fortune" and the game played with it see A. W. Reed in the Introduction to More's *Works, 1* (1931), 17. R. W. Chambers, *Thomas More* (1935), p. 92, says that these "metres" were "intended to add literary dignity to a parlour game."

13. In *The Rare Triumphs of Love and Fortune,* Act I; in Hazlitt's Dodsley, *6, 156,* there is a "show of Alexander" as an example of those slain by Fortune. His ghost is silent, but Mercury says that he "curseth fell Fortune, that did him delude."

4. THE TWO SIDES OF FORTUNE AND THE TREE, LADDER, AND HILL OF FORTUNE

1. James I, *The Kingis Quair,* ed. W. W. Skeat, STS (1884), stanzas 158–172.

2. "Devyse of a desguysing," ll. 682 f., in *Minor Poems,* EETS, Vol. 2.

3. *The Assembly of Gods,* ll. 316 f.

4. XVI, 10. The traditional attacks on Fortune are imitated in John Higgins' *The First parte of the Mirrour for Magistrates* (1574), but very frigidly and without novelty. Similarly, in William Wyrley's poem imitative of the *Mirrour* entitled "Lord Chandos," included in *The True Use of Armorie* (1592), Fortune is assailed as a "false turncoate," now smiling and now frowning with her "glosing face!"

5. *Reson and Sensuallyte,* ll. 50 f. See also Lydgate, *Troy–Book,* II, 10E, ivB. I resist the temptation to penetrate more deeply into Professor Patch's territory by discussing such concepts as those in the *Roman de la Rose,* ll. 7079 f., and John Gower, in the *Confessio Amantis,* ed. Reinhold Pauli, *3* (1857), 12.

6. *Hecatomgraphie* (Paris, 1543), sig. Ciii^v. Compare Cousin, *Le Livre de Fortune,* no. 125.

7. *An Humourous Day's Mirth,* Scene 15, ll. 182 f. At a "Lottery" held in 1602 as an entertainment for Queen Elizabeth the guests drew lots; most of these had to do with Fortune. See the text in Davison's *Poetical Rhapsody,* ed. Rollins, *1,* 242 f. and Rollins' notes, *2,* 202 f. Actually the goblet which Fortune sometimes holds, as in Dürer's engraving, is not to draw "posies" or lots from. It contains a stimulating drink for those who need and deserve it and contrasts with the bridle with which she checks the

over–zealous. Professor Panofsky informs me that Dürer's source is a Latin poem by Politian.

8. *Tragicall Legend of Robert, Duke of Normandy*, ll. 64 f.; in *Works*, ed. Hebel, *1*, 255 f. Note also Fortune's speech and Fame's reply, ll. 129 f.

9. For examples see Laborde, *Les Manuscrits*, *3*, pls. 54, 59, 64.

10. See Durrieu, *La Miniature flamande*, pl. 59.

11. *Of the newe landes and of the people founde by the messengers of the Kynge of Portyngale named Emanuel* (no place or date but probably Antwerp, ca. 1522). See Henry Harrisse, *Bibliotheca Americana Vetustissima* (New York, 1866), no. 116, where, however, the figure of Fortune is misnamed Justice. The same cut appears above the colophon of *A lyttell story that was of a trweth done in the lande of Gelders of a mayde that was named Mary of Memegen that was the divels paramoure by the space of vii. yere long* (John Duisbrowghe, Antwerp, n.d., early sixteenth century). The only known copy of this book is in the Huntington Library. It has been reproduced in facsimile with an introduction by H. M. Ayres and A. J. Barnouw (1932). These scholars offer no comment upon the figure of Fortune or upon the mysterious and unintelligible word in Greek letters below the figure. As the story of Mary of Mimmegen is possibly connected with the Faust legend and involves demonology, the Greek letters may be mere hocus pocus. The cut is reproduced in the *Britwell Court Sale Catalogue*, June 14, 1920, lot 207.

12. Engraving by one of the Van de Passe family in *Hortus Voluptatum* (Amsterdam, 1599) which I know from the reproduction in Franken, *L'OEuvre gravé des Van de Passe*, no. 1337.

13. Reproduced in D'Essling and Müntz, *Petrarque*, p. 93, where the Fortune is misnamed Reason.

14. Four wind–heads buffet four figures on the wheel in Hans Weiditz's title page of Petrarch's *Von der Artzney bayder Glück*, Augsburg, 1532.

15. Reproduced in *Verse*, *1* (1938), no. 2, p. 9.

16. Sig. Bvi^v. This copy is in the Print Room of the Metropolitan Museum of Art.

17. *Les Remèdes de l'une at l'autre fortune*, manuscript in Vienna, reproduced in Laborde, *Les Manuscrits*, pls. 54 and 55.

18. Giulio Cesare Capaccio, "Amico dell' una e dell' altra Fortuna," *Delle Imprese* (Naples, 1592), Bk. III, fol. 19^r.

19. Daniel Cramer, *Emblêmes des differens Etats de la Vie* (1630), no. 25. The motto is: "Sors potis est subito mutare in vincula coronam." The emblem is related to the famous tale of the man who buried his treasure, the second man who, having intended to hang himself, found the treasure, absconded with it, and left the rope behind, and the first man who, returning, found the treasure gone and hanged himself. Variants of the design appear elsewhere, notably in Peacham, *Minerva Britanna*, no. 153 with a poem telling the tale. See also "Sorte" in Ripa, *Iconologia*, and "Fortuna fatalis" in Cousin, *Le Livre de Fortune*, no. 162.

20. *Much Ado about Nothing*, II.3.64–67. But to the instability of the seas there is one exception: The Caspian neither ebbs nor flows and is

therefore emblematic of Constancy which is above the sway of Fortune. This is used by various emblematists, e.g. Peacham, *Minerva Britanna*, no. 27.

21. Robert White, *Masque of Cupid's Banishment*, in Nichols, *Progresses of James I*, *3*, 289.

22. *Arbasto, The Anatomy of Fortune* (1584); in *Prose Works*, 15 vols., ed. Alexander Grosart, *3* (1881–86), 171 f.

23. *Perymedes the Black Smith* (1588), ed. J. P. Collier (1870), p. 17.

24. *Rosalynde* (1590), ed. W. W. Greg (1907), p. 57. The passage is as follows: "Fortune . . . Thou standest upon a globe, and thy wings are plumed with Time's feathers, that thou mayest ever be restless: Thou art double–faced like Janus, carrying frowns in the one to threaten, and smiles in the other to betray: Thou profferest an eel, and performest a scorpion."

25. Simion [or Simon] Grahame, *The Anatomy of Humors* (Edinburgh, 1609), pp. 67–69. The assignment of Time's attribute to Fortune is interesting. The description is not illustrated. In André Frideric and Jacques de Zettre *Emblemes Nouveaux, esquels le Cours de ce monde est depeint et representé* (Frankfort, 1617), no. 62 (misnumbered 42), Occasion stands with one foot on an hourglass.

26. *A Fig for Fortune* (1596), p. 58.

27. *Delectable demaundes and Pleasant Questions, with their several Answers, in matters of Love: Natural Causes, with morall and politicke devises* (1566), ed. 1596, p. 133. This is an anonymous translation from the French. There seems to be some confusion here with the forelock of Occasion.

28. Pp. 42 f. The poem has been attributed to Samuel Rowlands or Nicholas Breton; I believe it is not by either.

29. *Emblemata Nobilitatis et vulgo scitu singularis historiis symbola adscripta* (Frankfort-a–M., 1593), no. 1. I know this very rare book only in the facsimile, ed. Friederick Warnecke, Berlin, 1895.

30. *Gilbert of the Haye's Prose Manuscript* (1456), ed. J. H. Stevenson, STS, *1* (1901), *The Buke of the Law of Armys or Buke of Bataillis*.

31. So in British Museum MS, Royal C viii. This design is reproduced full scale but without colors in Stevenson's edition of Gilbert of the Haye. This reproduction is labeled "Haye's Manuscript" but it is from the original French *Arbre*.

32. As in a manuscript of the *Arbre* reproduced in Meurgey, *Les Principaux manuscrits*, pl. 74.

33. *La Vere e Nove Imagini degli Dei*, ed. Lorenzo Pignoria (1615), p. 571.

34. *Fortunes Tennis–ball: . . . or, A Proviso for all those that are elevated to take heed of falling, for Fortune spights more the mightie then the poore* (1640), sig. Ci^v.

35. *Wits Theater of the little World* (1599), fol. 219^v–220^r. Allott, mentioning Timotheus, also notes that in antiquity Fortune was painted "holding in her hands a spreading net, where with–all shee caught Citties and Regions." Compare Guillaume Gueroult, *Le Premier Livre des Em-*

blemes (Lyons, 1550), no. 16, where Fortune catches the sleeping Timotheus in her net.

36. IV.4, in Hazlitt's Dodsley, *8*, 366. It is evident, since Fortune climbs to her "bower" and Prodigality uses a ladder to mount thereto, that a practicable scaffolding was erected for the performance before the Queen, equivalent to the upper stage of the public theaters.

37. Antonio Phileremo Fregoso, *Dialogo de Fortuna* (Venice, 1521); reproduced in Prince D'Essling, *Les Livres à figures venetiens*, *5* (Paris and Florence, 1907–14), 406.

38. *Ariosto's Satyres, in Seven Famous Discourses* (1608), Third Satire, p. 42.

39. "La vertue soutient las vertueux que la Fortune les abandonnent." In this design the ostentatious rich man and virtuous poor man are two contrasted individuals, not the same person in good and evil fortune.

5. FORTUNE ASSOCIATED WITH THE FATES, NEMESIS, JUSTICE, AND OPPORTUNITY

1. The cut is in *Das Narrenschiff* (Reutlingen, 1494); reproduced in Schramm, *Der Bilderschmuck der Frühdrucke*, *9*, nos. 524 and 543. See also the Basle edition (1495), fol. 43^v. There is a good copy among the woodcuts in Alexander Barclay, *The Ship of Fools* (Pynson, 1509); reproduced in the J. Pierpont Morgan *Catalogue of Manuscripts and Early Printed Books*, *3* (New York, 1907), 231. See also the edition of Barclay, *1* (Edinburgh, 1874), 186. The cut is also in the prose version, *The shyppe of fooles* (Wynkyn de Worde, 1509), fols. 56^v and 79^{vr}.

2. Reproduced in S. A. Strong, *Critical Studies* (ed. 1912), op. p. 90, and in outline in Salomon Reinach, *Répertoire de peintures*, *4* (Paris, 1905–23), 626.

3. Reproduced in Pauli, *Beham*, no. 143, and Van Marle, *Iconographie*, *2*, 200, fig. 226.

4. Reproduced in Bernard Berenson, *The Drawings of the Florentine Painters*, *3* (Chicago, 1938), no. 180, fig. 933. Here the mounting figure has a bird on his back, flapping its wings, that is, aspiring. The man prostrate on the ground holds a mirror. Is this the mirror of his fallen pride? Or has he learned prudence through misfortune? Or is this a "Mirror for Magistrates"?

5. *The Roaring Girl*, I.1.197–198.

6. 1.402; ed. J. A. Adams, Folger Shakespeare Library Publications no. 2 (Washington, D.C., 1937). The poem is a sort of sequel to Shakespeare's *Rape of Lucrece*. See further on Middleton's authorship a letter by Dr. James G. McManaway in *TLS*, April 16, 1938. Dr. Adams and Dr. McManaway thought there was confusion in Middleton's mind between the wheels of Fortune and the Fates.

7. "Time Goes by Turne," in *Saint Paters Complaynt* (1595), p. 39; *Recusant Poets*, ed. L. I. Guiney (1939), p. 294.

8. *The Gorgeous Gallery of Gallant Inventions* (1578), ed. H. E. Rollins (1926), p. 46.

9. Shackerley Marmion, *The Antiquary*, V.1, in Hazlitt's Dodsley, *13*, 514.

10. *As You Like It*, I.2.34–35.

11. *Anthony and Cleopatra*, IV.15.43–45.

12. *Henry V*, V.1.85–87.

13. Robert Recorde, *The Castle of Knowledge* (1556), pp. 113–114. Veronese's Fortune in the Doges' Palace has dice as an attribute. Other examples could be given.

14. For example, in the French Alciati, *Livret des Emblemes* (Paris, 1536), sig. Cii^v.

15. *The Tempest*, I.1.31–37.

16. *Franc. Baconi De Verulamio Historia Regni Henrici Septimi Angliae Regis Opus vere Politicum* (Leyden, 1642). The engraver of the title page is Cornelis van Dalen.

17. *The Third Part of the Countess of Pembroke's Ivy-Church* (1592), fol. 54^v.

18. Ed. L. A. Magnus, EETS, *1*. 1794.

19. *Emblemes* (Lyons, 1558 and 1566) and in other editions.

20. *Recueil d'Emblemes Divers* (Paris, 1638; not 1636 which is the date on the engraved title page), Bk. I, p. 324. Baudoin takes this emblem, he says, from Bacon. In his preface he makes a general acknowledgment to Bacon, who inspired in him the desire to write on emblems.

21. *Discours ou Traicté des Devises* (Paris, 1620), p. 122. This treatise, which contains no illustrations, was put together from the notebooks of François d'Amboise by his son Adrian. The snake does not seem to be a specially appropriate emblem for slowness unless with thought of its sluggishness in cold weather.

22. *Hecatomgraphie* (Paris, 1543), sigs. Fiiii^v–Fv^r.

23. R. B. McKerrow, *Printers' and Publishers' Devices*, no. 167.

24. Thomas Carew, *Coelum Britanicum* (1634), sig. D2^v. See also Nichols, *Progresses of James I*, *3*, 289. The stage direction with which Carew introduces Fortune is as follows: "Tiche enters, her head bald behind, and one great locke before, wings at her shoulders, and in her hand a wheele, her upper parts naked, and the skirt of her garment wrought all over with Crownes, Scepters, Bookes, and such things as expresse both her greatest and smallest gifts."

25. *The Fountaine of Ancient Fiction*, sig. Aaiv^v f.

26. Ibid., sig. Cci^v. Cf. the cut in Cartari, *Imagine* (Venice, 1571), p. 482.

27. Claude Paradin, *Devises heroiques* (Lyons, 1557), p. 161. Fortune is equated with Fate when she has as attributes a hammer and nails. In one emblem she drives a nail into the rim of her wheel, thus keeping it from rolling; see Sebastian de Covarubbias, *Emblemas Morales* (Madrid, 1610), First Century, no. 65. Ripa's Necessity holds a hammer and nails. The emblem of a prostrate man being pressed to death is labeled "Inevitabile Fatum" but here Fortune herself does not appear; see Gregory Kleppis, *Emblemata Varia* (1624), no. 42.

28. For example, Alciati, *Emblemata* (Lyons, 1554), p. 18, and Whitney,

Choice of Emblems, ed. Henry Green (Holbein Society, 1870), p. 181. Whitney's explanation that the razor informs men that Occasio "cuts on every side" is not lucid and seems to miss the point.

29. In Theodore Galle's engraving of "The Triumph of Patience," reproduced in Van Marle, *Iconographie,* 2, 149, fig. 172, the dejected and captive Fortune who follows the chariot of Patience holds a razor.

30. Laurence Haechtanus, *Mikrokosmos* (Antwerp, 1592). I have not seen this book and know the design only from Green, *Shakespeare and the Emblem Writers,* p. 263.

31. *Emblemes and Epigrams* (1600), EETS (1876), p. 10.

32. In *La Mascherata della Genealogia degli Dei;* reproduced in Allardyce Nicoll, *Stuart Masques and the Renaissance Stage* (New York, 1938), p. 187.

33. For example, in the German version of Sallustius' *Chronica* (Strassberg, 1534), reproduced in Weiss and Co's *Catalogus Librorum Rarorum,* 6 (Munich, 1930), no. 227. See Linche, *Fountaine,* sig. Bbiv^r. Martin Meyer, *Homo Microcosmos* (Frankfort, 1670) has an emblem, no. 21, labeled "Fortunae Natura," in which a footless Fortune has one ankle supporting her on a sphere, her other leg is in the air. Adrian Junius, *Emblemata* (1565) and other emblematists show footless Fortune. On "Fortuna sine pedibus" see further A. H. Gilbert in *MLN,* 52 (1937), 190 f.

34. Reproduced in Van Marle, *Iconographie,* 2, 190, fig. 215.

35. Cartari, *Imagini degli Dei* (ed. 1615), p. 433.

36. Nichols, *Progresses of James I,* 3, 285.

37. Peacham's Repentence, in *Minerva Britanna,* no. 46, holds a birch and a fish, to chastise herself and to fast.

38. For example, in a cut in Hawes, *The Example of Vertu* (1530), sig. Aii^r.

39. In a sixteenth–century Florentine drawing, reproduced in Van Marle, *Iconographie,* 2, 201, fig. 228.

40. So in Linche, *The Fountaine of Ancient Fiction,* sig. Ziii^r, and in one of Ripa's concepts of Fortune.

41. For example, Worldliness so appears as one of the enemies of the soul in Van Veen's *Amoris Divini Emblemata* (ed. 1660), p. 83; and the De Bry engraving in John Theodore and John Israel de Bry, *Emblemata Saecularia, Mira et Jucunda Varietate Saeculi huius Mores ita Exprimentia* (Frankfort, 1596), no. 2, reproduced in S. C. Chew, *Spenser's Pageant of the Seven Deadly Sins* (Princeton University Press, 1954), fig. 5.

42. Thomas Bastard, "In Fortunum [sic]," *Chrestolaros* (1598), Ipigram ii, 35.

43. Linche, *Fountaine,* sig. Bbiv^r and ^{v}.

44. *The Rare Triumphs of Love and Fortune,* in Hazlitt's Dodsley, 6, 152.

45. *Perymedes the Black Smith* (1588), ed. J. P. Collier, p. 18.

46. *Wittes Pilgrimage* (1605), sig. T3^v. Davies notes that the aphorism comes from "Publi," that is, the *Sententiae* of Publilius Syrus. See Wilhelm Meyer's edition of that work (Leipzig, 1880), p. 31. Davies' prolix poem has no personification of Fortune.

47. *Essayes . . . Newly corrected* (1632), no. 36, sig. T3ᵛ.

48. Jean Puget de la Serre, *The Mirrour which Flatters Not* (1639), p. 7. This translation from the French is by Thomas Cary.

49. Peter Flettner, "Dass Wankelhafte Glück" (ca. 1540).

50. "The gerful lady with her whel / That blynd is and seth nevr a del," Lydgate, *Reson and Sensuallyte*, 11.1358–9.

51. Pierre Michault's *La Danse aux Aveugles* was written about 1460. It is an allegory in prose and verse. Entendement guides the Author successively to three parks or enclosures where are the three blindfold divinities who preside over human destiny: Love, Fortune, and Death. Love is attended by Venus, Fol Appetit, and Oyeuse; Fortune by Heur and Malheur; Death by Age, Accident, and Sickness. Before them different classes of humanity dance. Fortune's face is one half fair the other black. Manuscripts of the *Danse* generally illustrate these scenes. See Laborde, *La Mort chevauchant un Boeuf* (Paris, 1923), pls. 9, 10, and 11. The allegory concludes with a colloquy between Entendement and the Author the upshot of which is: you may escape Love by retirement and serious occupation, and Fortune by despising grandeur and riches, but no one can escape Death.

52. For example, in an engraving by a member of the Sadeler family Error, blindfold and fallen from the sphere of Vainglory, lies on the ground below Wisdom. Reproduced in Chew, *The Virtues Reconciled*, pl. 12.

53. *The Bankette of Sapience* (1534), ed. 1542, sig. Diiiiᵛ.

54. Thomas Combe, *The Theatre of Fine Devices* (1614), no. 20, from La Perriere.

55. Patrick Hannay, *Songs and Sonnets* (1622), sonnet 16; in *Poetical Works*, Hunterian Club (1875), p. 250.

6. WHOM DOES FORTUNE FAVOR? WITH WHOM DOES SHE COLLABORATE? WHO TRIUMPH OVER HER?

1. *The First Parte, of The Eyghth liberall Science: Entituled, Ars adulandi, The Arte of Flatterie, with the confutation thereof . . . Newly corrected and augmented* (1579), especially sigs. Bᵛ f. and Biiᵛ. I have not seen the original edition of 1576. No second part seems to have been published.

2. Similarly, among the evils of the time lamented by John Lane in *Tom Tel–Troths Message, and his Pens Complaint. A worke not unpleasant to read nor unprofitable to be followed. Written by Io. La. Gent.* (1600), pp. 15 f., is the forlorn state of the Seven Liberal Sciences which even at Oxford and Cambridge "are now like Almesfolkes beggerly maintained." Lane devotes a stanza to the sad, neglected condition of each. After his complaint for the Arts comes a disappointingly unspecific lament for the decay of Poetry.

3. Humphrey King, *An Halfe–penny–worth of Wit, in a Penny–worth of Paper* (1613), pp. 28–29. This is "the third impression"; STC does not record copies of the first and second.

4. *In Praise of Folly*, translated by H. H. Hudson (Princeton, 1941), p. 103.

5. Sig. S2ᵛ. The original is still at Basle. I have used the facsimile edition, Basle, 1931.

6. *As You Like It*, II.7.19.

7. Ed. J. Sharman (1874), p. 131.

8. *Pierce Penilesse*, in *Works*, ed. R. B. McKerrow, *1* (1910), 158.

9. For example, the anonymous *Soliman and Persida*, II, in Hazlitt's Dodsley, *5*, 309; Ben Jonson, *Every Man Out of His Humour*, I.1.178, and elsewhere in Jonson; *Jack Drum's Entertainment*, I.258, in *The School of Shakespeare*, ed. Simpson, *2*, 144; Thomas Dekker and John Ford, *The Witch of Edmonton*, I.1.

10. *Times Curtaine Drawne, or the Anatomie of Vanitee* (1621), sig. N2ᵛ.

11. *Taylor's Motto* (1621), sig. Bᵛ.

12. This is in *Das Narrenschiff* (Reutlingen, 1494), reproduced in Schramm, *Der Bilderschmuck*, *9*, nos. 524 and 543; in ibid. (Basle, 1495), fol. 43ᵛ. There is a good copy in Barclay's *The Ship of Fools* (Pynson, 1509), reproduced in the J. Pierpont Morgan *Catalogue of Manuscripts and Early Printed Books 3*, 231. It is also in the prose *Shyppe of fooles* (Wynkyn de Worde, 1509), fols. 56ᵛ and 79ᵛ. Compare the wheel in the *Grand Nef des Fous* (Lyons, 1497), reproduced in A. Claudin, *Histoire de l'imprimerie en France*, *4* (Paris, 1910–1914), 298.

13. Reproduced in Schramm, *12*, no. 261, and *20*, no. 169. Compare ibid. *20*, no. 430, from a Horace *Opera* (Strassburg, 1498), and *18*, nos. 452 and 471, from *Das Narrenschiff* (Nurnberg, 1494) where the design is in reverse and reduced in size.

14. *1* (Augsburg, 1494), fol. CVᵛ; reproduced in Georg Hirth, *Kulturgeschichtliches Bilderbuch*, *1*, no. 356. The design is by Hans Weiditz.

15. Reproduced in Bayot, *Martin Le Franc*, pl. 21.

16. Catherine P. Hargrave, *A History of Playing Cards* (Boston, 1930), p. 33, no. 10.

17. Ibid., p. 228, no. 8 (misnumbered).

18. *Ariosto's Satyres, in Seven Famous Discourses* (1608), p. 98.

19. André Frideric and Jacques de Zettre, *Emblemes Nouveaux, esquels le Cours de ce monde est depeint et representé* (Frankfort–a–M., 1617), no. 43.

20. See Count Emiliano di Parravicino, "Three Packs of Italian Tarocco Cards," *Burlington Magazine*, *3* (1903), 237–243.

21. *Memoirs of Colonel Hutchinson* (ed. 1906), p. 298. The late Professor Godfrey Davies called my attention to this.

22. Horatian Emblems (Antwerp, 1607), p. 155. In the English version of Van Veen (1721), p. 100, the design is interpreted thus: "Fortune cannot give desert. . . . 'Tis not in her Power to disguise the Monkey she has crown'd so well." Van Veen's ape reappears, but without the accompanying figure of Fortune, copied precisely in Julius Wilhelm Zinkgref, *Emblematum Ethico–Politicorum Centuria* (Heidelberg, 1616), no. 47. The motto is: "Le singe ensceptré ne change de nature."

23. Cats, *Spiegel van den Ouden* (3rd ed. Dordrecht, 1635), Part III, p. 5. The first edition appeared in 1627.

24. These satires are included in Brathwaite's *The Honest Ghost or a voyce from the Vault* (1658) which contains nothing else to our purpose.

25. *The Fall of Princes*, ed. Bergen, *3*, 204–707.

26. *Le Livre de la Ruyne des nobles hommes et femmes* (Bruges, 1476), fol. 74; reproduced in Henri Michel, *L'Imprimeur Colard Mansion* (Paris, 1925), pl. 4.

27. Reproduced, ibid., p. 41, and in A. Claudin, *Histoire de l'imprimerie*, *1*, 223. Claudin misinterprets the illustration.

28. In some of the manuscripts of Laurent the fable is illustrated more simply than in the engravings and woodcuts. Thus, in the Rothschild MS we have not three episodes but only one: Fortune is supine and Glad Poverty kneels upon her; there is no violence, all is quite seemly not to say prim. See Sir E. Maunde Thompson, "The Rothschild Manuscript in the British Museum of 'Les Cas des Malheureux Nobles Hommes et Femmes,'" *Burlington Magazine*, 7 (1905), pl. 1, b. But there is violence in the scene of combat in a Huntington Library *Fall of Princes* (HM. 268) where Poverty is vigorously beating a prone Fortune. In a fifteenth–century French manuscript of the original *De Casibus* (Pierpont Morgan MS 342) there are two episodes: Fortune meets ragged Poverty, and Poverty bestrides Fortune, beating her.

29. *Visiones Rerum* (1623), Third Vision.

30. Maurice Scève, *Parvus Mundus*, No. 22, and Martin Meyer, *Homo Microcosmos*, p. 44, no. 22.

31. See various plates in Bayot's monograph on the Brussels MS. of the *Estrif*. Bayot reproduces scenes from various other MSS. of the *Estrif*. See especially pl. 19, where the castle behind Virtue and the ruins behind Fortune appear.

32. *Liberality and Prodigality*, in Hazlitt's Dodsley, *8*, 337.

33. Combe, *The Theatre of Fine Devices*, no. 28, from La Perriere.

34. For example, La Perriere, *La Morosophie*, no. 79. Here Fortune stands by the house built on the sand.

35. "Of the unconstant stay of Fortune's gifts," in *The Paradise of Daintie Devises* (1576), ed. H. E. Rollins (1927), p. 16.

36. See Rudolf Wittkower, "Chances, Time and Virtue," *Journal of the Warburg Institute*, *1* (1937–8), 318. See also Van Marle, *Iconographie*, *2*, 186, fig. 211.

37. D'Essling and Müntz, *Petrarque*, p. 94.

38. For example, Alciati, *Emblemata*, ed. 1551, p. 255, and ed. 1591, where Mercury is quadrifrons; Capaccio, *Delle Imprese* (1592), Bk. III, 58^v, where the design is labeled "Stabilta della Virtù"; Jean Baudoin, *Recueil d'Emblemes Divers* (Paris, 1638), Bk. II, no. 16.

39. *Emblems and Epigrames*, ed. F. J. Furnival, EETS, p. 8.

40. *The Widow's Tears*, V.3.45–6; *Chabot*, II.3.112 and III.1.191; *Caesar and Pompey*, III.1.26.

41. Laurent–Vibert and Audin, *Les Marques de libraires*, no. 61.

42. Wither, *Emblemes*, Bk. I, no. 6, Bk. II, nos. 19 and 47. In another emblem (Bk. II, no. 29) Wither does not set in opposition but combines the altar stone and the winged ball, thus suggesting that the solidity of true religion is the best foundation for life but that earthly fortune is not to be despised. The happy state is that in which great virtues are joined to great wealth, "God helpe us, then, poore soules, who scarce have either!" Wither ejaculates. In yet another emblem (Bk. IV, no. 31) he combines altar stone and winged ball with a spade in token that labor is needed for both virtue and prosperity.

43. *Le Livre de Fortune*, nos. 83, 85, 89, and 93.

44. *Hecatomgraphie*, sig. Mvii^v–Mviii.

45. Ibid., sigs. Gviii^v–H and Fviii^v–G.

46. Jean Jacob Boissard, *Emblematum Liber* (Frankfort-a-M., 1593), no. 51, p. 103. The engraving is by Theodore de Bry.

47. Florentius Schoonhovius, *Emblemata partim moralia, partim etiam Civilia* (Ghent, 1618), no. 2.

48. *La Morosophie*, no. 78.

49. Ibid., no. 68.

50. *General and Rare Memorials pertaining to the Perfect Art of Navigation*. This is the first part of an intended four volume work of which the rest was never published. This part is chiefly concerned with the establishment of a royal navy, with the encouragement and regulation of fisheries, and with visions of empire. The title page illustrates Dee's vision of the future allegorically. On the shore a skull and an inverted ear of wheat indicate famine overseas, but from "the Castle of Safety" Lady Opportunity (Occasion rather than Fortune in a more general sense) beckons to the Queen. The ship is labeled "Europe." An angel with the shield of St. George and a flaming sword hovers in the sky. The title page is reproduced in Charlotte Fell–Smith, *John Dee* (1909), facing p. 39, and is described in detail in J. Ames, *Typographical Antiquities*, ed. William Herbert, *1* (1785–90), 660–662. See also R. B. McKerrow and F. S. Ferguson, *Title-page Borders* (1932), no. 157.

51. *Magnificent Entertainment*, in *Dramatic Works*, *1*, 317–318.

52. *The Tragedy of Caesar and Pompey*, II.4.129–142.

53. Reproduced in Paul Kristeller, *Florentinische Zierstücke in Kupperstich aus dem XV. Jahrhundert* (Berlin, 1909), no. 29.

54. *Delectable demaundes* (1596), p. 216.

55. Laurent–Vibert and Audin, *Les Marques de libraires*, nos. 17–21, 40–42, 206, 207.

56. Achille Bocchi, *Symbolicarum Quaestionum . . . Libri Quinque* (1574), Bk. II, no. 51. In the Albertina in Vienna is a drawing by Heemskerck of Fortune attended by Diligence who is spinning, Parsimony who goes barefoot with her shoes hanging to her girdle to save shoe leather, and Labor who holds a "Feuerstein" in his hand. Reproduced in *Beschreibender Katalog der Handzeichnungen in der graphischen Sammlung Albertina*, *2*, no. 101.

57. *Le Imprese Illustri*, fol. 258^v.

58. Daniel Meisner, *Sciographia Cosmica* (Nuremberg, 1637), pl. D–3.

59. Van Havre, *Marques typographiques*, pp. 25–26. There are several versions of this.

60. *Le Imagine*, p. 479. Here Occasio is a masculine figure.

Chapter 4. The Spiritual Foes of Man

1. THE INFERNAL TRINITY

1. Morton W. Bloomfield, *The Seven Deadly Sins. An Introduction to a Religious Concept, with Special Reference to Medieval English Literature* (Michigan State College Press, 1952), p. 243. This is an admirable monograph on the origins and medieval development of the theme, but the Renaissance, except for a brief discussion of Spenser, is beyond his temporal limits. What follows in this chapter, and something of what has gone before, is a revised and greatly expanded form of my article, "Spenser's Pageant of the Seven Deadly Sins" in *Studies in Art and Literature for Belle da Costa Greene* (Princeton, 1954), pp. 37–54.

2. Chaucer, *The Tale of Melibeus*, § 39. These enemies enter the Heart through the "windows" of the Body. Skeat compares *Sawles Warde*, in Old English Homiles, ed. Rev. Dr. R. Morris, EETS First Series *29* (1867), p. 245, and *The Ayenbite of Inwyt*, ed. Rev. Dr. R. Morris, EETS, First Series *23* (1867), p. 263. Long afterwards, in Father David's *Veridicus Christianus* (Antwerp, 1601), pl. 66, a very surrealistic design has a man's head shaped like a house. The mouth is a door, the nostrils a gabled window, and the eyes and ears are windows. Death is climbing into the house. The Sense of Touch is not symbolized.

3. Passus XVI; cf. Passus VIII, 38 f.

4. 11.305 f., in *Digby Plays*, ed. F. J. Furnivall, EETS, 1896. When Christ pardons Mary Magdalene a stage direction (line 691) reads: "With this word vij dyllys xall de–woyde from the woman, and the bad angyll enter into hell with thondyr."

5. Ed. F. J. Furnivall and A. W. Pollard, EETS, 1904.

6. J. L. Lowes, "Spenser and the Mirour de l'Omme," *PMLA*, *29* (1914), 270–87; condensed in *The Works of Edmund Spenser, New Variorum Edition*, *1*, 411–13.

7. If, following some moralists, we assign Envy to Mundus instead of to Diabolus, the shift does not affect Spenser's pattern.

8. 11.878 f. The text is in *Specimens of the Pre–Shakespearean Drama*, ed. J. M. Manly, *2*, 1897. For the Sins in miracle plays and other moralities see W. R. Mackenzie, *The English Moralities from the Point of View of Allegory*, 1914.

9. Stephen Hawes, *The Example of Vertu* (Wynkyn de Worde, 1530), chaps. 10 and 11. The woodcut is opposite sig. f^r. The poem was written much earlier, probably 1594.

10. 1592, sig. B4^r. To the relative obscurity of a note may be consigned a reference to Stephen Bateman's grossly repulsive picture showing a pope issuing from the fundament of a seven–headed devil. See *The New Arival*

of the three Gracis into Anglia. Lamenting the abuses of this present Age (n.d., ca. 1573), sig. Eiii^v.

11. 1596; reprinted in Publications of the Spenser Society, *35*, 1883. See pp. 73 and 79 of the reprint.

12. Pl. 26. With the Seven Kings compare William Tyndall's translation (1533) of Erasmus' *Enchiridion*, sig. Bii.

13. Thomas Combe, *The Theater of Fine Devices* (1614), Emblem 99.

14. Design by Battista Pittoni in Lodovico Dolce, *Imprese di Diversi Prencipi* (Venice, 1562), no. 34. The Hydra might be introduced into political struggles. Leonard Gaultier's engraved portrait of Henri IV shows him with the Hydra at his feet; he has lopped off all its seven heads. See Eugène Bouvy, *La Gravure de portraits et d'allegories* (Paris, 1929), pl. 61.

15. Discussed and reproduced in Evelyn Underhill, "The Fountain of Life: an Iconographical Study," *Burlington Magazine*, *17* (1910), 99–109.

16. See J. D. Passavant, *Le Peintre–Graveur* (Leipzig, 1862), III.380.30, where this print is attributed to Holbein.

17. (1) *Cantica, Certen of the Songes of H. N. . . . Translated out of the Basealmayne* (no date, 1575?). The cut is at the end. (2) *Terra Pacis: A true Testification of the Spirituall Lande of Peace . . .* (no date). The cut is on the verso of the title page. (3) *The Prophetie of the Spirit of Love* (1574). The cut is on the verso of the title page; it varies from the other two, being heart shaped while the others are rectangular.

18. *Veridicus Christianus*, pls. 38 and 39. See also pl. 43 and p. 140.

19. In *Dat Narren Schyp* (Lubeck, 1497) the Devil is shown inciting with his bellows; reproduced in A. Schramm, *Der Bilderschmuck der Frühdrucke*, *12*, 246. In *Das Neue Narrenschiff* (Strassburg, 1497) a miser, dressed as a fool, contemplates his bags of money while the Devil blows his bellows at him; reproduced ibid., *20*, 188. In Dürer's famous engraving called "The Monk's Dream" or "The Doctor's Dream" the Devil is fanning the fires of lust with the same instrument. In John Day's *Peregrinatio Scholastica* (see Chapter 7 below) Luxuria is a fire kept blazing with the Devil's three pairs of bellows: wanton discourse, lascivious dalliance, and gawdy attire. The bellows of Lechery is commonplace. Elsewhere we find it with Discord. Daniel Cramer's fine "Discordia" holds a flaming brazier in one hand and bellows in the other. See *Emblêmes des differens Etats de la Vie* (1630), no. 42. Adrian Junius' Lis (Strife) holds a torch and stands on a bellows. See *Emblemata* (Antwerp, 1565), nos. 53 and 54. See also A. F. Doni, *Trattati Diversi* (Vinegia, 1557), p. 82. Professor J. L. Lievsay has informed me of a similar design by Giuseppe Porta in the Library of the University of Washington. This I have not seen. The first plate in Johannes Saubertius, *Emblematum Sacrorum Erster Theill* (Nuremberg, n.d., early seventeenth century) shows the Devil blowing his bellows against a Christian who grasps a spear let down to him from the hand of God. Unique, so far as I know, but probably taken from some source, is a design in the Trevelyon commonplace book, Folger Library, fol. 206^r, which despite its amateurishness is impressive. The Devil is applying a bellows to a man's ear; an arrow issues from the man's mouth. Inscriptions read: by the Devil, "I am the father of all lyes. / and and [sic] help all them that tales

dev[i]es"; and by the man: "Even as the devill gives it me. / So I the same committe to thee." This picture is labeled "Make Tale," that is malignant gossip, slander. Extra–illustrated copy of Alban Butler, *Lives of the Fathers, Martyrs and other principal Saints* (1779). There is a Devil with bellows, but a novel use. Copperplate of Saint Genevieve (S. Genovefa) who holds a candle which a serpent–tailed devil is trying to blow out with a bellows while an angel is lighting it again. Designed by Anthon. Caron. Engraved by G.E.?

20. *Les Emblemes d'Amour Divin et Humain Ensemble. Expliquez par des vers francais. Par un Pere Capucin* (Paris, 1631), no. 54.

21. *Amoris Divini, Emblemata* (ed. Antwerp, 1660), p. 83.

22. P. 28. The play on words is an allusion to the story, popular in Christendom, of Sultan Mahomet II and the Greek slave Irene or "Hiren." "As they are now called" is probably a reference to a passage in Thomas Middleton's play, *The Old Law*. See S. C. Chew, *The Crescent and the Rose* (New York, Oxford University Press, 1937), p. 483.

23. John Taylor the Water–Poet was inspired by *Wither's Motto* to write *Taylor's Motto. Et habeo, Et Careo, et Curo* (1621). A laboriously conceived and not very well executed engraved title page by Thomas Cockson is interpreted in "The Embleme Explained." A man (Taylor himself) stands upon a rock (Hope) in a sea of temptations. A crown marked "I.R." (Jacobus Rex) means "I have a master." Taylor holds an oar, to indicate his means of livelihood as a Thames water–man. In the other hand he holds an empty purse upside down. Between his legs a book rests upon a globe, because his satiric verse makes the world his hobby horse. He gazes upward at the Sun of Righteousness.

24. Joseph Fletcher, *The History of the Perfect–Cursed–Blessed Man: setting forth Man's Excellency, Misery, Felicity by his Generation, Degeneration, Regeneration* (1628); reprinted in Fletcher's *Poems*, ed. A. B. Grosart (1869), pp. 23–119. For an account of the poem see Chew, *The Virtues Reconciled*, pp. 55–58.

25. Daniel Sudermann, *Funfzig Schonen . . . Figuren* (1628), no. 35.

26. John Downame, *The Christian Warfare Against the Devil, World and Flesh. Wherein is described their nature, the maner of their fight and meanes to obtaine victorye* (1634). Reproduced as the frontispiece to William Haller's *The Rise of Puritanism* (1938).

27. John Vicars, *The last Trumpet: or, A Six–Fold Christian Dialogue . . . Translated from the elegant Latine Prose of Richard Brathwait Esquire into English Verse* (1635).

28. E. B., *A Description of an Annuall World, or, Briefe Meditations upon all the Holy–daies of the Yeere* (1641). The author draws analogies between the circle of the heavens and the cycle of the Christian year. Quite beautifully Saturn is associated with Good Friday, the Sun with Christmas Day, the fixed stars with All Saints' Day. Other parallels are drawn from the rainbow, a flower, a tree, and so forth. Many of the ideas are taken from *A Learned Summary Upon the Famous Poeme of William of Saluste, Lord of Bartas* (1621).

29. When Jenner's book was reissued in 1658 the sheets were trimmed,

the format was smaller, and consequently the plates had to be folded. The plates are "paged in," that is, included in the pagination by stamping the signature upon each impression. The design of "Francie" is at sig. D4^r. The work is a curious prose paraphrase of Sir John Davies' *Nosce Teipsum*.

30. *XL Emblemata miscella nova* (Zurich, 1622), no. 19.

2. THE DEADLY SINS AND THE PAGEANT IN *The Faerie Queene*

1. The mystic, esoteric, and recondite connotations of the number seven are well known to every inquirer into mythology, legend, folklore, religious thought, and other fields of the human imagination and fancy. To list here a considerable number of these associations will be found not without value. The Trinity and the four points of the compass (symbolizing the material cosmos) make up the number seven. Sir Thomas Browne has a discussion of the Ages which touches on speculations, theories, and beliefs regarding the numbers seven and nine. He notes the Psalmist's "three score and ten" (ten multiplied by seven), Christ's counsel of forgiveness till "seventy times seven," the seven stars in Ursa Major, in Ursa Minor, and in the Pleiades, the seven planets, the seven wonders of the world, the seven cities that claimed to be the birthplace of Homer, the seven wise men of Greece, and Virgil's phrase "O terque quarterque beati!" Sir Thomas Browne, *Pseudodoxia Epidemica* (1646), Bk. IV, chap. 12; in *Works*, ed. Geoffrey Keynes, *3* (1928), 52-72. Browne's catalogue is by no means exhaustive. There are the Seven Last Words from the Cross, the Seven Joys and Seven Sorrows of the Blessed Virgin Mary, the Seven Works of Mercy (both Corporal and Spiritual), the Seven Hills of Rome, the Seven Labors of Hercules, the Seven Sages of Rome, the Seven Gifts of the Holy Ghost, the Seven Virtues (the Three Christian Virtues and the Four Stoic Virtues), the Seven Deadly Sins (who may be the seven devils cast out of Mary Magdalene), the Seven Liberal Arts (or Sciences), the Seven Sleepers, the Seven against Thebes, the Seven Nations driven from Canaan by the Israelites, the Seven Champions of Christendom, and (more rarely) the Seven Blasphemies and the Seven Stupendous Signs. These last two are met with so infrequently that the plates illustrating them in Father Jan David's *Paradisus Sponsi et Sponsae* (Plantin, Antwerp, 1607), may be described. No. 40 shows the Seven Blasphemies. From the mouths of six men and a devil come arrows, along the shaft of each of which is a text (e.g. "He saved others," etc., "Thou that destroyest the temple," etc.). The arrows are aimed at seven tondi in which are scenes representing Christ's Humanity, Divinity, Power, Lineage, Majesty, Piety, and Mediatorship. No. 43 shows the Seven Stupendous Signs at the moment of Christ's death: the rocks split, the veil of the temple rent, the outcry at the moment of death (a swan), the sun obscured, the blood and water (flowing from a lamb), the earthquake, and the graves opened. Father David interprets the Seven Last Words also (no. 41), employing analogues from the Old Testament (e.g. "Father, into Thy hands I commend my spirit" is illustrated by Noah's Ark). Erasmus likens the Seven Deadly Sins ("captains of the hole hoost of vices") to the Seven Nations inhabiting Canaan. See

Tyndall's version of the *Enchiridion* (1533), sig. Bii^r. In Alain Chartier's *Delectable demaundes, and Pleasant Questions* (1596), Bk. II, there is a "pleasant question": "Why cannot the childe borne in the eigth moneth live, and the childe of the seventh moneth customably doth live?" Answer: "Because the number of seven is a perfect number."

2. Reproduced in Frederick Rogers, *The Seven Deadly Sins* (1907).

3. "Kitto" Bible, *36*, no. 6742.

4. *The Mirrour of Mutabilitie, or Principall part of the Mirrour for Magistrates. Describing the fall of divers famous Princes, and other memorable Personages. Selected out of the sacred Scriptures.*

5. The reader may like to be reminded that it was from a painting of this sort in Genoa that Flaubert derived the first suggestion for his *Tentation de Saint Antoine*. The Seven Deadly Sins appear in the first version of that masterpiece; Flaubert discarded them in the second and third (final) versions.

6. *Amoris Divini Emblemata* (1660), p. 83.

7. Hereafter referred to as Bavarian woodcut. Reproduced in P. A. Lemoisne, *Les Xylographies du XIVe et du XVe siècle au Cabinet des Estampes de la Bibliotheque Nationale*, 2 (Paris, 1930), pl. 102.

8. *A Monomachie of Motives in the Mind of Man: Or a Battell betweene Vertues and Vices of contrarie qualitie* . . .

9. Hind, *Early Italian Engraving*, E.III.4. See ibid., E.III.5, for a companion print of the Virtues.

10. The STC identifies "T.A." as Thomas Acheley. The poem is lively, interesting, and ingenious and deserves to be recalled to notice. According to the dedication "this youngling Poesie" is "the first fruites" of a young man's labors. It has the inexpertness but also the liveliness of youth. It begins with the theme of the Four Ages of the World. In the Golden Age life was idyllic and ideal; the description of it is what today we would call "Soft Primitivism." In the Silver Age agricultural labor and commerce on the seas commence. In the Brazen Age ignorance and warfare begin to afflict mankind. So far there are no personifications. But in the Iron Age Virtue is banished and Error, Envy, and Treason hold sway. As men begin to dig in the earth's "entralls" to them appears a woman who has escaped from the "blacke house of Styx." She is clothed in silver and is Pecunia. Avarus, gloating upon her beauty, bids her assume her place as mistress of the empire of the world. Prodigus then woos Pecunia, promising that with him she shall travel, ransom captives, replenish exhausted countries or, if she so desires, bribe judges and breed dissentions. Liberalis now takes his part in the debate. He is the mean between Avarus and Prodigus: "Ill ere goes double championed against good," he says. If Pecunia will live with him in his cottage, he promises to win countless friends, help the tenant at rent day, give abundant alms, support in court the just claims of the poor against their oppressors, pay physicians' fees, and do other charitable offices. Avarus denounces Liberalis: an encourager of idleness, a "feeder of riot," helping the base to encroach upon the privileged, and housing runagates. Having attacked Prodigus in like unmeasured terms, he urges Pecunia to reject them both and take shelter, hidden from the world, with him. In a long

speech Liberalis, the mean, scolds both extremes. Prodigus, he declares, is the supporter of courtesans and unnecessary artisans. He is the cause of dearth and does nothing of profit to the commonwealth. He wastes money on hunting and on fashionable clothes while the poor cry in vain at his door. As for Avarus, he would keep Pecunia in perpetual imprisonment. A rapid–fire and quite dramatic debate follows, the names of the three speakers being noted in marginal glosses. Avarus and Prodigus beg the Lady: "Choose me!" Liberalis says calmly: "Lady, choose whom thou wilt." No matter what the choice he will remain content. Pecunia rejects Prodigus as a waster and Liberalis as "a nice Puritaine," and she accepts "sweete Avarus" as her true lover. Whereupon Prodigus, enraged, attacks Avarus with his sword.

At this point (to the reader's surprise) three goddesses intervene. The first is Fortune, "Mistress of Chaunce, great Queene of destinie."

> On her right side stands
> A Nymph, that bore her ever turning wheele;
> On th'other side a King, who with his hand[s]
> Held out a globe, which like a bowle, did reele.
> Fortune had after her attendants three,
> The fatal sisters of the Destinie (sig. D2ᵛ).

These lines are reminiscent of the episodes in Thomas Dekker's *Old Fortunatus*, I.1 and II.2, where Fortune appears with Kings and with the Three Fates. The second goddess is Vice. Her nymphs carry a tree laden with fruit, but in every branch of it "the gazers eye might well behold a scoffe" (which seems to mean that the fruits of vice are a mockery). The third goddess is Virtue. Her dress is bespangled with stars and upon her head she wears not only garlands and a crown but also a coxcomb (an emblem of vigilance). Her nymphs carry a tree "halfe greene, halfe withered" (The meaning being apparently that half the human race is virtuous and the other half depraved). Virtue is weeping. Fortune boasts that she exalts whom she will: clowns, fools, and cowards, and gives gems to the dunghill cock; and she debases the brave and wise. "I turn fair learning out to beggerie." Vice makes a long speech, counseling Virtue to forego her opposition, quit "precisme" (being so precise), put on fine apparel, and "goe gay." She then describes her "scholars" who are none other than six of the Seven Deadly Sins (Wrath being omitted). The first is Avarice; the second Prodigality (who thus makes up the number seven). The third is Envy who holds poisonous snakes in his fist and in his "iron pawes" "balls of wild–fire." He keeps an owl, whose shrieks waken him to work revenge. The fourth is Idleness with snail–like pace and eyes sunk in his head. "Snorting he lies all night, dreaming all day." The fifth is Gluttony; "his house is nought but kitchin" and his followers are "smel-feasts." The sixth is Pride, clad like the morning sun and with ladies attending her. The seventh is "mine owne darling hight licentiousness" whose "brests lye open . . . the perfect mirrour of formositie." Virtue's nymphs urge their mistress to "chace hence this scumme" and Vice exclaims: "What a nice brawling keep these cattes precise!" Virtue remonstrates, listing her "counter–checks": Humility, Continence, Bounteousness, and Meekness. She defies not only Vice but also Pecunia. Fortune then speaks up, demanding that Virtue yield "obeysance" to her.

A challenge is issued, and Virtue as "the weaker combattant" has the right to choose the ground for the battle. She chooses England. Both sides solicit the favor and aid of the gods. Jove sends Mercury to assure Virtue of victory. Pallas supports Virtue; Venus and Mars are on Vice's side. Virtue, armed with the breastplate of Faith and the headpiece of Comfort, takes up her station in the fortress of Hope. Liberalis is a "warlike Collonell" in her army, which numbers many virtues and "troupes of soules." But the smallest wing of Vice's host is three times as large as all Virtue's forces. The battle is joined. Jove, hurling his thunderbolts, compels Fortune and Vice to yield to Virtue. Vice was imprisoned; they should have slain her, for she quickly corrupted the jailer's heart and made her escape. We are reminded of the inconclusive ending of Anthony Copley's *A Fig for Fortune*, 1596, where Doblessa, though routed, returns to the attack. So also at the close of *The Faerie Queene*, Bk. VI, the Blatant Beast breaks his chain and again ranges the world, working mischief: "Pecunia now to Vertues lappe y–lept, / Begging for pardon for her stubbornesse." Virtue entrusts her to the charge of Liberalis. Jove, departing, counsels Virtue to "set up her chiefest rest" in England. In that happy land "Pecunia is disposed thriftly" and England is "the perfect patterne of the golden age." The poem ends with a prayer that long life be granted to "Englands Beta." The entrusting of Pecunia to Liberalis is paralleled in one of the Van Veen's Horatian Emblems (pp. 119–120) where two men wearing liberty–caps tame Pecunia, one putting a yoke upon her shoulders while the other holds a chain that binds her. She holds another chain binding her kneeling devotees, the avaricious. In a design by Jacob Cats people pay homage to Pecunia, crowned and enthroned, surrounded by moneybags and treasure chests. See Cats, *Spiegel van den Ouden* (3rd ed. Dordrecht, 1635), Part II, p. 93.

Somewhat similar, though the Sins are not introduced, is Roger Bieston's *The bayte and snare of Fortune Wherin may be seen that money is not only the cause of mischefe and unfortunat endes: but a necessary mean to mayntayne a vertuous quiet life. Treated in a Dialoge betweene man and money.* The author's name does not appear on the title page but he signs himself in the initial letters of the lines of a concluding poem. The piece is undated; STC guesses 1550, because of the reverent tone of an allusion to the pope. I date it a little later, in the reign of Mary. The debate is in alternate octaves (ababcdcd), is conducted with dignity, and is lively and vigorous, each debater breathlessly catching up his opponent. Money boasts of his power. Man denounces him as the root of evil. Money argues that he brings honor to princes and has built fine cities. Not so, replies Man; cities are built by labor and prudence and experience. One would think, says Money, that lacking me men would be sinless, yet Adam and Eve, who had no money, sinned when Satan tempted them. "Shall I beare the blame for his abhomination?" Man admits "this is a fayer excuse," but nevertheless you cause infinite ills. Ambition and other evils, Money retorts, should bear much of the blame; it is cruel to blame me for all enormities. On the contrary, I bestow great substance on the Church of God.

> The poor have my saccour in hunger, frost, and snowe
> I feed both horse and man on holy pilgrimages,
> For fayer young lusty maydens I purchase mariages,
> When Churches and Chapels be fallying in dekay
> I must make reparation.

But unconvinced, Man reaches a climax of denunciation: "By thee the gentyll Jesus unto the doves was solde." Money disclaims responsibility, laying it upon Judas' avarice. Finally Man admits:

> If man with his money woulde be so reasonable
> To use it in vertue, and with a good entent,
> The usage therof shall never be damnable . . .
> So order we our money that God be not offended.

11. On these monstrous hybrids see F. Saxl in *Festschrift für Julius Schlosser* (Vienna, 1927), p. 104 and pl. 21; F. Saxl, "A Spiritual Encyclopaedia of the Later Middle Ages," *Journal of the Warburg and Courtauld Institutes*, 5 (1942), and pl. 21; Dodgson, *Catalogue of Woodcuts in the British Museum*, 2, no. 240, pl. 102; Paul Heitz, *Einblattdrucke des Fünfzehnten Jahrhunderts*, 50 (Strassburg, 1909 et. seq.), 5.

12. *The New Arival of the three Gracis* (ca. 1573), sig. F1ᵛ.

13. These both are in André Frideric and Jacques de Zettre, *Emblemes Nouveaux* (Frankfort, 1617), nos. 15 and 24.

14. In *Poems*, ed. John Small, EETS, 2 (1893), 117–121; in *Poems*, ed. W. M. Mackenzie (1932), pp. 120–3.

15. Stephen Hawes, ll. 5425–73.

16. *Visiones Rerum* (1623), Fourth Vision.

17. *Divine Meditations and Elegies* (1622), VI.

18. From a contemporary letter quoted by John Nichols, *Progresses . . . of King James the First*, 1, 92–3.

19. *Das buch granatapfel im latin genant Malogranatus* (Augsburg, 1510), sig. aaᵛ. (I have not seen the edition in Latin.)

20. Ibid., sig. cciiʳ. This design comes at the beginning of a set of sermons "Von den siben schayden."

3. THE DEADLY SINS AND THE PAGEANT IN *The Faerie Queene* CONTINUED.

1. Chew, *The Virtues Reconciled*, p. 146: 'Before the destruction of the "Painted Chamber" of Westminster Palace in the fire of 1834 C. A. Stothard had made drawings of the only two episodes of the thirteenth–century murals of the Psychomachia which were not too much decayed to be worth copying. Engravings from these drawings accompany Gage Rokewood's article on the "Painted Chamber" in *Vetusta Monumenta*, The Society of Antiquaries, 6 (1836), pl. 38. They are again reproduced in W. R. Letheby,

"English Primitives: The Painted Chamber and the Early Masters of the Westminster School," *The Burlington Magazine*, 7 (1905), 257–269, pl. 1. See ibid., *33* (1918), 5, for a water-colour "reconstruction" of the Chamber by Matthew Dawson, which shows the probable arrangement of the lost murals. Stothard's original drawings were shown in the Exhibition of English Primitives in 1924. "Largesse" (Charity, Generosity, Liberality), a woman, stands in triumph upon "Covoitise" (Avarice and Covetousness) and pours money into his mouth from a large purse.'

2. See C. E. Keyser, *A List of Buildings in Great Britain and Ireland having Mural or Other Painted Decorations of Dates Prior to the Latter Part of the Sixteenth Century* (3rd ed., 1883). Keyser's descriptions are brief and sometimes vague; for seven churches he gives no description. A few murals have been recovered from beneath whitewash or in the course of reconstruction since Keyser compiled his list.

3. John Piggott, Jr., "Notes on the Polychromatic Decoration of Churches, with special reference to a Wall Painting discovered in Ingatestone Church," *Transactions of the Essex Archaeological Society*, 4 (1869), 137–143. This contains a chromolithograph of a drawing of the mural by William Strutt.

4. Reproduced in Borenius and Tristram, *English Medieval Painting*, fig. 8.

5. M. R. James, "The Wall Paintings in Brooke Church," in *A Supplement to Blomefield's Norfolk*, ed. Clement Ingleby (1929), pp. 14–25.

6. E. T. Long, "Some Recently Discovered English Wall Paintings," *Burlington Magazine*, *56* (1930), 225–32 and pl. 33. A.

7. Paris, Bibliothèque Nationale, MS fr. 400; discussed and reproduced in Emile Mâle, *L'Art religieux en France, 3* (Paris, 1925), 329 f.

8. The German woodcuts are reproduced in Schramm, *Bilderschmuck*, *3*, nos. 213–226; the Dutch in ibid., *12*, 377–391. The Dutch series is expanded to fifteen, there being a preliminary illustration of the Sins drawn up in battle array under the leadership of Satan.

9. The Pierpont Morgan MS is described in H. Lehmann–Haupt, *Schwäbische Federzeichnungen* (Berlin, 1929), pp. 78 and 196.

10. See D. T. Wood, "Tapestries of the Seven Deadly Sins," *Burlington Magazine*, *20* (1912), 210–222, 277–289. The Hampton Court tapestries are related to sets in Continental collections. In a fifteenth–century German tapestry depicting the Psychomachia the Virtues stand erect but the Sins are mounted on beasts and have creatures or other devices on their helmets, shields, and banners; reproduced in Heinrich Göbel, *Tapestries of the Lowlands*, pl. 60. Of about the same date is a manuscript which twice depicts the Psychomachia. In one the Sins, with emblematic creatures on their helmets, assault the Castle of the Virtues. In the other they ride on emblematic creatures and have others on their helmets, shields, and banners. They are attacking two castles, one defended by the three Theological Virtues, the other by the four Stoic Virtues. See Saxl, "A Spiritual Encyclopaedia," pp. 103–4 and pl. 25a. Both engagements strikingly resemble the assault in *The Castle of Perseverance* (ca. 1425). See also E. H. Buschbeck, "The Vienna Tapestry Exhibition," *Burlington Magazine*, 37 (1920), 123–130.

11. Margaret Jourdain, "The Embroidery at Hardwick Hall," *Burlington Magazine*, 6 (1909), 97 f.

12. Jacques le Grand, *Sophologium*, was abbreviated as *Le Livre de bonnes meurs* (Paris, Antoine Caillaut, 1487). The first part of this work is on the Seven Deadly Sins and their opposing Virtues. The antithetical pairs are entirely normal. There is no personification in the text, but abundant examples from the Bible and ancient history, and quotations from Cicero, Seneca, Moralists, the Fathers, etc. The vices are subdivided. The French version of 1487 has woodcuts of the Sins riding upon animals: Pride on a lion; Lechery (who is a man) on a goat; Avarice on an ape, and so forth. Reproduced in A. Claudin, *Histoire dè l'imprimerie*, *1*, 303–7.

13. Reproduced in ibid., *1*, 321–3.

14. For the cuts in *Eguyllon de crainte divine*, appended to *L'Art de bien vivre et bien mourir* (1492 and subsequent editions), see ibid., *2*, 427 f.; and for the punishments in Guy Marchant, *Compost et Kalendrier des Bergers* (1491 and subsequent editions), ibid., *1*, 375 f. and Hind, *History of Woodcut*, *2*, 649–654. Antoine Vérard (who numbered Henry VIII among his patrons, was often in England, and may even have had a shop in London) printed in Paris, 1503, the English version, *The Kalendayr of Shyppars* (Facsimile edition, ed. H. O. Sommer, 1892). It bears neither his name nor device but contains many of the cuts from his *Bien vivre et bien mourir*, including the punishments. See Hind, *History of Woodcut*, *2*, 504.

15. Reproduced in Mâle, *L'Art religieux*, *3*, 338–341.

16. In many Books of Hours and Offices of the B.V.M. the Seven Deadly Sins illustrate the Penitential Psalms. Thus in *Offices* (Petrus Liechtenstein, Venice, 1545) there are six of the Sins (no Ira). Each is a tiny vignette. Each has a beast: Pride a dragon; the others traditional or unidentifiable. Reproduced in D'Essling, *Les Livres à figures venetiens*, *1*, 481. D'Essling has valuable tables of the principal subjects illustrated in *Offices of the B.V.M.*

17. Facsimile edition, Edinburgh, The Roxburghe Club, 1905. The English craftsman omitted the black backgrounds relieved with white dots (*nielli*) which so much enrich the effect of the original designs. Instead of one block for each combat, as in the originals, he made two, apparently expecting them to be used in different combinations and not realizing that each Sin is overthrown by an appropriate Virtue.

18. See S. C. Chew, "The Iconography of *A Booke of Christian Prayers* (1578)," *Huntington Library Quarterly*, 8 (1945), 293–305.

19. *A christall glasse of christian reformation, wherein the godly maye beholde the coloured abuses used in this our present tyme. Collected by Stephen Bateman Minister.* I have not thought it necessary to give references to signatures.

4. VANITY, FOLLY, AND THE BANQUET IN *The Faerie Queene*

1. *The Contention of Liberality and Prodigality*, in Hazlitt's Dodsley, *8*, 333. The play was published in 1602 but is of earlier date.

2. *Rosalynde* (1590); in *Works*, Hunterian Club, *1* (Glasgow, 1883), 12.

3. *Emblemata Anniversaria Academiae Altorfinae* (Nuremberg, 1597), fol. 69ʳ.

4. *King Lear*, II.2.39.

5. Marlowe, *The Jew of Malta*, II.2.39; Ben Jonson, *Volpone*, II.3.21, and *The Devil is an Ass*, I.1.42. Neither of these dramatists describes Lady Vanity.

6. *The Mariage of Wit and Wisedom*, not, however, the separate morality of that title but the fragment in *Sir Thomas More*, in *The Shakespeare Apocrypha*, ed. Tucker Brooke (Oxford, Clarendon Press, 1908). See especially IV.1.147 and 215.

7. In the second of Cornelis Anthonisz's six prints (ca. 1540).

8. Father Herman Hugo, *Pia Desideria Emblemata* (Antwerp, 1624), Bk. II, no. 20.

9. *Emblemes* (1635), Bk. I, no. 4. Cf. Bk. IV, no. 5. The designs, be it remembered, are not Wither's own invention.

10. *Iconologia*, ed. 1630, Part III, pp. 144–5.

11. Huntington Library "Kitto" Bible, *23*, no. 4288.

12. *The Voyage of the Wandering Knight*, translated from the French of Jean de Cartigny by W. Goodyear (1581 and several later editions). To this beautiful allegory we shall return in Chapter 7. On Spenser's possible indebtedness to it see Dorothy F. Atkinson, " 'The Wandering Knight,' the Red Cross Knight, and 'Miles Dei,' " in *Huntington Library Quarterly*, 7 (1944), 109–134.

13. *Mundus et Infans* (published 1522 but of earlier date), 11.168 f., 349 f., 460. Reprinted in John M. Manly, *Specimens*, *1*.

14. Reproduced in Raffaello Piccoli, "Veritas Derelicta," *Burlington Magazine*, *56* (1930), 244–55.

15. Jacques de Zettre, *Emblemes Nouveaux* (Frankfort, 1617), no. 43. This is a translation from the German of André Frideric. I have not seen the original. In the First Vision in Hagthorpe's *Visiones Rerum* (1623) the author tells how in a dream he met Moria (Folly) in the Palace of Cronos. Moria gets astride a reed (symbolizing insecurity), fits wings to his shoulders, breaks Time's hourglass, and scatters the sand "to be sure Time's glass should not run out." Compare the antics of the foolish fellows ("Fatui") who, oblivious of Time, play with his hourglass and scythe in Father Jan David, *Occasio Arrepta, Neglecta* (Antwerp, 1605), no. 3.

16. Reproduced in Hind, *History of Woodcut*, *1*, fig. 91, and in André Blum, *Les Origines de la gravure en France* (Paris, 1927), pl. 69. This picture may throw light upon the way in which the lost English *Paternoster Play*, or at any rate one episode in it, was produced at Beverley. It is known to have contained eight "pageants": one for Vicious and one for each of the Deadly Sins. There is a facsimile of the original edition of the *Exercitium*, Berlin, 1905.

17. *A Mirror of Monsters: Wherein is plainely described the manifold vices, and spotted enormities that are caused by the infectious sight of Playes, with the description of the subtile slights of Sathan, making them his.*

18. Fol. 4^v.

19. Fol. 7^v f.

20. One of the examples of Dissention (fol. 19^r) is "Ferrex and Porrex." Examples of blasphemy "of our owne present age" are omitted, but the introduction into plays of characters "calling on Mahomet" is cited as blasphemous. Is this an allusion to *Tamburlaine?*

21. Fol. 24^r.

22. In *Adams Complaint, The Olde Worldes Tragedie, David and Bathsheba* (1596), sig. D2^v f. There is no allegory in the first and third poem.

5. PRIDE

1. A wall painting in an English church shows Pride wearing a crown; another has Pride drawn to a larger scale than the other figures and she holds a scepter. In an Italian engraving (existing only as republished in 1569 but dating from ca. 1470–80) Regina Superbia, crowned, occupies a central place, the other Sins flanking her. She presides over seven Sins, not six, Vaingloria being the seventh. See Hind, *Early Italian Engraving,* I.e.iii.4. For another example of Pride crowned and sceptered, see Sigismondo Fanti, *Triompho di Fortuna* (Venice, 1527), carte xxviii^v.

2. Reproduced in Göbel, *Tapestries,* no. 60.

3. A. Feuillerat, *Revels at the Court of Edward VI and Mary,* p. 245.

4. Vainglory or Arrogance rather than Superbia Intellectualis is visualized in a German painting and a German engraving (both sixteenth–century) illustrating the proverb "Poverty sits upon the skirts of Pride." Here a poor man and his wife and child sit upon the ostentatiously trailing gowns of a rich man and woman. See R. Campbell Dodgson, "Two Illustrations of a German Proverb," *Burlington Magazine,* 26 (1915), 145–6 and pl. An English parallel, though not a close one, is F. T.'s *The debate betweene Pride and Lowliness, pleaded to an issue in Assise.* This is undated, probably ca. 1570. J. P. Collier suggested Francis Thynne, son of the Chaucerian editor, as the author. This *DNB* questions, but the very old fashioned quality of this tedious poem makes the identification plausible. In the month of May the Poet had a dream. Having walked through pleasant fields he found himself in a dale beside a brook. (The landscape has nothing to do with what follows.)

> An sodenly mee thought I had espied
> A thing come downe the hilward toward me:
> But not on foote, ne yet on horse dyd ryde,
> Which mee thought very strange there for to see.

It was "a goodly velvet breech," made of Granado silk, paned, and embroidered. Then another pair of breeches rolled down an opposite hill, made of cloth and unadorned. Velvet breeches is scornful of Cloth breeches; the latter argues that the same Workman fashioned them both. The poet tries to moderate between them. A jury is assembled, but presently the dreamer wakes.

5. John Theodore and John Israel de Bry, *Emblemata Saecularia, Mira*

et Jucunda Varietate Saeculi huius Mores ita Exprimentia (Frankfort, 1596), no. 2. The fifty vigorous plates in this book hold together in a logical sequence, as is explained at the beginning in a "succinct argument." It opens with Democritus and Heraclitus contemplating the World. The last two plates show Death exhibiting his hourglass to a man and a woman.

6. S.P. [Samuel Pordage?], *Mundorum Explicatio or The Explanation of a Hieroglyphical Figure: Wherein are couched the Mysteries of the External, Internal, and Eternal World, shewing the true progress of a Soul from the Court of Babylon to the City of Jerusalem; from the Adamical fallen state to the Regenerate and Angelical. A Sacred Poem* (1661), p. 115. Was this poem, with its conspirational council in hell under the presidency of Satan, known to Milton?

7. As in two seventeenth–century prints in Huntington Library "Kitto" Bible, *1*, 79, and *3*, 355. Eve's fall was brought about by her intellectual pride as was Adam's by sensuality.

8. Callot's exquisite series of the Sins is reproduced in J. Lieure, *Jacques Callot*, Part II, *1* (Paris, 1924), nos. 354–360. Numerous copies and imitations by later, inferior artists testify to the popularity of these engravings.

9. Trevelyon commonplace book (ca. 1608). Among the several hundred crude, colored illustrations is a sequence of the Sins, fols. 151^r–154^r, which is of interest as recording a popular concept of the theme in England very shortly after the time of Spenser. See further Chew, *The Virtues Reconciled*, pp. 127 and 153. Three of Trevelyon's Sins are reproduced for the first time in my article on "Spenser's Pageant," figs. 8, 15, and 16. Thomas Cheaste, *The Christian Path–Way* (1613), p. 26, without personifying Pride, likens this Sin to a pale horse: "Death rideth on it, for death is the wages of pride."

10. *VII Peccatorum Capitalium Imagines Elegantissime a Philip. Gallaeo Depictae et Aeri Incisae* (n.d., ca. 1600).

11. The series is reproduced in René van Bastelaer, *Les Estampes de Peter Brueghel l'Ancien* (Brussels, 1908), nos. 125–131.

12. Reproduced in *Britwell Court Catalogue*, March 12, 1923, lot no. 657. In this tedious satiric poem Taylor, while scourging Pride as expressed in riches, costly attire, worldly wisdom, and so forth, admits that by stimulating many trades it has become a "necessary evil."

13. *Doctor Faustus*, II.2.121.

14. Reproduced in W. G. Thomson, *Tapestry Weaving in England From the Earliest Times to the End of the XVIIIth. Century* (ca. 1915), fig. 5.

15. D'Essling, *Les Livres à figures venetiens, 1*, 481.

16. Ed. 1578, sigs. 43^v and 64^r. This is one of the cuts which disappear from later editions and reappear inappropriately in other books. See Chew, in *Huntington Library Quarterly, 8* (1945), 293–305.

17. *Itinerary, 4* (ed. Glasgow, 1907), 230. Compare the portrait of Mary, Countess of Dorset, by Marcus Gheeraerts the Younger, reproduced in H. K. Morse, *Elizabethan Pageantry* (1934), p. 59.

18. For Lechery with a mirror see a woodcut by Anthony Van Worms, ca. 1530. This is one of the cuts decorating the margin of a leaf torn from a book which I have not identified and know only from the detached

page in the Huntington Library extra–illustrated Bryan's *Dictionary*, *2*, Part V, after p. 622.

19. *The Virtues Reconciled*, pp. 14–15.

20. At the Royal Entry of Charles VII into Paris in 1437 the Seven Deadly Sins and the Seven Cardinal Virtues rode in the procession, "all clothed according to their characteristics." See Enid Welsford, *The Court Masque* (Cambridge, 1927), p. 52.

21. See S. C. Chew, "The Allegorical Chariot in English Literature of the Renaissance," in *De Artibus Opuscula XL*, Essays in Honor of Erwin Panofsky, New York University Press, 1961. In Thomas Timme's *A Plain Discoverie of ten English Lepers, verie noisome and hurtfull to the Church and commonwealth* (1592) only one of the "lepers" approximates personification: the proud man who rides in the chariot of Pride, see sig. E4^v.

22. Huntington Library "Kitto" Bible, *60*, 16, 833^v.

23. Mâle, *L'Art religieux*, *3*, 333–4.

24. *Wisdom*, in *The Macro Plays*, ed. F. J. Furnivall and A. W. Pollard, EETS, 1904. Unusually full stage directions afford an idea of costuming with interesting analogies to popular prints: The Vices who attend upon Mind (1.695) are Indignation, Sturdiness, Malice, Hastiness, Vengeance, and Discord: "with rede berdis, and lyouns rampaunt on here [their] crestis, and yche a warder in hys honde." (The red beards are suggestive of Judas and treachery; the lion crests of pride; the warders of their authority.) They are announced by a minstrel who sounds a trumpet. The Vices who attend upon Understanding (1.727) are six false Jurors, Wrong, Sleight, Doubleness, Falsehood, Ravine, Deceit: "with hodis abowt her [their] nekis, hattis of meyntenance . . . vyseryde dyversly; her mynstrell a bag–pype." The hoods are well known emblems of Fraud. "Maintenance" was a form of corruption in the courts, but what "hats of maintenance" may have looked like I do not know. The variegated visors probably refer to some emblem worn on the front of the helmet? Will, who has become Lechery, has also a crew of six (1.755): Recklessness, Idleness, Surfeit, Greed, Adultery, and "gentle" Fornication. Three are "dysgysyde as galontis, and iij as Matrones, with wondyrfull vysurs conregent; here [their] mystrell a hornepype." Which Vices are gallants and which matrons is not specified; nor do I know what "visors conregent" may have been. When the Soul has fallen into sin we have this stage–direction (11.906 f.): "Here Anima apperythe in the most horrybull wyse, fowlere than a fende. . . . Here rennyt out from undyr the horrybyll mantyll of the Soull, VI small boys in the lykness of Deevylls, and so retorne a–geyn."

25. II.2.172.

26. *Tom Tel–Troths Message, and his Pens Complaint. A worke not unpleasant to read nor unprofitable to be followed. Written by Io. La. Gent.*

27. *Peregrinatio Scholastica or Learneinges Pilgrimage Containeinge the straundge Adventurs and various entertainments he founde in his traveils towards the shrine of Latria . . . Composed and devided into morall Tractates.* This was first published, from British Museum Sloane MS 3150, in *Works*, ed. A. H. Bullen, *2* (1881), 35–80.

28. When each Age of Human Life is associated with a Sin appropriate

to the Age, Pride belongs with the prime of life and may be emblematized by a lion. Other examples are in *The Ancren Riwle*, Gower (and the French manuscript related to Gower), Lydgate, Bateman, the *Eruditorium Penitentiale*, the *Chasteau de Labour*, and Fanti. See also Thomas Nashe, *Christs Teares over Jerusalem*, in *Works*, ed. R. B. McKerrow, *2* (1910), 131.

29. Reproduced in Hind, *Early Italian Engravings*, A.II.20.

30. On the regality of the elephant see Dora and Erwin Panofsky, "The Iconography of the Galerie François Ier at Fontainebleau," *Gazette des Beaux–Arts*, Sept. 1958, pp. 131–3.

31. In Dirk Volckertszoon Coornhert, *Emblemata Moralia et Oeconomica* (Arnheim, 1609), sig. Ciii[v], and in the same author's *Recht Ghebruyck ende Misbruyck van Tydlicke Have* (Amsterdam, 1620), no. 8. In the French version of Ripa, *1* (1698), 472, and in the English version (1709), no. 26 Arrogance, which springs from Pride, has ass's ears.

32. *Iconologia* (ed. Padua, 1630), pp. 21, 94, 276, 339–340.

33. "Tromperie," in *Iconologie ou la Science des Emblemes, 2* (Amsterdam, 1698), 505–6; "Deceit," in *Iconologia or, Moral Emblems* (1709), p. 42.

34. In *Emblemata* (Frankfort–a–M., 1584), no. 64.

35. In *Emblematum Christianorum Centuria* (Zurich, 1581), no. 25.

36. In *The Metamorphosis of Pigmalions Image. And Certaine Satyres* (1598), Satire I, 136, in *Works*, ed. A. H. Bullen, *3* (1887), 268.

37. *Minerva Britanna*, nos. 197 and 47. Cf. Maurice Scève, Μικροκ ο σμος *Parvus Mundus* (Arnheim, ca. 1570). no. 20.

38. *The Gentlemans Exercise* (ed. 1612), p. 114.

39. In *Picturae Loquentes, Or Pictures Drawne forth in Characters* (1631), ed. 1635, sig. D9[v].

40. In *Emblêmes des differens Etats de la Vie* (1630), p. 73.

41. Dodgson, *Catalogue of Woodcuts in the Bri ish Museum*, *1*, 341–2. In Cornelis Anthonisz's "De Waarheyt" Truth's lips are padlocked.

42. "Of the Instabilitie of Fortune," *A Posie of Gilloflowers* (1580), sig. L2[v], in *Complete Poems*, ed. A. B. Grosart (1870), p. 92.

43. "The Bowge of Court," in *Poetical Works*, ed. Alexander Dyce, *1* (1843), 56; "Magnificence," ibid., *2*, 34.

44. In *The Paradise of Daintie Devises* (1576), ed H. E. Rollins (1927), p. 21: poem no. 18, with no title. See also Rollins' note, ibid., p. 197.

6. SLOTH OR IDLENESS

1. Horatian Emblems, p. 177; reproduced in my "Spenser's Pageant," fig. 11.

2. Ibid., p. 17; reproduced ibid., fig. 9.

3. Anonymous, *Emblemes d'Amour* (Paris, early seventeenth century), pl. 39. A similar design is in Otho Van Veen, *Amorum Emblemata* (Antwerp, 1612), p. 125: "Amor addit Inertibus Alas."

4. Gregory Kleppis, *Emblemata Varia* (1624), no. 15. A set of four curious designs shows Caro (a wider concept than Luxuria since it includes

Sloth and Gluttony also) as an ass. Homo Carnalis consorts with the creature, while Anima (his distressed Soul) looks on. In the first design he adorns with a headdress the ass labeled "Caro"; in the second he dines with the ass; in the third they are dancing together; in the fourth the ass is in bed and vomits into a basin held by Homo Carnalis. I found these in Jacob de Zetter, *Philosophia Practica* (Frankfort, 1644), a collection of nearly a hundred small etched copies of prints of earlier date. I have not seen the originals of these Caro prints and do not know the designer's name.

5. *King Lear*, I.4.94. The passage runs: "Hog in sloth, fox in stealth, wolf in greediness, dog in madness, lion in prey." Neither these five sins nor their animals conform to any tradition but the relationship is unmistakable!

6. Van Veen, p. 57; reproduced in Chew, "Spenser's Pageant," fig. 10.

7. On this pillow or cushion see Erwin Panofsky, *Studies in Iconology*, p. 88 and pl. 38, and Edgar Wind in *The Journal of the Warburg Institute*, *1* (1937–8), 62–63. In Chew, *The Virtues Reconciled*, p. 16, I have added Father David's Flesh with the cushion on her head and suggested the possibility of allusions to the theme when Chaucer's Pandarus enters the lovers' bedchamber carrying a pillow and when Falstaff puts a pillow on his head.

7. GLUTTONY

1. This emblem is not in the 1531 and 1542 editions of Alciati's *Emblemata* and first appears in the Lyons edition of 1558, pp. 112 and 115. Thereafter it is in other collections. For a late example see Jean Baudoin, *Recueil d'Emblemes Divers*, *1* (Paris, 1638), 188.

2. John Davies of Hereford, *Humours Heav'n on Earth* (1609), stanza 16. The repulsiveness of these greedy gullets is surpassed by an emblem in John Swan's *Speculum Mundi, or a Glasse Representing the Face of the World* (1635), p. 484, where the "Gulon" or "Jerf" represents Gluttony because of its nasty habit, the purpose of which need not be explained, of squeezing itself between two trees.

3. E. H. Buschbeck, "The Vienna Tapestry Exhibition," *Burlington Magazine*, 37 (1920), pp. 123–130 and pl. IIc.

4. *I Henry IV*, IV.2.24.

5. Judas Iscariot, who is of course often associated with Avarice and Despair, is once at least associated with Gluttony. In a church window at Great Malvern depicting the Last Supper he is secreting a fish under the tablecloth. This incident is said to derive from a fourteenth-century French Life of the Virgin where Judas is said to have behaved like a Glutton at the Last Supper and to have taken "the best fish" for himself. See G. McN. Rushforth, *Medieval Christian Imagery as illustrated by the Painted Windows of Great Malvern Priory Church* (Oxford, 1936), pp. 61–62.

8. LECHERY

1. Göbel, *Tapestries*, no. 72.

2. Hind, *Early Italian Engraving*, A.II.6. Hind is incorrect in saying

there are seven women. He thinks this print is based upon a lost original by the Master of the Banderoles.

3. On Lechery's helmet are birds in a chaplet of flowers, on her shield a siren, on her banner a basilisk. Similar but not identical is the emblematic scheme in a German metalplate in color (ca. 1480–1500), depicting the combat of Lust and Chastity. Lust rides a bear; on her helmet is a basilisk, on her shield a hog, on her banner a siren. There is a reproduction in color of this print in F. M. Haberditzel, *Die Einblattdrucke des XV Jahrhunderts in der Kupferstichsammlunger der Hofbibliothek zur Wien* (Vienna, 1920), pl. 107. See also W. L. Schreiber, *Handbuch der Holz– und Metallschnitte des XV Jahrhunderts, 4* (Leipzig, 1927), no. 1866.

4. See Max Geisberg, *Die Anfänge des Kupferstiches* (Leipzig, n.d.), pp. 38–39 and pl. 19. Reproduced also in Carl Zigrosser, *Six Centuries of Fine Prints* (New York, 1937), pl. 137.

5. *The Taming of the Shrew*, II.1.34.

6. Heitz, *Einblattdrucke*, 59, no. 14.

7. *The Faerie Queene*, II, 7, 39, and V, 12, 30.

8. Reproduced in Schreiber, *Handbuch, 4*, no. 1865a and in Heitz, *Einblattdrucke, 24, 20*.

9. AVARICE

1. Ralph Winterton, *The Considerations of Drexelius upon Eternity* (1636), p. 123. This is a translation of Henry Drexelius, *De AEternitate Considerationes* (Cologne, 1631). In the English version the illustrations are in reverse and a good deal simplified. For an early example of the motif, in which Christ stands beside a two–humped camel and the needle is on the ground, see *Geistliche Auslegung des Lebens Jesu Christi* (Ulm, ca. 1483), reproduced in Schramm, *Der Bilderschmuck der Frühdrucke, 5* (Leipzig, 1923, 1927), no. 356. John Swan, in *Speculum Mundi, or a Glasse Representing the Face of the World* (1635), p. 444, likens "the swelling pride and confidence of worldly men" to the camel's "bunch." In *The Penitent Publican* (1610), sig. B4ᵛ, Thomas Collins writes: "Thou that put'st Cammells through a needles eye, / For all their bunches of iniquitie."

2. This is a design by Battista Pittoni in Lodovico Dolce, *Imprese di Diversi Prencipi, Duchi, et d'Altri Personaggi et Huomini Letterati et Illustri* (Venice, 1562), no. 17.

3. Gabriele Simeone, *Le Sententiose Imprese* (Lyons, 1560), p. 60.

4. "The Evil Times of Edward II," in *The Political Songs of England*, ed. Thomas Wright, Camden Society, *6* (1839), p. 326.

5. See Schramm, *Der Bilderschmuck der Frühdrucke, 8* (1924), no. 341, from *Ars Moriendi* (Cologne, ca. 1475), and D'Essling, *Les Livres à figures venetiens, 1*, 263–264, from Venetian editions of the same.

6. In the *Eruditorium Penitentiale*. Without the purse the ape appears in the *Livre de bonnes meurs* and the *Chasteau de Labour*.

7. Mole or badger (in the French manuscript); hedgehog (Nashe and the Italian engraving in Hind, *I*, E.iii.4); squirrel (Morgan MS. 782, reproduced in Chew, "Spenser's Pageant," fig. 14); toad (in Fanti and Burgk-

mair). The tortoise in Furnius seems less appropriate. In the *Speculum Mundi*, John Swan, who is always prolific of suggestions for emblems from natural history (drawn from Topsell and other authorities), associates with Covetousness the "Swam–fisk," a very greedy fish of Norway (p. 373), the Kite (p. 394), and the Ferret (p. 459)—this last because "if at any time their prey shall be taken from them, they fall a squeaking and crying" as rich men wail over their losses. The she–ape is also (p. 474) an emblem of Covetousness. Often she "killeth with kindness" her favorite offspring by crushing it in her arms, while "the neglected one" is "glad to sit upon the back of his damme, open to all dangers," yet faring the better for want of "foolish cockering."

8. *Emblemata* (ed. 1531), sig. C6^r, and in later editions; Whitney, *Choice of Emblemes* (1586), Greene's facsimile, p. 18; Christoff Murer, *Emblemata* (Zurich, 1622), no. 16; Daniel Meisner, *Sciographia Cosmica* (Nuremberg, 1637), pl. A–25; and elsewhere. In the *Eruditorium Penitentiale* a confused conflation of emblem and sin emblematized makes the ass browsing among thistles emblematic not of Avarice but of Sloth.

9. Middleburg, 1618. The emblem is repeated in Cats, *Proteus* (Rotterdam, 1627). In *Vulgar Errors* (4th ed. 1658), Bk. VII, chap. 15, Sir Thomas Browne glances at the opinion that the crocodile "hath no period of increase, but groweth as long as it liveth."

10. Meisner, *Sciographia Cosmica*, pl. F–12.

11. André Frideric and Jacques de Zettre, *Emblemes Nouveaux* (1617), no. 60.

12. D. V. Coornhert, *Recht Ghebruyck ende Misbruyck* (Amsterdam, 1620), no. 20.

13. In a fourteenth–century MS of the *Roman de la Rose*, Pierpont Morgan MS. 185.

14. Mathias Holzwart, *Emblematum Tyrocinia: sive Picta Poesis latino-germanica* (Strassburg, 1581), no. 53.

15. Ed. L. A. Magnus, EETS (1905), 11.104, 113, 173, 319, 420, 752, 833 f., 1725 f.

16. *The Combat betweene Conscience and Covetousness in the Mind of Man* (1598), in *Complete Works*, ed. A. B. Grosart (1871), pp. 179 f.

17. Lyons, ca. 1486–7; reproduced in Claudin, *Histoire de l'imprimerie*, 2, 253.

18. "Kitto" Bible, 24, 4458. The engraving is signed "D."

19. Florentine Schoonhovius, *Emblemata partim moralia, partim etiam Civilia* (1618), no. 36. Compare Peacham, *Minerva Britanna*, no. 197: Pallas is caught in a net by Avarice and Fraud. These emblems appear elsewhere.

20. John Lane's Avarice is troubled with the dropsy; she drinks and drinks but cannot quench her thirst. See *Tom Tel–Troths Message*, p. 37 f.

10. ENVY

1. Envy "delights to hear evil" and to spread ill report of others. This is why she is so frequently shown impotently attacking or raging against

Truth or Good Fame. Detraction is consequently a form of Envy, or rather a manifestation of Envy. Is this connection brought out, or hinted at, in Spenser's delineation of Slander, the Blatant Beast? In Shakespeare's allusions to the "many–headed multitude" are there included suggestions of the mob's propensity to spread scandal and slander? In 1595 Dr. John Dee wrote, and in 1599 published *A Letter containing a most briefe Discourse Apologeticall*, a thin pamphlet protesting against the current accusation that the writer was a conjuror. This was reprinted in 1603 as *A Letter, Nine yeeres since, written and first published* (a curiously inaccurate statement). Both issues have a remarkable woodcut upon the title page, differing only in this, that certain phrases which are in Greek, Latin, or French in 1599 are put into English in 1603. The cut of 1603 (Fig. 92) is either from the reworked original block or else is a close but not identical copy after the original. The many–headed mob–monster with winged feet is definitely Slander and is described as "The Swift Sharpe Poysonable Tongued Monster of many heads that devoureth men." The Gentleman who is the victim of Slander kneels upon the cushion of Hope, Humilitie, and Patience, and prays "O God impute not this Sinnre unto them." Overhead are the eye, ear, and hand of God. The hand brandishes a sword over the mob–monster. But Dee, though he prays for his enemies, is no sheep to be devoured by the wolf, as the presence of these creatures upon the woodcut makes clear; and we remember that the wolf is occasionally the emblematic beast of Envy. The original title page is reproduced in *Autobiographical Tracts of Dr. John Dee*, ed. James Crossley, Chetham Society Publication, 24 (1851), 69. See further Charlotte Fell–Smith, *John Dee* (1909), pp. 255–256.

2. Thomas Middleton, *The Triumphs of Truth*, in *Works*, ed. Bullen, 7, 241.

3. *Speculum Mundi*, pp. 410 and 452. The peacock, he explains, is an emblem of Envy because it hides its dung, which is "very medicinal and useful to man in many ways." The lynx is similarly selfish: Its urine turns into a stone like amber and is of sovereign virtue, but the creature hides it in the earth.

4. In *A Godly prymer* (John Byddell printer, 1535), reproduced in Hodnett, *English Woodcuts, 1480–1535*, fig. 232, the flying, bat–winged demon who vomits upon Truth as Time brings her from the cave, is labeled Hypocrisy but is close to Envy; she holds four snakes in her hand. Compare Boissard's Hypocrisy with snaky locks, in *Emblemata* (1584), no. 64.

5. In *Piers Plowman*, Passus V, every word spoken by Envy "was of an addres tonge." In an English pageant of 1596 Envy had "haires of snakes." See Nichols, *Progresses of Queen Elizabeth*, 3, 405. In Richard Davies' *Chester's Triumph* (1610) she wore a wreath of snakes. See Nichols, *Progresses of James I*, 2, 295 and 302 f. Snakes are among the attributes of Envy in the Induction to Ben Jonson's *Every Man Out of His Humour*. See A. H. Gilbert, *The Symbolic Persons in the Masques of Ben Jonson* (1948), p. 87. Francis Sabie in *The Olde Worldes Tragedie* (1596) describes Envy's den as "adder–haunted." Thomas Milles, in *The Treasurie*

of *Auncient and Moderne Times* (1613), p. 37, makes the eel an emblem of Envy "because it never keeps company with other fishes"; but this is probably a mere misinterpretation of some illustration of a snake. It may be further noted that the snaky hair of Heresy in Father David's *Veridicus Christianus*, pl. 6, is borrowed from Envy because this Jesuit controversialist ascribes the hostility of Protestants to their envy of Roman Catholics.

6. Peacham, in *The Gentlemans Exercise*, p. 114, describes Dissimulation as "a lady wearing a vizard of Two faces, in a long Robe of changeable colour, in her right hand a magpie."

7. Boissard, *Emblematum Liber* (ed. 1593), p. 31, no. 15.

8. *The Christmas Prince* (anonymous), Malone Society, p. 286.

9. *Two Bookes of Epigrammes and Epitaphs* (1639), Bk. I, no. 202.

10. *The Magnificent Entertainment*, in *Works*, ed. Pearson, *1*, 318. Detraction, in the same show, has many of the characteristics of Envy.

11. "Fortune fawning she [Envy] frownes, frowning she smiles," writes John Norden in *The Labyrinth of Mans Life. Or Virtues Delight and Envies Opposite* (1614), sig. H4^v.

12. See the design in Meisner, *Sciographia Cosmica* (Nuremberg, 1637), A–25, where Envy rages against a fashionably dressed gentleman and takes no notice of a beggar.

13. Reproduced in D'Essling, *Les Livres à figures venetiens*, 3, 431–438.

14. *Emblematum Liber* (ed. 1593), p. 31.

15. "The Worth of Poesie," in *Arisbas: Euphues amidst his slumbers* (1594), sig. G1^v f.

16. Cats, *Spiegel van den Ouden*, Part III, p. 53.

11. WRATH

1. *Tom Tel–Troths Message*, p. 31 f.

2. For example see the *Horae* of Pigouchet for Simon Vostre (1502), Thielmann Kerver, *Horae* (1505), and Hardouyn, *Horae* (1514).

3. *Minerva Britanna* (1612), no. 128.

4. *Symbolorum et Emblematum ex Animalibus . . . Centuria Altera* (Nuremberg, 1595), no. 10.

5. Hellmouth may be the yawning jaws of a lion. See, for example, Hind, *Early Italian Engraving*, A.ii.20.

6. See, for examples of bears, a German woodcut (ca. 1480) in Schreiber, *Handbuch*, no. 1865a, a German tapestry in Göbel, *Tapestries*, no. 60; Trevelyon's design in Chew, "Spenser's Pageant," fig. 16; one of the pseudo–Brueghel prints, Ripa, Fanti, Martin de Vos, and elsewhere. For the boar see Gower, the French manuscript; Lydgate's *Assembly;* and Bateman. Nashe links Wrath with a wolf. In *Die Siben todsünden* Wrath rides on a camel. On her helmet is a sparrow–hawk and on her banner is a "merwund called Serta." So runs the accompanying text, but why a whale should be called "Serta" I cannot explain. On her shield should be a mad dog. The text gives this last detail but in the woodcut the shield is blank. The dog appears, however, on the shield in Pierpont Morgan MS 782.

7. See Chew, *The Virtues Reconciled*, p. 123 and references there given.

8. *The Seven Deadlie Sinnes of London*, p. 58.

9. *The Masque of Queens*, 1.131. Mathias Holzwart, *Emblematum Tyrocinia* (Strassburg, 1581), no. 18, pictures Peccatum as a horrid crone with a two–forked tongue masking a flame before her eyes. In some pictures of Ira there are flaming towns in the background.

10. *The Duchess of Malfi*, IV.2.190.

11. *Hymenaei* (1606), 906.

12. Francis White, *Replie to Jesuit Fishers Answere* (1624). The plate is perhaps by Renold Elstrak.

13. Richard Grafton's colophon, showing six of the Arts (Logic omitted), to John Merbecke's *The booke of Common praier noted* (1550). On the other hand, in Gregorius Reisch's famous *Margarita Philosophia* (Basle, 1583), p. 238, Rhetoric, enthroned, has a sword and a palm branch protruding from her mouth. But in Raffaello Borghini, *Il Riposo* (Florence, 1584), p. 4, where Liberal Art is associated with a planet and a part of the body, each Rhetoric is associated with Venus and "le parti vergognose."

14. *Love's Labour's Lost*, III.1.64. Cf. *The Rape of Lucrece*, 1027: "This helpless smoke of words," and *King John*, II.1.229: "Calm words folded up in smoke."

15. *The Triumphs of Truth*, in *Works*, 7, 241, 245. The theme recurs in Middleton's *The Sun in Aries*, in *Works*, 7, 348. Truth driving off Error with a fan of stars makes yet another appearance in Thomas Jordan's *The Triumphs of London* (1678). See F. W. Fairholt, *Lord Mayors' Pageants*, 2 (1844), 157.

12. THE PURPLE ISLAND

1. In *Poetical Works*, ed. F. S. Boas, 2 (Cambridge, 1908–9), 1–171.

2. *The Purple Island*, Canto VII, stanzas 52 and 83.

Chapter 5. The Spiritual Guardians of Man

1. PATIENCE

1. For example, Peacham, *Minerva Britanna*, no. 27.

2. Whitney, *A Choice of Emblemes*, p. 66.

3. This is found in many emblem books. See, for example, Joachim Camerarius, *Symbolorum et Emblematum ex Animalibus . . . Centuria* (Nuremberg, 1595), no. 24; Jacobus Boschius, *Symbolographia* (1702), Class I, table 39, no. 876.

4. *Youths Instructions* (second ed., 1613), p. 90.

5. *Delle Imprese*, Bk. I, fol. 35ʳ.

6. [Alain Chartier], *Delectable demaundes, and Pleasant Questions, with their several Answers, in matters of Love: Natural causes, with Morall and politicke devises* (1596), p. 227.

7. *The Worthy tract of Paulus Iovius, contayning a Discourse of rare*

inventions, both Military and Amorous called Imprese. Whereunto is added a Preface contayning the Arte of composing them, with many other notable devises. By Samuell Daniell late Student in Oxenforde (1585), sig. Eii^v.

8. John Lyly, *Euphues: the Anatomy of Wit;* in *Works*, 3 vols., ed. R. Warwick Bond, *1* (1902), 191. It is with the analogy of the palm in mind that Lyly in *Euphues and His England*, in *Works*, *2*, 76, writes: "So fast a roote hath true love taken in my hart, that . . . the more it is loaden the better it beareth."

9. *Believe As You List*, I.i. The image occurs elsewhere in Jacobean drama. In an anonymous play, *Revenge for Honour*, II.2.29, it is said that palm trees "flourish most when bow'd down fastest."

10. Barthelemy Aneau, ΑΛΕΚΤΩΡ. *The Cock* (1590), p. 150. This is a translation, probably by J. Hammond, from the French.

11. *The Song of Songs* (1621), p. 198.

12. *Emblemes*, Bk. I, no. 28.

13. Ibid., Bk. III, no. 38.

14. The detail of the weighted palm tree is reproduced, enlarged, in S. C. Chew, *The Crescent and the Rose* (New York, 1937), op. p. 15.

15. Samuel Daniel, *The Worthy tract of Paulus Iovius* (1585), sig. Eii^v; Gabriele Simeone, *Le Sententiose Imprese et Dialogo* (Lyons, 1560), p. 74; Giovanni Ferro, *Teatro d'Imprese* (Venice, 1623), Part II, p. 537, where, curiously, there is no weight on the tree; Ieronimo Ruscelli, *Le Imprese Illustri* (Venice, 1572), fol. 136^r.

16. Alciati, *Emblemata* (ed. 1531), sig. B3^r. Here the weight is not hanging but is a horizontal monolith on the top of a pollarded tree. Cf. La Perriere, *La Morosophie* (1553), no. 83.

17. François and Adrien d'Amboise, *Discourse ou Traicté des Devises* (Paris, 1620), p. 154.

18. On a printer's device; McKerrow, *Printers' and Publishers' Devices*, no. 428.

19. Nicolaus Taurellus, *Emblemata Physico-Ethica* (Nuremberg, 1595), sig. D6^r. Here a man hangs by his arms from the branches of a palm tree. The emblem, occasionally met with, of a man or boy climbing up a palm tree does not only teach resistance to adverse Fortune but Victory to be gained by effort. This is in many editions of Alciati. Jean Baudoin, *Recueil d'Emblemes Divers* (Paris, 1638), Part I, 510, using this design, combines the two ideas; the boy climbs "ce merveilleux Arbre, qui se roidit contre le fardeau qu'on luy oppose." So when Nicolaus Taurellus, *Emblemata* (Nuremberg, 1595), sig. D6^r; shows a man hanging from a palm tree the motto is "Sursum deflexa recurrat." Schoonhovius, *Emblemata* (1618), no. 74, has a man climbing a palm, the motto is "Ardua quae pulora."

20. Boschius, *Symbolographia*, Class III, no. 115.

21. William Drummond, *History of Scotland* (1655), p. 263. This was one of the emblems embroidered on Queen Mary's "bed of state." There also was an apple tree growing in a thorn, with the motto "Per vincula crescit." Zacharias Heyns, *Emblemata* (Rotterdam, 1625), p. 47, depicts a tall palm tree surrounded by a thicket of thorns; the motto is "Labore et perseverantia corona paratur."

22. The crest of the Alison family. See *Fairbairn's Book of Crests*, 2 (4th ed. 1905), pl. 143, no. 10.

23. *Speculum Mundi* (1635), p. 276.

24. *The Period of Mourning. Disposed into Six Visions* (1613), sig. B1ᵛ f. The simile in *Hamlet*, V.2.40: "As love between them like the palm might flourish" has nothing to do with the burdened palm tree; its bi–sexuality is an emblem of conjugal love. For parallels see Albert Flamen, *Devises et Emblemes d'Amour* (Paris, 1653), no. 57; Daniel de la Feuille, *Devises et Emblemes anciennes et moderne* (Amsterdam, 1691), pl. 16, no. 13, with the mottoes "Idem nos unit" and "The same affection joynes us." In the same author's *Livre Nouveau et Utile pour toutes Sortes d'Artistes* (Amsterdam, 1691), no. 4, this emblem has the motto "L'Amour les ioint." La Feuille was a professor of languages, the *Devises* contain mottoes in seven languages; his English is very accurate in the main. See also Chew, *The Virtues Reconciled*, p. 153, note 80.

25. *Minerva Britanna*, no. 167, with a marginal reference to Pliny.

26. Boschius, *Symbolographia*, Class III, no. 115.

27. Albert Flamen, *Devises et Emblemes d'Amour* (Paris, 1653), no. 31.

28. John Lyly, *Euphues: The Anatomy of Wit*, in *Works*, ed. Bond, *1*, 191. Bond notes that Lyly "pilfered" this from William Pettie's *Palace of Pleasure*: "As the hearbe Camamile, the more it is troden downe, the more it spreadeth abroade." See *I Henry IV*, II.4.441–3.

29. *Visiones Rerum* (1623), Third Vision, stanza 4.

30. *The Theater of Fine Devices* (1614), no. 97. The cut shows a man treading down a crop.

31. Peacham, *Minerva Britanna*, no. 113.

32. *Britanna's Pastorals*, Bk. II (1616), Song 3; in *Works*, ed. W. C. Hazlitt, *2* (1869), 36.

33. "Of Fortune, etc.," in *Belvedere, or the Garden of the Muses* (1600), ed. Spenser Society (1875), p. 153.

34. *The Parliament of Foules*, 242–3. See Chew, *The Virtues Reconciled*, p. 151, note 58.

35. [John Hall], *Emblems with elegant Figures* (1658), Bk. II, p. 104. Here the hourglass is winged and is surmounted by a skull.

36. See, for example, Heemskerk's "Triumph of Patience," reproduced in Van Marle, *Iconographie*, *2*, 149.

37. As in David's *Veridicus Christianus*, no. 60.

38. Reproduced in Pauli, *Beham*, no. 141.

39. William Cowper, Eighteenth Treatise, in *Workes* (2nd ed., 1629), p. 713.

40. Plate opposite sig. A4ᵛ. Here Patience has a group of pupils, each with an emblem: arrows, chain, cudgel, whip, the coarse straw of a prison cell, etc.

41. Van Bastelaer, *Les Estampes de Peter Brueghel*, pl. 124.

42. Johann Cogler, *Similitudines* (Wittenberg, 1561), fol. 24ʳ.

43. *Delle Imprese*, Bk. III, fol. 45ʳ.

44. A similar but simpler example of such balanced abstractions are the

bas–reliefs on the Thomas Sutton monument (1615) by Nicholas Stone in the Chapel of the Charterhouse. See W. L. Spiers, "The Note–book and Account Book of Nicholas Stone," Walpole Society, *1* (1918–1919), pl. 3. The reliefs are of Time and a Child blowing bubbles. Spiers interprets them as Youth and Old Age but they are obviously Time and Vanity.

45. The series is described in Kerrick's Heemskerk *Catalogue*, pp. 77 f.

46. Van Havre, *Marques typographiques*, p. 218.

47. In the English version of Henri Drexelius, *The School of Patience* (1640), opposite sig. A4ᵛ. On the title page of this work she stands by a column on which is perched a cock, emblem of watching and waiting for the dawn.

48. Van Bastelaer, *Les Estampes de Peter Brueghel*, no. 124. The attribution to Brueghel is erroneous.

49. Eighteenth Treatise, "In Praise of Patience," in *Workes*, p. 713.

50. Compare the curious punning emblem of Faith: a swan, with the motto: "[In] hoc cygno vinceo." See, e.g. [Henry Hawkins], *Partheneia Sacra, or the Mysterious and Delicious Garden of the Sacred Parthenes . . . By H. A.* [sic]. (Rouen? 1633), p. 271.

2. SEVERAL SERIES OF TRIUMPHANT VIRTUES

1. John Daye's son Richard (the "R.D." of the preliminary address "To the Christian Reader") may have been responsible for the expansions, omissions, and alterations which made the volume of 1578 essentially a new work. For the curious subsequent history of the cuts of four of the Virtues and for a study of the other designs in both books see my article in *Huntington Library Quarterly*, *8* (1945), pp. 293–305. The series of the Virtues occurs twice: sigs. 41ʳ–51ᵛ and 61ᵛ–72ʳ. It should be noted that a few of the personifications are not, strictly speaking, Virtues but the consequences of virtuous living. In my descriptions words placed within quotation marks are taken from the labels on the cuts.

2. For example, the Seven Virtues in *Horae*, Pigouchet for Simon Vostre, 1502, in most cases anticipate the concepts of the same seven in the English *Christian Prayers*.

3. Robert Withington, *English Pageantry*, *1* (1924), 169.

4. In a belated encomium on Henry VIII, a curious medley of verse and prose, Ulpian Fulwell tells how at the Battle of Bosworth Lady Concord descended from heaven to unite the Houses of York and Lancaster. She crowns Henry Tudor. See *The Flower of Fame. Containing the bright Renowne, and most fortunate raigne of King Henry the VIII* (1575), sig. Dʳ.

5. Sigs. K.iʳ–T.iiiᵛ.

6. The block from which Bateman's illustration was printed had a curious history; far down in the seventeenth century it was used, much worn and debased, to illustrate a popular love ballad. See "The Mariner's Misfortune" (ca. 1684), *Bagford Ballads*, ed. Ebsworth, *1*, 250.

7. The identification is based, needless to say, on John 14:6. In the pre-

liminary note on "The Names and Attyre of the Parsonages in Thissame Playe" in Henry Niklaes' *Enterlude of Myndes* (ca. 1575), "The Treuth" is a man "like an High–Priest or Christ."

8. [Richard Niccols], in *The Furies with Vertues Encomium or The Image of Honour. In two Bookes of Epigrammes Satyricall and Encomiasticke. By R. N.* (1614). With a fresh title page "Vertues Encomium" begins at sig. D4ʳ. The epigrams associating each part of the lady's body with a Virtue are deplorably crude and far fetched.

3. THE THREE CHRISTIAN VIRTUES

1. From the account of the Seven Virtues in this section and the following section I have omitted the Virtues who opposed the Sins in the German and Dutch treatises on the Sins (1474 and 1490). Like the Sins they ride on animals and have other animals on their helmets, shields, and banners. All these, however, are either obviously appropriate or else unintelligible. For reproductions see Schramm, *Der Bilderschmuck der Frühdrucke, 3*, nos. 213–226 and *12*, nos. 377–391 (alternate numbers). They appear also in Pierpont Morgan MS. 782. In all three series the Virtues are not precisely the "orthodox" Seven.

2. Thomas Adams, *The Three Divine Sisters* (1616), p. 2.

3. For example, in the so–called tarots of Mantegna; reproduced in Hind, *Early Italian Engraving*, E.I.40, a and b. See also Paul Kristeller, *Die Tarocchi. Zwei Italienische Kupperstichfolgen aus dem XV. Jahrhundert* (Berlin, 1910), no. 40.

4. Feuillerat, *Edward VI and Mary*, p. 245.

5. Van Bastelaer, *Les Estampes de Peter Brueghel*, no. 132.

6. Johann Cogler, *Similitudines* (Wittenberg, 1561), fol. 14ʳ. In this cut Faith holds a crucifix in her right hand, a chalice in her left, and is treading on a serpent.

7. Alain Chartier, *L'Esperance ou la consolation des trois virtues*, Pierpont Morgan MS. 438.

8. She is thus shown in Simon Vostre's *Horae* where she also holds the Tables of the Law.

9. Huntington Library "Kitto" Bible, *14*, 2480.

10. For example, Michel Baudier, *Histoire generale de la religion des Turcs* (1625), reproduced in Chew, *The Crescent and the Rose*, facing p. 446. The title page of Sir Richard Barckley's *The Felicitie of Man* (1598) is similar. See S. C. Chew, "Islam and England during the Renaissance," *The Moslem World*, October, 1941, pp. 15–16.

11. *Emblematum Tyrocinia* (Strassburg, 1581), unnumbered emblem at the end of the book.

12. Gregory Kleppis, *Emblemata Varia* (1624), no. 40. Here she has also a cross and a chalice.

13. *Emblems with elegant Figures* (1658), Bk. II, p. 80.

14. Sebastian de Covarrubias, in *Emblemas Morales* (Madrid, 1610), first "Century," no. 27.

15. *Two Gentlemen of Verona*, IV.4.1–65.

16. John Ruskin, *The Stones of Venice*, in *Works*, Library Edition, *10*, 339–40.

17. Reproduced in Colvin, *Early Engraving and Engravers*, p. 17, fig. 7. The date, some time in the fifteen–sixties, is uncertain, for in the unique surviving impression the last digit in the date "156–" has been torn off.

18. Van Bastelaer, *Les Estampes de Peter Brueghel*, no. 133.

19. Reproduced in Mâle, *L'Art religieux*, *3*, 319, fig. 172. Hope's hand rests on a spade in a French design, but in Jan David's *Veridicus Christianus*, no. 16, it is Charity who holds a spade.

20. Alciati's emblem of Hope is a storm tossed ship; *Emblematum Liber* (ed. 1531), sig. B6ᵛ. For the Ship of Hope see also the *impresa* designed by Ruscelli which is referred to in Chapter 3.

21. Francois Courboin, in *Histoire illustrée de la Gravure en France*, *1* (Paris, 1923), no. 234.

22. *The Gentleman's Exercise* (1612), p. 106.

23. Cut on the title page of Giovanni Andrea dell' Angvillara, *Edippo Tragedia* (Venice, 1565).

24. The phoenix is at the feet of Mantegna's Hope. See Hind, *Early Italian Engraving*, E.I.39, a and b; Kristeller, *Die Tarocchi*, no. 39.

25. Corrozet, *Hecatomgraphie* (1543), sigs. Iiᵛ–Iiiʳ.

26. Ibid., sig. Gviiiᵛ–Hʳ.

27. *Two Gentlemen of Verona*, III.1.246.

28. In the fresco of "The Marriage of Poverty" at Assisi Charity holds a heart. Love of God holds a heart in *A Booke of Christian Prayers*, sigs. 41ᵛ and 62ʳ, and in general a heart, though appropriate to Charity, is associated with Love in a wider sense. Giotto's Charity in the Arena holds a dish of loaves. Jan David's Charity, in *Veridicus Christianus*, no. 16, has a burning heart on her head and holds a key and a spade.

29. As in the design attributed to Mantegna, Hind, *Early Italian Engraving*, no. 38, a and b; Kristeller, *Die Tarocchi*, no. 38. The Largesse, of which the original mural was destroyed long ago, in the "Painted Chamber" of Westminster Palace, stood in triumph upon Avarice and poured money into his mouth from a large purse. See *The Virtues Reconciled*, p. 146, note 2.

30. She wears this garment in a sixteenth–century French manuscript of Chartier, *L'Esperance*, Pierpont Morgan MS. 438. I am not sure, however, that the boxes are for alms; they may contain a balm or healing ointment.

31. As in the Mantegna design. In the pseudo–Brueghel print she has a pelican on her head; see Van Bastelaer, *Les Estampes de Peter Brueghel*, no. 134.

32. *The Faerie Queene*, I, 10, 31.

33. A fine example may be seen in Heinrich Vogtherr the Younger's "The Death of the Righteous and the Death of the Unrighteous," where in the upper section are six medallions of the Works. In two of the scenes Christ appears with a halo. Goltzius did a large copperplate: Christ in the center with six vignettes of the Works around him. See "Kitto" Bible, *58*, 10568. On the authority of Christ's words the beneficiary of any of the

Works of Mercy is often identified with Him. There is nothing in Tudor–Stuart literature precisely corresponding to the series of paintings in the Vatican Gallery where each recipient of charity wears a halo in token that he is Christ. See further Chew, *The Virtues Reconciled*, pp. 102–3.

34. *The Song of Songs* (1621), pp. 162–163, stanzas 18–31.

35. Hind, *Early Italian Engraving*, *1*, B.III.8.2. Without personifications there are here seven episodes in a street. In the foreground is Savonarola preaching.

36. With the intention to edify and encourage, the Works of Mercy were frequently depicted on the walls of English churches; upwards of a dozen examples of such murals are extant. Sometimes they are displayed in opposition to the Seven Deadly Sins (where they do not properly belong). They may be arranged in the pattern of a wheel. In one series, now destroyed, there was inscribed over them the words, "For Jesu's Sake." In Wickhampton Church, Norfolk, a woman (Mercy or perhaps Dorcas) performs each Work, and here in the Visitation of Prisoners the recipient of the charitable act is sitting in the stocks. For details see the authorities cited in Chew, *The Virtues Reconciled*, p. 147, notes 12 and 13.

37. *The Faerie Queene*, I, 10, 36–43.

38. The Order of Trinitarians had been engaged in the merciful work for centuries; they came to be known as Redemptionists. The need to ransom captives from the Moors became most pressing about a quarter of a century after Spenser's death. See Chew, *The Crescent and the Rose*, pp. 368 and 385–386. A treatise by Julius Roscius Hortinus, whose title page is reproduced in Chew, *The Virtues Reconciled*, fig. 15, *Opera Misericordia ad Corpus Pertinentia* (Frankfort, 1596), with engravings by Theodore and Israel de Bry, exemplifies the Works of Mercy with appropriate incidents. The Fourth Work is the Redemption of Captives: "Redime Captivos."

39. Sigs. 52–54 and 72^v–74^v.

40. In the center of this engraving are the Last Judgment, the Resurrection of the Dead, and a hellmouth in which writhes a monster with seven heads. In medieval English murals the Works of Mercy were sometimes similarly associated (as the Gospel text warranted) with these eschatological subjects, for the "accursed" who have not performed the Works are doomed to everlasting fire.

41. I know this series only from a set in the "Kitto" Bible, *36*, 6786.

4. THE FOUR CARDINAL OR STOIC VIRTUES

1. Sig. Eii^v–Eiii^v.

2. This is a "lamentable complaint" in the manner of *The Mirrour for Magistrates*. At sig. Hiii^r there is a cut of Death snatching off King James' crown.

3. See photograph in K. A. Esdaile, *English Monumental Sculpture* (1927), op. p. 26.

4. Spiers, "The Note–book and Account Book of Nicholas Stone," *Walpole Society*, *1*, pls. 2 and 37^a.

5. In *Panacea: or Select Aphorismes Divine and Morall* (1630), sig. Ci^r f.

6. "Devyse of a desguysing," 281 f.; in *Minor Poems*, 2, 682 f.

7. Dedication to *The First parte of the Mirrour for Magistrates* (1574), sig. iiij; *Parts added to The Mirror for Magistrates*, ed. L. B. Campbell (Cambridge, 1946), pp. 32–33.

8. The signature on the recto of the first leaf is Aiii, a proof that not much has been lost before the point at which the fragment begins.

9. *Minerva Britanna*, no. 93.

10. A beautiful fifteenth–century example of Temperance is reproduced in Count Emiliano di Parravicino, "Three Packs of Italian Tarocco Cards," *Burlington Magazine*, 3 (1903), 237 f.

11. Hind, *Early Italian Engraving*, E.I.34, a and b; Kristeller, *Die Tarocchi*, no. 34.

12. Van Bastelaer, *Les Estampes de Peter Brueghel*, no. 138.

13. Reproduced in Mâle, *L'Art religieux*, 3, 313, fig. 168.

14. In *The Myrrour of good maners* (ca. 1520), introductory commendatory stanzas.

15. *Wits Theater of the little World* (1599), fol. 24^r f.

16. "Kitto" Bible, 24, 4510.

17. In the lost Edwardian interlude Wisdom was "a woman with to faces and in eache hand a glas." See Feuillerat, *Edward VI and Mary*, p. 245.

18. In Francesco de Alegri, *Tractato della Prudentia & Justitia* (Venice, 1508) Prudence has three faces. Reproduced in Prince D'Essling, *Livres à figures venetiens*, 4, 167. Mâle, 3, 321, mentions three examples.

19. Aneau, ΑΛΕΚΤΩΡ. *The Cock*, p. 167.

20. "Devyse of a desguysing," 139 f.; in *Minor Poems*, 2, 682 f.

21. For example, in Wither's *Emblemes*, Bk. II, no. 47. Prudence with the serpent was the device of William Jaggard. See, for example, the title page of John Swynnerton, *A Christian Love–Letter* (1606). Compare S. W. Roberts, *Printers' Marks*, pp. 81, 87, 88.

22. Gabriele Simeone, *Le Sententiose Imprese et Dialogo* (Lyons, 1540), p. 17.

23. In an early Italian niello print Prudence sits upon a dragon. Reproduced in A. M. Hind, *Nielli, Chiefly Italian of the Fifteenth Century . . . in the British Museum* (1936), no. 187.

24. Reproduced in Mâle, *L'Art religieux*, 3, 315, fig. 170. The discarded sack of coins which in this miniature lies at the feet of Prudence, who apparently cares not for mundane possessions, is by no means a usual attribute of this calculating Virtue.

25. Van Bastelaer, *Les Estampes de Peter Brueghel*, no. 136.

26. *Symbolicarum Quaestionum . . . Libri Quinque* (Bonn, 1574), Bk. IV, no. 108.

27. F. Herbet, "Catalogue de l'Œuvre de L.D.," *Les Graveurs de l'Ecole de Fontainebleau*, 1 (1896), no. 65.

28. Linche, *The Fountaine of Ancient Fiction*, sig. kiii^r.

29. *The Faerie Queene*, V, 1, 9. But later, V, 2, 49, a foolish giant em-

ployed other scales to distribute worldly goods not in proportion to merit and desert but with absolute equality. His were not the "righteous ballance" of Justice.

30. *The Example of Vertu* was written ca. 1494 though not published till 1530. The trial is narrated in chapters 6 and 7, and there the title page woodcut is repeated.

31. *The Myrrour of good manners*, sig. Diii^r.

32. [John Heath], "On Justice Ballance," *The House of Correction, or Certayne Satyricall Epigrams. Written by I. H. Gent.* (1619), sig. C6^v.

33. Aneau, ΑΛΕΚΤΩΡ, p. 166. This statue is made of gold, an incorruptible metal yet soft and pliable and therefore a symbolic indication that Justice should lean towards Mercy.

34. In the prose version, Wynkyn de Worde, 1509, fol. 99^v.

35. Saavedra Faxardo, *Idea Principio Christiano Politici Centum Symbolis Expressa* (Brussels, 1649), nos. 51 and 53. I have not seen the Spanish original of this work. Reduced and debased copies of the emblems are in the English version of Faxardo, *The Royal Politician*, translated by Sir James Astry (1700).

36. Reproduced in E. M. Tenison, *Elizabethan England*, *3* (1933), frontispiece, and less satisfactorily in *Connoisseur*, *118* (1944), 73, fig. 6.

37. *Emblemes*, Bk. III, no. 15.

38. This is the fine device of the Antwerp printer Guislain Janssens. The cock stands on a skull and holds an hourglass; the motto is "Vigilate quia nescitis diem neque horem." See Van Havre, *Marques typographiques*, *1*, 225–6. S. W. Roberts, *Printers' Marks*, p. 208. In the *Minerva Britanna* (no. 139) Peacham has the cock of Vigilance perched on a beacon.

39. [Nicholas Ling], *Politeuphuia: Wits Commonwealth* (1596), fol. 81^r.

40. The earliest (1543) visual renderings of personified abstractions in engravings on metal published in England are those on this title page. Reproduced in Colvin, *Early Engraving and Engravers*, pl. 1. The design reappears in the English translation of Vesalius (1553) and, somewhat altered, in the second edition of the translation (1559).

41. Dekker, *The Magnificent Entertainment*, in *Dramatic Works*, *1*, 317.

42. Quarles, *Emblemes*, Bk. III, no. 10.

43. Reproduced in Chew, *The Virtues Reconciled*, fig. 14. It is possible, but I do not think it likely, that the pillow on which rest the crown and scepter which a petitioner offers to Justice, may represent the softening of Justice. Beyond doubt the bed on which Justice sits in a French miniature indicates that merciful considerations should soften her. See Mâle, *L'Art religieux*, *3*, 314, fig. 169.

44. *Natures Embassie: or the Wild–Man's Measures: Danced by Twelve Satyres* (1621), p. 135.

45. *Susanna: or, the Arraignment of the Two Unjust Elders* (1622), one of Aylett's "sacred epics" in the manner of *A Learned Summary. . . . Lord of Bartas* (1621).

46. Iohannes Pierus Valerianus, *Hieroglyphica sive de Sacris Ægyptiorum* (ed. Lyons, 1552), p. 634.

47. Faxardo, *Idea*, no. 53.

48. The converse of this is seen when the scales of Justice are assigned to Death as a symbol of his impartiality. A crown and a scepter are shown to be of equal weight with a rake, a pitchfork, and an axe. See La Perriere, *La Morosophie* (1553), no. 99.

49. The third pageant in Elkanah Settle, *Glory's Resurrection, being the Triumphs of London Revived* (1698), p. 4. An accompanying engraving does not correspond to the description in the text.

50. *Veridicus Christianus*, pl. 23.

51. Petrus Costalius (Pierre Cousteau), *Pegma cum narrationibus philosophicis* (Lyons, 1555), sig. Aiv^r, and the French version, *Le Pegme de Pierre Cousteau* (Lyons, 1560), p. 7.

52. Van Havre, *Marques typographiques*, p. 86.

53. *The Song of Songs* (1621), pp. 132–133.

54. Giotto's Fortitude in the Arena holds a club. She holds a mace in the engraving attributed to Mantegna; Hind and Kristeller, both no. 34. So also in "Spiritus Fortitudinis" discussed below. An early sixteenth–century black–letter broadside called *The Cronycle of all the Kynges: that have Reygned in Englande* (n.d.) has crude cuts of the Seven Virtues. Only Fortitude has an unusual attribute: a block of wood with an axe in it.

55. Mathias Holzwart, *Emblematum Tyrocinia* (Strassburg, 1581), unnumbered emblem at end.

56. So, for example, in the "Mantegna" engraving and in the "Spiritus Fortitudinis."

57. Huntington Library "Kitto" Bible, *24*, 4265.

58. For a convenient account of the Nine Orders with the sources, functions, and iconography see G. M^cN. Rushforth, *Medieval Christian Imagery as illustrated by the painted Windows of Great Malvern Priory Church* (Oxford, 1936), p. 204.

59. "Kitto" Bible, *23*, 4377.

60. *Veridicus Christianus*, pl. 26.

5. THE PAULINE ARMOR

1. See G. R. Owst, *Literature and Pulpit in Medieval England* (Cambridge, England, 1933), p. 67.

2. In *Minor Poems*, *2*, 630 f.

3. *Reson and Sensuallyte*, 1187–1203. The allegorical interpretation of these three pieces of armor are additions by Lydgate to his French source.

4. Norwich play of *The Temptation of Man in Paradise*, 137 f.; *Non-Cyclical Miracles Plays*, EETS, p. 18.

5. On the influence of Erasmus upon Dürer's "Knight, Death, and Devil" see Panofsky, *Albrecht Dürer*, *1*, 152. An interesting early German visualization of the theme of the Christian Knight is found in *Der füsspfadt tzu der ewigen seligkeyt* (Heidelberg, 1494). On the title page a knight is

shown kneeling before a wayside crucifix. There follow, with illustrations, interpretations of his horse, saddle, bit, and bridle, and each piece of his armor. This series is reproduced in Schramm, *Der Bilderschmuck der Frühdrucke, 19,* nos. 589–614. For other versions of the Christian Knight and his enemies see R. Munther, *Die Deutsche Buchillustration der Gothik und Renaissance, 2* (Munich and Leipzig, 1884), pl. 169; G. Pauli, *Inkunabeln der Deutsche, und Niederlandischen Radierung* (Berlin, 1908), pl. 18.

6. *The assaute and conquest of heven translated out of frenche into englische* (1529), sigs. Aiv^v–Biii^v. I have not seen the French original.

7. Sig. Fiij^r.

8. In *Works* (1560–64), 2 (Cambridge University Press, 1843–44), fol. 140 f.

9. *Typus Totius Orbis Terrarum.* Part of, but not all, the illustration of the Christian Knight is reproduced in Colvin, *Early Engraving and Engravers,* fig. 19.

10. This compartment of the title page is labeled "Defiance to Death" and points to Cowper's eleventh Treatise (pp. 501–578) which has the same title. The treatise, however, has little bearing upon the Christian Armor theme and no allegory beyond the expansion of the metaphor of the body as the dwelling–place of the soul.

11. "Wiseman" is a pseudonym, possibly allegorical. The author, according to the STC, was William Fitch, according to the Huntington Library catalogue, Benedict Canfield.

12. *Mortalities Meditation: or A Description of Sinne,* stanzas 111–113, sig. D3^r.

13. *The Song of Songs* (1621), p. 177. Ephesians 6:15 seems here to be interpreted in the light of Romans 12:1: "Let us run with patience the race that is set before us."

14. *The Penitent Publican* (1610), sig. E4^v.

Chapter 6. The Path of Life

1. "ONE MAN IN HIS TIME PLAYS MANY PARTS"—*As You Like It*

1. This chapter is a revised and much expanded form of my article "This Strange Eventful History" in *Joseph Quincy Adams Memorial Studies* (Washington, D. C., The Folger Shakespeare Library, 1948), pp. 157–182.

2. *Comic Characters in Shakespeare* (1946), pp. 50–1.

3. See the notes on the passage in *As You Like It,* especially in the Halliwell–Phillipps, *New Variorum,* Arden, and Kittredge editions. Important older studies are J. W. Jones, "Observations on the Origin of the Division of Man's Life into Stages," *Archaeologia, 35* (1853), 167–189, and J. G. Waller, "Christian Iconography and Legendary Art; The Wheel of Human Life or the Seven Ages," *Gentleman's Magazine, 39* (1853), 494–502. Some years ago the quest of Shakespeare's "source" was renewed.

See J. W. Draper, "Jaques' 'Seven Ages' and Bartholomeus Anglicus," *M.L.N.*, *54* (1939), 273–6; A. H. Gilbert, "Jacques' 'Seven Ages' and Censorius," ibid., *55* (1940), 103–5; D. C. Allen, "Jaques' 'Seven Ages' and Pedro Mexia," ibid., *56* (1941), 601–3; J. W. Bennett, "Jaques' Seven Ages," *Shakespeare Association Bulletin*, *18* (1943), 168–174. In my opinion all four discussions fail to carry conviction.

4. Many authorities are cited in Pedro Mexia (Mejia), *Silva de varia leccion* (Seville, 1542) of which an English version of parts, from the French version by Claude Gruget (1552), was made by Thomas Fortescue, entitled *The Foreste or Collection of Histories, no lesse profitable, then pleasant and necessarie* (1571; reprinted, 1576). Of this Bk. I, chapter 17 is on "The distinction of the Age of Man, according to the opinion of most Astrologians." It includes the opinions of many other writers besides "astrologians." The material reappears in the great miscellany of erudition which was made for William Jaggard, probably by Thomas Milles, from Mexia and other Continental authors, and published as *The Treasurie of Auncient and Moderne Times* (1613). See Bk. IV, chapter 15, pp. 336–9: "The Ages of Man severally distinguished, according the [sic] enstructions of Astrologers." From resemblances between part of Mexia's discussion and Jaques' speech Professor Allen argued that Shakespeare must have known either the French version of Mexia or else have seen Milles' translation in manuscript. Neither hypothesis is necessary, for two editions of Fortescue's version were accessible—if Shakespeare relied upon Mexia at all, which I doubt.

5. In the anonymous fourteenth-century dream poem *The Parlement of the Three Ages* (ed. Israel Gollancz, 1915) Youth, Middle Age, and Old Age expound their several philosophies of life. For an account of this piece see Albert C. Baugh in *A Literary History of England* (1948), p. 241. The fifteenth-century Scottish poem *Ratis Raving*, ed. R. Girvan, STS, Third Series, *11* (1939), possibly by a certain David Rate, contains a long account of the Seven Ages (1104–1734) with much moralizing detail.

6. Following Saint Augustine and Bede and in line with the custom of paralleling the macrocosm and the microcosm, writers frequently bring together the two sequences of the Ages of the World and the Ages of the Life of Man. In accordance with the belief that the Seventh Age of the World will be ushered in at the Last Judgment, the *Promptorium Parvulorum* (ca. 1440), ed. Albert Way, Camden Society, Old Series no. 25 (1863–65), 7, assigns only six Ages to the transitory life of man because, as in the sequence of world history, "Septem erit in resurrectione finali." This is echoed by Swan in his *Speculum Mundi* (1635), pp. 15–18, where, following Du Bartas, he asserts: "The seventh age shall begin at the resurrection."

7. The whole of life is passed in swift review in the reliefs on the right-hand doorpost of the West Portal of the Baptistry in Parma (thirteenth century). These are based upon Saint Augustine's exposition of the parable of the Laborers in the Vineyard (Matthew 20) in terms of the Six Periods of World History and Six Ages of Human Life. The parable mentions the early morning, the third hour, the sixth, the ninth, and the

eleventh. The Vine meanders up the doorpost. The several episodes are not well differentiated, but inscriptions make identification possible. At the bottom one reads "Prima etas Seculi," corresponding to Infancy. Then come "Hora Tercia: Puericia"; "Hora Sexta: Adulescentia"; "Hora Nona: Iuventus"; and then Gravitas and Senectus share the eleventh hour between them. At the top the Master of the Vineyard, called "Pater Familias," is paying the laborers their wages.

8. In the main foyer of the hotel is a large rug designed by the French artist Louis Rigel. Its central medallion, eighteen feet in diameter, shows six Ages: the newborn babe with joyful parents and relatives; youth and friendship; the defeats and disasters in the struggle for life; domestic felicity and mature serenity; old age; and death. Between these groups are spaced smaller figures symbolizing the emotions appropriate to each Age. It is all rather Burne–Jonesian in style and does not conform closely to the iconographic tradition. Somewhat inexplicably, the design of the rug is repeated in marble mosaic tesserae (1939) in the floor of the Park Avenue foyer of the hotel. About 148,000 pieces of marble in 181 different shades are in this mosaic. Another twentieth–century example is the stained glass window of the reading room in the Folger Shakespeare Library. (This Library possesses a large collection of prints illustrating Jaques' speech.) Even an advertiser has been attracted by the theme. Charles Pfizer and Co., Inc. have circulated a folder urging the prescription of "Terramycin in the treatment of infectious Disease throughout the Seven Ages of Man." This displays two series of the Ages, one in Elizabethan costume, with quotations from Jaques, and one in modern dress. The brochure is not so offensive as those who have not seen it would imagine. Madison Avenue has often committed worse breaches of decorum! Miss Carol Biba kindly brought this item to my attention.

9. Reproduced in color in *Shakespeare in Pictorial Art* (Special Spring Number of *The Studio*, 1916). The painting is in the Victoria and Albert Museum. See also *Shakespeare's Seven Ages of Man Illustrated by Original Designs on Wood by William Mulready* (1848).

2. THE BRIDGE, THE STAIRWAY, AND THE CIRCLE AS SYMBOLS OF THE PATH

1. Reproduced in W. L. Schreiber, *Handbuch*, *4*, no. 1861 (labeled "Spiegel der vernuft") and no. 1861a (labeled "Speculum racionis"). There are subsidiary symbols such as an admonitory clock and the Tables of the Law. Beneath the bridge are three corpses—the spiritually dead.

2. Lines 276, 419, 1578, and 2483 f.

3. Reproduced in Van Marle, *Iconographie*, *2*, 192, fig. 217. There are similar windows in the cathedral of Basle and in the church of St. Stephen at Beauvais.

4. Reproduced, ibid., *2*, 164, fig. 189. See also *Mitteilungen der Gesellschaft für Vervielfaltigende Kunst* (1909), p. 8, no. 63.

5. The same idea appears in a woodcut by Hans Glaser (Nuremberg, ca. 1540–60) where Old Age moves feebly along in a "walker" pushed by a naked child. To the front of the machine are attached an hourglass

and a skull. Reproduced in Emil Reicke, *Der Gelehrte in der deutschen Vergängenheit* (Jena, 1924), fig. 50. Variations are played upon the motif of the infant's aspiring hand which we observe in Breu's print. In Whitney's *A Choice of Emblemes* (1586), p. 152, a man has a winged right hand and a left hand tied to a weight, representing, as Whitney phrases it, "Wish and Will" against "Want and Woe." Compare Mathias Holzwart, *Emblematum Tyrocinia: sive Picta Poesis latino–germanica* (Strassburg, 1581), no. 47. The theme occurs twice in a woodcut by Tobias Stimmer in Nicolaus Reusner, *Aureolorum Emblematum Liber* (Strassburg, 1587). No. 74: A man has both arms winged and aspiring but his ankles are bound to a money–bag. The motto is "Aut Deo, aut Mundo." No. 103: The same design with the motto "In Philoplutum." In Father Herman Hugo's *Pia Desideria* (Antwerp, 1624), Bk. III, no. 39, Psyche (the Soul) is chained by the heel to the world (a sphere) but lifts her arms in aspiration. In Quarles' *Emblemes*, Bk. II, no. 4, Heavenly Love has his arm raised while Earthly Love is bound by her ankle. See also Jean Baudoin, *Recueil d'Emblemes Divers*, (Paris, 1638), Part I, 610.

6. The convention of such animals was never firmly established, and their appropriateness is not always evident. In different versions we find them shifted about; the cat, for example, is sometimes emblematic of childhood because it likes to play and sometimes of old age because it likes to doze by the fire. Occasionally there is an effort to attach to an Age the animal emblematizing the Deadly Sin particularly perilous at that time of life: Childhood—Gluttony—pig; Youth—Lechery—goat; and so forth. But this scheme was necessarily limited to the Seven Ages since there were Seven Deadly Sins. Moreover confusion was inevitable because for one or another Age an animal might be selected to represent a characteristic that was not sinful.

7. Reproduced in A. Bertarelli, *L'Imagerie populaire italienne* (Paris, 1929), p. 35.

8. Compare (though not in a sequence of the Ages) an engraving in Jacob Cats, *Alle de Werken*, 2 (Amsterdam, 1726), 507, where Death reaches an hourglass across the desk of an aged scholar who continues his studies though one of his feet is in a grave that yawns by his side.

9. Reproduced in Bertarelli, p. 33 and in Van Marle, *Iconographie*, 2, p. 165, fig. 190.

10. "Man's Gradation," in *Two Bookes of Epigrammes and Epitaphs* (1639), Bk. I, no. 201.

11. Text and cut are reproduced in Halliwell–Phillipps' edition of *As You Like It*, in Shakespeare's *Works*, 6, 155.

12. I know this only from an impression in the Huntington Library extra–illustrated "Kitto" Bible, *1*, fol. 167ʳ. So far as I know, it has not been reproduced.

13. For a late eighteenth–century example, Italian but with texts in Spanish (for exportation), see Bertarelli, *L'Imagerie populaire*, p. 71.

14. This is by l'Humble Georgin and was published at Lille, ca. 1820. It is reproduced in Lucien Descaves, *L'Humble Georgin, Imagier d'Epinal* (Paris, 1932), following p. 18. See also Louis Duchartre and René Saulnier,

L'Imagerie populaire (Paris, 1925), p. ii. For another French example of about the same period see Meyer Schapiro, "Courbet and Popular Imagery," *Journal of the Warburg and Courtauld Institutes*, 4 (1940), p. 167 and pl. 39d.

15. For these versions see H. T. Peters, *Print–makers to the American People*, *1* (Garden City, New York, 1929–31), nos. 1080 and 1081. The same artists did a set of the "Four Seasons of Life": Childhood, the Season of Joy; Youth, the Season of Love; Middle Age, the Season of Strength; Old Age, the Season of Rest. See ibid., nos. 1076–1079. I am indebted to Mr. Franklin M. Biebel of the Frick Collection for calling my attention to Currier and Ives.

16. I do not know whether this has been reproduced. There is an impression in the Metropolitan Museum of Art.

17. British Museum, Arundel MS 83. Reproduced by J. W. Jones, in *Archaeologia*, *35* (1853) op. p. 177, and in Shakespeare, *Works*, ed. Halliwell–Phillipps, *5*, op. p. 154. Both reproductions are from tracings of the original.

18. Each of the ten tondi has a Latin inscription. That of the infant, for example, is: "Mitis sum et humilis, lacte vivo puro" and that of the tomb: "Versus sum in cinerem, vita me decrepit." Not all the inscriptions seem obviously appropriate.

19. Reproduced in E. I. Fripp, *Shakespeare; Man and Artist*, *2* (1938), op. p. 533, and elsewhere.

20. In these cases we have a panorama not of life but of the preparation for maturity. The earlier part of Hawes' poem *The Pastime of Pleasure* follows loosely this pattern. This preliminary adventure is sometimes symbolized as the steps or several storeys of the Tower of Learning—the *Graduus ad Parnassum*. See the well known woodcut in Gregorius Reisch, *Margarita Philosophica* (Freiburg, 1503), fol. 3^r, which has been often reproduced. The progress may even be limited to the first steps upon that ascent, as in an engraving of the "Tower of Grammar" by Heinrich Vogtherr (1548), where the child climbs steps labeled "alphabet," "syllabary," and so forth, and so ascends a tower whose storeys are named for the parts of speech. But the progress may be from childhood to early manhood. Thus, in the thirteenth–century sculptures on the external face of the first architrave of the Porta Principale of San Marco in Venice we observe the contrast between "Savage Education" and "Gentle Education." In the first sequence the woman at the bottom sitting upon a lion symbolizes untamed nature. Above her, children rob a bird's nest and quarrel with one another. Then a boy shoots with a bow and arrow. Then a grown man attacks a lion with a sword. Savage Education is complete. On the other side Gentle Breeding is symbolized by a boy sitting upon an ox, a domesticated animal. Above him, a child is receiving instruction from a patient tutor. Then a bearded father sends his son forth into the world. Then we see him setting out "on his own." Two episodes in the next roundel illustrate honest business and dishonest, furtive transactions. The final scene is a warning of the perils of life from which even a proper education cannot protect you: our hero is being attacked by an evil–doer

who creeps up upon him from behind. The contrast thus culminates: the savage man attacks a beast; the gentle man is attacked by a beastly savage. See Camillo Boito et al., *Basilica di San Marco in Venezia*, 6, pls. 128 and 128a,b,c. See also the English translation by F. H. Rosenberg (1889) of Part III of this work, pp. 522–525.

21. The only known example is in the British Museum. It was found by Panizzi pasted inside the cover of an old book. It is reproduced by Halliwell–Phillipps, edition of Shakespeare, 6, op. p. 126, and in Schreiber, *Handbuch*, no. 1883a. On the angel's shield is the Pythagorean Y, emblematic of the Choice of the Paths. Halliwell–Phillipps' note still possesses some value.

22. The original is in the Fitzwilliam Museum. It is reproduced in *The Illustrated London News*, May 28, 1932. The artist, William de Brailes, was identified by Sir Sidney Cockerell.

23. Gaspar is Youth, Balthazar Manhood, Melchior Old Age; Compare the conspicuous contrast in ages in Giorgione's "Three Philosophers" in Vienna.

24. For example, in Pierpont Morgan MS 324 (fifteenth century).

25. Reproduced in S. A. Strong, *Critical Studies* (ed. 1912), op. p. 90, and (in outline) in Salomon Reinach, *Répertoire de peintures*, 4, 626. The hourglass relates this painting to the Fortune–Opportunity–Time complex, and the cushion on which the king sits is perhaps intentionally symbolic of Luxury.

26. So they appear in a mural in Wickhampton Church in Norfolk. See M. R. James, "The Wall Paintings in Wickhampton Church," *Supplement to Blomefield's Norfolk* (1929), pp. 123–142. They may be so represented in a mural in Hurstbourne Tarrant Church in Hampshire, but the condition of the painting makes identification difficult. See W. F. Storck, "Aspects of Death in English Art and Poetry," *Burlington Magazine*, 21 (1912), 249–256, no. 25, and 314–319, pl. I. c. Also ibid., no. 13.

27. Balliol MS 354; published in *Songs, Carols, and Other Miscellaneous Poems*, ed. Roman Dyborski, EETS, Extra Series, 101, 93.

28. *The Sinner's Care*, in *The Bagford Ballads*, ed. Ebsworth, 1, 160. In John Vicars' *The last Trumpet: or, A Six–Fold Christian Dialogue . . . Translated from the elegant Latine Prose of Richard Brathwait Esquire, into English Verse* (1635), p. 9, we read:

> *Death* is the *child hood* of weake *infancie*,
> *Death* is the *lad–age* of our *childe–hoodry*,
> *Death* is the *youth* of our *lad–age* estate,
> *Death* is the *manly–hood* of *youthfull* fate,
> *Death* is the *old–age* of our *man–hood stout*,
> *Death* after *old age* doth *decrepid* flout.
> For *Death* is of *Decrepid–age* the *Death*.

This intolerable lugubriousness means that at any Age of Life Death may be the next stage in the sequence. Brathwaite's original work is *Novissima Tuba* (1632).

3. THE THREE AGES OF MAN

1. *Metropolis Coronata* (1615); reprinted in Nichols, *Progresses . . . of James I*, 3, 114.

2. See G. R. Owst, *Literature and Pulpit in Medieval England* (Cambridge, England, 1933), p. 70. A ship is a useful allegorical commonplace, and we have not only ships of the faithful or saints or the Church Fathers but of the damned and of course *The Ship of Fools*. In the polemical caricatures of the sixteenth century, whether directed against Roman Catholics or Protestants, it often occurs. The theme of the Voyage of Life appears in visual and verbal imagery down the centuries. On the level of sentimental but not displeasing romanticism the American landscape painter Thomas Cole painted this Voyage in four episodes, which, reproduced in steel engravings, were widely popular in the mid–nineteenth century. The babe in a boat issues from the Cave of Birth, accompanied by his guardian angel. The youth, with hands upraised, floats confidently down the stream. Clouds gather when the boat is in mid–stream, and the angel has disappeared. And at length the boat puts out to sea. Of slightly later date is a lithograph entitled "The Voyage of Life." The Four Ages are in a row boat: children in the prow; then young lovers; then husband and wife; and in the stern an aged couple. The masterful rower, a sturdy John–Bullish figure, is the Victorian equivalent—is he not?—of medieval personifications of Religion or Holy Church.

3. Henry Howard, Earl of Surrey, *Poems*, ed. F. M. Padelford (1928), pp. 95–6.

4. See Van Marle, *Iconographie*, 2, 159 and 160, figs. 184 and 185, and for a sequence at Foligno, ibid., 161 and 162, figs. 186 and 187.

5. The border containing this vignette first appeared in William Cunningham's *Cosmographical Glasse* (1559) and reappears in some seventeen books of later date. See R. B. McKerrow and F. S. Ferguson, *Title–page Borders* (1932), No. 99, where the design in question is described as "Time bringing Truth and Antiquity to light"—which is absurd. From H. Billingsley's *Elements of Geometrie* (1570) it is reproduced in E. M. Tenison's *Elizabethan England*, 2 (1933), 75. It is most familiar to us from the title page of Thomas Campion's *Booke of Ayres* (1601).

4. THE FOUR AGES OF MAN

1. Barthelemy Aneau, *Picta Poesis ut Pictura Poesis Erit* (Lyons, 1552), p. 26.

2. Thomas Tusser, *Five hundred pointes of good Husbandrie* (1573); ed. W. Payne and S. J. Herrtage, English Dialect Society (1878), pp. 65–6. This quatrain is transcribed in the Trevelyon commonplace book in the Folger Shakespeare Library, fol. 19^r.

3. *The XV, Bookes of P. Ovidius Naso, entytuled Metamorphosis* (1567), p. 190.

4. *Ovid's Metamorphosis Englished by G. S.* (n.d., 1628), pp. 309–310.

This version is quoted by Walter Colman in his poem *La Dance Machabre* (1633 ?), pp. 38–9.

5. *The Hierarchie of the Blessed Angels* (1635), p. 166. Heywood's discussion contains nothing that is novel.

6. See Pietro Toesca, "Gli Affreschi della Cattedrale di Anagni," *Le Gallerie Nationale Italiane* (1902), 129 f. Toesca traces the system back to classical sources in Galen, Hippocrates, and other writers. He accepted the erroneous attribution to Honorius of Autun of the *Sacramentarium* (*Patrologia Latina*, ed. Jacques Paul Migne, 72 [Paris, 1928–36], 773) whence the frescoes immediately derived. It is really by William of Conches. See Lynn Thorndike, *A History of Magic and Experimental Science*, 2 (1923), 56 f., and H. Licheschütz in *Vorträge der Bibliothek Warburg* (1923–4), p. 119. The relevant words are: "Homo est minor mundus. . . . Ex terra habet carnem, ex aqua sanguinem, ex aere spiritum, ex igne animan. . . . Quatuor tempora anni habet: ver, pueritiam; aestatem, iuventutem; autumnnum, senectutem; hiemen, aetatem decrepitam."

7. The only copy I have seen of this series is in the Library of Congress.

8. See Erwin Panofsky, *Albrecht Dürer*, *1*, 235.

9. The traditional solution is the Three Ages, but see W. B. and E. P., *A Helpe to Discourse or a Miscellany of Merriment* (1619), p. 192. Here it is said that "in his second childhood or decrepit age [Man] creepeth upon all 4 againe."

10. Thomas Tusser, *Five hundred pointes*, ed. Payne and Herrtage, English Dialect Society, p. 138. Trevelyon copied these lines also in his commonplace book, fol. 20ʳ.

11. *Wits Theater of the Little World* (1599), fol. 54ʳ.

12. R.C., *The Examination of mens Wits* (1604), pp. 11–12. This is a translation from Camillo Camilli's Italian version of Huarte's *Examen de ingenios para las ciencias* (1575).

13. *Workes . . . in the Englysh tonge* (1557), sigs. 22ᵛ–4ʳ.

14. C. S. Lewis, *The Allegory of Love* (1934), p. 296, note, remarks upon the resemblance of More's fifth, sixth, seventh, and eighth pageants to the impressive final episodes in Hawes' *Pastime of Pleasure*—the visions of Death, Fame, Time, and Eternity; but he does not note the indebtedness of both More and Hawes to Petrarch. The only parallel I have come across of More's conflation of the Ages and the Triumphs, a parallel very succinct and not very close, is in *Batman uppon Bartholome, his Booke De Proprietatibus Rerum, newly corrected, enlarged and amended* (1582), fol. 142ʳ, where Petrarch's personal story of his love for Laura is broadened and generalized into a history of human life.

15. Designed, engraved and published by Nicolas Guérard. Examples are in the Robert Bonnart collection in the Pierpont Morgan Library. Touched with worldliness, perhaps, but not with cynicism is a set of engravings by Crispin Van de Passe (1596) from designs by Martin de Vos. These have pleasantly jingling titles: "Adolescentia Amori," "Iuventus Labori," "Virilitas Honori," and "Senectus Dolori." In the first, Cupid shoots his arrow at a young couple. In the second, Minerva stands by a man who holds instruments of labor and science. In the third, Fame places

a crown upon the head of a richly dressed man. In the fourth, Time stands behind an old man who is contemplating a picture of the Triumph of Death. There is an extinguished lamp and the sand in an hourglass has run out. See D. Franken, *L'OEuvre gravé des Van de Passe*, nos. 1087–1090.

16. With this Age of Anxiety we may compare an early–eighteenth–century Italian version of the same theme. The man has a long ass's ear (he must patiently listen to his wife's behests). To his other ear is attached a bell (he must keep his appointments). Children clinging to his knee thwart the desire to escape symbolized by a winged foot. Time points to an open grave. Reproduced in Bertarelli, *L'Imagerie populaire*, p. 69. This picture is very likely one of a set of four similiar to the French series, but I have not seen the other three.

5. THE FIVE AGES OF MAN

1. The metaphor (or simile) is often met with. There is J. J. Boissard's *Theatrum Vitae Humanae* (Frankfort, 1596) where the first plate illustrates the theme: "Vita humana est tanquam Theatrum omnium miseriarum." In an epigram "Of Life" Anthony Sherley combines the metaphors of the theatre and the pilgrimage:

> It is a play that sadly doth begin,
> Continues tragicall, concludes in trouble. . . .
> Life is a pilgrimage, that every step
> Treades on a Coffin.

See *Witts New Dyall* (1604), sig. L4ʳ f. Sir William Cornwallys expands the simile, writing: "Zeale and Contemplation have likened the earth to a Theater, human natures to Actors, whose partes delivered, they deliver their stage to the next, witnessing by this, the shortness of mortalitie. Let me lengthen this suite made for the world, and resemble our knowledge to a common Players, who gets his part by hart without the knowledge of his heart, speaking, not understanding." See *Essayes* (1632), no. 44, sig. Bb3ᵛ.

2. In *Works* (ed. 1829), VIII, 704–5.

3. The date is a guess in STC where there is also a guess that the author may be Valentine Leigh.

4. *The pleasaunt playne & pythye Pathewaye* (1550), sigs. C1ʳ and ᵛ.

5. Manzoli's scholarly penname was Marcellus Palingenius Stellatus. The *Zodiacus Vitae*, a poetical inquiry into the *summum bonum* of which the intricacies are involved in astrological speculation and a fantastic allegory, had a great reputation in Protestant countries because of its attacks upon clericalism (it was put upon the Index).

6. *The Zodiake of life* (ed. 1588), Bk. VI, pp. 99–100.

7. *The Foreste* (1571), Fortescue's vision of Mexia's *Silva*, Part II, chap. 17; the pseudo–Platonic *Axiochus* (1592), pp. 46–48; the Milles–Jaggard *Treasurie* (1613), Bk. IV, chap. 15, pp. 336–9; Heywood's *Hierarchie* (1635), pp. 164–5. In an astrological treatise translated from the French a precise bodily temperature is supposedly typical of each of the Five Ages. See William Warde, *The most excellent, profitable and pleasant book of*

the famous Doctor and expert Astrologian Arcandam (ed. 1592), sigs. M2ʳ and ᵛ. Ripa, *Iconologia* (ed. 1630), p. 224, discusses the Five Ages but is chiefly concerned to relate the Four to the Four Elements and the Four Quarters of the Globe.

8. The engraver was Nicolas Guérard; the design seems to me to be not by him. A copy is in the Robert Bonnart collection in the Pierpont Morgan Library.

6. THE SIX AGES OF MAN

1. This is a series of vignettes on the title page of Cats' *Houwelick*, in the collected edition of his works, *Alle de Werken*, *1* (Amsterdam, 1726), 235.

2. *The Treasurie of Auncient and Moderne Times*, Bk. II, chap. 2, pp. 81 f. The first Age of the World is its "Child–hood or Infancy." The third is its "Adolescency or youthful yeares." The fourth is "the lusty and sprightly Age of the world, for in this time infinite occasions happened, wherewith all Histories are plentifully enriched." This fourth Age covers the span between the Captivity in Babylon and the Birth of Christ. No analogy is drawn to human life in the second, fifth, and sixth periods of history.

3. See Franken, *L'OEuvre gravé des Van de Passe*, nos. 1091–1097.

4. The instability of the iconography of the Ages is shown by the fact that in some other sequences cat and monkey accompany Old Age, the cat because it loves to doze by the fire, the monkey because it is foolish and avaricious.

5. *Mortalities Memorandum, with a Dreame Prefixed, imaginarie in manner, reall in matter*, p. 20.

7. THE SEVEN AGES OF MAN

1. I do not embrace within my survey medieval literary treatments of the Seven Ages such as that in the fifteenth–century Scotch poem *Ratis Raving*, possibly by a certain David Rate, ed. R. Girvan, STS, Third Series, *11* (1939), 1104–1754, which has much moralizing detail.

2. E. Panofsky and F. Saxl, *Dürers Kupferstich Melencolia I; Studien der Bibliothek Warburg*, *2* (Berlin and Leipzig, 1923), p. 56.

3. Four of Guariento's Ages and Planets are reproduced in Paolo d'Ancona's *L'Uomo e le sue opere nelle figurazioni italiane del medioevo* (Florence, 1923), pls. 8 and 9. In England vestiges of murals of the Seven Ages are extremely scanty. I know of only three and have seen none of them. One in the nave of Hardham Church, Sussex, is described as being in so bad a state of preservation that the subject is doubtful. See C. E. Keyser, *A List of Buildings . . . having Mural or Other Painted Decorations* (3rd ed., 1883), p. 122, and *Archaeological Journal*, *38*, 82, 95. Another, dating from the early seventeenth century, is in the gate–house of West Stow, Suffolk. See *The East Anglian, Notes and Queries 1* (1864), 7. A third series is among the murals in the tower at Longthorpe, near Peterborough. The Seven Ages, in a half circle above a window, are consider-

ably damaged but recognizable. See *The Illustrated London News*, Nov. 5, 1949, pp. 705–6, and fig. 4.

4. *Lives of the Most Eminent Painters, Sculptors, and Architects*, trans. by G. De C. Vere, 7 (1912–14), 131–137; Everyman's Library ed., 3, 227–231.

5. For a series of the Seven Ages associated with the Seven Liberal Arts see Schreiber, *Handbuch*, no. 1882.

6. *The History of the World* (1614), Bk. I, chap. 2, sect. 5, p. 31.

7. *La Morosophie* (Lyons, 1553), sig. B5ᵛ, nos. 1–7.

8. *Metropolis Coronata* (1615), in Nichols, *Progresses of James I*, 3, 114.

9. 7th ed. (1633), pp. 120–1.

10. "Annex," sig. Giᵛ f.

11. *The Differences of the Ages of Mans Life: Together with the Original Causes, Progresse, and End thereof*, pp. 117–120. Of his three principal divisions Cuffe says that Childhood is hot and moist, Middle Age "hot and dry, or rather moderately moist," and Old Age characterized by the decay of heats and moistures, yet between fifty and sixty–five "not so much but that there remaineth a will and readiness to be doing."

12. *Varieties: or, A Surveigh of Rare and Excellent Matters*, Bk. V, sect. 6, pp. 11–12 (second pagination).

13. The "hieroglyphikes" of the Ages occupy pls. 9–15.

14. *Resolved Meditations written by Ar: Warwicke. Libellus posthumous* (1637).

15. *Lychnocausia sive moralia facum emblamata. Lights Moral Emblems*, no. 57.

16. The flame of a candle is of course an old and obvious image of human life; it is found in many emblem books—not to mention famous lines in *Othello* and *Macbeth*. But both Quarles and Farley may have had especially in mind an emblem in Cats, *Spiegel van den Ouden* (Dordrecht, 1635), Part II, p. 137, where man's life is a candle melting in the sun and guttering in the wind. Among the accompanying quotations of which Cats is always so lavish is Ronsard's: "L'homme n'est rien qu'une vaine fumée."

17. This I have not seen; it is described in Thomas Corser, *Collectanea Anglo–Poetica*, 3 (1861), 203–6.

18. It is classed as spurious in F. M. Harrison's Bunyan *Bibliography* (1932). The "Scriptural Poems" and the prose meditations are also believed to be unauthentic.

19. It is also in the editions of the French translation, Lyons, 1486 and 1491. Reproduced in Claudin, *Histoire de l'imprimerie*, 3, 202 (where it is erroneously called a Four Ages) and in Hind, *An Introduction to a History of Woodcut*, 2, fig. 353.

20. Reproduced in the Kurt Wolff *Catalogue of Incunabula* (Frankfort-a–M., 1926), p. 19.

21. Trevisa's translation dates from 1398. The cut is in Wynkyn de Worde's edition (n.d., 1495 ?), sig M2ʳ.

22. *Batman uppon Bartholome, his Booke De Proprietatibus Rerum* (1582), pl. op. fol. 70ʳ.

23. Reproduced in Claudin, 4, 344, again with an error in the counting.

24. *Delectable demaundes and Pleasant Questions, with their several Answers, in matters of Love: Natural causes, with Morall and politicke devises,* p. 232.

8. THE AGES DIVIDED INTO EIGHT, NINE, TEN, ELEVEN, AND TWELVE STAGES

1. *The Touchstone of Complexions* (ed. 1581), fols. 29ʳ–30ᵛ.

2. Reproduced in Van Marle, *Iconographie,* 2.

3. This series I have not seen. Impressions are very rare; Franken, *L'OEuvre gravé,* nos. 1079–1086, was able to record only a set from which the first and eight members were missing.

4. In the card index of the Huntington Library it is attributed tentatively to Thomas Jenner and dated ca. 1656. The last plate is signed "Ja. v. L. fecit" (Jacob Van Langeren).

5. Is it possible that Milton knew of this image of Sin?

6. Reproduced in Dodgson, *Catalogue of Woodcuts in the British Museum,* 2, pl. 103; described in Schreiber, *Handbuch,* no. 1881.

7. I recall that when I was a small boy an aged relative used to say, after so shivering, "A goose flew over my grave." Compare Graham Greene, *The Confidential Agent:* "A goose went winging by somewhere above his grave—where? He shivered."

8. Reproduced in Van Marle, *Iconographie,* 2, 163 fig. 188.

9. In similar fashion (at a much earlier date) in the church of Saint Nizier at Troyes a woman representing Religion is engaged in a moral dialogue with each of the Seven Ages. To each she gives an appropriate emblem.

10. See Félix Soleil, *Les Heures gothiques* (Paris, 1882), pp. 31–37; Paul Lacombe, *Livres d'heures imprimés au XVᵉ et au XVIᵉ siècle conservés dans les bibliothèques publiques de Paris* (Paris, 1907), p. lxii; Mâle, *L'Art religieux,* 3, 303.

11. *Five hundred pointes of good Husbandrie* (1573), ed. Payne, note 45, supra, p. 138.

12. Boissard, *Emblemata* (1584), no. 22.

Chapter 7. Strangers and Pilgrims

1. PHILIPPIANS 3:20 AND HEBREWS 11:10–16

1. Bunyan's *Works,* ed. George Offer, 1852; John Brown, *John Bunyan: His Life, Times, and Work,* 1885 (revised by F. M. Harrison, 1928); J. B. Wharey, *A Study of the Sources of Bunyan's Allegories* (1904); G. R. Owst, *Literature and Pulpit in Medieval England.*

2. See Chew, *The Crescent and the Rose* (1937), chap. II.

2. THE CHOICE OF THE TWO PATHS

1. *Didache*, sections 1–6; *Epistle of Barnabas*, 18–20. Both books are reprinted in *The Apostolic Fathers*, ed. Kirsop Lake, Loeb Classical Library.

2. For the origins and ramifications of the myth see Erwin Panofsky, *Hercules am Scheidewege* (Leipzig, 1930), where an abundance of illustrations will be found.

3. *Choice of Emblemes*, p. 41, "Bivium virtutis et vitii."

4. *Parvus Mundus*, no. 49; also in Meyer, *Homo Microcosmos*, which derives from Scève.

5. *XL Emblemata miscella nova*, no. 39.

6. Corrozet, *Hecatomgraphie*, sigs. Kviii^v–L.

7. This "Dialogue" is in *The Shepherds Starre* (1591) which I have not seen and know only from Thomas Corser, *Collectanea Anglo–Poetica*, 2, 328–330. Corser does not quote any passage from the poem.

8. *Emblemes*, Bk. I, no. 22.

9. *The Pastime of Pleasure*, 83 f.

10. *The Doome warning all men to the Judgemente* (1581), p. 295.

11. Fleming, *The Diamond of Devotion* (ed. 1602), pp. 44 f.

12. *Emblemata*, no. 14.

13. Zacharias Heyns, *Emblemata. Emblemes Chrestienes et Morales* (Rotterdam, 1625), Part II, fol. 49^r.

14. Ludwig Volkmann, *Bilderschriften der Renaissance* (Leipzig, 1923), pp. 64 and 123. The design for Nicholas de Chemin is an example of the punning device: "Nicholas of the Path."

15. *Aureolorum Emblematum Liber* (Strassburg, 1587), nos. 74 and 103.

16. *Teatro d'Imprese* (Venice, 1623), Part II, p. 672.

17. I know this from an impression in the Huntington Library extra–illustrated Bryan, *Dictionary*, 3, Part IV, after p. 604.

18. Reproduced in the J. Pierpont Morgan *Catalogue of Manuscripts and Early Printed Books*, 3 (New York, 1907), 85.

19. Reproduced in Laborde, *Manuscrits à peintures*, 3, pls. 25 and 126.

20. Reproduced in F. M. Haberditzl, *Die Einblattdrucke des XV. Jahrhunderts in der Kupferstichsammlung der Hofbibliothek zu Wien*, 1, no. 168.

21. Jan David, *Veridicus Christianus*, no. 23.

22. William Browne of Tavistock, *Britannia's Pastorals*, Bk. I, Song 5.

23. Hieremia Drexel, S.J., *Heliotropium seu Conformatio humanae voluntatis cum divina*, Munich, 1627.

24. *Emblemata*, no. 35.

25. In *Emblemata Nobilitatis et Vulgo*, no. 6.

26. *Vertues Commonwealth: or the High–way to Honour*, sig. F4^v. The notion that in the relationship between Prince Hal and Falstaff and the Chief Justice Shakespeare intended to suggest the choice between Vice and Virtue or Ill and Good Fame seems to me to have nothing to recommend it.

3. FAME AND RUMOR

1. Opening lines of *Love's Labour's Lost*.

2. Thomas Fenne, *Fennes Fruites* (1590), first piece.

3. *Il Riposo* (Florence, 1584), p. 91.

4. *Tragicall Legend of Robert, Duke of Normandy*, lines 64 f. Fame is an attendant upon the Ghost of the Duke.

5. *Time's Journey* (1599), sig. C2^r.

6. The assumption of many editors that the tongues are painted on a garment is not fully borne out in the arts of design where the tongues (or eyes or ears) are sometimes on Fame's or Rumor's body.

7. *The Description of a Maske* (1614); in *Works*, ed. Percival Vivian (1909), p. 151. A "skin coat" was probably a tight fitting jacket or else, less probably, a coat made of leather.

8. *Æneid*, IV, 176–183.

9. Reproduced in Richard Muther, *Die Deutsche Büchillustration der Gothik und Frührenaissance*, 2 (Munich and Leipzig, 1884), 143.

10. *The Fountaine of Ancient Fiction* (1599), sig. Viii^v.

11. Peacham, *The Gentlemans Exercise* (ed. 1612), p. 117.

12. *Minerva Britanna*, no. 35. One of Peacham's "Visions" in memory of Henry Prince of Wales shows him in a chariot conducted by Fame. See *The Period of Mourning. Disposed into six Visions . . . In Memorie of the late Prince* (1613), sig. B3^r.

13. Cramer, *Emblemes* (1630 ?), no. 21.

14. *Recueil d'Emblemes Divers* (Paris, 1638), Part II, 146.

15. Raphael Holinshed, *Chronicle*, 3 (ed. 1587), 849.

16. Feuillerat, *Revels at the Court of Edward VI and Mary*, p. 142.

17. *The Plaie of Pacient Grissel* (ca. 1565–1568), ed. R. B. McKerrow and W. W. Greg, Malone Society (1909), 1671–87.

18. *Clyomon and Clamydes* (ca. 1570), ed. W. W. Greg, Malone Society (1913), 1197–1210.

19. Giovanni Felice Astolfi, *Della Officina Istorica . . . Libri IIII* (Venice, 1622), p. 82.

20. "The Legend of King Albanact," in *The First Parte of the Mirrour for Magistrates* (1574); *Mirrour for Magistrates* (1587), fols. 8^{r-v}.

21. *Chester's Triumph in Honor of Her Prince* (1610), in Nichols, *Progresses of James I*, 2, 293 f.

22. It is unnecessary to record these instances; consult the index to Robert Withington, *English Pageantry*. On one of the arches erected for the triumphal progress of James I through London in March 1604 there was a figure of Fame, "a woman in a watchet roabe, thickly set with open eyes and tongues, a payre of large golden winges at her back, a trumpet in her hand." Beneath her on five "mounts" were the Five Senses with scutcheons bearing "herogliphical bodyes to express their qualities." On a still lower level were Detraction holding "an open cuppe about whose brim a wreath of curled snakes were winding," and Oblivion with a black cup that was covered. The appropriateness of the presence here of the Five

Senses is not apparent. See Dekker, *Magnificent Entertainment,* in *Dramatic Works, 1,* 297–8; and Nichols, *Progresses of James I, 1,* 355.

23. *Herodian of Alexandria, His Historie of Twenty Roman Caesars and Emperors* (1635). At sig. A2ᵛ there is an interpretation of the title page in verse.

24. [or Scott], *Philomythie or Philomythologia wherin Outlandish Birds, Beasts, and Fishes, are taught to speake true English plainely* (1616), sig. B2ʳ.

4. LOVE

1. Meyer, *Homo Microcosmos,* no. 55, from Maurice Scève. The pretty notion is of course much older; cf. the explanations in the English version of Chartier's *Delectable demaundes,* p. 59, of the inscriptions: on Love's stomach: "Fane off and at hand," on his robe "Death and Life," on his forehead "Springtime and Sommer" (this last an odd antithesis).

2. For example, in Alciati, *Emblematum Liber* (ed. 1531), sig. B2ᵛ; Whitney, *Choice of Emblemes,* p. 65.

3. For example, in Alciati (ed. Paris, 1542), p. 54; (ed. Lyons, 1566), p. 195; Whitney, p. 65; J. T. and J. I. de Bry, *Emblemata Saecularia, Mira et Jucunda* (1596), no. 46.

4. For example, in Van Veen, *Amorum Emblemata* (1608), pp. 14–15; *Fons Amoris sive Emblemata Amatoria* (n.d.), no. 60.

5. In many editions of Alciati; also in Whitney.

6. Van Veen, *Amorum Emblemata,* pp. 114–115.

7. Jacob Cats, *Maechden–Plicht . . . Officium Puellarum, in castis Amoribus, Emblemata expressum* (Middelburg, 1618), no. 13.

8. *Delectable demaundes,* p. 35. But Ripa has an emblem of Love tamed by Time and Poverty.

9. The appropriate variant in Van Veen's religious series shows Divine Love and the Soul within the ring.

10. *Perymedes the Black Smith* (1588), ed. Collier, p. 50.

11. For example, in Alciati (ed. Paris, 1542), p. 40; but in Van Veen, *Fons Amoris* Love has a wing attached to the right foot and another to the left wrist.

12. Combe, *The Theater of Fine Devices* (1614), no. 77, from La Perriere.

13. Reproduced in Schreiber, *Handbuch, 4,* no. 1869.

14. For example, in Paulus Maccius (Paolo Maccio), *Emblemata* (unknown, 1628), no. 45.

15. De Bry, *Emblemata Secularia,* no. 8. Many of these plates are coarsely cynical on the subject of sexual attraction.

16. *A Midsummer Night's Dream,* I.2.169 f.

17. *Metamorphoses,* I, 466–471.

18. "The Lover to Cupid for Mercie," in Chalmers' *English Poets, 2* (ed. 1810), 605.

19. *Reson and Sensuallyte,* 5412–5518. See also Lydgate, *The Temple of Glasse,* 112–116.

20. *The Castle of Pleasure* (1518), sig. Aiii[r]. See Lewis, *The Allegory of Love*, pp. 253 f.

21. *Here begynneth a lytel treatyse called the Dysputacyon or complaynt of the herte thorughe perced with the lokynge of the eye* (colophon: Wynkyn de Worde; n.d.), sig. B[v].

22. Ed. Rollins, *1*, 6, no. 4.

23. Ibid., *1*, 253, no. 305.

24. Line 842; in Hazlitt's Dodsley, *4*, 224.

25. *A poore Knight his Pallace of private pleasures* (1579), sig. D[v]. This I have not seen; it is quoted in *A Paradise of Dainty Devices*, ed. Rollins, p. 260.

26. *Hekatompathia* (1582), ed. Arber, sonnet 63, p. 99.

27. *Roxburghe Ballads*, *3*, 530.

28. Other allusions to the theme may be found in Surrey's poems, in the *Paradise of Daintie Devises*, in Sidney's *Arcadia* (the Song at Bk. II, 14, 2), and in *The Virgin Martyr* by Dekker and Massinger.

29. Cupid appears in Lyly's *Gallathea* and in Beaumont and Fletcher's *Cupid's Revenge*; in both cases the treatment is conventional and uninteresting.

30. "Cupid's Golden Dart," in *Roxburghe Ballads*, *3*, 533.

31. *Cupid's Messenger or, A trusty Friend stored with sundry sorts of serious, witty, pleasant, amorous, and delightful Letters* (1629).

32. In Hazlitt's Dodsley, *7*, 27. Cupid recounts his triumphs over various celebrated victims of his power. For the date of this play (1566 and revised later), editions, and multiple authorship (revised by Robert Wilmot) see Chambers, *The Elizabethan Stage*, *3*, 514.

33. *Scillaes Metamorphosis* (1589), in *Works*, Hunterian Club, *1*, 21.

34. A French version is *Emblemes d'Amour. Illustrez d'une Explication en prose fort facille pour entendre le sens moral de chaque Embleme* (Paris, n.d., early seventeenth century). Here, differing from the original Van Veen, the verses and prose interpretations are engraved on the plates. With coarse and debased copies of the plates and with a tasteless triviality in the text Van Veen's book reappears in Philip Ayres' *Cupid's Address to the Ladies* (1683).

35. The only copy I have seen of this tiny book is in the Library of Congress. Place and date of publication are not given, but the imprint "Ex Officina Crispiani Passi" indicates Utrecht, early seventeenth century.

36. *Emblemes Sacrés avec leur Explications Nouvelles, ou sont exprimez les Differens etats de la vie spirituelle, & les Resolutions que l'Ame Fidele y doit prendre* (Auxerre, 1687). The pious canon addresses a lady, Philothée, who had desired ampler explanations than were given in the compact Latin verses. There are 119 copperplates, all familiar. He notes that the designs have for long been well known, for forty or fifty years, he says. He does not always follow the original interpretations, sometimes inventing new, especially when he can give to a secular subject an other worldly meaning.

37. In the French Alciati (Lyons, 1566), pp. 188–189, the commentary refers to the story in Jean le Maire de Belges.

38. Whitney, *Choice of Emblemes* (1586), p. 152, in his commentary on this emblem, which he takes from Alciati, paraphrases Joachim du Bellay's poem. See Green, *Shakespeare and the Emblem-Writers*, pp. 400–403.

39. *Viri Clarissimi D. Andree Alciati . . . Emblematum Liber* (1531), sig. D3^v. This is the second issue of the first edition by Henry Green (Holbein Society, 1870), no. 3. The woodcuts are ascribed to Hans Weiditz.

40. *Toutes les Emblemes de M. André Alciat* (Lyons, 1558), p. 191.

41. *Les Emblemes de Maistre André Alciat, . . . mis en rime françoise, avec curieuse correction* (Paris, 1542), p. 140.

42. Scève, *Parvus Mundus* (ca. 1570), no. 13: "De Morte et Cupidine"; Peacham, *Minerva Britanna*, no. 172, same title; Meyer, *Homo Microcosmos*, no. 13, same title.

43. *Godfrey of Bulloigne* (1600), II, 34.

44. *The Affectionate Shepherd* (1594), stanzas 6–9; in *Complete Poems*, ed. Alexander Grosart (1871), pp. 8–9.

45. *The Floating Island*, V, 2, in *Works*, ed. Bertram Dobell (1907), p. 221. The play dates from 1636 but was not published till 1655.

46. *The Old Couple*, II; in Hazlitt's Dodsley, *12*, 31.

47. James Shirley, *Cupid and Death* (performed 1653; published 1659), in *Works*, 6 (1833), 343 f. See Welsford, *The Court Masque*, pp. 261 f.

48. *Arisbas, Euphues amidst his slumbers: Or Cupids Journey to Hell . . . With the Triumph of True Love, in the foyle of false Fortune. By I.D.* (1594). "Cupid's Journey" is at sig. D3^r f.

5. THE FIVE SENSES

1. Reproduced in P. A. Lemoisne, *Les Xylographies du XIVe et du XVe siècle au Cabinet des Estampes de la Bibliothèque Nationale*, 2, pl. 102.

2. All five cuts in *La Nef des Folles* (Paris, Le Petit Laurens, ca. 1495) are reproduced in Claudin, *Histoire de l'imprimerie*, 2, 130–133.

3. Pp. 19, 38, 52, 60, and 71. After later sections on other forms of Folly—fine clothes, dancing, gluttony, voluptuousness, etc.—comes (p. 163) the contrasting Ship of the Church, steered by the Pope. A crucifix is in its midst. The author, labeled "Mestre Johan Drouin," waves an invitation to people on shore to come aboard.

4. As late as the time of Charles II the Senses occur on an embroidered panel, reproduced in *The Connoisseur*, *90* (1935), 321.

5. Reproduced in the Walpole Society's *Annual Volume*, *14* (1925–6), pl. 31. The tortoise is an attribute probably because it is so sensitive to a touch that in reaction to one it instantly withdraws its head. This creature is associated with Touch in the University play *Lingua*, to be discussed presently.

6. See E. C. Rouse's article on these murals, *Illustrated London News*, Nov. 5, 1944, pp. 705–706 and fig. 5. Opposite p. 705 the figure of Reason is reproduced in full color.

7. Dirck Volckertszoon Coornhert, *Recht Ghebruyck ende Misbruyck van Tydlicke Have* (Amsterdam, 1620), no. 20. This is the earliest Dutch edition of these emblems and poems I have seen; they had originally appeared

many years earlier. There is an attractive Latin version by Richardus Lubbaeus, *Emblemata . . . de Rerum Usu et Abusu, olim inventa et Belgicis Rithmis explicata a Theodore Cornhertis* (Arnheim, 1609).

8. The two series begin respectively at sigs. 55^r and 75^v. Father David, *Veridicus Christianus*, no. 42, also connected the Five Senses with passages in the Bible but in a different way, likening them as a group to the Five Rebel Kings, the Five Satraps of the Philistines, the Five Yoke of Oxen, the Five Porches of the Pool of Bethesda, and the Five Gates of a City.

9. The plates had already appeared in another work by Jenner of the same title but different text, dated 1563. A copy of this, which I have not seen, is in the British Museum. The Huntington Library volume, from which I take my description, is thought to be of somewhat later date since the plates show signs of wear. Here the plates are "paged in," that is, included in the book's pagination. The signatures are not printed from type or engraved but roughly stamped on the engraving or missing altogether. This irregularity makes one suspect that they may not originally have been intended for Jenner's book. A reprint of 1558 is in smaller format and the plates are folded.

10. In Hazlitt's Dodsley, *9*, 331-463.

6. THE SEVEN LIBERAL ARTS OR SCIENCES

1. *Minor Poems*, *2*, 630 f. See Withington, *English Pageantry*, *1*, 144.

2. *Minor Poems*, *2*, 724 f.

3. See H. A. Napier, *Historical Notices of the Parishes of Swyncombe and Ewelme in the County of Oxford* (Oxford, 1858), p. 125.

4. Hind, *Early Italian Engraving*, E.I, 21-26 and 29.

5. See *The Pastime of Pleasure*, ed. W. S. Mead, EETS (1928), introduction, pp. lxiv f. The cut has been often reproduced; see, for example, *The Legacy of the Middle Ages* (Oxford, 1926), op. p. 272; Withington, *English Pageantry*, *1*, op. p. 144; Plimpton, *The Education of Shakespeare*.

6. These cuts are scattered through the first 400 pages of the *Margarita Philosophica*; it is not necessary to give page references. The vast treatise goes on through another thousand pages, covering the entire range of knowledge; there are, however, no more personifications though there are many diagrams.

7. Reproduced in Schreiber, *Handbuch*, *4*, no. 1873. Also in Georg Steinhauser (ed.), *Die Deutschen Stände in Einzeldarstellung*, *7*: Emil Reicke, *Der Gelehrte*, nos. 27-29.

8. Reproduced in McKerrow and Ferguson, *Printers Devices*, no. 122, and in the *Britwell Court Catalogue*, March 28, 1927, lot no. 717.

9. Bartsch, *Le Peintre-Graveur*, *15*, 504, nos. 1-7. The date is on a tablet in the engraving of Arithmetic.

10. *Emblemata* (Antwerp, 1564), p. 142.

11. *Il Riposo*, p. 4.

12. Preceding the title page is a long explanation called "A Draught of the Frontispice" [sic], on a folded sheet. This curious arrangement suggests that the explanation was an afterthought.

13. *The Three Parnassus Plays*, ed. J. B. Leishman (1949) supersedes W. D. Macray's edition (1886). The *Pilgrimage* and the first part of *The Return from Parnassus* remained in manuscript till Macray's edition. The second part of the *Return* was published in 1606. The two parts of the *Return* have to do with the scholars' disappointments and failures to attract patrons and to make a living. Problems of authorship and of the many allusions to contemporary poets and other persons have been much debated. The latest contribution is Marjorie L. Reyburn, "New Facts and Theories about the Parnassus Plays," *PMLA*, 74 (1959), 325–335.

14. TEXNO AMIA: *or the Marriages of the Arts* (1618). A facsimile of the copy in the Folger Library, which has manuscript corrections apparently by the author, has been edited by Sister M. J. C. Cavanaugh (Washington, D.C., 1942).

7. THE LADDER OF LIFE

1. See Migne, *Pat. Lat.*, 6, 997.

2. Reproduced in Hind, *Early Italian Engraving*, A.V.1(i).

3. Reproduced in Schramm, *Der Bilderschmuck der Frühdrucke*, *19*, no. 910.

4. Reproduced in Hind, A.II.20. In a miniature in Herrade de Landsberg, *Hortus Deliciarum*, devils are shooting souls off the ladder. For an example of the two ladders, Celestial and Infernal, see the frontispiece to the EETS edition (Vol. 182) of the *Speculum Christiani*.

5. De Montanay, *Emblemes* (1571), no. 13.

6. Reproduced in Hind, *Early Italian Engraving*, B.IV.2.

7. Jacobus Bornitius, *Emblematum Ethico–Politicorum Sylloge posterior* (Heidelberg, 1664), First Series, no. 6. The man with the burden on his back appears again in no. 10.

8. I have left to the searchers after Bunyan's sources the heavy task of reading this enormously long narrative. I know it only from the photostat copy in the New York Public Library of MS 22,542 in the Sorbonne Library. Here there are a few miniatures showing the road along which the Pilgrim has his adventures.

9. This is well known for its woodcuts. Two are reproduced in Delen, *Histoire de la Gravure*, *1*, pl. 43. See also Hind, *History of Woodcut*, 2, 587–589.

10. On the title page this is described as "newlie altered and augmented," but apparently no earlier edition is known.

11. Reproduced in *Burlington Magazine*, *51* (1927), 69.

12. Barclay's version is *A Treatyse intitulyd the Myrrour of good maners* (ca. 1520).

13. *A plaine Path to perfect Vertue: Devised and found out by Mancinus, a Latine Poet, and translated into English by G. Turbervile Gentleman* (1568), sig. vii[r].

14. *Certain Selected Histories for Christian Recreations with their severall Moralizations* (1576), sig. Biiii[r].

15. *La Dance Machabre or Death's Duel* (1633 ?), p. 54, stanza 206.

16. *The Prodigals Teares: or His fare–well to Vanity* (1614).

17. *Here foloweth a compendyous story and it is called the exemple of vertu in the whiche ye shall fynde many goodly storys and naturall dysputacyons* . . . (Wynkyn de Worde, 1530). The poem was written long before, probably in 1494. In my summaries of this poem and of later versions of the Pilgrimage I have, with a few exceptions, not thought it necessary to give page references.

18. What does the poet mean by growing "two folde"? Does he mean that forty years of age is twice twenty, when his protagonist was Youth?

19. Of paraphrases the most interesting I have read is Gilles Corrozet, *Le Tableau de Cebes, Ancien Philosophe* . . . *Auquel est paincte* . . . *la vraye image de la vie humaine* . . . *exposé en Ryme Francoyse* (Paris, 1543).

20. This has been often reproduced. See, e.g. H. Knackfuss, *Holbein* (Bielefield and Leipzig, 1899), fig. 50, and for a detailed description of the cut, ibid., pp. 71–73.

21. It was closely copied by Z. A. Vavasore for the title page of the *Dictionarium Graecum* (Venice, 1525). The original and the copy are reproduced side by side in D'Essling, *Livres à figures venetiens*, 5, nos. 515 and 516.

22. In my summary all matter placed within quotation marks is from Poyntz's translation.

23. *Epictetus his Manuall. And Cebes his Table. Out of the Greeke originall* (1610).

24. Wharey, *Sources of Bunyan's Allegories*, pp. 125 f., discusses the possible indebtedness of Bunyan to Bateman.

25. This expression of loyalty is at least less extravagant than the conclusion of the anonymous play *Soliman and Persida* where Death declares that he has no power over the Queen.

26. *The Voyage of the Wandering Knight. Showing the whole course of Mans life, how apt he is to follow Vanitie, and how hard it is for him to attaine to Virtue.* There are several later editions, one in 1670. The translator was a merchant of Southampton. The original edition of 1581 has been reprinted with excellent notes by Dorothy Atkinson Evans (Seattle, 1951).

27. This is a striking example of the ease with which the theme of the Pilgrimage fuses with that of the Ages of Human Life.

28. *The Castell of Courtesie, Whereunto is adjoyned The Holde of Humilitie: with the Chariot of Chastitie thereunto annexed. Also a Dialogue betweene Age and Youth, and other matters herein conteined. By James Yates Servingman* (1582). The "Chariot," the "Dialogue," and the "other matters" have no connection with the "Castell" and the "Holde."

29. *The Pilgrimage to Paradise* . . . *compiled in verse.* The six line stanza riming *ababcc* is employed.

30. Reprinted in the Publications of the Spenser Society, No. 35 (1883) but without introduction or notes. This poem also is in the *ababcc* stanza.

31. *Humours Heav'n on Earth; with The Civile Warres of Death and Fortune. As also The Triumph of Death: Or, The Picture of the Plague, according to the Life; as it was in Anno Domini,* 1603 (1609), pp. 2–183; in *Complete Works,* ed. A. B. Grosart, *1* (1878), Section e.

32. With Time as Death's "master" compare Robert Aylett's characterization of Death: "Thou art but as a Servant unto time," in *Thrift's Equipage* (1622), p. 55. Quarles' "hieroglyphic" of Time staying Death from snuffing out the candle of Life has an accompanying vigorous dispute in which Time declares that Death has no power to strike "till Time shall please to say Amen." In *Hieroglyphikes of the Life of Man,* no. 6.

33. Henry Peacham may have taken from Davies suggestions for his "vision" of the dungeon of Death in *The Period of Mourning. Disposed into sixe Visions. In Memorie of the late Prince* (1613), sig. B2ʳ f. The walls of this dungeon were hung with "escotcheons" and epitaphs. There were monuments with defaced inscriptions. Bottles of tears were to be seen. Bores, spades, mattocks, etc. were on the ground, and dead men's wills and "pothecaries bills." On the floor lay a meager wretch that had wept his eyes out and had pined to a skeleton—Death. Death lamented that aiming his dart amiss he had struck Noblest Henry. He bade the poet hasten away for he was on dangerous ground.

34. It will be remarked that Time is not here precisely the discoverer of Truth; but Davies would scarcely have conceived of her as dwelling in the Cave of Time had he not had in mind the many visual images of Time leading forth Truth from a cave.

35. A long description of the torments of hell is introduced at this point, stanzas 157–194.

36. Bk. I, Songs 4 and 5; W. C. Hazlitt's edition, *1* (1868), 106 f. Also in the Muses' Library. See F. W. Moorman, *William Browne* (Strassburg, 1897). The wanderings of True Religion (who is practically equated with Truth) is the subject of a short poem called "Somnium" by "R.C." who was probably Richard Corbet. See R.C., *The Time's Whistle,* ed. J. M. Cowper, EETS, *48* (1871), 137–141. The piece is dated ca. 1615, that is, precisely contemporary with Browne's poem. In a dream True Religion appeared to the poet and narrated her adventures. Driven from Rome, she sought refuge in England, where Queen Mary pierced her heart. However, Queen Elizabeth revived her, and now under King James she rules "this Britaine empire." But she must still carry a sword and a torch, for she has an enemy as dark as night called Envy. Her torch is to disperse Envy's mists. (We are reminded of various emblems.) Moreover, of late her power has begun to decay, threatened as it is by a "hellish monster, damned Hypocrisie," that is (as she explains to the poet), the Puritan party. (We recall the variant of the Time–Truth design in which Hypocrisy is substituted for Envy and of the religious controversialists who ascribe their opponents' hypocrisy to envy of true religion.) With this denunciation of the Puritans the poem ends.

37. *Peregrinatio Scholastica or Learneinges Pilgrimage Containeinge the straundge Adventurs and various entertainements he founde in his traveils towards the shrine of Latria . . . Composed and devided into morall*

Tractates, in *Works,* ed. A. H. Bullen, *1* (privately printed, 1881), 35–80.

38. The stages are Lion–Drunk, Goat–Drunk, Fox–Drunk, and Swine–Drunk. The motive appears elsewhere. In *Pierce Penilesse* Thomas Nashe lists eight kinds, not stages, of drunkenness. The behavior of each Drunkard is described and an animal is assigned to each. See *Works,* ed. McKerrow, *1,* 207. In William Hornby's *The Scourge of Drunkennes* (1611), sig. B2ᵛ, a satiric and moralizing poem by a reformed drunkard, the four stages are associated with the ape, goose, lion, and swine. In "R.C.'s" *The Time's Whistle* (ca. 1615), Satire V, we have the apish, maudlin, lion–drunk, and swine–drunk stages. In *Philocothonista, or, the Drunkard, Opened, Dissected, and Anatomized* (1635), a curious mixture of erudition and moralizing, anonymous but ascribed to Thomas Heywood, a woodcut on the title page shows six men with animal heads sitting at a table and drinking. The hostess is bringing in two large tankards. The goose drinks quietly; the goat tosses off his pot; the hog is vomiting; the calf is smoking; the lion, at the quarrelsome stage, is about to strike with a big goblet the ass who shrinks away. The accompanying comment "Upon the Frontispiece" mentions only four stages, omitting the goose and the lion, while in the characterizations of the stages (pp. 2–6) seven are discussed: calf, ape, fox, hog, lion, goat, and goose. These contradictions are an example of the occasional lack of harmony between interpretations of emblematic title pages and the actual designs, as though the author and the artist had not consulted together. Three centuries later Currier and Ives, borrowing the pattern of the Nine Ages of Human Life with the stairway leading up and then down, produced a Nine Stages of Drunkenness. In the arch beneath the stairs are a weeping wife and her child.

ter 4.

39. For Day's description of each see my discussion of the Sins in Chap-

40. If, as seems likely, this is a topical allusion it dates the piece in or shortly after 1625. The coronation of James I had taken place too long before to give any point to the satire.

41. I have discussed Despair at ampler length in *The Virtues Reconciled,* pp. 110–118.

42. *Pathomachia; or, the Battell of the Affections* (1630), p. 7.

43. *Abuses Stript and Whipt* (1622), Bk. I, Satire 11; in *Works,* Spenser Society (1871–1882), p. 147.

44. *Franciscus Petrarca Von der Artzney bayder Glück* (Augsburg, 1532), Part II, fol. cxxvᵛ. See Dodgson, *Catalogue of Woodcuts in the British Museum,* 2, 144. Despair is occasionally figured in emblem books as a woman who has hanged herself. Daniel Cramer represents Despair as a woman with a noose round her neck; she is knotting the other end of the rope to a branch of the tree she has climbed. See *Emblêmes des differens Etats de la Vie* (ca. 1630), no. 37. The suicide of Judas Iscariot made the rope or halter the chief image of Despair. A Flemish Book of Hours (ca. 1500) in the Huntington Library (MS 1157) has a marginal miniature of the Via Dolorosa. Beside the road along which Jesus is carrying his Cross is a tree which Judas is climbing; Satan at the foot of the tree is handing a rope up to him.

45. Alexander Barclay, *The Ship of Fools*, ed. T. H. Jamieson, 2 (1874), 188. The cut is derived from the continental sources.

46. For reproductions see Claudin, *Histoire de l'imprimerie*, 2, 439, 3, 211–212, 4, 439–440, and Schramm, *Bilderschmuck der Frühdrucke*, 8, nos. 333–343. On the block–book *Ars Moriendi* and its successors see Hind, *History of Woodcut*, 1, 224–230.

47. In Cornelis Anthonisz's woodcut of the Prodigal Son eating husks among the swine, reproduced in Chew, *The Virtues Reconciled*, pl. 16, Disease, Famine, War, Death, the Devil, and Remorse of Conscience stand by the sinner. Despair is not personified, but the heart of Remorse is gnawed by a serpent labeled "Desperatio." Similarly, Ripa directs that Affano or Despair is to be personified as an old man through whose breast his heart is revealed devoured by serpents.

48. *Mundus et Infans*, ll. 855 and 874 f.

49. *Mankind*, ll. 784 f. and 813.

50. *Magnificence*, ll. 2285–2324.

51. *The Tyde tarryeth no Man. A Moste Pleasant, and merry commodym right pythie and full of delight* (1576), sig. Cjᵛ f.; reprinted in *Illustrations of Early English Popular Literature*, ed. J. P. Collier, 2, 1864.

52. *The First parte of the Mirrour for Magistrates* (1574), Legend of Cordelia. The "griesly Ghost" Despair appears in the shape of a woman beside whom lurks Death while Cordelia is subjected to temptation.

53. *A poor Knight his Pallace of private pleasures . . . Written by a student of Cambridge And published by J. C. Gent.* (1579), sig. Cʳ. For an account of the routing of Despair not by Mercy but by Reason in Barclay's *Castell of Labour* see Chew, *The Virtues Reconciled*, p. 116.

54. This was published anonymously; it is ascribed to Denny in Corser's *Collectanea, the DNB,* and elsewhere. It is not mentioned by Wharey, *Sources of Bunyan's Allegories;* there are, however, some striking analogies to *Pilgrim's Progress.*

55. In the third sub–division of this final canto, describing the Holy Hill, the stanzas are hill–shaped, the lines gradually lengthening from the first to the last. Such *tours de force* were fashionable in the seventeenth century.

56. Denny often employs the word "emblematical" in his interpretations; e.g. (p. 215): "This Stanza is altogether emblematical."

57. *Mundorum Explicatio or The Explanation of a Hieroglyphical Figure: Wherein are couched the Mysteries of the External, Internal, and Eternal World, shewing the true progress of a Soul from the Court of Babylon to the City of Jerusalem; from the Adamical fallen state to the Regenerate and Angelical. A Sacred Poem* (1661). See Wharey, pp. 128–131, for a discussion of Bunyan's possible indebtedness.

Chapter 8. The Journey's End

I. THE DANCE OF DEATH, THE THREE LIVING AND THE THREE DEAD

1. Anthony Sherley, *Witts New Dyall* (1604), sig. L4ʳ.

2. W. Parkes, *The Curtaine-Drawer of the Whole World* (1612).

3. Older inquiries such as Francis Douce's *Dissertation on the Dance of Death*, 1833, have been superseded. See, among many other authorities, W. L. Schreiber, *Der Totentänze* (Leipzig, 1900); F. P. Weber, *Aspects of Death and Correlated Aspects of Life in Art, Epigram, and Poetry* (3rd ed., 1918); Gert Buchheit, *Der Totentänz* (Berlin, 1926); P. S. Kozaky, *Geschichte der Totentänze* (Budapest, 1936); J. M. Clark, *The Dance of Death* (Glascow, 1950). To these and to other monographs and to various articles I am indebted. I have, however, added some other material.

4. Especially valuable for the treatment of *Les Trois Vifs et les Trois Morts* is W. F. Storck's article, "Aspects of Death in English Art and Poetry," *Burlington Magazine*, 21 (1912), 249–256. In a second contribution Storck supplies a catalogue and good bibliography, ibid., pp. 314–319.

5. Of this Dance Sir Thomas More wrote that loathly as the skeletons were they were not so grisly as the fantasies of Death engraven by the imagination in men's hearts. See Sir Thomas More, *The Four Last Things*, in *English Works*, 1 (1931), 468.

6. *The Daunce of Death*, ed. Beatrice White, EETS, 1931. Miss White's introduction is of great value.

7. Abundant illustrations of the Dance and of other aspects of Death will be found in the works cited in notes 3 and 4 above; in Claudin, Schramm, and Hind; in the relevant pages of Mâle's *L'Art religieux*, especially *3*; and in Van Marle's *Iconographie de l'art profane*, *2*. Save in a few cases I have not thought it necessary to give particular references.

8. One of Philippe Pigouchet's editions of the Book of Hours certainly influenced Daye's two prayer books discussed in the next paragraph, though the cuts are much daintier. See Claudin, *Histoire de l'imprimerie*, *2*, 52–53.

9. I am thinking of Thomas Rowlandson's *English Dance of Death*, 1816 and Richard Dagley's *Death's Doings*, 1826. Contemporary with these books was the vogue for little ceramic figures of the Dance.

10. See my article on these two volumes in *Huntington Library Quarterly*, 8 (1945), 297–8 and 300.

11. Walter Colman's *La Dance Machabre* (ca. 1633) contains, despite its title, no dance. He translates it "Death's Galliard" and rimes "macabre" with "labour." It is odd that though the adjective has remained in common usage, the English pronunciation never established itself. Many seventeenth-century cautionary ballads play variations on the theme of the Dance, often describing the types of humanity, high and low, to whom impartial Death comes. Sometimes there is an accompanying woodcut. See *Roxburghe Ballads*, ed. William Capell, *1* (1869), 239, 282 f., 330 f., 394. There was a ballad tune called "Death's Dance"; see ibid., *1*, 184.

12. See especially the illustrations in Storck's article "Aspects of Death," *Burlington Magazine*, 21, 1912, cited in note 4, above.

13. Reproduced in Storck, pl. II, J, and in R. Freyhan, "English Influence on Parisian Paintings of about 1300," *Burlington Magazine*, 54 (1929), 320 f.

14. See F. Saxl, "A Spiritual Encyclopaedia of the Later Middle Ages," *Journal of the Warburg and Courtault Institutes*, 5 (1942), 96.

15. British Museum MS 10 E. IV; reproduced in Storck, "Aspects of Death," *Burlington Magazine*, *21* (1912), pl. II, G.

16. Reproduced in Edward Hodnett, *English Woodcuts*, *1480–1535*, no. 378.

17. *This treatyse is called the doctrynale of dethe and is to be rede afore a man or a woman whan it semeth that they be in the artycle of deth.*

18. Reproduced in D'Essling, *Livres à figures venetiens*, Part I, 2, 41.

19. Reproduced in Van Marle, *Italian Schools of Painting*, *17* (1935), no. 53.

20. Reproduced in Heinrich Röttinger, "Hans Wechtlin," *Jahrbuch der Kunsthistorischen Sammlungen des Allerhöchsten Kaiserhauses*, 27 (1907), after p. 4.

21. De Bry, *Emblemata Nobilitatis* (1593), unnumbered, following no. 21.

22. De Covarrubias, *Emblemas Morales*, Bk. II, no. 88.

23. John Awdeley, *An Epitaph of Maister Fraunces Benison* (1570).

2. PERSONIFICATIONS OF DEATH

1. Hęlkiah Crooke, ΜΙΚΡΟΚΟΣΜΟΓΡΑΦΙΑ: *A Description of the Body of Man* (2nd ed. 1631), pp. 933 and 935.

2. Death seizes the woman by the wrist. His head is a hairy skull; his body still clothed in flesh. An inscription reads: "Omnem in homine venustatem mors abolet." Reproduced in Pauli, *Beham*, no. 151.

3. Huntington Library "Kitto" Bible, *18*, 3356.

4. Sambucus, *Emblemata* (ed. 1566), p. 99. The winged skull rests on a globe; above the skull is an hourglass and a book. A close copy of this is the device of the English printer W. Leake (McKerrow, *Printers' and Publishers' Devices*, no. 341) where the book bears the motto: "I live to dy. I dy to live." Leake used it, for example, in the edition of 1602 of Shakespeare's *Venus and Adonis* (of all places!) and in Robert Southwell's *Mary Magdalen's Funeral Tears* (1609).

5. In various paintings and prints of the Triumph of Death from Petrarch's *Trionfi* the Three Fates are substituted for Death. Lydgate, who seems to conceive of Atropos as masculine, imagines that he petitions Righteousness to serve the Lord of Light; the petition is granted and his name is changed to Death. See *Assembly of Gods*, especially line 1403.

6. Reproduced in Hind, *Early Italian Engraving*, B.II.3.I.

7. Gabriele Faerno, *Centum Fabulae ex Antiquis Auctoribus* (Antwerp, 1573), p. 22.

8. *The Gorgeous Gallery of Gallant Inventions* (1578), ed. Rollins, p. 119.

9. *Tottel's Miscellany* (1557), no. 158; ed. Rollins, *1*, 109.

10. *II Henry IV*, I.i.66.

11. Reproduced in Pauli, *Beham*, no. 150.

12. *Induction* to *The Mirrour for Magistrates*, stanza 41.

13. *Delia* (1592), sonnet 49.

14. *Two Bookes of Epigrammes and Epitaphs* (1639), Bk. II, no. 89.

In ibid., Bk. I, no. 199, Bancroft says that Death unwinds the human machine which is run by the weight of Reason.

15. *Prince Henries Obsequies* (ed. 1622?), Elegy 23; in *Works*, Spenser Society (1871–1882), p. 388.

16. R.C. (probably Richard Corbet), *The Time's Whistle* (ca. 1615), EETS, pp. 128 f.

3. THE MESSENGERS OF DEATH AND DEATH'S ARRIVAL

1. Lydgate's translation, *The Pilgrimage of the Life of Man*, EETS (1871), Part II, 646–652.

2. *A Thoroughfare of Woe*, in *Minor Poems*, 2, 822 f.

3. John Awdeley, *Remember Death, and Thou shalt never sin* (1569). In this ballad Death invites all men to come to his dance and proclaims himself to be the guide to heaven.

4. *I Henry VI*, II.5.5.

5. I know this quotation only from *Select Poetry, Chiefly Devotional, of the Reign of Queen Elizabeth*, ed. Farr, *1*, 158.

6. *Never too late to Mend*, in *Works*, ed. Grosart, *8*, 150.

7. *Politeuphuia. Witts Commonwealth* (ed. 1598), fol. 222^r.

8. "A briefe dialogue between sickness and worldly desire," in *A Gorgeous Gallery of Gallant Inventions* (1578), ed. Rollins, p. 95; "The fall of folly, exampled by needy Age," ibid., pp. 91–92. In an earlier collection, *Tottel's Miscellany* (1557), no. 212, ed. Rollins, *1*, 166, an anonymous poet tells how he saw "the harbinger of death" riding toward him. "The cough, the colde, the gaspyng breath, / Doth bid me to provide."

9. *Mortalities Memorandum* (1621), p. 33. The fact that in Michault's *Danse aux Aveugles* Death has, in addition to Sickness and Old Age, a third attendant named Accident may be merely a coincidence, but Rachel Speght was a learned lady and may have read Michault.

10. "Translated out of a Part of Petronius Arbiter's Satyricon," in *Poems and Songs* (4th ed., 1686), stanza XI; *Caroline Poets*, ed. George Saintsbury, *3* (1921), 316. Saintsbury calls this piece a "translation-amplification" and remarks that of part of this stanza there is not even a suggestion in the *Satyricon*.

11. Hawes, *The Pastime of Pleasure*, 5383 f.

12. Catherine P. Hargrave, *A History of Playing Cards* (Boston, 1930), pp. 31, 33, 228.

13. *Dialogue against the Fever Pestilence* (1564; 1578), EETS, pp. 114–117.

14. It seems to me less likely that the association of Death with the unicorn comes from the episode in the Barlaam and Josophat legend where the man who climbs the tree gnawed by the black and the white rat does so to escape the unicorn which symbolizes Death; but there is some connection or even an equation. This suggestion comes from Dr. S. Schönberger and was communicated to me by Professor Panofsky.

15. *La Mort Chevauchant un Boeuf. Origine de cette illustration de l'Office des Morts dans certains Livres d'Heures de la fin du xve siècle*

(Paris, 1923). It has been suggested that the idea may be traced back to the Hindu belief that Yama, the god of the dead, rides on a buffalo.

16. In the edition of the *Danse* (Paris, ca. 1495) of which an example believed to be unique is in the Pierpont Morgan Library, sig. D1^r, Death rides not a bullock but a horse and not blindfold. This is in direct contradiction to the text.

17. I know only from a reproduction in Paul Kristeller, *Early Florentine Woodcuts* (1897), no. 14, a curious cut in the anonymous *Historia della Morte* (Florence, ca. 1572). Death on a bull rides over four prostrate bodies. Behind him there stream out from his belt four pairs of shoes! Are these trophies? Has Death removed them from the four dead in order to make it more difficult for them to run away from him? Perhaps the text, which I have not seen, explains this strange piece of symbolism.

18. *II Henry IV*, III.2.38 f.

19. Valvasor's book is a series of engravings of the "Saltum Mortis" closely imitated from Holbein.

20. Hind, *Early Italian Engravings*, A.II.18.

21. Bartsch, *Le Peintre-graveur*, 7, 465, no. 16. Reproduced in W. Y. Ottley, *Collection of 129 Facsimiles of Scarce and Curious Prints* (1828), no. 92.

22. *Horae* (Geoffrey Tory, 1531), sig. Pviii.

4. DEATH CONQUERS ALL

1. This is by the Master B.R. with the anchor. I know it from an example in the Albertina.

2. Hind, *Early Italian Engraving*, A.II.18.

3. Engraving by Wierex, Huntington Library "Kitto" Bible, 3, 496.

4. *Sciographia Cosmica*, no. 80.

5. Reproduced in Schreiber, *Handbuch*, 4, no. 1897; Haberditzl, *Die Einblattdrucke*, no. 911.

6. Schreiber, 4, no. 1898; Heitz, *Einblattdrucke*, 19, 30. In sequences of the Ages of Human Life a falcon often appears with the figure of Young Manhood.

7. Schreiber, 4, no. 1897m; Heitz, 55, 5.

8. This is by the Master B.R. with the anchor. Reproduced in Max Lehrs, *Geschichte und Kritischer Katalog des deutschen, niederlandischen, und franzosichen Kupferstiche im xv Jahrhundert*, 6 (Vienna, 1908 f.), no. 440.

9. Sloane MS 1896; reprinted in *Old English Ballads*, ed. Rollins (1920), pp. 252 f. The ballad was entered for publication in 1563–4 (*Stationers' Register*, ed. Arber, 1, 237), but either it was not printed or else no copy is extant.

10. Huntington Library "Kitto" Bible, 4, 571.

11. Bartsch, *Le Peintre-graveur*, 9, p. 163, no. 2.

12. Reproduced in Burkhard, *Hans Burgkmair*, no. 23.

13. Reproduced in *Burlington Magazine*, 1 (1903), 199.

14. Many examples are in Van Marle, *Iconographie*, *2*. There is an engraving by Crispin de Passe in the "Kitto" Bible, *3*, 494. A fine drawing (1531) by Hans Leu of Zurich is reproduced in the Albertina *Catalogue of Drawings*, *4* (1933), no. 336. The subject of Death and the Lady is rarely found in emblem books. Once we have Death peeping from behind a lady; a baby is at her feet. The motto is: "Plorando nascimur, plorando morimur." See Mathias Holzwart, *Emblemata Tyrocinia* (1581), no. 22. Combined with the mirror theme and somewhat enlarged, it appears on low levels of popular English cautionary verse. "A Looking Glass for a Christian Family," in *The Shirburn Ballads*, ed. Andrew Clark (Oxford, 1907), is adorned with two woodcuts which draw the same lesson in different ways: one shows Death driving Mars and Venus before him; the other shows a warrior and two ladies with Death below them; both in token that Valor and Beauty alike descend to the grave.

15. *Romeo and Juliet*, V.3.102–5. Two passages in *Antony and Cleopatra* (I.2.147–9, and III.13.192–3) are not precise parallels. When Enobarbus says of Cleopatra: "I do think there is mettle in death, which commits some loving act upon her," he is speaking ironically and Death is not exactly personified. When Antony tells Cleopatra that the next time he fights he will make Death love him we obviously do not have the Death and Beauty theme. It is noteworthy that Professor Kittredge capitalizes "Death" in the second passage but not in the first.

16. Colman, *La Dance Machabre*, stanzas 77–78.

17. *Castara* (1634), p. 50.

18. In *Bagford Ballads*, ed. Ebsworth, *1*, 148 f.

19. Reproduced in Eugen Diedericks, *Deutsches Leben der Vergangenheit in Bildern*, *1* (1908), no. 618.

20. McKerrow, *Printers' and Publishers' Devices*, no. 337. The suggestion that this device may have been used on a plague–bill is McKerrow's, p. 131.

21. Reproduced in Charles A. Sawyer's *Catalogue*, No. 130 (1936), item 249, where this *Horae* was offered for sale.

22. Huntington Library MS 1165, fol. 105ᵛ.

23. Reproduced in K. Weinhold, "Glucksrad und Lebensrad," *Abhandlungen der Kgl. Akad, d. Wissenschaft zu Berlin* (Berlin, 1892), fig. 2.

24. "Kitto" Bible, *24*, 4454.

25. De Montenay, *Emblemes* (1571), no. 19.

26. In *Old English Ballads*, ed. Rollins, pp. 257 f. The number of ballads treating of Death with solemnity or with a sort of desperate jollity is very large. I include but a few examples. See in addition to those in the *Roxburghe Ballads*, the *Bagford Ballads*, and the *Shirburn Ballads*, and Child's great collection, several by Anthony Munday, from *Dainty Conseits* (1588), in the *Harleian Miscellany*, *9* (1812–13), 227, 230, 238, 252.

27. Schreiber, *Der Totentänze*, *4*, 1899m; Heitz, *Einblattdrucke*, *38*, nos. 16–18. For an unusual variant of Death the Reaper see Heitz, *70*, no. 49, where Death with a huge scythe has reaped four human heads: Pope, Cardinal, Kaiser, and Burger. The heads lie on the ground along the edge of the blade.

28. Fabio Glisenti, *Discorsi Morali contra il Dispiacer del Morire* (Venice, 1600). These discourses are in the *Ars Moriendi* tradition.

29. Gabriele Simeone, *Le Sententiose Imprese et Dialogo* (Lyons, 1560), p. 39.

30. Claude Paradin, *Heroical Devices*, translated by P.S. (1591), p. 273.

31. Wither, *Emblemes*, Bk. I, no. 48.

32. La Perriere, *La Morosophie* (1553), no. 99.

33. These lines, signed "T.P.," are on the title page of John More, *A lively Anatomie of Death* (1596).

34. *The Mirrour which Flatters Not*, translated by Thomas Cary (1639). The engraved title page shows an enthroned King Death, with many mortuary details.

35. In *Old English Ballads*, ed. Rollins, pp. 262 f., from Sloane MS 1896. Lydgate's "Timor Mortis Conturbat Me," in *Minor Poems*, 2, 828 f., contains a long list of Death's victims: famous men, fair women, Joy, Youth, the Seasons and so forth.

36. *Curtaine–Drawer of the Whole World* (1612), pp. 56–61. Westminster Abbey is not named in the poem, but a marginal gloss reads: "St. Peter's Church of West." There is no indication that the conclusion is spoken by Death, though it is obvious that he is the speaker. In the copy in the Huntington Library a marginal note in a seventeenth–century hand reads: "Epilogue by Death." Parkes' book is a heavy moralizing satire, part verse, part prose, on contemporary iniquities.

37. Rachel Speght, *Mortalities Memorandum, with a Dreame Prefixed, imaginarie in manner, reall in matter* (1621), p. 29. The spellings of the proper names are Mistress Speght's.

38. *Dood-Kiste voor de Levindige*, in *Alle de Werken*, 2, 490–1, 498, 507.

39. *The Example of Vertu* (1530), chapters 5 and 6.

5. DEATH AS GOD'S AGENT AND NATURE'S COMPANION

1. *The Considerations of Drexelius upon Eternitie*, translated by Ralph Winterton (Cambridge, 1636), op. p. 191.

2. By George Daniel Heuman (1691–1759), Huntington Library "Kitto" Bible, *24*, 4290.

3. Hawes, *The Pastime of Pleasure*, 5383 f. A cut shows Death on horseback, brandishing a dart and holding a spade and a coffin lid; hell-mouth is behind him. There follows, line 5473 f., the famous and impressive address by Death beginning "O mortall folke." Allusions to Death's weapon, spear or dart, are to be found times beyond number in late medieval and early Renaissance English literature; e.g. *The Court of Love*, 294: "Deth . . . me thirlith [pierceth] with his spere."

4. *Hyckscorner*, 535 f.

5. *The Scourge of Drunkennes* (1611), sig. B3^v.

6. *Mortalities Meditation: or, A Description of Sinne* (1624), stanzas 120–121.

7. *All Fooles* (1598; published 1603), I.2.77 f.

8. *The Blacke Rod and the White Rod* (1630), in *Plague Pamphlets*, ed. F. P. Wilson (1925), p. 202.

6. DEATH WITH PARCAE, FORTUNE, AND TIME

1. Pp. 445 f. and 1403.

2. This is ascribed to an artist in the circle of Pieter Coecke van Alost. See the *Beschreibender Katalogue*, 2, no. 55.

3. Göbel, *Tapestries of the Lowlands*, nos. 73 and 76.

4. Ibid., no. 85.

5. Boissard, *Emblematum Liber* (1593), no. 47.

6. The only known example is in a deplorable condition. Reproduced in Schreiber, *Handbuch*, no. 1884, and elsewhere.

7. This I saw in 1936; I was unable to obtain a photograph. I do not know whether it still exists.

8. *Humours Heav'n on Earth; With the Civile Warres of Death and Fortune.* As also the *Triumph of Death* (1609). The *Civile Warres*, which Davies calls a "Second Tale," occupies pp. 183–219. The third poem, *The Triumph of Death*, pp. 220–248, is a grimly vivid description of the plague in London in 1603. It contains no personifications except a very bad one of Despair "clad in a sable weede" and of Death who shouts his threats and denunciations and "like a Conqueror in Triumph rides." This simile and the poem's title are the only connections with the Petrarchan *Trionfi*.

9. Stanza 10: "for thou wanst Eyes," with the gloss: "Justice, Fortune, & Death are eielesse sith they have no respect of persons." Davies ignores the inconsistency of having Fortune reproach Death for his blindness when she is herself blind.

10. This leads into a long digressive story of how Death spared one man who repeatedly begged for a respite till he had risen from poverty to empire. This emperor is Death's only follower. The allegory is here cryptic to the point of unintelligibility. The description of Fortune's parasites gives Davies an opportunity for satire upon various social types. In this passage, at stanza 76, a propos of the misfortunes of stageplayers, occurs the famous, mysterious gloss: "W.S.R.B." whom Fortune "guerdond not to their desarts." Many scholars like to believe that the initials stand for William Shakespeare and Richard Burbage.

11. *Two Bookes of Epigrammes and Epitaphs* (1639), Bk. I, nos. 27 and 44.

12. On the title page of the anonymous *Epulario, or, The Italian Banquet* (1598), reproduced in *Britwell Court Catalogue*, March 30, 1925, lot no. 267.

13. "Allegorie op de Vergankelijkleid."

14. Bartsch, *Le Peintre-graveur*, 15 529–530.

15. *The Crums of Comfort with godly prayers*, compiled and published by M. Sparke (seventh edition, 1628).

16. Colophon: Printed at Dort by Henry Ash, 1639. Paget was for many years an English minister in Holland. A puzzling detail in this

design is that depending by a strap from Time's shoulder is an oblong object like a discus with the device of an arrow crossing an ellipse.

17. McKerrow, *Printers' and Publishers' Devices*, no. 424.

18. In *Roxburghe Ballads*, 4, 130.

19. Ibid., 7, 808 f. Compare also the cut of Time and Death in *Bagford Ballads*, 2, 747. There is an odd illogicality in another woodcut, for it shows Death striding before and Time following after. This cut illustrates "The Doleful Dance and Song of Death," *Roxburghe Ballads*, 3, 184 and "The Plotter Executed," ibid., 4, 125.

20. Robert Aylett, *Thrifts Equipage* (1622), Meditation 5, p. 55.

21. In *Works*, Hunterian Club, 1, 36 f.

7. DEATH AS A RELEASE FROM LIFE

1. *A Theater of Delightful Recreation* (1605), pp. 62 f.

2. *Spiegel van den Ouden* (3rd ed. Dordrecht, 1635), Part III, p. 150.

3. Herman Hugo, *Pia Desideria Emblematis* (Antwerp, 1624), Bk. III, no. 38; *Les Emblemes d'Amour Divin et Humain . . . Par un Pere Capucin* (1631); Quarles, *Emblemes*, Bk. V, no. 8; Brunet, *Emblemes Sacrés* (1667), no. 112. A crude woodcut of the same, from an unidentified Dutch book, is in the Huntington Library "Kitto" Bible, *58*, 10,515.

4. A variant in Quarles, Bk. V, no. 10, shows the Soul as a caged bird to which Divine Love brings food.

5. For example, in Brunet, *Emblemes Sacrés*, no. 8.

6. Ibid., no. 52.

7. Cramer, *Emblemes Sacrez*, p. 169.

8. "I.H.," *This Worlds Folly. Or a Warning–Peace discharged upon the Wickedness thereof* (1615), sig. D3ᵛ.

9. John More, *A lively Anatomie of Death* (1596).

10. La Perriere, *La Morosophie* (1553), sig. C4ᵛ.

11. Georgette de Montenay, *Emblematum Christianorum Centuria. Cent Emblemes Chrestiens* (Zurich, 1584), no. 89; and elsewhere.

12. *La Morosophie*, sig. O8ᵛ.

13. *An Epitaph upon the Death of Richard Price* (n.d.).

14. Claude Paradin, *Devices Heroiques* (Lyons, 1557), p. 258. The "Sprouting Tomb" must be distinguished from the "Speaking Tomb." Of the latter the best known example is Poussin's beautiful "Shepherds of Arcadia" in the Louvre. The inscription on the tomb reads: "Et in Arcadia Ego"; there is no verb. If the missing verb is "Fui" it is the dead man within the tomb who speaks: "I, too, was once in Arcadia." If it is "Sum," Death himself speaks: "Even in Arcadia am I." See Erwin Panofsky, "Et in Arcadia Ego," in *Philosophy and History. Essays presented to Ernst Cassirer* (Oxford, 1936), pp. 223 f.

15. *Emblemes*, Bk. I, no. 21.

16. Jean Mercier, *I. C. Emblemata* (1592), fol. 10ᵛ, no. 6.

17. McKerrow, *Printers' and Publishers' Devices*, no. 243. Recorded in three theological books published by J. Windet, 1585–91, and at the end of "First Tome" of Joseph Hall, *Works* (1628). That the writings of the

Wise and not only Holy Writ are not subject to Death is the theme of one of Schoonhovius' *Emblemata* (1618), no. 29. Death has his crown and scepter; beside him, however, are the circular serpent of Eternity and a book with a vine sprouting from it. The motto is: "Vivitur ingenio."

18. *Emblemes*, Bk. II, no. 14.

19. Reproduced in René Fülöp–Miller, *The Power and Secret of the Jesuits* (1930), pl. 8. Ripa's Humility carries a laden sack on her back: the burden of her sins.

20. *Emblematum Ethico–Politicorum Sylloge posterior* (Heidelberg, 1664), First Series, no. 6. Also in C. F. Lenestrier, *L'Art des Emblemes* (1684), pp. 42 and 413.

21. Braithwaite, *Lignum Vitae* (1658).

22. Following p. 22.

Appendix. Knowledge of the Arts

I. SOME ANALOGIES BETWEEN SHAKESPEARE AND THE FINE ARTS

1. Part of this Appendix is a revised and much expanded version of the first of a series of Alexander Lectures delivered at the University of Toronto. See Chew, *The Virtues Reconciled*, pp. 3–34.

2. *Microcosmos*, p. 215, and *The Civile Warres of Death and Fortune* (1609), p. 208.

3. All three epigrams are in *The Scourge of Folly* (1611).

4. *Wittes Pilgrimage* (ca. 1605), Sonnet 40.

5. The saying that dissemblers have "two faces in one hood" occurs frequently. See Rollins' note in his edition of *The Paradise of Daintie Devises*, p. 197.

6. "A table [picture] of the conyng perspective of death and a woman, done by Hilliarde." Lionel Cust, "The Lumley Inventories," *Sixth Annual Volume of the Walpole Society* (1917–18), p. 27.

7. *All Fooles*, I.1.47–48.

8. *Chabot*, I.1.68–72.

9. *The Alchemist*, III.4.87–99. Simpson's note evinces a misunderstanding of this passage.

10. *Every Man Out of His Humour*, IV.3.92. Simpson defines "piece of perspective" as a "peepshow."

11. *Richard II*, II.2.18–20. For other but less likely interpretations see note in the *New Variorum* edition.

12. *Twelfth Night*, V.1.223–4. See the inconclusive note in the *New Variorum* edition.

13. *All's Well that Ends Well*, V.3.48–52.

14. See A. H. R. Fairchild, *Shakespeare and the Arts of Design*, University of Missouri Studies, *12* (1937), Part III; M. F. Thorp, "Shakespeare and the Fine Arts," *PMLA 46* (1931); and the briefer treatment by Lionel Cust in *Shakespeare's England*, *2* (Oxford, 1917), chap. 17.

15. With the exception of Capell, commentators seem to have failed to understand this; they reprove Shakespeare for thinking that Giulio Romano

was a sculptor. See the long and for the most part fatuous note in the *New Variorum* edition. For the use of the verb "perform" in the sense of "complete" see *OED*.

16. *Pluto his Travailes, or, The Divels Pilgrimage to the Colledge of Jesuites. Lately discovered by an English Gentleman* (1612), p. 11.

2. MURALS AND PAINTINGS, RELIGIOUS AND SECULAR

1. For a striking example of the suppression of a very Romish subject, the *Pietà*, and the substitution of one warranted by Scripture see S. C. Chew, "The Iconography of *A Booke of Christian Prayers*, 1578," *Huntington Library Quarterly, 8* (1945), 299 and figs. 1–4.

2. See C. E. Keyser, *A List of Buildings in Great Britain and Ireland having Mural and Other Painted Decorations of Dates Prior to the Latter Part of the Sixteenth Century*, 3rd. ed., 1883. Subsequent discoveries have expanded this list.

3. *Macbeth*, II.3.83; II.2.55.

4. See the catalogue of examples (which supersedes Keyser's list) in W. F. Storck, "Aspects of Death in English Art and Poetry," *Burlington Magazine, 21* (1912), 249–256, 314–319.

5. The Prodigal Son as the type of penitent sinner is sometimes associated with the Seven Deadly Sins. See M. R. James, "The Wall Paintings in Brooke Church," in *A Supplement to Blomefield's Norfolk*, ed. Clement Ingleby (1929), pp. 14–25.

6. Donald Lupton, *London and the Countrey Carbonadoed* (1632), p. 127.

7. On the Hampshire murals see Margaret Jourdain, *English Decoration and Furniture in the Early Renaissance* (1924), pp. 90–91 and fig. 116. Here will be found examples of the Nine Worthies, the Five Senses, the Four Seasons, the Four Elements, and other subjects painted on walls, ceilings, chimneys, etc. The discovery of the Prodigal Son sequence was reported in the weekly edition of *The Times* (London), Nov. 5, 1935.

8. *I Henry IV*, III.3.37 and IV.2.27–28; *II Henry IV*, I.2.39 and II.1.157; *The Merry Wives of Windsor*, IV.5.8.

9. See P. M. Johnson, "Mural Paintings in Houses," *Journal of the British Archaeological Association, 37* (1931), 75–100.

10. In *The Letting of Humors Blood in the Head–Vaine* (ed. 1613), Satire 6, Samuel Rowlands writes of the "Nine Worthies on his Hostis wall." See H. C. Marillier, "The Nine Worthies," *Burlington Magazine, 61* (1932), 13–19, an article chiefly concerned with some tapestry specimens. When in the masque of the Nine Worthies in *Love's Labour's Lost*, V.2, Sir Nathaniel bungles the part of Alexander the Great, Costard says: "O, sir, you have overthrown Alexander the conqueror. You will be scrap'd out of the painted cloth for this." The use of the verb "scrape" confirms the view that the pictures of the Siege of Troy in *The Rape of Lucrece* are "painted cloths," not genuine tapestries, for Lucrece says she will scrape part of them and tapestries can not be scraped. Being used, like tapestries, to keep out cold and damp, they may supply a variant upon the

simile of the whited sepulchre. So in *Philotemus. The Warre betwixt Nature and Fortune* (1583), sig. U4^r, Brian Melebancke writes: "Wee see ragged walles have painted clothes when sound marble is naked." Shakespeare refers to them several times, twice noting the trite moral sentiments issuing as labels or "balloons" from the lips of figures. In *As You Like It*, III.2.90, Orlando says to Jaques: "I answer you right painted cloth." In *Troilus and Cressida*, V.10.46–47, Pandarus, having recited a bit of cynical doggerel, says: "Good traders in the flesh, set this in your painted cloth." In William Cartwright's play *The Ordinary*, I.3, in Hazlitt's Dodsley, *12*, 224, Andrew tells his tutor that he would "fain learn some religion," and the tutor replies:

> Yes, and become a martyr, and be pictur'd
> With a long label out o' your mouth, like those
> In Fox's book; just like a juggler drawing
> Riband out of his throat.

11. *Essayes* (ed. 1632), no. 22, sig. K^r.

12. *A Terrible Battell betweene Time and Death* (ca. 1606), in *Works*, Hunterian Club, *1*, 36.

13. *II Henry IV*, II.4.250–5.

14. *Ariosto's Satyres, in Seven Famous Discourses* (1608), p. 98. Published anonymously, but the translator was R. Tofte.

15. Thomas Heywood, *The English Traveller*, IV, in *Dramatic Works*, *4* (1874), 84. The figure of Fortune at the top of the fifth "Pegme" of the Arches of Triumph in 1604, nude and with bellying sail, probably gives a good idea of the figure outside the theatre. See William Kyp's engraving in Stephen Harrison, *The Arches of Triumph* (1604).

16. See J. F. A. Roberts, "English Wall–Paintings after Italian Engravings," *Burlington Magazine*, *78* (1941), 86–92.

17. John Weever, *Ancient Funerall Monuments* (1631), p. 584.

18. These were painted for the Guildhall in the Steelyard on a commission from the merchants of the Hanseatic League in 1552–3. When Queen Elizabeth expelled the merchants in 1598 the Steelyard fell into neglect. The two paintings were presented to Henry Prince of Wales in 1610; later (ca. 1627) they were in the Arundel collection; they passed to the Continent and are last heard of in Paris in 1666. To describe the surviving sketches in detail would take more space than we can afford. In "The Triumph of Riches" Plutus is drawn by emblematic animals; before him in his chariot sits Fortune; he is accompanied by famous wealthy men of antiquity and other appropriate personages. Poverty's cart is drawn by oxen and asses; in her retinue are Misery and Industry. See further A. B. Chamberlain, *Hans Holbein the Younger*, *2* (1913), 23–30.

19. See Cust, "Lumley Inventories," pp. 20 and 27.

20. Anonymous, *The London Chanticlers*, 2, in Hazlitt's Dodsley, *12*, 326.

21. William Rowley, *A Match at Midnight*, V.1, in Hazlitt's Dodsley, *13*, 88.

22. John Marston, *The Insatiate Countess*, I.1.339–41.

23. Robert Taylor, *The Hog Hath Lost His Pearl*, II, in Hazlitt's Dodsley, *11*, 447.

24. John Vicars' translation, *The last Trumpet* (1635), p. 3.

25. *Cymbeline*, V.4.184.

26. *Christ's Tears over Jerusalem*, in *Works*, ed. McKerrow, *2*, 69. Skulls lacking the lower jaw appear on various funeral monuments. Such a one is painted on the back of a portrait by Boltraffio at Chatsworth, reproduced by Sir Arthur Strong, *Critical Studies* (ed. 1912), op. p. 84. The fifth emblem in Peacham's *Minerva Britanna* shows a hand holding a like skull. Instances might be multiplied. The entire skull was of course (*pace* Nashe) often pictured, but the incomplete type was familiar in over-crowded graveyards and charnel houses.

27. *The Magnificent Entertainment* (1604), in *Dramatic Works*, *1*, 317. Dekker was dissatisfied with some of the costumes, remarking: "To describe what apparrell these Arts and Muses wore were a hard labour, and when it were done, all were but idle. Few taylors know how to cut their garments"—that is, the costumes for personifications, for tailors are not "great in their books." He adds that the performers in the pageant "go attirde in such thin clothes, that the winde everie minute is readie to blowe through them." The vivid detail calls to mind that in Middleton's Lord Mayors' Show, *The Triumphs of Truth*, in *Works*, ed. Bullen, *7*, 244, Truth was clad in a "close garment" (or, as we should say, flesh–colored tights) so that she might appear naked. In the "Epistle Dedicatory" of his translation of the *Odyssey*, Chapman sneers at Middleton: "A poor chronicler of a Lord Mayor's naked truth."

28. See in general Enid Welsford, *The Court Masque*, Allardyce Nicoll, *Stuart Masque and the Renaissance Stage*, and other writers on the masque.

29. *The Insatiate Countess*, II.1.33 f.

30. Tucker Brooke, *Life of Marlowe*, in *Works*, Arden Edition, *1* (1930), 107.

31. William Cartwright, *The Ordinary*, I.3, in Hazlitt's Dodsley, *12*, 224.

32. Robert Taylor, *The Hog Hath Lost His Pearl*, II, in Hazlitt's Dodsley, *11*, 447.

33. *The Antiquary*, I.1 and II.1, in Hazlitt's Dodsley, *13*, 429 and 450.

34. *Britannia's Pastorals*, Bk. II, Song 1, ed. Hazlitt, *1*, 184 f.

35. *The Barrons Warres*, VI, 30–41, in *Works*, ed. Hebel, *2*, 110 f.

36. *The City–Match*, V.7, in Hazlitt's Dodsley, *13*, 309.

37. *Englands Heroicall Epistles*, "Rosamond to Henry II," lines 93–97, in *Works*, ed. Hebel, *2*, 135.

38. *The Gentleman's Exercise* (ed. 1612), p. 9.

39. *Graphice. Or the Use of the Pen and Pensil* (1658), p. 27.

40. *The Gentleman's Exercise*, p. 58.

41. *Britannia's Pastorals*, Bk. II, Song 1, ed. Hazlitt, *1*, 175. Note that Browne employs the word "picture" for both painting and sculpture.

42. *Sacred Works* (1620), p. 211. The three brothers De Critz, John, Emmanual, and Thomas, were decorative painters. John, sergeant–painter to James I and Charles I, is probably the one to whom Sylvester refers.

See Rachael Poole, "An Outline of the History of the De Critz Family of Painters," *Second Annual Volume of the Walpole Society* (1913), pp. 45–68. Robert Peake was one of Vandyke's assistants. "Marcus" is Marcus Gheeraerts (or Garrard) the Younger, court-painter to James I. The three miniaturists are Nicholas Hilliard, Isaac Oliver, and Peter Oliver.

43. *The Letting of Humors Blood in the Head–Vaine* (ed. 1613), Epigram 29.

44. *Thalias Banquet: Furnished with an hundred and odde dishes of newly devised Epigrammes* (1620), Epigram 6.

45. "Democritus, Jr. to the Reader," in *The Anatomy of Melancholy*.

46. *Palladis Tamia* (1598), fol. 287^r.

47. *The Compleate Gentleman* (1622), p. 109.

48. *Graphice* (1658), p. 20.

49. *The Anatomy of Melancholy*, II, 11, 4. Half a dozen members of the Sadeler family were engravers. By "Vrintes" (which puzzled Colvin) Burton may mean Franz de Vrient (Frans Floris) the painter, who did a few etchings, or more probably, confusing names, Simon de Vries (Frisius) one of the most famous of early etchers.

3. TAPESTRIES

1. See W. G. Thomson, *Tapestry Weaving in England* which cites many inventories. See also the same writer's *History of Tapestry*, 1930.

2. For the inventory of Henry VIII see Thomson, *Tapestry Weaving in England*, pp. 34–41.

3. Ibid., fig. 5, facing p. 48. This piece is now in the Victoria and Albert Museum.

4. See Margaret Jourdain, "The Embroidery at Hardwick Hall," *Burlington Magazine*, *16* (1909), 97–99. The description is from the manuscript inventory made by Elizabeth of Hardwick, Countess of Shrewsbury.

5. See W. Cyril Wallis, "Sheldon Tapestries for the Royal Scottish Museum," *Burlington Magazine*, *51* (1927), 24–26.

6. *Cymbeline*, II.4.68–82. The "chaste Diana bathing" over the chimney in Imogen's room was carved, not painted, for the "cutter's" art is commended.

7. *The City–Match*, II.3, in Hazlitt's Dodsley, *13*, 233.

8. See Frederick Hard, "Spenser's Clothes of Arras and of Tours," *Studies in Philology*, *27* (1930), 162–195; summarized in the *Variorum Spenser*, *3*, 394–9.

9. Anonymous, *Law Tricks* (ed. 1604), sig. D4^v.

10. *The Ordinary*, III.3, in Hazlitt's Dodsley, *12*, 260.

11. *Orlando Furioso in English Heroical Verse* (1591), pl. illustrating Bk. 33. The plates are poor English copies of those by Girolamo Porro in the Venice edition of 1584.

12. John Fletcher, *The Woman's Prize*, III.3.

13. James Shirley, *The Lady of Pleasure*, I.2.

14. Robert Aylett, *Joseph, or, Pharaoh's Favorite* (1623), p. 33.

4. PRINTS

1. Hodnett, *English Woodcuts, 1480–1535,* provides much information on native work, importations, adaptations, loans, and other transfers, and on the descent of cuts from printer to printer.

2. See McKerrow and Ferguson, *Title–Page Borders,* no. 29.

3. Reproduced in Hind, *Introduction to a History of Woodcut,* 2, fig. 224.

4. Nichols, *Progresses of Queen Elizabeth,* 1, 105–6. Accounts of this incident are in J. A. Gotch, *Early Renaissance Architecture in England* (ed. 1914), p. 259 and in Fairchild, *Shakespeare and the Arts of Design,* p. 98, but in neither is the German vendor mentioned.

5. Colvin, *Early Engraving and Engravers,* pp. 4 and 38. At this point I should like to acknowledge my indebtedness to Colvin's book. I have, however, examined almost all the engravings I discuss, I add some details, and at a few points I am in disagreement with Colvin. Ryther's eleven plates were issued together with the title *Expeditionis Hispanorum Angliam vera descriptio Anno Do: MDXXXVIII.* They supplemented Ryther's translation of Petruccio Ubaldino's narrative of the Armada: *A Discourse concerning the Spanish Fleete* (1589).

6. Was the fictitious Mistress Philips' name suggested by "Phyllis"? The *lai* was illustrated by many German engravers. See Eugen Diederiche, *Deutsches Leben der Vergängenheit in Bildern,* 1, figs. 26, 27, 467, 468, 496; Burkhard, *Hans Burgkmair,* pl. 66; and examples in Van Marle, *Iconographie,* 2. The subject appears less frequently in Italian art. See Hind, *Early Italian Engraving,* A.i.79 and A.iv.20. Phyllis and her victim often appear among the captives of Love in Petrarchan Triumphs. Among English poets Gower, *Confessio Amantis,* lines 2705 f. and Hawes, *The Pastime of Pleasure,* lines 3570 f. tell the story. Aristotle and Phyllis are sometimes associated with Samson and Delilah, David and Bathsheba, and Solomon worshiping false gods at his wives' instigation.

7. See A. M. Hind, "Studies in English Engraving, IV. William Faithorne," *Connoisseur,* 92 (1933), 92–105.

8. Reproduced in Hind, *A History of Engraving and Etching* (1923), fig. 58.

9. *The Mysteries of Nature and Art* (ed. 1635), pp. 147 and 232.

5. CONTINENTAL EMBLEM BOOKS

1. See, among other authorities, L. Volkmann, *Bilderschriften der Renaissance* (Leipzig, 1923); Mario Praz, *Studies in Seventeenth Century Imagery* (1939); Rosemary Freeman, *English Emblem Books* (1948). R. J. Clements has published articles on special aspects of the subject in learned journals between 1944 and 1955. E. N. S. Thompson, "Emblem Books" in *Literary Bypaths of the Renaissance* (1924) is an attractive introduction to the subject. Much information is still to be had from various works by Henry Green. The enthusiasm with which in *Shakespeare and the Emblem Writers*

he carried the argument beyond the limits of the evidence has too much discredited him. The bibliography in *CBEL* is inaccurate and incomplete.

2. [William Camden], *Remaines of a Greater Worke, Concerning Britaine, the inhabitants thereof, their languages, Names, Sur–names, Empreses, Wise speeches, Poesies, and Epitaphs* (1605), p. 158 (misnumbered 851).

3. "I cannot imagine what he meant, which tooke for his devise," etc. (p. 170).

4. Thomas Jenner, *The Soules Solace; or Thirtie and one Spiritual Emblemes* (1631), sig. A2^r.

5. [Henry Hawkins], *Parthenia Sacra, or the Mysterious and Delicious Garden of the Sacred Parthenes . . . By H.A.* [sic] (Rouen ?, 1633), pp. 70 and 78.

6. Quarles, *Emblemes*, "To the Reader."

7. Thomas Blount, *The Art of making Devises: Treating of Hieroglyphicke, Symbols, Emblemes, Aenigma's, Sentences, Parables, Reverses of Medalls, Armes, Blazons, Cimiers, Cyphres, and Rebus. First Written in French by Henry Estienne* (1646), pp. 5–7, 30, 48, 52, and chaps. 7 and 8.

8. Estienne writes (Blount's translation, p. 62): "Ladies may also place their Devises on their Coaches, Cabinets, Beds, Hangings, Cushnnets, Carcanets, and on other parts of their ornaments and apparell." A beautiful impresa designed for Isabella Gonzaga and probably a wedding gift is in my own possession. It is described by Richard Bernheimer, *Wild Men in the Middle Ages* (Cambridge, Mass., 1952), p. 184 and note 17.

9. In the present book we shall have little or nothing to do with symbols and aenigmas in the pseudo–technical sense which Estienne attaches to them, and devices will interest us less than emblems because the rule was laid down (though often violated) that a device should not use the human form. It therefore offers few analogies on the level of personification, though many in the way of attributes.

10. Article "Embleme," *Enciclopedia Italiana*, *18*, 861.

11. For example, Reusner, *Emblemata partim ethica, partim vero historica, et hieroglyphica* (1581), p. 210.

12. On the title page of an English Bible published by Robert Parker in 1639 a small oval shows Christ standing in the wine press which presses down upon Him. Around it are the words of Isaiah, 63:3: "Ego torcular calcavi Solus." I have not come across any English rendering of the Spies and the Grapes, prototype of Synagogue, Church and Crucifixion.

13. The parable is a warning to the rich and a promise to the poor. The two Lazaruses of the New Testament are sometimes conflated in accordance with an old tradition, and the scene of Dives faring sumptuously and Lazarus begging at his table may occur at the beginning of the Office for the Dead (as in a Huntington Library *Horae* MS 1171 and a printed *Horae*, Paris, Hardouyn, 1514 or we may have the scene with Dives and the Resurrection of Lazarus together (as in Huntington Library MS 1101).

14. The relationship between this parable and the pattern of some English moralities has been recognized. Six prints (ca. 1540) ascribed to

Cornelis Anthonisz (Tennissen) are memorable. Here the Prodigal in his spendthrift days dines with Mundus, Caro, and other evil personifications; when eating with the swine, the serpent "remorse of Conscience" gnaws at his breast and near him stand the Devil and five terrible personifications; and on returning home he is greeted by his father and by joyful personifications. The banquet with Mundus is reproduced in my article "Spenser's Pageant of the Seven Deadly Sins" in *Studies in Art and Literature for Belle da Costa Greene*, pl. 4; the Prodigal at the swine's trough and the Prodigal welcomed home in Chew, *The Virtues Reconciled*, pls. 16 and 18.

15. *Veridicus Christianus* (1601), no. 62, facing p. 206.

16. Of many examples I note only a few. In De Montenay, *Emblematum Christianorum Centuria* (1584), no. 18, the beam is held in front of the man's eye by a hand reaching down from heaven. When the parable is illustrated in the Trevelyon commonplace book in the Folger Shakespeare Library, fol. 166^r, the beam juts out from a ruined wall and almost enters the eye of one brother and a splinter from it almost hits the eye of the other; an evident attempt at rationalization. See Domenico Fatti's painting reproduced on the cover of *Records of the Museum of Historical Art. Princeton University*, 2, Spring, 1943.

17. Ralph Winterton, *Considerations upon Eternity* (1636), p. 123. Reproduced in my Spenser article, pl. 13.

18. Francis Quarles, *Emblemes* (1635), Bk. V, no. 8, from Father Hugo.

19. Some of the woodcuts in Francesco Colonna's *Hypnerotomachia Polyphili* (1499) were influenced by Orapollo as were many of the recondite ornaments on Dürer's Triumphal Arch for the Emperor Maximilian I. See Erwin Panofsky, *Albrecht Dürer*, 1, 173–9 and 2, 98 and 101.

20. Both Orapollo and Valeriano were known in England. Ben Jonson refers to both. In Thomas Milles' huge translation and compilation *The Treasurie of Auncient and Moderne Times* (1613), p. 37, some hieroglyphics are interpreted in their manner. In *A Learned Summary Upon the famous Poeme of William of Saluste, Lord of Bartas . . . Translated out of French by T. L. D. M. P.* (1621), p. 14, there is a discussion of "the Portraits of Memphis" and it is stated that the Egyptians used "Figures of all sorts of creatures" to "express their conceptions." Reference is made to Horus Apollo and John Pierus who have expounded these "portraits."

21. Henry Green's *Andreae Alciati Emblematum Fontes Quatuor* (1870) brings together the editions of 1531, 1534, and 1546, and he considers the problem of the original collection of ca. 1522. His *Andreae Alciati Emblematum Flumens Abundans* (1871) contains the text of 1551 with later additions and variants. See also his *Andrea Alciati and his Books of Emblems: a Biographical and Bibliographical Study* (1872).

22. *Hecatomgraphie*, sig. Aiii^v.

23. Alciati had been known in England from an early date. Edward VI's copy, bearing the king's signature, of the Lyons edition of 1549 is in the British Museum.

24. There is a facsimile edition, Antwerp, 1901.

25. *The Schollers Medley, or, an Intermixt Discourse upon Historicall and Poeticall Relations* (1614), pp. 49–53.

26. Here are a few pleasant examples of Swan's love for his creatures. Of the squirrel (p. 453): "Such is the stately minde of this little beast, she tarrieth and saveth her selfe in the tops of tall trees, disdaining to come down." Of the cat (p. 463): "The common or vulgar *Cat* is a creature well known, and being young it is very wanton, and sportfull; but waxing older, very sad and melancholy. It is called Cat, from the Latine word *Cautus*, signifying wary; for a Cat is a watchfull and warie beast." Again (p. 466): Mice, says Swan, "make a voidance" of any old and ruinous building, taking flight "even as fast as their little legs will give them leave." The story of Bishop Hatto, popular in England at the time, follows.

27. Pp. 372 and 462. For contemporary allusions in English literature to the Dog of Nilus see Chew, *The Crescent and the Rose*, p. 20, note 4.

28. Ottavio Boldoni, *Theatrum Temporaneum Æternitati Caesaris Montii*, Milan, 1636.

29. Principio Fabricci, *Delle Allusioni, Imprese et Emblemi . . . sopra la Vita, Opera, et Attioni di Gregorio XIII, Pontefice Massimo Libri VI. Nei quali sotto allegoria del Drago, Arme del detto Pontefice, si descrive anco la vera forma d'un Principe Christiane; e altre cose*, Rome, 1588.

30. *The Institution of a Young Noble Man* (Oxford, 1607), pp. 226–7.

31. *Emblemata Anniversaria Academiae Altorfinae Studiorum inventutis Exercitandorum Causa Proposita et Variorum Orationibus Exposita*. This is anonymous.

32. To give a few examples: an owl surmounting a bit and bridle has the motto "Vigilis et moderatione" (fol. 35ᵛ); a winged tortoise on a book: "Et Labor et Virtus" (60ʳ); a peacock: "Vanitas" (69ʳ); a man climbing a tree to the top of which is attached a wreath teaches that victory is the reward of arduous endeavor (85ʳ).

33. For specimens of tarots see Hargrave, *A History of Playing Cards*, pp. 31, 33, 35, 228, 233. The article on "Carte da Giuoco" in the *Enciclopedia Italiana*, 9 (1931), contains excellent illustrations.

34. The *OED* records several instances from our period of the metaphorical use of "terrestrial triumph." "Triumph" of course means "trump," which is a derivative; but I have not been able to discover why the adjective "terrestrial" was employed.

35. G. de la Mothe, *The French Alphabet* (ed. 1615), p. 248. I have not seen the original edition of 1592.

36. For interpretations in terms of the Virtues see E. H. Richter, "The Tarocchi Prints," *Print-Collector's Quarterly*, 6 (1916), 37–38. St. Bernadino of Siena (quoted by Richter) advised that "little cards" be painted with allegories and suggested a series of Sins in the same order in which they appear in the tarot packs.

37. The most famous of all the packs are the two series of the so-called "Tarocchi Cards" of Mantegna, but whether they are genuine tarots and whether designed by Mantegna is very doubtful. For reproductions see Kristeller, *Die Tarocchi* and Hind, *Early Italian Engraving*, E.I.1–50. Dürer, probably with an assistant, made drawings from a pack engraved at Ferrara. See Panofsky, *Albrecht Dürer*, 2, Handlist, nos. 976–995. In three series painted in the fifteenth century by artists of the Paduan school there

is an exquisite combination of dignity, delicacy, and grace. All three series are incomplete. See Count Emiliano di Parravicino, "Three Packs of Italian Tarocco Cards," *Burlington Magazine, 3* (1903), 237–243.

38. *Roome for a Messe of Knaves* (1610).

39. Not to look further than England, France, and Antwerp, many examples of personifications used by printers are reproduced in Van Havre, *Marques Typographiques*; Roberts, *Printers' Marks*; McKerrow, *Printers' and Publishers' Devices*; and Laurent–Vibert, *Les Marques de libraires.*

6. ENGLISH EMBLEM BOOKS

1. *A Theatre wherein be represented as wel the miseries and calamities that follow the voluptuous Worldings, As also the greate joyes and pleasure which the faithfull do enjoy* (1569). The running title is "A Theatre for Worldings."

2. *The New Arival of the three Gracis* (undated; the STC dates it ca. 1580 but it may be not long after 1573), sig. F1ᵛ.

3. *A Choice of Emblemes, and other Devices, For the moste parte gathered out of sundrie writers, Englished and Moralized. And Divers Newly Devised . . . herein by the office of the eie and the eare, the minde maye reape dooble delighte*, Leyden, 1586. There is a facsimile edition with an introduction by Henry Green, 1866.

4. *The Worthy tract of Paulus Iouius, contayning a Discourse of rare inventions, both Military and Amorous, called Imprese. Whereunto is added a Preface contayning the Arte of composing them, with many other notable devises. By Samuell Daniell late Student in Oxenforde*, 1585. The original work is *Dialogo del imprese militari et amorose*, Lyons, 1559, and later editions.

5. *Insignium, Armorum, Emblematum, Hieroglyphicorum, et Symbolorum, quae ab Italia Impresa nominantur, explicatio*, 1588.

6. Lowndes first suggested Verstegen. I have dealt fully with this matter in "Richard Verstegen and the *Amorum Emblemata* of Otho van Veen," *Huntington Library Quarterly, 8* (1945), 192–9.

7. In 1627 Cats was in England as an emissary of the United Provinces and was knighted by Charles I. He was again in England in 1657 on diplomatic business with Cromwell.

8. *Silenus Alcibiades, sive Proteus, Vitae humanae ideam, Emblemate trifarium variato, oculis subijciens*, 1618. Sylvester's sonnet, praising the mingling of sweetness, learning, and divinity in this ingenious work, is in the preliminary matter. The *Silenus* has the alternative title *Proteus* because the emblems of human love in the first part are applied morally in the second and religiously in the third. Cats' *Self–Stryt*, 1620, a dramatic poem on Joseph and Potiphar's wife, was translated by John Quarles as *Self–Conflict: or, The powerful Motions between the Flesh and Spirit*, 1680. How long Cats' reputation lasted in England is evinced by an unattractive mid–Victorian volume entitled *Moral Emblems from Jacob Cats and Robert Farlie*, 1860, a clumsy conflation of material from several books. John Leighton "freely rendered" the original designs.

9. Thomas Heywood, *Pleasant Dialogues and Drammas . . . With sundry Emblems extracted from the most elegant Iacobus Catsius* (1637), pp. 203–230.

10. The English printers had some difficulty in adjusting the plates to the pages; occasionally the designs overlap the type. In what seems to be the earliest issue of the *Emblemes*, "London, Printed by A.M. for John Grismond," two designs were wrongly placed and corrections were made by pasting new impressions over those that were erroneous. See pp. 105–108 of that issue. The corresponding pages in the issue "A.M. for Richard Royston" have been normalized. For some further information about these plates see Franken, *L'Œuvre gravé des Van de Passe*, pp. 263–4.

11. *A Collection of Emblemes Ancient and Moderne* (1635), Bk. II, no. 49.

12. See Rosemary Freeman, *English Emblem Books*, pl. 22. The metal spinners attached to the paper easily tore loose and are missing in all copies I have seen.

13. See, in addition to Praz and Freeman, G. S. Haight, "The Sources of Quarles' *Emblems*," *Library*, Fourth Series, *16* (1935), 188–209.

14. Thus, in Bk. III, no. 14 picturing the Soul gazing on Death through a spy glass the personification of Flesh, a naked woman seated beside the Soul, does not appear in the original.

15. See Eleanor James, "The Imagery of Quarles' Emblems," *Studies in English*, The University of Texas (Austin, 1943), pp. 26–49.

16. *Complete Poems*, ed. Grosart, contains the poems and Biblical texts of the *Schola Cordis* but lacks the designs without which poems and texts are incomplete and not always comprehensible.

17. Miss Freeman, Appendix I, section B, has a list of such manuscripts but includes only one that is in the United States, and that without stating its whereabouts. This is the original manuscript of Francis Thynne's *Emblemes and Epigrams* (ca. 1600) in the Huntington Library (MS E L 34, B. 12). It is not autograph and has no illustrations but is beautifully written. F. J. Furnivall edited it for EETS (1876). The commonplace book (ca. 1600) in the Folger Shakespeare Library (MS 2058. 1.) probably made by Thomas Trevelyon contains along with much else some emblems and personifications. Also in the Folger (Smedley MS 20) is: *Emblemata Varia recens adinventa, suis Iconibus, unàq carmina Latino donato Authore Henrico Peachamo*. It is dedicated to Sir Julius Caesar and is in Peacham's autograph.

7. PERSONIFICATIONS AND EMBLEMS IN VARIOUS ARTS

1. William Drummond of Hawthornden, "Letter to his worthy Friend Master Benjamin Johnson," *The History of Scotland* (1655), p. 263; reprinted in *Ben Jonson*, ed. Herford and Simpson, *1*, 208–210. See Margaret Jourdain, "Sixteenth Century Embroidery with Emblems," *Burlington Magazine*, *11* (1907), 326–8, and J. L. Nevison, "English Domestic Embroidery Patterns of the Sixteenth and Seventeenth Centuries," *Walpole Society*, *28* (1940), 1–13 and plates.

2. See A. F. Kendrick, "The Hatfield Tapestries of the Seasons," *Walpole Society*, *2* (1913), pp. 89–97 and pls. 45–48; Thomson, *Tapestry Weaving in England*, pp. 59–62, with reproductions of the "Spring" and "Winter"; and a reproduction of the "Autumn" in *Burlington Magazine*, *64* (1934), p. 64.

3. *The Archs of Triumph Erected in honor of the High and mighty prince James the first . . . Invented and published by Stephen Harrison . . . and graven by William Kip*, 1604.

4. A Continental precedent of interest to us because Otho Van Veen, who designs the arches had English connections, is Johannes Bochius (Boch), *Descriptio Publicae Gratulationis* (Plantin, 1595), on the occasion of the reception at Antwerp of the Archduke of Austria.

5. Among Continental artists who made such designs for funerals were Guido Reni and Jacques Callot. See Bartsch, *Le Peintre–Graveur*, *18*, 306, 54–60, and J. Lieure, *Jacques Callot*, *1* (Paris 1924), nos. 124–144.

6. W. L. Spiers, "Note–book . . . of Nicholas Stone," pls. 2a, 3, 37a.

7. See M. Kathleen Martin, "Some Pictures by Marcus Gheeraerts the Younger, including two versions of the 'Perfect Wife,'" *Burlington Magazine*, *25* (1914), 137–144 and pl. 2.

8. Plutarch interprets the tradition recorded by Pausanias that Pheidias carved an Aphrodite with one foot on a tortoise. Alciati uses this emblem. In the French version (Lyons, 1539) Venus is nude, she has a foot on the tortoise, her doves are at her feet. In the Spanish version (Lyons, 1549) a draped Venus has the tortoise and Cupid is beside her. In Adrian Junius' *Emblemata* (1565) she stands squarely on the tortoise; in one hand are keys, the other is to her mouth. The presence of Adrian Junius in England for some years may have influenced the painter of the two portraits. The Pheidian theme is expounded in the English translation of Chartier's *Delectable demaundes and Pleasant Questions* (ed. 1596), p. 220. Analogous to the "Perfect Wife" are German designs of the "Wise Woman" by Anton Woensam (ca. 1525) and Cornelis Anthonisz (Tennissen) (ca. 1540). She has a key at her ear, a padlock on her lips, a dove in her breast, a serpent at her waist, and instead of human feet she has horse's hooves.

9. All three are reproduced in Lionel Cust, "The Painter HW ('Hans Eworth')," *Walpole Society*, *2* (1913), pls. 4, 14, 31b.

10. Reproduced in C. E. Collins Baker and W. G. Constable, *English Painting of the Sixteenth and Seventeenth Centuries* (1930), pl. 22.

11. Reproduced in Tenison, *Elizabethan England*, *1*, following p. 42.

12. Henry Peacham, *Minerva Britanna*, no. 44.

13. Reproduced in Colvin, *Early Engraving and Engravers*, pl. 5.

14. By Thomas Geminus on the title page of the third edition of his *Compendiosa totius Anatomiae delineatio* (1559). Reproduced in Hind, "Studies in English Engraving," *Connoisseur*, *91* (1933), 363, fig. 2.

15. This is a huge engraving by Geminus, reproduced in Colvin, fig. 17.

16. In the famous painting by Hans Eworth at Hampton Court. Reproduced in Cust, "The Painter HW," pl. 22; Tenison, *1*, after p. 22; E. C. Wilson, *England's Eliza* (1939), op. p. 238. Wilson also reproduces

(op. p. 366) the title page of *The Holi bible* (1569) where the Queen is crowned by Justice and Mercy while Fortitude and Prudence sit below.

17. This is the "Rainbow" portrait at Hatfield. Reproduced in Tenison, *3*, frontispiece, and in F. M. Kelly, "Queen Elizabeth and her Dresses," *Connoisseur, 113* (1944), 73, fig. 6. The Queen's hand rests on the rainbow, and the inscription is "Non sine Sole Iris"—not without the sun (Elizabeth) is there the rainbow (Hope). It has been suspected that in depicting a costume so weighed down with symbolism the artist drew upon his imagination, but there is nothing inherently unlikely in the supposition that in her immense wardrobe the Queen had such a dress. Such costumes may have been created for fancy-dress balls and similar occasions.

18. This is Eworth's painting known as "The Tudor Family." Henry VIII is enthroned with Mary and Philip on his right, Edward VI on his left, and Elizabeth in front of Edward. Elizabeth leads by the hand Peace, who treads upon armor, and behind her is Plenty with her cornucopia. Opposite, behind Mary and Philip, is Mars, representing War. An inscription commends all four sovereigns. The painting probably dates from the early years of Elizabeth's reign. Long afterwards William Rogers made an engraving after it, altering details but preserving the general arrangement. But an inscription is in striking contrast to the original quite guarded one. It is now declared that whereas Queen Mary "put down" Truth, Elizabeth has exiled Sorrow and defeated Care, Broils, and Falsehood. The painting is reproduced by Cust, pl. 22a; the engraving in *Connoisseur, 91*, 368, fig. 7.

19. Reproduced in Collins Baker and Constable, pl. 25; in Tenison, *2*, op. p. 152; in *Connoisseur, 113*, 75, fig. 9. The dog is not identified but I am sure his name is Fido. In only one other portrait of the Queen is there an animal: the charming one by Nicholas Hilliard at Hatfield (ibid., fig. 10), where the ermine of Chastity rests on her arm. The ermine prefers to be slain rather than soil itself with mud. The notion comes from the *Fiore di Virtu*, a book known to Leonardo da Vinci; hence the ermine in the famous Portrait of a Lady in the Czartoryski Gallery in Cracow. It sometimes occurs on Chastity's banner in Petrarchan Triumphs. John Fletcher uses the emblem three times: "That ermine honesty, unspotted ever" (*Monsieur Thomas*, IV.1); "Honour, Ermin-like, can never suffer / Spot or black soyle" (*The Knight of Malta*, II.5); "Ladies honours / Were ever, in my thoughts, unspotted ermines" (*Wit without Money*, IV.4). John Hall, *Emblems* (ed. 1648), p. 92, writes:

> The Ermine rather chose to die
> A Martyr to its purity,
> Than that one uncouth soile should stain
> Its hitherto preserved skin.

20. This is William Rogers' engraving entitled "Eliza Triumphans," done in celebration of the Armada and dated 1589. Reproduced in Colvin, *Early Engraving and Engravers*, p. 48, fig. 21. Colvin thought the pomegranate inappropriate "since this fruit was a special badge of Catherine of

Aragon and her daughter Queen Mary, and is not at all usually associated with Elizabeth." It was, however, an ancient symbol not to be claimed exclusively by any sovereign.

21. Reproduced in A. F. Johnson, *Catalogue of Engraved and Etched English Title-pages* (1934), W. Van de Passe, No. 1. Carleton's narrative, with about a score of vignettes by Frederick Van Hulsen (Hulsius), has to do with the escapes of Elizabeth and James I from conspiracies, attempted assassinations, and papal, Spanish, and Irish enemies. The original edition (1624) has no engravings.

22. Richard Brathwaite, *The Arcadian Princes; or The Triumph of Justice*, 1635.

23. McKerrow and Ferguson, *English Title-page Borders*, no. 222.

24. *A Learned Summary Upon the Famous Poeme by William of Saluste Lord of Bartas . . . Translated out of French by T.L.D.M.P.* (1621).

25. Reproduced in Johnson, *Catalogue*, Le Blon, no. 1.

26. Reproduced, ibid., Cecill, no. 22.

27. Reproduced, ibid., Cecill, no. 16, and in Colvin, pl. 31a.

28. This was W. C. Hazlitt's opinion, *Notes and Collections* (1876), p. 101.

29. Reproduced in Colvin, pl. 27.

30. Reproduced in Johnson, Hole, no. 14, in the Herford–Simpson *Ben Jonson*, and elsewhere.

31. Scholars who have attempted the "reconstruction" of the Tudor–Stuart theatres seem to have overlooked this bit of evidence. It is slight and lacking in detail, but views are so few that nothing should be disregarded, and this partial view of the "hut" is from an angle differing from all others. Hole's "Theatrum" was copied by Francis Delaram on his title page of Edmund Bolton's *New Caesar, or Monarchie Depraved* (1624).

32. *The Sanctuarie* was published in 1601 and revised and enlarged in 1607. In that year a second part appeared. The two parts were joined in the edition of 1616 which was the first to have the engraved title page.

33. Reproduced in Johnson, Hole, no. 15; in Hebel's edition of Drayton's *Works;* and elsewhere.

34. Reproduced in *Ben Jonson*, ed. Herford and Simpson, *8*, op. p. 177 (with Jonson's poem on pp. 175–6); in Jonson's *Poems*, ed. B. H. Newdigate (1936), p. 125; in Johnson, *Catalogue*, Elstrack, no. 6; and elsewhere. For the sources of the concept of history see Simpson's commentary.

35. Reproduced in Johnson, Vaughan, no. 6.

36. Reproduced, ibid., Marshall, no. 29.

INDEX

References to figures in this volume are denoted by the page number of the text on which they are first discussed, followed by the figure number in parentheses. References to discussions in the Notes section, pp. 299–402, are denoted by the page number of the TEXT to which the note is keyed (see running heads of the Notes section), followed by the number of the note in italics.

ILLUSTRATIONS

FIG. 2. The Fall of Man. Painting by the School of Lucas Cranach the Elder. (Page 2)

FIG. 3. The Fall of Man. Sixteenth–century woodcut by Hans Sebald Beham. (Page 2)

FIG. 1. The Garden of Eden. Miniature in a French *Horae*, ca. 1500. (Page 1)

FIG. 4. The Fall of Man.
Sixteenth-century engraving
by Hans Sebald Beham.
(Page 2)

FIG. 5. The Fall of Man. Engraving by Frans Floris in the
Huntington Library "Kitto" Bible. (Page 2)

FIGS. 6 and 7. The Fall of Man. Miniatures in a
manuscript of *The City of God*. (Page 2)

FIG. 8. The Seven Deadly Sins in the Tree of the Knowledge of Good and Evil. Frontispiece in Giovanni Boccaccio, *De Claris Mulieribus*, Louvain, 1487. (Page 2)

FIG. 9. The Tree of Sin. Engraving in Jan David, *Veridicus Christianus*, Antwerp, 1606. (Page 4)

FIG. 10. Death snaring the Soul. Engraving in Francis Quarles, *Emblemes*, London, 1635. (Page 6)

PECCATVM, EIVSQVE OCCASIO FVGIENDA. 24.

Quæ fugienda mihi mala funt, cane peius, et angue? Peccatum: Et quidquid peccato porrigit Anfam.

FIG. II. The Expulsion from Paradise. Woodcut in Raoul de Presles' translation of *La Cité de Dieu*, Abbeville, 1485. (Page 7)

FIG. 12. The Expulsion from Paradise. Seventeenth-century engraving signed "R.C." in the Huntington Library "Kitto" Bible. (Page 7)

FIG. 14. Engraving on title page in John Weever, *Ancient Funerall Monuments*, London, 1631. (Page 8)

FIG. 13. The Garden of Eden and the Garden of Christ. Engraving by Theodore Galle in Jan David, *Paradisus Sponsi et Sponsae*, Antwerp, 1607. (Page 7)

FIG. 15. Time in the Garden of Eden. Woodcut in Thomas Peyton, *The Glasse of Time, in the Second Age*, London, 1620. (Page 10)

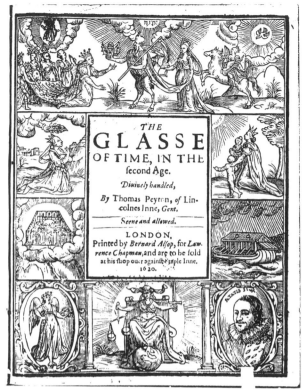

FIG. 16. Woodcut on title page in Thomas Peyton, *The Glasse of Time, in the Second Age*, London, 1620. (Page 10)

FIG. 17. Time the Destroyer. Engraving by Willem Swidden on title page in *Voornaamste Gebouwen Vande Tegenwoordige Stadt Romen*, anonymous, n.d., sixteenth century. (Page 14)

FIG. 18. Time the Destroyer. Engraving in Otho Van Veen, *Quinti Horatii Flacci Emblemata*, Antwerp, 1612. (Page 14)

FIG. 19. Love saving the *Acta Sanctorum* from devouring Time. Seventeenth–century engraving by Martin Tyroff. (Page 15)

FIG. 20. Love saving the *Acta Sanctorum* from devouring Time. Engraving on title page in the *Acta Sanctorum* of the Bollandists, Antwerp, 1643. (Page 15)

FIG. 21. Age, guided by Time, leaves behind the treasures of the World. Woodcut by Joannes Sambucus in *Emblemata*, Antwerp, 1564. (Page 16)

FIG. 22. Time with a bag on his back. Woodcut in an English antipapal broadside, "Poor Robin's Dream." (Page 17)

FIG. 23. Time brings consolation to Age. Engraving in Otho Van Veen, *Quinti Horatii Flacci Emblemata*, Antwerp, 1612. (Page 17)

A SCOVRGE

for Paper-Perfecutors.
OR

Papers Complaint, compil'd in ruthfull Rimes,
Againſt the Paper-ſpoylers of theſe Times.
By I. D.

WITH

A continu'd iuſt Inquiſition
Of the ſame ſubieƐt, fit for this ſeaſon.

Againſt PAPER-PERSECVTORS.
By A. H.

Witt.

nay vp with him if he were my brother.
if he will needs be a paper-ſpoyler

Time.

O couldſt Thou whip theſe Bedlams till they bleed
Thou whippſt in vaine : weele whip anon indeed.

Printed at London for *H. H.* and *G. G.* and are to be ſold at the
Golden Flower Deluce in Popes-head Alley. 1 6 2 5.

FIG. 24. Time as the whipping post for Folly. Title page in John Davies of Hereford, *A Scourge for Paper—Persecutors*, London, 1625. (Page 18)

EMBLEMA LIII.   59

Veritas tempore reuelatur, deſſidio obtruitur.

*Quid penniger Saturne in auras virginem nu-
    dam rapis?*
*Quid feminarum cœtus aggeſta obruit terra
    ſcrobem?*
Specu emicantē veritatē, tēporis natam, triplex
Obruere peſtis apparat; Lis, Inuidia, Calumnia.
                       Diſcor-

FIG. 25. Time with a Whip. Woodcut on title page
in Giovanni Andrea Gilio, *Topica Poetica*, Venice,
1580. (Page 18)

FIG. 26. Time rescuing Truth from a cave.
Woodcut in Adrian Junius, *Emblemata*,
Antwerp, 1565. (Page 19)

FIG. 27. Truth rising from a tomb. Engraving in Jacob Cats, *Spiegel van den Ouden ende Nieuven Tijt*, Dordrecht, 1635. (Page 19)

FIG. 28. Time and Truth reveal the Past. Engraving by John Droeshout on title page in *Truth Brought to Light and Discovered by Time,* anonymous, London, 1651. (Page 21)

FIG. 29. Time holding a mirror for Truth. Engraving on title page in Jacob Cats, *Spiegel van den Ouden ende Nieuven Tijt*, Amsterdam, 1635. (Page 21)

FIG. 30. Engraving on title page in Jacob Cats, *Tafereel van de Belacchende Werelt*, Amsterdam, 1635. (Page 21)

FIG. 31. Time. Drawing in Guillaume de la Perriere, *La Morosophie*, Lyons, 1553. (Page 21)

FIG. 32. Time and the Soul. Engraving in Francis Quarles, *Emblemes*, London, 1635. (Page 23)

FIG. 33. Time. Woodcut in Stephen Hawes, *The Pastime of Pleasure*, London, 1506. (Page 23)

FIG. 34. Time leading the Seasons. Engraving in Otho Van Veen, *Quinti Horatii Flacci Emblemata*, Antwerp, 1612. (Page 24)

FIG. 35. Time turning Fortune's Wheel. Earliest known Spanish copperplate, dating from before 1454. (Page 26)

FIG. 36. "Fortuna sive Occasionis Deus." Drawing in Jean Cousin, *Le Livre de Fortune*, Paris and London, 1883. (Page 26)

A. TEMPVS ego, sine quo nihil est quodcunque creatum est.
  Me sine nec cœlum, neq, cœlo sidera, nec sol
  Aureus irradient: sine me, nec terra, nec aquor,
  Et quidquid vasta Mundi compage tenetur,
  Existant: Sed enim, per me, velut omnia constant;
  Omnia sic rursum, per me, revoluta labascent.
B. Illa ego, quæ priscis OCCASIO cognita Seclis.
  Me quicunque catus non fastidiunt, amico
  Sed vultu acceptam tenuit, mandata capessens;
  Ille sibi, compos voti, decora ampla parauit.

FIG. 37. Engraving by Theodore Galle on title
page in Jan David, *Occasio Arrepta, Neglecta.
Huius Commoda: Illius Incommoda*, Antwerp,
1605. [Figs. 38–49 are also derived from this volume.] (Page 28)

FIG. 38. Time and Occasion. Engraving by Theodore Galle. (Page 29)

FIG. 39. Engraving by Theodore Galle. (Page 29)

FIG. 40. Five Imprudentes waste and mock Time.
Engraving by Theodore Galle. (Page 29)

A. Effluat in risum TEMPVS: quid rectius istam
  Ætatem deceat, quam ludere, quamque iocari?
B. Dum ver molle sinit, rapiat sua quemq voluptas.
C. Vnam ție multis mihi sit fas vellere pennam
  Gestamen capiti. D. Non pluma hac aptior vlla

FIG. 41. Five Imprudentes mock Time and Occasion. Engraving by Theodore Galle. (Page 29)

FIG. 42. Five Prudentes are greeted by Time, Occasion and an Angel. Engraving by Theodore Galle. (Page 29)

FIG. 43. Five Prudentes receive rewards from Occasion. Engraving by Theodore Galle. (Page 29)

FIG. 44. Five Prudentes grasp Occasion's forelock. Engraving by Theodore Galle. (Page 29)

DVM TEMPVS LABITVR. OCC... ...ONTE CAPILLATA REMORATVR. 7.

A. *Non vt vos fertis, post est Occasio calua.*
Ecce, capillatam obtendo, gaudete, tenete.
B. *Ad baratrum, ad baratrum sic sic raptentur inertes*

FIG. 45. Five Imprudentes lament lost Opportunity and wasted Time. Engraving by Theodore Galle. (Page 29)

FIG. 46. Five Imprudentes attempt to grasp Opportunity. Engraving by Theodore Galle. (Page 29)

FIG. 47. Five Imprudentes dragged towards hellmouth. Engraving by Theodore Galle. (Page 29)

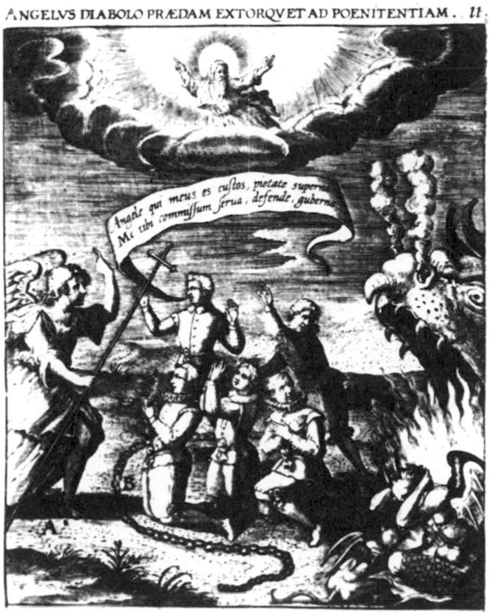

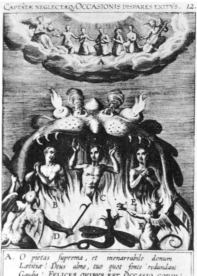

ANGELVS DIABOLO PRÆDAM EXTORQVET AD POENITENTIAM. 11.
Angele qui meus es custos, pietate superna
Me tibi commissum serua, defende, guberna
A.
B.

FIG. 48. An Angel rescues Five Imprudentes from hellmouth. Engraving by Theodore Galle. (Page 29)

CAPTATÆ NEGLECTÆQ. OCCASIONIS DISPARES EXITVS. 12.
A
B
C
D
E
F
A. O pietas suprema, et inenarrabile donum
Lætitiæ! Deus alme, tuo quot fonte redundant
Gaudia! FELICES, QVIBVS EST OCCASIO CORDI!

FIG. 49. Souls burn in hellmouth and are in bliss in heaven. Engraving by Theodore Galle. (Pages 29–30)

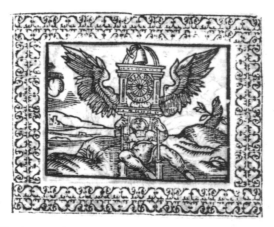

EMBLEME LXVIII.

When youth is in his flowring prime,
He cares not how he passe his time.

Redeeme the time, time dearer is then gold,
And time once gone can neuer be reclaimed,
He need begin betimes that would grow old,
If time be lost, our life is likewise maimed.
Yet greene yong heads disdaining to be told,
As though more priuiledge of yeres they claimed,
Do seem to pul the weights with all their sway,
And waste their time, and haste their dying day.

FIG. 50. Wasting Time. Woodcut in Thomas Combe, *The Theatre of Fine Devices,* London, 1614. (Page 30)

FIG. 51. Time turning the Macrocosm and the Microcosm. Engraving by Theodore de Bry on title page in Robert Fludd, *Metaphysica, Physica atque Technica Historia*, Oppenheim, 1617. (Page 34)

FIG. 52. Fortune at her Wheel. Sixteenth–century woodcut by George Pencz. (Pages 36, 39)

FIG. 53. Fortune at her Wheel. Woodcut by Hans Burgkmair in Petrarch, *De Remediis Utriusque Fortunae*, Augsburg, 1532. (Pages 36, 39)

FIG. 54. Many–handed Fortune. Woodcut in John Lydgate, *The Fall of Princes*, London, 1554. (Page 46)

fortuna sum sparges
munera multiceca

FIG. 55. Fortune. Anonymous sixteenth–century French drawing. (Page 49)

FIG. 56. Fortune. Drawing in Jean Cousin, *Le Livre de Fortune*, Paris and London, 1883. (Page 55)

FORTVNA
ROTANS
ROTA

The Castle of Knowledge.

The Sphere of Destinye.

Sphæra Fati

whose gouernour is Knowledge.

The wheele of Fortune.

Sphæra Fortunæ

QVO MODO SCANDIT · CORRVET STATIM ·

whose ruler is Ignoraunce.

TO KNOWLEDG is this Trophy set,
All learninges friendes will it support.
So shall their name great honour get,
And gaine great fame with good report.

Though spitefull Fortune turned her wheele
To staye the Sphere of Vranye,
Yet dooth this Sphere resist that wheele,
And fleeyth all fortunes villanye.
Though earthe do honour Fortunes balle,
And bytells blynde hyr wheele aduaunce,
The heauens to fortune are not thralle,
These Spheres surmount al fortunes chance.

FIG. 57. Fortune and Destiny. Woodcut on title page in Robert Recorde, *The Castle of Knowledge*, London, 1556. (Page 57)

FIG. 58. "Nemesis." Woodcut in Andrea Alciati, *Livret des Emblemes*,
Paris, 1536. (Page 57)

FIG. 59. "Occasio." Woodcut in Andrea Alciati, *Emblemata*, Lyons, 1554.
(Page 59)

FIG. 60. "Fortuna sine pedibus." Drawing in Jean Cousin, *Le Livre de
Fortune*, Paris and London, 1883. (Pages 59–60)

FIG. 61. Fortune. Engraving by Nicoletto da Modena. (Page 60)

FIG. 62. Fortune and the Nine Worthies. Woodcut in Stephen Hawes, *The Example of Vertu*, London, 1530. (Page 60)

FIG. 63. The Wheel of Fortune. Woodcut in *Das Narrenschiff*, Basle, 1495. (Page 63)

FIG. 64. Fortune favoring an ape. Engraving in Otho Van Veen, *Quinti Horatii Flacci Emblemata*, Antwerp, 1607. (Page 64)

FIG. 65. The House on the Rock and the House on the Sand. Lutheran antipapal engraving by Erhard Schoen. (Page 66)

FIGS. 66 and 67. Mercury (Arts) opposed to Fortune. Woodcuts in Andrea Alciati, *Emblemata*, Lyons, 1551 and 1591. (Page 66)

Franc. Baconi
DE VERULAMIO
HISTORIA REGNI
HENRICI SEPTIMI
Angliæ Regis
OPUS VERE POLITICUM.

LVG. BATAVOR.
Apud Franc. Hackium.
Anno 1642.

Cornelis v. Dalen sculp.

FIG. 68. Fortune and Flatterers, the Wise Man stays the Wheel. Engraving by Cornelis Van Dalen on title page in Francis Bacon, *Henry VII*, Leyden, 1642. (Page 67)

FIG. 69. The Death of the Righteous and the Death of the Unrighteous. Lower part of an engraving from a design by Heinrich Vogtherr the Younger. (Page 74)

FIG. 70. The World, the Flesh, and the Devil assault the Soul. Engraving in Jan David, *Veridicus Christianus*, Antwerp, 1601. (Page 75)

TRES CONIVRATI ANIMÆ HOSTES. 38

Quæ nos infeſto circumſtant agmire peſtes?
Mundus ouans: Sathanaſq; furens: Caroq; intimus hoſtis.

FIG. 71. "Amoris Securitas." Engraving in Otho Van Veen, *Amoris Divini Emblemata*, Antwerp, 1660. (Page 75)

FIG. 72. The Soul repudiates worldly possessions and is impervious to the Devil. Engraving by Renold Elstrack on title page in George Wither, *Wither's Motto. Nec habeo, nec Careo, nec Curo*, London, 1621. (Page 76)

Formæ naturâ, lue morum, morte fubactâ,
Almus eram, ater eo, mox tamen albus ero.

I wrestle not against flesh and blood only, but against principalities & powers.
Ephes. 6. 12.

CHRISTIANVS MILITANS

of the Spirit

of Truth

of Righteousnes

of Faith

of the preparation

of the Gospell

Cecill sculp.

All-spotlefs fair I formed was, But am by Sin deform'd ;
Yet truft ere long by Death to pafs, To glorious life conform'd.

FIG. 73. The Christian Knight. Engraving by Thomas Cecill on verso of title page in Joseph Fletcher, *The History of the Perfect–Cursed–Blessed Man*, London, 1628. (Pages 76–77)

FIG. 74. The Christian Knight. Engraving by John Payne on title page in John Downame, *The Christian Warfare Against the Devil, World and Flesh*, London, 1634. (Page 77)

FIG. 75. The Christian, assaulted by Deadly Sins, clings to the Crucifix. Engraving by Hieronimus Wierex. (Pages 83–84)

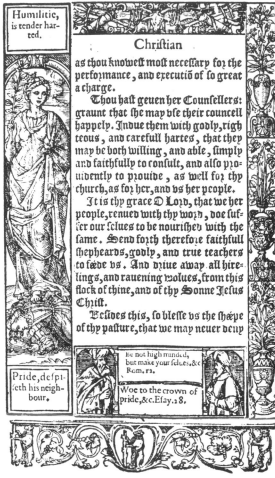

FIG. 76. Humility triumphs over Pride. Page from John Daye, *A Booke of Christian Prayers*, London, 1578. (Page 90)

FIG. 77. The Prodigal Son: Banquet of Sins. Engraving, probably by Cornelis Anthonisz (Tennissen), ca. 1540. (Pages 93, 94)

FIG. 78. Everyman dining with Pride, Gluttony, and Avarice. Woodcut in *Exercitium super Pater Noster*, Paris, n.d., fifteenth century. (Page 94)

VII
PECCATORVM CAPITA
LIVM IMAGINES ELE
GANTISSIME A PHILIP.
GALLAEO DEPICTAE
ET AERI INCISAE.

Ecce omnes animæ, meæ ſunt:
vt anima patris, ita et ani
ma filij, mea eſt. Anima
quæ peccaverit, ipsa
morietur.
Ezech. 18.

FIG. 79. Death and the Devil expose the Seven Deadly Sins. Engraving by Philip Galle on title page in *VII Peccatorum Capitalium Imagines Elegantissime,* ca. 1600. [Figs. 80–86 are also derived from this volume.] (Page 96)

FIG. 80. Pride. Engraving by Philip Galle. (Page 96)

Phls Galle invent et excud.

2 AVARITIA.

Hieron Wierx sculp.

FIG. 81. Avarice. Engraving by Philip Galle. (Page 96)

FIG. 82. Lechery. Engraving by Philip Galle. (Page 96)

FIG. 83. Envy. Engraving by Philip Galle. (Page 96)

FIG. 84. Gluttony. Engraving by Philip Galle. (Page 96)

FIG. 85. Wrath. Engraving by Philip Galle. (Page 96)

FIG. 86. Sloth. Engraving by Philip Galle. (Page 96)

FIG. 87. Divine Love and the Soul chastise Pride. Engraving in Otho Van Veen, *Amorum Emblemata*, Antwerp, 1606. (Page 96)

FIG. 88. The Chariot of Sin. Engraving in Jan David, *Veridicus Christianus*, Antwerp, 1601. (Page 97)

Dic: homini quâ non clades damnosior vlla est?
Peccatum; excussis in quo sibi plaudit habenis.

Welck is het quaetste quaet; en dat meer schade inheeft?
Der sonde boose daet; daer-gh'ongheduxht in leeft.

Dis moy, quelle peste, Soit la plus funeste, Et de plus d'effroy:
Du peché la tache, Au quel on se lache, Sans bride, et sans loy.

FIG. 89. "Woe, woe, woe!"—a boat with the Seven Deadly Sins falling over a cataract into Hell. Seventeenth-century engraving by Conrad Meyer in the Huntington Library "Kitto" Bible. (Page 98)

FIG. 90. The meeting with Lady Lechery. Woodcut in
Stephen Hawes, *The Example of Vertu*, London, 1530.
(Page 104)

DER·GOTLOSEN·SCHÄCZE·ZEND
KAIN·NVTZE·ABER·GERECHTI
GKAIT·ERRETT·VOM·TOD
C·X·V·2.

FIG. 91. Satan obscures from Avarice the sight of Justice and Death.
Seventeenth–century engraving signed "D" in the Huntington Library
"Kitto" Bible. (Page 108)

A LETTER,

Nine yeeres since, written and first published : Containing a most briefe Discourse Apologetical, with a plaine demonstration, and feruent Protestation, for the lawfull, sincere, and very Christian course, of the Philosophicall studies and exercises, of a certaine studious Gentleman : a faithfull Seruant to our late Soueraigne Lady Queene *Elizabeth*, for all the time of her Raigne : and (*Anno 1603. Aug. 9.*) sworne Seruant to the King his most excellent Maiestie.

But I gaue my selfe to prayer. Psalm. 109.

O God impute not this Sinne vnto them

He that maketh himselfe a Sheep } { The Wolfe will eate him.

The Swift Sharpe Poyson'd

Tongued Monster of many heads that spreadeth mischiefe, Persecuteth, that creepeth men,

For my friendship they were my aduersaries:

Hope. Humilitie. Patience.

A false witnesse shall not be vnpunished : and he that speaketh lyes, shall perish. *Prouerb. 19. verf. 9.*

FIG. 92. Slander: "The many–headed mob–monster." Woodcut on title page in John Dee, *A Letter, Nine yeeres since, written and first published*, London, 1603. (Page 109)

FIG. 93. The Weighted Palm Tree. Detail of engraving by William Marshall on frontispiece in Charles I, King of England, *Eikon Basilike*, London, 1649. (Page 117)

CRESCIT SUB PONDERE VIRTVS

Guil: M

FIG. 94. Faith and Infidelity (Mahomet). Engraving by an unknown artist, ca. 1580, in the Huntington Library "Kitto" Bible. (Page 128)

FIG. 95. The Works of Mercy. Engraving by Philip Galle on title page in *Septem Opera Misericordiae Corporalia*, 1577. (Page 132)

FIG. 97. Justice. Engraving in Francis Quarles, *Emblemes*, London, 1635. (Page 138)

FIG. 96. Justice. Woodcut on title page in Stephen Hawes, *The Example of Vertu*, London, 1530. (Page 137)

FIG. 98. Justice. Engraving by Johannes Galle. (Page 139)

ANGELIS SVIS DEVS MANDAVIT DE TE, VT CVSTODIANT TE IN OMNIBVS VIIS TVIS

FIG. 99. The Guardian Angel. Seventeenth–century Flemish engraving by an unknown artist in the Huntington Library "Kitto" Bible. (Page 140)

FIG. 100. The Christian Knight: Defiance to Death. Detail of engraving on title page in William Cowper, Bishop of Galloway, *Workes*, London, 1629. (Page 142)

Late sixteenth–century engravings by Christofero Bertello, or Bertelli. FIG. 101: The Nine Ages of Man (Page 148). FIG. 102: The Nine Ages of Woman (Pages 148–49).

FIG. 103. The Cycle of Life. A *Memento Mori* print by Hans Schäufelein, ca. 1517. (Pages 149–50)

FIG. 104. The Four Ages of Man subdivided into Eight. Miniature in the British Museum Arundel MS 83. (Page 150)

FIG. 105. Death and the Four Ages of Man. Engraving by Theodore de Bry on title page in J. J. Boissard, *Theatrum Vitae Humanae*, Frankfort, 1596. (Page 152)

FIG. 106. Death and the Four Ages of Man. Seventeenth-century woodcut in a broadside, "The Sinner's Care." (Page 153)

FIG. 107. Time and the Three Ages of Man. Detail of title page border in Thomas Campion, *Booke of Ayres*, London, 1601. (Page 154)

FIG. 108. Spring and the time of budding. Woodcut by Robert Vaughan in Robert Farley, *Kalendarium Humanae Vitae*, Milan, 1638. [Figs. 109–11 are also derived from this volume.] (Page 156)

FIG. 109. Summer and the seed–time. Woodcut by Robert Vaughan. (Page 156)

FIG. 110. Autumn and the harvest of ripened years. Woodcut by Robert Vaughan. (Page 156)

FIG. 111. Winter and chilly old age. Woodcut by Robert Vaughan. (Page 156)

L'adolescence. Age d'étude.

La peine suit tout les Emplois.
L'étude fait verser des larmes.
Cependant il faut dans les lois.

Les arts l'eglise ou les armes.
Prendre un parti qu'on doit choisir
Sagement pour d'un repentir

Se Vend a Paris chez N. Guerard Graveur rue St Jacques à la Reyne du Clergé proche St Yues. C.P.T.

Jeunesse. Age de la Joye.

Le Jeune homme qui a son bien.
Sans un tuteur pour se financer.
Se voit bien tôt réduit à rien.

Par les excez de sa dépence.
Le prodigant en insensé.
Il ressemble au panier percé.

Se Vend a Paris chez Guerard Graveur rue St Jacques à la Reyne du Clergé proche St Yues. C.P.R.

Adolescence.

Youth.

Manhood.

Old Age.

Virilité. homme en ménage.

On peut bien dire adieu bontemps.
Sitôt qu'on se met en ménage.
C'est un arrest depuis longtemps.

joint au contract de mariage.
Que l'homme doit finir son sort.
Dans le chagrin jusqu'à la mort.

Se Vend a Paris chez N. Guerard Graveur rue St Jacques à la Reyne du clergé   Avec Privilege du Roy.

Vieillesse. âge d'infirmité.

Le chaud, le froid et les voleurs.
Pauvreté, mort et maladie.
Causent d'éternelles frayeurs.

Au dernier âge de la vie.
Où toutes choses font souffrir.
Un vieillard qui craint mourir.

Se Vend a Paris chez Guerard Graveur rue St Jacques à la Reyne du clergé proche St Yues.   C.P.R.

FIG. 116. "Folie du Temps." The Five Experiences of Courtship. Late seventeenth-century French engraving published by Nicolas Guérard. (Page 161)

FIGS. 117–20. Savage Education and Gentle Education. Details from the architrave of the Porta Principale, San Marco Cathedral, Venice, thirteenth century. (Page 162)

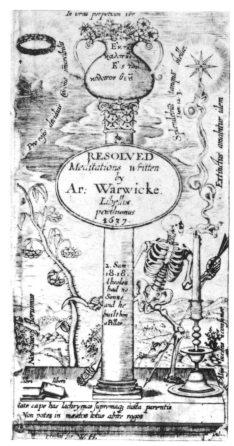

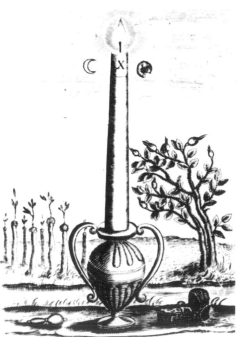

't Luna Infantia torpet .

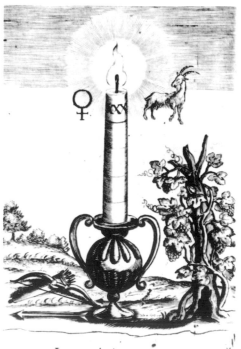

Iam ruit in Venerem .

FIG. 121. The Candle of Life. Title page devised by Francis Quarles in Arthur Warwick, *Resolved Meditations*, London, 1637. (Page 167)

FIG. 122. The Moon and the First Age. Engraving by William Marshall in Francis Quarles, *Hieroglyphikes of the Life of Man*, London, 1638. [Figs. 123–26 are also derived from this volume.] (Page 168)

FIG. 123. Venus and the Third Age. Engraving by William Marshall. (Page 168)

Et Martem spirat et arma .

Will. Marshall. sculpsit .

Invidiosa Senectus .

Will. Marshall. sculpsit .

FIG. 124. Mars and the Fifth Age. Engraving by William Marshall. (Page 168)

FIG. 125. Jupiter and the Sixth Age. Engraving by William Marshall. (Page 168)

FIG. 126. Saturn and the Seventh Age. Engraving by William Marshall. (Page 168)

Plumbeus in terram .

Will. Marshall. sculpsit

FIG. 127. The Seven Ages of Man. Woodcut in Bartholomeus Anglicus, *De Proprietatibus Rerum*, Lyons, 1482. (Page 169)

FIG. 128. The Seven Ages of Man. Woodcut in Bartholomeus Anglicus, *Boeck van den proprieteyten der dinghen*, Harlem, 1485. (Page 169)

FIG. 129. The Seven Ages of Man. Woodcut in Bartholomeus Anglicus, *Le Proprietaire des Choses*, Lyons, 1500. (Page 169)

FIG. 130. The Choice of Two Paths: Hercules at the Crossroads. Engraving in George Wither, *Emblemes*, London, 1634. (Page 176)

FIG. 131. The Choice of Two Paths: The Y of Pythagoras. Engraving in Zacharias Heyns, *Emblemata. Emblemes Chrestienes et Morales*, Rotterdam, 1625. (Page 177)

FIG. 137. Touch. Woodcut.
(Pages 192–93)

FIG. 138. The Hill of Virtue.
Engraving in Jan David, *Veridicus Christianus*, Antwerp,
1601. (Pages 201–02)

VIRTVTES, ATQVE OPERA MERENTIA CÆLVM. 31.

Quæ bona Chriſtiadis patranda,ediſsere paucis.
Omnigenum Pietatis opus: Mellitaq3 Virtus.

FIG. 139. The Christian Pilgrim and his Guide. Engraving by Francis Barlow on frontispiece in Sir William Denny, *Pelecanicidium: or the Christian Adviser against Self-Murder*, London, 1653. (Page 224)

FIG. 140. Death warns the Living. Miniature in a fifteenth–century Italian *Officium B.V.M.* (Page 230)

FIG. 141. Death triumphs over Lust of the Flesh, Lust of the Eyes, and Pride of Life. Engraving by Hieronimus Wierex in the Huntington Library "Kitto" Bible. (Page 239)

FIG. 142. Death and the Hopes of Youth. Woodcut in Daniel Meisner, *Sciographia Cosmica*, Nuremberg, 1637. (Page 239)

FIG. 143. Death parting a father from his family. Engraving in Otho Van Veen, *Quinti Horatii Flacci Emblemata*, Antwerp, 1612. (Page 242)

FIG. 144. Nature with Death behind her. Woodcut in Stephen Hawes, *The Example of Vertu*, London, 1530. (Page 245)

FIG. 145. Death turning Fortune's Wheel. Anonymous German woodcut, ca. 1470. (Page 247)

FIG. 146. "Allegorie op de Vergankelijkleid."
Engraving by Cornelis Anhonisz (Tennissen),
1537. (Page 248)

FIG. 147. The Soul under the Ribs of
Death. Engraving in Francis Quarles, *Em-blemes*, London, 1635. (Page 250)

lxxxix.

Suaue mori, quoties ſcelerum mens libera, nullũ
Judicis horreſcens iudicium refugit.
Suaue etenim Chriſto cõiungi: et corpus humatũ
Regno ſublime deſpicere athereo.

                                     B   *Adiutare*

FIG. 148. "Desiderans Dissolvi." In Georgette de Montenay, *Emblematum Chris-*
tianorum Centuria, Zurich, 1584. (Page 251)

FIG. 149. "Post Funera Virtus, Vivet Tamen." Engraving in Jean Mercier, *I. C. Emblemata*, London, 1592. (Page 251)

FIG. 150. The Soul discerns Death and Heaven. Engraving in Francis Quarles, *Emblemes*, London, 1635. (Page 251)

FIG. 151. The Christian Pilgrim. Engraving by Robert Vaughan on title page in Richard Brathwaite, *Lignum Vitae*, London, 1658. (Page 252)

FIG. 152. Nobody. Woodcut on title page of *Nobody and Somebody*, anonymous, London, 1606. (Page 257)

FIG. 153. "Heaping Coals of Fire." Engraving in Jan David, *Veridicus Christianus*, Antwerp, 1601. (Page 278)

NOBILE AC NOVVM VINDICTAE GENVS. 46 62.

Qua ratione meos vlciſcar plenius hoſtes?
Aggere candentes inimico in vertice prunas.

FIG. 154. Engraving by Thomas Cecill on title page in Sir William Corn-wallys, *Essayes*, London, 1632. (Page 294)

FIG. 155. "Theatrum." Engraving by William Hole on title page in folio edition of Ben Jonson, *Workes*, London, 1616. (Page 295)

FIG. 156. Engraving by William Hole on title page in John Haywarde, *The Sanctuarie of a Troubled Soule*, London, 1616. (Page 296)